LEGITIMACY IN EU CARTEL CONTROL

This book examines the laws enacted by the EU to control cartels. These laws are carefully documented and analysed against a standard of legitimacy which questions the EU's enforcement measures, its institutional structures, policy choices, substantive law, evidentiary standards, and procedures and sanctions. It includes a unique catalogue of over 150 EU cartel decisions, as well as novel analyses of difficult borderline issues such as mixed horizontal and vertical cartels, single-brand dealer cartels and buyer cartels. The effect on trade in cartel cases is analysed with reference to established law and deterrence theory. Throughout the book the author asks whether EU law also applies at the national level, or whether certain assessments need to be made according to national law. This approach makes the book particularly helpful for national authorities, courts and private practitioners. The book includes in-depth comparisons with US law, as well as a comprehensive survey of the secondary (academic) literature on cartels. As such it presents not only a comprehensive practical view, but also a sound theoretical framework for better understanding cartel law. This is a work which will be of utmost importance to those working in competition authorities and competition courts in the EU Member States, as well as those working for EU institutions and in private practice and academia.

Volume 20 in the series Modern Studies in European Law

Modern Studies in European Law

Volume 1: Soft Law in European Community Law *Linda Senden*

Volume 2: The Impact of European Rights on National Legal Cultures *Miriam Aziz*

Volume 3: Partnership Rights, Free Movement and EU Law *Helen Toner*

Volume 4: National Remedies Before the Court of Justice: Issues of Harmonisation and Differentiation *Michael Dougan*

Volume 5: The National Courts Mandate in the European Constitution *Monica Claes*

Volume 6: EU Environmental Law: Challenges, Changes and Decision-Making *Maria Lee*

Volume 7: European Union Law and Defence Integration *Martin Trybus*

Volume 8: Principles of European Constitutional Law *Armin von Bogdandy & Jürgen Bast*

Volume 9: EU International Relations Law *Panos Koutrakos*

Volume 10: Free Movement, Social Security and Gender in the EU *Vicki Paskalia*

Volume 11: The Regulation of the State in Competitive Markets in the EU *Erika Szyszczak*

Volume 12: European Administrative Law in the Constitutional Treaty *Eva Nieto-Garrido and Isaac Martín Delgado*

Volume 13: EU Food Law: Protecting Consumers and Health in a Common Market *Caoimhín MacMaoláin*

Volume 14: Legal Responses to Trafficking in Women for Sexual Exploitation in the European Union *Heli Askola*

Volume 15: Unfair Contract Terms in European Law: A Study in Comparative and EC Law *Paolisa Nebbia*

Volume 16: Energy Security: The External Legal Relations of the European Union with Major Oil and Gas Supplying Countries *Sanam S Haghighi*

Volume 17: EU Criminal Law *Valsamis Mitsilegas*

Volume 18: Effective Judicial Protection and the Environmental Impact Assessment *Áine Ryall*

Volume 19: Network-based Governance in EC Law: The Example of EC Competition and EC Communications Law *Maartje de Visser*

Volume 20: Legitimacy in EU Cartel Control *Ingeborg Simonsson*

Legitimacy in EU Cartel Control

Ingeborg Simonsson

·HART·
PUBLISHING

OXFORD AND PORTLAND, OREGON
2010

Published in North America (US and Canada) by
Hart Publishing
c/o International Specialized Book Services
920 NE 58th Avenue, Suite 300
Portland, OR 97213-3786
USA
Tel: +1 503 287 3093 or toll-free: (1) 800 944 6190
Fax: +1 503 280 8832
E-mail: orders@isbs.com
Website: www.isbs.com

Hart Publishing, 16C Worcester Place, Oxford, OX1 2JW
Telephone: +44 (0)1865 517530 Fax: +44 (0)1865 510710
E-mail: mail@hartpub.co.uk
Website: http://www.hartpub.co.uk

British Library Cataloguing in Publication Data
Data Available

ISBN: 978-1-84946-005-7

Typeset by Hope Services, Abingdon
Printed and bound in Great Britain by
TJ International Ltd, Padstow, Cornwall

Preface

In the late 1990s a malfunction in the European Community competition law system was recognised by the European Commission. It consisted of an enforcement deficit and a priority problem. A considerable part of the Commission's resources was spent on controlling vertical restraints such as reseller agreements, leaving many serious offences such as cartels untouched. Furthermore, the Member States were not actively involved in EC competition law control, while the Commission had insufficient resources to supervise competition in the EC single-handedly. The cure, brought into force in 2004, included increased involvement of Member States in competition law supervision, and a new focus on action against cartels. The malfunctions which the reform aimed to remedy may be classified as a legitimacy problem.

Legitimacy may be understood to presuppose two things: that the law rests on rational foundations, and that average compliance can be ensured.

This work explores the role of legitimacy in EC competition law, as regards the new policy focus on cartel control. Legitimacy must be distinguished from legality. By and large, there is seldom any reason to question that the law has been adopted in accordance with applicable constitutional principles. Legitimacy, on the other hand, is a more profound question: whether the law corresponds to deeper notions in society.

There are several different ways of evaluating legitimacy. One may look for empirical legitimacy, actual acceptance of the rules in society. One may look at normative legitimacy, whether the law can be reconstrued rationally. One may look for the democratic aspects of the process according to which the law is adopted. And then there is the matter of enforcement, to ensure that the law does not self-destruct from within the system.

Exploring legitimacy in EC competition law is a work-intensive exercise, given that not much of the law is codified in statutes; the massive bulk of law consists of administrative decision-making, soft law and case law. In order for it to be operative when applied in 27 Member States and by the Commission, it must possess some degree of internal rationality. Reflection must also be made on the institutional guarantees for average compliance; in other words, what will happen if all Member States do not apply the law in a uniform and effective way.

This book brings together all these strands: whether the Community's central policy against cartels is legitimate; how sanctions ought to be structured; whether the law is characterised by rationality; whether it is possible to envisage that Member States will respond favourably and ensure average compliance; and, ultimately, the role of legitimacy in public enforcement against cartels in the EC.

Ingeborg Simonsson
Stockholm, August 2009

Acknowledgements

Law is in a sense an ongoing dialogue where participation is of essence.

Thanks must go to my supervisor, Nils Wahl, for accepting me as a PhD candidate and for helping me escape velocity. To my co-supervisor, Steven Anderman, for being an extra parent to this work. To Stockholm University for financing this research. To my husband, Sven, for listening to my ideas and for gracefully accepting the substantive and long-term reduction of my salary brought about by the change of career path necessary for this project. To Louise Widén for helping me with my first work on cartels, an article published in a Swedish legal review in 2002. To Ida Otken Eriksson and Ulf Öberg—together we carried out several academic and commercial projects during our time as PhD candidates. To Vladimir Bastidas, Dan Eklöf, Lars Henriksson, Evelina Janunger, Peter Whelan and Mauro Zamboni for reviewing earlier draft chapters. To all my fellow colleagues at Stockholm University and other universities and public and private institutions for your generosity in adopting me into the academic community, and for excellent co-operation on various academic projects. And to my colleagues at Stockholm City Court for your encouragement and support during the project's final year. To Olav Kolstad who was the opponent when a previous version of this work was publicly defended as a PhD thesis in Stockholm, and to Ulla Neergaard, Lars Pehrson and Wouter Wils who jointly formed the examination board at the same occasion. Lastly, to Richard Hart, Jo Ledger and Mel Hamill at Hart Publishing.

Note to Reader

This book was written and prepared for publication prior to the entry into force of the Treaty of Lisbon. It retains the classic numbering of the provisions of the Treaty Establishing the European Community (the EC Treaty).

Although the Treaty of Lisbon amends and renames the EC Treaty—now the Treaty on the Functioning of the European Union—it does not introduce any new significant substantive content to the competition law provisions.[1] In short, the legal analysis in this book is not affected in any material way by the entry into force of the new Treaty.

As a matter of terminology, the Treaty amendments now require references to the *Community* to be read as *Union*, references to the common market as the *internal market* and references to the *Court of First Instance (CFI)* as the *General Court*.[2]

For the convenience of the reader, a table of equivalence for the provisions discussed or referred to in this book is provided below.[3]

Treaty on the Functioning of the European Union

Old numbering of the Treaty Establishing the European Community	**New numbering of the Treaty on the Functioning of the European Union**
Article 3, paragraph 1 (repealed)[4]	
Article 10[5]	Article 4.3 TEU
Article 81	Article 101
Article 82	Article 102
Article 83	Article 103
Article 192(2)	Article 225
Article 211[6]	Article 17 TEU
Article 226	Article 258

[1] Although Article 3(1)(g) EC, which provided for a system of undistorted competition in the internal market to facilitate the attainment of the Community objectives has now been repealed, the status of competition policy in the EU remains undiminished. According to Article 3(1)(b) TFEU, the Union retains the exclusive competence to establish the competition rules necessary for the functioning of the internal market, while the objective of maintaining undistorted competition reappears in *Protocol No 27 on the Internal Market and Competition.* The latter protocol expressly points out that the internal market set out in Article 3 of the Treaty on European Union includes a system ensuring that competition is not distorted.

[2] See Article 2 (2) of the Treaty of Lisbon amending the Treaty on European Union and the Treaty establishing the European Community, signed at Lisbon, 13 December 2007.

[3] For the complete table of equivalence, see [2008] OJ C 115/361.

[4] Replaced, in substance, by Articles 3 to 6 TFEU.

[5] Replaced, in substance, by Article 4, paragraph 3, Treaty on the European Union.

Article 230	Article 263
Article 234	Article 267
Article 250	Article 293
Article 251	Article 294
Article 252 (repealed)[6]	
Article 253	Article 296

[6] Replaced, in substance, by Article 17, paragraph 1, Treaty on the European Union

Summary Contents

Contents

Table of Cases

Introductory Note
The following list includes cases without page references. These entries were relied upon for research purposes, but not referred to explicitly in the text.

European Court of Justice

Court of First Instance

Commission horizontal cartel decisions (chronological order)

Commission horizontal cartel decisions, alphabetical order with description of infringement

Alloy Surcharge	21 January 1998	98/247/ECSC	OJ L/100	1/4/1998	55–71	Price fixing by stainless steel producers.	80, 174, 268, 337
Aluminium imports from eastern Europe	19 December 1984	85/206/EEC	OJ L/92	30/3/1985	1–76	Exclusionary practices between Western primary aluminium producers and trade organisations from the former East European republics, including purchasing quotas and export prohibitions.	100, 104
Amino Acids	7 June 2000	2001/418/EC	OJ L/152	7/6/2001	24–72	Price fixing, quotas and information exchange by producers of lysine.	290, 312, 313, 315, 319
Ansac	19 December 1990	91/301/EEC	OJ L/152	15/6/1991	54–60	Joint sales operation for natural dense soda-ash by producers in US Webb-Pomerene Association (export cartel).	155
AROW/BNIC	15 December 1982	82/896/EEC	OJ L/379	31/12/1982	1–18	Price fixing adopted by the national cognac industry board.	91, 104, 151

Association Syndicale Belge de la Parfumerie (ASPA)	30 June 1970	70/333/CEE	JO L/148	8/7/1970	9–12	Collective resale price maintenance and market sharing between producers, wholesalers and agents of perfume products.	91, 151
Austrian banks–'Lombard Club'	11 June 2002	2004/138/EC	OJ L/56	24/2/2004	1–75	Price fixing by banks.	138, 151, 152, 170
Beer cartel in the Netherlands	18 April 2007	IP/07/509				Price fixing by brewers.	151
Belgian Architects	24 June 2004	2005/8/EC	OJ L/4	6/1/2005	10–11	Recommended minimum prices adopted by the Belgian Architects Association.	104, 151, 321
Benelux flat glass	23 July 1984	84/388/EEC	OJ L/212	8/8/1984	13–22	Price fixing, market sharing and information exchange by glass producers.	
Bitumen Spain	3 October 2007	IP/07/1438				Price fixing, quotas, markets sharing and information exchange by bitumen suppliers.	
Bleaching chemicals	3 May 2006	IP/06/560				Information exchange resulting in limitation and/or controlling of production and capacities, allocation of market shares and fixing and monitoring of target prices by producers of hydrogen peroxide and sodium perborate.	337

Bomée-Stichting	21 November 1975	75/781/EEC	OJ L/329	23/12/1975	30–34	Exclusionary schemes and (until 1972) collective resale price maintenance by manufacturers and importers of perfumes, toiletry articles and cosmetics.	91, 104, 151
BP Kemi–DDSF	5 September 1979	79/934/EEC	OJ L/286	14/11/1979	32–52	Agreement between two producers of synthetic ethanol, where one would stop producing and instead buy its total requirements from the other, in addition they shared customers, applied the same prices, applied a quota and exchanged information.	96
Brasseries Kronenbourg Brasseries Heineken (French beer)	29 September 2004	2005/503/EC	OJ L/184	15/7/2005	57–59	Peace agreement ending intense acquisition/investment competition (ie a joint limitation on investment) between brewers, including 'balancing' of volumes.	151
British Midland v Air Lingus	26 February 1992	92/213/EEC	OJ L/96	10/4/1992	34–45	Participation in tariff consultation between airlines, outside Regulation (EEC) No 84/91.	
British Sugar, Tate & Lyle, Napier Brown and James Budgett Sugars	14 October 1998	1999/210/EC	OJ L/76	22/3/1999	1–65	Coordination of prices through information exchange on future pricing behaviour by sugar producers and sugar merchants.	151

Building and construction industry in the Netherlands	5 February 1992	92/204/EEC	OJ L/ 92	7/4/1992	1–30	Price fixing, bid-rigging and information exchange within the building and construction industry.	104, 151, 321
Carbonless paper	20 December 2001	2004/337/EC	OJ L/115	21/4/2004	1–88	Price fixing and market sharing by producers and distributors of carbonless paper.	89–91, 104, 141, 147, 174, 188, 202, 256, 278, 337
Carreaux céramiques	29 December 1970	71/23/CEE	OJ L/10	13/1/1971	15–23	Catalogue prices and rebates decided by industry association for producers of ceramic tiles.	100, 104, 151
Cartonboard	13 July 1994	94/601/EC	OJ L/243	19/9/1994	1–78	Price fixing and market sharing by producers of cartonboard.	104, 173, 209, 265, 314, 318, 337
Cast iron and steel rolls	17 October 1983	83/546/EEC	OJ L/317	15/11/1983	1–18	Price fixing and market sharing (including bid-rigging) by manufacturers of cast iron and steel rolls.	104
Cement	30 November 1994	94/815/EC	OJ L/343	30/12/1994	1–158	Market sharing (including export prohibitions) and information exchange by cement producers.	104, 120, 124–27, 130–31, 137–140, 144–45, 147, 171, 190, 196, 198, 210, 213, 222, 226, 229, 234, 252, 253, 254, 255, 265, 282, 307, 318, 321, 322, 337
Cementregelig voor Nederland	18 December 1972	72/468/CEE	OJ L/303	31/12/1972	7–17	Price fixing and quotas by cement producers.	104, 151

Centraal Bureau voor de Rijwielhandel	2 December 1977	78/59/EEC	OJ L/20	25/1/1978	18–27	Collective resale price maintenance and exclusionary tactics adopted by trade association organising bicycle manufacturers, wholesalers, intermediaries, retailers, repairers and dealers.	91, 100, 104, 151
Centraal Stikstof Verkoopkantor	20 July 1978	78/732/EEC	OJ L/242	4/9/1978	15–36	Joint sales operation, including quotas and prices, between manufacturers of fertilising products.	104
Cewal, Cowac and Ukwal	23 December 1992	93/82 EEC	OJ L/34	10/2/1993	20–43	Market sharing between shipping conferences.	154
Chloroprene rubber	5 December 2007	IP/07/1855				Price fixing, market sharing and information exchange by producers of chloroprene rubber.	
Chauffage central	20 October 1972	72/390/CEE	OJ L/264	23/11/1972	22–31	Exclusionary practice through reciprocal exclusivity by trade associations organising producers, wholesalers and entrepreneurs of heaters and radiators.	91, 100, 104, 151
Choline Chloride	9 December 2004	2005/566/EC	OJ L/190	22/7/2005	22–26	Price fixing and market sharing by producers of animal feed vitamins.	90, 91
Cimbel	22 December 1972	72/474/CEE	OJ L/303	31/12/1972	24–40	Quotas, price-fixing and market sharing by cement producers.	104, 151

Citric Acid	5 December 2001	2002/742/EC	OJ L/239	6/9/2002	18–65	Price fixing, quotas, market sharing, information exchange and predatory practices by producers of citric acid.	104, 139, 176, 204, 244, 278, 290, 295, 300, 301, 316, 317
CNSD	30 June 1993	93/438/EEC	OJ L/203	13/8/1993	27–33	National Council with government representative established tariff rates charged by customs agents following proposals by departmental councils where industry was represented.	104, 151, 320
Coapi	30 January 1995	95/188/EC	OJ L/122	2/6/1995	37–50	Price fixing for services relating to filing of patents, registration of trade marks, utility models and other industrial property procedures, among industrial property agents.	104, 151
COBELPA/ VNP	8 September 1977	77/592/EEC	OJ L/242	21/9/1977	10–19	Information exchange, *inter alia* on prices, mutual observance of business conditions as well as exclusionary tactics agreed between two national paper industry federations established in separate Member States.	104
Cold-rolled stainless steel flat products	18 July 1990	90/417/ECSC	OJ L/220	15/8/1990	28–41	Price fixing and quotas by producers of cold-rolled stainless steel flat product.	104, 107
Copper fittings	20 September 2006	IP/06/1222				Price fixing, market sharing and information exchange by producers of copper fittings.	

Copper plumbing tubes	3 September 2004	2006/485/EC	OJ L/192	13/7/2006	21–29	Price fixing, quotas and market sharing by producers of copper water, heating and gas tubes.	337
Decca Navigator System	21 December 1988	89/113/EEC	OJ L/43	15/2/1989	27–48	Market sharing by manufacturers of navigator systems. Vexatious litigation brought against competitor.	OJ L/366
Distribution of railway tickets by travel agents (UIC)	25 November 1992	92/568/EEC		15/12/1992	47–59	Trade association for railway companies recommended that travel agents be appointed on the basis of national borders, also recommended use of standard contract and uniform commission rates. Recommendations adhered to.	
Dyestuffs	24 July 1969	69/243/CEE	OJ L/195	7/8/1969	11–17	Price fixing by producers of dyestuffs.	78, 148
Electrical and mechanical carbon and graphite products	3 December 2003	2004/420/EC	OJ L/125	28/4/2004	45–49	Price fixing and exclusionary tactics by producers of carbon and graphite products.	104
Eurocheque: Helsinki Agreement	25 March 1992	92/212/EEC	OJ L/95	9/4/1992	50–67	Maximum and minimum interbank commission rates, aligned with competing means of payment, for Eurocheques.	151

Europe Asia Trades Agreement	30 April 1999	1999/485/EC	OJ L/193	26/7/1999	23–60	Limitation of capacity and information exchange between shipping lines.	
European producers of beams (Steel beams)	16 February 1994	94/215/ECSC	OJ L/116	6/5/1994	1–62	Price fixing, market sharing and information exchange by producers and distributors of steel beams.	80, 104, 107, 141, 142, 189, 226, 251, 277, 310, 337
European Sugar Industry (Suiker Unie)	2 January 1973	73/109/EEC	OJ L/140	26/5/1973	17–48	Price fixing, market sharing and exclusionary tactics by producers and sellers of sugar.	106, 153, 168
Euro-zone currencie—Germany Far East	11 December 2001	2003/25/EC	OJ L/15	21/1/2003	1–34	Price fixing by banks (reversed on appeal).	151, 208
Trade Tariff Charges and Surcharges Agreement (FETTCA)	16 May 2000	2000/627/EC	OJ L/268	20/10/2000	1–13	Price fixing between shipping lines.	80, 116, 197, 261, 263, 264, 277, 282, 313, 314
Far Eastern Freight Conference	21 December 1994	94/985/EC	OJ L/378	31/12/1994	17–36	Price fixing on inland transport services by members of a freight conference.	

Fasteners	IP/07/1362					Price fixing, market sharing and information exchange in four separate cartels by manufacturers of hard haberdashery products.	
Fatty Acids	2 December 1986	87/1/EEC	OJ L/3	6/1/1987	17–26	Information exchange on historic individual sales figures by producers of oleochemicals.	87, 104
FEG and TU (Dutch electro-technical)	26 October 1999	2000/117/EC	OJ L/39	14/2/2000	1–28	Collective exclusive dealing by importers and suppliers, and price co-ordination by wholesalers of electrotechnical equipment.	79, 83, 91, 104, 130, 151, 203, 205, 254, 309, 321
Fenex	5 June 1996	96/438/EC	OJ L/181	20/7/1996	28–36	Price fixing by providers of logistical services.	104, 151, 321
Ferry Operators—Currency Surcharges	30 October 1996	97/84/EC	OJ L/26	29/1/1997	23–33	Price fixing for ro-ro traffic by ferry operators.	153
Fine Art Auction Houses	30 October 2002	2005/590/EC	OJ L/200	30/7/2005	92–95	Price fixing between auction houses.	
Fire insurance	5 December 1984	85/75/EEC	OJ L/35	7/2/1985	20–34	Price fixing by fire insurers.	102, 104, 151
Flat glass	7 December 1988	89/93/EEC	OJ L/ 33	4/2/1989	44–75	Price collusion by producers of flat glass.	151

Flat glass producers	28 November 2007	IP/07/1781				Price fixing by flat glass producers.	
Floral	28 November 1979	80/182/EEC	OJ L/39	15/2/1980	51–63	Joint sales operation by fertiliser manufacturers.	151
Food flavour enhancers	17 December 2002	2004/206/EC	OJ L/75	12/3/2004	1–31	Price fixing, market sharing and information exchange by producers of nucleotides.	
Franco–Japanese ball-bearings agreement	29 November 1974	74/634/EEC	OJ L/343	21/12/1974	19–26	Price fixing by ball-bearing manu-facturers.	104
French beef	2 April 2003	2003/600/EC	OJ L/209	19/8/2003	12–41	Price fixing and import restrictions by federations representing farmers and slaughterers in the beef sector.	104, 151, 165, 166, 168, 321
French inland waterway charter traffic	10 July 1985	85/383/EEC	OJ L/219	17/8/1985	35–44	Price fixing by introduction of a uniform levy through agreement between association of self-employed waterway carriers and federation of inland waterway forwarding agents.	104, 151
French-West African shipowner's committees	1 April 1992	92/262/EC	OJ L/134	18/5/1992	1–35	Exclusionary practices to reserve freight traffic to the participants.	154

Gas insulated switchgear	24 January 2007	IP/07/80				Price fixing, market sharing (including bid-rigging) and information exchange by producers active in distribution and installation of gas insulated switchgear.	337
Gas water-heaters and bath-heaters	3 July 1973	73/232/EEC	OJ L/217	6/8/1973	34–38	Collective limitation of distribution channels and joint setting of rebates by manufacturers and importers of gas water-heaters and bath-heaters.	151
GB-Inno-BM/ Fedetab	20 July 1978	78/670/EEC	OJ L/224	15/8/1978	29–45	Collective resale price maintenance and exclusionary practices adopted by industry association organising manu-facturers, wholesalers and retailers of tobacco products.	91, 101, 104
German scrap iron	21 January 1970	70/118/CECA	OJ L/29	6/2/1970	30–36	Purchase price fixing and quotas by steel producers.	104
GISA	22 December 1972	72/478/CEE	OJ L/303	31/12/1972	45–49	Price fixing and exclusionary practices by wholesalers in sanitary equipment.	104, 151
Glass containers (IFTRA)	15 May 1974	74/292/EEC	OJ L/160	17/6/1974	1–17	Price collusion, including information exchange, by manufacturers of glass containers.	
Graphite Electrodes	18 July 2001	2002/271/EC	OJ L/100	16/4/2002	1–42	Price fixing and market sharing by producers of graphite electrodes.	143, 174, 240, 255, 256, 257, 258, 266, 268, 276, 293, 294, 308, 314, 316, 318

Greek Ferries	9 December 1998	1999/271/EC	OJ L/109	27/4/1999	24–50	Price fixing by ferry companies.	153, 315
HOV SVZ/ MCN	29 March 1994	94/210/EC	OJ L/104	23/4/1994	34–57	Joint sales operation among national railroad companies for carriage of seaborne containers.	
IFTRA rules (aluminium)	15 July 1975	75/497/EEC	OJ L/228	29/8/1975	3–16	Price collusion by producers of aluminium.	
IJsselcentrale and others	16 January 1991	91/50/EEC	OJ L/28	2/2/1991	32–46	Exclusionary practice; collective import and export exclusivity among electricity generating companies, extended to distributors.	91, 151
IMA Rules	18 September 1980	80/1071/EEC	OJ L/318	26/11/1980	1–22	Collective exclusionary practices by agents, importers and processors of plywood.	91, 100, 104, 151
Industrial and medical gases	24 July 2002	2003/207/EC	OJ L/84	1/4/2003	1–16	Price fixing and market sharing by producers and suppliers of industrial and medical gases.	104, 151, 310, 337, 340
Industrial bags	30 November 2005	IP/05/1508				Price fixing, quotas, market sharing (including bid-rigging) and information exchange by producers of industrial plastic bags.	104
Industrial thread	14 September 2005	IP/05/1140				Price fixing, market sharing and information exchange by producers of industrial thread.	

Industrial copper tubes	16 December 2003	2004/421/EC	OJ L/125	28/4/2004	50–53	Price fixing and market sharing by producers of copper tubes.	104
Industrieverband Solnhofener Natursteinplatten	16 November 1980	80/1074/EEC	OJ/ L318	26/11/1980	32–39	Price fixing and exclusionary practices by producers of limestone slabs.	151, 154
Interbrew and Alken-Maes	5 December 2001	2003/569/EC	OJ L/200	7/8/2003	1–58	Price fixing, market sharing and information exchange by brewers.	104, 107, 151, 320
IPTC Belgium	5 December 1983	83/667/EEC	OJ L/376	31/12/1983	7–10	Decision complementing the *NAVEWA-ANSEAU* decision.	
Italian cast glass	17 December 1980	80/1334/EEC	OJ L/383	31/12/1980	19–26	Quotas and information exchange by producers of cast glass.	151
Italian flat glass	28 December 1981	81/881/EEC	OJ L/326	13/11/1981	32–43	Price fixing, quotas, market sharing, information exchange and exclusionary practices by producers, wholesalers and processors of flat glass.	104, 151
Julien/Van Katwijk	28 October 1970	70/487/CEE	OJ L/242	5/11/1970	18–21	Market sharing; mutual agreement between producers of carton tubes not to sell in each others' geographic areas.	

Kali & Salz	11 May 1973	73/212/EEC	OJ L/217	6/8/1973	3–6	Quotas and joint sales activities between producers of potassium products.	100
Kali & Salz/ Kali Chemie	21 December 1973	74/17/EEC	OJ L/19	23/1/1974	22–26	Joint sales operation between producers of potassium products.	
Kraanver-huurbedrijf	29 November 1995	95/551/EC	OJ L/312	23/12/1995	79–89	Price fixing and exclusionary practices by undertakings that hire out mobile cranes.	104, 151, 321
LdPE	21 December 1988	89/191/EEC	OJ L/74	17/3/1989	21–44	Price fixing and market sharing by petro-chemical producers.	232
Lifts and escalators	21 February 2007	IP/07/209				Price fixing, market sharing (including bid-rigging) and information exchange by companies active with sale, installation, maintenance and modernisation of lifts and escalators.	
Luxemburg Brewers	5 December 2001	2002/759/EC	OJ L/253	21/9/2002	21–41	Market sharing by brewers, including exclusionary tactics.	151, 340
MELDOC	26 November 1986	86/596/EEC	OJ L/348	10/12/1986	50–65	Price fixing, quotas, bid-rigging and exclusionary practices within the dairy industry.	151, 168
Methacrylates	31 May 2006	IP/06/698				Price fixing and information exchange by producers of acrylic glass.	

Pabst & Richarz/BNIA	26 July 1976	76/684/EEC	OJ L/231	21/8/1976	24–29	Decision collectively to stop sales (reduce supply on the market) adopted by trade association organising Armagnac producers, co-operatives, wholesalers, distillers and brokers.	104, 151
Papier peints de Belgique	23 July 1974	74/431/EEC	OJ L/237	29/8/1974	3–11	Price fixing and exclusionary tactics by wallpaper manufacturers.	104, 151
Peroxygen products	23 November 1984	85/74/EEC	OJ L/35	7/2/1985	1–34	Market sharing and quotas by producers of hydrogen peroxide and sodium perborate, also bilateral price fixing.	104
Plasterboard	27 November 2002	2005/471/EC	OJ L/166	28/6/2005	8–11	Information exchange aimed at ending price wars as well as concerted price increases by producers of plasterboard.	
Polypropylene	23 April 1986	86/398/EEC	OJ L/230	18/8/1986	1–66	Price fixing, quotas and market sharing between producers of polypropylene.	81, 114, 120, 131, 133, 143, 348
Pre-insulated Pipe Cartel (District Heating Pipes)	21 October 1998	1999/60/EC	OJ L/24	30/1/1999	1–69	Price fixing, market sharing including bid-rigging and exclusionary practices among producers of district heating pipes.	104, 140, 173, 174, 210, 258, 297, 304, 311, 312, 337
Preserved mushrooms	8 January 1975	75/77/EEC	OJ L/29	3/2/1975	26–30	Price fixing and quotas by manufacturers of preserved mushrooms.	104

Publishers Association—Net Book Agreements	12 December 1988	89/44/EEC	OJ L/22	26/1/1989	1–35	Collective resale price maintenance by publishers.	104, 151, 320
PVC I	21 December 1988	89/190/EEC	OJ L/74	17/3/1989	1	Price fixing and market sharing by petrochemical producers.	
PVC II	27 July 1994	94/599/EC	OJ L/239	14/9/1994	14–34	Re-adoption; price fixing and market sharing by petrochemical producers.	81, 119, 148, 149, 197, 198, 206, 240–45, 248, 251–52, 281
Quantel International–Continuum/ Quantel SA	27 July 1992	92/427/EEC	OJ L/235	18/8/1992	9–18	Following the sale of a company, seller and purchaser agreed on a geographic market sharing that was unlimited in time and designed to protect the seller from the purchaser.	
Quinine	16 July 1969	69/240/CEE	OJ L/192	5/8/1969	5–22	Price fixing, quotas and markets sharing by quinine and quinidine producers.	81
Raw Tobacco Italy	20 October 2005	IP/05/1315				Purchase price fixing and market sharing by tobacco processors.	83, 104, 107, 151, 321
Raw Tobacco Spain	20 October 2004	IP/04/1256				Purchase price fixing and purchase quotas by tobacco processors.	83, 104, 151, 321

Reinforcing bars	17 December 2002	2006/894/EC	OJ L/353	13/12/2006	1–4	Price fixing and quotas by producers of concrete reinforcing bars (reversed on appeal).	151
Road bitumen NL	13 September 2006	IP/06/1179				Price fixing by suppliers and purchasers of road bitumen.	91, 151, 337
Rolled steel products	8 February 1980	80/257/ECSC	OJ L/62	7/3/1980	28–38	Price fixing by ex-stock sellers (ie dealers, some of them vertically integrated with producers) of rolled steel products.	104, 151
Rolled zinc products and zinc alloys (CRAM and Rheinzinc)	14 December 1982	82/866/EEC	OJ L/362	23/12/1982	40–52	Market sharing, bilateral sales and production agreements and information exchange by producers of zinc products.	77, 199, 207
Roofing felt	10 July 1986	86/399/EEC	OJ L/232	19/8/1986	15–33	Price fixing and quotas by producers of roofing felt.	104, 129, 151
Rubber chemicals	21 December 2005	IP/05/1656				Price fixing and information exchange by rubber chemical producers.	
SAS Maersk Air	18 July 2001	2001/716/EC	OJ L/265	5/10/2001	15–41	Market sharing between airlines.	279, 320, 337
Scottish Salmon Board	30 July 1992		OJ L/246	27/8/1992	37	Price fixing between Norwegian and Scottish salmon farmers.	104
Seamless steel tubes	8 December 1999	2003/382/EC	OJ L/140	6/6/2003	1–29	Market sharing by steel producers.	107, 190, 210–13, 225, 239, 248, 261, 281

Siemens/Fanuc	18 December 1985	85/618/EEC	OJ L/376	31/12/1985	29–38	Competing manufacturers of numerical control computers entrusted each other exclusively with distribution rights in connection with R&D agreement and this amounted to market sharing.	99
Soda-ash–Solvay/CFK I	19 December 1990	91/298/EEC	OJ L/152	15/6/1991	16–20	Market sharing between producers of soda-ash.	118, 207
Soda-ash–Solvay/CFK II	13 December 2000	2003/5/EC	OJ L/10	15/1/2003	1–9	Re-adoption.	
Soda-ash–Solvay/ ICI	19 December 1990	91/297/EEC	OJ L/152	15/6/1991	1–15	Market sharing by producers of soda-ash.	
Sodium Gluconate	2 October 2001	IP/01/1355				Price fixing, quotas and market sharing by producers of sodium gluconate.	146, 176, 254, 263, 283, 294
Sorbates	1 October 2003	2005/493/EC	OJ L/182	13/7/2005	20–25	Price fixing and quotas by producers of chemical preservatives.	
Specialty Graphite	17 December 2002	2006/460/EC	OJ L/180	4/7/2006	20–24	Price fixing, information exchange and market sharing by producers of specialty graphites.	92, 140

Stichting Sigaretten-industrie	15 July 1982	82/506/EEC	OJ L/232	6/8/1982	1–38	Price fixing, collective resale price maintenance and quotas agreed between manufacturers, importers, wholesalers and retailers of cigarettes.	91, 100, 101, 104, 107, 151
Stoves and Heaters	3 June 1975	75/358/EEC	OJ L/159	21/6/1975	22–28	Collective resale price maintenance and exclusionary scheme by manufacturers, importers, wholesalers and retailers of heating appliances.	91, 100, 104, 151
Sugar beet	19 December 1989	90/45/EEC	OJ L/31	2/2/1990	32–45	Collective industry agreements between beet growers and sugar refineries, including purchase price fixing and sharing of supply, and production quotas.	104, 151, 168, 320
Synthetic rubber	29 November 2006	IP/06/1647				Price fixing and market sharing by producers and traders of synthetic rubber.	91
Toltecs–Dorcet	15 December 1982	82/897/EEC	OJ L/379	31/12/1982	19–29	Market sharing under disguise of a trademark agreement.	91, 104, 151
Trans-Atlantic Agreement	19 October 1994	94/980/EC	OJ L/376	31/12/1994	1–56	Price fixing and capacity agreements by shipping lines.	
Trans-Atlantic Conference Agreement	16 September 1998	1999/243/EC	OJ L/95	9/4/1999	1–112	Price fixing by members of a shipping conference agreement.	79, 105, 254, 261, 337

VBBB/VBVB (Flemish books)	25 November 1981	82/123/EEC	OJ L/54	25/2/1982	36–50	Collective resale price maintenance agreed between trade associations organising publishers.	91, 100, 104, 153
Vegetable parchment	23 December 1977	78/252/EEC	OJ L/70	13/3/1978	54–68	Price fixing, market sharing and information exchange by manufacturers of vegetable parchment.	104
Vereeniging van Cementhan-delaren	16 December 1971	72/22/CEE	OJ L/13	17/1/1972	34–43	Horizontal price-fixing by cement producers.	100, 151
Videotape producers	20 November 2007	IP/07/1725				Price fixing and information exchange by videotape producers.	
Vimpoltu	13 July 1983	83/361/EEC	OJ L/200	23/7/1983	44–51	Price fixing and information exchange on tractors adopted by trade association for agricultural machinery.	100, 104, 151
Vitamins	21 November 2001	2003/2/EC	OJ L/6	10/1/2003	1–89	Price fixing and quotas by producers of vitamins.	202, 262, 301, 316
WANO Schwarzpulver	20 October 1978	78/921/EEC	OJ L/322	16/11/1978	26–35	Joint production and sales operation between manufacturers of blackpowder.	96
Welded steel mesh	2 August 1989	89/515/EEC	OJ L/260	6/9/1989	1–44	Price fixing, quotas and market sharing by producers of welded steel mesh.	98

White lead	12 December 1978	79/90/EEC	OJ L/21	30/1/1979	16–24	Price fixing, quotas and information exchange by manufacturers of white lead.	
Wirtschafts-vereinigung Stahl	26 November 1997	98/4/ECSC	OJ L/1	3/1/1998	10–21	Information exchange in the German steel industry.	87, 207
Wood pulp	19 December 1984	85/202/EEC	OJ L/85	26/3/1985	1–52	Price concertation by producers of wood pulp.	82, 117, 118, 129, 131, 132, 148, 149, 155, 200, 207
Zinc phosphate	11 December 2001	2003/437/EC	OJ L/153	20/6/2003	1–39	Price fixing and market sharing by producers and suppliers of zinc phosphate.	104, 146, 276, 278, 316
Zinc producer group	6 August 1984	84/405/EEC	OJ L/220	17/8/1984	27–45	Price fixing, quotas, market sharing and exclusionary practices by zinc producers.	

Other Commission Decisions

Advocate-General Opinions

US Case Law

Table of Legislation

International Agreements

1

The Method

COMPETITION LAW ENFORCEMENT and supervision in the EC used to be a primary responsibility of the European Commission. Following a paradigm shift introduced in May 2004, EC competition law is based on decentralised enforcement. Decentralisation is built on a combination of Community law and national law.

I. WHY LEGITIMACY IS NEEDED IN EC COMPETITION LAW

The functioning of the EU is dependent on loyal co-operation by national legislators, courts and authorities. If EC law is *produced* through legislation and jurisprudence, it must be *reproduced* time and time again by national authorities and courts in order to be operative. Unless they carry out the duties specified in EC law, the law will remain a paper product.

The tools available for EC institutions to make sure that EC law is supervised and enforced by national authorities and courts are blunt. Under Article 226 EC, the Commission can bring action against a Member State that fails to fulfil its obligations, but for pragmatic reasons this can be done only in high-profile cases of great importance. It is unworkable as a way to ensure that the day-to-day management of EC law is carried out by any given national authority or court in any of the 27 Member States. One could of course rely on the principle of supremacy of EC law, in the hope that a national judiciary will carry out its duties out of loyalty. Loyalty makes sense if we take the view that all Member States gain advantages through their membership of the EU, and should therefore readily accept the obligation to protect EU law. This is more or less a social contract view, where Member States comply because they have agreed to do so and because of the joint interest of all participants to ensure compliance. However, reliance entirely on the inter-State contractual aspect of EC law leads to a risk that we ignore the question of deeper legitimacy of the law: how the law is perceived by society.

Articles 81 and 82 EC have direct effect, as do general principles of EC law. In cases of conflicting laws, EC law prevails. A duty of loyal co-operation is stipulated in Article 10 of the Treaty. But hinging decentralisation on direct effect, supremacy and loyalty implies that courts and authorities alike in Member States will accept unquestioningly the law as it is. Furthermore, it will be unworkable unless the law is very clear and without complications, since otherwise even loyal co-operation will result in a given frequency of incorrect applications. If national legislators, authorities and courts are to regard EC law as sound and system-friendly, the law must present such features. This aspect can also be seen as pedagogic in the sense that the law must be possible to understand, at least for a qualified practitioner. Of crucial importance, furthermore, are the institutional arrangements. The best of intentions within the judiciary will not compensate for the absence or scarcity of enforcement capacity. Taking the reasoning one step further, acceptance of the legislation in the business community and in the legal community presupposes that enforcement of the legislation is perceived as efficient.

It follows that if decentralisation is to be successful, the law must be rational and we must have a system that generates average compliance. Competition law in the EC must be structured so as to convince national legislators, courts and authorities about its internal logic and inherent qualities. If the law is rationally persuasive then we can expect it to be applied (and correctly applied) by the enforcers and, as a second step, by the business community. Looking at enforcement, uneven supervision will be inefficient and generate its own legitimacy problems. This means that the institutional structure must be appropriate to ensure efficient administrative enforcement.

II. BASIC METHODOLOGY

A. The discussion of legitimacy in contemporary European law and its application to this work

Given that I explore decentralised enforcement of the Community's central competition law policy—in particular how Member States can be expected to respond to their new responsibilities—a perspective that allows for a systemic view is necessary. This is to be found in the contemporary scholarly discussion on legitimacy. I will take as a starting point the discussion in 1989 between Tuori and Habermas on rational collective will-formation,[1] via Habermas's work *Between Facts and Norms*, and then proceed to Scharpf's work in 1999 and some of the discussion it has generated.

Tuori suggests three dimensions of legitimacy. First there is *internal rationality of law*, problems or crisis tendencies in the internal systematic of the legal order. Secondly comes the relationship between the law and its subject of regulation, that is the *subject rationality of law*. Thirdly, there is the problem concerning either actual acceptance or acceptability of legal norms. This last sense Tuori refers to as *normative rationality of law*.

[1] Habermas, Jürgen, 'Towards a Communication-Concept of Rational Collective Will-Formation. A Thought Experiment' (1989) *Ratio Juris* (2) 144; Tuori, Kaarlo, 'Discourse Ethics and the Legitimacy of Law' (1989) *Ratio Juris* (2) 125.

Habermas recognises that we cannot be sure that we arrive at a correct result just because we follow prescribed procedures: 'Juridical and argumentative procedures presumably promote correct results, but they cannot guarantee that this is the case'.[2] And he continues to explain how this 'holds true even more for juridical procedures, which place modes of argumentation under the local, social and temporal constraints of the pressure for decision-making'.[3] Habermas still places reliance on court procedures which are 'tailored to the logic of a discourse of application'.[4] He concludes that

> Whether the laws presumed to be valid in the legal discourse are also valid in the more demanding terms of practical reason depends on the rationality of the legislative praxis . . .[5]

Moving forward to the democratic procedure, he evaluates the representative democracy necessary in complex societies and finds that it 'satisfies conditions for equal participation at least indirectly to the extent that it remains open and sensitive to a public opinion arising from the grass roots'.[6]

Now, if we accept Habermas's view, at least as a working hypothesis, we are left wondering how we should understand it in relation to EC law, where the democratic link is weaker than in a 'normal' democratic Western State. Admittedly, Tuori's and Habermas's discussion was not specifically on Community law, and therefore they did not address the problems related to the democratic and institutional structure of the EU. Scharpf, on the other hand, has provided a coherent theory on this particular subject.[7] Scharpf discards the idea of one singular anchoring point for legitimacy and builds a theory of anchoring legitimacy on several points at the same time. The traditional '*input-oriented legitimisation*', Scharpf says, often relies on the rhetoric of participation and of consensus.[8] This justification would be plausible for dealing with local problems where all persons affected, or their representatives, could meet and find solutions to which all can agree.[9] He then introduces the concept of majority voting and explains why, given that a majority can impose rules to the detriment of the minority, a democracy with majority voting must be based on a common feeling of trust that our fellow citizens will behave benevolently. Such reliance can be found in pre-existing commonalities of history, language, culture and ethnicity.[10] This commonality, precisely, is, however, missing in the EU, says Scharpf.[11]

2 Habermas, above n 1, at 150.
3 *Ibid.*
4 *Ibid.*
5 *Ibid*, at 151.
6 *Ibid*, at 153.
7 Scharpf, Fritz Wilhelm, *Governing in Europe: Effective and Democratic?* (Oxford, Oxford University Press, 1999).
8 *Ibid*, at 7.
9 *Ibid.*
10 *Ibid*, at 8.
11 *Ibid*, at 9.

Scharpf proceeds to develop his theory on *output legitimacy*, which allows for a much wider variety of legitimising mechanisms than reliance on democratic functions. Output legitimacy, or 'Government for the people',

> derives legitimacy from its capacity to solve problems requiring collective solutions because they could not be solved through individual actions, through market exchanges, or through voluntary cooperation in civil societies . . .[12]

Scharpf's view is that the legitimacy of politically salient European decisions depends on their effectiveness in achieving consensus goals.[13] But this poses specific problems when it comes to the substantive content of competition law. Scharpf points out how the combined doctrines of direct effect and supremacy have constitutionalised competition law and placed the conclusions of specialists 'beyond even the control of parliamentary super-majorities at the national level'.[14]

The Court of Justice of the European Communities ultimately interprets the substance of Articles 81 and 82 EC. Court adjudication is normally separated from the control of democratically elected representatives. This can be explained by reference to the need to ensure the independence of judges. By contrast, it can also be explained as a way to separate the judiciary from the legislator, to prevent courts from programming themselves, a classic separation of power doctrine.[15] We consider judge-made law legitimate on the presumption that the legislator would move to change dysfunctions.[16] However, a change of legislation in response to incorrect decisions adopted by the Commission and the Community courts is more or less unavailable as a remedy when it comes to the interpretation and application of Articles 81 and 82 EC. We cannot expect that these Treaty provisions would be changed even if the institutions responsible were to produce unrealistic judgments. Secondary legislation (Directives and Regulations) can be changed, of course, but it is doubtful how much could be accomplished this way. Furthermore, the Commission sets the agenda for secondary legislation adopted by Council as a result of its prerogative to propose legislation. We are consequently facing an instance where the legitimising power of (passive) acquiescence by the EC legislator is weak.[17]

The discussion about a democracy deficit in the EU law seems well established by now.[18] We will have to live with certain shortcomings when it comes to democratic legitimacy in the more traditional sense of Community court-made competition law. This raises the question whether we can find any other source of legitimacy. It has already been explained how much of the law consists of jurisprudence. The procedure before the Community courts is particularly interesting here. Gormley

[12] *Ibid*, at 11 ff.

[13] *Ibid*, at 21 ff.

[14] *Ibid*, at 54.

[15] Habermas, Jürgen, *Between Facts and Norms* (Cambridge, Polity Press, 1996), at 172.

[16] Scharpf, above n 7, at 15.

[17] See generally *ibid*, at 22.

[18] Dougan, Michael, *National Remedies before the Court of Justice—Issues of Harmonisation and Differentiation* (Oxford, Hart Publishing, 2004), at 197 ff.

suggests that legitimacy of the Court of Justice flows from the principle of every Member State being represented in the Court. Yet he sets out in detail how this notion has been transformed as a result of changes in the procedure which makes plenary sessions a rare exception rather than the default rule.[19] Indeed, it seems difficult to derive legitimacy of judge-made law solely from the fact that Member States appoint one judge each, especially given the dilution of powers resulting from the expansion of the Union to 27 Member States. There are, of course, other ways for Member States to exert influence. Soft law created by the Commission is nowadays subject to public consultation at the drafting stage. Decisions by the Commission are preceded by consultation with the Advisory Committee on Restrictive Practices and Dominant Positions, where the competition authorities of the Member States are represented.[20] Still, all consultation requires resources from those that take part, and intervention is arduous, especially for smaller Member States. In addition, legislative power has been delegated to the Commission to declare Article 81(1) of the Treaty inapplicable to certain categories of agreements, decisions by associations of undertakings or concerted practices.[21]

I agree with Scharpf that input-legitimacy would require some more specific political legitimisation by Member States in the gradual development of competition law principles than the original agreement when the Treaty was drafted or when new Member States acceded.[22] A contractarian approach is insufficient as a model of explaining legitimacy.[23] Above all, contractarian theories will not produce effective enforcement. Dismissing EC competition law as altogether illegitimate from a legal theoretical perspective would, however, be inexplicable in so far as we are discussing a bulk of law which has been in operation for a considerable time. Not least, it is largely consistent with other major competition law systems in the world. This brings me back to Tuori's view that we can search either for *empirical legitimacy*, that is acceptance of the law by society, or *normative legitimacy*, that is acceptability of the law. I agree with Tuori that empirical legitimacy is not conclusive, but I take the view that it will at least provide a good indication.

Habermas holds that if the law is to be legitimate, it must not only produce foreseeable results based in existing law. It must also be rationally grounded 'so that all

[19] Gormley, Laurence W, 'The Judicial Architecture of the European Union after Nice' in Arnull, Anthony, and Wincott, Daniel (eds), *Accountability and Legitimacy in the European Union* (Oxford, Oxford University Press, 2002), at 135.

[20] Article 14 of Council Regulation (EC) No 1/2003, [2003] OJ L/1/1.

[21] Regulation No 19/65/EEC of 2 March of the Council on application of Article 85(3) of the Treaty to certain categories of agreements and concerted practices, [1965] OJ 36/533, amended by Council Regulation (EC) No 1215/1999; Regulation (EEC) No 2821/71 of the Council of 20 December 1971 on application of Article 85(3) of the Treaty to categories of agreements, decisions and concerted practices, [1971] OJ L/285/46; Council Regulation (EEC) No 1534/91 of 31 May 1991 on the application of Article 85(3) of the Treaty to certain categories of agreements, decisions and concerted practices in the insurance sector, [1991] OJ L/143/1; Council Regulation (EEC) No 479/92 of 25 February 1992 on the application of Article 85(3) of the Treaty to certain categories of agreements, decisions and concerted practices between liner shipping companies (consortia), [1992] OJ L/55/3.

[22] Scharpf, above n 7, at 70–71.

[23] Arnull and Wincott (eds), above n 19, at 4.

participants can accept them as rational decisions'.[24] However, the arena in which Habermas pictures the discussion and participation to take place must be understood primarily as the democratic process in Western society. In EC competition law, in enforcement of Articles 81 and 82 EC in particular, there are two central arenas, neither of them the standard Western democratic process. The first is the procedure taking place before the Community courts. As explained, this procedure allows for participation of the addressees of the decision, of the Commission and of Member States. But the procedure is not open to all participants in society, or to the legal community. Judgments produced by the Community courts can, however, open up this deficit if drafted in a transparent way.

This leads us to the only arena open to the public in a wider sense, which is the dialogue between the Community courts and the legal community, taking place in the context of court litigation and in scholarly writing. National courts take part in this dialogue when they study Community law, apply it and make references pursuant to Article 234 EC. Decentralisation *invites* national courts and authorities to participate. Legitimacy of EC competition law must consequently be sought primarily in this dialogue. The ultimate benchmark for the judge-made interpretations of Articles 81 and 82 EC, and other legislation such as soft law, is their reception in the legal community.

Scharpf indeed recognises the need for critique by the expert community, but does not seem to hang legitimacy on the outcome of such critique but rather on the (democratically elected) legislator's capacity to amend undesirable outcomes in case law.[25] My view places greater emphasis on the control function exercised by scholars and by national courts. This is not because I consider this an ideal solution; rather, I am adjusting to a real-life phenomenon in EC competition law.

It is ultimately to Tuori's and Habermas's views that I turn, to determine from an outside perspective whether the decentralisation is rationally grounded. Habermas's theory allows for relying either on the legislative process *or* at least justification from pragmatic, ethical and moral points of view.[26] Admittedly it is doubtful whether it is possible to rely on Habermas to find that a law is legitimate if it is accepted (or can be expected to be accepted) by the legal community. While Tuori seems more inclined towards the idea that the law must be rationally persuasive, Habermas advocates that the forms of communication need be legally institutionalised themselves to assume legal shape.[27] Whether the thin layers of participation in the EU allow for this can be questioned. Nevertheless, a constitutional court has the ability to include the actors in the community in its decision-making practice by explicitly engaging in a dialogue *in the judgments*. It is thus submitted here that a constitutional court (such as the Court of Justice) is able to *increase* legitimacy through a transparent dialogue with the legal community, or with the community at large:

[24] Habermas, above n 15, at 198.
[25] Scharpf, above n 7, at 16.
[26] Habermas, above n 15, at 30.
[27] *Ibid*, at 455.

> By exposing their reasoning, judges and commentators are subjected to each others' critical analyses, which in turn can lead to better understanding for the future . . .[28]

The method chosen means that, in order to arrive at a conclusion about the legitimacy of decentralised enforcement, the law must be analysed in depth. The law is legitimate if it is rational; enforcement is legitimate only in so far as a rational law is enforced.[29]

However, an additional aspect must be added, which is the need to ensure that enforcement is not sporadic, temporary or inconsistent, a practice which will result in a perceived arbitrariness among the public. Credible enforcement will depend on consistency, effectiveness and efficiency. Habermas indeed points to the stabilising function of the State's enforcement of the law.[30] The law, and ultimately the development of the constitutional State, is otherwise challenged by 'legally uncontrolled social power that penetrates law *from the outside*'.[31]

> Modern societies are integrated not only socially through values, norms, and mutual understanding, but also systemically through markets and the administrative use of powers . . .[32]

The regulatory competence fails if the law is ineffective in its implementation or gives rise to disintegrating effects.[33] Habermas summarises:

> A legal norm has validity whenever the state guarantees two things at once: on the one hand, the state ensures average compliance, compelled by sanctions if necessary; on the other hand, it guarantees the institutional preconditions for the legitimate genesis of the norm itself, so that it is always at least possible to comply out of respect for the law.[34]

B. Comparative legal studies: US antitrust law

There is a conflict or contradiction in the relation between EC competition law and US antitrust law, in so far as it would seem natural for EC law to source legitimacy from the more mature US system; however, that seldom seems to happen. Competition law in the EC has developed in a way very similar to US antitrust law, although it must be said that US law is often several decades ahead. There are differences in the approach adopted by the US and Community courts respectively. Comparative studies of EC law and US antitrust law form a normal way of approaching difficult competition law issues.[35] References to US antitrust law and

[28] Areeda, Phillip E, Hovenkamp, Herbert et al, *Antitrust Law—An Analysis of Antitrust Principles and Their Application*, 2nd edn (New York, Aspen Publishers, Wolters Kluwer Law and Business, 2003), Vol VII, § 1500, at 338.

[29] Habermas, above n 15, at 27–29.

[30] *Ibid*, at 37.

[31] *Ibid*, at 39.

[32] *Ibid.*

[33] *Ibid*, at 386.

[34] *Ibid*, at 448.

[35] Elhauge, Einer, and Geradin, Damien, *Global Competition Law and Economics* (Oxford, Hart Publishing, 2007).

legal doctrine are sometimes made by the Advocates-General of the Community courts in their Opinions.[36] The problems encountered on each side of the Atlantic are often identical: burden of proof; standard of proof; the impact of State interference; and how to address information exchanges between competitors. Possible problems of methodology are not so much inherent in the comparisons as such.

The purpose of studying US antitrust law and using it (here) is to see whether US law could be used to a greater extent as a source of legitimacy for EC competition law.

[36] A-G Fennelly's Opinion in Joined Cases C-395/96 P and C-396/96 P *Compagnie Maritime Belge* [2000] ECR I-1365 at fn 92; A-G Poiares Maduro's Opinion in Case C-109/03 *KPN Telecom* [2004] ECR I-11273 at fn 16; A-G Jacob's Opinion in Case C-53/03 *Syfait and Others v GlaxoSmithKline* [2005] ECR I-4609 at fn 40.

2

The Role of Legitimacy in Decentralisation

I. EXPLORING LEGITIMACY

A. Modernisation sought to remedy a legitimacy deficit

A STRUCTURAL LEGITIMACY DEFICIT was identified in the discussion preceding decentralisation of EC competition law. The Commission was overburdened with notifications and had painted itself into a corner by focusing on vertical restraints rather than cartels. A radical administrative shift was required: 'Freed from the burden of having to process notifications, the Commission for its part could concentrate on taking action against the most serious infringements'.[1] Furthermore, an undercurrent in the preparatory works was the need to involve the (until then) rather disengaged Member States in EC competition law supervision and enforcement.

One might ask how this lack of interest was created. Possible explanations lie in the way in which Member State competition authorities were not considered important enough, and how the Commission 'sought to locate knowledge . . . in Brussels, creating few incentives for Member State decision makers to acquire such knowledge'.[2] In 1999, only eight out of 15 Member States had empowered their national competition authorities to apply Community law.[3] The passive attitude of Member States to EC competition law was not directly commented upon in the legislative process, although the Commission said at one point that 'the decision-making bodies should be brought closer to the individual so as to disseminate more widely a common competition culture and to foster the acceptance of Community rules'.[4] The Council actually held that increased involvement of national competition authorities and courts was the cornerstone of the proposal.[5]

[1] White Paper, *Modernisation of the rules implementing Articles 85 and 86 of the EC Treaty* [1999] OJ C/132/1, ch II, at 72 in fine.

[2] Gerber, David J, *Law and Competition in Twentieth Century Europe: Protecting Prometheus* (Oxford, Oxford University Press, 1998), at xiv.

[3] White Paper, above n 1, ch II, at 94.

[4] IP/00/1064.

[5] Discussions at Council 14/5/2001–15/5/2001, Session 2349, C701/181.

Attempts at remedying the problem of insufficient application of the EC competition rules at national level had been made previously through the older Commission Notices on co-operation with national courts and authorities.[6] The second of those Notices set out the Commission's conviction that an enhanced role of national competition authorities would boost the effectiveness of Articles 81 and 82 of the Treaty, and strengthen the application of Community competition rules. But application of Articles 81 and 82 EC in Member States remained low. For instance, the Green Paper on antitrust damages revealed a remarkably low frequency of private litigation based on EC competition law.[7] In spite of the direct effect of Articles 81(1) and 82 EC, national judiciaries continued to rely on national law. This evidences an insufficient legitimacy of EC competition law, in a deeper sense, prior to modernisation. The centralised enforcement system caused Member State judiciaries to experience insignificant attachment to EC competition law. But this is not to say that competition was unprotected. Member States instead relied on national competition laws of varying content.

Later in this book it will be explained that the Commission, as well as the European Parliament and the Council, was working from the assumption that substantive EC competition law was legitimate, and that it was only enforcement that was lacking. It will also be clear that such a view can be questioned—shortcomings in substantive law were at least a contributing factor to the enforcement deficit.

B. Uniformity as a cornerstone of Regulation 1

1. The travaux préparatoires

Uniformity is in essence a matter of the rule of law, in contrast to discretionary exercise of justice and *ad hoc* judgments.[8] But in the context of Community law, the concept of uniformity embodies yet another aspect, because it tells us something about of the choice of law. It should be kept in mind that in the absence of Community law, we could assume the existence of national laws instead. The rule of law would still prevail, but it would be through a variety of national laws rather than one Community law. Uniformity is very strongly connected to the goal of integration between Member States.

Uniform interpretation and application is considered to be of the essence in Community law. This has been recognised repeatedly by the Court of Justice, *inter*

[6] Commission Notice on co-operation between national courts and the Commission in applying Articles 85 and 86 of the EEC Treaty [1993] OJ C/39/6; Commission Notice on co-operation between national competition authorities and the Commission in handling cases falling within the scope of Articles 85 or 86 of the EC Treaty [1997] OJ C/313/3.

[7] COM (2005) 672 Green Paper, *Damages actions for breach of the EC antitrust rules*, 19/12/2005.

[8] On the rule of law see, especially, Arnull, Anthony, 'The Rule of Law in the European Union' in Arnull, Anthony, and Wincott, Daniel (eds), *Accountability and Legitimacy in the European Union* (Oxford, Oxford University Press, 2002), at 240.

alia in cases on Article 234 EC.[9] As regards uniform application of competition law, the Court held in *Walt Wilhelm* that application of national law must not prejudice the uniform application of Community law on cartels.[10] The Court based this finding on the objective of respect for the ultimate general aim of the Treaty and the character of its rules on competition. A reinforcement of this case law was made in *Simmenthal*, where the Court held that direct applicability means that rules of Community law must be applied fully and uniformly in all the Member States.[11] Notably, in *Eco Swiss*, the Court underlined the manifest interest of the Community legal order that, in order to forestall differences of interpretation, every Community provision should be given a uniform interpretation, irrespective of the circumstances in which it is to be applied.[12]

The move from a centralised to a decentralised system made uniformity a focal point in the process of modernising the competition rules. An account of the arguments made during the legislative process is given in the following paragraphs. Since uniformity is a principle of Community law, the arguments made in the preparatory works really do not add anything, whether or not one considers *travaux préparatoires* as a source of interpretation. The fact that Community institutions, as well as several qualified observers, have identified uniformity as a key issue does, however, confirm the importance of uniformity as an essential theme for the purpose of EC competition law research.

In the Commission 1999 White Paper on modernisation, uniform application of law and policy development throughout the EU was emphasised as one of the objectives to be met.[13] It was considered important that decentralisation should not compromise uniform interpretation of Community law, or result in contradictory decisions by national authorities in one and the same case.[14] The Commission was endeavouring to create a structure that would ensure consistency of application by the Commission, national competition authorities and courts.[15] The idea presented in the 1999 White Paper, later realised in Regulation 1, was to let the Commission continue to have a special role in the determination of Community competition policy and legislation.[16] The Commission would retain its monopoly to propose legislation and soft law, and would 'act whenever necessary in order to ensure consistency and uniformity in the application of the competition rules'.[17] Reference was also made to the Treaty mechanisms in Articles 230 and 234. Under Article 230, the Commission can bring Member States to the Court of Justice for infringements of Community law. Article 234 requires

[9] Case 166/73 *Rheinmühlen-Düsseldorf* [1974] ECR 33, at para 2; Case C-221/88 *Busseni* [1990] ECR I-495, at paras 13–16.

[10] Case 14/68 *Walt Wilhelm* [1969] ECR 1, at paras 4–6.

[11] Case 106/77 *Simmenthal* [1978] ECR 629, at para 14.

[12] Case C-126/97 *Eco Swiss China Time Ltd* [1999] ECR I-3055, at para 40.

[13] White Paper, above n 1, at 11.

[14] *Ibid*, at 47.

[15] *Ibid*, at 51.

[16] *Ibid*, at 83.

[17] *Ibid*, at 84.

national courts of last instance to refer questions of interpretation of Community law to the Court of Justice for preliminary rulings. However, these procedures were considered insufficient for the day-to-day co-operation between competition authorities. Information and co-operation mechanisms were proposed to fill the perceived lacunae.[18]

The White Paper was well received during the legislative procedure, although some fears were expressed. In particular, the Economic and Social Committee was concerned about consistent implementation:

> . . . [W]ithout appropriate measures, there is little or no chance that the national courts will react in basically the same way to the reform. The danger is that it will prove impossible to implement the reform in a uniform manner throughout the Community, and that the unity of the system will thus be jeopardised.
>
> . . . The varying situations in individual countries may also lead to inconsistencies and differences in interpretation, which the more mobile companies (and those located in the countries with the most favourable conditions) could exploit to the detriment of others and of the coherence of the entire system.
>
> . . . In view of the nature of the Commission proposal, safeguarding the unity and coherence of the system will be the area carrying the greatest risks.
>
> . . . The danger of fragmentation of the single market and the 'renationalisation' of competition law are particular sources of concern.[19]

Unconvinced by the Commission's structural proposals to remedy the uniformity problem, the Economic and Social Committee recommended adoption of 'robust preparatory and accompanying measures'.[20] A right to appeal national judgments to a supranational court of law with full powers of examination was suggested as a remedy against conflicting or inconsistent decisions or errors of judgement.[21]

The European Parliament welcomed the Commission's proposal as a sound, but still insufficient, basis for discussion of reforms.[22] It stressed that modernisation must not impair legal certainty or the consistent application of competition rules,[23] and underlined that the reform should not lead to a renationalisation of competition policy and a calling into question of the primacy of Community law.[24] It called for a concentration on specialised courts in all the Member States, in the interest of consistent application of the law in cartel proceedings.[25]

[18] *Ibid*, at 104.

[19] Opinion of the Economic and Social Committee on the 'White Paper on modernisation of the rules implementing Articles 81 and 82 of the EC Treaty—Commission programme No 99/027' [2000] OJ C/51/55, at paras 2.3.2.1, 2.3.2.2, 2.3.2.3, 2.3.5.1 and 2.3.5.6.

[20] *Ibid*, at para 2.3.5.6.

[21] *Ibid*, at para 2.3.5.11.

[22] European Parliament Resolution on the Commission White Paper on modernisation of the rules implementing Articles 81 and 82 of the EC Treaty (COM (1999) 101—C5-0105-1999–1999/2108(COS)), [2000] OJ C/304/66, at 2.

[23] *Ibid*, at 6.

[24] *Ibid*, at 16.

[25] *Ibid*, at 18.

In its proposal for a Council Regulation, the Commission recognised the importance of consistency as put forward by the European Parliament and the Economic and Social Committee. Industry associations and lawyers had expressed similar concerns during the consultation process.[26] Here, the Commission emphasised Articles 11, 15 and 16 of the draft regulation as measures to address the danger of inconsistent application effectively.[27] Article 11 is the formal basis for establishing the European Network of competition authorities. The Commission envisaged close co-operation with national authorities, as well as certain formal mechanisms.[28] Article 15 concerns co-operation between the Commission and national courts, including a right for the Commission to submit written observations to national courts on its own initiative when coherent application of Article 81 or Article 82 so requires. Under Article 16 of Regulation 1, national courts cannot take decisions running counter to a decision adopted by the Commission in an individual case. They must also avoid giving decisions which would conflict with a decision contemplated by the Commission. The Commission undertook to provide further guidelines to promote consistency.[29]

These measures were apparently not sufficient for the Economic and Social Committee, which repeated its concerns about consistency. The Committee was worried about the lack of harmonisation of competition procedures, and the absence of a single appeal authority.[30] The European Parliament questioned whether the duty of national competition authorities to provide the Commission with information before proceedings begin would be sufficient to prevent divergent and inconsistent application of the rules.[31]

2. *What is uniformity?*

Calls for consistent interpretation and application of EC competition law soon came to dominate the academic debate on the modernisation.[32] Lenaerts and Gerard recognise the concerns relating to the competence of national courts and their acquaintance with the concepts underlying the application of competition law provisions. They suggest that the key is to provide national judges with

[26] COM(2000) 582 Final, Explanatory Memorandum, at 3.

[27] *Ibid*, at 22–23.

[28] *Ibid*, at 9.

[29] *Ibid*, at 8.

[30] Opinion of the Economic and Social Committee on the 'Proposal for a Council Regulation on the implementation of the rules on competition laid down in Articles 81 and 82 of the EC Treaty—Commission programme No 99/027 ' [2001] OJ C/155/73.

[31] Report on the proposal for a Council regulation, Session document of the European Parliament 21 June 2001, A5-0229-2001, at 25.

[32] Venit, James S, 'Brave New World: The Modernization and Decentralization of Enforcement under Articles 81 and 82 of the EC Treaty' (2003) 40 *CML Rev* 545; Coyet, Johan, Fellenius-Omnell, Caroline, and Landström, Charlotte, 'Modernizing EC Competition Law: Will a System of Parallel Application of EC and National Competition Laws Ensure Convergence' in Hawk (ed), *International Antitrust Law & Policy: Fordham Corporate Law* (New York, Juris Publishing, 2002).

sufficient guidance, which is primarily a task for the Commission.[33] Gilliams is not optimistic, and concludes that decentralisation is

> likely to result—certainly in an initial period—in less efficient enforcement by national courts and competition authorities, a significant degree of inconsistency in the application of Community competition law, and increased costs for business . . .[34]

Gerber and Cassinis analyse the structural prerequisites for consistency and find that '[t]he effectiveness of this system depends on the interactions of the many institutions now fully competent to apply Community competition rules'. They highlight the soft factors which will determine the success of the system:

> a delicate balancing of forces among the interacting institutions, but . . . also . . . the determination of those within those institutions to co-operate with each other and earn each other's trust . . .[35]

The academic debate on the prospects of coherent application of competition rules mirrors concerns expressed by scholars about a general enforcement deficit in Community law.[36] Rather than being a unique challenge for competition law supervision and enforcement, achieving consistent application is at the core of Community law in general.

It appears that the legal community, as well as the business community, will be happy with the modernisation, provided it leads to uniform results in the Member States. So what precisely do we mean when we refer to 'uniformity'? Anyone who has studied law would answer that there is uniformity when the same set of facts is judged in the same way by different courts or authorities. Those who apply the law must share the same view on what the law means and how to apply it to a given combination of circumstances.[37] This is another way of referring to the rule of law.

Perhaps one should not expect identical assessments but at least a very high level of similarity. In the words of Mario Monti: 'Consistent application requires that the rules are sufficiently clear and that the approaches followed in their application are sufficiently similar'.[38] Notably, Wahl suggested decentralisation already in 1994, and distinguished in this context between formal uniformity and functional uniformity. Formal uniformity would require identical legal assessments, while

[33] Lenaerts, Koen, and Gerard, Damien, 'Decentralisation of EC Competition Law Enforcement: Judges in the Frontline' (2004) 27(3) *World Competition* 313, at 329.

[34] Gilliams, Hans M, 'Modernisation: From Policy to Practice' (2003) 28(4) *EL Rev* 451, at 473.

[35] Gerber, David J, and Cassinis, Paolo, 'The Modernisation of European Community Competition Law: Achieving Consistency in Enforcement: Part 2' (2006) 27(2) *ECLR* 51, at 57.

[36] On the latter debate, see Dougan, Michael, *National Remedies before the Court of Justice—Issues of Harmonisation and Differentiation* (Oxford, Hart Publishing, 2004), at 97.

[37] Gerber and Cassinis distinguish between 'systemic consistency', by which they mean consistency in outcomes among different cases within the system, and 'single-case consistency', which relates to the treatment of a single set of facts by multiple institutions: Gerber, David J, and Cassinis, Paolo, 'The Modernisation of European Community Competition Law: Achieving Consistency in Enforcement: Part 1' (2006) 27(1) ECLR 10, at 14.

[38] Monti, Mario, 'The Modernisation of EC Antitrust Policy, opening speech', in Ehlermann, Claus Dieter, and Atanasiu, Isabella, *European Competition Law Annual 2000: The Modernisation of EC Antitrust Policy* (Oxford, Hart Publishing, 2001), at 7.

functional uniformity means that the interest is focused on supervision and enforcement of the large bulk of competition restrictions. One might then have to accept that all competition restrictions are not treated identically, provided there is a common minimum standard. Wahl explains how the requirement of formal uniformity cannot be neglected, while at the same time the need for functional uniformity cannot be ignored, hence a decentralisation must observe these two somewhat conflicting interests.[39] Indeed, if only a few competition restrictions are rigorously pursued and sanctioned while other equally serious infringements remain untouched for mere enforcement reasons, the system would fail to produce uniform results in terms of enforcement.

But we could also apply a legitimacy perspective on uniformity—going back to Habermas's insistence that legitimacy requires (in addition to a legitimate genesis of the law) that the State can ensure average rules compliance. Rule compliance is not just a matter of using administrative force to bring companies and natural persons into line with the law. A more basic requirement, which must necessarily come first, is that courts and authorities understand and apply the law in the same way. Otherwise we will end up with enforcement of a widely varying set of rules, depending on how the individual judge or official understands the law. Furthermore, conformity can be expected to reduce costs by reducing the number of appeals and legislative action.[40]

The idea that competition law and its enforcement must be *consistent* (the level playing field argument) should generally be viewed with some scepticism; inconsistent conditions for competition can result from any regulatory system that is not coherent in the EU, whether it is environmental law, health and sanitary requirements or competition law. From an economic perspective the level playing field argument is not viable because partial harmonisation will only shift competition to non-harmonised parts, and it will not in any event compensate for non-legal factors such as access to raw material or climate conditions.[41] Unless we want to harmonise every aspect of all regulatory systems in the Union, we must accept that there will exist divergences which can benefit some undertakings and put others at a disadvantage. Still, consistency can be desirable for undertakings because it can reduce their costs for operation on transnational markets. Gerber points at the misallocation of resources that can result from significant differences and uncertainties.[42] This is a valid point. If interpretation and enforcement of competition law differ between Member States, companies operating in the EU will have to spend money on advice to check how Articles 81 and 82 EC are understood and applied in each Member State, and then adapt their business strategies

[39] Wahl, Nils, *Konkurrensförhållanden* (Stockholm, Juristförlaget, 1994), at 514.

[40] Wahlgren, Peter, *Lagstiftning—Problem, teknik, möjligheter* (Uppsala, Norstedts, 2008), at 42.

[41] Van den Bergh, Roger J, and Camesasca, Peter D, *European Competition Law and Economics: A Comparative Perspective*, 2nd edn (London, Thomson Sweet & Maxwell, 2006), at 432.

[42] Gerber, David J, 'Consistent Application of Competition Laws Across System Border: Rethinking the Issues' in Andersson (ed), *Parallel and Conflicting Enforcement of Law* (Stockholm, Norstedts, 2005), at 171–72.

accordingly; or they will have to ignore such differences and thus expose themselves to risks of regulatory incompliance. In the alternative they can seek a lowest denominator and adjust their business behaviour to the toughest standards, thus bearing the costs associated with over-deterrence. A uniformity requirement shifts this cost to the governments—they will have to allocate resources to ensure that their authorities and courts adhere to Community law standards. Looking at the legal system, uniformity through a sophisticated set of rules can be expected to decrease the number of legal proceedings which would arise in a system characterised by arbitrary outcomes.[43] On balance, this speaks in favour of uniformity. In all likelihood, the cost for a number of authorities and courts to keep themselves informed about competition law is by far lower than the cost for cross-border business operators to keep themselves informed about regulatory varieties in 27 Member States.

Uniformity hence emerges as stemming from the integration objective. If we accept, as a work hypothesis, that competition law enhances welfare, then uniformity should have welfare effects too, although this effect is more indirect and indeed difficult to verify with reference to economic theory. The most valid economic argument is that uniformity can be expected to reduce costs.

3. *Defining the relation between EC law and national law*

The first step in an analysis of uniformity is to define the precise content of EC law, if that is at all possible. It is often taken for granted in the debate that the Community courts have long since achieved consistent and uniform application, while some detailed analysis will (as will be seen) contradict such a view.

Furthermore, how does one define the border between national law and Community law in the field of competition law enforcement? The answer is not entirely straightforward. As described, modernised public competition law enforcement is based on the application of Community competition law, through national procedure. In a perfect world, there would be a symbiotic interplay between national procedure and EC law, to achieve optimal enforcement. In the real world, there will be anything from outright conflicts of law, when national procedure will have to be set aside as a result of the precedence of Community law,[44] to situations when national law will affect the outcome of a competition proceeding, although without any actual conflict of laws. As a result of the decentralisation, it is necessary to define the actual scope of application of EC competition law.[45]

[43] Wahlgren, above n 40, at 42.

[44] Case 14/68 *Walt Wilhelm* [1969] ECR 1, at para 6.

[45] Lenaerts and Gerard, above n 33, at 316 in fine: 'to define precisely the domains of application of, respectively, national and EC competition laws'.

C. Effectiveness as the other cornerstone of Regulation 1

The legal basis for the requirement of effective enforcement of Community law is often Article 10 of the Treaty (the principle of loyal co-operation), but effectiveness also constitutes a general principle of EC law.[46]

The situation prevailing before the modernisation led to calls for increased participation of national authorities and courts as a way to achieve the full effect of EC competition law.[47] References to effectiveness were made in the preparatory works of the modernisation regulation,[48] but at the time it did not appear as a central argument underpinning the reform. In choosing between the various options for reform, the Commission explained that '[t]he need to ensure a balance between effectiveness of policy and simplification of control must therefore be the guiding principle'.[49] Decentralisation would allow Community law to 'be implemented by the body that was able to do so most effectively'.[50] The reform would serve the purpose of 'continuing to safeguard competition effectively'.[51] More intelligible, effective supervision was connected to the possibility of detecting the most serious infringements.[52] Brief references to effectiveness were made concerning the role of national courts[53] and the primacy of Community law.[54] Notably, effectiveness was the leading argument for strengthening the Commission's powers of inspection.[55] Similarly, the Commission argued that removal of immunity from fines for notified practices would render the prohibition in Article 81 EC more effective since the dissuasive effect would be increased.[56]

In the final product, effectiveness was upgraded.[57] The objective of Regulation 1 is to allow Community competition rules to be applied effectively.[58] This is repeated in the preamble to the Regulation, where effective enforcement or application is referred to as a reason for regulating burden of proof,[59] extending the

[46] Tridimas, Takis, *The General Principles of EU Law*, 2nd edn (Oxford, Oxford University Press, 2006), at 418; Dougan, above n 36, at 53.

[47] See especially Wahl, above n 39, at 67, 512 ff.

[48] White Paper, above n 1.

[49] *Ibid*, ch II, at 41 in fine.

[50] *Ibid*, at 47.

[51] *Ibid*, at 71.

[52] *Ibid*, at 77.

[53] *Ibid*, at 99.

[54] *Ibid*, at 101.

[55] *Ibid*, ch III, at 109–16.

[56] *Ibid*, at 123.

[57] Wesseling observes that 'The motivation for the Commission's "modernisation plans" has shifted from pure administrative concerns (disposing of excessive workload), via constitutional objectives (bringing enforcement of EC antitrust law in line with the subsidiarity principle) to, now, enhancing the protection of competition (increasing effectiveness)': Wesseling, Rein, 'The Draft-regulation Modernising the Competition Rules: The Commission is Married to One Idea' (2001) 26(4) *EL Rev* 357.

[58] Council Regulation (EC) No 1/2003 [2003] OJ L/1/1(hereinafter 'Regulation 1'), the preamble, at 1 and 34.

[59] *Ibid*, preamble, at 5.

powers of national authorities,[60] obliging national authorities and courts to apply Articles 81 and 82,[61] establishing a network of competition authorities,[62] extending the Commission's fact-finding powers[63] and enabling national authorities to assist one another with fact-finding measures.[64] Furthermore, Article 35 of Regulation 1 obliges Member States to designate the competition authorities responsible for the application of Articles 81 and 82 EC in such a way that the provisions of the Regulation are complied with effectively.

There are two reasons for the legislator's seemingly unconditional support for effectiveness. First, Article 83(2)(b) of the Treaty forms part of the legal basis for Regulation 1. Accordingly, the Council can adopt Regulations or Directives which will be designed in particular to lay down detailed rules for the application of Article 81(3), taking into account the need to ensure *effective supervision*, on the one hand, and to simplify administration to the greatest possible extent on the other. Secondly, effectiveness is a principle of Community law, according to well-established case law.[65]

Unlike uniformity, the rudiments of which every lawyer can understand more or less intuitively, effectiveness is a less straightforward concept. Dougan expands on the way in which this concept has undergone several different manifestations. Depending on whether the case concerns individual rights enforced against a Member State, rights enforced against other private parties, protection of the general interest, or application of the Article 234 preliminary reference procedure, there are diverging interpretations of the principle of effectiveness.[66] Moving from Dougan's meta analysis to a more specific analysis of Regulation 1, it even seems unlikely that effectiveness means the same thing when referred to in various parts of the Regulation. Effectiveness of fines must be interpreted in relation to the case law on sanctions as developed by the Community courts. When effectiveness is used as the legal basis for regulating burden of proof and fact-finding in Regulation 1, it must be understood in the light of the abundant case law on rights of the defence. Effectiveness is one thing when investigations are carried out by the Commission,[67] possibly another when carried out by a national authority. In the latter situation, effectiveness must be interpreted with reference to the principles of national procedural and institutional autonomy.[68] In the context of co-operation between the Commission and national authorities in the European

[60] Preamble, at 6.
[61] Preamble, at 8.
[62] Preamble, at 15.
[63] Preamble at 25 and 26.
[64] Preamble at 28.
[65] Set out comprehensively in Lenaerts, Koen, Arts, Dick, Maselis, Ignace, and Bray, Robert (eds), *Procedural Law of the European Union*, 2nd edn (London, Sweet & Maxwell, 2006), ch 3.
[66] Dougan, above n 36, at 26–52.
[67] Joined Cases C-204/00 P, C-205/00 P, C-211/00 P, C-213/00 P, C-217/00 P and C-219/00 P *Aalborg Portland and others v Commission* [2004] ECR I-123, at para 61.
[68] Accetto, Matej, and Zleptnig, Stefan, 'The Principle of Effectiveness: Rethinking Its Role in Community Law' [2005] *European Public Law* 375, at 394.

Competition Network (ECN), the meaning of effectiveness has yet to be defined, since this constitutes a novel form of institutional governance.[69]

Wahl discusses different ways of measuring effectiveness and opts for 'the possibility that the obligation to apply Community law weeds out rulings according to national law that would run counter to Community law'.[70] This view connects effectiveness to uniformity, and thus, indirectly, to integration. Linda Senden reasons along the same line, and finds that effectiveness concerns 'the extent to which society can be moulded through law, or in other words the realisation of the internal market and the Community objectives through the adoption of legislation'.[71]

Reasoning on effectiveness can be expected to shape the development of the Court's case law on cartels. It follows that systematic appraisals of the meaning of effectiveness for the purpose of cartel law enforcement will be made throughout this study. There is no manual available for determining what effective enforcement of EC law is. The final word on numerous points has yet to be made by the Court of Justice.

D. Efficiency

Efficiency is a matter of enforcement success, where 'any economic approach to antitrust must employ a kind of cost–benefit analysis of how limited enforcement dollars are to be spent'.[72]

Enforcement efficiency was addressed sporadically in the documents which paved the way for the modernisation. Some statements were made, for instance in the White Paper: 'Our Community requires a more efficient and simpler system of control'.[73] Efficiency was related to enlargement, and the Commission noted how

> In a European Union with more than 20 Member States, the rules for implementing Articles 85 and 86 must be modernised if competition policy is to continue to operate efficiently . . .[74]

When presenting the proposal for a new regulation, the Commission explained that there would be increased enforcement through more enforcers (the Member States), by allowing the Commission to focus on the most serious infringements and by increasing the Commission's powers of investigation.[75] The ambiguity is

[69] The point on institutional governance is made in the European Parliament Report, 21 June 2001, A5-0229/2001, at 39.

[70] Wahl, Nils, 'To What Extent Has the Modernisation Reform Been Successful at the National Level?', *Europarättslig Tidskrift* No 3, 2006, 490, at 494.

[71] Senden, Linda, *Soft Law in European Community Law* (Oxford, Hart Publishing, 2004), at 93, footnote omitted.

[72] Areeda, Phillip E and Hovenkamp, Herbert, *Antitrust Law—An Analysis of Antitrust Principles and Their Application*, 3rd edn (New York Aspen Publishers, Wolters Kluwer Law and Business), Vol I, § 112, at 134.

[73] White Paper, above n 1, Executive summary, at 10 in fine.

[74] *Ibid*, Introduction, at 7 in fine.

[75] COM(2000) 582 Final, Explanatory Memorandum, at 5–7.

amply illustrated by the Commission Notice on co-operation within the Network of Competition Authorities,[76] where the words 'efficient' and 'effective' are used repeatedly and interchangeably, without any apparent effort to explain what it means for the purpose of competition law enforcement. Some of the confusion can be resolved if one understands that effectiveness relates to more than one goal and must be distinguished from efficiency, which is a matter of enforcement success. In fact, most of the statements made in the preparatory works of Regulation 1 relate to enforcement success in a wider sense and not to the principle of effectiveness as developed in case law.

If the analysis is to be meaningful it must be based on an idea of what efficiency is in this context. Yeung distinguishes between effectiveness and efficiency. Effectiveness concerns the extent to which a regulatory scheme is successful in achieving its collective goal or goals, while efficiency refers to the relationship between resources and outcomes.[77] Temple Lang makes a similar distinction: 'Effectiveness means the extent to which the law achieves the objectives which it can fairly be expected to have,' including in this notion 'an assessment of the efficiency of each national competition authority'.[78] He considers that the ease with which victims get redress is the result of the efficiency of court or competition authority procedures, while the ease with which a competition authority proves and stops practices when it suspects them is the result of the size, efficiency, and legal powers and economic expertise of the competition authority.[79] According to Posner,

> effective enforcement of a body of law requires effective sanctions for violators and an institutional structure that enables violations to be detected with reasonable accuracy and promptitude and at reasonable costs . . .[80]

The question of what constitutes efficient competition law supervision will be addressed further in this chapter and in chapter eight.

E. Action against hard-core infringements as a top priority

Regulation 1 came into force on 1 May 2004.[81] The major novelty was to make the provision on exemption in Article 81(3) EC directly applicable.[82] Under Article

[76] Commission Notice on co-operation within the Network of Competition Authorities [2004] OJ C/101/43.

[77] Yeung, Karen, *Securing Compliance—A Principled Approach* (Oxford, Hart Publishing, 2004), at 30.

[78] Temple Lang, John, 'General Report on the Application of Community Competition Law on Enterprises by National Courts and National Authorities', FIDE Congress 1998, available at http://ec.europa.eu/comm/competition/speeches/text/sp1998_027_en.html., at 48.

[79] *Ibid.*

[80] Posner, Richard A, *Antitrust Law*, 2nd edn (Chicago, University of Chicago Press, 2001), at 266.

[81] Art 45 of Regulation 1.

[82] Art 1.2 of Regulation 1 provides: 'Agreements, decisions and concerted practices caught by Article 81(1) of the Treaty which satisfy the conditions of Article 81(3) of the Treaty shall not be prohibited, no prior decision to that effect being required.'

81(3) EC, the prohibition in Article 81(1) can be declared inapplicable for agreements, decisions and concerted practices the pro-competitive effects of which outweigh their negative effects, as defined in the conditions of that paragraph. Before the enactment of Regulation 1, only the Commission had the power to grant such exemptions.

The basic prohibition against competition restrictions (including cartels) in Article 81(1) EC, however, was directly applicable prior to Regulation 1.[83] Member State courts could apply Article 81(1) EC as from the entry into force of the Treaty, or from any later date of accession of each Member State. So could national authorities, provided their national law has conferred the necessary powers on them.[84] As for the division of power between the Commission and national authorities in individual cases, Article 9(3) of Regulation 17 allowed Member State authorities to apply Article 81(1) EC as long as the Commission had not initiated a procedure.[85] The possibility for an undertaking to halt national proceedings by filing a notification with the Commission, often referred to as the major obstacle against national application,[86] was largely theoretical for hard-core infringements. Cartels and hard-core vertical restrictions seldom, if ever, qualify for exemption under Article 81(3), and participants would be extremely reluctant to notify their practices.[87] Thus, one may ask what the modernisation has actually brought about in terms of novelty in the control of hard-core infringements.

An analysis of Regulation 1 and its preparatory works shows that this piece of legislation in fact affects enforcement fundamentally, by introducing certain new elements of law and policy, and these will be described in the following subsections.

1. *A choice of law provision*

Pursuant to Article 3 of Regulation 1, Member States' competition authorities and courts shall apply Article 81 of the Treaty to agreements, decisions by associations of undertakings or concerted practices within the meaning of Article 81(1) of the Treaty where they apply national competition law and there is an effect on trade. They are not allowed to prohibit agreements and practices which do not restrict competition within the meaning of Article 81(1) EC, or which fulfil the conditions for exemption under Article 81(3). Neither are they allowed to prohibit agreements or practices which are covered by a block exemption regulation for the application of Article 81(3). Further, Member State competition authorities and

[83] Case 127/73 *BRT* [1974] ECR 51, at para 16: 'As the prohibitions of Articles 85(1) and 86 tend by their very nature to produce direct effects in relations between individuals, these articles create direct rights in respect of the individuals concerned which the national courts must safeguard.'

[84] See the now outdated Commission Notice on co-operation between national competition authorities and the Commission in handling cases falling within the scope of Articles 85 or 86 of the EC Treaty, [1997] OJ C/313/3, at 4–5.

[85] EEC Council Regulation No 17, First Regulation implementing Articles 85 and 86 of the Treaty, [1962] OJ P/13/204.

[86] White Paper, above n 1, at 100.

[87] Riley, Alan, 'EC Antitrust Modernisation: The Commission Does Very Nicely—Thank You! Part 1: Regulation 1 and the Notification Burden' (2003) 24(11) *ECLR* 604, at 612.

national courts shall apply Article 82 of the Treaty when they apply national competition law to any abuse prohibited by Article 82.

The mandatory requirement to apply Articles 81 and 82 EC when national competition law is applied and there is an effect on trade resolved a long-lasting situation of legal uncertainty. Prior to the introduction of Article 3 of Regulation 1, the application of Community competition law was to a large extent dependent on the choices of the national legislator. The Court of Justice held in *Van Schijndel* that Community law does not require national courts to raise of their own motion issues concerning breaches of Community law, where that would oblige the courts to abandon the passive role assigned to them by going beyond the ambit of the dispute defined by the parties themselves and relying on facts and circumstances other than those raised by the parties.[88] In other words, the national court is not obliged to apply EC competition law *ex officio* if the national procedure prescribes a passive role for the court, which is the normal situation in private litigation.[89] On the other hand, the Court repeated, with references to previous case law, the obligation for national courts to raise of their own motion EC law when national procedure included an obligation or a discretionary power to do so.[90]

In 1999, the Court of Justice established in *Eco Swiss* that Article 81 EC is a matter of public policy, which meant that a national court must, on application, annul an arbitral award if it considers that the award is in fact contrary to Article 81 EC, where its domestic rules of procedure require it to grant an application for annulment founded on failure to observe national rules of public policy.[91] *Eco Swiss* has been interpreted by the Court not to reverse *Van Schijndel*—there is still no unconditional EC law requirement on national courts to apply Article 81 EC *ex officio*.[92]

When the White Paper was published in 1999, only eight out of 15 Member States had empowered their national competition authorities to apply Community law.[93] Subsequent case law has emphasised the obligation for national authorities to apply Community competition law, but there is still the matter of what mandate has been granted to the national authority by the national legislator.[94] Consequently, there was no single choice of law rule for the application of Articles 81 and 82 EC in the national context. Instead, it was left as a matter of how the national procedure was

[88] Joined Cases C-430/93 and C-431/93 *Van Schijndel* [1995] ECR I-4705, at paras 19–22.

[89] Discussed by Jacobs, Francis G, 'Enforcing Community Rights and Obligations in National Courts: Striking the Balance' in Lonbay, Julian and Biondi, Andrea (eds), *Remedies for Breach of EC Law* (New York, Wiley, 1997), at 26.

[90] *Van Schijndel*, above n 88, at paras 13–14.

[91] Case C-126/97 *Eco Swiss China Time Ltd* [1999] ECR I-3055, at para 41.

[92] Joined Cases C-222/05 to C-225/05 *van der Weerd and others* [2007] ECR I-4233, at para 41; see also Gustafsson, Magnus, 'What are the prospects for enhanced private antitrust litigation? A Swedish perspective' (2005) 30(4) *EL Rev* 490. Andersson, on the other hand, considered it unlikely that competition rules should be treated like other rules of EC law under the *Van Schijndel* case law, and that national courts would be prevented from enforcing of agreements that violate competition law, regardless of the content of national procedural rules: see Andersson, Torbjörn, *Dispositionsprincipen och EG:s konkurrensregler* (Uppsala, Iustus, 1999), at 201.

[93] White Paper, above n 1, ch II, at 94.

[94] Case C-198/01 *CIF* [2003] ECR I-8055, at paras 49–50.

structured and what powers had been granted to national authorities in each specific Member State. Article 3 of Regulation 1 untied this knot by forcing national courts and competition authorities to apply these Treaty rules when national competition law is applied and there is an effect on trade.

Against this background, the introduction of a choice of law provision must be seen as a major achievement, and as a prerequisite for national supervision and enforcement of EC cartel law, even though the provision did not go as far as the Commission originally intended. The Commission had proposed that application of Articles 81 and 82 EC should exclude application of national competition law,[95] but this met some opposition in the Council.[96] Article 3(1) of Regulation 1 retains the possibility of parallel application of national and Community competition law, as was the case before modernisation.

2. Engaging national authorities in EC competition law supervision

As explained, not all Member States had granted their national authorities the power to supervise Articles 81 and 82 of the Treaty prior to the modernisation. According to Article 5 of Regulation 1, the competition authorities of the Member States have the power to apply Articles 81 and 82 EC in individual cases. They may require that an infringement be brought to an end and order interim measures. They may also accept commitments and impose sanctions provided for in their national laws.

The Commission considered, in the proposal for a modernisation regulation, that national authorities were generally well equipped to deal with Community competition law cases, that they had the necessary resources and were close to the markets.[97] The idea was to bring more enforcers into the arena, where the Commission and the national competition authorities should form a network and work closely together.[98] For this purpose, mechanisms for information exchange and co-operation were enacted in Articles 11, 12 and 22 of Regulation 1. However, one may question what exactly the Commission had in mind—national enforcers were busy enforcing national competition law even before modernisation. It is not as if unemployed resources were suddenly utilised when national authorities and courts were obliged to apply EC law. The argument of bringing more enforcers into the arena can thus be questioned. Rather, the paradigm shift lies in the application of one law instead of many; in other words, it is once again a question of uniformity, or integration through law.

Simultaneously with the adoption of Regulation 1, the Council and the Commission issued a joint statement on the functioning of the ECN.[99] It is

[95] COM(2000) 582 final, [2000] OJ C/365 E/284, draft Art 3.

[96] 2394th Council meeting—Energy/Industry, Brussels, 4 and 5 December 2001, PRES/01/452, 4/12/2001.

[97] COM(2000) 582 Final, Explanatory Memorandum, at 6.

[98] *Ibid.*

[99] Available on http://ec.europa.eu/comm/competition/ecn/more_details.html.

recognised in the statement that all Network members have full parallel competence to apply Articles 81 and 82 of the Treaty. Still, the members of the Network will ensure that cases are adequately allocated and assessed. 'Cases will be dealt with by a single competition authority as often as possible,' where the Network will seek to agree on which authority is best placed to act. The Commission will be particularly well placed if more than three Member States have been affected.

The Commission subsequently adopted a Notice on co-operation within the Network of Competition Authorities,[100] addressing among other issues division of work principles and mechanisms for co-operation. The Commission describes the Network as

> the framework for the close co-operation mechanisms of Council Regulation 1/2003. At the same time it is a discussion forum dealing with a variety of topical issues of interest to its member authorities . . .[101]

The merits of the co-operation within the Network will be analysed further in this chapter. For present purposes it suffices to observe that co-operation within the Network is a complete novelty established in connection with Regulation 1.

3. *Strengthened investigative powers of the Commission*

Regulation 1 strengthened the Commission's powers of investigation. In particular, the Commission obtained in Article 20 of the Regulation the right to inspect premises other than those of the undertakings concerned, including the homes of directors, managers and other members of staff. Another innovation was the power in Article 19 to take statements from natural and legal persons who consent to be interviewed. Moreover, Article 24 allows for periodic penalty payments to be imposed on undertakings, amounting to 5 per cent of the undertaking's average daily turnover.[102]

F. Preliminary conclusion: output orientated legislation

The discussion preceding the modernisation was output orientated, as will be clear from the analysis above. The idea that EC law should be applied uniformly, effectively and efficiently throughout the Community represents a traditional 'integration through law' approach.[103] Dougan offers a critical analysis of this approach—'an untenable ideal of integration'. He suggests a sectoral approach, where the demand for uniformity is relative, changing according to the field of Community activity in question. Still, he identifies competition law as a sector

[100] Commission Notice on co-operation within the Network of Competition Authorities [2004] OJ C/101/43.
[101] Information on http://ec.europa.eu/comm/competition/ecn/faq.html.
[102] On these innovations, see esp Riley, above n 87, at 604–15.
[103] Dougan, above n 36, at 69, 389–90.

where uniformity remains a valid goal. Uniformity and effectiveness, essential for the functioning of Community competition law, were primary concerns of the modernisation Regulation, repeatedly emphasised in the legislative process leading up to this reform. So was the fight against hard-core restrictions.

II. A FOCUS ON HARD-CORE RESTRAINTS AS A STUDY OBJECT

The present work comprises an in-depth study of cartels. Admittedly another field of competition law, such as abuse of dominance, could have been chosen, given that the only objective of the in-depth study of substantive law is to provide a laboratory in which legitimacy is tested. It is impossible to be encyclopaedic and go through all aspects of Articles 81 and 82 EC. The choice of hard-core restraints is appropriate, however, since it represents the overriding policy objective in EC competition law.

In its 2002 Report on competition policy, the Commission explained that the first pillar of EU competition policy is 'vigorous enforcement of the antitrust rules', an activity which

> focuses increasingly on preventing the most serious forms of anticompetitive behaviour by market players, such as such as price-fixing or market-sharing cartels, from disrupting effective competition . . .[104]

Now, why would an antitrust agency in today's world need to communicate explicitly its rather self-evident mission of combating cartels? The explanation lies in the shift in enforcement policy brought about by the modernisation. At the drafting stage, the Commission described the modernisation as 'a fundamentally different enforcement system'.[105]

In its 1999 White Paper on modernisation, the Commission explained how its role has changed over time. In 1962 there were only six Member States, in 1999 there were 15, and the enlargement of the EU to 25 Member States was due in 2004. There had been, over time, a move from establishing rules on restrictive practices which interfered directly with the goal of market integration, to detecting and stopping cross-border cartels and maintaining competitive market structures.[106] Harding and Joshua record this development and conclude that the Commission's actions against cartels were maintained at a low profile during the 1960s, when the Commission would quietly negotiate termination or revision of unlawful arrangements and use fines as a last resort. This all ended in the 1970s, when the Commission opted for vigorous litigation in a series of major cartel cases.[107] In the late 1990s the Commission decided to put major emphasis on the

[104] XXXIInd Report on Competition Policy 2002, SEC (2003) 467 final, at 19.
[105] COM(2000) 582 Final, Explanatory Memorandum, at 3.
[106] White Paper, above n 1, at 8.
[107] Harding, Christopher, and Joshua, Julian, *Regulating Cartels in Europe—A Study of Legal Control of Corporate Delinquency* (Oxford, Oxford University Press, 2003), at 112 and 128.

fight against cartels. Resources were reallocated for a crack-down on cartels, leading to the adoption of 10 cartel prohibition decisions annually in 2001 and 2002.[108] (This should be compared with a record of some two or three cartel decisions annually in the years before.) Still, the burden of the notification system prevented the Commission from using its resources for the detection and punishment of serious infringements.[109] In the White Paper, reform was promised to allow the Commission to focus on the most serious infringements.[110]

The enlargement of the EU, as well as globalisation, made it necessary to strengthen competition policy with regard to cartels.[111] The Commission considered it necessary to refocus and use its resources to combat cartels, particularly in concentrated markets and in markets which were being liberalised.[112] Whether this was actually a radical reform can be questioned, and Riley has made the point that 'the abolition of the notification procedure is merely a removal of an already irrelevant procedure, with marginal impact on the operation of EC competition rules'.[113] At least, cartel enforcement remained a strong argument in support of the reform all through the legislative process.[114]

Although it is still too early to evaluate the long-term success of this shift, some substantive results are already visible. The OECD observed the results in its 2005 survey of competition law and policy in the EU, noting a shift over the previous 10 years from control of vertical restraints to horizontal cartels.[115] The diminishing role of enforcement against vertical restraints is well documented.[116] This policy change will be discussed further below.

III. JUDICIAL CO-OPERATION AND LEGITIMACY

The present analysis goes back to Habermas's view that not only must the law have a legitimate genesis, but also the State must guarantee average compliance, compelled by sanctions if necessary.[117] Here we can observe how the Community's competition law enforcement suffered from a legitimacy deficit prior to modernisation. That was because many of the Commission's resources were spent on relatively uncontroversial issues and not on combating hard-core horizontal restrictions. Moreover, there was evidence of a legitimacy deficit in so far as

[108] Guersent, Olivier, 'The Fight Against Secret Horizontal Agreement in the EC Competition Policy' in Hawk (ed), *International Antitrust Law & Policy: Fordham Corporate Law* (New York, Juris Publishing, 2003), at 43–44.

[109] COM(2000) 582 Final, Explanatory Memorandum, at 2.

[110] White Paper, above n 1, Executive Summary, at 13.

[111] *Ibid*, ch I, at 7 and 8.

[112] *Ibid*, ch II, at 45.

[113] Riley, above n 87, at 604.

[114] COM(2000) 582 Final, Explanatory Memorandum, at 6 and 7; Press release IP/00/1064; see also Guersent, above n 108, at 45.

[115] OECD, *Competition Law and Policy in the European Union* (OECD, 2005), at 65.

[116] Gerber, above n 2, at 389.

[117] Habermas, Jürgen, *Between Facts and Norms* (Cambridge, Polity Press, 1996), at 448.

Member States were not actively carrying out supervision and enforcement of EC competition law (in spite of being largely empowered to do so) but continued to rely on national competition law. Following decentralisation, national competition authorities and courts are empowered to apply EC competition law in parallel with each other and with the Commission. Co-ordination of these efforts is carried out through the ECN. We now turn to the prerequisites for this enforcement system, with focus on the institutional aspects.

Scharpf's distinction between input legitimacy and output legitimacy may be recalled as we turn our attention to the matter of efficient enforcement. According to Scharpf:

> under modern conditions centralized-unitary as well as decentralized-fragmented decision structures have become less effective in dealing with the diversity, variability, and complexity of interests, problems, and solutions in societies that are at the same time more differentiated and more interdependent than ever. Hence more loosely structured, flexible, and informal networks of communication and interaction may indeed have a necessary role to play in the development of effective solutions to the characteristic policy problems of the present age.[118]

Scharpf is indeed optimistic about network co-operation, and he finds that

> all varieties of effective decision-making will be strengthened in their legitimacy by their coexistence with open policy networks in which problems and potential policy choices can be explored in wide-ranging or narrowly focused deliberation . . .[119]

However, his view seems to be based more on the prospects of creating well-designed policies than on creating efficient enforcement. It will be clear from this presentation that I am considerably less hopeful.

IV. PREREQUISITES FOR ENSURING AVERAGE COMPLIANCE

The analysis in this chapter has touched upon how the principle of effectiveness influences the impact or prevalence of EC law in individual situations arising in national courts and national authorities. But it is important to keep in mind that when the Court of Justice is given an opportunity to solve a problem on effectiveness, it is in a concrete case pending in a national court and not in the context of designing a Europe-wide efficient system for Community law supervision. Paradoxically, we may have a system that ensures effectiveness (that EC law has sufficient impact in a singular case when Articles 81 and 82 EC apply in a national court or authority) without ensuring average compliance. For instance, Member State authorities and courts may be meticulous in ensuring effective application *once a case is brought*, but can, on the other hand, take a lax view of competition

[118] Scharpf, Fritz Wilhelm, *Governing in Europe: Effective and Democratic?* (Oxford, Oxford University Press, 1999), at 20, footnotes omitted.

[119] *Ibid*, at 21.

law enforcement in general by allocating insufficient resources to this quest or by prioritising other matters. Thus a few infringements are pursued vigorously while the vast majority are left untouched. A more realistic perspective on decentralisation is offered, however, by the observation that there will be considerable difficulties in achieving even partial successes. This is what has happened in telecom regulation, where, according to the Commission, there have been inconsistent regulatory approaches by 27 national regulatory authorities.[120]

The classic idea of institutional efficiency derives from the relation between costs and output. Nicolaides describes efficient policy implementation as achieving a certain objective or amount of value at the lowest cost possible, or achieving the largest possible amount of value from constant costs.[121] The view adopted here is, however, less economically orthodox and centres around the question whether we can ensure, under EC law, that competition law infringements are pursued with a reasonable detection rate, and when they are, that this is done uniformly, with regard to the principle of effectiveness and with appropriate sanctions.

A. Importance of institutional structure and human resources

If we assume that there is a genuine spirit of co-operation among Member States, so that they wish to ensure uniform, effective and efficient competition law enforcement, then what is needed to accomplish this task? And if we are less idealistic and take into account national favouritism and local champions, what would ultimately be needed to ensure compliance? It has been pointed out elsewhere that it is to be expected that Member States will agree on common rules and then depart from them at the implementation stage, so that EU policies can be applied effectively only when they contain provisions regarding implementation and the performance of the bodies responsible.[122]

As with any legal system, EC competition law is not settled in all respects, especially as regards the interface between national law and Community law. Even on the points of law that are well settled, it is quite plain that application is a know how-intensive business. Just understanding the law can be an arduous exercise, and in actual litigation the facts, evidence and procedure complicate things exponentially. It will be explained below that national authorities and courts must proceed from a dual understanding both of their own procedural system *and* general principles developed in EC law, which makes national cases more complicated than those litigated in the Community courts. And national procedures cannot

[120] COM(2007) 699 rev 2, Proposal for a Regulation of the European Parliament and of the Council establishing the European Electronic Communications Market Authority.

[121] Nicolaides, Phedon, *From Graphite to Diamond—The Importance of Institutional Structure in Establishing Capacity for Effective and Credible Application of EU Rules* (Maastricht, European Institute of Public Administration, 2002), at 29.

[122] Nicolaides, Phedon, Geveke, Arjan and den Teuling, Anne-Mieke, *Improving Policy Implementation in an Enlarged European Union—The Case of National Regulatory Authorities* (Maastricht, European Institute of Public Administration, 2003), at 43.

necessarily be conducted in one language only, given that there may be an obligation to provide translations for foreign companies.

Temple Lang considered enforcement success in drafting the 1998 General Report to FIDE on the modernisation.[123] He emphasised in particular that national authorities must have sufficient staff and adequate procedures. For decisions to be generally accepted by companies, economists and lawyers, national authorities must have a sufficient degree of independence, professionalism and objectivity.[124]

The OECD evaluates national competition law regularly with reference to a variety of factors, including how the national competition law institutions work. The professional skills of the institution's staff are a key aspect of an authority's performance.[125] There seems to be wide consensus among scholars on this point, namely the key importance of skilled people.[126] Quoting Kovacic, 'effectiveness of competition agencies depends on establishing intellectual leadership'.[127] Regulatory agencies will come up against the most qualified professionals in defending their cases, and will consequently need to attract a small but highly competent body of professionals, and apply pay scales that are comparable with those of private firms.[128] Nicolaides *et al* find that 'Effective policy application and enforcement depends on institutions that are empowered, sufficiently independent and fully accountable'.[129] Capacity, say the authors, depends on knowledgeable staff, sufficient resources and incentives to act.[130] Gerber's prognosis is focused on the know-how factor, and he emphasises that the success of the decentralisation depends on what judges and decision-makers learn and how fast they learn it.[131]

The experiences in the field of European telecom regulation point in the same direction. In its proposal for the establishment of a European electronic communications market authority, the Commission points to the inconsistent application of EU rules and the regulatory fragmentation of the market. Despite harmonisation, there have been inconsistent regulatory approaches by the 27 national regulators, which vary significantly in terms of competences, independence, and

[123] Temple Lang, John, 'General Report on the Application of Community Competition Law on Enterprises by National Courts and National Authorities', FIDE Congress 1998, available at http://ec.europa.eu/comm/competition/speeches/text/sp1998_027_en.html.

[124] *Ibid*, at 6–7.

[125] See OECD, *Regulatory reform in Sweden* (OECD, 2007), at 51.

[126] Nicolaides, above n 121; Trebilcock, Michael J, and Iacobucci, Edward M, 'Designing Competition Law Institutions' (2002) 25(3) *World Competition* 361; Serebrisky, Tomás, 'What Do We Know about Competition Agencies in Emerging and Transition Countries? Evidence on Workload, Personnel, Priority Sectors and Training Needs' (2004) 27(4) *World Competition* 651.

[127] Kovacic, William E, 'Achieving better practices in the design of competition policy institutions' (2005) 50(3) *The Antitrust Bulletin* 511, at 515.

[128] Mateus, Abel M, 'Why Should National Competition Authorities be Independent and How Should They be Accountable?' (2007) 3(1) *European Competition Journal* 17, at 24.

[129] Nicolaides *et al*, above n 122, at 107.

[130] *Ibid*, at 100.

[131] Gerber, above n 2, at xvi.

financial and human resources.[132] A new European authority, it is said, would act as a centre of expertise.[133]

On the whole, the ingredients necessary for successful enforcement are not unknown to people in the trade. Tentatively, there must be sufficient resources, adequate procedures, know how and co-ordination in the Member States if the modernisation is to be efficient. To this can be added a policy perspective—that Member States set correct priorities in their enforcement, based on analyses of the competition problems in their territory. For instance, abuse of dominance by existing or former monopolists may be the prevailing problem in certain sectors of economy, while cartels are frequent in other sectors or Member States. Further, the authorities and courts must make correct assessments of the practices they examine. Finally, the sanctions imposed on hard-core infringements must be severe enough to ensure deterrence.

B. The principle of institutional autonomy and Regulation 1

As explained in the previous section, the modernisation of EC competition law results in all sorts of practical requirements as regards the institutional structure in Member States, more precisely on how to organise and equip national competition authorities and courts. However, Community law does not *actually* require anything of the sort. The Court held, as early as in 1971, that Member States enjoy institutional autonomy. In the wording of the Court:

> When provisions of the Treaty or of regulations confer power or impose obligations upon the States for the purposes of the implementation of Community law the question of how the exercise of such powers and the fulfilment of such obligations may be entrusted by Member States to specific national bodies is solely a matter for the constitutional system of each State.[134]

Advocate-General Jacobs stated in *DEI*[135]:

> According to the system of the division of powers established by the EC Treaty, in the absence of applicable Community rules, the responsibility for the implementation, application and enforcement of Community rules falls upon the Member States in accordance with their national legal systems, subject, of course, to the constraints of the principle of effectiveness as developed by the Court.

A sharp contrast can be seen when the institutional requirements (or, rather, the absence thereof) are compared with the requirements of effectiveness and uniformity in individual cases. Member State competition authorities and courts have all kinds of obligations under EC law, once there is a competition law case before

[132] COM(2007)699 rev 2, above n 120, Explanatory memorandum, at 2.

[133] *Ibid.*

[134] Joined Cases 51 to 54/71 *International Fruit Company* [1971] ECR 1107, at paras 3–4.

[135] Opinion of Advocate-General Jacobs delivered on 24 February 2005 in Case C-394/02 *Commission v Greece* [2005] ECR I-4713 at 27.

them. On a more general level, the Court of First Instance pointed out in *Automec* that, unlike the civil courts, whose task is to safeguard the individual rights of private persons in their relations inter se, an administrative authority must act in the public interest.[136]

Did Regulation 1, then, introduce anything to set aside or qualify the principle of institutional autonomy in relation to Articles 81 and 82 EC? Article 11(1) of the Regulation provides that the Commission and the competition authorities of the Member States shall apply the Community competition rules in close co-operation. Further, Member States have an obligation under Article 35 of Regulation 1 to designate competition authorities in such a way that the provisions of the Regulation are complied with effectively. Now, does the obligation to engage in close co-operation and to designate competition authorities imply that Member States must secure the necessary resources for efficient cartel fighting? Prerequisites would include sufficient staff, procedures that ensure that cases are completed or closed within a reasonable time, independence from the government, sufficient know how among the employees and judges, and capacity to co-operate on the national and international level.

A comparison may be made with implementation of Directives. Effective transposition of an EC Directive requires that the competent authority for the grant of such rights be clearly designated and that transparent administrative procedures be established to implement them. Even if the Member States are free to delegate powers to their domestic authorities as they consider fit, and to implement Directives by means of measures adopted by various authorities, the fact remains that individuals must be made fully aware of their rights.[137] It follows that a clear designation of a competent authority is required, and the establishment of transparent administrative procedures. This is also what the modernisation requires, in so far as Member States must, under Article 35 of Regulation 1, designate competition authorities in such a way that the Regulation is complied with effectively. Still, the question of allocating sufficient resources in terms of staff, know how etc, seems to be a matter left entirely at the Member States' discretion. Although inconvenient, this is probably the law as it stands. The experience in the telecoms regulatory sector points in the same direction.[138]

V. EFFICIENCY: ECN AND THE COMMISSION'S CENTRAL SUPERVISION AND ENFORCEMENT MECHANISMS

A. ECN co-operation

According to Article 11(1) of Regulation 1, the Commission and the competition authorities of the Member States shall apply the Community competition rules in

[136] Case T-24/90 *Automec v Commission* [1992] ECR II-2223, at para 85.
[137] Case C-97/01 *Commission v Luxembourg* [2003] ECR I-5797, at paras 36–37.
[138] COM(2007) 699 rev 2, above n 120, Explanatory memorandum, at 8.

close co-operation. When Regulation 1 was adopted, the Council and the Commission issued a joint statement on the functioning of the ECN.[139] The members of the ECN will ensure that cases are adequately allocated and assessed. Cases will be dealt with by a single competition authority as often as possible, where the ECN members will seek to agree on which authority is best placed to act. The Commission will be particularly well placed if more than three Member States have been affected. The accompanying Notice on co-operation addresses division of work principles and mechanisms for co-operation.[140] The Commission describes the ECN as the

> framework for the close co-operation mechanisms of Council Regulation 1/2003. At the same time it is a discussion forum dealing with a variety of topical issues of interest to its member authorities . . .[141]

Networked governance is used in several policy areas within the EU. The potential and problems of these networks have been examined by Jordan and Schout in relation to environmental policies, in particular on what is needed to ensure that these new modes function effectively at national and at European level.[142] Networks are informal relationships between essentially equal agents, where co-ordination is built on trust and loyalty rather than administrative commands.[143] The authors explore whether co-ordination has been supported with adequate resources to ensure implementation. They suggest that the EU should be more sceptical about the long-term co-ordinating potential of networks.[144] This view is reinforced by the (discouraging) experiences of network co-ordination in the electronic communications sector.[145]

Perhaps failures in other policy areas can be explained (at least in part) by reference to the grand scale of the attempted co-ordination. Control of Articles 81 and 82 EC, on the other hand, is an outright enforcement activity where administrative co-ordination seems like a workable prospect. In spite of the grey zones identified on the interpretation of EC law, the law seems sufficiently well established for networked governance to work. Obviously we do not know the answer to every possible question, but creases can be ironed out through references to the Court of Justice, or through the cases pursued by the Commission in the Community courts. Unlike deregulated areas such as telecoms, policies do not have to be worked out from scratch, and control takes place retrospectively, thereby avoiding all the problems with ex ante regulation. Still, we should pay due attention to the fact that national competition authorities, as well as the Commission, have a wide range of

[139] Available on http://ec.europa.eu/comm/competition/ecn/more_details.html.

[140] Commission Notice on co-operation within the Network of Competition Authorities [2004] OJ C/101/43.

[141] Information on http://ec.europa.eu/comm/competition/ecn/faq.html.

[142] Jordan, Andrew, and Schout, Adriaan, *The Coordination of the European Union—Exploring the Capacities of Networked Governance* (Oxford, Oxford University Press, 2006).

[143] *Ibid*, at 16.

[144] *Ibid*, at 275.

[145] COM(2007) 699 rev 2, above n 120.

tasks. Their resources must be divided between merger control, abuse of dominance cases, vertical restrictions, sector inquiries, general competition advocacy and cartels. By and large, though, co-operation should not (as such) be the major obstacle. The experiences so far are promising.[146] Rather, the problems present themselves at the national level of application, ie the national authorities' and courts' capacity to deal with these very complex cases, which are made even more complex by the existence of dual procedural requirements, since both national procedure and EC procedural principles apply.

B. The Commission's powers in relation to national competition authorities and courts

Several rules have been enacted in Regulation 1 for the purpose of co-operation between the Commission and Member States. This discussion will focus on the Commission's abilities to ensure that the national authorities carry out competition law enforcement uniformly, effectively and efficiently.

The Commission's steering mechanisms are of two kinds: obligations for Member State competition authorities to provide information about their cases; and ultimately a power for the Commission to step in and thereby relieve the national authority of its jurisdiction to handle the case.

According to Article 11(3) of Regulation 1, Member State competition authorities have a duty to inform the Commission in writing before or without delay after commencing the first formal investigative measure. Article 11(4) contains further obligations on national authorities to inform the Commission in advance about decisions they intend to adopt. They must provide the Commission with a summary of the case and the envisaged decision, or, in the absence thereof, any other document indicating the proposed course of action. On request, the national authority must make available to the Commission other documents it holds which are necessary for the assessment of the case. In addition to these obligations, there are voluntary options for the Commission to provide Member State competition authorities with information, and for national competition authorities to exchange information between themselves.

According to Article 11(6) of Regulation 1, the initiation by the Commission of proceedings for adoption of a decision shall relieve the competition authorities of the Member States of their competence to apply Articles 81 and 82 EC. This power applies only in relation to national competition authorities, not in relation to courts. Finally, if there is already a Commission decision on an agreement, a decision or a practice, Article 16(2) prohibits national competition authorities from taking decisions which would run counter to the decision of the Commission.

146 Dekeyser, Kris, and Jaspers, Maria, 'A New Era of ECN Cooperation—Achievements and Challenges with Special Focus on Work in the Leniency Field' (2007) 30(1) *World Competition* 3.

However, the Commission's powers vis-à-vis national *courts* are extremely limited in cases on Articles 81 and 82 EC. Under Article 15(2) of Regulation 1, Member States must provide the Commission with a copy of any written judgment of national courts deciding on the application of Article 81 or 82 EC, without delay after the parties have been notified of the judgment. There is thus an obligation on Member States to inform the Commission retrospectively. The Commission can act under Article 15(3) of Regulation 1 by submitting, on its own initiative, written observations to the courts of the Member States, and, with the permission of the court in question, make oral observations. There is no obligation for the national court to follow the Commission's advice, but it can be assumed that, for practical purposes, observations will exert an influence as a result of the Commission's authoritative and central role in cartel enforcement. Lastly, Article 15(1) provides that national courts cannot take decisions running counter to decisions adopted by the Commission. This extends to an obligation to avoid giving decisions which would conflict with a decision contemplated by the Commission, in which case the national court may assess whether it is necessary to stay its proceedings.

Given the division of work carried out within the ECN, it seems unlikely that there will be concurrent and non co-ordinated handling of one and the same case by the Commission and national authorities, save in exceptional circumstances. The obligation to avoid conflicting decisions is consequently of little practical use. For the purpose of day-to-day activities, the Commission will have to rely on a combination of information from the Member States and its own ability to step in and initiate proceedings itself, as a steering mechanism. The latter alternative is open only if the case is pending with a national authority, without having proceeded to a national court. There is no power for the Commission to relieve national courts of their competence, and no rule in Regulation 1 on standing for the Commission in national courts.

The present analysis has shown that there are really no hard rules in Regulation 1 which the Commission can employ to ensure, on a larger and systematic scale, uniform, effective and efficient competition law supervision in Member States. *Investigation* must be made by Member States at the Commission's request, according to Article 22 of Regulation 1. Other than this, the Commission will have to choose between carrying out all detection, decision-making and litigation itself, or relying essentially on the goodwill of the 27 Member States. The realities will tend to be somewhere in between: if, according to the information provided by Member States, everything is working out fine, the Commission will leave things to the Member States; otherwise, it can ask for information and, if all else fails, initiate its own proceedings. But it should be kept in mind that central monitoring through reception of information is extremely complex for the Commission. Information may be available in all the official languages of the Member States, and will have to be understood against the background of national administrative and procedural law. Member States may be expected to filter the information, if nothing else, to make it easier to access. It seems implausible, on the face of it, to expect that the Commission should be able to ensure uniformity, effectiveness and efficiency in this way.

1. *Enforcement priorities following decentralisation*

With reference to the Community interest, the Commission enjoys a margin of discretion in setting its enforcement priorities.[147] In its 2005 Report on Competition Policy, the Commission explains that it has insufficient resources to investigate every problem brought to its attention. Priorities will be set according to a list of criteria intended to determine the Community interest.[148] The self-imposed criteria are very approximate and will allow for nearly any policy. Magnitude at least is of central importance: the size of the infringement matters, geographically, by reference to the turnover on the market and the size of the players involved. The availability of national enforcement is another determining aspect. Complainants can choose to file complaints with national authorities.

The matter of distribution of work within the ECN will not be addressed here—the question asked for the purpose of the present chapter is whether national competition authorities are under an obligation to duplicate the Commission's enforcement priorities, for instance by focusing on cartels. Documents produced by EU institutions are silent about the enforcement focus of national competition authorities. This is because each national competition authority in the EU will set its own priorities on how to use its resources. There is no firm support yet for the idea of forcing national authorities to act by entitling private parties to require such action under EC law. Eilmansberger comments that

> it is downright astounding that there is no clear statement of the Court yet with regard to the availability of offensive Community remedies aiming at ensuring the correct application of EC law by national *public authorities*. . .[149]

VI. LENIENCY AND SETTLEMENT PROCEDURES LEAD BACK TO CENTRALISED ENFORCEMENT

There is no single mailbox in Europe for companies that wish to file leniency applications (seek immunity from or reduction of cartel fines). The absence of harmonisation or centralised procedures in this regard has been identified as a major problem.[150] Although a one-stop shop would be very attractive for business, there is as yet no such procedure. For cartels with significant cross-border effects within

[147] See especially Kerse, Christopher, and Khan, Nicholas, *EC Antitrust Procedure*, 5th edn (London, Sweet & Maxwell, 2005), at 92 ff.

[148] European Commission, *Report on Competition Policy 2005*, at 26–27; see also Koeck, Heribert Franz, and Karollus, Margit Maria (eds), *The Modernisation of European Competition Law—Initial Experiences with Regulation 1/2003* (Linz, FIDE XXIII Congress, facultas.wuv, 2008), at 396–97.

[149] Eilmansberger, Thomas, 'The relationship between rights and remedies in EC law: In search of the missing link' (2004) 41 *CML Rev* 1199, at 1229.

[150] See especially Kerse and Khan, above n 147, at 275.

the EU, the Commission is presently seen as the most logical recipient of a leniency application.[151] This is partly because the parties may initially not know the precise extent of the cartel, and partly because of the uncertainties related to how national authorities will handle information submitted under leniency applications.[152]

The Commission introduced settlement procedures in 2008 in order to achieve faster handling of cartel cases.[153] In the context of settlement discussions, the Commission can make an early disclosure of matters such as the facts alleged, the classification of those facts, the gravity and duration of the alleged cartel, the attribution of liability, an estimation of the range of likely fines, the evidence and the potential fines. If this leads to a common understanding about the potential objections and range of likely fines, an expedited procedure will apply, provided that the party makes a formal request to settle. The Commission can decide to reward settlements by a 10 per cent reduction of the fine, on top of any leniency award.[154]

To conclude, as long as the Commission acts as a magnet for larger cartels, as a result of its leniency programme and settlement procedures, this effectively centralises cartel enforcement within Brussels.

VII. INSTITUTIONAL ASPECTS

A. The Commission's role in EC competition law

It remains to be seen what role the Commission will assume following decentralisation. An outline is presented in the following sections. As can be seen, the Commission would be heavily occupied even if it did not pursue a single infringement. If anything, decentralisation has increased the Commission's workload. This was not unexpected. Gerber commented in 1998 on how

> orchestrating such a relationship entails high levels of uncertainty and complexity, and these, in turn, may be expected to impose significant additional costs on the Commission as well as interfere with its capacity to control efforts to protect competition in the EU.[155]

The Commission's increased workload is evidenced in the 2008 FIDE Report, and can be explained with reference to the switch from notification-based work to cartel decisions which are more time-consuming and resource-intensive.[156]

[151] Reynolds, Michael J, and Anderson, David G, 'Immunity and Leniency in EU Cartel Cases: Current Issues' (2006) 27(2) *ECLR* 82, at 86.

[152] *Ibid.*

[153] Commission Regulation (EC) No 622/2008 of 30 June 2008 amending Regulation (EC) No 773/2004, as regards the conduct of settlement procedures in cartel cases [2008] OJ L/171/3, at 3–5, http://ec.europa.eu/comm/competition/cartels/legislation/settlements.html.

[154] Commission Notice on the conduct of settlement procedures in view of the adoption of Decisions pursuant to Article 7 and Article 23 of Council Regulation (EC) No 1/2003 in cartel cases [2008] OJ C/167/1, at 1–6, http://ec.europa.eu/comm/competition/cartels/legislation/settlements.html.

[155] Gerber, above n 2, at 398.

[156] Koeck and Karollus, above n 148, at 388.

1. To be the primary force in EC competition law control

With a record of some 150 cartel decisions (from the 1960s through 2007), the Commission has by far the most extensive experience of cartel cases in the EU. The picture is similar when it comes to control of vertical restraints and abuse of dominance. It is crucial that the Commission continues to handle difficult and complex cases, and litigate them before the Community courts. This way, it has the opportunity to retain the expert knowledge it needs as a policy maker. If competition law control was a relatively easy job, the ideal situation would be to allow Member States to carry out the huge bulk of it, leaving only the largest or most difficult cases to the Commission. Such a solution would correspond to the Commission's present capacity when it comes to cartel enforcement, which is limited to around 10 decisions a year, at its best, with little prospect of obtaining more resources.[157]

2. To co-ordinate decentralised enforcement

Co-ordination of decentralised EC cartel control includes the processing of significant volumes of information. This is a result of the obligations on Member State competition authorities to keep the Commission informed about ongoing cases, and the voluntary options for further information exchange between authorities and the Commission.

From May 2004 until 31 December 2006, some 670 cases were reported in the ECN case-management system.[158] When global or EC-wide infringements are being detected and investigated, there may be dawn raids in several Member States simultaneously, carried out by national authorities pursuant to Article 22 of Regulation 1. These must, of course, be co-ordinated in advance, and the ECN can work to establish such routines. Increased filing of leniency applications by companies contributes to the ECN's workload, given the division or work principles established. There may also be a need to discuss and solve issues of common interest,[159] such as how to address questions about professional secrecy and access to files. All this must be done with due attention to the fact that there are over 20 official languages in the EU. The need for network management is recognised as crucial in network governance, and the most obvious candidate for this job is the Commission.[160]

157 Guersent, Olivier, 'The EU Model of Administrative Enforcement Against Global Cartels: Evolving to Meet Challenges' in Ehlermann, Claus Dieter, and Atanasiu, Isabela, *European Competition Law Annual 2006: Enforcement of Prohibition of Cartels* (Oxford, Hart Publishing, 2007), at 216.

158 Dekeyser and Jaspers, above n 146, at 7.

159 *Ibid*, at 11.

160 Jordan and Schout, above n 142, at 269.

3. To supervise the guarantees in Member States for well-functioning competition law enforcement

Article 226 EC empowers the Commission to bring infringement proceedings against Member States before the Court of Justice where it considers that a Member State has failed to fulfil an obligation under Community law. Failure to fulfil Community law can derive not only from national legislation, but also from administrative practices and national case law.[161]

Theoretically Article 226 proceedings could be a way to correct national outcomes in cases that violate Articles 81 or 82 EC, or fundamental principles of Community law. However, the practicalities of competition law cases will make it very difficult for the Commission to define and make credible a failure committed by a Member State. Obviously no one would want a complex national case effectively to be re-litigated before the Court of Justice unless some exceptional circumstances justified it. It seems more likely that the Commission will confine itself to taking action in more clear-cut cases of failure, for instance if a Member State competition authority refused to provide information pursuant to Article 11 of Regulation 1, or if there would be no legal provisions on competition law sanctions in a Member State. For many of the possible infringements of Community law that could occur, there will be local enforcers in so far as the matters can be expected to be raised by the parties to the proceedings. Undertakings can be expected to be alert to infringements of fundamental rights, and competition authorities should be sensitive to attempts from the national judiciary to raise the standards of proof to intolerable levels. Even counting on the assistance of private parties and national enforcers alike, though, a certain amount of work will be left to the Commission.

4. Article 234 cases referred to the Court of Justice and amicus curiae observations

A number of the cases litigated before national courts are bound to be referred to the Court of Justice for preliminary rulings pursuant to Article 234 EC. Possible questions may include the interpretations of Articles 81 and 82 EC and Regulation 1, fundamental rights, standard of proof or effectiveness of sanctions. Once a referral is made by a national court, the Commission is able to provide the Court with written observations, and the Commission does this systematically in order to ensure the coherency of EC law. Decentralisation may be expected to result in an increased number of referrals, keeping the Commission occupied.

In addition, the Commission's self-imposed role as a friend of the national courts (amicus curiae) pursuant to Article 15 of Regulation 1, will further increase the Commission's workload when it is asked to provide information or submit observations.

[161] See Lenaerts *et al*, above n 65, at 132–33.

5. *Peer pressure and benchmarking*

Evaluation programs can contribute to the performance of national competition authorities. The OECD has emphasised that routine evaluations can form part of a discussion about the rationales for and contributions to competition policy.[162] Looking at central European agencies in particular, Geradin comments on the absence of mechanisms to evaluate their regulatory activities. He suggests that the impact of all regulatory activity should be examined periodically, with a view to establishing whether the existence of the agency is justified and whether it is functioning efficiently.[163] This reasoning applies generally.

Self-assessment is the most realistic option in the EU, given the absence of any competence for Community institutions to evaluate the performance of national bodies. Perhaps some centralised scheme can be worked out by the ECN though consensus. Calls for periodic peer or expert reviews of the performance of regulatory agencies have been voiced both in the EU and in the US.[164] Such reviews are entirely optional, however, and Member States may do what they please with the results. This means that performance reviews are not the answer to efficient enforcement of EC law. Still, they can be a valuable tool for examining and verifying which national competition authorities are most efficient in the EU. Those authorities should be entrusted with the more complex cases in the framework of co-operation of the ECN, provided, of course, that they wish to take on such tasks. The Commission is the most logical institution for designing and co-ordinating evaluations.

6. *International co-operation*

International co-operation is constantly increasing in competition law. Since infringers often operate cross-border, enforcers must do the same. This has resulted in a body of law and practice relating to co-operation between authorities worldwide.

The OECD noted a significant increase in international co-operation from 1999 to 2003, including close working relationships between the Commission and the US.[165] In a 2005 follow-up, the OECD concluded that the trend had continued, and noted an unprecedented level of international co-operation in discovering, investigating and prosecuting international cartels. Enforcement co-operation included co-ordinated inspections and exchange of information, all through international agreements.[166]

[162] OECD, *Evaluation of the actions and resources of competition authorities* (OECD, 2005).

[163] Geradin, Damien, 'Development of European Regulatory Agencies' (2004) (11) *Columbia Journal of European Law* 1, at 50–51.

[164] Nicolaides *et al*, above n 122, at 104; Kovacic, above n 127.

[165] OECD, *Hard Core Cartels, Recent Progress and Challenges Ahead* (OECD, 2003), at 31–32.

[166] OECD, *Hard Core Cartels, Third Report on the Implementation of the 1998 Recommendation* (OECD, 2006), at 29–38.

The EU has concluded international agreements on co-operation on antitrust matters with Japan, Canada and the US,[167] and under the EEA agreements. As a result of international co-operation, the Commission has a central role in co-ordinating with foreign jurisdictions.

7. Law and policy development

The Commission has a virtual monopoly over proposing legislation in the EC. This follows from the third indent of Article 211 of the Treaty, which stipulates that the Commission shall 'participate in the shaping of measures taken by the Council and by the European Parliament'. Admittedly it is difficult to understand the Commission's sole power to propose legislation from a literal reading of Article 211, but if read in conjunction with Articles 192, 250, 251 and 252 of the Treaty, it communicates that only the Commission can propose legislation. Save for exceptional situations, legislation cannot be proposed by the European Parliament, nor by Member States. The Commission cannot be compelled to submit proposals and is entitled to withdraw draft legislation at any time.[168]

Agenda-setting is often (and correctly) described as a powerful tool, but in the context of a systemic view of cartel control, it must also be understood as an administrative and legal–political burden on the Commission. Not only is there the task of producing draft legislation, but there is also a delegation of powers according to which the Commission can adopt block exemptions.[169] In the year 2004 alone, the Commission generated a proposal for application of Articles 81 and 82 EC to maritime transport, adopted amended rules on liner shipping consortia, pursued a consultation process on new rules for air transport and adopted a preliminary draft block exemption in this field, and saw the entry into force of new rules for motor vehicle distribution.[170] This only on application of Articles 81 and 82 EC, leaving aside State aid.

[167] Agreement between the European Community and the Government of Japan concerning co-operation on anti-competitive activities [2003] OJ L/183/12; Agreement between the European Communities and the Government of Canada regarding the application of their competition laws [1999] OJ L/175/50; Agreement between the European Communities and the Government of the United States of America on the application of positive comity principles in the enforcement of their competition laws [1998] OJ L/173/28.

[168] Lenaerts, Koen, Van Nuffel, Piet, and Bray, Robert (eds), *Constitutional Law of the European Union*, 2nd edn (London, Sweet & Maxwell, 2005), at 577ff.

[169] Regulation No 19/65/EEC of 2 March of the Council on application of Article 85(3) of the Treaty to certain categories of agreements and concerted practices [1965] OJ 36/533; Council Regulation (EC) No 1215/1999 of 10 June 1999 amending Regulation No 19/65/EEC on the application of Article 81(3) of the Treaty to certain categories of agreements and concerted practices [1999] OJ L/148/1; Regulation (EEC) No 2821/71 of the Council of 20 December 1971 on application of Article 85(3) of the Treaty to categories of agreements, decisions and concerted practices [1971] OJ L/285/46; Council Regulation (EEC) No 1534/91 of 31 May 1991 on the application of Article 85(3) of the Treaty to certain categories of agreements, decisions and concerted practices in the insurance sector [1991] OJ L/143/1.

[170] *Report on Competition Policy 2005*, above n 148, at 19–22, available on http://ec.europa.eu/comm/competition/annual_reports/.

Even so, secondary legislation is only a small part of the Commission's policy workload. Soft law has come to represent the major challenge for the Commission's Competition Directorate. Preparatory documents (such as COM-documents preparing legislation), informative instruments such as action plans, communications, notices, discussion papers and the like have become the predominant mode of producing competition policy. An example from 2004 illustrates this point. In that year the Commission issued a Discussion Paper on the application of the EU competition rules on abuse of dominance, to promote a debate on the law relating to exclusionary conduct. Furthermore, it adopted a Notice on the rules for access to the Commission file in merger and antitrust cases. It also adopted impact assessment guidelines to improve the regulatory environment in the EU. Not least, it adopted a Green Paper on antitrust damages actions.[171]

The general understanding is that a regulatory power for the Commission to issue interpretative documents follows from the implementing powers given to the Commission, in particular in Article 211 EC.[172] It can also be observed that Article 85 EC obliges the Commission to ensure the application of the principles laid down in Articles 81 and 82. Advocate-General Geelhoed addressed the principal importance of Commission communications in *Vulcan Silkeborg*. The case concerned block exemptions for motor vehicle distribution and accompanying brochures published by the Commission about the said regulations. According to the Advocate-General, the importance of Commission communications for policy-making and administration of justice in the Member States has increased following decentralisation. Thus:

> Legal certainty and unity of law in the application of and compliance with those rules, and the effectiveness thereof, are ensured if the Commission provides clear guidance on the application of the components of those rules . . .[173]

The 'non-binding character' of informal communications, often referred to, may be questioned. It is by now settled that notices are not devoid of any binding legal obligation. For an example, reference may be made to the Court of First Instance's judgment in *SEB/Moulinex*, where it held that

> the Commission is bound by notices which it issues in the area of supervision of concentrations . . . Moreover, the Commission cannot depart from rules which it has imposed on itself . . .[174]

Such judicialisation of soft law further heightens the qualitative requirements of communications issued by the Commission, and can be expected to result in a

[171] *Ibid*, at 19–29.

[172] Senden, Linda, *Soft Law in European Community Law* (Oxford, Hart Publishing, 2004), at 313.

[173] Opinion of A-G Geelhoed, delivered on 27 April 2006 in Case C-125/05 *Vulcan Silkeborg* [2006] ECR I-7637 at 36.

[174] Case T-119/02 *Royal Philips Electronics v Commission* [2003] ECR II-1433, at para 242 with references.

need for more participation by Member States and the legal community at large, all co-ordinated by the Commission.

It follows that it was quite correct for the authors of the White Paper on modernisation to conclude that, notwithstanding modernisation, the Commission has a special role in the determination of Community competition policy and legislation.[175] The point made here is merely that by making the Commission the engine in law and policy development, a huge administrative burden has been placed on this institution, and it will risk detracting from the Commission's other functions in enforcement of EC competition law.

VIII. A ROADMAP

In Regulation 1 and its preparatory works, as well as in subsequent Notices published by the Commission, reference is made repeatedly to the importance of effectiveness and uniformity in EC competition law supervision. There is, however, less information about the precise nature of these concepts and the consequences to be drawn from them. Similarly, competition lawyers are united in their call for uniformity, although without questioning whether uniformity ought to be a top priority in this context. On closer scrutiny, uniformity and effectiveness are exposed as integration goals and not as based on competition law theory. The main economic value lies in reduction of costs, given that it will be less expensive for authorities and courts in Member States to inform themselves about EC law, than for economic operators to inform themselves about 27 different national laws.

At least the preparatory works, as well as the academic discussion, support the view that the modernisation was *output orientated legislation*, intended to make Articles 81 and 82 EC less of a paper product and more of an enforced reality. The vagueness of the discussions on effectiveness and uniformity, prevalent when the modernisation was enacted, may be understood better if seen as a call for legitimacy, especially the need to ensure average compliance. The method employed in this work, however, builds on the need, in a legitimacy analysis, to look not only for average compliance but also for a legitimate genesis of the law. This can be described as a sense of scepticism regarding the idea that EC competition law has long since achieved 100 per cent rationality and that it was only proper enforcement that was lacking prior to modernisation.

It cannot be excluded from start that the enforcement problems experienced before modernisation were symptoms of a deeper legitimacy crisis, which has not been fully addressed nor remedied. Furthermore, the present analysis has revealed low levels of central enforcement mechanisms. There is a dependence on the goodwill of Member States to ensure average compliance. The fragmented enforcement structure created results in a crucial need for a rational law that can

[175] White Paper, above n 1, at 83.

be understood and applied by lawyers in a large number of legal cultures and subcultures. Whether the law fulfils this need will be tested here with reference to a relatively detailed examination of several aspects of EC law. The rationale for the policy against hard-core infringements will be tested, as well as central jurisprudence on horizontal hard-core infringements, evidentiary rules, procedure and fines. The method serves to avoid generalisations and short-cuts, and will provide a thoroughly underpinned evaluation of the role of legitimacy in decentralised EC cartel control.

3

Testing Legitimacy of the Policy Pursued

THE PARADIGM SHIFT in EC competition law enforcement policy from vertical restrictions to cartels, brought about by the modernisation, will be evaluated in this chapter, to see whether the new enforcement policy corresponds to conceptions prevailing in society. It has already been explained in chapter two that the modernisation of EC competition law was driven by the objective of creating better output in terms of antitrust control. The method was to make the pursuit of hard-core horizontal restraints rather than vertical restrictions a priority, and to engage Member States in competition law enforcement. It was also explained that enforcement could be legitimate only as long as a legitimate law was enforced.[1] Addressed in this chapter is the question whether the change in enforcement focus brought about by modernisation is rational, and thus legitimate in a deeper sense.

The present chapter aims at extracting legitimacy from an outside perspective to see whether competition policy corresponds to deeper notions in society or common goals that can be fulfilled only jointly. In other words, can the law be rationally reconstructed?

Majone's reflections on the legitimacy of EC law may be of help. He connects the legitimacy question to the fact that the EU is lagging behind in economic growth, and continues:

> Legitimacy involves the capacity of a political system to engender and maintain the belief that its institutions are the most appropriate ones for the society. It follows that a serious crisis may develop if a new system is unable to produce the results expected by major social groups for a period long enough to develop new sources of legitimacy. While prolonged effectiveness—which today means primarily a satisfactory level of economic growth—may give legitimacy to a new political system, a breakdown of effectiveness for a long period will endanger even a legitimate system's stability. It is this connection between effectiveness, legitimacy, and systemic stability which makes the poor economic performance of the EU over the last 30 years so worrisome.[2] (footnote omitted)

Majone clearly has a point: the EU must generate economic welfare if it is to be seen as legitimate among citizens. Here, competition law will not be the only

[1] Habermas, Jürgen, *Between Facts and Norms* (Cambridge, Polity Press, 1996), at 27, 29.

[2] Majone, Giandomenico, 'Legitimacy and Effectiveness: A Response to Professor Michael Dougan's Review Article on Dilemmas of European Integration' (2007) 32(1) *EL Rev* 70, at 75.

solution, but it can definitely contribute. Competition law can set up obstacles to actions that will restrict competition.

To avoid an inbred, EC law-based view of these phenomena, I will look primarily at sources outside EC law and build the analysis on economics, US law and the experiences from global forums such as the Organisation for Economic Co-operation and Development (OECD), the International Competition Network (ICN) and the World Trade Organisation (WTO). Economics in particular require careful consideration. As stated by Areeda and Hovenkamp: 'Economic theory provides significant help but is not determinative. The theorists themselves are often in dispute'.[3]

From a legal theoretical perspective, the analysis in this chapter leans heavily on law and economics. Given that the comparative legal analysis is of US law, which is influenced in large part by law and economics, the comparisons ultimately are also drawn from law and economics.

The Treaties contain several provisions which in principle opt for economic growth and market economy. According to Article 2 of the Treaty on the European Union, one of the Union's objectives is to promote economic progress. Article 3(g) of the EC Treaty provides that the activities of the Community shall include a system ensuring that competition in the internal market is not distorted. Furthermore, Article 4 EC states that the activities of the Member States and the Community shall include adoption of an economic policy, 'conducted in accordance with the principles of an open market economy with free competition'. However, the Treaties as such do not contain any predetermined views or definitions of concepts such as economic growth, open market economy, or competition. The significance of this is as follows: the Treaties express a certain openness towards economics, given the references in the Treaties to economic growth, economic progress, open market economy and competition. The Treaties are not closed systems but retain, for the purpose of interpretation and application, a certain curiosity or inquisitiveness in relation to economics. This represents a dynamic which calls for continuous evaluation and development of competition policy in relation to new insights in economic theory, and in relation to real-world developments in the global economy and the economy of Member States.

I. WHETHER THE FIGHT AGAINST CARTELS IS LEGITIMATE IN A DEEPER SENSE

The following discussion targets two distinct questions: whether a cartel prohibition is justified as such, and whether it is justified to spend scarce public resources on combating cartels instead of other restrictions.

[3] Areeda and Hovenkamp, *Antitrust Law—An Analysis of Antitrust Principles and Their Application*, 2nd edn (New York, Aspen Publishers, Wolters Kluwer Law and Business), Vol VII, § 1500, at 337.

A. Cartels: an introduction

There is no clear-cut international agreement on what a cartel actually is, or on what is the best way to prohibit it.[4] The OECD defines a hard-core cartel as

> an anticompetitive agreement, anticompetitive concerted practice, or anticompetitive arrangement by competitors to fix prices, make rigged bids (collusive tenders), establish output restrictions or quotas, or share or divide markets by allocating customers, suppliers, territories, or lines of commerce . . .[5]

The ICN notes widespread consensus on the basic statutory elements, which are: an agreement between competitors to restrict competition, with price-fixing, output restrictions, market allocation and bid-rigging as archetypes of hard-core conduct.[6]

As explained, the Commission has limited its use of leniency (that is, immunity from or the reduction of fines) to cartels, defining cartels as follows:

> agreements and/or concerted practices between two or more competitors aimed at co-ordinating their competitive behaviour on the market and/or influencing the relevant parameters of competition through practices such as the fixing of purchase or selling prices or other trading conditions, the allocation of production or sales quotas, the sharing of markets including bid-rigging, restrictions of imports or exports and/or anti-competitive actions against other competitors.[7]

The Notice defines cartels solely for the purpose of immunity from or reduction of administrative fines imposed by the Commission, and consequently does not add any qualification or extra layer to the prohibition in Article 81 EC. Given the wide discretion the Commission enjoys in setting fines, it may well change its cartel definition in future leniency notices. National authorities are, of course, free to choose their own definitions for the purpose of fines or leniency under national competition law.

European Community courts and institutions frequently use the term 'cartel'. However, there is no definition of the term as such in the EC Treaty, where the relevant provision is Article 81(1). This prohibits all agreements, decisions by associations of undertakings and concerted practices which may affect trade between Member States, and which have as their object or effect the prevention, restriction or distortion of competition within the common market.

[4] Marsden, Philip, *Exclusionary Anti-Competitive Practices, their Effects on Competition and Development, and Analytical and Remedial Mechanisms,* Report prepared for UNCTAD (Geneva, United Nations, 2005), at 14, available at www.unctad.org.

[5] Recommendation of the OECD Council Concerning Effective Action against Hard Core Cartels, reproduced in OECD, *Hard Core Cartels, Third Report on the Implementation of the 1998 Recommendation* (OECD, 2005), Annex 1, Section 1.A.2.a).

[6] ICN Working Group on Cartels, *Defining Hard Core Cartel Conduct, Effective Institutions, Effective Penalties* (European Communities, ICN, 2005), at 10.

[7] *Commission Notice on immunity from fines and reduction of fines in cartel cases* [2006] OJ C/298/17.

For the purpose of this study, it is noteworthy that examples of prohibited practices are listed in Article 81(1)(a), (b) and (c) EC: direct or indirect fixing of purchase or selling prices or any other trading conditions, the limitation or control of production, markets, technical development or investment, and the sharing of markets or sources of supply. These are all classic representations of cartel behaviour. The provision encompasses all sorts of anticompetitive behaviour, ranging from agreements that have pro-competitive effects, eligible for exemption under Article 81(3) EC, to hard-core non-exemptible restrictions such as price-fixing. Article 81(1) EC makes no conceptual difference between cartels and other restrictions on competition.[8] As will be argued later in this chapter, it is likely, although not verifiable, that Article 81(1) *in combination with* Article 81(3) EC distinguishes cartels as competition law restrictions that are normally too harmful to qualify for exemption.

B. Empirical legitimacy: international discussions, experiences and policies

Looking at the *empirical legitimacy* of the fight against cartels, cartels are recognised internationally as a threat to competition. In *Trinko*, the US Supreme Court described collusion as the supreme evil of antitrust.[9] Ruling on the appeal in *SAS and Maersk*, the Court of First Instance spelled out that cartels counteract the EC Treaty's main objective of integrating the Community market.[10] The European Commission seems less inclined to consider the integration aspect as a leading theme and has made the following policy statement, which is clearly based on economics:

> Cartels are among the most serious violations of competition rules. What distinguishes them from all other anticompetitive practices is that they are secret agreements or concerted practices between competitors. It is due to this characteristic that they are considered 'cardinal sins'. Cartels are particularly harmful to European industry and consumers. They diminish social welfare, create allocative inefficiency and transfer wealth from consumers to the participants in the cartel by modifying output and/or prices in comparison with market-driven levels. Cartels are harmful also over the long run. Engaging in cartels to avoid the rigours of competition can result in the creation of artificial, uneconomic and unstable industry structures, lower productivity gains or fewer technological improvements and sustained higher prices. Furthermore, the weakening of competition leads to a loss of competitiveness and threatens sustainable development.[11]

[8] Joshua, Julian M, and Jordan, Sarah, 'Combinations, Concerted Practices and Cartels: Adopting the Concept of Conspiracy in European Community Competition Law' (2004) 24(3) *Northwestern Journal of International Law and Business* 647, at 651.

[9] *Verizon Communications Inc v Law Offices of Curtis V Trinko, LLP*, 540 US 398, 124 S Ct 872, Jan 13, 2004.

[10] Case T-241/01 *Scandinavian Airlines System v Commission* [2005] ECR II-2917, at para 85.

[11] XXXIInd Report on Competition Policy 2002, SEC (2003) 467 Final, at 28.

The Commission continues:

> For all these reasons, the detection, prosecution and punishment of secret hardcore cartel agreements is one of the central elements of the Commission's competition policy . . .[12]

The OECD initiated an anti-cartel programme in the late 1990s and adopted a Recommendation on effective action against cartels.[13] The Recommendation condemned hard-core cartels as 'the most egregious violations of competition law' which

> injure consumers in many countries by raising prices and restricting supply, thus making goods and services completely unavailable to some purchasers and unnecessarily expensive to others . . .

As stated in the Recommendation, 'effective action against hard core cartels is particularly important from an international perspective', and member countries are called upon to ensure that their competition laws effectively halt and deter them. In particular, their laws should ensure adequate legal prohibitions, effective sanctions, enforcement procedures and investigation tools.[14]

In a 2005 follow-up publication about the ongoing fight against cartels, the OECD noted that, since the adoption of the above Recommendation, the OECD Competition Committee had considered the anti-cartel effort as one of its top priorities.[15]

The WTO's Working Group on the interaction between trade and competition policy produced a background note in 2002, finding that

> hardcore cartels are the most pernicious type of anticompetitive practice from the point of view of trade and development as well as of competition law enforcement; that they can have the effect of undermining the benefits that should flow from international trade liberalization, and hence are an important concern for the multilateral trading system . . .[16]

In 2004, the ICN established its Cartel Working Group, with a view to addressing the challenges of anti-cartel enforcement, both domestically and internationally.[17] In a Report prepared for its 2005 Conference, the ICN positioned itself by declaring that '[s]ecret cartel agreements are a direct assault on the principles of competition and are universally recognised as the most harmful of all types of anticompetitive conduct'.[18]

Turning to the empirical legitimacy of spending scarce government resources on cartel enforcement, it is recognised that cartels differ, from an enforcement

[12] *Ibid.*

[13] Recommendation, above n 5, Annex 1.

[14] *Ibid*, Section I.A.1.

[15] OECD, *Hard Core Cartels, Third Report on the Implementation of the 1998 Recommendation*, above n 5, at 7.

[16] World Trade Organisation Working Group on the Interaction between Trade and Competition Policy, 'Provisions on Hardcore Cartels', WT/WGTCP/W/191, at 3, available at www.wto.org.

[17] Mandate for the ICN Cartels Working Group, available at www.internationalcompetitionnetwork.org.

[18] ICN Working Group on Cartels, above n 6, at 5.

perspective, from other competition law infringements. For the purpose of analysing the legitimacy of the pursuit against cartels, it is worthwhile to observe that policymakers consider cartels extremely harmful and particularly difficult to expose and bring to justice. Detection, evidence and procedure are at the core in cartel work. In effect, cartel law is different from the perspective of the practitioner. Bringing cartel participants to justice entails a battery of specific problems related to fact-finding, legal assessments, burden of proof, standard of proof, sanctions, leniency and rights of the defence.

Although similar difficulties are encountered, at least in part, in other types of infringement cases, such as abuse of dominance and vertical restraints, cartel cases have gradually distinguished themselves as a separate category for the purpose of enforcement. Their distinctive character has been recognised in academic contributions,[19] and also by the OECD in the following terms:

> cartel operators know that their conduct is unlawful and they operate their conspiracies in secret. In some cases they devise elaborate schemes for concealing their arrangements. When competition authorities do learn of a possible cartel and begin an investigation the conspirators do not willingly co-operate with it. Thus, cartels are unique among the various types of anticompetitive conduct, and unique investigative methods are required to combat them.[20]

The ICN explains:

> The pursuit of cartels requires certain specialist skills which differ from the skills required for the investigation and prosecution of other infringements of competition law. Cartel offences such as price-fixing, volume quotas, market sharing or collusive tendering are considered in many jurisdictions as *per se* infringements for which it is almost universally accepted that they restrict competition. Hence, the focus lies on proving the existence of the arrangement itself rather than demonstrating its impact on the market in economic terms.[21]

The ICN observes that an increasing number of competition agencies have set up special cartel branches, to build up centres of excellence.[22] This is certainly true for the EC, where the Commission set up a new cartel unit in 2005[23] (its first cartel unit had been created in 1998, the second in 2002).

Cartel enforcement shows marked administrative law and public law features, and is also closely related to criminal law. This makes it different from other fields of competition law, which are often more related to economics and contract law.[24]

[19] Harding, Christopher, and Gibbs, Alun, 'Why go to court in Europe? An analysis of cartel appeals 1995–2004' (2005) 30(3) *EL Rev* 349, at 354.

[20] OECD, *Hard Core Cartels, Recent progress and challenges ahead* (OECD, 2003), at 19.

[21] ICN Working Group on Cartels, above n 6, at 23.

[22] *Ibid*, at 47.

[23] Saarela, Anna, and Malric-Smith, Paul, 'Reorganisation of cartel work in DG Competition' (2005) *Competition Policy Newsletter*, No 2, Summer, at 43: 'Cartel work has a strong legal focus, both in investigation and development of a case, and in the need to apply correct procedures and ensure that rights of the defence are respected.'

[24] Harding, Christopher and Joshua, Julian, *Regulating Cartels in Europe—A Study of Legal Control of Corporate Delinquency* (Oxford, Oxford University Press, 2003), at 3–4.

Cartel behaviour constitutes a criminal offence in many jurisdictions, notably in the US, Canada and the UK. Whether criminal sanctioning is a necessary element in public enforcement is often debated.[25]

In summary, there is consensus, at least in industrialised countries, about the harmful nature of cartels and the need to combat them. Tentatively, the policy in the EC is (in recent years) based on the adverse welfare effects of cartels rather than on the integration objective. The reasons for this will be explored next, with reference to economics.

C. Economic perspectives and some facts and figures on cartels and cartel law enforcement

There is no available information—not even estimates—about how many cartels exist worldwide or in any particular jurisdiction. Neither are there any statistics on the chances of detecting cartels and bringing them to justice. Similarly, there is no simple rule of thumb to quantify the profits cartels make or, alternatively, the losses they cause to society. The participants in these secret unlawful arrangements are unlikely to volunteer information to enlighten us.

Given the considerable information deficit just outlined, how do we know that cartels are harmful to society, and how can we justify allocation of public resources to enforcement? Presented here are some economic perspectives that will provide understanding of why competition law should be particularly stringent in prohibiting cartels and controlling such prohibition.

1. Allocative inefficiencies resulting from cartels

Competition will push companies on the market to produce at the lowest cost available. Inefficient companies will (after a while) have to leave the market, to be replaced by more efficient competitors. This is known as operating efficiency. Allocative efficiency occurs when price equals marginal costs in the market, which presupposes a sufficiently large number of companies in operation, buying and selling, as well as resource mobility. There is then efficient use of resources both on the production side and on the buyer or consumer side, where welfare is maximised because each buyer pays the value of the product.[26] Another logical consequence of a competitive economy is that companies will seek efficiency by improving products and production.

Economic theory predicts that cartels (for the time being understood as involving price-fixing, bid-rigging, quotas and market-sharing) generate allocative

[25] Wils, Wouter P J, *The Optimal Enforcement of EC Antitrust Law—Essays in Law and Economics* (The Hague, Kluwer Law International, 2002), ch 8.

[26] Generally see Areeda and Hovenkamp, *Antitrust Law—An Analysis of Antitrust Principles and Their Application*, 3rd edn (New York, Aspen Publishers, Wolters Kluwer Law and Business), Vol IIB, § 402, at 6 ff.

inefficiencies as well as additional inefficiencies in society caused by *weakened* competition. That is because cartels, like monopolies, reduce output and increase prices. Posner presents the basic problem as follows:

> When market prices rises above the competitive level, consumers who continue to purchase the sellers' products at the new, higher price suffer a loss . . . exactly offset by the additional revenue that the sellers obtain at the higher price. Those who stop buying the product suffer a loss . . . not offset by any gain to the sellers. This is the 'deadweight loss' from supracompetitive pricing. . . .[27]

The allocative inefficiency is the welfare loss resulting from customers having less money to spend on the things that they would prefer. More money is spent on the cartelised product. Alternatively, there is a loss because the customers do not buy the products at all at the higher price.

Deadweight loss consists of the reduced benefits to society caused by the non-occurrence of transactions that would otherwise happen. 'The deadweight loss reflects the inefficiency from the sales that did not take place.'[28] Any cartel that reduces output will cause deadweight loss.[29] The deadweight loss includes not only the loss of certain transactions, but also the fact that some consumers will turn to substitute products which they value less.[30]

Cartels can be created quickly and without all the competition and investment that is required to build up a monopoly position. Driving out rivals from the market is a costly business, while invitations to them to join in monopoly profits can be made at short notice and at relatively low cost. Because of its quick and low-cost creation, much lower profit levels are sufficient to make the cartel profitable. This mechanism is recognised in US law as the main reason for heightened concern about cartels.[31] The relationship between cartel control and other forms of competition restriction will be examined later on in this chapter.

2. X-efficiency and social costs resulting from cartels

As explained above, higher prices, reduced output, welfare transfers and deadweight loss are often referred to as the major objections to cartels. However, there is another and even more compelling reason for antitrust intervention. Cartels generate a long-term impact on the market. For instance, investment decisions will tend to be optimised in relation to the cartel arrangement, which means that the cost structure of the participants will be altered.[32] More particularly, cartels can be

[27] Posner, Richard A, 'The Social Costs of Monopoly and Regulation', *Journal of Political Economy*, Aug 75, Vol 83, Issue 4, at 807.

[28] Leslie, Christopher R, 'Antitrust damages and deadweight loss' (2006) 51(3) *The Antitrust Bulletin* 521, at 530.

[29] *Ibid*, at 525.

[30] *Ibid*, at 535.

[31] Areeda and Hovenkamp, above n 26, Vol XII, § 2002, at 16–17.

[32] Konkurransetillsynet, 'Sanksjonering—er verdt prisen? Om sanksjonering under konkurranseloven', *Skrifter fra Konkurransetillsynet* 1/2001, at 29.

expected to operate with higher costs. Given that a cartel is a loose co-operation, participants will be reluctant to close down inefficient production units and will rather negotiate joint output reductions, maintaining production in high-cost units. Cartelists may thus have significantly higher costs than monopolies.[33] Cost savings realised by secret joint bidding are not considered relevant in this context, because costs for tendering are seen as normal costs for competition.[34] Industry structure may be affected as such by cartels, since the unlawful conduct will insulate the participants from normal structural measures such as the closing down of unprofitable businesses. In an unlawful cartel, 'cartelists may be afraid to reduce their productive capacity to the level that is optimal for the cartel's reduced output, since competition may break out at any time'.[35] Supra-normal profits can induce market entry, but conversely the cartel can engage in building entry barriers.

Economic theory predicts that undertakings will be less efficient as a result of weaker exposure to competition. Leibenstein studied this phenomenon in 1966 and called it X-efficiency.[36] Challenging the theory of the firm that depended on the assumption of cost minimisation, Leibenstein demonstrated that the degree of competitive pressure, as well as other motivational factors, affected productivity and cost:

> In situations where competitive pressure is light, many people will trade the disutility of greater effort, of search, and the control of other people's activities for the utility of feeling less pressure and of better interpersonal relations . . .[37]

Leibenstein highlighted the risk that reduced competition would result in managerial slack and a corresponding unwillingness by management to seek cost-improving production methods.[38] The data available suggested that the impact of X-efficiency, or X-inefficiency more properly labelled, is considerably larger than that of welfare transfers resulting from monopoly output and prices.

Indeed, prospects of easy profits can cause productive inefficiencies because of the reduced incentives to keep production costs down, and reduce the incentive to innovate.[39]

Posner analyses social costs, defined as deadweight loss plus additional costs. Monopoly profits (including cartel profits) tend to transform into higher costs for the industry, without a corresponding consumer surplus. Cartelists and monopolists have an incentive to engage in rent-seeking activities, intended to maintain or acquire monopoly power: 'an opportunity to obtain a lucrative transfer payment in the form of monopoly profits will attract real resources into efforts by

33 Areeda and Hovenkamp, above n 31, Vol IIB, § 405, at 29.

34 Areeda and Hovenkamp, above n 3, Vol XII, § 2002, at 14.

35 Posner, Richard A, *Antitrust Law*, 2nd edn (Chicago, University of Chicago Press, 2001), at 16.

36 Leibenstein, Harvey, 'Allocative Efficiency vs "X-Efficiency"' (1966) 56 *American Economic Review* 392.

37 *Ibid*, at 413.

38 *Ibid*, at 408.

39 Van den Bergh, Roger J, and Camesasca, Peter D, *European Competition Law and Economics: A Comparative Perspective*, 2nd edn (London, Thomson Sweet & Maxwell, 2006), at 155.

sellers to monopolize . . .'.[40] In response, customers can be expected to spend resources on preventing being charged monopoly prices.[41] Secondly, Posner observes *inter alia* that constraints on price competition can lead to improvements of non-price competition such as levels of service, although the value of improved service is less than its cost.[42] Applying a model for estimating the social costs, Posner finds levels of social costs roughly corresponding to, or even exceeding, the cartel price increases.[43] Although some consumer benefits can accrue, the net effect is substantive welfare losses to society.

X-inefficiency and social costs emerge as the principal problems caused by cartels. There is every reason to take stringent measures against cartels simply in order to prevent X-inefficiency and the welfare losses resulting from the transfer of cartel profits into social costs, quite independent of the losses for consumers.

3. *Cartel frequency and geographic impact*

There are no official figures on the number of detected cartels. Estimates can be found in academic writing, and occasionally from other sources. Aggregated data are scarce and the academic findings in the field are difficult to compare since there is no uniform standard, either for the basis of estimates or on how to present them.

Connor and Helmers identified 283 modern private international cartels as having been detected throughout the world from January 1990 to the end of 2005, and found that in the early 2000s about 35 such cartels were uncovered each year.[44]

In a large-scale survey the ICN identified 117 public enforcement penalty decisions in cartel cases in the year 2003 alone, involving 174 companies that were fined.[45] During the same year, 30 individuals were sentenced to prison for cartel crimes, for a total of over 500 months.[46] The survey included Australia, Brazil, Canada, the EU, France, Germany, Hungary, Ireland, Japan, Mexico, Pakistan, Russia, South Africa, Spain, Sweden, Switzerland, the United Kingdom, the US and Venezuela.

According to the European Commission, it adopted 66 cartel decisions from 1969 to 2002.[47] There is no available information on how the Commission arrived at this figure, which demonstrates a grave case of institutional amnesia. In fact the Commission's record is twice as good as its own estimate. My own case studies include approximately 150 formal Commission decisions from 1969 to 2007

[40] Posner, above n 35, at 13–14.
[41] *Ibid.*
[42] Posner, above n 27, at 810–11.
[43] Posner, above n 35, at 304.
[44] Connor, John M, and Helmers, C Gustav, 'Statistics on Modern Private International Cartels, 1990–2005', The American Anitrust Institute AAI Working Paper No 07-01.
[45] ICN Working Group on Cartels, above n 6, at 56. Figures for the years 2002 and 2001 were also presented.
[46] *Ibid.*
[47] Lowe, Philip, 'What's the Future for Cartel Enforcement', Speech presented at the Conference *Understanding Global Cartel Enforcement*, Conrad Hotel, Brussels, 11 February 2003.

under Article 81 EC and Article 65 ECSC against horizontal cartels,[48] out of which some 120 fall within the period 1969–2002.

The number of cartel decisions is subject to various and contradicting estimates: Guersent finds a total of less than 80 Commission decisions against hard-core cartels during the period 1969 to 2003,[49] and Jephcott finds 87 major Commission cartel decisions during the same period.[50] Sakkers and Ysewyn address 96 decisions until 2007.[51] The reason for this confusion is the absence of a cartel concept on which everyone can agree.

Schinkel, in his study of detected cartels, finds 181 anticompetitive horizontal agreements, including 14 cases where negative clearance was given and 24 exemption decisions. He refers to all these as cartels, arguing that a considerable number of notifications obtained negative clearance or exemptions in the 1960s for practices that would have raised suspicions today.[52] For the purpose of legal analysis I find some methodological problems with this approach. Admittedly, cases that were tried 40 years ago could have another outcome if they were tried today, but it is hardly workable to reassess and reclassify over 40 years of Commission decision-making practices. Secondly, there can exist such decisions that have actually been tried on appeal and upheld. This reminds us that Commission decisions are not at the top of the hierarchy of sources of Community law. Authority on EC cartel cases must ultimately be sought in the jurisprudence of the Court of Justice. The Court of First Instance is the second-highest authority, and must be considered the expert court given its assessments of both law and facts, while Commission decisions must be seen as the starting point for what has in the last decade effectively become cartel proceedings in three instances (the Commission, the Court of First Instance and the Court of Justice).

On recent enforcement, Geradin and Henry identify 48 decisions under Article 81 EC during the period 1998 through 2004,[53] of which most are cartel decisions. Veljanovski reports 39 cartel decisions between 1999 and 2004.[54]

The US stepped up its cartel enforcement in the 1990s following a long period of limited activity in this area.[55] There seem to be no official figures available on the total number of cartels detected in the US. A table setting out violations

[48] Table of Cases.

[49] Guersent, Olivier, 'The Fight Against Secret Horizontal Agreement in the EC Competition Policy' in Hawk (ed), *International Antitrust Law & Policy: Fordham Corporate Law* (New York, Juris Publishing, 2003), at 47.

[50] Jephcott, Mark, *Horizontal Agreements and EU Competition Law* (Richmond, Richmond, 2005).

[51] Sakkers, Ewoud, and Ysewyn, Jordan, *European Cartel Digest* (The Netherlands, Wolters Kluwer, 2008).

[52] Schinkel, Maarten Pieter, 'Effective Cartel Enforcement in Europe' (2007) 30(4) *World Competition* 539, at 540.

[53] Geradin, Damien, and Henry, David, 'The EC fining policy for violations of competition law: An empirical review of the Commission decisional practice and the Community Courts' judgments' (2005) 1(2) *European Competition Journal* 425.

[54] Veljanovski, Cento, 'Penalties for Price-fixers: An Analysis of Fines Imposed on 39 Cartels by the EU Commission' (2006) 27(9) *ECLR* 510–13.

[55] Klein, Joel I, Speech at the International Anti-Cartel Enforcement Conference, 30 September 1999, available at http://www.usdoj.gov/atr/public/speeches/3727.htm.

yielding a corporate fine of $10 million or more, presented on the website of the US Department of Justice, indicates some 25 convicted cartels for 1995 through 2005.[56] The figures are not exhaustive. Many cartel cases are handled under the heading 'civil non-merger enforcement' as opposed to 'criminal enforcement'.[57] In one single year, the US reported civil action taken four times by the Department of Justice, and six times by the Federal Trade Commission, against cartel practices.[58] A recent estimate of the Federal Trade Commission's enforcement against horizontal restraints shows 84 orders issued from 1993 through 2003.[59] The US Department of Justice communicated in 2004 that about 50 grand juries were investigating suspected international cartel activity.[60] The public enforcement figures, if we had them, could not be expected to represent all detected cartels in the US. Given the role of private enforcement in the US (ie private plaintiffs suing for damages), there should be several more cases.

Evenett, Levenstein and Suslow identify 40 international price-fixing cartels as having been detected successfully by the US and/or EC during the 1990s.[61] The typical international cartel of the 1990s involved firms from two or three countries and had an average duration of six years.[62] In a further study, Levenstein and Suslow demonstrate the impact of international cartels on developing countries, finding that in 1997, developing countries imported over $51 billion in goods from industries where there had been international cartel activity at some point during the 1990s.[63] The annual overcharge must be substantial. Additional negative effects could be envisaged, such as exclusionary practices adopted by cartelists to block developing country participants from the market.[64] An analysis by Jenny of reports on *domestic* anticompetitive practices in developing countries, drawn from numerous public sources, demonstrates how consumers and industry in developing countries are affected by domestic cartels.[65] Numerous reports of cartel behaviour were found in several developing countries, in several economic sectors,

[56] available at http://www.usdoj.gov/atr/public/criminal/220752.htm.

[57] The Federal Trade Commission, in a report covering 2002 to March 2006, describes action taken against approximately 46 instances of what could be described as domestic cartels: 'Antitrust Enforcement Activities Fiscal Year 2002–March 15, 2006', presented at the ABA Antitrust Section Spring Meeting 2006, available at http://www.ftc.gov/bc/anncompreports.htm.

[58] *Annual Report on Competition Policy Developments in the United States from October 1, 2004, to September 30, 2005* (OECD, 2006, DAF/COMP(2006)7/07), at 11–14, available at http://www.ftc.gov/bc/anncompreports.htm.

[59] Langenfeld, James A, and Silvia, Louis, 'Federal Trade Commission horizontal restraint cases: an update' (2004) 49(3) *The Antitrust Bulletin* 521.

[60] 'Status Report: A Summary Overview of the Antitrust Division's Criminal Enforcement Program', available at http://www.usdoj.gov/atr/public/guidelines/202531.htm.

[61] Evenett, Simon J, Levenstein, Margaret C, and Suslow, Valerie Y, 'International Cartel Enforcement: Lessons from the 1990s' [2001] *World Economy* 1221.

[62] *Ibid*, at 1225–26.

[63] Levenstein, Margaret, and Suslow, Valerie Y, 'Contemporary international cartels and developing countries: Economic effects and implications for competition policy' (2004) 71(3) *Antitrust Law Journal* 801.

[64] *Ibid*, at 821.

[65] Jenny, Frédéric, 'Cartels and Collusion in Developing Countries: Lessons from Empirical Evidence' (2006) 29(1) *World Competition* 109.

including agriculture, food and beverages, transportation, fuel, construction materials, professional services, insurance, telecom and industry products. This survey, together with the work of Levenstein and Suslow, shows that the cartel problem is not restricted to developed economies but has a profound impact on developing countries as well.

On the whole, there is surprisingly little information available on the total number of cartels detected worldwide. The absence of official aggregated data is puzzling, since it strongly indicates a lack of awareness by leading antitrust agencies of their own enforcement records against cartels. This ultimately stems from the absence of a cartel concept on which everyone can agree. But at least it is obvious that cartels exist, possibly in all jurisdictions worldwide.

Some cartels are domestic, while others are international in scope. The problem persists over decades (indeed centuries), in spite of existing prohibitions. Following increased awareness and enforcement, more and more cartels surface. A safe assumption is that the number of cartels in operation has been significantly higher than those sentenced thus far. This is illustrated by the race to the courthouse brought about by adoption of leniency programmes. Following the adoption of its 2002 Leniency Notice, the Commission received over 200 leniency applications in four years, from companies seeking immunity from or the reduction of fines for cartel participation.[66] The US Department of Justice has received more than one amnesty application per month since the adoption of its 1993 Leniency program.[67] Available data thus confirm the importance of allocating public resources to the fight against cartels, since their occurrences are frequent enough and quantitative enough to cause disturbances to the economy.

4. *Empirical studies on cartel duration*

What is the duration of a typical cartel? If cartels are inherently unstable[68] then public enforcement need not be very strong. If, on the other hand, cartels are successful in achieving stability, enforcers must be well organised too in order to detect them. Variations in duration could also help in focusing enforcement activities on areas where cartels seem most persistent—for instance, if international cartels prove to have a longer duration than domestic cartels, or if certain markets appear more prone to harbour stable cartels.

Levenstein and Suslow analyse cartel duration with reference to several studies.[69] They find an average cartel duration of between 3.7 and 7.5 years. Highlighting the

[66] Lowe, Philip, 'Commission's enforcement record in 2006', *Competition Policy Newsletter* 2007, No 1, Spring.

[67] Status Report: An Overview of Recent Developments in the Antitrust Division's Criminal Enforcement Program, p 8, 2/1/2004, available at http://www.usdoj.gov/atr/public/guidelines/202531.htm.

[68] Arbault, Francois, and Sakkers, Ewoud, 'Cartels' in Faull, Jonathan, and Nikpay, Ali (eds), *The EC Law of Competition* (Oxford, Oxford University Press, 2007), at paras 8.12, 8.64, 8.80, 8.90.

[69] Levenstein, Margaret C, and Suslow, Valerie Y, 'Studies of Cartel Stability: A Comparison of Methodological Approaches' in Grossman, Peter Z (ed), *How Cartels Endure and How They Fail, Studies of Industrial Collusion* (Cheltenham, Edward Elgar Publishing, 2004).

variation in outcomes, they observe *inter alia* that a significant number, between 12 and 37 per cent, lasted more than 10 years: 'Some cartels can barely get off the ground, while others last for decades.'[70] A crucial finding is the difficulty in measuring duration, because cartels appear to break down and reshape several times. In a subsequent study of 80 contemporary cartels existing in 1990 or later, the authors find an average duration of 7.5 years and a median of 6 years.[71]

In a study of over 200 international cartels discovered from January 1990 to July 2004, Zimmerman and Connor find an average duration of 6.3 years and a median of 4.4 years.[72] They find that increased use of antitrust leniency programmes has had a significant negative impact on cartel duration. The study indicates that cartels in highly concentrated sellers' markets tend to be longer-lived, and the same applies in industries with high barriers to entry.

In summary, available studies on cartel duration strongly contradict the idea that cartels will self-destruct more or less automatically shortly after formation. With an average life span of four to seven years, cartels will have time to inflict considerable damage before they break down. Recent research on why some cartels are stable while others are not will be presented in the sections below. The view that public resources should be allocated to the fight against cartels is thus reinforced by studies of cartel duration.

5. *Probability of detection*

Available studies on convicted cartels provide essential information about the cartel problem, but without revealing the actual number of cartels active in the past or present. There must be cartels out there that are never detected.

A method for estimating probability of detection was suggested by Bryant and Eckard in 1991.[73] Out of a sample of 184 cartels, they found that the average duration was five to seven years. The probability of getting caught in a given year was concluded to be between 13 and 17 per cent. This method does not seem to have gained any widespread use in the legal or economic communities. Although the authors suggest that one can extrapolate duration of non-detected cartels from those that are detected, there is still an unresolved sample selection issue. For instance, can we even be sure that the authorities managed to expose the full duration of the cartels that were brought to justice? Another problem is the absence of adaptation of the method to changes in enforcement policy. In other words, increased enforcement activities may be expected to generate a higher probability

[70] *Ibid*, at 17.

[71] Levenstein, Margaret C, and Suslow, Valerie Y, *Determinants of International Cartel Duration and the Role of Cartel Organization*, Ross School of Business Working Paper 1052, available at http://papers.ssrn.com/sol3/papers.cfm?abstract_id=936912.

[72] Zimmerman, Jeffrey E, and Connor, John M, 'Determinants of Cartel Duration: A Cross-sectional Study of Modern Private International Cartels', available at www.agecon.purdue.edu/staff/connor/papers/.

[73] Bryant, Peter G, and Eckard, E Woodrow, 'Price Fixing: The probability of getting caught' (1991) 3 *Review of Economics and Statistics* 531.

of detection.[74] But more fundamentally, estimates of duration involve methodological problems, as demonstrated by Levenstein and Suslow.[75] It appears that cartels are cyclical, in the sense that the arrangements go through different stages, break down partially and are renegotiated. To illustrate this point, suppose a cartel is established, covering one product in two national markets. The cartel evolves and eventually covers five products worldwide. Meanwhile, several renegotiations and adjustments have taken place. When the cartel is eventually detected, are we dealing with one cartel of, say, 10 years' duration, or several cartels of shorter duration? Slight variations in the approach taken by the authorities and the courts can have an impact on the calculation of probability of detection, if average duration is used as a base.

Connor and Lande make the well-informed observation that 'Of course, no one knows the per centage of cartels that are detected and proven'.[76] The absence of verifiable estimates of the probability of detection is also confirmed by Wahl in a study on competition law sanctions.[77] Further studies and the development of economic models will be needed to clarify cartel frequency and the probability of detection.

In summary, available studies of the total number of detected cartels worldwide from time to time, and their geographic impact and duration, have provided support for the view that allocation of public resources for cartel fighting is a worthwhile cause. Attempts at estimating the total number of cartels (including both detected and undetected) are inconclusive, however, and give no solid indications about either the need for public resources or how sanctions should be quantified.

6. *On cartel profits and overcharges*

The present analysis does not address whether parties injured by competition restrictions are entitled to damages, and how such damages should be calculated. Nevertheless, an understanding of overcharges is relevant for determining whether a cartel prohibition is legitimate in a deeper sense and whether scarce public resources should be available for enforcement. And it is relevant, at least indirectly, to the proper structuring of a deterrent system of sanctions.

Assuming that the rationale behind cartel formation is profits for the participants,[78] measuring cartel profitability should be fundamental to the purpose of

[74] Studies that take this into account are the ones by Zimmerman and Connor (above n 72), comprising a sample of cartels discovered from January 1990 to July 2004, and the 2006 study by Levenstein and Suslow (above n 71).

[75] Levenstein and Suslow, above n 69, at 14.

[76] Connor, John M, and Lande, Robert H, 'How High do Cartels Raise Prices? Thinking Creatively About Remedies' (2005) 80(2) *Tulane Law Review* 513, at 519.

[77] Wahl, Nils, *Optimala sanktioner inom svensk konkurrensrätt* (Konkurrensverkets uppdragsforskning 2006:3), at 66, available at www.konkurrensverket.se.

[78] This assumption is probably over-simplistic and the motives can be more complex: see Parker, Christine, 'The "Compliance" Trap: The Moral Message in Responsive Regulatory Enforcement' (2006) 40(3) *Law and Society Review* 591, at 607–08.

public enforcement. However, it appears that cartel profitability is not an entirely straightforward concept. At their simplest, cartel profits equal cartel prices compared to the prices that would have prevailed in the absence of the cartel; but when we take a second look, does this layperson's definition hold true?

Price increases by cartelists are not always equal to cartel profits. As suggested by Posner, monopoly profits tend to be transferred into costs, normally referred to as social costs.[79] Standard social costs may involve expenses for organising the infringement and for legal assistance.[80] In a study covering over 40 international cartels fined by the European Commission, Levenstein and Suslow identify patterns of regular meetings and information exchange.[81] In the cartels studied, top executives met two or three times per year, while lower-level executives communicated more frequently.[82] Monthly information exchanges were standard procedure for the cartels in the markets for beer, citric acid, lysine, cartonboard, vitamins A, E and B5, and zinc phosphate.[83] The cost of organising meetings and information exchanges must be substantial.

Occasionally, the administration of the cartel was outsourced to a third party,[84] a measure that might be explained as expenses either for organising the cartel or for concealing it. There might be further costs for upholding the position achieved by the cartel, such as for arranging exclusionary practices, or for joint lobbyism with the aim of obtaining State interference through legislation, trade policies or anti-dumping measures,[85] not to mention the costs of company internal investigations and legal assistance once the cartel has been detected. All these expenses represent efficiency losses without any transfer of real wealth to the cartelists. There is thus an inherent, and perhaps irresolvable, difficulty in isolating cartel profits from social costs.

If there are difficulties in measuring cartel overcharges, such claims are at least litigated and made subject to expert testimony. As stated in the Ashurst study, the courts have simply refused even to allow standing for claims on compensation for deadweight loss.[86] Leslie has made the same observation.[87] Leaving the subject of damages claims aside, it would still be relevant for the purpose of public enforcement to quantify deadweight loss in order to construct credible and deterrent sanctions. But is this possible? The US Sentencing Guidelines include a proxy of 10 per cent deadweight loss. This proxy is now widely considered unsupported by

[79] Posner, above n 35, at 13–18, 299ff.

[80] Wahl, above n 77, at 14.

[81] Levenstein, Margaret C, and Suslow, V, 'Cartel bargaining and monitoring: The role of information sharing', in *The Pros and Cons of Information Sharing* (Stockholm, Konkurrensverket, 2006), at 35–74, available at www.konkurrensverket.se.

[82] *Ibid*, at 42.

[83] *Ibid*, at 49.

[84] *Ibid*, at 51.

[85] Evenett *et al*, above n 61.

[86] Ashurst, report prepared by Clark, E, Hughes, M. and Wirth, D., 'Study on the conditions of claims for damages in case of infringement of EC competition rules', 31 August 2004, at 12, available on http://ec.europa.eu/comm/competition/antitrust/others/actions_for_damages/study.html.

[87] Leslie, above n 28, at 527.

empirical data, which is why the Antitrust Modernization Commission (AMC) has recommended that it be re-evaluated (see further below). As for the calculation of deadweight loss on a case-by-case basis, Leslie argues that it should be possible to achieve reasonable estimates.[88] Calculations would include five elements:

a) market output with the infringement;
b) the amount of overcharge;
c) what the market output would have been in the absence of the infringement;
d) the price that would have been charged but for the violation; and
e) the shape of the demand curve.[89]

The determination of these variables is subject to approximations and it can be made only on a case-by-case basis in relation to a specific infringement on a specific market. It would appear that the structuring of a proxy for administrative public enforcement could (in theory) be based on a study of a statistically significant sample of such case studies. But as a result of the absence of court rulings on damages for deadweight loss, we have no access to data that could be used to determine an average.

Moving our focus to the calculation of overcharges or damages, there are several alternative methods to employ. The Ashurst study[90] describes the most commonly claimed antitrust damages as overcharges or lost net profits. At the extreme, exclusionary practices can drive a company out of business, in which case damages are likely to be equal to the value of a terminated business as a going concern. The principle underpinning damages calculations is what is called the 'counterfactual', in other words, what would have happened if the infringement had not occurred. This is also referred to as the 'but-for' approach, when one tries to measure whether the prices would have been lower but for the cartel. A basic problem is to isolate the effects of the infringement from other market effects. Five models are outlined in the study:

a) the before-and-after approach;
b) the yardstick approach;
c) the cost-based approach; and
d) two econometric models called 'price prediction' and 'theoretic modelling'.

The methodologies are described as complementary to each other, and they all have various benefits and drawbacks.[91]

On the same theme, Alfter and Young discuss economic analysis of cartel impact in particular, pointing out several factors that are crucial for accurate

[88] *Ibid*, at 542.
[89] *Ibid.*
[90] Ashurst, above n 86, at 43ff.
[91] *Ibid*, at 28–29, in particular the conclusion at para 3.37: '. . . assessing damages for overcharging cases (eg cartels) may be far from straightforward, with the analysis ranging from the relatively simple (ie before and after, and yardstick approaches) to the complex (ie theoretic simulation models and econometric modelling to predict but for prices). This will inevitably lead to some judgment being required as to which presumptions are the most plausible given the data available . . .'

estimations.[92] They recommend econometric modelling as the most systematic and comprehensive approach to estimating cartel effects, and highlight that the quality of econometric analysis will depend on the quality of the available input data.[93]

Damages may be restricted to losses caused to direct purchasers, and there may also be statutory limitation periods preventing claims. A plaintiff may be under an obligation to mitigate his loss.[94] As regards the losses for customers and consumers, it is generally accepted that a pass-on effect will often occur, from the level of trade immediately affected by the cartel to the next level of trade. The costs for transfer of wealth to the cartel participants will thus be fragmented over a large number of victims, at several levels of trade, making damages calculations extremely complicated. All of this does not necessarily pose problems for the purpose of public enforcement to which this study is limited, because deterrence does not presuppose adequate reparation for a correctly defined category of victims. It suffices to make infringements non-profitable for actual or potential offenders.

Studies on harm caused by cartels confirm the theoretical and practical complications of calculating cartel profits. It appears more accurate to use *overcharges* for the purpose of measurement. For the optimisation of enforcement, information on harm caused by only a few individual cartels will be insufficient, and a comprehensive picture must be drawn on the basis of an empirically sound sample selection. The question posed here is whether we have access to this type of information.

In 2002, the OECD carried out a survey on cartel impact. The OECD pointed out that the worldwide economic harm from cartels is clearly substantial, although difficult to quantify. A conservative estimate was many billions of US dollars each year.[95] Perhaps the most striking finding in the report was the complexity—or impossibility—of quantifying the harm caused by cartels. The OECD concluded that accurate quantification of the harm from hard-core cartels was not possible at the time of the report.[96] Estimates of harm caused by individual cartels, in terms of affected commerce, ranged from 3 per cent to 65 per cent, with a median of 15–20 per cent.[97] However, the sample in which calculations had been made was very narrow, comprising only 14 out of 133 cartels.

Similar findings were made by the ICN in 2005. It was convincingly clear that national competition authorities did not normally use gains from cartels as a base for calculating penalties, because of the difficulties in assessing such gains.[98] As a matter of fact, competition authorities will work on the basis of proxies for cartel gains rather than engaging in calculations.

[92] Alfter, M and Young, J, 'Economic Analysis of Cartels—Theory and Practice' (2005) 26(10) *ECLR* 546.

[93] *Ibid*, at 553.

[94] Wahl, Nils, *Konkurrensskada* (Stockholm, JureCLN AB, 2000), at 308.

[95] OECD, *Report on the nature and impact of hard core cartels and sanctions against cartels under national competition laws* (OECD, 2002, DAFFE/COMP(2002)7), at 2.

[96] *Ibid*, at 16.

[97] *Ibid*, at 9.

[98] ICN Working Group on Cartels, above n 6, at 54, 59.

Since 1987, the United States Sentencing Guidelines have addressed price-fixing by way of proxies:

> It is estimated that the average gain from price-fixing is 10 per cent of the selling price. The loss from price-fixing exceeds the gain because, among other things, injury is inflicted upon consumers who are unable or for other reasons do not buy the product at the higher prices. Because the loss from price-fixing exceeds the gain, subsection (d)(1) provides that 20 per cent of the volume of affected commerce is to be used in lieu of the pecuniary loss. . . .[99]

After nearly 20 years of application of the Guidelines, the AMC reviewed the proxies of 10 per cent gain and 20 per cent of the volume of affected commerce. As a result, the AMC urged Congress to encourage the Sentencing Commission to re-evaluate and explain the rationale for the use of the 20 per cent harm proxy.[100] Furthermore, the AMC intends to recommend that the Sentencing Commission amends the Sentencing Guidelines to make explicit that the 20 per cent proxy may be rebutted by proof by a preponderance of evidence that the actual overcharge was higher or lower.[101] The direction taken by the AMC seems to have been prompted by the insistence of qualified observers that the 20 per cent proxy was, and still is, unsupported by empirical data.[102]

The European Commission's 2006 fining guidelines are based on a proxy as well, where a level up to 30 per cent of the value of sales will be used as a base for determination of fines.[103] It is not entirely clear whether, like the US Sentencing Guidelines, this proxy includes not only expected gains but also the welfare loss resulting from cartels.[104] Presumably the Commission was guided by the discussions in the US when adopting the new method.

7. *Empirical studies of overcharges*

The most comprehensive studies on cartel overcharges, available when the present work was drafted, are those by Connor and Lande in 2005[105] and 2006.[106] Based on an analysis of 489 cartel episodes from the years 1780 to 2004, the authors found a median cartel overcharge of 25 per cent. For the 30 post-1990 observations in the study, the estimated overcharge was 24.5 to 26.2 per cent.

[99] United States Sentencing Guidelines, § 2R1.1. Bid-Rigging, Price-Fixing or Market-Allocation Agreements Among Competitors, Commentary, Pt 3.

[100] Antitrust Modernization Commission Report and Recommendations April 2007, at 295, available at http://www.amc.gov/report_recommendation/toc.htm.

[101] *Ibid.*

[102] AMC Criminal Remedies Discussion Memorandum of May 4, 2006, at 13–14, available at http://www.amc.gov/commission_documents.htm#may9.

[103] *Guidelines on the method of setting fines imposed pursuant to Article 23(2)(a) of Regulation 1/2003* [2006] OJ C/210/2, at 21.

[104] *Ibid*, recital 6: '. . . an appropriate proxy to reflect the *economic importance of the infringement*' (emphasis added).

[105] Connor and Lande, above n 76, at 519.

[106] Connor, John M, and Lande, Robert H, 'The size of cartel overcharges: Implications for US and EU fining policies' (2006) 51(4) *The Antitrust Bulletin* 983.

International cartels were more effective over time in raising prices: 30 to 33 per cent, as compared to 17 to 19 per cent for domestic cartels.[107] Unsuccessful cartels were rare, only about 7 per cent of the observations.[108]

Analysing the impact of the method of calculation on the overcharge estimates, the authors found that the before-and-after method generated higher overcharge estimates than econometric methods, and that cost-based and yardstick methods also generated relatively high estimates.[109] In a subsequent study, European cartel overcharges were found to be in the 28 per cent to 54 per cent range.[110]

Further findings were made by Connor and Helmers in 2007, when they estimated that aggregate cartel overcharges for 283 modern private international cartels detected anywhere in the world from January 1990 to the end of 2005, amounted to $300 billion, measured in real 2005 money.[111]

In a Discussion Paper of 2003, Werden reviews studies of criminally prosecuted cartels in existence in the US after 1974.[112] A total of 13 studies are included, estimating average price increases ranging from 6.5 per cent to 36 per cent.

Studies of cartel overcharges demonstrate considerable variations between individual cartels. Quoting Levenstein and Suslow: 'Some cartels are very successful at increasing prices while others are dramatic failures.'[113] When analysing cartel success in cross-section studies, economists often use data ranging from the 1800s to recent years.[114] Historic data on cartel overcharges are less useful, however, for understanding how cartels work in the 2000s. Increased enforcement activities and sanctions will expose cartels to a higher probability of detection. A case study on the *Vitamin* cartel indicates that a cartel operating in a jurisdiction with active antitrust enforcement will attempt to fly under the radar by raising prices less.[115] Werden argues: 'The price effects of cartels at earlier times may have been substantially different because sanctions were less severe'.[116] Conversely, new communications techniques can simplify cartel organisation and monitoring, and conceal the activities.[117] For the purpose of analysing the need for enforcement or appropriate sanctions in today's world, recent figures are needed. This is indeed recognised by Connor and Lande, who find, over time, a downward trend in cartel profitability. Average estimated overcharges for international cartels have fallen

[107] Connor and Lande, above n 76, at 559.
[108] *Ibid*, at 544.
[109] *Ibid*, at 550–51.
[110] Connor and Lande, above n 106.
[111] Connor and Helmers, above n 44.
[112] Werden, Gregory J, *The Effect of Antitrust Policy on Consumer Welfare: What Crandall and Winston Overlook*, Economic Analysis Group Discussion Paper EAG 03-2, January 2003, with accompanying references, available at http://papers.ssrn.com/sol3/papers.cfm?abstract_id=384100.
[113] Levenstein and Suslow, above n 69, at 14.
[114] *Ibid*, at 51.
[115] Clarke, Julian L, and Evenett, Simon J, 'The deterrent effects of national anticartel laws: evidence from the international vitamins cartel' (2003) *The Antitrust Bulletin*, Fall, 689.
[116] Werden, above n 112 *ibid*.
[117] For an illustration, see the Commission's press release of 24 January 2007, IP/07/80, on the insulated switchgear cartel. The cartel participants were reported to have used sophisticated measures, including anonymous e-mail addresses and encryption for sending messages.

to 25 per cent since 1990.[118] They suggest that the explanation is the influence of effective anti-cartel enforcement, supporting the view that cartelists find it increasingly difficult to hide their activities.[119] Alternatively, greater antitrust scrutiny could prevent cartelists from charging full monopoly prices.[120]

As mentioned above, the US stepped up its cartel enforcement in the 1990s, while the EC effort gained speed a few years later. It takes considerable time (up to five years in the EC) from the beginning of the investigatory phase to the adoption of a decision, several more years for appeals. Follow-on suits on damages for harm caused to private parties take their time to make it through the courts or, alternatively, settle. In the EC, the frequency of private litigation has been remarkably low. In the Ashurst study, only 11 damages cases were reported from the Member States.[121] The chances of obtaining information on cartel overcharges from judgments by Member State courts are consequentially remote, unless some very significant increase in litigation were to occur. Settlements are often confidential. The Commission's cartel decisions are uninformative about cartel overcharges, and confidential business information is normally deleted from the decisions and other publicly available documents. If we want to obtain reliable data on the harm caused by cartels since the 1990s, there is an obvious sample selection problem to be dealt with[122]; and that is even before we take into account the sample selection bias resulting from the fact that only detected cartels are being analysed. Nevertheless, even in the absence of reliable data on the harm caused by cartels in the EC, the US experience gives ample support for the view that a cartel prohibition is supported by empirical observations on the harm caused to society.

8. *Cartel formation and cartel stability*

In the absence of a clear understanding of concepts such as cartel frequency, cartel profitability and the probability of detection, it is a great challenge for both enforcers and the scientific community to understand the mechanisms behind cartel formation and cartel stability. Knowledge could help us determine whether and to what extent public resources should be allocated to combating cartels.

Cartels are illegal in developed economies. In the EU, agreements that are prohibited under Article 81 are automatically void according to Article 81(2) EC. A cartel agreement cannot be enforced in court; consequently, the parties must find their own ways to ensure that they all adhere to the arrangement. Not only is there a risk of cheating; cartels are also subject to pressures from the outside world. A single factor, such as fluctuation in exchange rate levels, can cause asymmetries in costs and profits for the cartel participants, and thus create tensions within the cartel.[123]

[118] Connor and Lande, above n 76, at 560.
[119] *Ibid*, at 541.
[120] *Ibid.*
[121] Ashurst, above n 86, at 43ff.
[122] The same problem identified in the US; see Connor and Lande, above n 76, at 551–52.
[123] Alexander, Barbara J, 'The Impact of Exchange Rate Levels and Changes on International Cartels: Implications for Liability and Overcharge' (2003) 70(3) *Antitrust Law Journal* 819.

In an effort to obtain information on the economic and structural factors that contribute to the formation, maintenance or detection of cartels, the UK Office of Fair Trading commissioned a study on how to predict cartels, published in 2005.[124] The authors identify three basic requirements for cartel formation: product, level of volatility, and company criteria. First, cartels are much more likely to form in industries with homogeneous products, while considerable product differentiation has the opposite effect.[125] Secondly, cartels are more likely in markets where the output and market conditions are normally stable, and less likely in volatile markets. Thirdly, large market shares and relatively constant market positions among the leading players lead to a higher likelihood of cartels; conversely, significant changes in market shares and regular exit and entry make cartels less likely.[126] Several collaborative factors are identified as well, including *inter alia* market transparency, barriers to entry and evidence of excess capacity.[127]

If a market has the fundamental background and strong collaborative factors, it appears that an additional factor—a catalyst—is still needed for the formation of a cartel. The authors call it the 'why and when', and continue:

> There are two categories where there is good evidence: (i) where there has been a long run decline in demand and/or prices affecting all or almost all companies and, (ii) where there is a sudden market shock that affects all companies in the market.[128]

The correlation between negative market shock and cartel formation is further emphasised:

> What is clear, however, is that cartel formation is generally linked with a decline in prices; indeed, this finding is so widespread across the cases, that it is almost a stylized fact. This price decline can take many forms, notably (i) an abrupt price plunge . . . or (ii) a gradual price decline.[129]

Price declines in turn appear to be connected to excess capacity, which can emerge as a result of prolonged demand downturn, or because of actions aimed at acquiring or capturing market shares.[130]

Once a cartel is formed, what will make it stable and successful? Levenstein and Suslow analyse cartel stability in depth with reference to several variables.[131] In an important leap, they move the focus from traditional explanations of external market factors, to the internal organisation of cartels,

[124] Grout, Paul A, and Sonderegger, Silvia, *Predicting Cartels*, Economic Discussion Paper, March 2005, Office of Fair Trading.

[125] *Ibid*, at 15.

[126] *Ibid*.

[127] *Ibid*, at 15–16.

[128] *Ibid*, at 16.

[129] *Ibid*, at 59.

[130] *Ibid*, at 66.

[131] Levenstein and Suslow, above n 69.

> such as the distribution of power within the cartel, its voting structure, the sophistication of mechanisms for detecting and deterring cheating, and the ability of the cartel itself to create barriers to entry . . .[132]

Through further studies the authors have confirmed that 'cartels with a sophisticated internal organization are more likely to endure, all else equal'.[133]

Inherent instability because of cheating is often referred to as the major obstacle for cartels.[134] When a cartel collectively decides to raise prices or reduce output, an individual undertaking can increase its revenues at the expense of others by secretly applying higher output or lower prices.[135] There is a conviction in economic scholarly writing that cartels will face instability as a combined result of cheating and counter-actions in terms of price wars directed against the cheaters to enforce the cartel agreement. Theory remains inconclusive as to whether cheating is more likely to occur when there is a downturn in demand or an upturn, or if unstable markets lead to unstable cartels.[136]

Nevertheless, empirical studies have somewhat contradicted the idea of cheating as the primary cause of cartel breakdown. Cross-section studies may confirm the role of cheating as the most common cause of breakdown,[137] but case studies indicate that only one-tenth of the cartels in a sample came to an end due to cheating, market entry and internal bargaining problems causing most of the breakdowns.[138] Contemporary cartelists are well aware of the risk of cheating and make precautions to avoid that particular problem. This is done through communication and monitoring. Communication is carried out at meetings and through phone-calls and other means, while monitoring includes sophisticated information exchange systems on sales volumes, prices and customers.

A reluctance to accept that cartels are inherently unstable as a result of cheating has been expressed by US scholars, who in addition point out that even cartels of relatively short duration can be profitable to the members and costly to society.[139] Moreover, even if we could find empirical support for cheating as a cause for instability and breakdown of cartels, the large number of actual and durable cartels discovered (in the EC around 150 from the 1960s to 2007) means that we cannot rely on instability as a cartel control mechanism. For policy purposes, the theory on cheating is of low significance as long as there are actual cartels around to deter.

It follows that cartels can occur in virtually all industry sectors under certain conditions. At its simplest, the formation of a cartel is typically preceded by a

[132] *Ibid*, at 43.
[133] Levenstein and Suslow, above n 81, at 41.
[134] Arbault and Sakkers, above n 68, at paras 8.12, 8.64, 8.80, 8.90.
[135] Alfter and Young, above n 92, at 548.
[136] Ashenfelter, Orley, and Graddy, Kathryn, 'Anatomy of the Rise and Fall of a Price-fixing Conspiracy: Auctions at Sotheby's and Christie's' (2005) 1(1) *Journal of Competition Law and Economics* 3, at 14.
[137] Levenstein and Suslow, above n 69, at 27.
[138] *Ibid*, at 36.
[139] Areeda and Hovenkamp, above n 3, Vol XII, § 2002, at 20–21.

longer decline in prices, or a market shock, in a not so dynamic industry with homogeneous products, among competitors with relatively stable market shares. Once formed, the stability of a cartel is determined partly by market factors, but perhaps primarily by how successful the cartel is in its internal organisation. This gives us an indication about enforcement strategies. Cartels are industry-related rather than related to poor competition cultures in certain Member States. There is also a strong learning factor involved, which explains why a successfully organised cartel can expand its activities to new products and new geographic markets. If a sector in the economy is in crisis, we can expect to find cartels in virtually all Member States where industry is affected. National borders provide little logic here for the purpose of enforcement, and there is a strong indication that enforcement should be carried out centrally by the EU rather than nationally.

In summary, studies of cartel formation and stability provide further support for the view that public resources should be allocated to the fight against cartels. The problem will not go away by itself, and the cartels are stable enough to cause harm to society.

D. Moral aspects of cartel behaviour

Transfer of wealth from consumers to producers as a result of supra-competitive pricing is considered neutral in welfare economics, because it will not alter the total wealth in society, only its distribution between classes.[140] For the consumers or customers who pay a cartel or monopoly mark-up, however, the practice may appear similar to theft.

A view where consumer welfare is at the centre is indeed represented in competition policy.[141] Gerber observes how, in the post-war decades, 'Europeans had become markedly less willing to acquiesce in distributive arrangements that favoured existing social and economic elites'.[142] A strong argument can be made in favour of penalising hard-core competition law infringements primarily on the basis that the offenders are taking it into their hands to redistribute wealth without the approval (or even knowledge) of those concerned.

Public communications on cartel enforcement often have moral overtones. Cartels have been described as the 'supreme evil of antitrust' by the US Supreme Court, as a 'cardinal sin' by the European Commission, as 'a direct assault on the principles of competition' by the ICN and as 'the most egregious violations of competition law' by the OECD. Commissioner Neelie Kroes has said that 'Cartels strike a killer blow at the heart of healthy economic activity'.[143] Historically,

[140] Van den Bergh and Camesasca, above n 39, at 37.

[141] *Ibid.*

[142] Gerber, David J, *Law and Competition in Twentieth Century Europe: Protecting Prometheus* (Oxford, Oxford University Press, 1998), at 167.

[143] Delivering on the crackdown: recent developments in the European Commission's campaign against cartels, SPEECH/06/595, 13 October 2006.

cartels were regarded as morally neutral in Europe.[144] Now, an argument could be made that the ultimate objective of enforcement activities directed against cartels is to create a moral standard which prevents individuals and undertakings from engaging in cartel activities. That may be precisely what enforcement officials are attempting to do when referring to cartels as morally objectionable. Leslie describes the creation of moral norms in this field as follows:

> By criminalizing price-fixing agreements, antitrust law communicates the seriousness of the offense. . . . The antitrust-based social norm of not committing crimes can overcome a countervailing social norm of cooperation among competitors. . . . Antitrust laws may help create a social norm in which refusing to participate in a cartel is not seen as being overly competitive or uncooperative with one's fellow businessman, but as being law-abiding.[145]

The reasoning referred to carries some weight, but I am still disinclined to believe that morality is sufficient as a value basis for prohibiting cartels and other hard-core competition law infringements. Moral outrage is based precisely on the presumed economic effects of the activities in question; hence, if economic theory and analysis were to show us that cartels, monopolies, resale price maintenance or territorial restrictions were neutral or insignificant when it came to the creation and redistribution of wealth in society, the reasoning based on morality would lose all its force. This shows that the real underlying logic is economics, not morality.

Looking at substantive law, Yeung argues that issues of fairness and morality have little or no role to play in determining whether the relevant conduct is unlawful.[146] But if one evaluates whether the existing substantive law reflects values in society, the opposite can hold true. Per se prohibitions may be legitimate precisely with reference to moral reasoning, as illustrated by Hovenkamp and Areeda, who argue that cartelists have little moral standing in claiming that their market power was too insignificant for the cartel to be successful.[147] Yeung's arguments are nevertheless viable: '. . . regulatory law is primarily concerned with achieving economic and social goals, rather than to express moral outrage at the proscribed conduct'.[148] She argues that regulatory wrongs are situated in a grey zone between civil and criminal law.[149]

McCulloch further highlights this moral ambiguity of the public perception of cartelists, where the line between, on the one hand, risk taking and entrepreneurship and, on the other hand, dishonest profit maximisation, cannot be expected to

144 Joshua, Julian M, and Jordan, Sarah, 'Combinations, Concerted Practices and Cartels: Adopting the Concept of Conspiracy in European Community Competition Law' (2004) 24(3) *Northwestern Journal of International Law and Business* 647, at 651.

145 Leslie, Christopher R, 'Trust, Distrust and Antitrust' (2004) 82(3) *Texas Law Review* 515, at 631.

146 See Yeung, Karen, *Securing Compliance—A principled approach* (Oxford, Hart Publishing, 2004), at 102.

147 Hovenkamp, H, and Areeda, PE, *Fundamentals of Antitrust Law* (Kluwer, looseleaf), at 15–38.

148 Yeung, above n 146, at 102.

149 *Ibid*, at 251.

be entirely clear to juries.[150] His position illuminates a problem with basing competition law prohibitions on morality: will morality ultimately tell us where, precisely, to draw the line between lawful and unlawful conduct? Here again, we are better served by economics than by morality.

The preceding discussion has demonstrated that it is difficult to base competition law prohibitions entirely on morality. Even so, morality provides some support for the view that certain types of conduct should be prohibited.

II. CONTRASTING PERSPECTIVES

A. Cartels versus tacit collusion

In a market with only a few sellers, those sellers will be able to observe each other's behaviour and adapt their own market behaviour accordingly.

A certain tension may be observed between law and economics when it comes to tacit collusion, since economic theory does not distinguish between tacit and explicit collusion. Economic literature places less emphasis on formal agreements and more on the prerequisites for firms to find strategies for co-ordinating their behaviour.[151] A viable argument has been made that

> from a welfare point of view, prohibiting explicit collusion does not solve all the problems. Coordination may also take the form of tacit collusion . . .[152]

Posner argues emphatically for including certain instances of tacit collusion in the prohibition set out in section 1 of the US Sherman Act. For this purpose he distinguishes between avoidable and unavoidable tacit co-ordination. Price reactions in response to external shocks (an increase of the price of raw material is given as an example) should be inevitable and unobjectionable. Tacit agreements to limit output and charge a higher price than the competitive price should, on the other hand, be unlawful.[153] While this signifies a departure from prevailing US law, Posner sees it as more of a change in evidentiary requirements to infer a meeting of minds on non-competitive prices.[154] Even so, there seems to be agreement that tacit collusion is not altogether easy to accomplish, or at least that it is more difficult than express agreements.

Tacit collusion can be undermined by factors such as monitoring and matching problems, differences in cost structures among competitors, product differentiation, existence of non-price competition, volatile markets, entry of new competitors and buyer power.[155] Furthermore, tacit collusion can take as its base several

[150] MacCulloch, Angus, 'Honesty, Morality and the Cartel Offence' (2007) 28(6) *ECLR* 355, at 362.
[151] Areeda and Hovenkamp, above n 3, Vol XII, §2002 at 15.
[152] Van den Bergh and Camesasca, above n 39, 163.
[153] Posner, above n 35, at 95.
[154] *Ibid*, at 98.
[155] Areeda and Hovenkamp, above n 26, Vol IIB, § 404 at 15ff.

different factors, such as either price or the preservation of existing market structures. Co-ordination based only on observations of how competitors behave will consequently be highly imperfect.[156] Neven goes so far as to say that without communication, collusion is difficult to achieve, except in very simple market environments and with only two firms and a lot of experience.[157] Then again, cartels can be more or less successful as well.[158] This last point, comparing imperfect tacit collusion with moderately successful cartels, is, however, contradicted by the recent empirical studies on cartel overcharges, referred to earlier in this chapter. It appears that, empirically, cartels are nearly always harmful in terms of overcharges. No similar data are available on tacit collusion.

The primary objection against antitrust rules prohibiting tacit collusion, however, lies not in the lower precision of tacit collusion, but in the severe enforcement problems that would arise. Haphazard outcomes and wrong convictions are clear possibilities if tacit collusion is made unlawful.[159] Posner recognises this problem but argues that it is exaggerated.[160] Areeda and Hovenkamp, on the other hand, consider, on balance, that there are practical obstacles to prohibiting tacit collusion.[161] They highlight that a prohibition on tacit collusion involves saying that a company ought to ignore its rivals' behaviour.[162] A problem with a prohibition against tacit collusion is how to design an appropriate remedy: if companies are to ignore each other's behaviour then courts become involved in active price control, for which they are unsuited.[163] The authors instead opt for controlling tacit collusion by a policy that prevents mergers and similar practices which threaten to create oligopolistic market structures, and by making facilitating practices difficult.[164]

Legal theory about tacit collusion is reflected in EC law. Tacit collusion as such is *lawful* and outside Article 81(1) EC. Economic operators are entitled to adapt themselves intelligently to the existing and anticipated conduct of their competitors, provided there are no direct or indirect contacts between them to this effect.[165] The same holds true for US law, where, in *Brooke Group*, the Supreme Court held that

> Tacit collusion, sometimes called oligopolistic price coordination or conscious parallelism, describes the process, not in itself unlawful, by which firms in a concentrated market might in effect share monopoly power, setting their prices at a profit-maximizing, supracompetitive level by recognizing their shared economic interests and their interdependence with respect to price and output decisions[166]

[156] Van den Bergh and Camesasca, above n 39, at 164.
[157] Neven, Damien J, '"Collusion" under Article 81 and the Merger Regulation' in *Fighting cartels—why and how* (Stockholm, Konkurrensverket, 2001), at 65.
[158] Areeda and Hovenkamp, above n 3, Vol VI, at § 221.
[159] Van den Bergh and Camesasca, above n 39, at 164.
[160] Posner, above n 35, at 98–99.
[161] Areeda and Hovenkamp, above n 3, Vol VI at §§ 1428–36, at 205ff.
[162] *Ibid*, § 1432, at 231.
[163] *Ibid*, at 233.
[164] *Ibid*, at 234.
[165] Case C-49/92 P *Commission v Anic Partecipazioni* [1999] ECR I-4125, at para 117.
[166] *Brooke Group Ltd v Brown & Williamson Tobacco Corp*, 509 US 209, 227 (1993).

On tacit collusion, we can consequently observe that EC law follows legal theory and is analogous to US law.

B. Cartels versus merger control and abuse of dominance

Cartels are very similar to monopolies or dominant positions, but with two major exceptions. First, the existence of monopolies and dominant positions is well known, while cartels are operating secretly. This makes the detection and enforcement of cartels more difficult and costly for enforcers. Secondly, whereas we may expect similar losses of welfare flowing from monopolies and cartels, as well as from dominant positions and cartels, there are considerable costs and barriers connected with the establishment of a monopoly or dominant position. To acquire dominance, either an undertaking must grow organically to enjoy extreme market shares, a practice which entails (if nothing else) considerable investment and countervailing rivalry; or it must grow by acquisitions, which includes both significant investment and regulatory control. Developed economies employ merger control, and have empowered their competition agencies to stop mergers and concentrations which create or strengthen dominant positions.

Mergers and other forms of concentrations are very time-consuming and require the approval of all parties involved—owners, management (at least to some extent), banks and other creditors. Stock market rules must be complied with, as well as antitrust regulation. Structural changes come at considerable cost and are more or less irreversible, thus one can expect the parties involved to have made some sort of profitability analysis beforehand. By contrast, cartels can be put together in very short time, with little investment and without the opposition of rivals.[167] If the practice is kept secret, there will be no regulatory control in operation. Given that no permanent structural changes are involved and that the parties believe that they can reverse the cartel at any time, one should not expect any elaborate profitability analysis to have been drawn up. Even if there is a profitability analysis, it will not have been subject to control by the owners and by the market. Moreover, parties that are merging can be expected to realise some cost savings by streamlining their production and administration, while cartels have low incentives and opportunities to do the same, given that no permanent structural changes are taking place. Different costs, capacities or expectations will make it difficult for cartel members to agree on price, and the resulting compromises may be sub-optimal from a market perspective. Cartels may have higher costs than monopolies, even if we discount the costs of cartel management.[168]

Merger control aims at checking (in case of very high market shares resulting from the concentration) that there are real efficiencies involved which justify the transaction, but no such checks will be made in the context of a cartel, given that

[167] Areeda and Hovenkamp, above n 3, Vol XII, § 2002, at 16.
[168] Areeda and Hovenkamp, above n 26, Vol IIB, § 405, at 29.

it is a non-transparent collusion activity. Whereas mergers can generally be expected to come about as a result of long-term strategic considerations, cartels are opportunistic organisations. It would be contradictory to set up stringent regulatory control against concentrations, and at the same time adopt a *laissez-faire* attitude towards cartels. In particular, increased regulatory control of concentrations could tempt market actors to migrate from mergers to cartels if the former activity is subject to intense scrutiny while the latter is not. Enforcement policies regarding concentrations and cartels consequently should complement and reinforce one another.

Comparing cartel enforcement to enforcement against abuse of dominance, there is considerable harmony between these concepts. Behaviour that would be classified as unlawful if carried out jointly by competitors, is also prohibited when carried out unilaterally by a dominant undertaking. If a dominant company sells below cost to undercut its rivals and drive them out of the market, this is prohibited under Article 82 EC. The same would apply if done jointly by competitors.[169] If a market-dominant firm were to apply different prices to its customers without reason and without objective justification, this would be prohibited under Article 82 EC as price discrimination. The same applies under Article 81 EC if competitors share out customers or markets between themselves, or engage in bid-rigging, all classic examples of market-sharing. Refusal to supply can occasionally be prohibited as an abuse of dominance under Article 82 EC, and joint boycotts have indeed been condemned under Article 81 EC. When it comes to excessive pricing, there is not much of a difference in theory between Articles 81 and 82 EC, since cartel practices are considered to raise prices and, similarly, excessive pricing can be prohibited under Article 82 EC.[170] There is, however, a practical difference, given that excessive pricing is difficult to prove under Article 82 EC,[171] while no proof of higher prices need be provided under Article 81 EC. In summary, the differences between Articles 81 and 82 in this respect lie primarily in the treatment of exploitative abuses. Exploitation is considered inherent when there is a cartel, while it must be proved on a case-by-case basis for dominant undertakings. As for exclusionary abuses, the parallels are, on the other hand, obvious.

C. Cartels versus vertical restraints

There is relative consensus internationally not to include outright vertical restrictions (for example between manufacturer and retailer) in applicable cartel concepts.[172] The reasons for this will be examined next.

[169] For a practical example, see Joined Cases C-395/96 P and C-396/96 P *Compagnie Maritime Belge Transports and Others v Commission* [2000] ECR I-1365.

[170] Case 27/76 *United Brands v Commission* [1978] ECR 207.

[171] Case COMP/A.36.568/D3, *Scandlines Sverige AB v Port of Helsingborg*, at 217–18.

[172] ICN Working Group on Cartels, above n 6, at 14.

It was said at the beginning of this chapter that cartels are prohibited because they are similar to monopolies (although such similarity is often incomplete, given the difficulties faced in involving 100 per cent of competitors in a cartel). Monopoly theory does not apply as such to vertical restrictions. The concern is typically that vertical restrictions of competition between resellers of the same brand limits rivalry among them.[173] An argument can be made, though, that hard-core vertical restrictions within sales networks are just methods of organising cartels among those who trade in one and the same brand—a *collusion theory on vertical restraints.* According to this line of reasoning, resellers jointly press the supplier to enforce a collusive price or other restrictive conditions. This would decrease the manufacturer's incentive to lower upstream prices, and also facilitate collusion, at least in concentrated markets. The likelihood of this risk is played down, however, in both economic theory[174] and legal theory. The manufacturer has a general interest in preventing excess reseller profits, preferring maximum competition among resellers. The reduced quantities sold if resellers were to conspire to fix prices would otherwise affect the manufacturer negatively, leading to lower aggregate profits.[175]

If we take the view that price-fixing and market-sharing are prohibited regardless of market power, it is certainly tempting to reason by way of analogy and create a policy where the designation of sales territories and price restrictions among sellers of the same brand are prohibited. Such analogies were made in US law,[176] but that law has recently been reversed. Notably, the US Supreme Court in 2007 reversed previous case law and ruled that vertical agreements to fix minimum resale prices can have both pro-competitive and anticompetitive effects, depending on circumstances, and thus it cannot be stated with confidence that such agreements always, or almost always, tend to restrict competition and decrease output.[177]

A prohibition on vertical restrictions by way of analogy to horizontal restrictions means a move away from the very reason why naked price-fixing, market-sharing and quotas are prohibited, ie because they duplicate monopolies and do not produce any countervailing benefits. The fact that those practices are prohibited regardless of market share (*if* we apply a per se prohibition) is an *adjustment* of the theory on the effect of monopolies. A per se approach (see chapter four) is intended to reflect the administrative and procedural difficulties in demonstrating market power, and the strong deterrence message in having a clear and straightforward prohibition that does not allow for counter-evidence on the absence of such power. It makes little sense for competitors to cartelise in the absence of market power, hence market power can be presumed. We accept that this may lead to over-deterrence against small, insignificant cartels without market power, but the

[173] Areeda and Hovenkamp, above n 3, Vol VIII, § 1600, at 7.
[174] Van den Bergh and Camesasca, above n 39, at 208ff.
[175] Areeda and Hovenkamp, above n 3, Vol VIII, § 1600, at 33.
[176] *Ibid*, at 7.
[177] *Leegin Creative Leather Products, Inc v PSKS, Inc* 127 S Ct 2705, US 2007.

value of having a clear-cut rule justifies an outright prohibition against naked horizontal restraints.

With vertical restrictions, however, there is no such presumption; on the contrary, it is possible to establish the approximate market share of a manufacturer and its reseller organisation, and see whether there is monopoly power. Vertical restrictions do not necessarily expand that market share. The fact that vertical restraints on dealer prices and territories do not expand market power should alone justify significantly more lenient treatment for vertical agreements than for horizontal agreements.[178] In the absence of monopoly power (or very high market shares) there is no reason to assume that (for instance) the allocation of geographic sales territories and exclusive dealing within one and the same brand would lead to monopoly results in terms of lower output and higher prices.

The strong policy resemblance in EC law between the prohibition on hard-core vertical restrictions such as absolute territorial protection and resale price maintenance, on the one hand, and horizontal cartels, on the other, cannot be explained with reference to economic or legal theory. It must instead be understood as an outflow of the integration objective which has been instrumental in EC law. Then again, it may be another example of close resemblance to US law, applied but not explicitly referred to by the Community institutions.

The Commission's Leniency Notice is limited to agreements and/or concerted practices between two or more *competitors*, without distinguishing in principle between vertical and horizontal agreements. In the Explanatory Notes to the ECN Model Leniency Programme, however, vertical restrictions are considered ineligible for leniency and outside the cartel concept.[179]

As explained, vertical restrictions in the traditional sense relate mainly to intra-brand competition, that is, competition between parties working with one and the same brand. Those restrictions will often be connected to pro-competitive effects such as the promotion of investments and efficient distribution. Surely vertical restrictions can have inter-brand effects as well? For example, an exclusive purchasing obligation seals off a particular distribution channel for other manufacturers.

Cartels, on the other hand, relate to inter-brand competition—competition between parties engaged in the sale of different brands. The pro-competitive effects of such co-operation are generally very difficult to establish; and the restrictions (indeed, elimination of competition) flowing from horizontal co-operation will be more far-reaching, since it can directly cover a whole industry rather than just one brand. The difference between cartels and vertical competition restrictions thus lies partly in the likelihood of countervailing pro-competitive effects, partly in the magnitude of the (likely) restrictions, where cartels can typically be expected to mirror monopolies.

[178] Areeda and Hovenkamp, above n 3, Vol VI, § 1402, at 9.

[179] ECN Model Leniency Program, Explanatory Notes, at 14, available at http://ec.europa.eu/comm/competition/ecn/documents.html.

From an enforcement perspective it is far more difficult to expose horizontal co-operation than vertical restrictions. That is because traders facing the imposition of vertical restraints—such as resale price maintenance, export bans and market-sharing—will have a business incentive to challenge the restraints by reporting to the relevant authorities, or by taking action themselves in court. The chances of obtaining first-hand evidence on vertical restrictions are thus relatively good, while participants in unlawful horizontal co-operation, on the contrary, have the opportunity and incentive to keep their practices secret. This indicates that control of vertical restraints can, to a greater extent than control of cartels, be carried out through private enforcement rather than public enforcement.

III. COLLAPSING THE CARTEL CONCEPT

A. Horizontal behaviour with the object of restricting competition

The purpose of this section is to explore whether there is a cartel concept which might serve to distinguish horizontal hard-core competition restrictions, in other words the straightforward cases, from the cases where a more elaborate balancing of restrictive and pro-competitive effects is required.

An intellectual dilemma presents itself upon examination of this question: as at the end of 2007 there were some 150 Commission cartel decisions in which, in the vast majority, cartels were considered to have as their object the restriction of competition.[180] Many of those decisions have been appealed, but for the most part the Commission has been very successful in defending its cases before the Community courts. It may be recalled that appellants often choose not to dispute their participation in cartel arrangements as such.[181] Although some 25 per cent of EC cartel cases are reversed in part by the Community courts, reversals are often made on the basis of procedural mistakes made by the Commission, or because of incorrect calculations of fines. The Commission has seldom lost major cartel cases because of failure to establish the infringements. So where does one find the cases where the Community courts make guiding statements about what types of agreements have as their object the restriction of competition? And what is the theoretical framework for such assessments?

A common way to approach the object question is to make no clear distinction as whether it is the Commission, the Court of First Instance or the Court of Justice that has produced a statement on a given issue.[182] In the present analysis, however, the court hierarchy will be observed. Furthermore, the development of this question over time must be accounted for—as will be seen, it is quite possible that older case law is unreliable.

[180] The Commission horizontal cartel decisions are listed in the Table of Cases.

[181] Annual Report 2004, Proceedings of the Court of First Instance, at 89, available at http://curia.europa.eu/en/instit/presentationfr/index.htm.

[182] For such an approach, see especially Siragusa, Mario (ed), *EU Competition Law—Volume III Cartel Law* (Leuven, Claeys & Casteels, 2006), at 41ff; Jephcott, above n 50.

When adjudicating on the appeal against the Commission's decision in *Rolled Zinc Products*, the Court of Justice favoured a test according to which

> in order to determine whether an agreement has as its object the restriction of competition . . . it is . . . a question of examining the aims pursued by the agreement as such, in the light of the economic context in which the agreement is to be applied.[183]

Reasoning on a cartel for dishwashing machines in Belgium, the Court considered 'the purpose of the agreement, regard being had to its terms, the legal and economic context in which it was concluded and the conduct of the parties'.[184]

These older judgments indicate that the method is that of a case-by-case analysis, having regard to the legal and economic context, and the specific situation in which the agreement or concerted practice applies. But there has been some development since the 1980s. In *Cement*, the Court seems to have accepted, as a matter of principle, that quotas, market-sharing and price-fixing will harm competition.[185] And according to the Court of First Instance, price-fixing, market-sharing and control of outlets are obvious restrictions of competition.[186]

A rather basic question is whether each individual undertaking's behaviour must restrict competition in order to be prohibited, or if suffices that the restriction flows from the agreement or concerted practice as such. It turns out that in EC law the latter answer is correct: the relevant test is whether the alleged infringement restricts competition. It is irrelevant whether the individual participation of the undertaking concerned could restrict competition, notwithstanding its small scale.[187] This is consistent with the economic perspective that cartels duplicate monopoly power. But no such references are made by the Community courts—on the contrary, they say that this outcome is based on a textual reading of Article 81 EC.[188]

Furthermore, an agreement may be regarded as having a restrictive object even if it does not have the restriction of competition as its sole aim but also pursues other legitimate objectives.[189]

The analysis will now proceed to a more detailed examination of various types of classic cartels and the theoretical basis for deeming them to have the object of restricting competition.

183 Joined Cases 29/83 and 30/83 *Compagnie Royale Asturienne des Mines SA and Rheinzink GmbH v Commission* [1984] ECR 1679, at para 26.

184 Joined Cases 96–102, 104, 105, 108 and 110/82 *NV IAZ International Belgium and others v Commission* [1983] ECR 3369, at para 25.

185 Joined Cases C-204/00 P, etc *Aalborg Portland and others v Commission* [2004] ECR I-123, at para 53.

186 Joined Cases T-374/94, etc *European Night Services and Others v Commission* [1998] ECR II-3141, at para 136.

187 Case T-17/99 *KE KELIT* v *Commission* [2002] ECR II-1647, at para 58.

188 *Ibid*, with references.

189 Case C-551/03 P *General Motors BV v Commission* [2006] ECR I-3173, at para 64.

1. *Price-fixing*

By *price-fixing*, competitors can jointly act very much like a monopoly and influence price and output. As a result of the joint market power created by the cartel, it can charge a price that is significantly higher than the marginal cost of production. This can be done either by price-fixing, or by reducing the quantity that is produced or sold. By increasing price and minimising output, a cartel can maximise its profits to a tipping point. This occurs at a price level where a further increase would cause a proportionally greater reduction in demand on the market.[190]

Economics does not allow for the conclusion that all price-fixing increase prices. Price-fixing can prove ineffective as a result of large buyers on the market, or because of cheating by the cartel participants.[191] But such outcomes are more occasional than regular; indeed, the empirical studies of cartels, referred to in this chapter, demonstrate that detected cartels nearly always raise prices.

In this context we may consider what would happen if parties were allowed to justify price-fixing with reference to the reasonableness of the price they decided on. Courts would then become price controllers, in order to establish what a reasonable price is and whether the cartel price deviated from it.[192] The net social benefits from price cartels can be expected to negligible. Cartels can be expected to achieve their means only when they have joint market power, and that power is more likely used to advance their own interests than those of the consumers.[193]

In the early 1970s price-fixing was condemned in *Dyestuffs*. The Court held that

> the function of price competition is to keep prices down to the lowest possible level and to encourage the movement of goods between the Member States, thereby permitting the most efficient possible distribution of activities in the matter of productivity and the capacity of undertakings to adapt themselves to change.[194]

The Court is mixing two objectives in the *dicta*. It explicitly refers to price competition and the 'most efficient possible distribution of activities in the matter of productivity and the capacity of undertakings to adapt themselves to change'. But furthermore, price competition was considered to encourage integration, more particularly 'direct access by consumers to the sources of production of the whole community'.[195] It is difficult to tell which is the chicken and which is the egg. Tentatively, the Court was trying to say that competition would further integration. Earlier jurisprudence generally seeks legitimacy in the integration imperative.[196]

Some 32 years later, in *Cement*, an economic approach was taken, although with a reminder of the integration goal. The Court held that

[190] Posner, above n 35, at 11.
[191] Van den Bergh and Camesasca, above n 39, at 182.
[192] Areeda and Hovenkamp, above n 3, Vol VII, § 1509a, at 397.
[193] *Ibid*, at 400.
[194] Case 48/69 *ICI v Commission* [1972] ECR 619, at paras 115 ff.
[195] *Ibid*, at para 116.
[196] See Gerber, above n 142, at 358.

> Participation by an undertaking in anticompetitive practices and agreements constitutes an economic infringement designed to maximise its profits, generally by an intentional limitation of supply, an artificial division of the market and an artificial increase in prices. The effect of such agreements or of such practices is to restrict free competition and to prevent the attainment of the common market, in particular by hindering intra-Community trade. Such harmful effects are passed directly on to consumers in terms of increased prices and reduced diversity of supply.[197]

On the other hand, on appeal by a Dutch cartel for electrotechnical fittings, the Court more recently upheld the findings of the Court of First Instance, according to which the object of an information exchange on prices was to endeavour to keep the market calm and maintain prices,

> manifestly an object prohibited by Article 81(1) EC since it was intended to substitute for the undertakings' individual decisions the results of their collusion on prices . . .[198]

There, the wording implies a freedom of action idea (that each trader should independently decide its own policy) rather than monopoly theory. It is submitted here that this particular wording should not be understood to reflect a theory discussion; rather, it hinges on the line of reasoning adopted for concerted practices, which will be discussed further in chapter four.

Nevertheless, an objective to protect the freedom of economic actors has existed in EC competition law. Gerber points out that

> an important strand of German thought and scholarship has continued to emphasize the goal of economic freedom as a value in competition law decisions . . .[199]

The influences of German ordoliberal foundations, with their emphasis on individual freedom of action, are well documented.[200] In *Bloemenveilingen Aalsmeer*, a decision adopted in 1988, the Commission evaluated an alleged competition restraint as follows:

> The proper yardstick for judging whether VBA tenants are subject to anticompetitive agreements is the unrestricted freedom of choice enjoyed by a dealer under perfect competitive conditions.[201]

The co-operation in question was essentially vertical, but included horizontal elements in so far as there was a horizontal co-operation between Dutch flower auctions.

The Court of First Instance emphasised in *TACA* that horizontal price-fixing agreements are clear infringements of Article 81(1) EC.[202] Reference was made to

[197] *Aalborg Portland and others v Commission*, above n 185, at para 53.

[198] Case C-105/04 P *Nederlandse Federatieve Vereniging voor de Groothandel op Elektrotechnisch Gebied v Commission* [2006] ECR I-8725, at para 142.

[199] Gerber, above n 142, at 418.

[200] Van den Bergh and Camesasca, above n 39, at 89.

[201] *Bloemenveilingen Aalsmeer* [1988] OJ L/262/27, at 116.

[202] Joined Cases T-191/98 and T-212/98 to T-214/98 *Atlantic Container Line and others v Commission* [2003] ECR II-3275, at para 498.

the express prohibition in Article 81(1)(a) EC, but no theoretical basis was provided in the judgment. In *FETTCA*, the Court of First Instance considered that an agreement that prohibited the parties from granting their customers discounts on the published rates of charges and surcharges, had as its object the restriction of competition by indirectly fixing prices. Then again, the ratio was that the parties had mutually deprived themselves of the freedom to grant their customers discounts.[203] This implies a freedom of action idea rather than monopoly theory. Fixing part of the price was considered prohibited under Article 81(1)(a) in *Alloy Surcharges*, but it is not clear whether this was done as a matter of principle, given that the Court of First Instance engaged in a discussion about the agreement's effect on the final price of the products.[204] An agreement not to increase prices may also constitute a price-fixing agreement, said the Court of First Instance in *Steel beams*, although this was stated without any attempt at suggesting a theory base.[205]

We can thus see a development over time, where the Community courts tend to be increasingly inclined to follow economic theory while paradoxically often seeking legitimacy in the wording of Article 81(1) EC and in earlier jurisprudence. Over time it seems that the mixed goals of integration, freedom of action and economics have gradually been replaced by more outright competition analysis of price-fixing, at least if *Cement* is seen as the leading case.

2. *Quotas and other output limitation*

On *output reduction*, quotas and output limitation produce the same effect as price-fixing. If supply is limited, some people will value the product more and bid up the price. Conversely, if there are more products on the market, prices will fall. By limiting supply, producers can increase the price.[206] Furthermore, sales and production quotas can be indispensable to making a cartel work, since an increase in price will reduce demand for the product; a price-fixing scheme will then have to be coupled with a joint decision on how to reduce production.[207] Not only production of units is covered by this logic; limitations of advertising and opening hours can also result in higher costs for consumers and cause deteriorating product quality and diversity.[208]

Output refers to packages of products, services and information, rather than just the number of items produced. It is not always a clear concept, since undertakings normally produce and offer goods, services, trademarks and advertising as packages rather than separate parts.[209]

[203] Case T-213/00 *CMA CGM and others v Commission* [2003] ECR II-913, at para 175.

[204] Joined Cases T-45/98 and T-47/98 *Krupp Thyssen Stainless and Acciai Speciali Terni v Commission* [2001] ECR II-3757, at paras 156–57.

[205] Case T-141/94 *Thyssen Stahl v Commission* [1999] ECR II-347, at para 227.

[206] Posner, above n 35, at 9.

[207] *Ibid*, at 66.

[208] Van den Bergh and Camesasca, above n 39, at 155.

[209] Areeda and Hovenkamp, above n 3, Vol VII § 1503, at 351.

Limitations or control of production are expressly listed in the prohibition in Article 81(1) EC. Quotas were addressed in the *Quinine* cartel. The Court of Justice reversed the Commission's decisions on sales quotas, but did so because of insufficient evidence and not because sales quotas would have been lawful.[210] Production quotas were tried as well, and it was held that a gentlemen's agreement prohibiting a group of French undertakings from manufacturing synthetic quinidine clearly had the object of restricting competition. However, the ratio of the decisions covered the stringency of the restrictions, the fact that they were imposed on undertakings from one Member State for the benefit of undertakings in other Member States, and the importance of the undertakings on the market in question.[211] Concessions to the freedom of action doctrine were made twice in this connection.[212]

Several years later, in *Polypropylene*, the Court nevertheless rejected a rule of reason approach to 'a restrictive arrangement involving producers accounting for almost all the Community market and concerning price targets, *production limits* and sharing out of the market' (emphasis added).[213] Quota systems were exposed and fined in *PVC II*, where the Commission's decision was ultimately upheld by the Court of Justice.[214]

In *Cement*, intentional limitation of supply was classified as an economic infringement designed to maximise the undertakings' profits.[215]

The hard cases on output limitation are those on advertising restrictions and opening hours. In *Doulamis*, the Court of Justice took a permissive attitude.[216] This shows that not all output limitation must necessarily be seen as hard-core, or even as restrictive of competition. Most of all, the case displays the reluctance in Community law to rely on US law as a legitimacy base. The mature discussion in US law[217] was not commented upon by either the Advocate-General or the Court of Justice.

3. *Market sharing including bid-rigging*

Market sharing constitutes an effective way of reducing or altogether eliminating competition between the participants. Markets may be shared with reference to geography, customers or products.

Bid-rigging is the same as an output restriction or market sharing.[218] The aim may be to find a substitute for price-fixing in situations in which the cartelists

[210] Case 41/69 *ACF Chemiefarma v Commission* [1970] ECR 661, at paras 145 ff.
[211] *Ibid*, at para 155.
[212] *Ibid*, at para 157, 161.
[213] Case C-235/92 P *Montecatini v Commission* [1999] ECR I-4539, at para 133.
[214] Joined Cases C-238/99 P, etc *Limburgse Vinyl Maatschappij and others v Commission* [2002] ECR I-8375.
[215] *Aalborg Portland and others v Commission*, above n 185, at para 53.
[216] Case C-446/05 *Doulamis* [2008] ECR I-1377.
[217] See especially Areeda and Hovenkamp, above n 3, Vol XII, § 2023, at 184ff.
[218] *Ibid*, § 2006, at 77.

experience problems agreeing on a common price because of different cost structures, or when a fixed price would be difficult to monitor and enforce.[219] It can also be driven by the objective to discriminate on price, or in other words to exploit the elasticity of demand for the product. If the price for a product increases then customers have an incentive to switch to other products. Conversely, if the price decreases, more products will be sold. However, not all customers have the same preference, and they do not place the same value on the product. This can be exploited by a cartel. If the members of a cartel do not have to agree on one single price, but can differentiate their prices depending on the customer to which or the geographic market on which they are selling, then each customer will be paying what it considers to be the value of the product. Market forces will not level out price at a market price level; instead, all customers are compartmentalised and forced into a large number of isolated sale and purchase channels, where each seller can set its own profit-maximising price for designated transactions.[220] Perfect price discrimination will exclude the deadweight loss described in the previous section. At the same time, it will further increase cartel profits.[221] Perfect price discrimination is unfeasible, but some level of price discrimination will increase cartel profits.

In *Woodpulp*, producers were prohibited from applying, in contracts for the sale of wood pulp, clauses prohibiting buyers from exporting and reselling pulp. On appeal, the Court upheld the decision in this regard, finding that

> a clause designed to prevent a buyer from reselling or exporting goods he has bought *is liable to partition the markets* and consequently to affect trade between Member States . . . (emphasis added)[222]

This reasoning finds its root in the integration objective.

Market sharing—an artificial division of the market—was considered an anti-competitive practice in *Cement*, an economic infringement designed to maximise profits, the effect of which is to restrict free competition and to prevent the attainment of the common market, where harmful effects are passed directly on to consumers in terms of increased prices and reduced diversity of supply.[223] The reasoning is limited but implies a more economic approach.

In *Seamless steel tubes*, the Court of First Instance held that agreements which involve mutual respect of domestic markets pursue the object of restricting competition and fall within a category of agreements expressly prohibited by Article 81(1) EC.[224] No particular arguments were put forward to justify this conclusion, save for a reference to the Court's equally non-communicative judgment in *Cement*[225] and to the wording of Article 81(1) EC.

219 *Ibid*, § 2031, at 217.
220 *Ibid*, § 2031, at 218.
221 Posner, above n 35, at 292.
222 Joined Cases 89/85, etc *Ahlström Osakeytiö and others v Commission* [1988] ECR 5193, at para 176.
223 *Aalborg Portland and others v Commission*, above n 185, at para 53.
224 Case T-67/00 *JFE Engineering v Commission* [2004] ECR II-2501, at para 184.
225 Joined Cases T-25/95, etc *Cimenteries and others v Commission* [2000] ECR II-491, at para 1088.

Product market sharing and geographic market sharing were considered to have the object of restricting competition in the *Haberdashery* cartel.[226] However, the Court of First Instance occasionally wavers. When the *Seamless steel tubes* decision was appealed, it found that contracts that divided up the requirements of one producer between three other European producers, stipulating the price to be set according to a mathematical formula, had the

> object and/or, at the very least, the effect . . . to substitute a negotiated allocation of the profits to be obtained from sales . . . for the risks of competition . . .[227]

Back on track, although with reference to that ruling, the Court of First Instance held in *Luxembourg brewers* that a market-sharing practice had the object of restricting competition:

> As the object of the Agreement was to maintain the parties' respective clienteles in the Luxembourg on-trade and to impede penetration of that sector by foreign brewers, its existence made sense only if its object was to restrict competition in this sector appreciably, that is to say in a manner commercially useful to them.[228]

In summary, the Community courts have not often had to express themselves on horizontal market sharing, but when given the opportunity they justify a prohibition with reference to a combination of sources. The ultimate effects for consumers constitute one limb, the integration objective another.

4. *Buyer cartels*

Buyer cartels are not as frequent in Community competition law jurisprudence as other forms of cartels. The Commission has fined buyer cartels on several occasions,[229] but there used to be a vacuum when it came to authoritative rulings from the Court of Justice. *Exclusionary* buying schemes have been tried, and so has one *exploitative* scheme.

In 2006, as regards the *electrotechnical* cartel, the Court clarified that a collective exclusive dealing arrangement pursued an anticompetitive object, consisting of maintaining prices at a supra-competitive level, *inter alia* by lessening the competitiveness of undertakings seeking to operate on the wholesale market and thereby to compete with members of the cartel.[230] The practice was one of exclusion: to prevent supplies to those that did not belong to the cartel. I see no reason why a joint exploitative effort such as joint setting of purchase prices should be treated differently. Direct or indirect fixing of purchase prices is explicitly covered by Article 81(1)(a) EC, but one can still question the theory basis.

[226] Case T-30/05 *Prym and Prym Consumer v Commission* [2007] ECR II-107, at para 129.

[227] Case T-44/00 *Mannesmannröhren-Werke v Commission* [2004] ECR II-2223, at paras 158–59.

[228] Joined Cases T-49/02 to T-51/02 *Brasserie Nationale and others v Commission* [2005] ECR II-3033, at paras 140–41.

[229] Notably *Raw Tobacco Spain* IP/04/1256 and *Raw Tobacco Italy* IP/05/1315. Generally on buyers' cartels, see Arbault, Francois, and Sakkers, Ewoud, 'Cartels' in Faull, Jonathan, and Nikpay, Ali (eds), *The EC Law of Competition* (Oxford, Oxford University Press, 2007), at 759.

[230] Case C-113/04 P *TU v Commission* [2006] ECR I-8831, at para 180.

In the *French beef* case, the Court of Justice examined an argument raised by the appellants that a scale of minimum purchase prices was not anticompetitive. The Court confirmed that such a scheme had the object of restricting, preventing or distorting competition.[231] It may be improper, however, to refer to the *French beef* case as purchase price-fixing, since the purchasers (slaughterers) were forced by the suppliers (farmers) to apply minimum prices. Then again, this illustrates how vendor price-fixing may be construed as purchase price-fixing if suppliers are given the opportunity to put pressure on purchasers.

United States law certainly prohibits buyer cartels. The logic behind this is that buyer cartels reduce business incentives among the cartels' suppliers. Acceptance of buyer cartels would accordingly amount to 'the simple error of thinking lower prices were good even though they deprived suppliers of the normal fruits of their enterprise'.[232] The Commission takes a similar view and states in its horizontal guidelines that a high degree of buying power over the suppliers of a market may bring about inefficiencies such as quality reductions, the lessening of innovation efforts, or ultimately sub-optimal supply.[233] Interestingly, however, the Commission does not see this as the primary concern, but instead focuses on the risk that lower prices derived from buyer power are not passed on to customers further downstream. This may cause exclusionary effects when suppliers try to recover price reductions for one group of customers by increasing prices for other customers or competitors.[234]

Further, the Commission is not at all clear on how to distinguish a buyer cartel from an acceptable joint purchasing operation.[235] In its horizontal merger guidelines, on the other hand, the Commission considers that a merger that creates or strengthens the market power of a buyer may significantly impede effective competition. The merged firm may be in a position to obtain lower prices by reducing its purchase of inputs. Here, however, the Commission immediately adds that this in turn may lead to lower output *in the final product market*, and thus harm consumer welfare.[236]

We can consequently observe a situation where there is a low frequency of case law, as a result of a relatively low frequency of administrative enforcement against buyer cartels. In the alternative, the situation could be interpreted as evidence of only the sporadic existence of buyer cartels. Empirical studies actually indicate that single buyers can control suppliers to a great extent. It is evident that retailers that have a gate-keeper role through their influence over a large consumer base, can

[231] Joined Cases C-101/07 P and C-110/07 P *Coop de France Bétail and Viande v Commission* [2008] ECR I-0000 at paras 87–88.

[232] Areeda *et al*, above n 3, Vol VII, § 1504, at 360.

[233] Commission Notice, *Guidelines on the applicability of Article 81 of the EC Treaty to horizontal co-operation agreements* [2001] OJ C/3/2, at 126.

[234] *Ibid.*

[235] *Ibid*, at 124–26.

[236] *Guidelines on the assessment of horizontal mergers under the Council Regulation on the control of concentrations between undertakings* [2004] OJ C/31/5, at 61.

dictate or negotiate preferential terms with their suppliers.[237] Perhaps buyers do not generally have an acute need to collude on their buying strategies?

In summary, there may be problems with drawing the line between, on the one hand, acceptable joint purchasing operations, where functions such as administration and logistics are brought together to create efficiencies, and, on the other hand, outright purchase price-fixing. Absent production efficiencies, there are convincing arguments for treating purchase price-fixing as a per se infringement.[238]

5. *Boycotts and other joint exclusionary conduct*

Cartels reduce output and raise prices, thus customers can be expected to migrate to other sources of supply. At the same time, the supra-competitive prices created by the cartel can attract new market entry. Cheating among the cartel participants is another apparent risk when prices increase and there is remaining excess production capacity. In addition to disciplining cheaters, it makes perfect sense for the cartel to engage in activities to prevent market entry, market expansion, or even market existence by competitors outside the cartel.

Exclusionary practices such as boycotts are driven by the business rationale of eliminating 'additional lower-cost, higher-quality, or more innovative output from the market'.[239] Joint exclusionary schemes will thus reduce market output and, as a result, increase prices. Boycotts cause wasteful defensive measures by the victims and wasteful expenses by cartelists.[240]

Boycotts are very diverse phenomena and can be grouped into several different categories depending on whether they, for instance, are orchestrated by competitors or by vertically related firms. The existence of investments could change the picture further as a result of pro-competitive effects. Parties that have jointly built an infrastructure may wish to keep it for themselves rather than allowing what they perceive as free riders.

Distinctions can be made between exclusionary boycotts that enforce a collusive scheme, rival-directed boycotts and boycotts directed at non-rivals.[241] A valid point can be made that boycotts do not always involve joint exclusionary conduct, but can just as well comprise an outflow of joint exploitative practice.

One must still question what is the purpose or value in differentiating between one type of boycott and another. Hovenkamp points out that the distinction between price-fixing and joint exclusionary conduct 'should not be exaggerated, for exclusion is typically nothing more than the way a cartel is enforced'.[242]

[237] Dobson, Paul W, 'Buyer-Driven Vertical Restraints', in *The Pros and Cons of Vertical Restraints* (Stockholm, Konkurrensverket, 2008).

[238] See especially Kokkoris, Ioannis, 'Purchase Price Fixing: A Per Se Infringement' (2007) 28(9) *ECLR* 473.

[239] Areeda and Hovenkamp, above n 3, Vol XIII, § 2203, at 272.

[240] Van den Bergh and Camesasca, above n 39, at 156.

[241] Glazer, Kenneth L, 'Concerted Refusals to Deal under Section 1 of the Sherman Act' (2002) 70(1) *Antitrust Law Journal* 1.

[242] Areeda and Hovenkamp, above n 3, Vol XII, § 2008, at 91.

Whether the same restraint is litigated as a self-limitation on output (ie a quota) or as a concerted refusal to deal is not a matter of principle but rather depends on circumstances prior to litigation.[243] Hovenkamp suggests that the crucial issue is whether the parties that are accused of a boycott or similar practice are engaged in any significant integration of production or distribution. If not, the 'only rationale for the restraint is the elimination of additional lower-cost, higher-quality, or more innovative output from the market'.[244] The joint action should then be treated as a naked restraint.

A collective boycott was considered to have as its object the restriction of competition in *Pre-insulated pipes*.[245] No particular arguments were put forward by the Court to justify this conclusion. In fact, the Court had established already in *Tournier* that Article 81 EC must be interpreted as prohibiting any concerted practice having as its object or effect collective refusals to deal.[246] Similarly, no reasoning accompanied this conclusion. In *French beef*, the Court of Justice upheld the findings of the Court of First Instance that a commitment to suspend imports had the purpose of sealing off the French internal market and thus of restricting competition.[247] Once again, there was no reasoning to explain this finding, which, by and large, seems dictated by integration objectives.

Under US law, agreements between two or more actual or potential competitors to refuse to deal with another firm or firms will be prohibited without a full competition analysis provided that any such agreement is unlikely to have purposes other than the reduction of output or increase of price (for a comprehensive discussion about per se and quick look prohibitions, see chapter four).[248] The US Supreme Court held in *General Motors* that

> where businessmen concert their actions in order to deprive others of access to merchandise which the latter wish to sell to the public, we need not inquire into the economic motivation underlying their conduct . . .[249]

Prohibition without a full competition analysis does not, however, apply to refusals to deal carried out by vertically related firms.[250]

European Community law is consequently very similar to US law on collective boycotts. The Court of Justice has not gone to great lengths to legitimise its approach.

[243] *Ibid*, Vol XIII, § 2203, at 274.

[244] *Ibid*, at 272.

[245] Joined Cases C-189/02 P, etc *Dansk Rørindustri and others v Commission* [2005] ECR I-5425, at paras 144 ff.

[246] Case 395/87 *Ministère Public v Jean-Louis Tournier* [1989] ECR 2521, at para 23.

[247] *Coop de France Bétail and Viande v Commission*, above n 231, at paras 83ff.

[248] Areeda and Hovenkamp, above n 3, Vol XIII, § 2203, at 267.

[249] *US v General Motors Corp* 384 US 127, 146.

[250] Areeda and Hovenkamp, above n 3.

6. Facilitating practices including information exchange

Whether information exchange falls within the definition of a cartel, as set out in the Commission's Leniency Notice, is not entirely clear. The most probable answer is that it depends on the circumstances.

Information exchanges can range from pro-competitive or uncontroversial co-operation, to practices that strongly resemble outright quotas or price-fixing.[251] Further, different legal standards apply to information exchanges in general, and to information exchanges that underpin or facilitate cartel agreements.

In late May 1996, the German steel industry trade association and 16 of its members notified an information exchange system to the Commission. The Commission rapidly sent a warning to the association and a request for information. Subsequently a decision was adopted prohibiting the information exchange.[252] On appeal, however, the decision was annulled.[253] The German steel industry claimed that the system concerned only data on quantities, as opposed to information on prices or future conduct. The Commission argued that

> the observation of competitors' behaviour and past performance is at the root of all the agreement's restrictive effects, because the more accurate and recent the information on quantities sold and market share, the greater is its impact on undertakings' future market behaviour.

This view was affirmed by the Court of First Instance,[254] which nevertheless made a distinction between various parts of the information exchange system. It turned out that the Commission had erroneously assumed that several questionnaires were covered by the information exchange, while in reality one questionnaire fell outside the system and had not been put into circulation. That particular questionnaire was the one asking for detailed information on deliveries of steel on the national market, according to qualities and specified for 28 different consumer sectors, likely to reveal the strategy of different producers. The questionnaires that were in use were limited to data on the sales of the participating undertakings, without distinguishing between the different consumer sectors, allowing market shares to be calculated only approximately. The Court of First Instance reiterated that information exchange agreements are not generally prohibited automatically but only if they have certain characteristics relating, in particular, to sensitive and accurate nature of recent data exchanged at short intervals.[255]

To determine whether a system of information exchanges infringes EC competition law, the Commission focuses its analysis on[256]:

[251] For an example of the latter, see *Fatty Acids* [1987] OJ L/3/17, at 39.
[252] *Wirtschaftsvereinigung Stahl* [1998] OJ L/1/10.
[253] Case T-16/98 *Wirtschaftsvereinigung Stahl and others v Commission* [2001] ECR II-1217.
[254] *Ibid*, at para 29.
[255] *Ibid*, at para 44.
[256] Commission Discussion Paper on the review of Regulation 4056/86 applying EC competition rules to maritime transport, para 183, available at http://ec.europa.eu/competition/consultations/2005_reg_4056_86/index.html#130705.

(a) The characteristics of the information exchange itself, namely

—The nature and type of information exchanged
—The level of aggregation of information
—The period to which the information relates and the frequency of exchange
—The institutional structure of the system, ie the collection by one of the participating firms, by a trade association or by a completely independent organisation and if and with whom the information is subsequently shared

(b) and the structural characteristics of the market on which the exchange takes place.

When examining whether an information exchange infringes Article 81(1) EC, the crucial point is whether it reduces or removes the degree of uncertainty as to the operation of the market by affecting and appreciably reducing the participants' decision-making independence.[257] A restriction of competition stems partly from the fact that an information exchange is intended only for the undertakings participating in the exchange, to the exclusion of their competitors and of consumers.[258] The Court has, however, played down the importance of market structure, holding that 'the only general principle applied in relation to the market structure [is] that supply must not be atomised'.[259]

The need to carry out a case-by-case analysis for information exchanges has been emphasised by the Court of Justice. For instance, credit information exchange systems do not have, by their very nature, the object of restricting or distorting competition within the common market within the meaning of Article 81(1) EC.[260] However, the principles of analysis just referred to relate to autonomous information exchanges, without any connection to cartel agreements.[261] When, on the other hand, an information exchange underpins a cartel agreement, another and different legal standard applies. The Court has held that even though the information exchanged is in the public domain or related to historical and purely statistical prices, its exchange infringes Article 81(1) EC where it underpins another anticompetitive arrangement. According to the Court:

> That interpretation is based on the consideration that the circulation of price information limited to the members of an anticompetitive cartel has the effect of increasing transparency on a market where competition is already much reduced and of facilitating control of compliance with the cartel by its members.[262]

It follows that we must distinguish between, on the one hand, information exchanges in general, where a case-by-case analysis is required with reference to

[257] Case C-194/99 P *Thyssen Stahl v Commission* [2003] ECR I-10821, at paras 81, 89; Case C-7/95 P *John Deere v Commission* [1998] ECR I-3111, at paras 89–90.

[258] *Thyssen Stahl*, above n 257, at para 85.

[259] *Ibid*, at para 86.

[260] Case C-238/05 *Asnef-Equifax v Ausbanc* [2006] ECR I-11125, at para 48.

[261] For a comprehensive discussion, see Bissocoli, Eugenio F, 'Trade Associations and Information Exchange under US and EC Competition Law' (2000) 23(1) *World Competition* 79; Capobianco, Antonio, 'Information Exchange under EC Competition Law' (2004) 41(5) *CML Rev* 1247.

[262] *Aalborg Portland and others v Commission*, above n 185, at para 281.

the type of information exchanged, periodicity, institutional structure and market structure, and, on the other hand, information exchanges that are facilitating devices for cartel agreements. In the latter case, the competition authorities and courts can find infringements of Article 81(1) EC even if the information exchanged is of the kind that would normally be permissible.

Naturally there will be the occasional borderline case. *Carbonless Paper* was such a situation, where it was not entirely clear whether the practices were unlawful as such, or because they underpinned an anticompetitive agreement or facilitated the conclusion of agreements. There were meetings where the participants did not arrive at a consensus or an agreement, although attempts were made to that effect. The participants were moved to exchange individual information on their prices and/or sales volumes, and the Court of First Instance concluded that the meetings functioned as a framework for concerted action contrary to Article 81(1) EC. There were also information exchanges and discussions on customers and the prices they were charged, which amounted to concerted practices.[263]

An approach where one prohibits as a matter of principle information exchange that facilitates collusion, while allowing efficiency reasoning on other types of information exchange, can be seen as compatible with an economic approach as understood in US law.[264] The need to distinguish between different sorts of information exchange is evident from US law, where the primary concern is that such arrangements may facilitate oligopoly or collusion.[265] Once again we have an instance of similarity between EC law and the economic approach, and between EC law and US law, although without explicit references to US law in the case law of the Community courts.

7. *Mixed horizontal and vertical cartels*

A question that has not been considered much in European handbooks on competition law is how to address restrictions that have both horizontal and vertical elements. During the period when policy and enforcement against vertical restraints were as tough as the policy against cartels (or indeed tougher), it would have made little difference whether a practice was classified as vertical or horizontal. Given the lower priority and more permissive attitude towards vertical arrangements, the matter becomes more problematic. In spite of a large number of cases, theory on mixed horizontal and vertical cartels remains undeveloped.

The Court of Justice held in *Grundig and Consten* that no distinction can be made in principle under Article 81 EC between vertical and horizontal agreements.[266] Still, it is clear that there is a distinction which is more than philosophical, for a number of reasons. First, the leniency rules would normally apply only

[263] Joined Cases T-109/02, etc *Bolloré and others v Commission* [2007] ECR II-947, at para 290 ff.

[264] Posner, above n 35, at 169.

[265] See generally Areeda and Hovenkamp, above n 3, Vol XIII, § 2111, at 47ff.

[266] Joined Cases 56 and 58/64 *Consten and Grundig* [1966] ECR 299, at 339, English special edition 299.

to cartels. Secondly, the analysis on agreements (see chapter four) shows that the Community courts tend to require more express acceptance by dealers in vertical relations with their supplier than by competitors that meet and exchange views. Further, the rules on evidence, set out in chapter five, will tend to require higher standards for vertical agreements as a result of the relative difficulties in proving a horizontal infringement.

Among the Commission's cartel decisions there are at least 20 examples of collective practices involving more than one level of trade. Before the adoption of the Commission's 1996 Leniency Notice there was no legal–technical reason to distinguish between cartels and other infringements. The word 'cartel' does not figure in the decisions on mixed horizontal and vertical infringements preceding 1996. A certain caution can be observed in *FEG and TU*, an infringement brought to the Commission's attention in 1991 and fined in 1999, where the Commission did not refer to the behaviour as a cartel.[267] No party applied for leniency. Since 1996, however, the Commission has (up to 2007) classified five mixed horizontal and vertical infringements as cartels.

First, in 2001, came *Carbonless paper*, explicitly referred to as a Europe-wide cartel, the decision belonging to a 'long line of decisions against cartels of all kinds'.[268] Second came *Needles*, in 2004, a cartel decision which was described as unique in the sense that it concerned a pure product and geographic market-sharing agreement. It was a cartel between manufacturers, facilitated by a concerted practice by a manufacturer/wholesaler/distributor. There the Commission granted Entaco full immunity under the 1996 Leniency Notice.[269] Third was *Choline chloride*, a producer cartel where measures were taken to control buyers, subcontractors and distributors.[270] The Commission applied its 1996 Leniency Notice and gave BASF, UCB and Akzo Nobel fine reductions.[271] Fourth was *Road bitumen NL*, a cartel between eight suppliers and six purchasers.[272] The Commission applied its 2002 Leniency Notice and granted full immunity to BP and a reduction to Kuwait Petroleum. Lastly, *Synthetic rubber*, a price-fixing cartel. The Commission applied its 2002 Leniency Notice and granted full immunity to Bayer and a reduction to Dow.[273]

Both the 1996 Notice and the 2002 Notice applied only to cartels.[274] Not every infringement of Article 81 EC involves a cartel, however, and outright vertical restrictions have not qualified thus far. Indeed, in the Explanatory Notes to the ECN Model Leniency Programme, vertical restrictions are considered ineligible

[267] See esp IP/99/803.
[268] IP/01/1892.
[269] IP/04/1313.
[270] IP/04/1454.
[271] *Choline Chloride* [2005] OJ L/190/22, at 236–37.
[272] IP/06/1179.
[273] IP/06/1647.
[274] Commission Notice on the non-imposition or reduction of fines in cartel cases [1996] OJ C/207/4; Commission notice on immunity from fines and reduction of fines in cartel cases [2002] OJ C/45/3.

for leniency and outside the cartel concept.[275] This apparently did not apply to *Needles*. When the decision was appealed, the Court of First Instance went ahead and considered whether one of the parties would have been entitled to a fine reduction under the 1996 leniency guidelines. The Court expressly referred to the infringement as a cartel. It refused a fine reduction because the undertaking in question did not fulfil certain requirements in the guidelines, but implicitly accepted that the guidelines applied as such and thus that the infringement was covered by the cartel concept.[276] Perhaps one should not draw too much from this, however, given that no party had claimed that the practice did not qualify for leniency. The borderline between cartels and other infringements will be tested for real only when a party applies for leniency and is denied immunity or reduction of fines by the Commission, not because the party was last in line but because the practice is classified as something other than a cartel.

Mixed horizontal and vertical cartels are considered to have as their *object* the prevention, restriction or distortion of competition.[277] But the Commission has often, in these cases, added some reasoning (albeit limited) about the *effects* of the practices. On one occasion a collective import and export scheme was considered to have as its effect the restriction of competition.[278] Over a dozen cases have been appealed and upheld in substance as regards the object of restricting competition.[279] Theoretically, it is logical that if we prohibit competitors from adopting

[275] ECN Model Leniency Program, Explanatory Notes, at 14, available at http://ec.europa.eu/comm/competition/ecn/documents.html.

[276] Case T-30/05 *Prym and Prym Consumer v Commission* [2007] ECR II-107.

[277] *ASPA* [1970] JO L/148/9; *Chauffage central* [1972] OJ L/264/22; *Stoves and heaters* [1975] OJ L/159/22; *Bomée-Stichting* [1975] OJ L/329/30; *Centraal Bureau voor de Rijwielhandel* [1978] OJ L/20/18; *GB-Inno-BM/Fedetab* [1978] OJ L/224/29, at 80; *IMA Rules* [1980] OJ L/318/1, at 59; *VBBB/VBVB* [1982] OJ L/54/36, at 40 ff; *NAVEWA–ANSEAU* [1982] OJ L/167/39, at 41 ff *Stichting Sigarettenindustrie* [1982] OJ L/232/1, at 99; *AROW/BNIC* [1982] OJ L/379/1, at 604; *FEG and TU* [2000] OJ L/39/1, at 105 ff; *Carbonless paper* [2004] OJ L/115/1; *Choline Chloride* [2005] OJ L/190/22, at 32, 64, 68; *Needles* IP/04/1313; *Road bitumen NL* IP/06/1179; *Synthetic rubber* IP/06/1647.

[278] *Ijsselcentrale and others* [1991] OJ L/28/32, at 25–26.

[279] Joined Cases 209–215 and 218/78 *van Landewyck and others v Commission* [1980] ECR 3125, at paras 109, 134, 146, 154 and 161–62 (joint setting of trade margins, rebates, payment terms); Joined Cases 43 and 62/82 *VBVB and VBBB v Commission* [1984] ECR 19, at paras 45–46 (collective resale price maintenance for books); Joined Cases 96–102, 104, 105, 108 and 110/82 *V IAZ Int Belgium and others v Commission* [1983] ECR 3369, at para 25 (collective impediment of parallel trade in dishwashing machines through a system of mandatory certification); Joined Cases 240, 241, 242, 261, 262, 268 and 269/82 *Stichting Sigarettenindustrie and others v Commission* [1985] ECR 3831 (collective setting of trade margins); Joined Cases T-5/00 and T-6/00 *FEG and TU v Commission* [2003] ECR II-5761, at paras 277, 295, 300, 322ff, on appeal Case C-105/04 P *FEG v Commission* [2006] ECR I-8725, at paras 125, 143, 160, 163 and 179, and Case C-113/04 P *TU v Commission* [2006] ECR I-8831, at para 184 (collective exclusive dealing arrangement intended to prevent supplies to undertakings not belonging to the FEG, binding decisions on fixed prices, price guidelines and provision of a forum for its members to discuss prices and discounts); Joined Cases T-109/02, etc *Bolloré and others v Commission* [2007] ECR II-947, at para 200 (price-fixing in a complex cartel); Case T-30/05 *Prym and Prym Consumer v Commission* [2007] ECR II-107, at para 129, and Case T-36/05 *Coats Holdings and Coats v Commission* [2007] ECR II-110 (cartel between manufacturers, facilitated by concerted practice of manufacturer/wholesaler/distributor); Joined Cases T-101/05 and T-111/05 *BASF and UCB v Commission* [2007] ECR II-4949, at para 200 (cartel between producers, where measures were taken to control buyers, subcontractors and distributors).

collective practices on prices, output, market-sharing, tenders or other conditions of trade, or exclusionary tactics, it would make little or no sense to deem such practices lawful in situations when they manage to involve yet another level of trade. Moreover, horizontal cartels have occurred time and time again in industries with a high level of vertical integration, such as building and construction, air traffic, steel, tobacco, banking and agriculture. Perhaps we should not be too surprised about substitution of both horizontal and vertical integration at the same time through a cartel. But this reasoning applies primarily to 'classic' cartels between competitors where, incidentally, another level of trade is involved, and is inconclusive for separating the hard cases from the straightforward ones.

In *Specialty graphites*, the distributor Intech was found to have participated together with the suppliers and producers.[280]

District heating pipes was another cartel that comprised more than one level of trade. On appeal, one of the undertakings that had participated insisted that it was merely a reseller, unable to implement measures decided at cartel meetings. The Court held that the participation in the cartel of dominant or particularly powerful undertakings in a position to take retaliatory measures against other, much less powerful, participants had no effect on the liability of those undertakings. It may, however, have consequences in the determination of the level of the penalty.[281]

A Spanish distributor denied its participation in *Carbonless paper*.[282] The Court of First Instance merely pointed out that in order for a cartel to operate properly on the Spanish market, it had to include the distributors.[283]

Jurisprudence seems, in a sense, consistent with legal theory on probability of dealer cartels, where the general understanding is that two levels of trade must normally be involved in order for a retail cartel to be successful.[284] But the opposite would not necessarily hold true, ie that producers must involve resellers.

In *Italian Flat Glass*, the Court of First Instance set aside the Commission's decision as regards the participation of two producers in a scheme designed to influence the purchasing and selling policies of the main wholesalers. But this quashing was not due to a view that such collective action would be lawful, but because the evidence the Commission had presented was insufficient.[285]

Looking at cases weighted towards the vertical aspects, it can be observed *inter alia* that a mixed horizontal and vertical agreement on car sales prices in Belgium was fined in *Mercedes-Benz*.[286]

[280] Joined Cases T-71/03, T-74/03, T-87/03 and T-91/03 *Tokai Carbon and others v Commission* [2005] ECR II-10, at para 76.

[281] Joined Cases C-189/02 P, etc *Dansk Rørindustri and others v Commission* [2005] ECR I-5425, at para 150.

[282] Joined Cases T-109/02, etc *Bolloré and others v Commission* [2007] ECR II-947, at paras 203–04.

[283] *Ibid.*

[284] See generally Areeda and Hovenkamp, above n 3, Vol VIII, § 1604.

[285] Joined Cases T-68/89, T-77/89 and T-78/89 *Società Italiano Vetro SpA and others v Commission* [1992] ECR II-1403, at para 250.

[286] *Mercedes-Benz* [2002] OJ L/257/1, 139–42, at 177, this part of the decision upheld on appeal, Case T-325/01 *DaimlerChrysler v Commission* [2005] ECR II-3319.

The question on how to distinguish vertical from horizontal restrictions from a legal theoretical perspective, or under an economic approach, is not addressed in European scholarly writing. Under US law, the courts have considered whether a 'mixed' practice is essentially horizontal or vertical. For instance, if a dealer has imposed collusion on other dealers, this can be said to be concertation between them, and it has been treated as essentially horizontal.[287] A practical example is when a powerful reseller forces the supplier to impose resale price maintenance on the other resellers, and on the supplier's own resale division. Similarly, if a supplier has imposed price-fixing on dealers, while at the same time being a competing dealer itself, it resembles horizontal price-fixing more than resale price maintenance.[288] And an agreement between competing producers or distributors to fix resale prices or to require their resellers to apply those prices would be horizontal price-fixing, regardless of whether it concerns goods, services, licences or other sales.[289]

This reasoning enables us to look at the specific facts of the case to determine whether the alleged infringement is more horizontal than vertical.[290] But classifying an agreement or collusion as essentially horizontal or vertical can cause confusion and effectively conceal what assessment the court or authority is actually making, thereby failing to expose the underlying reasoning.[291] There is consequently good reason to avoid formalism and look at the facts of each case.

Generally, economic theory is not relied on explicitly by the Community courts when they classify these infringements. Tentatively, the key question could be whether a merger or sales joint venture between the alleged cartel participants would be accepted. If the answer is negative, there is no reason to accept co-operation. Moreover, it should be kept in mind that absent the efficiencies realised by a permanent change in structure, collusive co-operation will be more detrimental than a merger.

One may generally ask whether mixed horizontal and vertical cartels should be treated differently in so far as there may be some efficiency-enhancing aspects. In *Seamless steel tubes*, a claim that vertical aspects of the cartel should be assessed under block exemption regulations was rejected by the Court of Justice on formalistic grounds.[292] But in *Jahrhundertvertrag*, a combined buyer and seller's cartel was exempted. The case concerned a joint commitment by electricity supply companies acting in concert towards the coalmining industry, to make long-term purchases of pre-defined amounts of German coal. The Commission found that the buyers had deprived themselves of the possibility of using coal from other origins, or other primary energy sources. Furthermore, electricity imports from other Member States were precluded to the extent that electricity was generated from the coal purchased. Nevertheless, the agreement was exempted. It promoted the

[287] Areeda and Hovenkamp n 3, Vol XII, § 2004, at 67.

[288] *Ibid.*

[289] *Ibid*, § 2003, at 58.

[290] Horizontal arrangements have been found when upstream firms are associations made up by downstream firms; see *ibid*, Vol XII, § 2033, at 229ff.

[291] *Ibid*, Vol VIII, § 1604, at 52.

[292] Case C-411/04 P *Salzgitter Mannesmann v Commission* [2007] ECR I-959, at paras 53 ff.

security of energy supplies in Germany, and the security of supply benefited electricity users. The arrangements were necessary to ensure certainty at the planning stage. Other domestic and imported energy sources could still be used for the remaining amount of electricity, and direct imports were not excluded either.[293] The case illustrates that what we may refer to as mixed horizontal and vertical cartels may create efficiencies and consequently qualify for exemption under Article 81(3) EC.

8. Single brand dealer cartels

Suppose a number of retail dealers of the same brand collude to fix prices, share markets or reduce output. To illustrate this point, we can see how the Swedish Market Court fined a cartel among Volvo dealers in 2008.[294] For the purpose of leniency applications, should such a collusive scheme properly be labelled a cartel? And should we apply a full-scale per se prohibition against it, and thus ignore market power and effects?

The Commission considers agreements between actual or potential competitors on price-fixing, output restrictions and market-sharing to be black-list infringements, never eligible for a de minimis defence.[295] It seems likely that retail dealers of the same brand would fit the Commission's description of either actual or potential competitors,[296] and consequently that dealer cartels would be considered hard-core by the Commission; but this type of formalism tells us nothing about the rationale for treating (or not treating) dealer price-fixing arrangements, market-sharing or output reduction like producer cartels.

A general observation derived from US scholarly writing is that dealer cartels will have problems achieving the intended cartelisation without involving the manufacturer or wholesaler.[297] The interests of the manufacturer do not necessarily coincide with those of the dealers. If dealers are seeking a quiet life or supranormal profits, this can affect sales detrimentally for the manufacturer, unless the manufacturer is included in the deal and allowed to share in the cartel profits. If dealers of the same brand collude to raise prices, share markets, prevent market entry or reduce output (this last objective can be achieved by agreeing on opening hours or advertising), this may be difficult to accomplish at all given the terms of their contracts with the manufacturer. Monitoring compliance and enforcing the scheme can also be difficult without the active assistance of the manufacturer or supplier. And if the dealers manage to collude secretly, the manufacturer can counter by including more dealers in its sales network, or by favouring existing

293 *Jahrhundertvertrag* [1993] OJ L/50/14.

294 MD 2008:12 Konkurrensverket mot Aktiebolaget Bil-Bengtsson m fl et v.v., www.marknadsdomstolen.se.

295 Commission Notice on agreements of minor importance which do not appreciably restrict competition under Article 81(1) of the Treaty establishing the European Community (de minimis) [2001] OJ C/368/07.

296 Fn 4 of the De Minimis Notice.

297 See generally Areeda and Hovenkamp, above n 3, Vol VIII, § 1604.

dealers that are performing well. Furthermore, the outside competitive pressure of competing brands will make a single-brand dealer cartel difficult to maintain. The best chances of creating and maintaining a dealer-induced cartel should consequently arise when powerful dealers are engaged in multi-brand distribution and jointly put pressure on one manufacturer at a time.[298]

This indicates that the chances of realising a (pure) dealer cartel are relatively low, and the chances of detection good. On detection, efficient dealers should have an incentive to stay outside the cartel or report it, while manufacturers that are put under pressure should have an incentive either to refuse or to report. We should consequently be sceptical about allegations of outright dealer cartels; in other words, the standard of proof could tentatively be higher for those cases. Strong arguments could be made for the opposite view, however; manufacturers may obtain something in return for complying and not reporting, and enforcement of the cartel may be carried out centrally by the manufacturer.[299] But these arguments are premised on the participation of the manufacturer. The prediction that single-brand dealer cartels are difficult to realise without involving the manufacturer seems to be supported by the absence of outright dealer cartels in EC competition law jurisprudence.

Leaving aside the matters of probability and detection, once a dealer cartel is found, US scholars argue that there is every reason to prohibit it. While dealers may horizontally collude to impose only what the supplier would otherwise impose (such as geographic market-sharing), one should be less generous towards dealer-induced restrictions than towards similar vertical restrictions. Dealers have an incentive to create excess profits for themselves, whereas a manufacturer cannot increase market power through a vertical restraint and has every reason to 'prevent excess dealer profit beyond that necessary for effective distribution'.[300] And a claim by the dealers that single-brand competition must be reduced in order for distribution to work efficiently should be viewed with doubt, since if that was the case the manufacturer could have realised that efficiency itself through its distribution system.[301] Resale price maintenance should be unlawful regardless of market power.[302] Classification as horizontal or vertical should not be decisive. A better option is to engage in a policy discussion.

Crucial issues outlined by US scholars include whether a restraint motivated by dealer interest instead of manufacturer's interest is justified or not. Another key point is whether the fact that a restraint can be explained only with reference to dealer power excludes the possibility of justification. Yet another is whether the inherent likelihood of anticompetitive effects is so high that it should be condemned without looking at market shares or effects.[303] The US Supreme Court

298 *Ibid*, at 41.
299 *Ibid*, at 44–45.
300 *Ibid*, at 43.
301 *Ibid*.
302 *Ibid*, at 51.
303 *Ibid*, at 52.

viewed a horizontal dealer cartel as illegal per se in *General Motors*,[304] but once again it is important to observe that the manufacturer was actively involved in that infringement.

The low probability of single-brand dealer cartels, without the manufacturer's involvement, highlighted in US scholarly writing, is reflected by an absence of such cartels in EC law. At least, I have not been able to find any cartels that are limited to resellers only, without the involvement of another level of trade and between resellers that are only resellers and not vertically integrated.

B. Cartels as naked restraints without redeeming virtues

It is well documented that co-operation that is on balance pro-competitive is accepted in EC competition law.[305] It may then seem logical to assume that cartels represent co-operation which archetypically produces only negative effects. The idea of cartels as naked restraints without redeeming virtues will be tested next.

1. Article 81(3) EC and cartels

Following the adoption of Regulation 1, national competition authorities and courts will have to consider whether cartels can be exempted pursuant to Article 81(3) because they bring about pro-competitive effects which outweigh their negative effects on competition.[306] According to Article 1(2) of Regulation 1, agreements, decisions and concerted practices caught by Article 81(1) EC which satisfy the conditions of Article 81(3) shall not be prohibited, no prior decision to that effect being required.

Exemptions under Article 81(3) EC used to be in the Commission's exclusive competence, and once in a while the Commission exempted restructuring or crisis cartels.[307] Such exceptional decisions were generally motivated by a need to carry out closure of obsolete production facilities in industries with structural overcapacity.[308] At the same time, there are examples of producers that reduced their capacity and instead entered into purchase agreements with their competitors, practices that were considered to restrict competition and were denied exemption.[309] Following a policy shift, the chances of qualifying for exemption are very limited, or nearly excluded.[310]

304 *US v General Motors Corp* 384 US 127.

305 See esp Faull and Nikpay (eds), above n 229, ch 7.

306 Generally on this subject, see Siragusa, above n 182, at 92–104.

307 *Synthetic fibres* [1984] OJ L/207/17; *Enichem/ICI* [1988] OJ L/50/18; *Bayer/BP Chemicals* [1988] OJ L/150/35; *Stichting Baksteen* [1994] OJ L/131/15.

308 For a comprehensive presentation, see Van Bael, Ivo, and Bellis, Jean-Francois, *Competition Law of the European Communities*, 4th edn (The Hague, Kluwer Law International, 2005), at 449 ff.

309 *WANO Schwartzpulver* [1978] OJ L/322/26; *BP Kemi–DDSF* [1979] OJ L/286/32.

310 Arbault and Sakkers, above n 229, at 748.

The Commission explains its policy in the guidelines for the application of Article 81(3)[311]:

> [S]evere restrictions of competition are unlikely to fulfil the conditions of Article 81(3). Such restrictions are usually black-listed in block exemption regulations or identified as hardcore restrictions in Commission guidelines and notices. Agreements of this nature generally fail (at least) the two first conditions of Article 81(3). They neither create objective economic benefits nor do they benefit consumers. For example, a horizontal agreement to fix prices limits output leading to misallocation of resources. It also transfers value from consumers to producers, since it leads to higher prices without producing any countervailing value to consumers within the relevant market. Moreover, these types of agreements generally also fail the indispensability test under the third condition. . . . Any claim that restrictive agreements are justified because they aim at ensuring fair conditions of competition on the market is by nature unfounded and must be discarded. The purpose of Article 81 is to protect effective competition by ensuring that markets remain open and competitive. (footnotes omitted)

Concerning exemptions for secret hard-core cartels, the Community courts were previously able to dismiss arguments about the application of Article 81(3) because the cartels had not been notified.[312] Now, though, there is an automatic exemption in Article 1(2) of Regulation 1, and from a procedural point of view cartelists may well claim that they have self-assessed their co-operation and concluded that it satisfies the requirements for exemption. However, while there are no agreements which are inherently incapable of qualifying for an exemption,[313] it will be extremely difficult to demonstrate in substance that Article 81(3) applies to cartels.

As explained in this chapter, the formation of a hard-core cartel is normally preceded by declining demand and overcapacity, often in a mature market. If the application of Article 81(3) EC is to be a matter of substance rather than just procedure, it is hardly viable to justify exemptions of crisis cartels with reference to the market situation. An alternative approach would be to justify them with reference to the self-imposed limitations of the parties, ie that they only co-operate on the closing down of obsolete production capacity, as opposed to fixing prices and sharing markets. But the theoretical soundness of allowing collusion in response to decline and recession has been questioned.[314] One would have to find and substantiate (with reference to economic analysis) a fundamental difference between quotas on the one hand and permanent capacity reductions on the other hand. There is in addition the matter of spill-over effects; in other words, the suspicion that the acceptable co-operation spills over into other activities, markets or lines of business. For instance, in *Welded Steel Mesh*, the arrangements on the German

[311] Communication from the Commission, Notice, *Guidelines on the application of Article 81(3) of the Treaty* [2004] OJ C/101/97, at 46–47.

[312] See, eg, Case C-411/04 P *Salzgitter Mannesmann v Commission* [2007] ECR I-959, at paras 53ff, and Joined Cases T-259/02 to T-264/02 and T-271/02 *Raiffeisen Zentralbank Österreich AG and others v Commission* [2006] ECR II-5169, at para 213.

[313] Case T-17/93 *Matra Hachette SA v Commission* [1994] ECR II-595, at para 85.

[314] Areeda and Hovenkamp, above n 26, Vol IIB, § 413, at 66–67.

market had their origin in a crisis cartel authorised by the German federal cartel office.[315]

Perhaps a more viable defence would be to invoke other objectives recognised by the Community, such as the achievement of social, environmental,[316] regional and cultural goals. In *FEG and TU*, the Court struck down a submission relating to social objectives. The cartel participants had agreed on uniform discount rates of 35 per cent to schools, and claimed that the practice had had a special social reason and special social justification. The Court rejected this argument:

> Since it was established by the Court of First Instance that the collusion on the standard discounts granted to schools had an anticompetitive object, neither the unique nature nor the social object of those discounts could protect the agreement relating to them from the application of Article 81(1) EC.[317]

This reasoning was derived from Article 81(1) and not from Article 81(3) EC. However, in *Matra Hachette*, arguments concerning the contribution to social progress and regional progress, as well as exceptional circumstances relating to public infrastructure and employment, were held irrelevant in relation to Article 81(3) EC.[318] Whether this was mainly for procedural or policy reasons is not entirely clear, but it is recognised that a broader approach to Article 81(3) EC than pure efficiency reasons is possible.[319] Nonetheless, the modernisation has brought about a need for less discretion and more proper legal standards, which means that the scope for considering other policies may be narrower than before.[320]

In practice there is hardly any scope left for Article 81(3) EC in relation to hardcore cartels. Crisis cartels were addressed by the Court of Justice in *Beef Industry Development Society and Barry Brothers*.[321] The Irish Beef Industry Development Society raised the argument that a joint industry production capacity reduction programme did not come within the category of infringements by object but should be analysed in the light of its actual effects on the market. It argued that the production capacity reductions did not have an anticompetitive purpose and did not entail injurious consequences for consumers or, more generally, for competition. This argument was not accepted by the Court, which held that

> even supposing it to be established that the parties to an agreement acted without any subjective intention of restricting competition, but with the object of remedying the effects of a crisis in their sector, such considerations are irrelevant . . .[322]

The Society argued for a narrow interpretation of Article 81(1). In response to the various arguments raised by the Society, the Court replied that it was apparent that

[315] *Welded steel mesh* [1989] OJ L/260/1.

[316] *CECED* [2000] OJ L/187/47.

[317] Case C-105/04 P *Nederlandse Federatieve Vereniging voor de Groothandel op Elektrotechnisch Gebied v Commission* [2006] ECR I-8725, at para 126.

[318] Case T-17/93 *Matra Hachette SA v Commission* [1994] ECR II-595, at paras 107, 139.

[319] Whish, Richard, *Competition Law*, 5th edn (LexisNexis, 2003), at 152 ff.

[320] *Ibid*, at 155.

[321] Case C-209/07 *Beef Industry Development Society and Barry Brothers* [2008] ECR I-0000.

[322] *Ibid*, at para 21.

the object of the arrangements was to change, appreciably, the structure of the market through a mechanism intended to encourage the withdrawal of competitors.[323] The intention was to

> enable several undertakings to implement a common policy which has as its object the encouragement of some of them to withdraw from the market and the reduction, as a consequence, of the overcapacity which affects their profitability by preventing them from achieving economies of scale.[324]

That type of arrangement patently conflicted with the concept inherent in the EC Treaty provisions relating to competition.[325] The indication in the judgment is that chances of obtaining exemption are limited. The Court hinted at this by referring to the possibility of exemption as something that could happen 'at the most'.[326]

It follows that the main problem is not how to treat outright price-fixing, market-sharing and quotas, including production capacity reductions, under Article 81(3) EC. The hard cases would centre around the question of whether to allow integration objectives to dictate the outcome, even when there were investments or some other efficiency enhancing such as improved distribution,[327] or research and development.[328] It may be observed that integration objectives have sometimes led to a harsh view on co-operation that includes pro-competitive aspects. In particular, auctions that are perceived to seal off a Member State have been treated without much generosity.[329] The establishment of auction houses (or perhaps in today's world, Internet auction sites) for goods like agricultural products entails substantive investment, and can be an efficient way to channel sales by multiple small and medium-sized firms. Exclusivity can, at least for some time and to some degree, be the only way to make the investment viable. There would also be obvious distribution advantages. If the establishment and maintenance of auction houses restrict competition at all, it ought to be possible to exempt them.

2. *The decision-making on exemptions for cartels*

Cartels can be said to differ from most other forms of restrictive agreements in one respect: they produce no countervailing benefits for competition. Cartels produce less and earn more.[330] Cartels restrict competition in the sense of Article 81(1) EC, and only in exceptional circumstances—perhaps never—will they qualify for

[323] *Ibid*, at para 31.
[324] *Ibid*, at para 33.
[325] *Ibid*, at para 34.
[326] *Ibid*, at para 39.
[327] *Cafeteros de Colombia* [1982] OJ L/360/31.
[328] *Siemens/Fanuc* [1985] OJ L/376/29.
[329] *FRUBO* [1974] OJ L/237/16; *Cauliflowers* [1978] OJ L/21/23, *Hudson's Bay–Dansk Pelsdyravlerforening* [1988] OJ L/316/43; *Bloemenveilingen Aalsmeer* [1988] OJ L/262/27.
[330] Monti, Mario, 'Why should we be concerned with cartels and collusive behaviour', in *Fighting Cartels–why and how?* (Stockholm, Konkurrensverket, 2001), at 15.

exemption under Article 81(3) EC. However, this line of reasoning has not been acknowledged as a matter of principle by the Community courts.

Before 1 May 2004, cartels had to be notified to the Commission to have any chance of obtaining exemption. For obvious reasons cartels will normally prefer to keep their existence secret. The Commission and the Community courts alike have often been able to dismiss arguments about pro-competitive effects without trying them in substance, with reference to the fact that no notification had been made. For instance, in *Seamless steel tubes*, a claim that vertical aspects of the cartel should be assessed under block exemption regulations was rejected by the Court of Justice on formalistic grounds, one of the reasons being that a block exemption had not entered into force at the time of the infringements.[331]

The occasional exemptions for crisis cartels blur the picture further. If we go back to the 1960s, 1970s, and even the 1980s, however, companies were apparently entertaining hopes about exemption, and there are several examples of cartels that were actually notified, but then prohibited by the Commission and denied exemption. The Commission would at that time refrain from imposing fines.[332] This presumably reduced incentives to appeal. We will next look at some cases that were nevertheless appealed.

3. *Cases before the Community courts where cartels were notified and tried under Article 81(3) EC*

In the *Flemish Books* case, a notification was made for an agreement that publishers must fix a single retail price for each title they published, without allowing for sales below this price. There was also a collective exclusive dealing agreement. The Commission refused an exemption.[333] On appeal, the publishers argued that fixed prices allowed the publishers, as a result of the profit realised on successful titles, to cross-subsidise more difficult and less profitable works. Distributors in their turn would be encouraged to keep more extensive stocks, and to serve their customers better by helping in this way to disseminate a greater number of varied works.[334] The Court of Justice did not accept this view and upheld the Commission's refusal to grant exemption, but it did so on a reasoning that was case-specific and cautious.[335]

Eleven years later, in *Net Book Agreements*, the Court set aside a Commission decision that had been upheld by the Court of First Instance, for a joint arrange-

[331] Case C-411/04 P *Salzgitter Mannesmann v Commission* [2007] ECR I-959, at paras 53 ff.

[332] *Carreaux céramiques* [1971] OJ L/10/15; *Vereeniging van Cementhandelaren* [1972] OJ L/13/34; *Chauffage central* [1972] OJ L/264/22; *Kali & Salz* [1973] OJ L/217/3; *Gas water-heaters and bath-heaters* [1973] OJ L/217/34; *Stoves and heaters* [1975] OJ L/159/22; *Centraal Bureau voor de Rijwielhandel* [1978] OJ L/20/18; *IMA Rules* [1980] OJ L/318/1; *VBBB/VBVB* [1982] OJ L/54/36; *Stichting Sigarettenindustrie* [1982] OJ L/232/1 (where fines were imposed); *Vimpoltu* [1983] OJ L/200/44; *Aluminium imports from eastern Europe* [1985] OJ L/92/1.

[333] *VBBB/VBVB* [1982] OJ L/54/36.

[334] Joined Cases 43 and 62/82 *VBVB and VBBB v Commission* [1984] ECR 19.

[335] *Ibid*, at paras 59 ff.

ment by publishers to sell books on standardised conditions.[336] The standardised conditions had been worked out by a Publishers Association representing 70 to 80 per cent of publishers in the United Kingdom. According to this Net Book Agreement, a 'net book' was not allowed to be sold at less than the net published price. The net published price referred to a practice where the publisher marketed a book at a net retail price. There were several exceptions to the prohibition against sales at less than the net price, including specified rules on discounts to such libraries, book agents and quantity buyers as had been previously authorised by the Association. Discounts were also allowed for book club editions and for the annual national book sales. The Court of Justice quashed the Court of First Instance's refusal to grant an exemption under Article 81(3) EC and distinguished the case from the *Flemish Books* case. The decisive difference, according to the Court, was that the Net Book Agreement applied only if a publisher chose to market a book as a net book. This reasoning is unconvincing.

A nationwide system for joint setting of trade margins, rebates and payment terms for tobacco products was considered in *GB-Inno-BM/Fedetab*.[337] Notification to the Commission was made after complaints had been filed. The Commission refused exemption. On appeal, the Court of Justice confirmed that exemption could not be granted, but the reasoning was once again case-specific. While the Court acknowledged that the collective agreement had the object of restricting competition, it made the refusal to grant an exemption hinge ultimately on the very large market shares of the parties involved.[338]

In *Stichting Sigarettenindustrie*, the Commission then denied exemption for a nationwide system for the collective setting of trade margins.[339] On appeal the applicants submitted *inter alia* that the agreements were intended to protect the structure of the distribution network and were therefore of benefit to consumers. There was also an argument relating to distortions due to national legislation. The case was not clear-cut when it came to notification, since only some of the restrictive practices had been notified. The Court denied exemption and said that

> even if exemption could have been granted in the absence of notification, it would necessarily have been refused on the ground that the price agreements benefited only the manufacturers and importers and were of no benefit to consumers . . .[340]

This statement is close to a declaration in principle that naked price-fixing inherently disqualifies for exemption.

Finally, in *Fire insurance*, the Commission denied exemption for a recommendation by a trade association that insurance premiums should be set (and indeed

[336] Case C-360/92 P *The Publishers Association v Commission* [1995] ECR I-23.
[337] *GB-Inno-BM/Fedetab* [1978] OJ L/224/29.
[338] Joined Cases 209–215 and 218/78 *van Landewyck and others v Commission* [1980] ECR 3125, at para 189.
[339] *Stichting Sigarettenindustrie* [1982] OJ L/232/1.
[340] Joined Cases 240, 241, 242, 261, 262, 268 and 269/82 *Stichting Sigarettenindustrie and others v Commission* [1985] ECR 3831.

raised) in a certain way.[341] The industry claimed that the recommendation was objectively necessary to re-establish the profitability of insurance companies whilst safeguarding the interests of those insured. The scheme included collective, fixed-rate and across-the-board increases in premiums. The Court of Justice held that the increases in premiums were general and undifferentiated, and encompassed not only cover for the expenses resulting from insurance claims but also the operating costs of the insurance companies. Given that there were considerable differences in the level of operating costs between different insurance companies, the Court said that the global nature of the increase was likely to result in restrictions on competition going beyond what was necessary to achieve the intended objective.[342] Once again, we have a case where price-fixing is denied exemption not as a matter of principle, but with reference to a case-specific and fact-specific reasoning.

We may consequently observe that the Court of Justice had a window of opportunity in the 1970s and 1980s to define price-fixing cartels as arrangements that restrict competition without producing any countervailing benefits, and that that opportunity was not exploited by the Court.

By contrast, the US Supreme Court, in *FTC v Indiana Federation of Dentists*, indicated that an analysis under the Sherman Act restraint of trade provisions targeted measures that impair the ability of the market to advance social welfare, so that in the absence of some countervailing pro-competitive virtue such measures cannot be accepted.[343] Defining naked restraints as restrictions that are objectively intended to increase price or reduce output seems firmly rooted in US law.[344]

C. Conclusion: cartel control as a structural remedy

We have looked at cartels from a variety of perspectives. First we looked at the common perceptions about cartels in the Western industrialised world, where cartels are generally considered very harmful to society. Next came the economic perspectives on cartels, which provide strong theoretical and empirical support for the need to prohibit cartels and use public resources to combat them. Thirdly, cartels were analysed with reference to other impediments to competition, such as tacit collusion, mergers, abuse of dominance and vertical restrictions. Lastly, cartels were defined by contrasting them with agreements and practices which have pro-competitive effects.

While the literature on cartels focuses primarily on the behavioural aspects of cartels and the results they produce, the survey just undertaken here reveals that cartel control may be seen as orientated towards preventing the creation of *forums* where competitors can meet or otherwise expressly communicate on prices, output and market conditions. By impeding the emergence of secret or open power forums, the

[341] *Fire insurance* [1985] OJ L/35/20.
[342] Case 45/85 *Verband der Sachversicherer eV v Commission* [1987] ECR 405, at para 60.
[343] *FTC v Indiana Federation of Dentists* 476 US 447 (1986).
[344] Areeda and Hovenkamp n 3, Vol XI, § 1906, at 235 ff.

authorities can effectively prevent the type of behaviour that may be expected to result. In the absence of such forums, no public intervention is made, which is evidenced by the prevailing view that tacit collusion is not liked but accepted.

Cartel control is theoretically related to merger control and the prohibition against abuse of dominance. Merger control takes place *ex ante*, while cartel control takes place *ex post*, but this does not reflect any difference in principle, only the realities of enforcement given that mergers must necessarily happen in the open while cartelists are inclined to keep their actions secret.[345] Moreover, it is not altogether unthinkable that the same companies that would merge if merger control were lenient or non-existent, will migrate to cartel formation if merger control is stringent. Migration of an industry from cartels to mergers has indeed been observed, although not studied systematically.[346] Cartels can be created quickly and at low cost, which is one of the reasons why they are detrimental. Unlike mergers, they will not realise volumes of scale, because of the absence of permanent integration of production. This implies that cartel control must be at least as effective as merger control, and this in spite of the secret nature of cartels.

Looking at cartels as *forums*, rather than as behaviour, actually makes the law easier to understand. Cartels as forums are indeed recognised (although marginally) by leading US scholars:

> Moreover, cartel institutions create a forum for continued exhortation toward compliance, for negotiation or adjustment of dissatisfactions that might lead to defections, and for the chastisement and repentance of cheaters before the self-help of escalating defections.[347]

Among European scholars, Neven also reasons along this line, and considers that 'the Commission should focus on the existence of effective *vehicles* of concertation between firms and pay only little attention to circumstances that are meant to favour co-ordination'.[348] Factors that may be evaluated with confidence are, according to Neven, ownership and access to information-sharing mechanisms in an industry, functions performed by industry associations and the public announcements they make. Structural links between firms, cross-shareholdings and cross-representations on boards, as well as simultaneous involvement in external organisations, should be scrutinised too.[349]

1. *Trade associations*

Neven's view that we ought to focus on trade associations and other vehicles for concertation gains support when we look at the role of trade associations in detected cartels.

345 See Neven, above n 157, at 62.

346 Evenett *et al*, above n 61, at 1229; Schoneveld, Frank R, 'Cartel Sanctions and International Competition Policy: Cross-Border Cooperation and Appropriate Forums for Cooperation' (2003) 26(3) *World Competition* 433, at 453.

347 Areeda and Hovenkamp, above n 3, Vol VI, § 1432, at 225.

348 Neven, above n 157, at 57 ff, emphasis added.

349 *Ibid*, at 68.

According to my findings, trade associations have been involved to a greater or lesser extent in at least 59, equalling nearly 40 per cent, of the Commission's cartel cases.[350] In early cartel decisions the borderline could be somewhat blurred between, on the one hand, trade associations and, on the other hand, cartels given legal form through establishment of a corporation. In the extreme, a trade association was set up precisely to monitor the cartel arrangement.[351] Though there may be borderline examples, this survey demonstrates the central role of trade associations for the creation and maintenance of cartels in Europe, and how the problem persists over time.

From a policy perspective, the figures on the involvement of trade associations indicate that 'soft' enforcement directed towards trade associations, and development of best practices, would have the potential to improve compliance significantly. Best practices might include a model where trade associations operate independently, without being staffed and administered by members. An independent trade association would possess a higher degree of integrity, and have less incentive to function as a forum for cartels.

2. *Permitted forums for concertation—shipping cartels*

Acceptance of forums where competitors can engage in outright negotiation of market conditions has been tried EC law in at least two ways: in the maritime sector, and as a result of government intervention. Both experiences have been discouraging but will briefly be accounted for here, to illustrate the point that a cartel prohibition may be seen as structural.

[350] *German scrap iron* [1970] OJ L/29/30; *Carreaux céramiques* [1971] OJ L/10/15; *Chauffage central* [1972] OJ L/264/22; *GISA* [1972] OJ L/303/45; *Papier peints de Belgique* [1974] OJ L/237/3; *Franco-Japanese ball-bearings agreement* [1974] OJ L/343/19; *Preserved mushrooms* [1975] OJ L/29/26; *Stoves and heaters* [1975] OJ L/159/22; *Bomée-Stichting* [1975] OJ L/329/30; *Pabst & Richarz/BNIA* [1976] OJ L/231/24; *COBELPA/VNP* [1977] OJ L/242/10; *Centraal Bureau voor de Rijwielhandel* [1978] OJ L/20/18; *Vegetable parchment* [1978] OJ L/70/54; *GB-Inno-BM/Fedetab* [1978] OJ L/224/29; *IMA Rules* [1980] OJ L/318/1; *Rolled steel products* [1980] OJ L/62/28; *Italian flat glass* [1981] OJ L/326/32; *VBBB/VBVB* [1982] OJ L/54/36; *NAVEWA/ANSEAU* [1982] OJ L/167/39; *Stichting Sigarettenindustrie* [1982] OJ L/232/1; *Cafeteros de Colombia* [1982] OJ L/360/31; *AROW/BNIC* [1982] OJ L/379/1; *Vimpoltu* [1983] OJ L/200/44; *Cast iron and steel rolls* [1983] OJ L/317/1; *Peroxygen products* [1985] OJ L/35/1; *Fire insurance* [1985] OJ L/35/20; *Aluminium imports from eastern Europe* [1985] OJ L/92/1; *French inland waterway charter traffic* [1985] OJ L/219/35; *Roofing felt* [1986] OJ L/232/15; *Fatty Acids* [1987] OJ L/3/17; *Publisher's association* [1989] OJ L/22/12; *Sugar beet* [1990] OJ L/31/32; *Cold-rolled stainless steel flat products* [1990] OJ L/220/28; *Building and construction industry in the Netherlands* [1992] OJ L/92/1; *UK Agricultural Tractor Registration Exchange* [1992] OJ L/68/19; *Scottish Salmon Board* [1992] OJ L/246/37; *CNSD* [1993] OJ L/203/27; *European producers of beams* [1994] OJ L/116/1; *Cartonboard* [1994] OJ L/243/1; *Cement* [1994] OJ L/343/1; *Coapi* [1995] OJ L/122/37; *Kraanverhuurbedrijf* [1995] OJ L/312/79; *Fenex* [1996] OJ L/181/28; *Pre-insulated pipe cartel* [1999] OJ L/24/1; *FEG and TU* [2000] OJ L/39/1; *Citric Acid* [2002] OJ L/239/18; *Luxembourg brewers* [2002] OJ L/253/21; *Interbrew and Alken-Maes* [2003] OJ L/200/1; *Zinc phosphate* [2003] OJ L/153/1; *Carbonless paper* [2004] OJ L/115/1; *Industrial and medical gases* [2003] OJ L/84/1; *French beef* [2003] OJ L/209/12; *Industrial tubes* [2004] OJ L/125/50; *Belgian architects* [2005] OJ L/4/10; *Raw Tobacco Spain* IP/04/1256; *Raw Tobacco Italy* IP/05/1315; *Industrial Bags* IP/05/1508.

[351] *Cast iron and steel rolls* [1983] OJ L/317/1, at 10.

A liner conference (or consortia) may be explained as a legal cartel operating on the markets for maritime transport services. Former block exemptions allowed competitors to co-operate on several aspects, including standards, transport capacity, rates and conditions. Competitors were allowed to regulate carrying capacity and allocate cargo and revenues.[352] While accepting those arrangements as a matter of policy, the Commission encountered severe difficulties in monitoring compliance with the limitations imposed by law on the liner conferences. In *TACA*, it brought an action under Article 82 EC against a liner conference. The allegation was neutralisation of potential competition, in particular by inducing competing parties to join. It was alleged that TACA had offered competing parties allocation of market shares provided they joined the conference, thereby systematically inducing potential competitors to join by allowing them to become conference members on terms other than those proposed to existing members.

The Court of First Instance quashed the Commission's decision on a combination of points of law and points of fact.[353] One of the decisive points was that under the liner shipping block exemption, market-sharing agreements entered into between the members of a liner conference were not necessarily prohibited.[354] The case evidences how hard it would be to restrict a group of competitors from expanding that group, and hence its aggregate market power, once we allow competitors to meet and agree on market conditions.

Similarly in *Compagnie Maritime Belge*, the Commission had to deal with joint exclusionary conduct by shipping companies. It consisted of a practice where competitors jointly offered lower prices on ship freight, on the particular dates and routes where they met competition. The practice was a joint exclusionary one, where the objective was (presumably) to recapture the costs once the competition had been eliminated. The Commission struck it down as an abuse of dominance and won the case, but only after two instances of litigation in the Community courts.[355] One of the problems was to determine when a liner conference might legitimately, on a case-by-case basis, adopt lower prices than those of its advertised tariff in response to a competitor's lower prices. Another was to decide on the exact scope of the expression 'uniform or common freight rates' in Article 1(3)(b) of Regulation 4056/86. However, the Court of Justice found that it was not necessary to rule on those issues, given that the liner conference had a 90 per cent market share and that the purpose of the conduct was to eliminate the only competitor.[356] This was prohibited as an abuse of dominance. The case nevertheless illustrates the

[352] See especially Arts 2 and 3 of Council Regulation (EEC) No 4056/86 of 22 December 1986 laying down detailed rules for the application of Articles 85 and 86 of the Treaty to maritime transport [1986] OJ L/378/4.

[353] Joined Cases T-191/98 and T-212/98 to T-214/98 *Atlantic Container Line and others v Commission* [2003] ECR II-3275, at paras 1279 ff.

[354] *Ibid*, at para 1302.

[355] Joined Cases C-395/96 P and C-396/96 P *Compagnie Maritime Belge Transports and Others v Commission* [2000] ECR I-1365.

[356] *Ibid*, at para 119.

problems regulators encounter once they provide an arena for competitors to co-operate on prices and other competitive conditions.

Acceptance of such forums will require constant monitoring by authorities, and will entail all sorts of problems in drawing the line between what is lawful and what is not.

The continued existence or abolition of exemptions in the shipping sector was discussed, assessed and evaluated in a lengthy legislative procedure. Among commentators, Townley concluded that the conferences increased static inefficiencies as well as productive inefficiencies, and encouraged rent-seeking activities.[357] A report published in 2005, drafted by external experts for the Competition DG, made several conclusions in favour of abolishing the exemption.[358] The theoretical model applied by the experts showed that conferences led to excess capacity (over-investment) or excess pricing, and endangered service reliability. Withdrawal of the system would always lead to lower prices, and a prohibition on conferences would remove excess capacity. There were no indications that competition between carriers would lead to inherent instability on the market. With or without conferences, there could be market volatility.[359]

In 2006 the Council adopted secondary legislation to repeal a block exemption.[360] This measure corresponded to serious concerns expressed in the legal community. Full application of Article 81 EC to liner conferences can, in my view, be seen as a structural remedy—liner conferences are organisations which will have to be dismantled or reshaped in response to the withdrawn exemption.

3. Cartels stemming from sector regulation and other forms of government intervention

Another argument for seeing the cartel prohibition as a way to prohibit forums for collusion rather than prohibiting competitor behaviour, can be found in the cartels stemming from sector regulation and other forms of government intervention.

There is evidence in the Commission's cartel decisions that sector regulation has provided a framework for cartels or, when abolished, has been replaced by collusion. National market organisations which provided *inter alia* for sales territories pre-dated the emergence of the *Sugar cartel* in the 1970s. The Commission said that 'This explains a tendency for old practices to become a habit'.[361] An intricate

[357] Townley, Chris, 'The Liner Shipping Block Exemptions in European Law: Has the Tide Turned?' (2004) 27(1) *World Competition* 107.

[358] Final Report 26 October 2005, *Application of Competition Rules to Liner Shipping*, produced by Global Insight, Berlin University of Technology (WIP) and the Institute of Shipping Economics and Logistics (ISL), available on http://ec.europa.eu/comm/competition/antitrust/legislation/maritime/.

[359] *Ibid*, at I-7, para 40.

[360] Council Regulation (EC) No 1419/2006 of 25 September 2006 repealing Regulation (EEC) No 4056/86 laying down detailed rules for the application of Articles 85 and 86 of the Treaty to maritime transport, and amending Regulation (EC) No 1/2003 as regards the extension of its scope to include cabotage and international tramp services [2006] OJ L/269/1.

[361] *European Sugar Industry* [1973] OJ L/140/17.

government system for taxes and statutory prices formed the background of the *Dutch Cigarette cartel.* There, the industry claimed that the reason for the arrangement was the Dutch Government's wish to deal with a single spokesman for the industry.[362] Crisis measures for the European steel industry, including quotas adopted by the Commission, were the background to a cartel for *cold-rolled stainless steel flat products.*[363] Delivery and production quotas and minimum prices imposed by the Commission as anti-crisis measures in the steel industry in the 1980s were later replaced by a *steel beams* cartel.[364] A voluntary export restraint concluded between the Commission and the Japanese Government in 1972 was also replaced by a cartel in *Seamless steel tubes.*[365] A cartel on the market for beer in Belgium originated at least partly in the price control exercised by Belgian authorities, where the trade association was allowed to file applications on behalf of the industry.[366] Similarly, Spanish market regulation for tobacco, which encouraged joint negotiations between producers and buyers on sales conditions, formed the basis for the emergence of a cartel for raw tobacco.[367] Along the same lines, the *Raw Tobacco Italy* cartel was preceded by national legislation aiming at determining in advance prices of products or the criteria for price determination.[368]

Once again, these examples show that once the legislator accepts or recommends a forum where competitors are allowed to discuss and agree on market conditions, it signifies the creation of organisations which take on a life of their own. Here, too, Article 81 EC can be seen as structural, because it hinders the creation and maintenance of such forums.

4. *Summing up on cartel control as structural rather than behavioural*

The main difference between merger control and cartel control is that, provided a per se or quick look-approach is applied, there is no or little need to look into market power in cartel control, unlike merger control where market power is the central issue. Does this objection undermine the idea of cartel control as structural? Or, conversely, does it imply that we ought to examine market shares in cartel control?

It is submitted here that refraining from examining market shares in cartel control is an enforcement policy decision adopted for deterrence purposes, more than a different theoretical perspective. Less money will be spent on supervision and litigation, hence more cartels can be pursued for less if we discard the market power inquiry. And cartels make little sense in the absence of market power. Mergers may happen because of volumes of scale and cost savings, but such synergies are seldom, if ever, realised in cartels.

362 *Stichting Sigarettenindustrie* [1982] OJ L/232/1, at 35.
363 *Cold-rolled stainless steel flat products* [1990] OJ L/220/28.
364 *European producers of beams* [1994] OJ L/116/1, at 308.
365 *Seamless steel tubes* [2003] OJ L/140/1, at 27.
366 *Interbrew and Alken-Maes* [2003] OJ L/200/1, at 10, 171, 247 ff.
367 *Raw Tobacco Spain,* Commission decision of 20 October 2004, at 53 ff.
368 *Raw Tobacco Italy* IP/05/1315, Commission decision of 20 October 2005, at 315 ff.

Furthermore, structural changes such as mergers and other concentrations are transaction specific. Each time, the authorities try only one particular transaction. Merger control is burdensome enough, but can nevertheless be seen as light when compared to the administrative problems that would be encountered if we allowed defences based on low market shares in cartel cases. Constant market monitoring would then be necessary in cartel-prone sectors, to distinguish cartels with low market power from those with high aggregate power. While we should be sceptical about allowing defences based on low market shares in cartel cases, the insights gained from a comparison with mergers could, on the other hand, be used for policy priority purposes and for sanctions—it is quite possible that cartels with low market shares are not as important and do not deserve fines as high as the larger cartels.

The analogy with mergers also raises the question whether we should allow efficiency defences for cartels. Given the solid theory on the general absence of efficiencies for price-fixing, quotas and market-sharing (including bid-rigging), such reasoning would seem futile for those infringements. Boycotts, on the other hand, are not a unitary concept, and it would seem possible that situations with efficiencies would exist, where an exemption could be granted. Purchase price-fixing is another candidate for exemptions—provided there is low market power, we cannot rule out the possibility of efficiencies. The same goes for mixed horizontal and vertical cartels, as set out in section III.A.7 above.

D. Defining cartels

There is no unitary view in European publications about what constitutes a cartel. Consider, as an illustration of the point just made, that the *European Cartel Digest* lists 96 cartel decisions adopted by the European Commission,[369] as compared with the 150 or so listed in the present work. The absence of a legal term, with content we can all agree on, is problematic because the debate risks becoming confused.

Looking at the idea of cartels as a *legal* concept, it has been explained in detail in this chapter that, within that category, the treatment of different infringements is not exactly the same. While price-fixing, quotas and market-sharing including bid-rigging are treated much the same, a more case-by-case approach may be observed for boycotts, where legal theory advocates different treatment depending on the circumstances. Information exchange is clearly approached on a case-by-case basis, unless it underpins price-fixing, quotas and market-sharing, in which case it is hard-core. Even price-fixing contains some unevenness, since buyer cartels have not been pursued much in EC law, and cases on dealer cartels (without the involvement of producers and wholesalers) are difficult to find at all. On quotas, a more tolerant approach may be observed as regards opening hours or other

[369] Sakkers, Ewoud, and Ysewyn, Jordan, *European Cartel Digest* (The Netherlands, Wolters Kluwer, 2008).

joint outlet restrictions than on outright production restrictions. The distinction between vertical and horizontal arrangements, used as an analytical tool by the Commission in its notices and guidelines, is altogether inconclusive given the large number of leading cases on mixed vertical and horizontal hard-core infringements. There, theory is not developed much at all.

In summary, trying to find a definition of cartels as a way to classify legally a certain category of practices, tends to be a fruitless exercise. And it risks detracting from the very reasons why these infringements are pursued. Normatively, the analysis should be based on theoretical and empirical observations about the effects *typically* produced by price-fixing, quotas and market-sharing. For boycotts, mixed cartels and information exchange, a combination of the effects typically produced and the facts of the case should be decisive.

Looking at the idea of cartels as cartels a *matter of enforcement priorities*, the empirical observations accounted for in the present chapter (at section I.C) indicate that there are considerable variations in the harm caused by cartels. More precisely, global cartels are far more harmful than domestic ones. Cartels with large market shares and large turnovers are more detrimental than cartels with low market shares or low turnover. And there will be situations where there can be countervailing efficiencies that must be taken into consideration (in particular for joint boycotts and information exchange). The term 'cartel' reflects an approximate idea of the worst infringements of Article 81 EC, but within that concept there are large discrepancies. This means that the term is too vague to allow for conscious enforcement policy choices. A more sophisticated approach is necessary if public resources are to be spent in a meaningful way. The rule of thumb suggested here is that, for enforcement priority purposes, we should look at cartels as if they were mergers, adjusting for the fact that they are secret and do not bring about structural efficiencies.

IV. SUMMARY AND CONCLUSIONS

The analysis in the present chapter has generated a strong imperative for a prohibition against cartels and for spending public resources on cartel control. Absent a well-functioning system for cartel control, there will be a considerable number of cartels in operation in society. This view is firmly underpinned by empirical observations: once the US and the EU took up cartel control seriously in the 1990s, a large number of cartels were unearthed.

Even with a well-functioning system for cartel control, the chances are that a certain number of cartels will be at work anyway because of the evident financial incentives. As explained, recent empirical observations indicate that international cartels generate 25 per cent overcharges. Domestic cartels are less prosperous but still generate considerable overcharges. A complete extinction of cartels is presumably out of reach. The aim for a well-functioning cartel control system is consequently to keep the number of cartels, and the size of each cartel in terms of duration, overcharges and geographic scope, at the lowest level possible. Absent cartel control, cartels will cause enormous welfare losses in society. Estimates indicate that the scope of those welfare losses are such that we ought to spend resources at combating them.

Conversely, cartel control generates better welfare, because it reduces or eliminates the overcharges, deadweight losses, X-inefficiency and involuntary welfare distribution that would otherwise be caused by cartels. Prohibition and enforcement against cartels improve welfare in society.

Not surprisingly, there is wide support in the legal community and in the business community for cartel control. Empirical legitimacy—or, if you wish, cultural legitimacy—is very strongly in favour of cartel control. Once we examine the cartel concept in depth, however, it turns out that it harbours several different practices which typically generate similar, but not identical, economic effects. Whereas sales price-fixing, quotas and market-sharing (including bid-rigging) are seen as hard-core infringements which always, or nearly always, produce negative effects, a more nuanced approach may be observed for buyer cartels, single-brand dealer cartels, boycotts, and mixed horizontal and vertical cartels. Information exchange is looked upon as either a prohibited practice (if it underpins a cartel agreement), or as a matter of balancing pro-competitive and negative effects (absent the cartel context).

If a common theoretical framework is to be established then, tentatively, cartel control can be seen as structural rather then behavioural. This view is developed in the present chapter and allows us to understand some long-lived frustrations that have occurred when, exceptionally, forums for cartels are tolerated.

The role of economic theory and empirical observations as a legitimacy base in EC jurisprudence is somewhat illusive. On the one hand, the case law seems to follow economic theory relatively closely. On the other hand, very few explicit references are made to economic theory or empirical observations in case law. Economic theory finds its way into EC cartel control very much through the administrative practices of the Commission—in other words, through its enforcement priorities. This raises the question how 27 Member State authorities and courts can be expected to respond in their own enforcement.

4

Legitimacy of Substantive Cartel Law

THE DISCUSSION IN the previous chapter established that the Commission's policy shift from control of vertical restraints to control of cartels makes sense in relation to economic and legal theory, and corresponds to conceptions prevailing in society. The examination now turns to the rationality of substantive EC law on cartels.

Decentralised enforcement means that the law, created in a specific setting, namely the procedure before the Commission and the Community courts, will now to a great extent be tried in all the systems and subsystems of the 27 Member States, before their authorities and courts, and in accordance with the procedural systems applicable there. All those actors must abstract the law from the setting where it was developed and make it work in their own systems. If, indeed, the Community courts have managed to create rational law with a high level of internal consistency, an EU-wide application in a variety of legal–cultural traditions should not be a problem. If, on the other hand, there are shortcomings in rationality from the start, or internal inconsistencies in the Community law, they will manifest themselves in inconsistent decentralised enforcement. Gerber explains that 'consistency in enforcement must be based on and follow from conceptual consistency—ie that conceptual consistency must precede enforcement consistency'.[1] If we want rational and consistent outcomes, we must have recourse to rational and consistent law as a starting point.

The adoption of the modernisation Regulation could hypothetically be seen as a retroactive legitimisation by the then present Member States of EC competition law and policy. However, such a view is far-fetched given the fears, expressed when modernisation was enacted, that national judges and officials would not have the necessary knowledge and skills to apply EC competition law. Indeed, the Commission has addressed this by allocating funding for competition law training for national judges. There is no support whatsoever for seeing EC competition law as legislation flowing from well-established notions in Member States. Let us consider a different hypothesis. If we assume that national judges and public officials in Member States are perfectly able to understand any rational law, is EC competition law then understandable when it comes to cartels?

[1] Gerber, David J, 'Consistent Application of Competition Laws Across System Borders: Rethinking the Issues' in Andersson (ed), *Parallel and Conflicting Enforcement of Law* (Stockholm, Norstedts, 2005), at 170.

The studies undertaken in this chapter will reveal whether some central notions in Article 81 EC have been interpreted in a way that is rational, internally consistent and possible to understand, given that systemic consistency and predictability are important prerequisites for uniform application. The analysis is limited to cartels, given that it would be impossible to cover all aspects of Articles 81 and 82 EC. As explained in chapter two, one of the primary aims of modernisation was precisely to focus enforcement on hard-core horizontal restraints. If enforcement becomes more intense, this tests the theoretical underpinning for the law as it stands.

This analysis targets the dialogue function of judgments from the Community courts—the judgments are communicating the law, and must consequently be sufficiently clear and precise if they are to be understood and accepted by the national authorities and courts entrusted with its application, and by the legal community at large. Before modernisation, the arena where this communication was taking place was for all practical purposes limited to certain actors: the Community courts, the Commission, the addressees of decisions, and a small group of attorneys and legal scholars. Decentralised enforcement brings more actors into the arena, given that national authorities and courts will now have to apply Articles 81 and 82 EC. Those actors have not been involved in the cases, and this calls for increased awareness of how judgments from the Community courts are drafted. Similarly, the legal community will be larger, given that lawyers (judges, officials, attorneys, academics) in Member States have every reason to participate in the dialogue when entrusted with the application of the rules.

More fundamental, however, is the need for a solid theoretical underpinning for the law. The ultimate test is consequently the theoretical basis for the law.

I. PER SE OR NOT PER SE

A. What is a per se prohibition?

European scholarly writing contains all sorts of statements about per se prohibitions against cartels. There are authors who insist that cartels constitute per se infringements in EC law.[2] But is this conclusion firmly underpinned by jurisprudence? The opposite view, noting the absence of a per se approach in EC law, is equally well represented.[3] Authors can occasionally be observed taking shortcuts,

[2] Arbault, Francois, and Sakkers, Ewoud, 'Cartels' in Faull, Jonathan, and Nikpay, Ali (eds), *The EC Law of Competition* (Oxford, Oxford University Press, 2007), at paras 8.03, 8.22, 8.49, 8.505.

[3] Van Bael, Ivo, and Bellis, Jean-Francois, *Competition Law of the European Communities*, 4th edn (The Hague, Kluwer Law International, 2005), at 389; Joshua, Julian M, and Jordan, Sarah, 'Combinations, Concerted Practices and Cartels: Adopting the Concept of Conspiracy in European Community Competition Law' (2004) 24(3) *Northwestern Journal of International Law and Business* 647, at 651.

for example to conclude that since Article 81 EC explicitly prohibits price-fixing, there is a per se prohibition.[4]

It is appropriate first to provide an explanation of the expression 'per se infringement'. This concept derives from the ruling of the US Supreme Court in 1958 in *Northern Pacific*:

> [T]here are certain agreements or practices which because of their pernicious effect on competition and lack of any redeeming virtue are conclusively presumed to be unreasonable and therefore illegal without elaborate inquiry as to the precise harm they have caused or the business excuse for their use. This principle of per se unreasonableness . . . avoids the necessity for an incredibly complicated and prolonged economic investigation into the entire history of the industry involved, as well as related industries, in an effort to determine at large whether a particular restraint has been unreasonable—an inquiry so often wholly fruitless when undertaken. Among the practices which the courts have heretofore deemed to be unlawful in and of themselves are price fixing . . . division of markets . . . group boycotts . . . and tying arrangements . . .[5]

By defining a category of practices that are always, or almost always, harmful to competition, courts avoid lengthy case-by-case analysis of market conditions and the actual impact on competition in a given case. The meaning of a per se illegality is that courts need not define a relevant market or establish the parties' market shares in order to find that a restraint is unlawful. Harmful effects are presumed and need not be proven. Further, courts will be very restrictive in accepting defences brought forward by defendants.[6] 'In fullest flower, a per se rule condemns conduct without proof of power, effect or purpose and without hearing claims of legitimate objectives.'[7]

The point of applying a per se rule lies in savings in judicial administration and in a reduction in the number of anticompetitive restraints.[8] The first aspect is thus one of procedural economy. Such beneficial effects are not limited to the individual proceedings but will (on a larger scale) enable the antitrust authorities to spend less time on each infringement and thus produce more aggregate enforcement. The second aspect concerns the value of having clear and unambiguous rules with which it is easy to comply. A per se approach is consequently deterrence-based, since it increases the likelihood of conviction, liberates resources in judicial administration and puts pressure on undertakings to comply.

[4] Siragusa, Mario (ed), *EU Competition Law—Volume III Cartel Law* (Leuven, Claeys & Casteels, 2006), at 41.

[5] *Northern Pacific* 356 US 1, 78 S Ct 514, references omitted.

[6] Areeda and Hovenkamp, *Antitrust Law—An Analysis of Antitrust Principles and Their Application*, 2nd edn (New York, Aspen Publishers, Wolters Kluwer Law and Business), Vol XI, § 1910, at 280.

[7] *Ibid*, Vol VII, § 1509a, at 396.

[8] *Ibid*, Vol XI, § 1910, at 281.

B. The development towards a per se prohibition in EC law

The following analysis will demonstrate that the Community courts are gradually moving towards a per se prohibition against cartels. It will be equally clear, though, that the jurisprudence contains several gaps and contradictions.

In *Polypropylene*, the Commission pushed the Court of Justice to accept a per se prohibition against agreements to fix prices, limit production and share out markets. The Commission referred to the highly damaging nature of such an infringement, and took the position that there is no need to inquire whether there are positive circumstances counterbalancing the negative effects. In Europe, said the Commission, as in the United States of America, horizontal agreements on prices are prohibited, even when undertakings are operating at a loss.[9] The Court of Justice responded by rejecting the rule of reason, but without embracing a per se approach.[10]

1. De minimis for hard-core restraints?

Is it possible to claim that agreements or concerted practices between competitors establishing price-fixing, bid-rigging, market sharing, quotas or boycotts do not have an appreciable effect on competition, quantitatively or qualitatively? The Court of First Instance has explicitly rejected application of the de minimis doctrine in cartel cases.[11] This is consistent with the view adopted by the Commission in its De Minimis Notice.[12] A reservation must be made, however, for the ruling in *Bagnasco*. There the Court found that a concerted practice, which excluded the right for economic operators to adopt a fixed interest rate, did not have an appreciable restrictive effect on competition.[13]

The Court of Justice has not yet decided whether a de minimis defence is viable in cartel cases. A further reservation must be made for the ruling in *Asnef-Equifax*. There the Court of Justice reiterated, with reference to *Völk*,[14] that an agreement will fall outside the prohibition in Article 81 EC if it has only an insignificant effect on the market.[15] It is interesting that the Court makes references to *Völk* in cases that concern restrictions which can have both pro-competitive and anticompetitive effects, such as systems for credit information and information exchange.[16] One cannot infer, *a contrario*, however, that the outcome would be the opposite in a hard-core horizontal case.

[9] Case C-235/92 P *Montecatini v Commission* [1999] ECR I-4539, at para 132.
[10] *Ibid*, at para 133.
[11] Case T-44/00 *Mannesmannröhren-Werke v Commission* [2004] ECR II-2223, at para 130.
[12] Commission Notice on agreements of minor importance which do not appreciably restrict competition under Article 81(1) of the Treaty, [2001] OJ C/368/13, at 11 ('the De Minimis Notice').
[13] Joined Cases C-215/96 and C-216/96 *Bagnasco* [1999] ECR I-135, at para 35.
[14] Case 5/69 *Völk v Vervaecke* [1969] ECR 295, at para 7.
[15] Case C-238/05 *Asnef-Equifax v Ausbanc* [2007] ECR I-11125, at para 50.
[16] Case C-7/95 P *John Deere v Commission* [1998] ECR I-3111, at para 77.

Whish describes the jurisprudence on this issue as 'somewhat confused and confusing',[17] a characterisation with which I agree. He suggests that there could be an opening for price-fixers to argue that their agreements quantitatively do not appreciably affect competition.[18] There is some support for this view in the present case law from the Court of Justice, and conversely an absence of support from the Court of First Instance. However, for the reasons set out below, I take the position that a de minimis defence should not generally be available.

A comparison with US law shows that this issue is not unique to European law. In *NCAA v Board of Regents*, the National Collegiate Athletic Association argued that its television plan had no significant anticompetitive effect since the Association had no market power. The US Supreme Court rejected the Association's argument, stating[19]:

> As a matter of law, the absence of proof of market power does not justify a naked restriction on price and output. To the contrary, when there is an agreement not to compete in terms of price or output, 'no elaborate industry analysis is required to demonstrate the anticompetitive character of such an agreement.'

Even if the participants would clearly lack any market power whatsoever, US scholars conclude that a per se rule is appropriate, provided the alleged conduct is a naked restraint without any redeeming virtues. A per se prohibition avoids elaborate and costly inquiries into market power. If an inquiry into market power is acceptable when there is an obvious lack of such power, it will also have to be carried out in different cases when absence of power is not so obvious. Further, there are pedagogic advantages to a clear-cut rule which does not allow defences based on lack of market power.[20] Prohibiting cartels that were fruitless from start because they had no market power produces few adverse effects if we accept the view that cartels have no redeeming virtues. Costs of compliance with an outright prohibition against price-fixing are low.[21] A naked restraint is rational only if the participants have collective market power, since in its absence they would not engage in the practice.[22]

Based on the US experience, it seems that the Court of First Instance and the Commission are justified in their view that the de minimis defence should not be viable as regards the fixing of sales prices, quotas and market-sharing. To this can be added a moral aspect: Hovenkamp and Areeda argue that cartelists have little moral standing in claiming that their market power was too insignificant for the cartel to be successful.[23]

[17] Whish, Richard, *Competition Law*, 5th edn (LexisNexis, 2003), at 111.

[18] *Ibid.*

[19] *National Collegiate Athletic Association v Board of Regents* 468 US 85, 104 S Ct 2948, reference omitted.

[20] Areeda and Hovenkamp, above n 6, Vol XI, § 1910, at 284.

[21] *Ibid*, at 282.

[22] *Ibid*, § 1906a, at 236.

[23] Hovenkamp, H, and Areeda, PE, *Fundamentals of Antitrust Law* 3rd edn (New York, Kluwer, looseleaf), at 15–38.

2. Whether market definitions are necessary in cartel cases

Closely related to the question whether a de minimis defence is viable in a cartel case is the question whether the plaintiff (normally the competition authority) must provide a correct market definition. The purpose of such a definition would be to determine whether the parties had any market power, and this of course would be necessary only if they were able to defend themselves by claiming that their practice did not appreciably affect competition. Further, low or insignificant market power could have an impact on the assessment of effect on trade, in other words, the jurisdiction of Community law.

Subject to the reservations expressed in the previous subsection, the current trend in EC law is that a market definition, and calculation of market shares, is not necessary in cartel cases *in so far as it relates to appreciable effect on competition.* It may be relevant for the purpose of establishing effect on trade, though; and the parties remain free to refer to market conditions as a way to prove their cause of action.

In *Italian flat glass*, the Court of First Instance declared in a rather dogmatic fashion that 'the appropriate definition of the market in question is a necessary precondition of any judgment concerning allegedly anticompetitive behaviour'.[24] The position has changed over the years, however, to a point where the same same Court held in *Seamless steel tubes* that if the actual object of an agreement is to restrict competition by market-sharing, it is not necessary to define the geographic markets in question precisely. That is

> provided that actual or potential competition on the territories concerned was necessarily restricted, whether or not those territories constitute 'markets' in the strict sense . . .[25]

The Court referred to *European Night Services*,[26] although it must be said that is very difficult to find support for the reasoning in that particular case.

In *FETTCA*, reference was made again to *European Night Services* as support for the view that when applying Article 81 EC there is an obligation to define the relevant market only where it is impossible, without such a definition, to determine whether the contested behaviour is liable to affect trade between Member States and has as its object or effect the prevention, restriction or distortion of competition within the common market.[27] This case in turn lent support to the same conclusion in *Luxembourg breweries*.[28] But then in *Euro-zone currencies—Germany*, the Court of First Instance observed, contrary to the Commission's view, that the arguments relating to the evaluation of market shares affected the likelihood of

[24] Joined Cases T-68/89, T-77/89 and T-78/89 *Società Italiano Vetro SpA and others v Commission* [1992] ECR II-1403, at para 159.

[25] Case T-44/00 *Mannesmannröhren-Werke v Commission* [2004] ECR II-2223, at para 132.

[26] Joined Cases T-374/94, T-375/94, T-384/94 and T-388/94 *European Night Services and Others v Commission* [1998] ECR II-3141.

[27] Case T-213/00 *CMA CGM and others v Commission* [2003] ECR II-913, at para 206.

[28] Joined Cases T-49/02 to T-51/02 *Brasserie Nationale and Brasserie Battin v Commission* [2005] ECR II-3033, at para 144.

existence of a horizontal price-fixing agreement in so far as the absence of sufficient market power would render such an agreement less likely.[29] In conclusion, it seems that evidence and arguments on market conditions are not entirely irrelevant, and can, at any rate, be used as a defence.

Although crucial for the methodology of bringing cartels to court, the question whether market definition is necessary in cartel cases is unresolved by the Court of Justice. In *Welded steel mesh*, the Commission had defined a market for welded steel mesh in general. This was upheld on appeal.[30] The appellant then submitted that the Court of First Instance had not given an adequate statement of reasons in the part of the judgment dealing with the definition of the relevant market. The Court tried this ground and found that the Court of First Instance had indeed explained its market definition to the requisite legal standard.[31]

The case concerned a cartel which included quotas and price-fixing. Both the Commission and the Community courts addressed the case on the implied assumption that a market definition was necessary. Possibly, this case should be seen as obsolete in this part, and the reasoning of the courts may be an outflow of the fact that the Commission considered itself (at the time) bound to produce a market definition. Even so, the existence of a case such as *Welded steel mesh* makes it difficult to establish the law.

3. *Assessment in the legal and economic context for hard-core restraints?*

The point of analysing an alleged competition restriction in its legal and economic context is to establish whether there are external factors which could explain the parties' behaviour. Government interventions and regulations would be typical examples of such explanations. Seen over time, the significance of economic analysis of alleged cartel behaviour is steadily decreasing in public enforcement cases. Parties can still make a valid point by referring to pressure from government intervention, but that escape route is very narrow. A brief account of this development will be given here.

Economic analysis was used in *Woodpulp*, where the Court of Justice accepted that there were plausible explanations other than concertation for the undertaking's parallel market behaviour.[32] Two year later, in *Soda-ash*, the Court of First Instance was much inspired by this ruling. There was an alleged concerted practice on the European soda-ash market which, according to the Commission, was due to a continuation of a market-sharing agreement concluded in the 1940s between Solvay and ICI. Although the agreement had been terminated formally in 1972, the Commission claimed that the practice had in fact continued. The Court of First Instance noted that the market-sharing agreement was lawful until the entry into force of Regulation 17 in 1962, and had not been formally challenged by

[29] Joined Cases T-44/02, etc *Dresdner Bank and others v Commission* [2006] ECR II-3567, at para 85.
[30] Case T-145/89 *Baustahlgewebe v Commission* [1995] ECR II-987, at para 36–43.
[31] Case C-185/95 P *Baustahlgewebe v Commission* [1998] ECR I-8417, at para 96–101.
[32] Joined Cases 89/85, etc *A Ahlström Osakeytiö and others v Commission* [1993] ECR I-1307.

the Commission under the adversarial procedure provided for by Regulation 17. Reiterating the standard of evidence required in *Woodpulp*, the Court of First Instance concluded[33]:

> On account of the weakness of the documentary evidence relating in particular to 1973 and the years immediately following it, the Commission should, in order to demonstrate to the requisite legal standard the concerted practice alleged against the applicant, have therefore been prompted to make, in the statement of objections, an overall and detailed economic assessment, in particular of the relevant market and the size and conduct of the undertakings active on that market.

The Court of First Instance furthermore referred to the cases pending at the time when Solvay and ICI had abused their dominant positions by rebate schemes, designed to foster loyalty among their customers, and hinted that this might be an explanation of the parallel behaviour. Even so, the Court's view appears surprising given that there was (according to the Commission's decision) evidence of regular meetings every two months or so between Solvay and ICI.[34] One may ask whether the ratio behind this case is now entirely obsolete, especially since it was established in 1999 that if an agreement or a concerted practice has the object of preventing, restricting or distorting competition, no analysis of its effects is required in relation to Article 81(1) EC.[35] This also applied to Article 65 ECSC.[36] Further, if the Commission produces documents which show that the practices were the result of an agreement or a concerted practice, the Court of First Instance will nowadays refuse to engage in examination of alternative explanations.[37]

What, then, is the present position of the Court of Justice? In *Distribution of Opel vehicles* the Court's reasoning strongly implies that an assessment in the actual context is necessary only for practices that are prohibited by reason of the distortion of competition which is their effect, as opposed to practices where the object is to prevent, restrict or distort competition.[38] But in *Seamless steel tubes* the Court was more cautious and said (with reference precisely to *Distribution of Opel vehicles*) that 'assessment of the conformity of conduct with Article 81(1) EC must, admittedly, be made in its economic context'.[39] The Court then proceeded to quash the argument of the cartel participant by saying that

> even on the assumption that the appellant's allegations were correct, they would not be capable of proving that the economic context precluded any possibility of effective competition . . .[40]

[33] Case T-30/91 *Solvay v Commission* [1995] ECR II-1775, at paras 70–76.

[34] *Soda-ash–Solvay, ICI* [1991] OJ L/152/1, at 6.

[35] Case C-49/92 P *Commission v Anic Partecipazioni* [1999] ECR I-4125, at paras 123–24.

[36] See esp Joined Cases T-45/98 and T-47/98 *Krupp Thyssen Stainless and Acciai Speciali Terni v Commission* [2001] ECR II-3757, at para 154.

[37] Joined Cases T-305/94, etc *Limburgse Vinyl Maatschappij and others v Commission* [1999] ECR II-931, at paras 722 ff.

[38] Case C-551/03 P *General Motors BV v Commission* [2006] ECR I-3173, at para 72.

[39] Case C-407/04 P *Dalmine v Commission* [2007] ECR I-829, at para 121.

[40] *Ibid.*

In other words, the economic context is still relevant, but only in so far as it would produce evidence that all possibilities of competition were excluded even prior to the anticompetitive practice.

It should be kept in mind that there are markets in Europe where competition is severely distorted as a result of historical and present government regimes, involving anything from price control to control of outlets. This applies in particular to the sale of pharmaceuticals. Regulated professions (medical practitioners, lawyers, auditors, etc) are complex markets in which the Community courts proceed with caution. It is possible that the Court was trying to address these concerns in *Seamless steel tubes*.

4. *Use of economic analysis in hard-core restraint cases*

The Court of Justice has established that its review of complex economic appraisals made by the Commission is limited. More precisely, the Court will verify whether the relevant rules on procedure and on the statement of reasons have been complied with, whether the facts have been stated accurately, and whether there has been any manifest error of appraisal or misuse of powers.[41] Is there any scope at all, though, for economic analysis in cartel cases in the first place?

In cases where there is evidence of collusion, there is no point in arguing that economic analysis could provide an alternative explanation for the behaviour of the undertakings, such as lawful parallel behaviour on a concentrated market. This follows explicitly from the Court of First Instance's *PVC II* judgments.[42] The work of Alfter and Young in 2005 confirms that the role of economic analysis in cartel cases is mainly to assess 'the impact of a cartel whose existence has been established'.[43] The Court of First Instance has been consistent in holding that a finding of an economic advantage is not necessary to establish participation in a cartel.[44] Profitability may nevertheless be relevant for the purpose of establishing an appropriate level of fines.

Desai carried out a study in 2002 on economic analysis in EC competition law proceedings, including three cartel cases.[45] His study shows that attempts to use economics to rebut the Commission's findings of fact in cartel cases have been unsuccessful, as was an attempt to rely on economic studies to prove that the cartel had no actual market impact.[46] Desai observes certain risks connected to the use of antitrust economics. Studies may be (and have been) used as swords against

[41] Case C-194/99 P *Thyssen Stahl v Commission* [2003] ECR I-10821, at para 78; see also Joined Cases C-204/00 P, etc *Aalborg Portland and others v Commission* [2004] ECR I-123, at para 279.

[42] Joined Cases T-305/94, etc *Limburgse Vinyl Maatschappij and others v Commission* [1999] ECR II-931, at para 726, confirmed on appeal in Joined Cases C-238/99 P, etc *Limburgse Vinyl Maatschappij and others v Commission* [2002] ECR I-8375.

[43] Alfter, M, and Young, J, 'Economic Analysis of Cartels—Theory and Practice' (2005) 26(10) *ECLR* 546.

[44] Joined Cases T-71/03, T-74/03, T-87/03 and T-91/03 *Tokai Carbon and others v Commission* [2005] ECR II-10, at para 81.

[45] Desai, Kiran S, 'Limitations on the Use of Economic Analysis in EC Competition Law Proceedings: Part 1' (2002) 23(10) *ECLR* 524.

[46] *Ibid*.

the parties relying on them. When questioned at the oral hearing, the author of a study can be forced to make concessions beyond what is in the study, possibly to the detriment of the party. Speculative and much criticised economic theories can be rebutted easily by the Commission. A study will have to be backed up by background material in order not to appear biased, and assumptions used as a basis in a study must be well-founded.[47]

5. *Analysis: per se prohibition or effects-based approach?*

Having split up the per se question in different pieces and analysed them one by one, the analysis now turns back to the overall question of what the position is in EC law on a per se prohibition against cartels. There is no unitary view on this in EC law, but the present analysis will at least contribute to an in-depth discussion. In one of the *Polypropylene* cases, the Court explicitly rejected a rule-of-reason approach to cartels.[48] Some caution is called for in so far as the Court based the finding not only on the practices (price-fixing, quotas and market-sharing), but also explicitly on the market position of the participants ('producers accounting for almost all the Community market'). While rejecting a rule-of-reason test for cartels, has the Court in later cases embraced a per se prohibition?

In *Cement*, the reasoning indicates that the Court has decided, as a matter of principle, that quotas, market-sharing and price-fixing necessarily have the effect of restricting competition:

> Participation by an undertaking in anticompetitive practices and agreements constitutes an economic infringement designed to maximise its profits, generally by an intentional limitation of supply, an artificial division of the market and an artificial increase in prices. The effect of such agreements or of such practices is to restrict free competition and to prevent the attainment of the common market, in particular by hindering intra-Community trade. Such harmful effects are passed directly on to consumers in terms of increased prices and reduced diversity of supply.[49]

The Court went on to say that there is no need to take account of the actual effects of an agreement once it appears that its aim is to restrict, prevent or distort competition within the common market.[50] The reasoning was based on *Sandoz*, a case where the Court actually went a step further and stated that

> In such a case the absence . . . of any analysis of the effects of the agreement from the point of view of competition does not constitute a defect capable of justifying a declaration that [the decision] is void.[51]

The same holds for concerted practices.[52]

[47] *Ibid*, at 529.
[48] Case C-235/92 P *Montecatini v Commission* [1999] ECR I-4539, at para 133.
[49] *Aalborg Portland and others v Commission*, above n 41, at para 53.
[50] *Ibid*, at para 261.
[51] Case C-277/87 *Sandoz prodotti farmaceutici SpA v Commission* [1990] ECR I-45, summary, at 3.
[52] Case C-49/92 P *Commission v Anic Partecipazioni* [1999] ECR I-4125, at paras 123–24.

It may, on the other hand, be necessary to analyse effects in outright cases of allegedly restrictive information exchanges, absent cartel monitoring. In *Steel Beams*, the Court upheld a finding of restrictive effects of an information exchange. The extensive reasoning included several factors:

a) The figures exchanged were confidential and had been sent only to a certain number of manufacturers.
b) The products in question were homogeneous.
c) The structure of the market was oligopolistic.
d) The information made it possible for the undertakings to know very precisely the market share of each of their competitors and, therefore, made it possible to monitor the activities of those competitors.
e) Lastly, the figures gave rise to discussions and criticism, and were up-to-date.[53]

Similarly, there may be other instances of concerted practices which do not have the object of restricting competition, and where the effects must be analysed.

The law has consequently moved in the direction of a per se prohibition against traditional price-fixing, quotas and market-sharing, but not for boycotts and purchase price-fixing. Even for price-fixing, quotas and market-sharing, though, there is some lingering uncertainty as to whether the Commission and national competition authorities can refrain from carrying out market analyses. Can we refrain from assessing such alleged infringements in their legal and economic context, and satisfy ourselves with proving their existence? Can cartel participants claim that the activities did not affect competition appreciably?

The Court of First Instance has, in recent years, consistently treated price-fixing, quotas and market-sharing according to a per se prohibition doctrine. As outlined in the subsections above, the Court of First Instance has held that those cartel participants cannot defend themselves by claiming that their practice did not appreciably restrict competition. They cannot demand that the Commission provides market definitions. Neither can they demand that their agreement or concerted practice is assessed in its legal and economic context. There is no requirement, for establishing liability, that the enforcer demonstrates that the practice generated profits for the participants. Application of Article 81(1) EC to those cartels is a legal exercise in the eyes of the Court of First Instance, as opposed to an economic exercise.

As demonstrated, the Court of Justice is inclined to treat price-fixing, quotas and market-sharing under a per se doctrine, but is otherwise either silent on the per se question or wavering between opposing views. Further, it has brought economics into the analysis by saying that it is necessary to examine an arrangement in its legal and economic context to assess whether it has an appreciable effect on trade.[54] This

[53] Case C-179/99 P *Eurofer v Commission* [2003] ECR I-10725, at para 44.
[54] Case C-238/05 *Asnef-Equifax v Ausbanc* [2007] ECR I-11125, at para 35.

means that the procedural efficiencies, indeed deterrence, that would follow from a more per se-orientated approach are not fully realised.[55]

My conclusion is that a definitive position has not yet been taken in Community law on the principles underpinning application of Article 81(1) EC to various types of cartels—whether it is a clear per se prohibition, or whether a more elaborate analysis should be applied in certain cases. Whish suggests that the only opening for price-fixers is to argue that their agreements quantitatively do not appreciably affect competition or affect trade between Member States, or, in the alternative, that they qualify for exemption under Article 81(3).[56]

Given the confusion in Community jurisprudence on this subject, it might be helpful to look across the Atlantic for theory building. In *Texaco Inc v Dagher*, the US Supreme Court held that under US law per se liability is reserved for those agreements that are so plainly anticompetitive that no elaborate study of the industry is needed to establish their illegality. Accordingly, the Supreme Court expressed reluctance to adopt per se rules where the economic impact of certain practices is not immediately obvious.[57]

In *PolyGram Holding*,[58] the US Court of Appeals, District of Columbia Circuit, observed that the Supreme Court had

> steadily moved away from the dichotomous approach—under which every restraint of trade is either unlawful per se, and hence not susceptible to a pro-competitive justification, or subject to a full-blown rule-of-reason analysis—toward one in which the extent of the inquiry is tailored to the suspect conduct in each particular case.

The Court further explained that the Supreme Court had adopted an intermediate inquiry—the 'quick look'—to evaluate horizontal restraints. The Court of Appeal found that the Supreme Court had 'backed away from any reliance upon fixed categories and toward a continuum'. An adaptation of the inquiry to the type of infringement that is alleged, through a step-by-step analysis, has been promoted by the US Federal Trade Commission as well.[59]

United States jurisprudence illustrates the problem connected to a per se prohibition: where to draw the line between per se prohibited activities and activities which (seen in the EC context) could be exempted pursuant to Article 81(3) EC. Having said that, it is worthwhile to observe that the US courts have (so far) insisted that horizontal price-fixing and output limitation are normally illegal per se. In *NCAA v Board of Regents*, the Supreme Court held that

[55] Areeda and Hovenkamp, *Antitrust Law—An Analysis of Antitrust Principles and Their Application*, 3rd edn (New York, Aspen Publishers, Wolters Kluwer Law and Business), Vol IB, § 266, at 202 ff.

[56] Whish, above n 17.

[57] *Texaco Inc v Dagher*, 126 S Ct 1276, 164 L Ed 2d 1, 2006-1 Trade Cas (CCH) P 75143 (US 2006).

[58] *Polygram Holding, Inc v FTC*, 416 F 3d 29, 367 US App DC 367, decided 22 July 2005.

[59] See opinion of the FTC in the *Matter of Polygram Holding, Inc; Decca Music Group Limited; UMG Recordings, Inc; and Universal Music & Video Distribution Corp*, July 2003, http://www.ftc.gov/os/caselist/d9298.shtm.

> Horizontal price fixing and output limitation are ordinarily condemned as a matter of law under an 'illegal per se' approach because the probability that these practices are anti-competitive is so high; a per se rule is applied when 'the practice facially appears to be one that would always or almost always tend to restrict competition and decrease output' . . . In such circumstances a restraint is presumed unreasonable without inquiry into the particular market context in which it is found.[60]

The refusal in US law to accept pro-competitive justification for naked cartels is confirmed by the Antitrust Modernization Commission (AMC) in its 2007 Report, where it is concluded that 'A consensus exists that such conspiracies almost invariably inflict harm on consumers and the economy'.[61] Reference is also made in the Report to established case law of the US Supreme Court which condemns the raising, depressing, fixing, pegging or stabilising of prices as illegal per se. The same applies to agreements to allocate territories, where there is no need to inquire into their 'business or economic justification, their impact on their marketplace, or their reasonableness'.[62]

To my mind, the established economic theory on cartels, together with the results of quantitative studies of their impact and the extensive experience of cartel cases in US and European courts, provide a sufficient basis for concluding that certain practices are always or almost always harmful to society. This should apply to price-fixing, market-sharing (including bid-rigging) and quotas, as a result of the welfare losses and inefficiencies created and the absence of pro-competitive effects. In the 'quick look' category we may place buyer cartels, facilitating practices, mixed horizontal and vertical cartels, and single-brand dealer cartels. Information exchange absent cartel monitoring require more elaborate analysis. Furthermore, market analysis will occasionally be necessary to analyse whether an exemption can be granted pursuant to Article 81(3) EC. In this context the difference between US law and EC law on cartels is more than academic, since under EC law a cartel can, at least in theory, be exempted under Article 81(3) EC. In that situation, however, it is then the cartel participant that must bring forward evidence to show that there are conditions justifying an exemption.

There is certainly support for the opposite view. Odudu argues that it is problematic to create an object category, and claims that 'there is no pre-defined conduct or type of agreement that always satisfies the object criterion'.[63] But this view is difficult to reconcile with theory and empirical evidence on the impact of cartels.

[60] *National Collegiate Athletic Association v Board of Regents* 468 US 85, 104 S Ct 2948, reference omitted.

[61] Antitrust Modernization Commission Report and Recommendations, April 2007, at 293, available at http://www.amc.gov/report_recommendation/toc.htm.

[62] *Ibid*, at 297, footnote omitted.

[63] Odudu, Okeoghene, 'Interpreting Article 81(1): The Object Requirement Revisited' (2001) 26(4) *EL Rev* 379, at 389.

II. AGREEMENTS AND CONCERTED PRACTICES, DECISIONS BY ASSOCIATIONS OF UNDERTAKINGS

A. Agreements

In order for there to be an agreement within the meaning of Article 81(1) EC, it is sufficient that the undertakings in question have expressed their joint intention to conduct themselves on the market in a specific way.[64]

Agreements may be entered into expressly, tacitly or passively. As for tacit acceptance, the Court held in *Cement* that

> a party which tacitly approves of an unlawful initiative, without publicly distancing itself from its content or reporting it to the administrative authorities, effectively encourages the continuation of the infringement and compromises its discovery. That complicity constitutes a passive mode of participation in the infringement which is therefore capable of rendering the undertaking liable in the context of a single agreement.[65]

The deterrence theory underlying this position is clear from the wording of the Court, but becomes even more obvious when we contrast cartels with vertical restraints. In *Volkswagen*, the car manufacturer was fined for imposing price discipline measures on its dealers. The Commission maintained that an agreement could be construed with reference to the dealership agreement between Volkswagen and its dealers, in combination with the unilateral price calls made by Volkswagen. The calls, said the Commission, formed part of a set of continuous business relations governed by a general agreement drawn up in advance. This reasoning was rejected by the Court. There must be a concurrence of wills on the part of the parties to the dealership agreement in each specific case.[66] The Court repeatedly emphasised the need for an *expression* of that concurrence of wills.[67] Further, the will of the parties may result not only from the clauses of the dealership agreement, but also from *the conduct of the parties, and in particular from the possibility of there being tacit acquiescence by the dealers.*[68]

Remaining with vertical agreements, the requirement for tacit approval is that an invitation is made—'a manifestation of the wish of one of the contracting parties to achieve an anticompetitive goal'—which will 'constitute an invitation to the other party, whether express or implied, to fulfil that goal jointly'.[69] The invitation must be matched by some sort of response which is communicated to the other party,[70] the result of which is the existence of a meeting of minds.[71] It follows that

[64] Case 41/69 *ACF Chemiefarma v Commission* [1970] ECR 661, at para 112.
[65] *Aalborg Portland and others v Commission*, above n 41, at para 84.
[66] Case C-74/04 *Commission v Volkswagen* [2006] ECR I-6585, at para 36.
[67] *Ibid*, at para 37.
[68] *Ibid*, at para 39.
[69] Joined Cases C-2/01 P and C-3/01 P *BAI and Commission v Bayer* [2004] ECR I-23, at para 102.
[70] *Ibid*, at para 122: '. . . the wholesalers wished to give Bayer the impression that, in response to its declared wish, they were proposing to reduce their orders to a given level'.
[71] *Ibid*, at para 123.

when a vertical restriction is suspected, the parties must express their concurrence of wills, in writing or through their conduct, the concept of conduct including tacit acquiescence. Some sort of response is required.

Conversely, when we look at horizontal agreements, *tacit approval* can consist of taking part passively in a meeting where an anticompetitive agreement is concluded. Presence at such meetings amounts to complicity, which constitutes a passive mode of participation in the infringement.

Agreements do not have to be realised to be illegal.[72] The Court held in *Cement* that even if an undertaking does not act on the outcome of a meeting having an anticompetitive purpose, it is not relieved from responsibility for participation in a cartel, unless it has publicly distanced itself from what was agreed in the meeting.[73] Furthermore, this applies to the cartel as a whole—even if it does not go ahead with the plan, there is still an infringement.[74] Consequently, a higher degree of mutual expression of a concurrence of wills is required in vertical agreements than in cartels; in the cartel context, concurrence of wills is simply implied from the presence at meetings where anticompetitive agreements are concluded. This view is deterrence-based, according to the Court of Justice.

The concept of an agreement does not require any precise terms. The fixing by economic operators of *rules of the game* applicable to their conduct on the market constitutes an agreement.[75] It is not necessary that it constitutes a valid and binding agreement under national law.[76] Applying these principles in the *Methionine* case, the Court of First Instance found that following two meetings between competitors, there was a joint intention among the participants to carry out a price increase according to certain terms. There was consequently an agreement.[77]

European Community case law on the notion of anticompetitive agreements may consequently be seen as deterrence-based.

1. *Decision-making meetings; opt-out necessary*

According to settled case law, it is sufficient to show that an undertaking participated in meetings at which anticompetitive agreements were concluded, without manifestly opposing them, to prove that the undertaking participated in the cartel.[78] The Court of Justice has formulated an *opt-out principle* for those occasions, according to which

[72] Joined Cases C-238/99 P, etc *Limburgse Vinyl Maatschappij and others v Commission*, above n 42, at para 509.

[73] *Aalborg Portland and others v Commission*, above n 41, at para 85.

[74] Case C-105/04 P *Nederlandse Federatieve Vereniging voor de Groothandel op Elektrotechnisch Gebied v Commission* [2006] ECR I-8725, at paras 155 ff, where the participants claimed that the cartel agreement had been a 'dead letter'.

[75] *Ibid*, at para 248.

[76] *Sandoz prodotti farmaceutici SpA v Commission*, above n 51, summary, at 2.

[77] Case T-279/02 *Degussa v Commission* [2006] ECR II-897, at para 142 ff.

[78] *Aalborg Portland and others v Commission*, above n 41, at para 81 with references.

> it is for that undertaking to put forward evidence to establish that its participation in those meetings was without any anticompetitive intention by demonstrating that it had indicated to its competitors that it was participating in those meetings in a spirit that was different from theirs.[79]

The reason for applying an opt-out principle to meetings where anticompetitive agreements are adopted is explicitly deterrence-based—to give the undertakings an incentive to discourage the continuation of the infringement and facilitate its discovery.[80]

As is evident from the relevant case law, the opt-out principle applies only to meetings or other contacts through which anticompetitive decisions are adopted.[81] The principle that an undertaking must opt out in order to avoid liability for agreements adopted at a meeting also applies in the context of complex agreements (combinations of agreements and concerted practices).[82] It will be demonstrated later on that the opt-out principle does *not* apply to mere concerted practices, including information exchange. A tough deterrence-based approach is consequently applied only for the worst infringements.

It remains uncertain how an opt-out must be made or formulated in order to be effective. There seems to be general consensus that leaving a cartel meeting, having openly declared to the others that the undertaking one represents does not wish to participate, is a valid opt-out.[83] But what about more subtle forms of communication? The Court of First Instance has demanded that an undertaking 'express a view which would have left the other undertakings in no doubt that it was distancing itself from the idea,' and has refused to accept vagueness as a defence, since that is 'akin to tacit approval which effectively encourages the continuation of the infringement and compromises its discovery'.[84]

Subsequent actions are telling as well. In *Industrial and medical gases* again, there was some doubt as to the actions of a Westfalen director at a meeting in October 1994. More decisively, there was no public distancing at a subsequent meeting in November the same year. The Court of First Instance considered it apparent that, having participated in a first meeting which was clearly anticompetitive, the applicant participated only a little more than a month later in a second collusive meeting without publicly distancing itself from it.[85] According to the Court of First Instance, 'the notion of public distancing as a means of excluding liability must be interpreted narrowly'. The Court nevertheless points out the possibility for an undertaking to distance itself in writing after the meeting.[86]

The Court of Justice hints in *Cement* that an opt-out may be made by reporting the infringement to the administrative authorities. This hinges on the very reason

[79] *Ibid.*
[80] *Ibid*, at para 84.
[81] See esp Case T-36/05 *Coats Holdings and Coats v Commission* [2007] ECR II-110, at paras 91 ff.
[82] *Aalborg Portland and others v Commission*, abvoe n 41, at para 83.
[83] Van Bael and Bellis, above n 3, at 55.
[84] Case T-303/02 *Westfalen Gassen Nederland v Commission* [2006] ECR II-4567, at para 84.
[85] *Ibid*, at para 101.
[86] *Ibid*, at para 103.

for applying an opt-out principle to meetings where anticompetitive agreements are adopted: to give the undertakings an incentive to discourage the continuation of the infringement and facilitate its discovery.[87] Nevertheless, undertakings frequently report to the authorities under applicable leniency programmes without being considered free from liability, although they can indeed obtain immunity from fines. The Court presumably meant in *Cement* that such reporting must be made immediately after a meeting. Or perhaps the Court was referring to the occasions when, for instance under US law, a party has reported to the authorities and is taking part in cartels meetings in order to gather evidence for the authority's investigation.

In *Greek Ferries*, the opt-out principle was applied to fax and telefax correspondence, to the detriment of the cartel participant.[88]

Whether the opt-out principle is applicable in national cartel proceedings when there is an effect on trade will be discussed in chapter five. It suffices to conclude here that it is deterrence-based.

B. Decisions by associations of undertakings

Three principal questions emerge in relation to associations of undertakings:

a) Can they be held responsible for infringements of Article 81 EC?
b) Can actions taken by them be attributed to the members?
c) Conversely, can action by members be attributed to the association?[89]

With regard to the first question, associations of undertakings can indeed be held responsible for infringements of Article 81 EC.

A few decades ago trade associations would produce decisions that were binding on their members. There was consequently some sort of integration, although loose, between the associations and their members, and therefore indirectly between the members themselves. Those days are gone, and enforcers now have to show that whatever was discussed at the trade association's meeting amounted to a *decision* in the sense of Article 81 EC. When an association produces only non-binding recommendations, there is an infringement of Article 81(1) only *if* the members proceed to implement them.

The Court of First Instance held in *DaimlerChrysler v Commission* that a measure may be categorised as a decision of an association of undertakings even if it is not binding on the members concerned, at least to the extent that the members to whom the decision applies comply with its terms.[90] Enforcers must consequently find not only a protocol or other evidence of a recommendation adopted at the

[87] *Aalborg Portland and others v Commission*, above n 41, at para 84.
[88] Case T-56/99 *Marlines v Commission* [2003] ECR II-5225, at paras 34–41.
[89] Art 65(5) of the ECSC Treaty does not provide for trade associations to be fined, IP/02/1908.
[90] Case T-325/01 *DaimlerChrysler v Commission* [2005] ECR II-3319, at para 210.

trade association's meeting, but also evidence to the effect that at least some of the members complied with those terms.

This judgment may be compared with older case law. The Court of Justice found in *Fire insurance* that there had been a decision by an association of undertakings, in spite of the claims of those concerned that it was only a non-binding recommendation. However, the reasoning in *Fire insurance* is not entirely straightforward. The Court started by saying that

> it is sufficient that the recommendation is in conformity with the association's statutes and that it was brought to the notice of its members as a statement of the policy of the association of undertakings in the manner laid down therein.[91]

The Court nevertheless then proceeded to support its argument by recourse to the facts: the insurers had a common interest in price increases given the market situation; the recommendation laid down in mandatory terms a collective, flat-rate and across-the-board increase in premiums; and the insurers actually complied with it by including new terms in their standard contracts.[92] It is still questionable whether these circumstances were sufficient. Decisive for the outcome was that the statutes of the association empowered it to co-ordinate the activities of its members, especially in relation to competition, including co-ordination of the members' premium rates policy, and that the decisions or recommendations were deemed to be definitive unless an internal appeal function was exercised.[93] *Fire insurance* was consequently a case where recommendations were binding according to the statutes; in addition, the members had actually had a motive *and* complied.

It is telling that the Court of First Instance did not refer to *Fire insurance* in *DaimlerChrysler*; instead, it relied on the judgment in the *Belgian dishwasher machine cartel*. There, the Court of Justice had looked at the associations' own activities or, in the alternative, those of the undertakings affiliated, as well as at compliance with the recommendation by the undertakings to which it was addressed.[94] Reference was also made to the *Belgian tobacco cartel*, where the Court rejected a submission that a recommendation was non-binding. There it was more obvious from the reasoning that there may be a decision of associations of undertakings on two alternative grounds: either because the association's statutes make it mandatory to adhere to its rules of conduct, or because the undertakings actually comply.[95]

Another borderline situation arises when the enforcers seek to establish what has been done by member undertakings and the trade association respectively. The Commission or national competition authority must demonstrate, in order to find that an association and its members have participated in one and the same

[91] Case 45/85 *Verband der Sachversicherer eV v Commission* [1987] ECR 405, at para 26.

[92] *Ibid*, at paras 29–30.

[93] *Ibid*, at para 31.

[94] Joined Cases 96–102, 104, 105, 108 and 110/82 *V IAZ Int Belgium and others v Commission* [1983] ECR 3369, at para 20.

[95] Joined Cases 209/78 to 215/78 and 218/78 *Van Landewyck and others v Commission* [1980] ECR 3125, at paras 88–89.

infringement, conduct on the part of the association which is separate from that of its members.[96] In *Woodpulp I*, the actions of the export association KEA were not distinguishable from those of its members. At KEA meetings, members could adopt price agreements binding for those who were absent, but only if each member was informed in advance and provided that the unanimous agreement of the members present was achieved. The association KEA was considered not to have played a separate role in the infringement committed by its members.[97]

The next question is whether members can be held responsible for actions of the association? Mere affiliation to a trade association does not automatically imply that the various types of conduct of that association must be imputed to an undertaking.[98]

There are three ways of tying an undertaking to anticompetitive actions by an association:

a) conferral of power;
b) compliance with the practices adopted by the association; or
c) attendance at meetings where anticompetitive agreements are concluded.

Occasionally an association has drafted agreements that are binding on its members. In *Eurocheque Helsinki*, the Court of First Instance examined an agreement between two associations. With reference to *BNIC v Clair*,[99] the Court found that membership of the association entailed, by virtue of the document constituting the association, adhesion by its members to the decisions adopted.[100] If the association is entitled to adopt binding decisions on behalf of its members, no further examination is necessary.

Some decades ago the articles of trade associations were routinely drafted as binding contracts under which the members undertook to follow the rules and subject themselves to arbitration or other private conflict resolution.[101] Given the binding nature of those arrangements (often coupled with fines or other private enforcement mechanisms), it was a straightforward exercise to establish responsibility for the members. However, cartels have since gone underground, and enforcers must find evidence to tie undertakings to the infringements. The Court of First Instance said in *FEG & TU* that the Commission had to demonstrate personal participation of a member or its support for the unlawful conduct.[102] In

[96] Opinion of A-G Juliane Kokott in Case C-105/04 P *FEG v Commission*, at para 84, which was referred to by the Court of Justice in its judgment in Case C-105/04 P *Nederlandse Federatieve Vereniging voor de Groothandel op Elektrotechnisch Gebied v Commission* [2006] ECR I-8725, at para 200. See also Joined Cases T-25/95, etc *Cimenteries and others v Commission* [2000] ECR II-491, at para 1325.

[97] Joined Cases 89/85, etc *A Ahlström Osakeyhtiö and others v Commission* [1988] ECR 5193, at paras 26–27.

[98] Case C-113/04 P *Technische Unie v Commission* [2006] ECR I-8831, at para 115.

[99] Case 123/83 *BNIC v Clair* [1985] ECR 391.

[100] Joined Cases T-39/92 and T-40/92 *CB and Europay v Commission* [1994] ECR II-49, at para 76.

[101] See especially *Roofing felt* [1986] OJ L/232/15, on appeal Case 246/86 *Belasco* [1989] ECR 2117.

[102] Joined Cases T-5/00 and T-6/00 *Nederlandse Federatieve Vereniging voor de Groothandel op Elektrotechnisch Gebied and Technische Unie v Commission* [2003] ECR II-5761, at para 355.

Cement, the Court of First Instance rejected the idea that mere capacity as member of a trade association would suffice to render an undertaking liable for manifestly unlawful decisions adopted at trade association meetings which it never attended. It was necessary to examine whether its conduct demonstrated such consent.[103]

The question of *indirect members* of trade associations was also raised in *Cement*. There, some undertakings were members in Cembureau only by virtue of their membership in national associations which in turn were members of Cembureau. The Court of First Instance did not accept responsibility simply as a result of indirect membership; it emphasised that indirect members could be liable only if they had participated in one or more measures implementing the agreement.[104]

Lastly, members who participated at meetings where anticompetitive agreements were concluded cannot escape responsibility. This follows from *Cement*, where several of the undertakings were present at the meetings of Cembureau where manifestly anticompetitive schemes were worked out.[105]

The discussion so far has focused on the responsibility of associations and their members. In addition, actions by members can occasionally be attributed 'backwards' to a trade association. This particular situation arose in *FEG & TU*, a Dutch cartel for electrotechnical fittings. During the operation of the cartel, pressure was put on external suppliers to refuse supplies to parties that were not members of the cartel. The trade association FEG argued that it should not have to bear responsibility for concerted practices put into effect by its members. However, the Court of First Instance imposed responsibility on FEG on the basis of three factors.[106] First, the practices were very much at the core of the infringement. Next, the persons involved held management posts within the FEG. Several members were, during the duration of the infringement, represented on the board of the FEG and participated directly in the approaches made to suppliers. The Court of First Instance also noted that a large number (11–26) of members of the FEG had acted in concert and formed delegations that visited suppliers for the benefit of all the members of the association. The Court summarised:

> Since the actions at issue pursued the same object, shared the same beneficiaries and were implemented by the members and certain executives of that association, it must be considered that the Commission was right to conclude that the responsibility for the approaches thus made by FEG members to suppliers not belonging to NAVEG could also be attributed to the FEG.[107]

On appeal, the findings were upheld by the Court of Justice.[108] The judgments show that there is no automatic attribution of liability from members to the trade

[103] Joined Cases T-25/95, etc *Cimenteries and others v Commission* [2000] ECR II-491, at para 1413.

[104] *Ibid*, at para 1310.

[105] *Ibid*, at para 4237.

[106] *Nederlandse Federatieve Vereniging voor de Groothandel op Elektrotechnisch Gebied and Technische Unie v Commission*, above n 102, at paras 390 ff.

[107] *Ibid*, at para 393.

[108] Case C-105/04 P *Nederlandse Federatieve Vereniging voor de Groothandel op Elektrotechnisch Gebied v Commission* [2006] ECR I-8725, at paras 194–200.

association—a careful assessment of the circumstances of the individual case must be made.

To conclude, the law on liability for associations is consistent with the idea put forward in chapter three at section III.C., that cartel control may be seen as a structural complement to merger control. In the absence of structural ties between an association and its members, such as an obligation for the members to follow recommendations or decisions issued by the association, the relation is treated more or less as with impositions of vertical restraints by a manufacturer, where the authorities must find some evidence that the demands were accepted or adhered to.

C. Concerted practices

Due to the expansion of other legal concepts, the role of concerted practices as a stand-alone ground for challenging collusion is steadily decreasing in EC law.

It has been explained in chapter three that there are, since *Cement*, two separate legal standards for information exchange. One is for information exchange which does not underpin a cartel arrangement, where a weighing of pro-competitive and anticompetitive effects must be made. The other is for information exchange that underpins an anticompetitive agreement. According to the Court, the circulation of price information limited to the members of an anticompetitive cartel has the effect of increasing transparency on a market where competition is already much reduced, and of facilitating control of compliance with the cartel by its members.[109] It will be explained that the Court of Justice has accepted a combined notion of agreements and concerted practices.

For pragmatic purposes, the need in cartel control to place something in the category of concerted practices is limited to:

a) discovery of a cartel in its infancy, where the parties have not yet properly reached a cartel agreement; and
b) various 'sidetrack' collusions happening on the periphery of a cartel, when such practices cannot be attributed to an overall cartel agreement.

Concerted practices constitute separate infringements of Article 81(1) EC if they affect trade and have as their object or effect the prevention, restriction or distortion of competition.

There are half a dozen leading cases on concerted practices.[110] A theoretical foundation for the interpretation of the concept of concerted practices was laid down in the 1970s judgment in *ICI*. A concerted practice is a

[109] *Aalborg Portland and others v Commission*, above n 41, at para 281.

[110] Case 48/69 *ICI v Commission* [1972] ECR 619; Joined Cases 40–48/73 *Suiker Unie and Others v Commission* [1975] ECR 1663; Joined Cases C-89/85, etc *Ahlström Osakeyhtiö and others v Commission* [1993] ECR I-1307 (*Woodpulp*); Case C-49/92 P *Commission v Anic* [1999] ECR I-4125, Case C-199/92 P *Hüls v Commission* [1999] ECR I-4287 and Case C-235/92 P *Montecatini v Commission* [1999] ECR I-4539 (the *Polypropylene* judgments); and Case C-194/99 P *Thyssen Stahl v Commission* [2003] ECR I-10821.

> form of co-ordination between undertakings which, without having reached the stage where an agreement properly so-called has been concluded, knowingly substitutes practical co-operation between them for the risks of competition.[111]

The Court condemned

> conduct of the applicant, in conjunction with other undertakings against which proceedings have been taken . . . designed to replace the risks of competition and the hazards of competitors' spontaneous reactions by co-operation . . .[112]

The reasoning seems based more on economics than anything else at this early point in the concept's development.

One may then ask whether a freedom of action idea permeated the case law over the next few years. The Court held in *Suiker Unie* that

> each economic operator must determine independently the policy which he intends to adopt on the common market including the choice of the persons and undertakings to which he makes offers or sells . . .[113]

It may be recalled that the objective of protecting the freedom of economic actors has existed in EC competition law[114] as a result of the influences of German ordoliberal foundations with their emphasis on individual freedom of action.[115] In *Bloemenveilingen Aalsmeer*, a decision adopted in 1988, the Commission evaluated an alleged competition restraint with reference to 'the unrestricted freedom of choice enjoyed by a dealer under perfect competitive conditions'.[116]

The actual meaning of 'concertation' remains illusive, in spite of all the case law. The closest we come to a definition is in *Suiker Unie*, where the Court established that

> Although it is correct to say that this requirement of independence does not deprive economic operators of the right to adapt themselves intelligently to the existing and anticipated conduct of their competitors, it does however strictly preclude *any direct or indirect contact between such operators, the object or effect whereof is either to influence the conduct on the market of an actual or potential competitor or to disclose to such a competitor the course of conduct which they themselves have decided to adopt or contemplate adopting on the market.* (emphasis added)[117]

This was reiterated in *Woodpulp* in 1993.[118]

When ruling on the *Soda-ash cartel*, the Court of First Instance summarised the case law in the following terms:

[111] Case 48/69 *ICI v Commission* [1972] ECR 619, at para 64.

[112] *Ibid*, at para 119.

[113] *Suiker Unie and Others v Commission*, above n 110, at para 173.

[114] Gerber, David J, *Law and Competition in Twentieth Century Europe: Protecting Prometheus* (Oxford, Oxford University Press, 1998), at 418.

[115] Van den Bergh, Roger J, and Camesasca, Peter D, *European Competition Law and Economics: A Comparative Perspective*, 2nd edn (London, Thomson Sweet & Maxwell, 2006), at 89.

[116] *Bloemenveilingen Aalsmeer* [1988] OJ L/262/27, at 116.

[117] *Suiker Unie and Others v Commission*, above n 110, at paras 173–74.

[118] *Ahlström Osakeyhtiö and others v Commission*, above n 110, at para 63.

> [A] concerted practice is characterized by the fact that it substitutes for the risks of competition co-operation between undertakings, which lessens each undertaking's uncertainty as to the future attitude of its competitors. If that uncertainty is not lessened, there is no concerted practice.[119]

When adjudicating on *Methionine* in 2006, the Court of First Instance went back to this position:

> [I]n order to prove that there has been a concerted practice, it is not necessary to show that the competitor in question has formally undertaken, in respect of one or several others, to adopt a particular course of conduct or that the competitors have colluded over their future conduct on the market . . . It is sufficient that, through its declaration of intention, the competitor has eliminated or, at the very least, substantially reduced the uncertainty as to the conduct to be expected from it on the market.[120]

A decisive development of the concept of concerted practices occurred in 1999 in the *Polypropylene* judgments. The Court referred to its previous case law and held that a concerted practice implies, *besides undertakings concerting together, conduct on the market pursuant to those collusive practices, and a relationship of cause and effect between the two.*[121] Further, the Court established a presumption for concerted practices:

> [S]ubject to proof to the contrary, which it is for the economic operators concerned to adduce, there must be a presumption that the undertakings participating in concerting arrangements and remaining active on the market take account of the information exchanged with their competitors when determining their conduct on that market, particularly when they concert together on a regular basis over a long period.[122]

Whether that presumption applies when national authorities and courts apply Article 81 EC will be discussed in chapter five.

The *Polypropylene* judgments are crucial for understanding the concept of concerted practices. The Community courts took different views on whether it included both concertation and subsequent market behaviour. Three conflicting views were advocated. The Court of First Instance considered that if a party had eliminated uncertainty about the future conduct of its competitors in advance, it could not fail to take account, directly or indirectly, of that information, and similarly the competitors were bound to take into account the information about the party's future market conduct in determining the policy which they intended to follow.[123] Advocate-General Cosmas, on the other hand, thought an infringement could be established solely on the basis of co-ordination between the undertakings, independent of any effect on or activity in the market.[124] Both options were implicitly rejected by the Court of Justice. The Court created a rebuttable

119 Case T-30/91 *Solvay v Commission* [1995] ECR II-1775, at para 66.
120 Case T-279/02 *Degussa v Commission* [2006] ECR II-897, at para 133.
121 *Commission v Anic*, above n 110, at para 118.
122 *Ibid*, at para 121.
123 Case T-6/89 *Enichem Anic SpA v Commission* [1991] ECR II-1623, at para 201.
124 Opinion of A-G Cosmas delivered on 15 July 1997 in *Commission v Anic*, above n 110, at para 27.

presumption that concertation results in subsequent market behaviour. Wessely observes that the Court

> nonetheless provides the undertakings concerned with the possibility to refute this presumption by showing that their market conduct has not been influenced by the previous contacts between them, but was determined by other factors or considerations . . .[125]

The Court of First Instance found in the *haberdashery* cartel that 'the mere fact of being informed about an anticompetitive agreement cannot give rise to liability for the infringement'.[126] Reception of such information is highly incriminating, though, and

> the fact that an exchange of information involves information which an independent operator scrupulously preserves as business secrets is sufficient to demonstrate the existence of an anticompetitive intention.[127]

If the undertaking which has been made aware of the cartel contributes by its own conduct to the achievement of that objective (for instance, by taking steps to facilitate the cartel), this will be considered a concerted practice.[128]

Further, and of central importance for cartel litigation, concerted practices are prohibited, regardless of their effect, when they have an anticompetitive object:

> Although the very concept of a concerted practice presupposes conduct by the participating undertakings on the market, it does not necessarily mean that that conduct should produce the specific effect of restricting, preventing or distorting competition.[129]

The interpretations and justifications in case law for the concept of concerted practices are difficult to understand. The concept has taken on a life of its own, and could be seen as a move away from economic theory and analysis. Whether the parties are acting in a way that allows them to duplicate a monopoly is a question that is not posed by the courts, at least not explicitly. Then again, what we can observe is a policy where the Community courts condemn practices where companies are acting as if they were engaging in in-house information exchange within a group of companies, while actually being competitors. A prohibition against such practices is consistent with an idea that we should act against forums for collusion. If we leave aside all the conflicting wording presented by the Community courts, this can perhaps be seen as an outflow of monopoly theory. We can infer from systematic exchange of sensitive, company-specific information that the competing undertakings are effectively considering themselves as a unit. There is also an inherent deterrence message, in so far as the policy makes it easier for the authorities to prove an infringement.

[125] Wessely, Thomas W, 'Case C-49/92 P *Commission v Anic etc*' (2001) 38(3) *CML Rev* 739, at 747, 751–54.

[126] Case T-36/05 *Coats Holdings and Coats v Commission* [2007] ECR II-110, at para 105.

[127] *Ibid*, at para 113.

[128] *Ibid*, at paras 114–18.

[129] *Commission v Anic*, above n 110, at paras 123–24.

1. Opt-out not possible for concerted practices, including information exchange

In *Industrial and Medical Gases*, the undertaking Westfalen sought to prove that it had publicly distanced itself from the cartel, and that it should consequently not be held liable. As far as that argument related to anticompetitive agreements, the Court of First Instance accepted it in law but quashed it on an examination of the facts. Further, the Court refused, on points of law, to accept public distancing as an argument in relation to a concerted practice. Instead, it reiterated that it was for Westfalen to adduce evidence that it had not taken account of the unlawful concerted practice, in which it participated at the meeting, when determining its own conduct on that market.[130]

Moreover, the Court of First Instance has on at least two occasions quashed, on points of law, arguments that undertakings had opted out of information exchange.[131] This view is consistent with the reasons why information exchange is considered, in certain circumstances, to restrict competition. Given that exchange of qualified types of information will have effects downstream, when the participating undertakings are determining their business policy, it is virtually impossible for an undertaking to avoid that happening by making declaratory statements that it does not wish to be involved, once it has engaged in that very same information exchange. It can also be considered consistent with the view that a requirement to opt out is made only for the worst types of infringements, a category where information exchange does not normally belong, being the subject of the weighing of pro-competitive and negative effects.

The consistency ends there, though—information exchange that facilitates cartel agreements is considered hard-core regardless of whether only publicly available information is exchanged. The reason is deterrence-based—circulation of price information limited to the members of an anticompetitive cartel has the effect of increasing transparency on a market where competition is already much reduced, and of facilitating the control of compliance with the cartel by its members.[132]

If we place facilitating practices in the hard-core category, we should also accept defences based on opt-out.

D. Complex infringements

When there is a complex cartel of long duration, the competition authority is not obliged to treat every single Article 81 infringement as a separate occurrence. Authorities and courts are allowed to refrain from clearly defining each element as either an agreement or a concerted practice.

[130] Case T-303/02 *Westfalen Gassen Nederland v Commission* [2006] ECR II-4567, at paras 131 ff.

[131] Joined Cases T-202/98, T-204/98 and T-207/98 *Tate & Lyle and others v Commission* [2001] ECR II-2035, at paras 64–66 (*British Sugar*); Case T-3/89 *Atochem v Commission* [1991] ECR II-1177, at para 54.

[132] *Aalborg Portland and others v Commission*, above n 41, at para 281.

The Court confirmed in *Anic* the possibility of operating from a combined notion of agreements/concerted practices when assessing complex cartels:

> [I]n view of their identical purpose, the various concerted practices observed and the various agreements concluded . . . part of systems of regular meetings, target-price fixing and quota-fixing . . . those schemes were part of a series of efforts made by the undertakings in question in pursuit of a single economic aim, namely to distort the normal movement of prices on the market.[133]

The Court added that there was

> continuous conduct, characterised by a single purpose . . . consisting of a number of separate infringements . . . an integrated set of schemes constituting a single infringement, which progressively manifested itself in both unlawful agreements and unlawful concerted practices.[134]

The reasoning can be understood as a rare and important example of explicit monopoly theory application in EC cartel control. If undertakings are acting as a single entity through their market behaviour, they should accept liability for a hard-core infringement of Article 81 EC.

Looking at the single purpose, is it sufficient that one of the parties, for example the ringleader, has this purpose; or must the purpose be shared by two or more cartel participants? According to the wording used by the Court in *Anic*, there must be a series of efforts made by *the undertakings in question* in pursuit of a single economic aim.[135] The purpose must consequently be shared by at least two participants, possibly by all infringers. This is consistent with the basic understanding that cartels duplicate monopolies.

Must a single infringement have an anticompetitive object, or does an effect suffice? The Court's findings in *Anic* demonstrate that there must be an anticompetitive object.[136] Importantly, agreements or concerted practices that have no anticompetitive object but only effects, fall outside the notion of complex cartels.

From a systematic perspective the notion of agreement/concerted practice is not entirely without its problems. The definition of an agreement is that the parties have faithfully expressed their joint intention to behave in a certain way on the market. Whether they actually implement the agreement is irrelevant. The definition of a concerted practice is concertation, pursuant market behaviour, and a relation of cause and effect between the two, although, as explained, market behaviour is presumed. A combination of these two concepts into a single infringement (agreement/concerted practice) appears to some extent paradoxical, since agreements do not require any pursuant market behaviour while concerted practices do. Moreover, the notion of agreement/concerted practice is difficult to reconcile with the opt-out principle. In order to avoid liability for agreements,

[133] *Commission v Anic*, above n 110, at para 197.
[134] *Ibid.*
[135] *Ibid.*
[136] *Ibid*, at para 203.

undertakings must publicly distance themselves; but an opt-out is impossible when it comes to concerted practices, where the only escape is to demonstrate that the undertakings took no account of the information exchanged with their competitors when determining their conduct on that market.

Although the theory is shaky, the agreement/concerted practice concept is probably the only pragmatic way of addressing complex cartels. The alternative would be to require authorities and courts retrospectively to define and prove every element in a complex cartel of long duration as either an agreement or a concerted practice. Given that cartels are forums and organisations rather than anything else, and that they develop their tactics and strategies as they go along, it seems perfectly consistent under monopoly theory to see their actions as a process rather than a series of singular unlawful occurrences. The case law of the Community courts here has been considered substantially the same as that developed by US courts in relation to the notion of conspiracy.[137] Further, it should be recalled that the Court has held that agreements and concerted practices catch forms of collusion having the same nature, and are distinguishable from each other only by their intensity and the forms in which they manifest themselves.[138]

While resolving some difficulties, the concept of agreement/concerted practices introduces yet other legal classification problems, notably, how liability relates to various degrees of involvement by different undertakings. The first step is obviously to establish the existence of a single infringement; the second is to establish which undertakings can be tied to that infringement. The test devised by the Court is as follows:

> [A]n undertaking which has participated in a single infringement, such as in this case, by its own conduct, which met the definition of an agreement or concerted practice having an anticompetitive object within the meaning of Article [81(1)] of the Treaty and was intended to help bring about the infringement as a whole, may also be responsible for the conduct of other undertakings followed in the context of the same infringement throughout the period of its participation in the infringement. *That is the case where it is proved that the undertaking in question was aware of the unlawful conduct of the other participants, or could reasonably foresee such conduct, and was prepared to accept the risk.* (emphasis added)[139]

Drawing from *Anic*, the Court reiterated this in *Cement* in slightly different terms by establishing that an undertaking is responsible if it intended to contribute by its own conduct to the common objectives pursued by all the participants, and was aware of the actual conduct planned or put into effect by other undertakings in pursuit of the same objectives, or could reasonably have foreseen it, and that it was prepared to take the risk.[140]

[137] Joshua, Julian M, and Jordan, Sarah, 'Combinations, Concerted Practices and Cartels: Adopting the Concept of Conspiracy in European Community Competition Law' (2004) 24(3) *Northwestern Journal of International Law and Business* 647.

[138] *Commission v Anic*, above n 110, at para 131.

[139] *Ibid.*

[140] *Aalborg Portland and others v Commission*, above n 41, at para 83.

The notion of complex infringements has been tried in relation to the personal nature of responsibility for infringements of that provision, the applicable rules of evidence and the rights of the defence.[141] There can be no doubt whatsoever that it applies when national authorities and courts apply Article 81 EC to alleged cartels.

In *Cement*, one of the undertakings argued that the concept of single agreement presupposes conduct that is single, uninterrupted and continuous in time, and that given that there was a gap of 14 months between two meetings, there was no single agreement. This view was rejected by the Court.[142] In *Lombard Club*, there were three levels of round table meetings between competing banks. Some of the banks claimed an absence of a link between the top meetings and the regional meetings. This argument was quashed by the Court of First Instance with reference to the evidence presented by the Commission.[143]

In *Choline Chloride*, the Commission considered arrangements concluded at worldwide level and at European level as a single complex and continuous infringement concerning the EEA, in which North American producers participated for a certain time and European producers participated over a longer period. On appeal, however, this part of the decision was set aside and the arrangements were characterised as two separate infringements.[144] Two practices will not amount to a single complex infringement just because they both distort competition in one and the same market.[145] The Commission thought that the two arrangements (one European and one global) were closely linked, and put forward that European arrangements could be regarded as a continuation by European producers of what had been originally agreed at a global level, but this theory failed on the facts.[146] The Court of First Instance noted that there was no temporal overlap between the two arrangements, that they pursued different objectives, that they were implemented by dissimilar methods and that the Commission had not demonstrated that European producers had intended to adhere to the global arrangements in order to share the EEA market.

The precise methodology of analysis for complex infringements has not been settled by the Community courts. A possible approach would be to start the analysis at the centre of gravity of the cartel—that is the initial ringleader(s) and/or the geographic centre or the date when the cartel began—and then continue in chronological order, or any other order that appears logical. It should be observed that such an analysis leads to adverse results for participants who joined at a later point in time, or whose involvement was limited to certain geographic markets or certain products. Once the existence of a single infringement has been established,

[141] *Commission v Anic*, above n 110, at para 204.

[142] *Aalborg Portland and others v Commission*, above n 41, at para 256.

[143] Joined Cases T-259/02 to T-264/02 and T-271/02 *Raiffeisen Zentralbank Österreich AG and others v Commission* [2006] ECR II-5169, at paras 114–26.

[144] Joined Cases T-101/05 and T-111/05 *BASF and UCB v Commission* [2007] ECR II-4949.

[145] *Ibid*, at para 180.

[146] *Ibid*, at paras 181–210.

any later participants or marginal players will be swept up into the single infringement. But is that a problem? If an undertaking joins a well-organised, unlawful scheme, it seems legitimate that it will eventually have to face the full legal consequences. Various degrees of involvement, as well as different periods of participation, will have to be addressed when fines or other sanctions are imposed.

To conclude, the notion of complex infringements, comprising agreements and concerted practices, can be understood as underpinned by monopoly theory given that it targets joint attempts at duplicating monopoly conditions. It can furthermore be seen as deterrence-based, since it saves administrative and judicial costs, hence liberating scarce resources for cartel control.

1. Opt-out necessary for complex infringements

If an undertaking participates in a meeting where there is an agreement/concerted practice—in other words, a complex infringement—an opt-out is necessary to avoid liability. This principle was first established in *Hüls*[147] and reiterated in *Cement.*[148] The undertaking must then show that its participation in the meetings was without any anticompetitive intention, by demonstrating that it had indicated to its competitors that it was participating in those meetings in a spirit that was different from theirs.[149] It now seems to be well-established practice to require an undertaking to opt out in order to escape liability for complex infringements.[150]

E. One or several cartels?

It has been explained that complex infringements are dealt with under the heading 'agreement/concerted practice'. In spite of this invention, which, as explained, brings EC cartel law closer to the US concept of conspiracy, there will be instances when there is more than one cartel in operation. This situation arose in *Citric acid*, where the Commission found that there were separate product markets with only limited substitutability and in effect two separate cartels.[151] As a result of the guidelines applicable at the time, the classification of two cartels instead of one resulted in higher fines. Likewise in *Choline chloride*, there were two separate cartels instead of one, but the older cartel was time-barred for the purpose of fines.[152] On the basis of the 2006 fining guidelines, where fines are calculated on the basis of the turnover on the markets, it should make less difference whether there are one or several cartels.

[147] *Hüls v Commission*, above n 110, at para 155.
[148] *Aalborg Portland and others v Commission*, above n 41, at para 83.
[149] *Ibid*, at para 81.
[150] See esp Case T-279/02 *Degussa v Commission* [2006] ECR II-897, at paras 134–37.
[151] Case T-43/02 *Jungbunzlauer v Commission* [2006] ECR II-3435, at para 310.
[152] *BASF and UCB v Commission*, above n 144.

F. Small, marginal players

While the centre of a cartel will consist of the instigators and ringleaders, there will often be smaller participants as well, who are not involved in the planning, whose participation in cartel meetings is irregular, and whose implementation of the cartel arrangements is less strict. The Community courts have consistently refused to accept absence of liability on the basis of such circumstances. Instead, a lesser degree of regular participation and of completeness of implementation of the measures agreed may be reflected in the severity of the penalty.[153] In *Cement*, the Court went as far as to say that

> the fact that an undertaking has not taken part in all aspects of an anticompetitive scheme or that it played only a minor role . . . must be taken into consideration only when the gravity of the infringement is assessed and if and when it comes to determining the fine.[154]

This view sends a strong deterrent message—small players have an incentive to stay outside the cartel or to report it.[155]

One may ask whether this is unfair towards small, marginal players. My impression is that the position taken by the Community courts is not surprising and could be in line with (for instance) national penal law. It is not unthinkable that national courts would act in a corresponding way when faced with organised crime, or gang-crimes such as robberies carried out by a group of delinquents.

1. *Parties forced to join*

In European jurisprudence parties have occasionally argued that specific standards should apply when collective actions involve more than one level of trade, *inter alia* by attempting to exonerate themselves from liability by claiming that they were in a vertical relationship, under pressure from a supplier to participate. In *Specialty graphites*, the participating distributor Intech argued that it was economically dependent on the producer Ibiden, which, in addition, exerted pressure on Intech. The Court of First Instance rejected that argument, holding that Intech could have refused to take part instead of being, as a distributor, a party to a horizontal agreement in which its supplier Ibiden also participated.[156] A similar argument was raised and rejected in *District heating pipes*.[157] On appeal, one of the

[153] Joined Cases C-238/99 P, etc *Limburgse Vinyl Maatschappij and others v Commission* [2002] ECR I-8375, at para 510.

[154] *Aalborg Portland and others v Commission*, above n 41, at para 86.

[155] This position has been taken in US law when a company claims that it has been compelled to participate: see Areeda and Hovenkamp, above n 6, Vol VI, § 1408, at 46; on 'throwaway' bids see *ibid*, Vol XII, § 2005, at 72.

[156] Joined Cases T-71/03, T-74/03, T-87/03 and T-91/03 *Tokai Carbon and others v Commission* [2005] ECR II-10, at para 76.

[157] Case T-17/99 *KE KELIT v Commission* [2002] ECR II-1647, at para 50.

undertakings that had participated insisted that it was merely a reseller, unable to implement measures decided at cartel meetings. The Court of Justice noted that ABB, one of the cartel participants present at the meeting, was indeed dominant, and yet another participant was much more powerful than the reseller. Nevertheless, the Court held that the participation in the cartel of dominant or particularly powerful undertakings in a position to take retaliatory measures against other, much less powerful, participants has no effect on the liability of those undertakings although it may have consequences for the determination of the level of the penalty.[158]

A Spanish distributor tried to argue in *Carbonless paper* that 'for a small distributor such as itself to have attended meetings of producers defies all logic,' an argument put forward in the context of denying participation in the cartel.[159] The Court of First Instance merely pointed out that a cartel

> necessarily had to include the distributors in order to operate properly on the Spanish market, which was characterised by extensive, integrated networks of production and distribution, such that a number of producers were also distributors . . .[160]

The approach seems consistent with what has been suggested by US scholars, who point out that if a competitor is compelled by threats to participate in a cartel, it should nevertheless be considered a conspirator. This may sound harsh, but it is motivated by the likelihood that coerced parties will either refuse or will inform the authorities.[161] The deterrent approach is obvious.

G. Unilateral versus joint market conduct

Although a cartel is normally a joint project to distort competition, borderline situations will arise when it is difficult to determine, on the facts, whether there is an agreement or a concerted practice, or unilateral conduct. Unilateral conduct is not encompassed by Article 81 EC, but can be prohibited as an abuse of dominance under Article 82 EC.

The principles applicable for distinguishing between joint and unilateral conduct have been outlined in *Bayer*,[162] *Steel beams* and *British Sugar*. According to the Court, 'an agreement cannot be based on what is only the expression of a unilateral policy of one of the . . . parties, which can be put into effects without the assistance of the others'.[163] Further, an anticompetitive agreement

158 Joined Cases C-189/02 P, etc *Dansk Rørindustri and others v Commission* [2005] ECR I-5425, at para 150.

159 Joined Cases T-109/02, etc *Bolloré and others v Commission* [2007] ECR II-947, at paras 203–04.

160 *Ibid.*

161 Areeda and Hovenkamp, above n 6, Vol VI, § 1408, at 46.

162 For a comprehensive analysis of *Bayer*, see Wickihalder, Urs, 'The Distinction between an "Agreement" within the Meaning of Article 81(1) of the EC Treaty and Unilateral Conduct' (2006) 2(1) *European Competition Journal* 87.

163 Joined Cases C-2/01 P and C-3/01 P *BAI and Commission v Bayer* [2004] ECR I-23, at para 101.

cannot be implied into an existing lawful contractual relationship, merely because one party tried to induce the other.[164]

Nevertheless, the distinction between one-way communication and co-operation is not entirely clear, and it might indeed be impossible to formulate an abstract principle that will solve the matter once and for all. In *British Sugar*, there was a series of meetings in which British Sugar informed its competitors, Tate & Lyle and Napier Brown, of the conduct which it intended to adopt on the sugar market. The information was found to constitute business secrets. The Commission had classified the content of the meetings as an agreement and/or concerted practice. The Court of First Instance considered that participation in meetings with an anticompetitive purpose is prohibited, even though it is limited to the mere receipt of information concerning the future conduct of competitors, and held:

> By participating at one of those meetings, each participant knew that during the following meetings its most important competitor, the leader in the industry concerned, would reveal its future price intentions. Independently of any other reason for participating in those meetings, there was always one at least which was to eliminate in advance the uncertainty concerning the future conduct of competitors. Moreover, by merely participating in the meetings, each participant could not fail to take account, directly or indirectly, of the information obtained during those meetings in order to determine the market policy which it intended to pursue.

It should be noted that the Court of First Instance qualified its assessment in a number of ways.[165] The wording indicates that the mere participation in a first meeting where information on future price intentions is transmitted is insufficient for a finding of an infringement. The dicta in *British Sugar* are based on the understanding that, having participated in a first meeting where such information was revealed, the competitors came back to a second meeting, knowing that price intentions would be revealed once again by the industry leader. A pattern was thus established between the participants, of providing and receiving information respectively, information which would mould the market policy of each participant.

In *Steel Beams* there was a cartel meeting in which British Steel announced to the other undertakings that it would be increasing its prices in the United Kingdom and called on them to follow that increase. The Commission managed to prove that British Steel and its competitors had acted in concert in regard to prices, this having already resulted in a number of price-fixing agreements for Continental ECSC markets to which British Steel had been a party. The Court of First Instance held that British Steel's action could not be regarded as unilateral conduct. Since British Steel had accepted, at numerous previous meetings, to bind itself, at least 'morally', to the Continental prices, it could reasonably expect its

[164] *Ibid.*

[165] Joined Cases T-202/98, T-204/98 and T-207/98 *Tate & Lyle and others v Commission* [2001] ECR II-2035, at paras 58 ff, on appeal Case C-359/01 P *British Sugar v Commission* [2004] ECR I-4933, this particular question not subject to appeal.

competitors to comply with its call that they respect its new prices in the United Kingdom.[166] In addition, the Court found that the competitors had indeed complied with the call. It can be inferred from the case that invitations to join in agreements or concerted practices will be contrary to Article 81 if:

a) there is an institutionalised cartel context; or
b) the competitors actually comply.

My view is that the case law shows that reciprocity is required if there is to be an infringement. This is consistent with the idea that cartels attempt to duplicate monopoly conditions. However, the reciprocity need not concern performance of the same type. For instance, one party can perform by providing information, and the other party can perform by adapting his behaviour to the information received.

H. 'No authority to bind the principal' argument

When facing a decision on penalties for cartel participation, undertakings have occasionally tried the 'rogue employee' argument, claiming that their representative did not have the necessary authority to attend meetings, etc. The Community courts have not been impressed so far. In one of the *Polypropylene* cases, ICI tried to describe the participation at cartel meetings of one of its employees as unofficial, but this did not relieve ICI of responsibility.[167] In *Greek ferries*, an argument was made that the owners of the ships which the applicant managed never gave it authority to conclude cartel agreements. According to the Court of First Instance, that was not an exculpatory factor.[168] Furthermore, it held in *Graphite electrodes* that

> The Commission's power to impose a sanction on an undertaking where it has committed an infringement presumes only the unlawful action of a person who is generally authorised to act on behalf of the undertaking . . .[169]

This was drawn from the judgment of the Court of Justice in *Musique diffusion Française*.[170] There, the Court emphasised the Commission's power to impose fines on undertakings or associations of undertakings, and held that it was

> not necessary for there to have been action by, or even knowledge on the part of the partners or principal managers of the undertaking concerned; action by a person who is authorized to act on behalf of the undertaking suffices.

[166] Case T-141/94 *Thyssen Stahl v Commission* [1999] ECR II-347, at paras 219–20; same outcome in Case T-151/94 *British Steel v Commission* [1999] ECR II-629, at paras 200 ff, this particular issue not tried on appeal to the Court of Justice.
[167] Case T-7/89 *Hercules Chemicals v Commission* [1991] ECR II-1711, at paras 103–04.
[168] Case T-56/99 *Marlines v Commission* [2003] ECR II-5225, at para 60.
[169] Case T-236/01 *Tokai Carbon v Commission* [2004] ECR II-1181, at para 277.

Although the Court refers to Regulation 17, the actual implication is that Article 81 EC applies regardless of any awareness by the management of an undertaking.

There was a similar story in *FEG & TU* concerning the question whether members of one association of undertakings, as agents, were authorised by their principals to conclude an exclusive dealing arrangement with another trade association. The Court of First Instance found the question irrelevant, and pointed out that the 'only relevant issue, with regard to the contested decision, is whether that agreement existed'.[171] In *Cement*, a number of applicants claimed that the cartel agreement did not fall within the scope of the activities authorised in the trade association's statues or in the statutes of the various national trade associations involved, and that the head delegates had no authority, but this was rejected by the Court of First Instance.[172]

European Community law seems to be the same as US law on this point. In *Hydrolevel*, a trade association was implicated in a scheme to discourage customers from buying Hydrolevel's product. The US Supreme Court held the trade association liable for acts of its agents within their apparent authority. It referred to the common law notion of business expediency, that is the desire that third persons should be given reasonable protection in dealing with agents. This intention was deemed consistent with the congressional intent to encourage competition, and led the Court to interpret 'the antitrust private cause of action to be at least as broad as a plaintiff's right to sue for analogous torts'.[173] Areeda *et al* comment:

> To be sure, an employee might take a step that restrains trade in violation of his employer's instructions, but this fact hardly lifts him out of the employer's entity . . .[174]

Deterrence objectives seems to be one limb of the law—an employer that is liable for infringements of its employees will have an incentive to educate or discipline its organisation to ensure compliance with the law.

I. Collaborators

Undertakings which make it their business to support cartels can find themselves being parties to the infringement, even though they are not active on the cartelised market. The breakthrough for this policy was relatively recent, in *Organic peroxides*, where the Commission fined the Swiss entity AC Treuhand (formerly Fides) which performed a number of tasks to enable the cartel to operate.[175] The

[170] Joined Cases 100/80 to 103/80 *Musique diffusion française and others v Commission* [1983] ECR 1825, at para 97.

[171] Joined Cases T-5/00 and T-6/00 *Nederlandse Federatieve Vereniging voor de Groothandel op Elektrotechnisch Gebied and Technische Unie v Commission* [2003] ECR II-5761, at para 147.

[172] Joined Cases T-25/95, etc *Cimenteries and others v Commission* [2000] ECR II-491, at paras 923–28 and 1312.

[173] *American Society of Mechanical Engineers v Hydrolevel*, 456 US 556 (1982).

[174] Areeda and Hovenkamp, above n 6, Vol VII, § 1472, at 268.

[175] *Organic Peroxides* [2005] OJ L/110/44, at paras 331 ff.

Commission imposed only a symbolic fine on AC Treuhand, but sent the message that 'organisers or facilitators of cartels, not just the cartel members, must fear that they will be found and heavy sanctions imposed from now on'.[176] The decision was appealed to the Court of First Instance, which upheld the Commission's decision.[177]

This recent development seems largely consistent with US law. There we can find theory-building concerning subordinate 'pawns' that perform tasks for a principal. Pawns are understood as mere assistants, not as competitors of the principal, nor as market actors whose buying or selling is being controlled. Their only role, for the purpose of antitrust scrutiny, is to assist the principal actor's market behaviour. Areeda *et al* conclude that

> no conspiracy with a pawn should be found unless the behaviour itself violates the law. Apart from that issue there are three prerequisites for finding a conspiracy with a pawn. *First*, the pawn must have knowledge of the principal's objective to restrain trade. *Second*, the pawn must not only facilitate the principal's restraint but must also intend to restrain trade. This usually means that the pawn must have a stake in the restraint, as distinct from merely selling its own services for their usual market price. *Third*, the pawn must contribute materially to the restraint. Materiality will usually be absent where he brings no special resources or talents that the principal could not as easily accomplish through its own employees. Unless these requirements are satisfied, the pawn should be deemed an independent actor pursuing his own lawful business rather than a conspirator with the principal.[178]

Although it is apparent that the Commission is attempting to introduce a new deterrence model, it is also clear from the considerations in US law that deterrence must be coupled with a strong focus on justice, to avoid unfair outcomes.

J. Legal requirements for withdrawing from a cartel

In spite of nearly 40 years of jurisprudence, it is not quite settled what an undertaking must do in order to be considered to have withdrawn from a cartel. Although withdrawal cannot liberate an undertaking from responsibility for past infringements, it puts an end to its involvement, and consequently to the period for which fines can be imposed.

In *Cement*, the Court of Justice explained that in cases of tacit approval of an unlawful initiative, there is liability unless an undertaking is 'publicly distancing itself from its content or reporting it to the administrative authorities,' since otherwise there is participation which 'effectively encourages the continuation of the infringement and compromises its discovery'.[179] Although the statement relates to

[176] IP/03/1700.
[177] Case T-99/04 *AC Treuhand v Commission* [2008] ECR II-0000.
[178] Areeda and Hovenkamp, above n 6, Vol VII, § 1474, at 290.
[179] *Aalborg Portland and others v Commission*, above n 41, at para 84.

establishment of liability, I see no reason why it should not be applicable as a legal test to see whether an undertaking has ended its involvement.

From the wording it appears that the two grounds are alternative: an undertaking can either distance itself publicly, or report to the authorities. In reality, though, the only foolproof method is perhaps to report to the authorities. As will be shown below, several undertakings have argued in vain that they distanced themselves from anticompetitive practices.

In *Zinc Phosphate*, it was common ground that Union Pigments participated in a cartel from March 1994 to March or April 1995, and from August 1995 to May 1998, but it claimed to have withdrawn during an intermediary period from March 1995 until 1 August 1995. The Court of First Instance noted that there were indeed indications that the undertaking withdrew from the cartel for a time. It had stated by fax that it 'was pulling out of the Zinc Phosphate Producers Association' and that, for that reason, it would no longer be forwarding statistics. There was in addition an internal note, written by the sales director to the management, containing a recommendation for withdrawal from the cartel. Further, Union Pigments did not communicate its statistics to the other undertakings concerned between April and August 1995. Even so, the Court held the undertaking responsible for the infringement during the alleged break, finding that it did not resume a genuinely autonomous policy in the market during that period:

> The benefit it obtained from access to the statistics from other members did not cease to exist on the day the applicant withdrew from the cartel. It presumably took account of information already exchanged with its competitors, including at the meeting . . . in determining its conduct on that market during its alleged withdrawal.[180]

It should also be observed in this context that the undertaking rejoined the cartel because it urgently needed information concerning the market.

In *Organic peroxides*, the Court of First Instance rejected an undertaking's arguments regarding withdrawal from a cartel. The undertaking claimed that it had not attended any meetings after a certain date, and that the director who was the contact person for the cartel activities had been dismissed a month after the last meeting. The Court found that the undertaking had continued to benefit from an information exchange after that date, and had furthermore failed to distance itself from the cartel, which could have been done by letting the other participants know that the director had been dismissed.[181]

In *Sodium gluconate*, ADM claimed that it had openly disassociated itself and withdrawn from the agreement at a meeting in October 1994. At that meeting, ADM's representatives informed the other participants that it would leave the group if outstanding issues on quotas were not resolved. No agreement was reached and ADM's representatives left. It also ceased reporting sales figures to the cartel. Nevertheless, the Court of First Instance found that ADM's conduct at that meeting was a 'negotiating strategy designed to obtain more concessions from

180 Case T-62/02 *Union Pigments v Commission* [2005] ECR II-5057, at para 39.
181 Case T-120/04 *Peróxidos Orgánicos v Commission* [2006] ECR II-4441, at para 64.

the other members of the cartel rather than as an end to its involvement in that cartel'.[182]

An example of a company which successfully managed to withdraw from a cartel may be found in *Carbonless paper*. There, the Commission had intended to fine Zanders for an infringement which lasted until March 1997. With reference to several measures undertaken, Zanders demonstrated that the participation had ended in September 1995. Those measures were as follows:

a) A letter from the CEO addressed to all employees in the group drew their attention to the fact that the group attached the highest importance to observing laws and ethics.
b) There was a meeting with the aim of impressing upon managerial staff the need to observe competition law.
c) A compliance programme was drawn up and (perhaps decisive for the outcome) a declaration was made in public by the president, after his accession to the presidency of the association, that the undertaking had ceased any collusive activities.[183]

The impression derived from the judgments of the Community courts is that internal communication within an undertaking may serve as a complementary means of evidence, to establish that it did indeed put an end to its participation in an infringement, but it has no independent significance. Still, the picture is not clear. Was the decisive point in *Carbonless paper* that Zanders' CEO made a public statement that Zanders had ended its collusive activities? As explained, the Court of Justice held in *Cement* that a decision to end the involvement must be communicated to the other cartel participants, or be manifested in a report to the authorities. Nevertheless, it would seem that there ought to be instances when an undertaking has in fact withdrawn from an unlawful arrangement and, after some time, has ceased to derive any benefits from its past participation.

K. Conclusion: a deterrence-based substantive policy

It follows that the theory underlying the central notions in EC cartel control is deterrence-based. This applies in particular to the notion of agreements, the opt-out rules for cartel meetings, and the established practice to sweep up smaller players into the infringement and differentiate their role only when it comes to fines.

III. JURISDICTION

When foreign (non-EU) companies engage in cartels, there is the matter of extraterritorial application of Article 81 EC. The Court of Justice has based

[182] Case T-329/01 *Archer Daniels Midland v Commission* [2006] ECR II-3255, at paras 242–47.
[183] Joined Cases T-109/02, etc *Bolloré and others v Commission* [2007] ECR II-947, at paras 96 ff.

jurisdiction on two grounds in these situations: either by attributing conduct of an undertaking to its parent; or by applying the implementation doctrine.

Dyestuffs was about co-ordinated price increases on dyes and pigments in the Community. The producer ICI was established in the UK, at the time outside the Community. The Court first found that the price increases were put into effect within the Common Market and concerned competition between producers operating within it. It then held ICI liable by attributing the conduct of the subsidiaries, located inside the Community, to the parent company.[184]

In *Woodpulp*, the alleged infringement was committed by producers based in Canada, the US, Sweden, Finland, Norway, Portugal and Spain, all with their offices outside the EC when the alleged infringement took place and when the Commission's decision was adopted. They argued that the Commission had misconstrued the territorial scope of Article 81 EC. In addition, they claimed that it would be contrary to public international law to apply Article 81 EC to conduct adopted outside the territory of the Community. The Court found that Article 81 EC applied since the producers had concerted on prices to be charged to their customers in the Community. They had put that concertation into effect by selling at prices that were actually co-ordinated.[185]

Addressing the claim relating to public international law, the Court held that an infringement of Article 81 consists of conduct made up of two elements: the formation of the agreement, decision or concerted practice; and the implementation thereof. The decisive factor for applicability of Article 81 was the place where the agreement, etc was implemented.[186] Since the producers had implemented their pricing agreement within the Common Market, the Community's jurisdiction was covered by the territoriality principle as recognised in public international law.[187]

Under the US Foreign Trade Antitrust Improvements Act, the Sherman Act will as a general rule not apply to conduct involving trade or commerce with foreign nations.[188] It still applies to foreign commerce other than import commerce if the conduct has a direct, substantial and reasonably foreseeable effect on US commerce and such effects give rise to a Sherman Act claim. An effects doctrine similar to that applicable in the US has been endorsed by the Commission and by Advocates-General several times, but has not yet been adopted by the Court of Justice.[189]

Subsequent developments in case law have made the reasoning on extraterritoriality in *Woodpulp* awkwardly detached from the concepts of agreements and concerted practices in Article 81 EC. In *PVC II*, the Court held that for the purposes of applying Article 81(1) EC, it is sufficient that the aim of an agreement is

[184] Case 48/69 *ICI v Commission* [1972] ECR 619.

[185] Joined Cases 89, 104, 114, 116, 117 and 125 to 129/85, *Ahlström Osakeytiö and others v Commission* [1988] ECR 5193, at para 13.

[186] *Ibid*, at para 16.

[187] *Ibid*, at para 17.

[188] 15 USCA § 6a.

[189] Jones, Alison, and Sufrin, Brenda, *EC Competition Law*, 2nd edn (Oxford, Oxford University Press, 2004), at 1248 ff; Van Bael and Bellis, above n 3, at 152 ff; Whish, above n 17, at 436.

to restrict, prevent or distort competition, irrespective of the actual effects of that agreement. Consequently, an undertaking which participates in meetings where agreements between competitors are reached, with knowledge of their aim, is liable *even if it did not proceed to implement any of the agreed measures.*[190]

Moving to concerted practices, the Court held in *Anic* that a concerted practice implies concertation, market conduct, and a relationship of cause and effect between the two.[191] However, the market conduct can be presumed, and it is for the undertaking to rebut this presumption.[192] Thus, for agreements no implementation is required; for concerted practices it may be presumed.

Nevertheless, the courts must occasionally check whether those agreements and concerted practices have been implemented in order to ensure that the jurisdiction criterion does not come into conflict with international law principles. This apparent dualism shows the theoretic weakness of the Court's approach in *Woodpulp*. Given the rulings in *PVC II* and *Anic*, it would now seem appropriate to separate the analysis of the jurisdictional application of Article 81 EC from the substantive interpretation of this Treaty provision. In other words, extraterritoriality should be analysed on its own merits and not with reference to implementation of agreements and concerted practices (which, as explained, do not have to be implemented or can be presumed to be implemented). Absent further development in case law, a national court facing this problem would benefit from requesting a preliminary ruling pursuant to Article 234 of the Treaty.

IV. EFFECT ON TRADE

The effect on trade concept is a jurisdictional criterion, as established in *Hugin*: '. . . the purpose of that condition . . . is to define . . . the boundary between the areas respectively covered by Community law and the law of the Member States'.[193] This was even more clearly articulated in *Alsatel*, where, according to the Court, 'the interpretation of that condition . . . must be based on its purpose, which is to determine the scope of application of Community competition law'.[194] Member State courts and authorities are not entitled to engage in their own interpretation of the effect on trade concept; the Court of Justice must ultimately make interpretations of the Treaty.[195]

The theory base for effect on trade is riddled with conflicts. More particularly, the conflict is between a free movement approach to effect on trade, or a competition welfare approach. I will outline the conflict and propose a solution.

[190] *Limburgse Vinyl Maatschappij and others v Commission*, above n 153, at paras 508–09.
[191] *Commission v Anic*, above n 110, at para 118.
[192] *Ibid*, at para 121.
[193] Case 22/78 *Hugin v Commission* [1979] ECR 1869, at para 17.
[194] Case 247/86 *Alsatel* [1988] ECR 5987, at para 11.
[195] The Swedish Market Court carried out a very individual interpretation of the effect on trade concept in the petrol cartel case, MD 2005:7. See Simonsson, Ingeborg, and Öberg, Ulf, 'Bensinkartelldomen MD 2005:7—fördragsstridig tillämpning av EG:s konkurrensrätt?, *Svensk Juristtidning* 1/2006 s 23.

A. Jurisprudence on effect on trade

1. *Some basic aspects*

It is not necessary to show that each separate undertaking's actions had an effect on trade. According to a consistent line of case law, it is sufficient that the infringement as a whole affected trade. In *ICI*, the Court of First Instance found that the Commission had established that the infringement in which ICI had participated was apt to affect trade between Member States. Thus it was unnecessary for the Commission to demonstrate that ICI's individual participation affected trade.[196] This formula has subsequently been relied on by the Court of First Instance in cartel cases.[197]

Other inventive approaches have been launched as well by undertakings accused of cartel activity, although without much success. In *Lombard Club*, several undertakings sought to argue that effect on trade should be evaluated separately for each relevant market, but this argument was rejected.[198] In *Pokémon*, one undertaking tried to introduce a temporal approach to the effect on trade concept, by arguing that the infringement was of very short duration (10 months). The Commission found an effect on trade without any reasoning on that point.[199]

2. *Cross-border infringements*

Establishing an effect on trade in cartel cases which involve several Member States is standard practice. In *Seamless steel tubes*, the Court of Justice held that the sharing of domestic markets in the Community is capable of significantly affecting the pattern of trade between Member States.[200] As for global cartels, the crux is whether they fall within EC jurisdiction as set out in the previous subsection.

3. *Domestic practices*

When assessing whether domestic cartels effect trade between Member States, it is helpful to recall that about one-third of the Commission's cartel decisions concern cartels confined to single Member States only. I have found that out of some 150 cartel decisions adopted between 1969 and 2007, approximately 50 are outright

[196] Case T-13/89 *ICI v Commission* [1992] ECR II-1021, at para 305.

[197] Case T-17/99 *KE KELIT v Commission* [2002] ECR II-1647, at para 58; Joined Cases T-259/02 to T-264/02 and T-271/02 *Raiffeisen Zentralbank Österreich AG and others v Commission* [2006] ECR II-5169, at para 196.

[198] *Raiffeisen Zentralbank Österreich AG and others v Commission*, above n 197, at para 172.

[199] Commission Decision of 26-05-2004 COMP/C-3/37.980 Souris–Topps, non-confidential version published on DG COMP's website http://ec.europa.eu/competition/antitrust/cases/index/by_nr_75.html#i37_980, at 129–32.

[200] Case C-407/04 P *Dalmine v Commission* [2007] ECR I-829, at para 91.

domestic, although with an effect on trade.[201] The Commission's reasoning on inter-State trade varies significantly between these cases, and it is near impossible to find a common analytical framework. However, there is at least one common denominator: the products were traded between Member States, or could potentially be traded.

Numerous domestic cartels have been set up specifically to seal off national markets from imports from other Member States, or in order to reserve the national market as far as possible to the established traders.[202] In other cases there was an effect on trade since cartelised products were to a significant extent imported into the Member State.[203] Yet other cases concern price-fixing and other measures for products sold cross-border to other Member States.[204]

Some relatively far-fetched cases with only potential trade effects may be observed as well. In the *Dutch mobile crane* case,[205] the cartel participants did not engage in intra-Community activities at the time of the decision, but the Commission observed that it was perfectly possible to move mobile cranes and that the system therefore constituted a potential restriction of intra-Community trade. On appeal, the Court of First Instance upheld the Commission's decision and stated that 'it is common ground that mobile cranes have an operating radius of roughly 50 kilometres. Inter-State trade can therefore develop in the frontier regions of the Netherlands'.[206]

[201] *ASPA* [1970] JO L/148/9; *Carreaux céramiques* [1971] OJ L/10/15; *Vereeniging van Cementhandelaren* [1972] OJ L/13/34; *Chauffage central* [1972] OJ L/264/22; *GISA* [1972] OJ L/303/45; *Gas water-heaters and bath-heaters* [1973] OJ L/217/34; *Papier peints de Belgique* [1974] OJ L/237/3; *Stoves and Heaters* [1975] OJ L/159/22; *Bomée-Stichting* [1975] OJ L/329/30; *Pabst & Richarz/BNIA* [1976] OJ L/231/24; *Centraal Bureau voor de Rijwielhandel* [1978] OJ L/20/18; *Floral* [1980] OJ L/39/51; *IMA Rules* [1980] OJ L/318/1; *Industrieverband Solnhofener Natursteinplatten* [1980] OJ L/318/32; *Rolled steel products* [1980] OJ L/62/28; *Italian cast glass* [1980] OJ L/383/19; *Italian flat glass* [1981] OJ L/326/32; *NAVEWA-ANSEAU* [1982] OJ L/167/39; *Stichting Sigarettenindustrie* [1982] OJ L/232/1; *AROW/BNIC* [1982] OJ L/379/1; *Vimpoltu* [1983] OJ L/200/44; *Fire Insurance* [1985] OJ L/35/20; *French inland waterway charter traffic* [1985] OJ L/219/35; *Roofing felt* [1986] OJ L/232/15; *MELDOC* [1986] OJ L/348/50; *Flat glass* [1989] OJ L/33/44; *Publisher's Association—Net Book Agreements* [1989] OJ L/22/12; *Sugar beet* [1990] OJ L/31/32; *Ijsselcentrale and others* [1991] OJ L/28/32; *Building and construction industry in the Netherlands* [1992] OJ L/92/1; *UK Agricultural Tractor Registration Exchange* [1992] OJ L68/19; *Eurocheque: Helsinki Agreement* [1992] OJ L/95/50; *CNSD* [1993] OJ L/203/27; *Coapi* [1995] OJ L/122/37; *Kraanverhuurbedrijf* [1995] OJ L/312/79; *Fenex* [1996] OJ L/181/28; *British Sugar, Tate & Lyle* [1999] OJ L/76/1; *FEG and TU* [2000] OJ L/39/1; *Luxemburg brewers* [2002] OJ L/253/21; *Interbrew and Alken-Maes* [2003] OJ L/200/1; *Euro-zone currencies—Germany* [2003] OJ L/15/1; *Austrian banks—'Lombard Club'* [2004] OJ L/56/1; *Industrial and medical gases* [2003] OJ L/84/1; *Reinforcing bars* [2006] OJ L/353/1; *French beef* [2003] OJ L/209/12; *Belgian Architects* [2005] OJ L/4/10; *Brasseries Kronenbourg, Brasseries Heineken* [2005] OJ L/184/57; *Raw Tobacco Spain* IP/04/1256, *Raw Tobacco Italy* IP/05/1315, *Road bitumen NL* IP/06/1179, *Beer cartel in the Netherlands* IP/07/509.

[202] Amongst others, *GISA* [1972] OJ L/303/45; *Stoves and Heaters* [1975] OJ L/159/22; *Centraal Bureau voor de Rijwielhandel* [1978] OJ L/20/18; *IMA Rules* [1980] OJ L/318/1; *NAVEWA-ANSEAU* [1982] OJ L/167/39; *MELDOC* [1986] OJ L/348/50; *Sugar beet* [1990] OJ L/31/32; *FEG and TU* [2000] OJ L/39/1; *Luxemburg brewers* [2002] OJ L/253/21; *French beef* [2003] OJ L/209/12.

[203] *Stichting Sigarettenindustrie* [1982] OJ L/232/1; *Vimpoltu* [1983] OJ L/200/44.

[204] *Pabst & Richarz/BNIA* [1976] OJ L/231/24; *Floral* [1980] OJ L/39/51; *Industrieverband Solnhofener Natursteinplatten* [1980] OJ L/318/32; *AROW/BNIC* [1982] OJ L/379/1.

[205] *Kraanverhuurbedrijf* [1995] OJ L/312/79.

[206] Joined Cases T-213/95 and T-18/96 *SCK and FNK v Commission* [1997] ECR II-1739, at para 177.

The Commission's assessments on the effect on trade in domestic cases have, as a standardised fact, been upheld on appeal.[207] The threshold seems to be rather low: for intermediate products, the Court held in *BNIC* that any agreement the object or effect of which is to restrict competition by fixing minimum prices for an intermediate product is capable of affecting intra-Community trade, even if there is no trade in that intermediate product between the Member States, where the product constitutes the raw material for another product marketed elsewhere in the Community.[208] It is very rare that a Commission cartel case is overturned on appeal on the basis of lack of effect on trade, although it happened in *Belgian wallpapers.*[209] The Court did not exclude the possibility that the restrictive practice of the wallpaper manufacturers' association had an effect on trade, but considered that the Commission should have supplied a more detailed statement of the grounds for this finding.[210]

Unless we want to question the fundamentals of nearly 40 years of adjudicative practices of the Commission and the Community courts, it seems fairly safe to assume that cartels covering an entire Member State will affect trade. Indeed the Court of First Instance has adopted this approach as a matter of principle.[211] For instance, in *Lombard Club* there was an effect on trade since a national bank cartel was deemed to have maintained barriers of access to the market, and preserved national market structures and consumers' habits.[212] The Court of Justice reiterated in *Manfredi* that

> An agreement, decision or concerted practice extending over the whole of the territory of a Member State has, by its very nature, the effect of reinforcing the partitioning of markets on a national basis, thereby holding up the economic interpenetration which the Treaty is designed to bring about.[213]

[207] See esp Case 8/72 *Vereeniging van Cementhandelaren v Commission* [1972] ECR 977, at para 29; Joined Cases 209–215 and 218/78 *van Landewyck and others v Commission* [1980] ECR 3125, at para 172; Joined Cases 96/82, etc *V IAZ Int Belgium and others v Commission* [1983] ECR 3369, at paras 27–28; Joined Cases 240/82, etc *Stichting Sigarettenindustrie and others v Commission* [1985] ECR 3831, at para 48; Case 45/85 *Verband der Sachversicherer eV v Commission* [1987] 405, at paras 49–50; Case 246/86 *Belasco and others v Commission* [1989] ECR 2117, at paras 32–38; Case T-29/92 *Vereniging van Samenwerkende Prijsregelende Organisaties in de Bouwnijverheid and others v Commission* [1995] ECR II-289, at paras 226 ff; Case T-61/89 *Dansk Pelsdyravlerforening v Commission* [1992] ECR II-1931, at paras 141–43; Joined Cases T-49/02 to T-51/02 *Brasserie nationale and Brasserie Battin v Commission* [2005] ECR II-3033; and Joined Cases T-217/03 and T-245/03 *FNCBV, FNSEA, FNB, FNPL and JA v Commission* [2006] ECR II-4987, at paras 63–68.

[208] Case 123/83 *BNIC v Clair* [1985] ECR 391, at para 29.

[209] Case 73/74 *Papier peints de Belgique and others v Commission* [1975] ECR 1491.

[210] *Ibid*, at para 33.

[211] Case T-325/01 *DaimlerChrysler v Commission* [2005] ECR II-3319, at para 212, with accompanying references.

[212] Joined Cases T-259/02 to T-264/02 and T-271/02 *Raiffeisen Zentralbank Österreich AG and others v Commission* [2006] ECR II-5169, at paras 165 ff, 185.

[213] Joined Cases C-295/04 to C-298/04 *Manfredi and others* [2006] ECR I-6619, at para 45.

4. Local practices

Even relatively local practices have been deemed to effect trade between Member States, but only when there have been clear cross-border aspects.[214] As a rule of thumb, local (or regional) cartels covering only part of a Member State will not be encompassed by Article 81 EC.

The Court established in *Hugin* that conduct, the effects of which are confined to the territory of a single Member State, is governed by the national legal order.[215] This jurisprudence is reflected in the absence of such cases in the Commission's cartel decisions. The Commission's Notice on effect on trade is also modelled on this view.[216] The Commission takes the position that agreements that are local in nature are not in themselves capable of appreciably affecting trade between Member States, even if the local market is situated in a border region.[217] For agreements covering only part of a Member State, the Commission suggests that geographic coverage and market share of the parties are important elements in the assessment, the best indicator being the share of the national market in terms of volume that is being foreclosed.[218] This is consistent with the Court's position that the effect which an agreement may have on trade is to be appraised in particular by reference to the position and the importance of the parties on the market for the products concerned.[219]

5. Export cartels

If undertakings restrict competition in markets *outside the Community*, some careful analysis will be required to check if there is an effect on trade. The Commission has established effect on trade for export cartels on a few occasions, although the aggregate number of cases remains low.

In *European Sugar Industry*, the Commission held that although the action at issue related to exports of sugar to countries outside the Community, it nevertheless allowed the export of sugar produced inside the Community. Competition within the Community had thus been prevented, restricted or distorted.[220] On appeal the Court upheld the Commission's finding.[221] The Court held that since the undertakings concerned had their place of business in France and Belgium, countries having a large sugar surplus, there was no doubt that,

[214] *VBBB/VBVB* [1982] OJ L/54/36, on appeal Joined Cases 43/82 and 63/82 *VBVB and VBBB v Commission* [1984] ECR 19, at paras 47–48; *Ferry Operators—Currency surcharges* [1996] OJ L/26/23; *Greek Ferries* [1999] OJ L/109/24.

[215] Case 22/78 *Hugin v Commission* [1979] ECR 1869, at para 17.

[216] Commission Notice, *Guidelines on the effect on trade concept contained in Articles 81 and 82 of the Treaty* [2004] OJ C/101/81.

[217] *Ibid*, para 91.

[218] *Ibid*, para 90.

[219] Case 99/79 *Lancôme and Cosparfrance Nederland v Etos* [1980] ECR I-2511 p 24.

[220] *European Sugar Industry* [1973] OJ L/140/17.

[221] Joined Cases 40–48, 50, 54 to 56, 111, 113 and 114/73 *Suiker Unie and others v Commission* [1975] ECR 1663, at paras 579–86.

> had it not been for the concerted action at issue, some at least of these undertakings would have been awarded smaller quantities than they were in fact awarded and would thus have been induced to sell more sugar in the other Member States, and these sales could not only modify the pattern of intra-community trade but also intensify competition within the common market.[222]

In *Bulk Oil*, however, the Court adopted the opposite position and held that a measure which is specifically directed at exports to a non-Member country is not in itself likely to restrict or distort competition within the Common Market.[223] Admittedly the case centred around the question whether a Member State was prohibited from adopting a policy restricting or prohibiting exports of oil to a non-Member country, but the Court's statement was unambiguous.

French-West African shipowners' committees concerned the sharing of markets for liner vessel cargo between French and African ports. The Commission found an effect on trade because the agreements aimed at partitioning the trade between the Community and the 11 African States concerned by giving French shipping lines privileged access to certain routes.[224] Similarly in *Cewal, Kowac and Ukwal*, the Commission found an effect on trade for agreements on liner shipping routes between Community ports and the coast of West Africa. In the Commission's view, artificial barriers were created, since carriers operating in the North Sea agreed to serve only some Community ports, and competition between various Community ports was influenced by altering the catchment areas and activities located in those areas, disturbing trade patterns.[225] The Commission's findings were upheld on appeal.[226]

For export cartels *inside the EC*, there is no doubt as to the application of Article 81. A cartel for floor coverings which set prices for sales outside Germany was found to violate Article 81 EC. However, since the cartel had existed prior to the entry into force of Regulation 17 and had been notified to the Commission, the prohibition did not apply.[227] In *Milchförderungsfonds*, several German entities, including the German Farmers' Union and the Central Association of Private Dairies, had set up a Milk Promotion Fund. The Fund's resources eventually came to be spent on promoting exports of milk and dairy products to relieve pressure on the domestic market. Part of the Fund's money was for exports to other Member States, and part for exports to non-Member countries. The Commission held that the activities had the object and effect of distorting competition, 'in so far as the undertakings which benefit are directly enabled to reduce their selling prices'.[228] While the Commission was primarily concerned about the private export subsidies

[222] *Ibid*, at para 580.

[223] Case 174/84 *Bulk Oil (Zug) AG v Sun International Limited and Sun Oil Trading Company* [1986] ECR 559, at para 44.

[224] *French-West African shipowners' committees* [1992] OJ L/134/1, at 42.

[225] *Cewal, Kowac and Ukwal* [1993] OJ L/34/20, at 39–40.

[226] Joined Cases T-24/93, T-25/93, T-26/93 and T-28/93 *Compagnie Maritime Belge and others v Commission* [1996] ECR II-1201, at para 202.

[227] *Industrieverband Solnhofener Natursteinplatten* [1980] OJ L/318/32.

[228] *Milchförderungsfonds* [1985] OJ L/35/35, at 29.

for sale of products in other Member States, it also condemned 'support for exports to Community and non-member countries, producing a further distortion of competition'.[229] The decision prohibits the granting of supports for exports within the Common Market. It does not seem to address the point whether joint schemes for private subsidies for exports to non-Member countries are prohibited.

As for *incoming export cartels*, US Webb-Pomerene export cartels active within trade with the EC have been found by the Commission to infringe Article 81(1) EC, without qualifying for exemption under Article 81(3) EC.[230]

In the vertical context, prohibitions on exporting *from* a country outside the EC have been considered to have the object of restricting competition *in third countries*, as opposed to restricting competition *within the Community*. The analysis of restrictions on competition within the EC consequently turns around the question of their effects in the EC rather than their object.[231] Being outside the 'object-box', vertical export restrictions must be assessed in their legal and economic context, and not according to a per se prohibition doctrine. However, an application of this reasoning to horizontal arrangements would be a classic example of stretching an analogy too far. An export prohibition could be part of a market-sharing practice if set up jointly by competitors.

In principle, whether competition law should address *outgoing* cartels (cartels where the planning and presence is within the territory, but where the effects are in a geographic area elsewhere) is a question which may be answered in more than one way. Notably, export cartels are permitted under US law. In contrast to the implicit acceptance of export cartels under EC law, the US policy is deliberate and based on a twofold theory. Export cartels are devised to overcome structural problems relating to market entry in a foreign territory, and to produce pro-competitive effects by allowing companies to work together.[232] Looking at EC law, it has been explained in relation to *Bulk Oil* (above) that the effect of trade criterion is normally not met for pure export cartels.

The positions in EC law and US have been severely criticised. Becker describes a 'remarkable leniency towards restrictions of competition having effects on a market outside the regulating state'. He finds it 'questionable, if not immoral, that a state should allow or support behaviour to the disadvantage of foreign markets that is strictly prohibited on the domestic market'.[233] Levenstein and Suslow analyse export cartel regulation in 55 jurisdictions and find *inter alia* that

> If we have a general consensus that price fixing harms consumers, then export exemptions benefit a nation only to the extent that they harm foreign consumers. The policy is one of enriching oneself at the expense of one's trading partners.[234]

229 *Ibid*, at 36.

230 *Woodpulp* [1985] OJ L/85/1; *Ansac* [1991] OJ L/152/54.

231 C-306/96 *Javico* [1998] ECR I-1983, at paras 20–22; *Junghans* [1977] OJ L/30/10, at 24.

232 Becker, Florian, 'The Case of Export Cartel Exemptions: Between Competition and Protectionism' (2007) 3(1) *Journal of Competition Law and Economics* 97.

233 *Ibid*, at 100, 114.

234 Levenstein, Margaret C, and Suslow, Valerie Y, 'The Changing International Status of Export Cartel Exemptions' (2005) 20(3) *American University International Law Review* 785, at 813.

They suggest that international co-operation could rationalise these policies and promote competition more effectively.[235]

Concluding on the position in EC law on export cartels, it is clear that Article 81 EC by its very wording prohibits only actions that affect trade between Member States and which have their object or effect the prevention, restriction or distortion of competition within the Common Market. Pure outgoing export cartels will normally be outside Article 81 EC, but can occasionally affect trade and restrict competition within the Common Market as a result of their indirect or spill-over effects.

6. The conflict between classic integration and welfare economics in the present case law

Jurisprudence on the effect-on-trade criterion in EC law has been analysed in the preceding subsections with reference to a number of possible situations (global cartels, regional, local and export cartels). The discussion now moves on to look at whether a rational analytical framework can be established for assessing effect on trade. No such framework is immediately evident in the case law.

European Community law rests on the premise of furthering integration between Member States, and the policy is based on the assumption that competition law will serve this purpose. Even if we accept this as a starting point, we have no empirical or theoretical support whatsoever to say *to what extent* competition law furthers integration. Will integration best be served by eliminating national competition laws altogether and applying EC law even to local practices? Or is it best served if we stop at some point and allow national law to rule? The analysis here will demonstrate that there is a reluctance in jurisprudence to say what is most important here: economics, or integration. There is a general lack of awareness about what might happen if domestic practices were left to national law.

As touched upon above, the Commission has sought to clarify the concept of 'effect on trade' in its Guidelines. For cartels covering several Member States, the Commission, with reference to the case law of the Court of First Instance, concludes that they, by their very nature, are capable of affecting trade.[236] On cartels covering a single Member State the position is less clear. With reference to *Wouters*,[237] the Commission holds that horizontal cartels covering a whole of a Member State are normally capable of affecting trade.[238] This position is taken without any explicit analysis of what is normal in this context and what is not. The Commission goes on to discuss at length possible scenarios: The cartel can take actions against competitors from other Member States. It can monitor foreign competition. The cartel can induce competitors from other Member States to join,

[235] *Ibid*, at 816.
[236] *Guidelines*, above n 216, at para 64 (footnote omitted).
[237] Case C-309/99 *Wouters* [2002] ECR I-1577, at para 95.
[238] *Guidelines*, above n 216, at para 78.

or place them at a competitive disadvantage.[239] The focus seems to be very much on the actual or potential actions by the cartel against competitors from other Member States and vice versa, in other words, the foreclosure effects of cartels. This approach is confirmed when the Commission suggests that guidance on effect on trade may be derived from Article 82 EC:

> Agreements that . . . have the effect of hindering competitors from other Member States from gaining access to part of a Member State, which constitutes a substantial part of the common market, should be considered to have an appreciable effect on trade . . .[240]

The Commission's interpretations derive from *Belasco* and *Bagnasco*. In the former case, the Court of Justice upheld the Commission's finding of an effect of trade for a roofing-felt cartel in Belgium.[241] However, the Court's reasoning implied that the outcome was a derogation from a general assumption of no effect on trade for domestic cartels. The Court stated that

> the fact that a cartel relates only to the marketing of products in a single Member State is not sufficient to exclude the possibility that trade between Member States might be affected . . .[242]

It found an effect on trade as a result of the protective and defensive measures undertaken by the cartel against foreign undertakings, 'although the contested agreement relates only to the marketing of products in a single Member State'.[243]

In *Bagnasco*, the Court upheld a finding of the Commission of no effect on trade of standard bank conditions imposed by the Italian Banking Association.[244] The Court referred to the Commission's finding that the banking service in question had a very limited impact on trade between Member States and that the participation of the subsidiaries or branches of non-Italian financial establishments was limited. During the proceedings the Commission had made clear that the standard conditions were not a factor of decisive importance in the choice made by foreign banks to establish themselves in Italy. The Court noted that the Commission's findings had not been called in question in the proceedings.[245]

It seems that the Commission concluded from *Belasco* and *Bagnasco* that effect on trade should be assessed through an integration approach where the key issue is whether a national market will be sealed off by the restrictive practice. There is, however, no apparent reason why foreclosure should form the sole theoretical basis for an examination of the effect on trade of hard-core competition restrictions. The Court held in *Stichting Sigarettenindustrie* that 'it must be emphasized that the partitioning of the market is only one example of the effects on trade

[239] *Ibid*, at paras 79–82.
[240] *Ibid*, at para 92.
[241] Case 246/86 *Belasco* [1989] ECR 2117.
[242] *Ibid*, at para 33.
[243] *Ibid*, at 34–38.
[244] Joined Cases C-215/96 and C-216/96 *Bagnasco* [1999] ECR I-135, at para 51.
[245] *Ibid*.

between Member States covered by Article [81(1)] of the Treaty'.[246] A view that focuses on foreclosure disregards most of the adverse effects of cartels. European Community competition law aims at promoting competition and integration respectively.[247]

It may be recalled from chapter three that the reason why cartels are considered harmful to society is because they create welfare losses by reducing output and increasing prices. Welfare losses consist of overcharges and deadweight loss. Furthermore, cartels generate other long-term market impact: X-inefficiency and social costs. Investments decisions, cost structure and industry structure in general may be altered as a result of collusion. Naturally, supra-normal prices and inefficiency will give others an incentive to enter the market, and cartels can generally be expected to take measures to protect themselves against such competition. The question raised by *Belasco* and *Bagnasco*, as interpreted in the Commission's Guidelines, is whether the effect on trade concept should be interpreted to apply only when matters have proceeded to a stage when one can observe or foresee such actions, foreclosing a particular Member State. Must we wait until the patient is dying? Should we interpret the effect on trade concept narrowly with reference to integration between Member States? Such a view may be compared with case law prevailing 30 years ago.

In *Metro I*, the Court held that

> the requirement contained in Articles 3 and [81] of the Treaty that competition shall not be distorted implies the existence on the market of workable competition, that is to say the degree of competition necessary to ensure the observance of the basic requirements and the attainment of the objectives of the Treaty, in particular the creation of a single market achieving conditions similar to those of a domestic market.[248]

Arguably, the Court's expressions relating to 'existence . . . of workable competition' and a 'degree of competition necessary to ensure . . . conditions similar to a domestic market' mean that we cannot limit the very application of Article 81 EC to situations characterised by actual or potential foreclosure effects. We must go further and protect competition as such, that is, if we stay with the idea that integration is best achieved through competition, development towards a single market.[249] Odudu finds a shift in favour of efficiency, at the expense of integration: 'The formal completion of the internal market diminishes the extent to which integration as an ideological constituent of the conception of competition can be supported'[250] (footnote omitted). Further, Article 81 EC does not protect competition in general—the requirement of a potential effect on inter-state trade implies that a

[246] Joined Cases 240, 241, 242, 261, 262, 268 and 269/82 *Stichting Sigarettenindustrie and others v Commission* [1985] ECR 3831, at para 48.

[247] Wahl, Nils, *Konkurrensförhållanden* (Stockholm, Juristförlaget, 1994), at 60.

[248] Case 26/76 *Metro v Commission* [1977] ECR 1875, at para 20.

[249] On the latter criterion, see Opinion of A-G Trabucchi delivered on 22 October 1975 in Case 73/74 *Papier Peints v Commission* [1975] ECR 1516, at 1523: '. . . keeping competition in a healthy state in terms of the common market'.

[250] Odudu, Okeoghene, *The Boundaries of EC Competition Law—The Scope of Article 81* (Oxford, Oxford University Press, 2006), at 21.

distortion of competition *at Community level* must occur.[251] Burnley finds that the substance of the analysis is to establish whether an element of inter-State trade is involved, and concludes:

> [W]here the relevant product market (or a market directly dependent on that market) involves actual or potential interstate trade (according to the natural development of the market), there is a de facto presumption that an alleged anticompetitive conduct which takes place on that market will affect interstate trade.[252]

The strong parallels between free movement thinking and delimitations of Article 81 EC have indeed been recognised in academic writing.[253]

Recent rulings may be understood as a move back towards acceptance of two alternative grounds for effect on trade: market partitioning *or* competition distortion. In *Manfredi*, the Court holds (as before) that it must be possible to foresee with a sufficient degree of probability, on the basis of a set of objective factors of law or of fact, that there may be an influence, direct or indirect, actual or potential, on the pattern of trade between Member States.[254] In addition, it emphasises that Community law covers any agreement or any practice which is capable of affecting trade between Member States in a manner which might harm the attainment of the objectives of a single market between the Member States.[255] This applies in particular to agreements and practices which:

a) seal off national markets; or
b) affect the structure of competition within the common market.[256]

The Court has consequently opted for both alternatives: effect on trade may be found either on integration grounds, or with reference to the competitive structure within the common market. Moreover, the threshold is relatively low. Only insignificant influences on the pattern of trade are outside Article 81 EC.[257] Unfortunately, the specific guidance given by the Court to the Italian national court in the following paragraphs of *Manfredi* is inconsistent with the principles just stated: the Court falls back into a one-sided integration approach.[258] Never is the conflict between an integration approach (or, if one so wishes, a free movement approach) and a welfare approach so obvious as in *Manfredi*. The Court was unable to come to terms with its own law.

In *Asnef-Equifax*, the Court was given the opportunity to expand further on the effect on trade concept.[259] The Court had begun the analysis in *Manfredi* and

[251] Burnley, Richard, 'Interstate Trade Revisited—The Jurisdictional Criterion for Articles 81 and 82 EC' (2002) 23(5) *ECLR* 217, at 221.
[252] *Ibid.*
[253] O'Loughlin, Rosemary, 'EC Competition Rules and Free Movement Rules: An examination of the Parallels and their Furtherance by the ECJ Wouters Decision' (2003) 24(2) *ECLR* 62.
[254] Joined Cases C-295/04 to C-298/04 *Manfredi and others* [2006] ECR I-6619, at para 42.
[255] *Ibid*, at para 41.
[256] *Ibid.*
[257] *Ibid*, at para 42.
[258] *Ibid*, at paras 46–52.
[259] Case C-238/05 *Asnef-Equifax v Ausbanc* [2007] ECR I-11125.

previous cases, and proceeded to find that it is necessary to examine an arrangement in its legal and economic context to assess whether it has an appreciable effect on trade.[260] This finding was drawn from the judgment in *Almelo*.[261] In *Almelo*, a case which concerned an exclusive purchasing clause, the Court referred to *Delimitis*[262] and *Brasserie de Haecht*[263] to explain why effect on trade must be determined by an assessment it in its economic and legal context, taking account of any cumulative effect resulting from the existence of other exclusivity agreements.

The Court's reasoning may be justified in cases where the key issue is whether a practice has the effect of preventing, restricting or distorting competition, but what about the cases where the *object* is such a restraint? In other words, how far does the method hold when a court is to determine effect on trade in hard-core cartel cases? Generally, the scope for analysing cartel arrangements in their legal and economic context is limited when it comes to the substantive application of Article 81 EC.[264] This shows that the theory chosen by the Community courts (which should not even properly be labelled a theory, given its shortcomings) does not provide answers to various situations that may arise under Articles 81 and 82 EC.

B. Presenting a deterrence theory on effect on trade

Evidently, the law on effect on trade has not been developed with a view to establishing enforcement priorities. A cartel that covers a Member State with a few million citizens is placed on par with a worldwide cartel. Time and time again, the Commission is asked to enforce EC law on purely domestic practices.

In what follows, I suggest a legal theoretical framework for analysing effect on trade. This framework starts from the premise that EC competition law protects competition and integration. Integration may be understood in more than one way. A free movement-orientated approach is visible in the case law, as shown in the previous subsections. The key issue has often been whether a good (or occasionally a service) is being moved across borders, or could potentially be moved. Such a free movement philosophy leads to a situation where nearly all competition restrictions should be covered by Articles 81 and 82 EC, because there will nearly always be a good or a service that can cross a border. United States law is largely similar.

Nevertheless, there are some problems with a free movement idea of effect on trade when it comes to cartels. Restrictions on free movement are only incidental,

260 *Ibid*, at para 35.
261 Case C-393/92 *Almelo* [1994] ECR I-1477, at para 37.
262 Case C-234/89 *Delimitis* [1991] ECR I-935.
263 Case 23/67 *Brasserie de Haecht* [1967] ECR 525.
264 Case C-407/04 P *Dalmine v Commission* [2007] ECR I-829, at para 121.

and not at all central, to the policy against cartels. Given that cartels are poor replicas of monopolies, the same can be said about abuse of dominance. Certainly, cartels and dominant undertakings compartmentalise markets and raise entry barriers in order to preserve their market position. Through quotas they can artificially direct production and sales to one Member State or the other, or indeed outside the EU. Competition law, though, hinges on the welfare losses and redistribution caused by restrictions of competition. This happens to coincide to a considerable extent with the political objective of integration in the EU. Still, integration in the classic free movement fashion provides no firm theory base for determining effect on trade. This view is reinforced by the haphazard patterns created in jurisprudence. While we can understand the law reasonably well, we cannot understand why it has developed the way it has, and how to build on further when new problems arise. The law is even more inexplicable once we consider that the effect on trade concept is not connected to other important EC law aspects. We cannot realistically bargain on a case-by-case basis with requirements such as uniformity and effectiveness, since that would undermine the credibility of EC law in general, but we can have a more restrictive application of effect on trade.

We may view integration as a matter of enhancing legitimacy of the EU through better welfare created by competition law, provided of course that the law is enforced so that average compliance is ensured. If this welfare idea of integration is accepted, the central question is whether cartels of a certain size will threaten welfare to an extent that can cause problems for the EU. Empirical observations of cartel overcharges are relevant here. Apparently, local cartels generate lower average overcharges and (because of their smaller footprint) lower aggregate losses than international or large regional cartels. The competitive pressure from outside is heavier the smaller the cartel is. This in turn means that benchmarking and detection risks increase if customers can observe price differences between one Member State and the other. It is plain that small cartels are detrimental to society, but at least they cause less welfare losses than larger cartels. Even the existence of numerous small local cartels would presumably not undermine welfare more than locally. The legal–political rationale is consequently to make sure that we have efficient enforcement against the larger cartels.

Enforcement in the EC is still primarily based on public action. Does a deterrence approach, then, provide any indications as to how the authorities should use their resources? With reference to deterrence theory, the key question is to ask what is efficient. The strongest reasons for having uniform rules is to decrease costs for business to keep themselves informed about 27 legal systems in Europe, and to create better competition by eliminating to the greatest extent over- or under-deterrence resulting from disparate competition law systems in parallel operation.

The cost argument obviously applies only to business that takes place in more than one jurisdiction. Local or purely national companies will normally have to bother about only one set of rules. Cost aspects thus point in the direction of reserving application of Articles 81 and 82 EC to situations where we can expect multinational companies to be involved, or companies with a significant amount of inter-State trade.

The over-deterrence problem is present primarily when multinationals try to find a standardised business policy that can work in Europe. There is a risk that the most visible and toughest system will be the benchmark. Like cost aspects, over-deterrence problems point in the direction of reserving Articles 81 and 82 EC to situations when multinationals may be expected to be involved. Local over-deterrence resulting from overly stringent national competition laws is a problem for the competitiveness of the Member State in question and its inhabitants, but not for the Community. This type of situation should not be solved by the EC. National lobby groups can be expected to react when their members experience less freedom than their European neighbours, in which case EC law provides an obvious reference point.

Under-deterrence (for practical purposes, leaving cartels undetected or insignificantly punished), on the other hand, may arise for two reasons—slackness in the law or in its enforcement. Here we may observe that the decentralised enforcement system aims specifically at higher efficiency as a result of co-operation between Member States and the Commission. The following should be kept in mind, though: if we say that a certain category of practices does not affect trade then we have opted out of the ECN co-operation, sharing of evidence and information, joint investigations and Article 234 references to the Court of Justice for that category of infringements. There will be no supervision or policy-making by the Commission either for that category. Is that good or bad? Without doubt, the co-operation created by Regulation 1 and the ECN has increased the chances of combating serious infringements. It has, on the other hand, increased costs, given the administrative burden of co-ordination and information. Not only is the Commission burdened by all its new responsibilities (see chapter two), but Member States are burdened as well with complying with substantive law, evidentiary standards and procedure (see the present chapter and chapters five and six). We are able to be tougher, but this is at a cost.

The insight from this is that there should be an effect on trade in each and every situation when co-operation between Member States, or between a Member State and the Commission, may be expected to be useful. If, on the other hand, co-operation is unnecessary and can only be expected to increase costs, there should be no effect on trade. Opting for effect on trade sets a huge bureaucracy in motion in terms of the information obligations in Regulation 1, the obligation to follow EC law and the possibilities of Article 234 references.

Nowadays there will normally be a fall-back through *national* competition law in the Member States, laws that can be expected to be largely similar to EC competition law. Even in the absence of an effect on trade, there is no reason to expect that cartels will be lawful under national laws, or remain ignored by the national competition authorities. Further, national laws can provide possibilities for injured parties to sue for damages as well.

My model for analysing effect on trade may be summarised as follows. Thinking along the lines of free movement when considering integration leads nowhere for the purpose of theory-building on effect on trade in EC competition law, and must be discarded from start to afford room for a contemporary and flexible approach. A modernised view, where integration in competition law is a matter of improving legitimacy for the EU through welfare, leads to the tentative result that small-scale restrictions should be outside the effect on trade concept, even if cartels or other hard-core restrictions are at hand. ('Small-scale' is to be understood as infringements that do not threaten welfare throughout the EU but only locally, and consequently which do not challenge public confidence in the Union.) Cost aspects and over-deterrence concerns point in the direction of reserving application of Articles 81 and 82 EC to situations in which we may expect multinational companies to be involved, or companies with a significant amount of inter-State trade. Under-deterrence concerns, lastly, determine that there should be an effect on trade in each and every situation when co-operation between Member States, or between a Member State and the Commission, enabled by Regulation 1, may be expected to be of use. If, on the other hand, co-operation is unnecessary and can only be expected to increase costs, there should be no effect on trade.

Applying this deterrence-based theory of effect on trade, it immediately becomes obvious that the finding of an effect on trade just because a practice covers a whole Member State (this is a very strong theme in the case law) serves no purpose whatsoever. Does a national cartel or other practice affect welfare in the EU? Normally it does not, unless, for instance, there is a concentration of an industry in that Member State, or if it is a large Member State. Welfare in the Member State in question is of course affected, but this can be addressed by national law. Public confidence in the EU will not be affected either, since presumably nationals of Member States will see it as a task for their national authorities and courts to solve their national problems.

The cost aspects of law compliance may be more or less relevant depending on what sector of the economy we are discussing. For sectors in which business is local or regional, diverging national laws will not cause many problems as long as the operators can normally comply by knowing their national law. Costs of compliance will consequently differ between different lines of business, and the need for uniform rules manifests itself in trades which are international in character, or which at least have significant cross-border effects. Over-deterrence concerns follow the same line of reasoning.

Under-deterrence concerns tell us that we should insist that there is an effect on trade for situations in which, as a standardised matter, there could be a value in having access to the co-operation available through Regulation 1 and the Article 234 reference system. In the absence of such values for a given category of infringements, we should keep in mind that uniformity is a costly apparatus for the Commission and Member States alike, and we should then find no effect on trade. A solid counter-argument can be made that the effect on trade rule ought to be characterised by administrative simplicity in order to be operative, and thus encompass all trade, whether or not a good passes a border.[265] But the administrative efficiency from such an all-encompassing rule is, as explained, consumed in EC law by the administrative burdens resulting from application of EC competition law rather than national law.

V. WHEN DO ARTICLES 81 AND 82 EC APPLY TO CARTELS?

A. Parallel application

1. National competition law and Community competition law

Application of Community competition law does not exclude application of national competition law. It is settled that they can apply in parallel.[266] Nevertheless, the Court also held in *Walt Wilhelm* that parallel application of national competition law can be permitted only in so far as it does not prejudice the uniform application of the Community rules on cartels or the full effects of the measures adopted in implementation of those rules.[267] In cases of conflict there is thus a principle of primacy of Community competition law, which requires any provision of national law which contravenes a Community rule to be disapplied, regardless of whether it was adopted before or after that rule.[268]

Article 3 of Regulation 1 retains the possibility of parallel application, and adds an extra layer of compulsory application of Article 81(1) EC where national competition law applies and there is an effect on trade.

B. Undertakings

Articles 81 and 82 EC apply only to undertakings and associations of undertakings. The concept of an undertaking encompasses all entities engaged in an economic activity.[269] This applies regardless of the legal status of the entity and the way in which it is financed.[270] The activity does not have to be profit-making to classify as an undertaking[271]; it suffices that it could, at least in principle, be carried out by a private actor in order to make profits.[272] Any activity consisting of offering goods and services on a given market is an economic activity. This entails receiving

[265] Areeda and Hovenkamp, above n 55, Vol IB, § 266, at 202ff.

[266] Case 14/68 *Walt Wilhelm* [1969] ECR 1, at para 3; recently reiterated in Joined Cases C-295/04 to C-298/04 *Manfredi and others* [2006] ECR I-6619, at para 38 and in Case C-238/05 *Asnef-Equifax v Ausbanc* [2007] ECR I-11125, at para 20 (references omitted).

[267] *Walt Wilhelm*, above n 266, at para 4.

[268] Case C-198/01 *CIF* [2003] ECR I-8055, at para 48.

[269] Case C-41/90 *Höfner and Elser* [1991] ECR I-1979, at para 21.

[270] *Ibid.*

[271] Case C-67/96 *Albany* [1999] ECR I-5751, at para 85.

[272] Opinion of A-G Jacobs in Case C-218/00 *Cisal* [2002] ECR I-691, at para 38; Case C-475/99 *Ambulanz Glöckner* [2001] ECR I-8089, at para 20.

payment and assuming a financial risk.[273] The concept of an undertaking does not require that the economic entity has legal personality.[274]

While these principles have been clearly articulated, their actual application can often be difficult, given the vast variety of public service financing that has arisen in the Member States. Private initiatives and privatisations have become frequent, resulting in a grey zone where activities may be carried out on a market but also in the public sphere. It has been observed in scholarly writing that, for instance, health care and education may be economic activities as well as non-economic, depending on who is performing them.[275]

The murkiness of the application of the concept of an undertaking is acknowledged as a problem when entities (private or public) provide services that are connected to public or statutory social security or insurance systems.[276] Market imperfections and the fact that these services are mainly financed by tax money have led to difficulties with the classification of particular entities as undertakings or not for the purpose of competition law. One can easily imagine situations where, for instance, publicly-owned schools or hospitals would engage in collective boycotts, collective bargaining or collective establishment of trading conditions.[277] Whether or not this would constitute an infringement of Article 81 is partly a matter of establishing whether at least two of the participants are undertakings in the sense of Article 81, since only undertakings are subject to this Treaty provision.

Trade associations, unions and other associations will often be classified as undertakings or associations of undertakings pursuant to Articles 81 and 82 EC. The matter is addressed by the Commission and the Community courts with reference to the entities the particular association represents.[278] If those entities are undertakings then the association representing them is an association of undertakings. The Court has taken a functional approach by holding that Article 81(1) 'also applies to associations in so far as their own activities or those of the undertakings belonging to them are calculated to produce the results which it aims to suppress'.[279]

In a case concerning mobile cranes, the Court of First Instance held the certification institute SCK to be an undertaking. The Court observed that SCK was a body governed by private law which set up a certification system for crane-hire

[273] Joined Cases C-180/98 to C-184/98 *Pavel Pavlov* [2000] ECR I-6451, at paras 75–76.

[274] Joined Cases C-189/02 P, etc *Dansk Rørindustri and others v Commission* [2005] ECR I-5425, at para 113.

[275] Kleis, Maria, and Nicolaides, Phedon, 'The Concept of Undertaking in Education and Public Health Systems' (2006) 3 *European State Aid Law Quarterly* 505.

[276] Lasok QC, K P E, 'When is an Undertaking not an Undertaking' (2004) 25(7) *ECLR* 383.

[277] In 2003 a number of Swedish regional municipalities considered a collective boycott against temporary staffing services, as a way to decrease costs for health care: see *Dagens Medicin* 2003-03-11 'Bra att Landstingsförbundet inte vill ha totalbojkott mot hyrläkare'.

[278] *French beef* [2003] OJ L/209/12, at 104 ff; upheld on appeal Joined Cases T-217/03 and T-245/03 *FNCBV and others v Commission* [2006] ECR II-4987, at paras 48–60.

[279] Joined Cases 209/78–215/78 and 218/78 *Van Landewyck and others v Commission* [1980] ECR 3125, at para 88.

firms to which affiliation was optional. The SCK established independently the criteria which the certified firms must satisfy, and issued certificates only on payment of a subscription. This sufficed to demonstrate that SCK was engaged in an economic activity and should be regarded as an undertaking.[280]

In spite of the struggling jurisprudence, the concept of an undertaking as developed in the case law of the Court of Justice seems well suited to address the difficulties arising in cartel law cases, without any need for tailored solutions. It may be observed in particular that individuals can be undertakings in the sense of Articles 81 and 82 EC, if they engage in economic activities.[281] Moreover, organisations of professionals have repeatedly been held to constitute undertakings. The practice of a regulatory body of a profession constitutes an economic activity, even when legislation has entrusted the body with certain regulatory functions.[282]

1. Outside Articles 81 and 82 EC: collective agreements, authorities, social security systems and certain purchasers

The concept of an undertaking does not include organisations involved in the management of public social security systems, which fulfil an exclusively social function and perform an activity based on the principle of national solidarity which is entirely non profit-making.[283] As an outflow of this, such organisations do not act as undertakings when purchasing what they require in order to perform those tasks. In *FENIN*, the Court settled that the nature of the purchasing activity must be determined according to whether or not the subsequent use of the purchased goods amounts to an economic activity.[284] Thus the managing of the Spanish health system did not constitute an economic activity.

In *Albany*, the Court made clear that agreements concluded in the context of collective negotiations between management and labour must be regarded as falling outside the scope of Article 81(1).[285] It should be noted that the Court's decision to bring collective labour market agreements outside Article 81(1) is not based on an analysis of the concept of undertaking; instead, collective agreements are brought outside Article 81(1) because of their social policy objectives and thus 'by virtue of their nature and purpose'.[286] Whether an employee, an organisation for employees or an organisation for employers is an undertaking will be determined with reference to the principles referred to above in section V.B.. In *French beef*, French trade unions argued in vain that they did not constitute undertakings.[287]

[280] Joined Cases T-213/95 and T-18/96 *SCK and FNK v Commission* [1997] ECR II-1739, at paras 121–22.

[281] Members of the Bar were held to be undertakings when providing legal services for a fee and taking the financial risk for the activity: Case C-309/99 *Wouters* [2002] ECR I-1577, at para 48.

[282] *Wouters*, above n 281, at paras 58–59.

[283] Joined Cases C-159/91 and C-160/91 *Poucet and Pistre* [1993] ECR I-637, at para 18.

[284] Case C-205/03 P *FENIN* [2006] ECR I-6295, at para 26.

[285] Case C-67/96 *Albany* [1999] ECR I-5751, at paras 59–60.

[286] *Ibid.*

[287] *French beef* [2003] OJ L/209/12, at 104 ff; upheld on appeal Joined Cases T-217/03 and T-245/03 *FNCBV and others v Commission* [2006] ECR II-4987, at paras 48–60.

The exercise of public authority is outside the concept of an undertaking in Articles 81 and 82 EC,[288] as are activities 'connected with the exercise of the powers of a public authority'.[289] In *Eurocontrol*, the Court held that Eurocontrol, an international organisation which provided air navigation control facilities and services, was a public authority acting in the exercise of its powers and not an undertaking.[290]

The Court of First Instance made a more elaborate examination of Eurocontrol's activities in a subsequent case. It found that the activity whereby Eurocontrol provided assistance to national administrations was an economic activity and that, consequently, Eurocontrol, in the exercise of that activity, was an undertaking within the meaning of Article 82 EC.[291]

Odudu neatly summarises the case law as follows: '. . . the Court seems to recognize three activities that do not involve the offer of goods and services to the market place. These are work, consumption, and regulation.'[292]

2. *Severability between economic activities and other activities*

In *Aéroports de Paris*, the Paris airports tried to argue that their administration of publicly-owned property was not an economic activity. This argument was rejected by the Community courts. The Court of First Instance had distinguished between the Paris airports' purely administrative activities, in particular supervisory activities, and activities which were remunerated by commercial fees. Accordingly, the management of airport infrastructures and the determination of procedures and conditions for ground-handling services were not in the exercise of official powers by a public authority. These findings were upheld by the Court of Justice.[293] In the words of the Court,

> the fact that, for the exercise of part of its activities, an entity is vested with official powers does not, in itself, prevent it from being characterised as an undertaking . . .[294]

There is consequently no immunity conferred on a public entity just because it is involved with the exercise of public authority: each activity must be assessed on its own merits. This model of analysis follows from *Höfner and Elser*[294a] since it is activities that are to be assessed, not entities. Whish summarises:

> . . . a particular entity might be acting as an undertaking when carrying out certain of its functions but not acting as an undertaking when carrying out others . . .[295]

[288] Case 30/87 *Bodson* [1988] ECR 2479: Article 81 'does not apply to contracts for concessions concluded between communes acting in their capacity as public authorities and undertakings entrusted with the operation of a public service'.

[289] *Wouters*, above n 281, at para 57.

[290] Case C-364/92 *SAT Fluggesellschaft mbH v Eurocontrol* [1994] ECR I-43, at paras 28–30.

[291] Case T-155/04 *SELEX v Commission and Eurocontrol* [2006] ECR II-4797, at para 92.

[292] Odudu, above n 250, at 27.

[293] Case C-82/01 P *Aéroports de Paris v Commission* [2002] ECR I-9297, at paras 74–83.

[294] *Ibid*, at para 74.

[294a] Above n 269.

[295] Whish, above n 17, at 82.

C. Agriculture

According to Article 2(1) of Council Regulation No 26,[296] there are some limits to the application of Article 81 as regards agricultural products:

> Article [81(1)] of the Treaty shall not apply to such of the agreements, decisions and practices referred to in the preceding Article as form an integral part of a national market organisation or are necessary for attainment of the objectives set out in Article [33] of the Treaty. In particular, it shall not apply to agreements, decisions and practices of farmers, farmers' associations, or associations of such associations belonging to a single Member State which concern the production or sale of agricultural products or the use of joint facilities for the storage, treatment or processing of agricultural products, and under which there is no obligation to charge identical prices, unless the Commission finds that competition is thereby excluded or that the objectives of Article [33] of the Treaty are jeopardised.

An example of acceptable restrictions was given in *DLG*. A provision in the statutes of a co-operative purchasing association, forbidding its members to participate in other forms of organised co-operation in direct competition with it, was not caught by the prohibition in Article 81(1) of the Treaty, so long as it was restricted to what was necessary to ensure that the co-operative functioned properly and maintained its contractual power in relation to producers.[297]

However, the Commission has consistently applied Article 81 EC to cartels and other agreements in agricultural products.[298] The precise scope of Regulation 26 was tested in *French beef*. There, French farmers' federations had concluded a series of agreements in 2001 which had the object of suspending imports of beef into France and fixing a minimum price for certain categories of cattle. On appeal, the federations claimed *inter alia* that the agreements were necessary to attain the objectives of the common agricultural policy. The Court of First Instance dismissed this argument. With reference to *Milk Marque*,[299] the Court explained, first, that Community competition law applies in the agriculture sector.[300] Further, that Article 2(1), first sentence of Regulation 26 must be interpreted restrictively, and is applicable only if the measures are necessary to meet all the objectives in Article 33 EC.[301] The Court then went on to examine the criteria in Article 33 EC and found, among other things, that the agreements did not ensure

[296] Regulation No 26 applying certain rules of competition to production of and trade in agricultural products [1962] OJ 30/993.

[297] Case C-250/92 *Gøttrup-Klim ea Grovvareforeninger v Dansk Landbrugs Grovvareselskab* [1994] ECR I-5641.

[298] *European Sugar Industry* [1973] OJ L/140/17; Case 71/74 *FRUBO v Commission* [1975] ECR 563; *Cafeteros de Colombia* [1982] OJ L/360/31; *Milchförderungsfonds* [1985] OJ L/35/35; *MELDOC* [1986] OJ L/348/50; *Sugar beet* [1990] OJ L/31/32; *French beef* [2003] OJ L/209/12; *Raw Tobacco Spain*, Commission Decision of 20 October 2004; *Raw Tobacco Italy*, Commission Decision of 20 October 2005.

[299] Case C-137/00 *Milk Marque and National Farmers' Union* [2003] ECR I-7975, at paras 57–58.

[300] Joined Cases T-217/03 and T-245/03 *FNCBV, FNSEA, FNB, FNPL and JA v Commission* [2006] ECR II-4987, at para 197.

[301] *Ibid*, at para 199.

that supplies reached consumers at reasonable prices, given that import restrictions would lead to higher prices.[302] The judgment of the Court of First Instance in *French beef* has been upheld on appeal.[303]

D. State action defence

Undertakings can find themselves squeezed between requirements made by the national legislator on the one hand, and the prohibitions in Articles 81 and 82 EC on the other hand. Sometimes there are conflicting norms in so far as national law allows or encourages infringements. The Community courts have struggled over the years to strike a balance.

Consorzio Industrie Fiammeriferi, an Italian match cartel created under the auspices of national legislation, claimed before the Court that Article 81 EC applies only to anticompetitive conduct engaged in by undertakings on their own initiative. It should not apply to anticompetitive conduct required of undertakings by national legislation. Neither should it apply if national legislation creates a legal framework which itself eliminates any possibility of competitive activity on their part. In response, the Court reiterated that Article 81 EC, read in conjunction with the Member States' duty to co-operate in Article 10 EC, requires Member States not to introduce or maintain in force measures, even of a legislative or regulatory nature, which may render ineffective the competition rules.[304] Member States' obligations continue to exist, and therefore the national competition authority remains duty-bound to disapply the national measure at issue.[305]

The Court was innovative and held that until the point in time when such disapplication is made, the national law constitutes a justification which shields the undertakings concerned from all the consequences of an infringement of Article 81 EC, and does so vis-à-vis both public authorities and other economic operators.[306] From the moment when disapplication of national law becomes definitive, the undertaking is exposed to the full consequences of its actions as regards penalties.[307] If a national law merely encourages or makes it easier for undertakings to engage in autonomous anticompetitive conduct, the undertakings may incur penalties, also in respect of conduct prior to the decision to disapply national law.[308] However, the national law is then a mitigating factor for the purpose of fines.[309]

302 *Ibid*, at para 205.

303 Joined Cases C-101/07 P and C-10/07 P *Coop de France Bétail and Viande v Commission* [2008] ECR I-0000.

304 Case C-198/01 *Consorzio Industrie Fiammeriferi* [2003] ECR I-8055, at para 45.

305 *Ibid*, at para 51.

306 *Ibid*, at para 54.

307 *Ibid*, at para 55.

308 *Ibid*, at para 56.

309 *Ibid*, at para 57.

Nonetheless, one important qualification must be made. The *CIF* case relates only to national legislation which is contrary to Articles 81 and 82 EC. In the absence of binding regulatory provisions imposing anticompetitive conduct, the undertakings will be deemed to have infringes Article 81 EC unless

> it appears on the basis of objective, relevant and consistent evidence that that conduct was unilaterally imposed upon them by the national authorities through the exercise of irresistible pressure, such as, for example, the threat to adopt State measures likely to cause them to sustain substantial losses.[310]

The mere knowledge or political support of the Member State is no defence in substance for infringers. In *French beef*, the fact that the conduct was known, authorised or even encouraged by national authorities had no bearing on the applicability of Article 81 EC.[311] However, in *Lombard Club*, the action or support of an authority was considered an attenuating circumstance when fines were set.[312] In *Seamless steel tubes*, the actual cartel duration was from 1977 to 1994, although trade agreements between the Community and Japan precluded fines from 1977–90.[313]

In *DaimlerChrysler*, the Court of First Instance took into account the national legislation on agency in Germany and on car leasing in Spain to determine whether the contracts between Mercedes-Benz (subsequently DaimlerChrysler) and its dealers restricted competition. It concluded that the alleged competition restriction derived from the Spanish legislation.[314]

E. Conclusion: delimiting Article 81 EC is not deterrence-based

It follows from the analysis in the preceding subsections that delimitation of Article 81 EC is not essentially based on deterrence. While the definition of the concept of an undertaking seems more economic-orientated, jurisdiction, effect on trade, the border against welfare systems and the State action defence seem directed more towards defining the borders of competition law as regards other fields of EC law and, indeed, Member State law. Unsurprisingly, and analogous with US law,[315] EC competition law is operating in a space where it must co-exist with other Treaty provisions and other legal systems.

310 Case T-65/99 *Strintzis Lines Shipping v Commission* [2003] ECR II-5433, at para 122.

311 *FNCBV, FNSEA, FNB, FNPL and JA v Commission*, above n 300.

312 Joined Cases T-259/02 to T-264/02 and T-271/02 *Raiffeisen Zentralbank Österreich AG and others v Commission* [2006] ECR II-5169, at para 261.

313 Joined Cases C-403/04 P and C-405/04 *Sumitomo Metal Industries and Nippon Steel v Commission* [2007] ECR I-729.

314 Case T-325/01 *DaimlerChrysler AG v Commission* [2005] ECR II-3319, at para 156.

315 Areeda and Hovenkamp, above n 55, Vol I, § 112, at 129 ff.

VI. RESPONSIBILITY FOR RELATED COMPANIES: LIFTING THE CORPORATE VEIL

Infringements of Article 81 EC made by undertakings are often attributed to their parent companies, or to other undertakings within the same group. As has been explained in section III. above, the Community courts have found jurisdiction if a legal entity (often a subsidiary) within the EC has infringed Article 81 EC, by attributing its behaviour to the parent which resides outside the EU.

Calculation of fines used to be affected (under previous guidelines) by the size of the undertakings involved, so attribution of liability had an impact on the level of sanctions. Furthermore, the 'naming and shaming' factor is sometimes held to be essential from a deterrence perspective. Further down the road the attribution of liability may affect liability in damages, and jurisdiction for that purpose. It is consequently natural that enforcers will struggle to find the parent companies guilty. The parent companies will in their turn struggle to point at a subsidiary as a scapegoat. But the subsidiary may no longer be part of the same group of companies. By the time a fine is imposed a subsidiary might have been sold, or, in the extreme, liquidated or put into bankruptcy. This raises the question of succession of liability when companies or assets are sold. The Court held in *Cement* that

> the Commission may be faced with difficulties inherent in the complex structures of certain operators, with restructuring and with changes in the legal personality of undertakings . . . It is appropriate, in that context, to observe that Article [81] of the Treaty refers to the activities of undertakings. For that provision to apply, a change in the legal form and name of an undertaking does not necessarily have the effect of creating a new undertaking free of liability for the anticompetitive behaviour of its predecessor when, from an economic point of view, the two are identical . . .[316]

The importance of the case law on this subject is enhanced by the modernisation, because it might determine the allocation of cases within the ECN. Finding which competition authority is best placed to act will, at least in part, depend on how the Commission and national competition authorities perceive the circle of infringers—are they all in the same Member State, or in several? Where is the centre of gravity of the cartel? For this reason it is important to find some standardised approach.

A. Responsibility for subsidiaries and other related companies

It seems obvious that parent companies are not necessarily aware of what their subsidiaries are doing, especially in large, multinational corporations. Should liability then be based on structural ties, regardless of whether control is exercised? Or should liability be excluded, provided that the parent refrains from encouraging the

[316] *Aalborg Portland and others v Commission*, above n 41, at paras 58–59.

subsidiary to engage in cartel activity? Is attribution of liability an expression of a structural test, or a matter of what influence was actually exercised?

If the starting point is that the jurisprudence should foster the kind of behaviour that is optimal from the legal point of view, we might speculate on the following policy choice: a presumption that a parent company is liable for the cartel activities of its undertakings, allowing the parent to rebut that presumption with reference to evidence that it took active steps to prevent cartel participation by subsidiaries. Such steps could include an explicit policy that no company in the group is to engage in cartels, and the existence of corporate compliance programs to this effect. The obvious advantage of this idea is that it internalises competition law compliance within the group. A parent company can contribute to a genuine competition culture by requiring that the companies within the group comply with competition law, and allocate sufficient resources for this purpose and establish workable routines. However, the theory presents one gap. A parent company may, indirectly, foster cartel behaviour among its subsidiaries by setting goals and objectives which the subsidiaries must seek to attain, the achievement of which is difficult or nearly impossible without recourse to unlawful means. This opens up for window-dressing corporate policies about compliance with competition law, combined with business policies which pursue other objectives. It will be very difficult for a competition authority to show this.

If, conversely, a structural test is applied, the crucial question is whether there is a corporate relationship and what criteria we apply to determine this. Competition authorities will seek to prove such links, and defendants will try to demonstrate their absence. Therefore, a structural test is not based on an objective of fostering a certain type of behaviour within a group, but is implicitly based on considerations of procedural economy. Ownership and other links are relatively easy to establish or rebut, as opposed to evidence relating to behaviour. This signifies a different kind of deterrence theory, where the focus is on the need to ensure that administrative enforcement is not spent unnecessarily on lengthy proceedings.

It is plain that none of the theories will produce correct results in all situations. If parent companies know for certain that they will always be liable when their subsidiaries take part in cartels, this should act as a strong deterrent and lead those parent companies to allocate resources with a view to preventing infringements. Nevertheless, although such a policy would greatly benefit a parent company which knew that it started out fresh, free from any kind of hidden or overt cartel activity within the group, many parent companies are not in such a fortunate position. They will have to work with the possibility (or even knowledge) of a subsidiary's active cartel participation.

A structural test would induce the parent to distance itself from a subsidiary which behaved in a questionable way, rather than promoting policies and education aimed at compliance with the law. It is crucial to keep in mind that deterrence must work not only from the perspective of those who consider entering into a cartel, but also in relation to those who are already implicated and seek to make rational choices about their future behaviour.

This leads us to the question of whether there is any point at all in holding parent companies liable, save for in situations when the subsidiary has been liquidated, sold or declared bankrupt. A parent company will always be adversely affected when a fine is imposed on its subsidiary, without any need to attribute liability to the parent itself unless it actually took part in the cartel. Perhaps the enforcers wish to have a high degree of freedom in attributing liability, but unless we can come up with a sound theory for this, the end result will be excessive litigation without any countervailing benefits. As is clear from the following account of relevant cases, the Community courts have not managed to build a robust theory so far.

In one of the *Cartonboard* cases, the Court held that

> the anticompetitive conduct of an undertaking can be attributed to another undertaking where it has not decided independently upon its own conduct on the market, but carried out, in all material respects, the instructions given to it by that other undertaking, having regard in particular to the economic and legal links between them.[317]

But to which instructions is the Court referring? Instructions to engage in cartel activity, or instructions about general market conduct? In other words, is the key point the structural capacity to direct the conduct of the other undertaking, or the content of such actual direction? As will be seen, a parent company will normally be held liable even though it did not encourage its subsidiary to take part in the cartel.

In *Stora*, yet another of the *Cartonboard* cases, the Court implied (although not explicitly) that a 100 per cent shareholding might be an insufficient basis for attribution of liability. There, the decisive factors were that the parent company did not dispute that it was in a position to exert an influence on its subsidiary's commercial policy, and that it had produced no evidence to support its claim that the subsidiary was autonomous. The Court established a presumption that, for wholly-owned companies, the parent company in fact exercised a decisive influence over its subsidiary's conduct.[318]

However, the presumption of attribution of liability to parents for the actions of wholly-owned companies does not tell the whole story. In *District Heating Pipes*, the Court said that if two separate commercial companies are, under Community competition law, a single economic unit, the actions of one company may be attributed to the other, and that one can be held liable to pay the fine for the other. Seen in isolation, this statement implies that it is the structural links that matter. However, the Court also established that the mere fact that the share capital of two separate commercial companies is held by the same person or the same family is insufficient.[319] The Court upheld the findings of the Commission and the Court of First Instance about a series of elements which established that a natural person

[317] Case C-294/98 P *Metsä-Serla and Others v Commission* [2000] ECR I-10065, at para 27.

[318] Case C-286/98 P *Stora Kopparbergs Bergslags v Commission* [2000] ECR I-9925, at paras 28–29.

[319] Joined Cases C-189/02 P, etc *Dansk Rørindustri and others v Commission* [2005] ECR I-5425, at paras 116 ff.

controlled the companies concerned. So, we find ourselves effectively back to a test of actual direction of the controlled undertaking's activities.

Perhaps the approach the Court is devising in *District Heating Pipes* is that a structural test and a direction test are not mutually exclusive but complementary. One would then be able to attribute liability on the basis of either a rebuttable presumption derived from the principle of a single economic unit—that is, structural capacity to exercise control—*or* evidence that the parent or related company engaged in the business activities. This conclusion is supported by *Graphite Electrodes,* where a subsidiary claimed that fines should have been imposed on the parent company instead. The Court of First Instance rejected this claim. The fact that the subsidiary may have formed an economic unit with its parent, so that it was unable to take autonomous decisions, would have been relevant only if the Commission had used its power to impose a sanction on the parent company for the subsidiary's conduct.[320]

If the complementary approach were adopted, the Commission, or indeed national competition authority, would thus have a discretionary power to address a decision to either the subsidiary or the parent. Given the parallel power of national courts and authorities to apply Article 81 EC and the case allocation within the ECN, some flexibility may be called for. It seems that the Court has endorsed this view in *Alloy surcharges,* by holding that the 'undertaking's anticompetitive conduct *may be* attributed to its parent company' and 'where undertakings in a group participating in a cartel have acted autonomously, the Commission *may* impose a fine on each of them, using a flat-rate amount as a starting point' (emphasis added).[321]

The Court of First Instance held in *DaimlerChrysler* that 'The imputation to the parent company of its subsidiary's conduct is always dependent on a finding that management power was actually exercised'.[322] This brings us back to the question asked previously: whether the key point is the exercise of management power to encourage participation in the cartel, or the exercise of management power in general. Drawing from the Opinion of Advocate-General Mischo in *Stora,*[323] the Court of First Instance tackled this problem in *Carbonless paper:*

> Something more than the extent of the shareholding must be shown, but this may be in the form of indicia. It need not necessarily take the form of evidence of instructions given by the parent company to its subsidiary to participate in the cartel.[324]

[320] Case T-236/01 *Tokai Carbon v Commission* [2004] ECR II-1181, at para 279.

[321] Joined Cases C-65/02 P and C-73/02 P *Thyssen Krupp Stainless and others v Commission* [2005] ECR I-6773, at paras 66–67; see also A-G Léger's Opinion in the same case at para 87: '. . . the imputation of responsibility for the infringement to the parent company should merely be a straightforward option available to the Commission. Any other solution would be tantamount to depriving the Commission of the considerable degree of latitude which the legislature and the Community judicature have recognised in its favour in relation to fines'.

[322] *DaimlerChrysler v Commission,* above n 314, at para 218.

[323] Opinion of A-G Mischo in Case C-286/98 P *Stora Kopparbergs Bergslags v Commission* [2000] ECR I-9928, at paras 17–62.

[324] Joined Cases T-109/02, etc *Bolloré and others v Commission* [2007] ECR II-947, at para 132.

It is consequently possible to discard the idea that actual encouragement to participate in a cartel is a prerequisite for liability. It is still not clear, though, whether imputation of liability is in essence a structural or a behavioural test. Further, as discussed above, the two theories are mutually incompatible because they aim at different objectives (fostering responsible behaviour *or* producing procedural economy).

In *Choline chloride*, the Court of First Instance clearly opted for a structural test. Nevertheless, with what can be read as apparent distrust of its own theoretical approach, it proceeded to a detailed test of the actual direction of the subsidiary's business. The Commission had made the parent company, Akzo Nobel, jointly and severally liable with its subsidiaries. Akzo Nobel denied that it had given instructions with regard to price-fixing and market-sharing. It said that a parent company of more than 1,000 legal entities cannot materially instruct even one of its subsidiaries with regard to pricing policy or commercial behaviour. The Commission, said Akzo Nobel, had failed to prove that Akzo Nobel was aware of or directly involved in the infringement, or that it had instructed its subsidiaries to commit it. In its view the evidence did not relate to its subsidiaries' commercial policy in the strict sense. Ultimately Akzo Nobel's cause of action was based on the view that the product unit in question was largely commercially autonomous. The Commission ought to have proved that Akzo Nobel had exercised a decisive influence on the commercial policy.

The Court of First Instance began its analysis by stating that there is a simple presumption that a parent company exercises a decisive influence over the conduct of its subsidiary.[325] The parent company must rebut that presumption by adducing evidence to establish that its subsidiary was independent.[326] According to the Court of First Instance, the parent company must prove that the subsidiary does not, in essence, comply with the instructions which it issues and, as a consequence, acts autonomously on the market; in fact the parent company must show that it does not form an economic entity with the subsidiary.[327]

An examination of the decision-making procedure within the group further revealed that the parent company was involved in strategy, operational planning, investments, acquisition/divestment, restructuring plans, general policies on functional issues, finance, control/accounting, human resources, legal affairs, risk and insurance management, technology and environment, informational technology and a subject headed 'miscellaneous'.[328] The Court of First Instance concluded that the competent personnel, and in particular the management of Akzo Nobel, played a significant role in several essential aspects of the strategy of the subsidiaries in question. The parent had reserved to itself the power of final decision with respect to a range of matters that defined the subsidiaries' course of conduct on the market.[329]

325 Case T-112/05 *Akzo Nobel and Others v Commission* [2007] ECR II-5049, at para 60.
326 *Ibid.*
327 *Ibid*, at paras 61–65.
328 *Ibid*, at paras 69–79.
329 *Ibid*, at para 82.

The theoretical underpinning here is that it is the economic and legal organisational links between the parent company and its subsidiary that matter. The key is to establish that the parent exercises an influence over the subsidiary's strategy, as opposed to proof that the parent company influences its subsidiary's policy in the specific area in which the infringement occurred.[330] Still, it remains difficult to make any sense of this distinction—what is the difference between legal and organisational links on the one hand, and actual policy influence on the other hand? It would seem, on the face of it, that it is difficult to have one without the other. As for the subsidiary's 'strategy', a concept that became central in the ratio of the above case, what precisely does that mean? One can understand that day-to-day activities and detailed market conduct is too specific to be included in the concept of strategy, but even so, the explanation offered by the Court of First Instance only raises further questions.

For jointly-owned companies, it seems that a case-by-case approach is applied. In *Sodium gluconate*, Avebe claimed that it had not been aware of the cartel participation of a subsidiary which was owned jointly with Akzo. The Court of First Instance consulted the joint venture agreement between the two parent companies and held, as a matter of fact, that Avebe must have been aware of the anti-competitive practices. As a matter of principle, the unlawful conduct of the subsidiary may be imputed to the parent companies, which become liable by virtue of the fact that they in reality control its marketing policy.[331]

The matter of attribution of liability for a sister company was addressed in *Steel beams*. The Court overturned a Commission decision, which had been upheld by the Court of First Instance. Two sister companies had been held jointly and severally liable for a single fine at a level calculated by reference to their combined turnover, although the Commission demanded payment of that fine from one of the sister companies alone. The Court deemed the Commission's reasoning incomprehensible, and set it aside because of failure to state reasons.[332]

The problem was revisited in *Citric acid*, where Jungbunzlauer denied liability for the actions of its sister company. Here the Court of First Instance observed that the Commission had not relied on the presumption of attribution of liability to parents for wholly-owned subsidiaries, but had relied on the information provided by Jungbunzlauer on the decision-making structure within the group. It noted that the management responsibilities for citric acid within the group had been placed on Jungbunzlauer, and that the sister company abided by its instructions.[333] Once again, we have a case that is obscure in the sense that it does not clarify whether the decisive point was instructions to engage in cartel activities, or management instructions in general.

[330] *Ibid*, at para 83.
[331] Case T-314/01 *Avebe v Commission* [2006] ECR II-3085, at para 141.
[332] Case C-196/99 P *Siderúrgica Aristrain Madrid v Commission* [2003] ECR I-11005, at paras 91 ff.
[333] Case T-43/02 *Jungbunzlauer v Commission* [2006] ECR II-3435, at paras 125 ff.

The ambiguous nature of the Community courts' jurisprudence has been highlighted in academic writing, as has the incoherence in the Commission's practice of attributing liability.[334]

B. Change of ownership: acquirer's and seller's responsibility

Acquiring an undertaking, knowing that it participated in a cartel, is not sufficient to establish responsibility of the new parent for actions undertaken before the acquisition.[335] The liability of the new parent will arise from the date of the acquisition.[336] The Court has established that

> It falls, in principle, to the legal or natural person managing the undertaking in question when the infringement was committed to answer for that infringement, even if, when the Decision finding the infringement was adopted, another person had assumed responsibility for operating the undertaking.[337]

A new owner may nevertheless be affected since the subsidiary itself can be held liable.[338] As has been discussed above, the Commission and national competition authorities enjoy some discretion as regards the attribution of liability between parent and subsidiary. Change of ownership may consequently be addressed in three separate ways:

a) fining the subsidiary (a measure that indirectly affects its new owner); or
b) fining the former parent company; or
c) fining both the subsidiary and the former parent company.

Following a reference for a preliminary ruling relating to an Italian cigarette cartel, the Court repeated the default position that the entity that infringes the competition rules is to answer for that infringement according to the principle of personal responsibility.[339] The question referred related to manufacturing and sales activities in the tobacco sector by an undertaking owned by the Government. From a certain date those production and sales activities ceased; but they were continued by another public body, which was subsequently privatised.

The Court expanded on its previous case law by explaining that an entity that is not responsible for an infringement may nevertheless be penalised if the entity that committed the infringement has ceased to exist, either in law or economically. The rationale underlying this is that a penalty imposed on an undertaking that has

[334] Montesa, Aitor, and Givaja, Ángel, 'When Parents Pay for their Children's Wrongs: Attribution of Liability for EC Antitrust Infringements in Parent–Subsidiary Scenarios' (2006) 29(4) *World Competition* 555.

[335] Joined Cases C-65/02 P and C-73/02 P *Thyssen Krupp Stainless GmbH and ThyssenKrupp Acciai speciali Terni SpA v Commission* [2005] ECR I-6773, at para 69 with references.

[336] Case C-279/98 P *Cascades SA v Commission* [2000] ECR I-9693, at paras 77 ff.

[337] *Ibid*, at para 78.

[338] *Ibid*, at para 79.

[339] Case C-280/06 *ETI and Others* [2007] ECR I-10893, at para 39.

ceased economic activity is likely to have no deterrent effect.[340] If it were otherwise, undertakings could escape penalties by changing their identity through restructurings, sales, or other legal or organisational changes, which would jeopardise the objective of suppressing anticompetitive conduct and preventing its recurrence by means of deterrent penalties.[341] The fact that the decision to transfer the activity had been taken by the legislature in view of a privatisation was held irrelevant with reference to the effectiveness of Community law.[342] Moreover, the newly-established entity was considered to have continued the economic activities of the previous entity, and could therefore be classified as its economic successor.[343]

Further, and perhaps decisively, the Court noted that when two entities constitute one economic entity, the competition authority can choose to impose penalties on the economic successor, even though the former entity still exists.[344] This, said the Court, is particularly permissible where those entities have been subject to control by the same person within the group and have therefore carried out, in all material respects, the same commercial instructions.[345]

Consequently, if the legal entity engaged in cartel activity has ceased to exist, the new owner may exceptionally be liable for past infringements if there is otherwise no responsible legal entity.[346] This is a matter of avoiding circumvention of liability.[347] Even if the cartel participant still exists, its economic successor may be held liable if they belong to the same economic entity.[348] The logic behind this is obviously that the old entity might have been emptied of contents and thus be incapable of paying any fines or submitting to other sanctions, something that should be prevented.

C. Liability when two or more companies in the same group participate

Where undertakings that belong to the same group have participated in a cartel although acted autonomously, the Commission may impose a fine on each of them, using a flat-rate amount as a starting point.[349]

[340] *Ibid*, at para 40.
[341] *Ibid*, at para 41.
[342] *Ibid*, at para 44.
[343] *Ibid*, at para 45.
[344] *Ibid*, at para 48.
[345] *Ibid*, at para 49.
[346] This line of cases began with Case C-49/92 P *Commission v Anic Partecipazioni* [1999] ECR I-4125, at para 145; see, for a comprehensive analysis, Dyekjaer-Hansen, Karen, and Hoegh Katja, 'Succession of Liability for Competition Law Infringements with Special Reference to Due Diligence and Warranty Claims' (2003) 24(5) ECLR 203.
[347] See also *Raiffeisen Zentralbank Österreich AG and others v Commission*, above n 312, at paras 323 ff.
[348] Case C-280/06 *ETI and Others* [2007] ECR I-10893, at paras 48–49.
[349] *Thyssen Krupp Stainless and others v Commission*, above n 335, at para 67.

D. Conclusion: attribution of liability is deterrence-based

It follows that attribution of liability is essentially deterrence-based. However, there is a need to define more clearly the type of deterrence at which the policy the aimed. Efficiency, in the sense of making sure that there is always a company on which to impose fines, may have to be balanced against the efficiency concern flowing from lengthy administrative proceedings and appeals.

VII. CONCLUSIONS

The central law on cartels is deterrence-based. A deterrence policy must be nuanced to reflect the different categories of infringements. This problem has reached a more mature stage in US law, but is still being addressed in a cautious way by the Court of Justice, in the context of whether condemning certain types of infringements per se.

The law on responsibility for companies within a group is essentially deterrence-based but displays a considerable number of ambiguities.

The law which delimits application of Article 81 EC, by defining jurisdiction, what an undertaking is, what 'effect on trade' is and when a State action defence may be used, does not seem deterrence-based but is directed towards placing Article 81 EC within its context in the Treaty, and in relation to the law of Member States.

Jurisprudence on the effect on trade seems orientated more towards a free movement policy than towards economic theory.

The modernisation was based on the assumption that the law was fairly settled. The White Paper on modernisation stated that

> The result of those first years of efforts is remarkable: a comprehensive policy, abundant case law, clearly established basic principles and well-defined details . . .[350]

The present chapter has provided reasons to reconsider this statement. The law is not settled but is in need of certain development. Inconsistencies or grey zones in the law are not necessarily a problem as such, however, at least not more than in any legal system. The point of having a supreme court is precisely to provide an institution which can solve problems in principle. Nevertheless, jumping from one theory base to another, depending on which notion of Article 81 EC is being analysed, must be considered problematic. At the very least, it requires a thorough understanding of the principles involved. Moreover, there is a tendency in the judgments to avoid a discussion in principle, and instead to justify the outcomes with reference to previous case law.

[350] White Paper on Modernisation of the Rules Implementing Articles 85 and 86 of the EC Treaty [1999] OJ C/132/1, at 6.

At a time when Member States are supposed to take a more active role in EC cartel control, there is a need for the Community courts to be pedagogic in order to illustrate the rational foundations of the law to all actors.

Another observation is that the law has developed in a way very similar to US law in a number of respects. Presumably, a pooling of experiences could only be beneficial in this complex field, and the Community courts could increase legitimacy by relying more openly on analogies with US law in their judgments.

5

Legitimacy and Evidentiary Standards

THE UNIFORM AND effective application of Articles 81 and 82 EC is to be carried out not only by the Commission and Community courts, but also by and in parallel with Member State authorities and courts, under the respective procedural and institutional systems of the 27 Member States. Burden of proof and evidentiary standards are crucial for upholding notions of fairness and justice. If there is no balanced approach then the legal community, and the community at large, may begin to question the rationality of the system. Predictability, transparency and legal certainty are at the core here—while the levels of fines may differ (see chapter seven), we would not accept a system where the burden of proof and standard of proof were allowed to vary in an arbitrary way from one case to another. Burden of proof and evidentiary standards should increase the chances of substantively correct outcomes. The importance of how evidence is evaluated is increased by the dramatic fines and other possible legal consequences in competition cases. This means that legitimacy is ever-present, at least implicitly, in a discussion of burden of proof, presumptions and standard of proof.

The relation between national law and Community law on evidence in cartel cases will be addressed in this chapter, together with the legal theoretical basis for Community law on evidence. On the latter question, the Community courts try to derive support from a combination of the European Convention of Human Rights (ECHR) and deterrence concerns.

I. THE RELATION IN PRINCIPLE BETWEEN COMMUNITY LAW AND NATIONAL LAW ON EVIDENCE

A. Uniformity, effectiveness, fundamental rights and procedural autonomy—a balancing act

The Court of Justice has put great emphasis on the uniform application of EC competition law.[1] However, the supervision and enforcement of Articles 81 and 82

[1] Case 14/68 *Walt Wilhelm* [1969] ECR 1, at paras 4–6; Case 106/77 *Simmenthal* [1978] ECR 629, at para 14.

EC have been decentralised, although without any harmonisation of the Member States' national competition procedures.

According to Article 2 of Regulation 1, the burden of proof is on the party alleging that an infringement of Article 81(1) or of Article 82 EC has taken place. A party claiming the benefit of Article 81(3) EC bears the burden of proving that the conditions of that paragraph are fulfilled. Apart from this, nearly all aspects of national supervision and enforcement of Articles 81 and 82 EC are governed by national law. Annual surveys undertaken by law firms specialising in competition law illustrate the wide variety of institutional and procedural competition law enforcement systems in the Member States.[2] According to settled case law, in the absence of Community rules it is for the domestic legal system of each Member State to designate the courts and tribunals having jurisdiction, and to lay down the detailed procedural rules governing actions for safeguarding rights which individuals derive from Community law. This is provided that such rules are not less favourable than those governing similar domestic actions (the principle of equivalence) and that they do not render virtually impossible or excessively difficult the exercise of rights conferred by Community law (the principle of effectiveness).[3]

The principles just referred to seem slightly at odds with strong effectiveness cases such as *Simmenthal* and *Factortame*, where the norm is the *full effect* of EC competition law. National courts have been obliged to set aside any provision of a national legal system and any legislative, administrative or judicial practice which even *might impair* the effectiveness of Community law.[4] Are there two different standards of effectiveness? Or is there a general erosion of the principle of national procedural autonomy, where we will see even more stringent requirements to the effect that Community law must be given full effect?[5]

When ruling on State aid under the ECSC Treaty, the Court of Justice took as a starting point that it is for the national courts to interpret, as far as is possible, the provisions of national law in such a way that they can be applied in a manner which contributes to the implementation of Community law. Given that such a Community-friendly interpretation of national law was not sufficient to solve the problem, the Court then referred to the full effect of Community law to set aside national procedural provisions. Those would otherwise 'frustrate the application of Community law in so far as it would make it impossible to recover State aid that was granted in breach of Community law'.[6]

[2] Rowley QC, J William, and Low QC, Martin, *Cartel Regulation 2006* (London, Global Competition Review, 2006).

[3] Joined Cases C-222/05 to C-225/05 *van der Weerd and Others* [2007] ECR I-4233, at para 28 with references.

[4] Case 106/77 *Simmenthal* [1978] ECR 629, at paras 21–24; Case C-213/89 *Factortame and Others* [1990] ECR I-2433, at paras 19–21.

[5] Accetto, Matej, and Zleptnig, Stefan, 'The Principle of Effectiveness: Rethinking Its Role in Community Law' (2005) 11(3) *European Public Law* 375, at 396.

[6] Case C-119/05 *Lucchini Siderurgica* [2007] ECR I-6199, at paras 59 ff.

It seems that the 'full effect' doctrine is applied mainly to solve outright conflicts of law.[7] The 'other' principle of effectiveness, that national rules must not render virtually impossible or excessively difficult the exercise of rights conferred by Community law, is relied on when national procedure merely exerts an influence on the case, without actually frustrating the outcome. The further steps in the analysis of the interplay between EC competition law and national procedure will be based on such a reading of the case law. I will consequently proceed from an understanding that effectiveness must be balanced against national procedural autonomy.

How, then, is this balancing supposed to be carried out? The Court has established, when interpreting a Community regulation, an obligation for national courts to interpret their national law within the limits set by Community law, in order to achieve the result intended by the Community rule in question.[8] When ruling in a case on a Community regulation in the agricultural sector, the Court accepted reliance on the rules of evidence of national law, *provided that the effectiveness of Community law was not undermined.*[9] It is obvious that national authorities and courts must be prepared to apply their national procedure in a flexible manner, with a view to achieving the objectives laid down in Community law. Tridimas comments on the development:

> The principle of effectiveness bypasses national standards and grants Community law a quasi-constitutional status . . . It prompts national courts to view the domestic rules of remedies from a different perspective . . .[10]

Further support can be found in *Commission v Greece*, where the Court held that national law must ensure that infringements of Community law are penalised under *procedural conditions*

> which are analogous to those applicable to infringements of national law of a similar nature and importance and which, in any event, make the penalty effective, proportionate and dissuasive . . .[11]

Lenaerts and Gerard conclude that

> Member States remain, however, autonomous in designing their own set of procedural rules, which may thus be significantly different from one to the other, regarding evidentiary rules for example . . .[12]

Yet another interface between national law and Community law exists, however. It is settled that where national legislation falls within the field of application of

[7] Flynn, Leo, 'Enforcement of EC Law: Protection of Individual's Rights in National Courts' (2007) 10(2) *Europarättslig Tidskrift* 294, at 316: '. . . disapplication of national law is reserved for these situations where it was not possible to read the national law in conformity with the requirements of EC law'.

[8] Case C-60/02 *Rolex and Others* [2004] ECR I-651, at para 59.

[9] Case C-279/05 *Vonk Dairy Products* [2007] ECR I-239, at para 43.

[10] Tridimas, Takis, *The General Principles of EU Law*, 2nd edn (Oxford, OUP, Oxford EC Law Library, 2006), at 423.

[11] Case 68/88 *Commission v Greece* [1989] ECR 2925, at para 24.

[12] Lenaerts, Koen, and Gerard, Damien, 'Decentralisation of EC Competition Law Enforcement: Judges in the Frontline' (2004) 27(3) *World Competition* 313, at 337.

Community law, the national court must observe fundamental rights in order to assess the compatibility of that legislation with the fundamental rights.[13] If the cause of action in a national procedure falls within the field of EC law, fundamental rights will automatically be applicable and must be observed, as far as possible, by the national court.[14] In particular, the Court of Justice has established that in all proceedings in which sanctions, especially fines or penalty payments, may be imposed, observance of the rights of the defence is a fundamental principle of Community law, which must be complied with even if the proceedings in question are administrative in nature.[15]

It must be considered well established by now that Member States, when acting within the scope of Community law, must comply with fundamental rights.[16] Tridimas finds additional arguments in support of the application of fundamental rights when national authorities initiate proceedings in accordance with Regulation 1:

> [I]n such cases, the national authorities act within the scope of a Community law and therefore are bound to respect the general principles of law as protected by the ECJ and the Community legal order. It also derives from Article 35(1) of Regulation 1/2003 which states that the Member States must designate the competent authorities responsible for the application of Articles 81 and 82 . . . It would be incongruous and contrary to the notion of equal treatment if undertakings were subject to a lower level of procedural protection where proceedings are initiated against them by national competition authorities rather than the Commission.[17]

B. Ascertaining the facts and determining the relevance of facts of a case—a division of functions

Under Article 3 of Regulation 1, national courts are to apply Articles 81 and 82 EC when they apply national competition law and there is an effect on trade. But the Regulation affects neither national rules on the standard of proof, nor the obligations of national competition authorities and courts of the Member States to ascertain the relevant facts of a case, provided that such rules and obligations are compatible with general principles of Community law.[18]

In national antitrust litigation (as well as in Community competition procedure), law and facts will be addressed without any procedural separation between

[13] Case C-159/90 *The Society for the Protection of Unborn Children Ireland* [1991] ECR I-4685, at para 31; Case C-299/95 *Kremzow* [1997] ECR I-2629, at para 15; Case C-94/00 *Roquette Frères* [2002] ECR I-9011, at para 25.

[14] See Case C-292/97 *Karlsson and Others* [2000] ECR I-2737, at para 37: '. . . it should be remembered that the requirements flowing from the protection of fundamental rights in the Community legal order are also binding on Member States when they implement Community rules. Consequently, Member States must, as far as possible, apply those rules in accordance with those requirements'.

[15] Case C-176/99 P *ARBED v Commission* [2003] ECR I-10687, at para 19.

[16] Lenaerts, Koen, Van Nuffel, Piet, and Bray, Robert (eds), *Constitutional Law of the European Union*, 2nd edn (London, Sweet & Maxwell, 2005), at 723.

[17] Tridimas, above n 10, at 395.

[18] Regulation 1/2003, preamble, at 5.

the two. For the clarity of this analysis, though, I will reason as if law and facts were clearly distinguishable, and properly sorted and labelled in different boxes. One might then say that a national authority or court examines the evidence, makes its findings on the facts and then applies the law to the facts that have been established. The process is actually a lot more sophisticated, of course, since a thorough understanding of the law is a prerequisite for determining *what* facts it will be relevant to establish. In other words, the law determines the whole mechanism of ascertaining the relevant facts of the case.

Lenaerts and Gerard emphasise the important role of the Court of Justice in qualifying the facts reported in an order for reference with regard to Community law, and how the Court 'is definitely entitled to determine whether a specific fact is relevant or not for the determination of the antitrust offences covered by Articles 81 or 82 EC'. The authors go on to explain that rulings of the Court of Justice in competition cases are generally preceded by very fact-intensive reasoning.[19] Nevertheless, the Court of Justice has underlined, with reference to the separation of functions between the national courts and the Court of Justice, that it is not for the Court of Justice to apply Community law to the dispute before the national court, or to assess the facts in the national proceedings.[20] And it has recurrently made clear the need for precision with regard to the factual and legislative context in the area of competition, which is characterised by complex factual and legal situations.[21] It has even (although exceptionally) refused to answer references of preliminary rulings when national courts have not managed to present the cases with a minimum level of precision.[22]

The relation between Community law and national law when it comes to ascertaining the facts in cartel cases is consequently as follows. It is utterly clear that the ascertaining of facts in cases on Articles 81 and 82 EC is a matter for national authorities and courts when such cases are initiated at the national level. Nevertheless, Community law ultimately determines what facts are relevant, through the interpretations given by the Community courts.

C. Burden of proof and presumption of innocence

According to Article 2 of Regulation 1, the burden of proof in any national or Community proceeding is on the party alleging that an infringement of Article 81(1) or Article 82 EC has taken place, while a party claiming the benefit of Article 81(3) EC bears the burden of proving that the conditions of that paragraph are fulfilled. This piece of legislation codifies the case law on burden of proof[23] and the

[19] Lenaerts and Gerard, above n 12, at 339.

[20] Case C-198/01 *CIF* [2003] ECR I-8055, at para 62.

[21] See especially Case C-238/05 *Asnef-Equifax v Ausbanc* [2007] ECR I-11125, at para 23.

[22] Order of the Court in Joined Cases C-438/03, C-439/03, C-509/03 and C-2/04 *Cannito* [2004] ECR I-1605.

[23] Case C-185/95 P *Baustahlgewebe v Commission* [1998] ECR I-8417, at para 58.

presumption of innocence derived from the case law of the European Court of Human Rights.[24] The burden of proof for showing that Article 81(3) EC applied was also settled prior to the entry into force of Regulation 1.[25]

The relation between Community law and national law is thus clear when it comes to the burden of proof in competition law cases, since the matter is regulated in the directly applicable Regulation 1. If cases were to arise concerning activities taking place before the entry into force of Regulation 1, the general principles of Community law on burden of proof and presumption of innocence would apply where there was an effect on trade.

What precisely, though, is the meaning of the concept 'burden of proof'; in other words, where does one draw the line as against the 'standard of proof'? According to the Court of First Instance, the burden of proof extends to a duty to establish that an undertaking acted as ringleader or instigator of the cartel.[26] It cannot be presumed that market leaders are ringleaders.[27] It is necessary to distinguish between the concept of leader in and that of instigator of an infringement, and to carry out two separate analyses to check whether the applicant was one or the other.[28] Similarly, the Commission has the burden of proof as regards the duration of a cartel.[29]

The reasoning above suggests that it is not self-evident what should be included in 'burden of proof 'and what is a matter regarding 'standard of proof'. This will be discussed further below.

1. Opt-out principle and presumption of pursuant market behaviour—the nature of the rules created by the Court of Justice

As described in chapter four, the Community courts have devised several rules for establishing liability in competition law cases, including the opt-out principle for cartel meetings and the presumption of pursuant market behaviour in cases of collusion. The theoretical basis of these rules will be examined next. Are they interpretations of Article 81(1) EC, general principles of Community law, or just pragmatic ways of solving the cases before the Court? Furthermore, the Court of Justice has not gone to any great lengths to distinguish between the burden of proof and the standard of proof. Why would such a distinction be important, then?

According to its 5th preamble, Regulation 1 affects neither national rules on the standard of proof, nor the obligations of national competition authorities and courts of the Member States to ascertain the relevant facts of a case, provided that such rules and obligations are compatible with general principles of Community

[24] Case C-199/92 P *Hüls v Commission* [1999] ECR I-4287, at para 150.

[25] Case T-65/98 *Van den Bergh Foods v Commission* [2003] ECR II-4653, at para 136 with references.

[26] Case T-15/02 *BASF v Commission* [2006] ECR II-497, at para 294.

[27] *Ibid*, at para 298.

[28] *Ibid*, at para 316.

[29] Joined Cases T-25/95, etc *Cimenteries and others v Commission* [2000] ECR II-491, at paras 4027, 2802 and 4109; Case T-59/99 *Ventouris v Commission* [2003] ECR II-5257, at para 181.

law. In essence, the burden of proof is subject to directly applicable secondary legislation, while there is still a discretionary power of national authorities and courts as regards the ascertaining of facts and the standard of proof.

So what is the nature of these presumptions? Looking at the question without prejudice, it could be that the presumptions developed by the Court of Justice are interpretations of Article 81(1) of the Treaty. Or they could be interpretations of the concept of 'burden of proof', now regulated in Article 2 of Regulation 1. It is also possible that they are general principles of Community law flowing from the rights of the defence. In the extreme, they could be nothing but outflows of the Community competition procedure under Regulation 17, Regulation 1 and the procedural rules of the Community courts.

The first of the prevalent rules is the opt-out principle: an undertaking is considered liable for an infringement if it has participated at meetings where anti-competitive decisions were adopted. It must be considered a conclusive presumption—if an undertaking has taken part in a meeting where anti-competitive decisions were adopted, it is liable for an infringement unless it *actually* indicated to its competitors that it was participating in those meetings in a spirit that was different from theirs, *or* it reported the meeting to the authorities soon after it occurred.[30] The undertaking itself must prove that it took the step necessary to free itself from the presumption of cartel participation. In *Hüls* this was explicitly connected to the burden of proof.[31] The reference to the Commission's burden of proof was equally clear in *Anic*,[32] and in *Montecatini* it was further connected to the presumption of innocence.[33]

The references to the burden of proof in the cases above mean that through Article 2 of Regulation 1, which regulates burden of proof, the opt-out principle applies in national Article 81 procedures in the Member States, whether public enforcement or private litigation. It is also a fundamental principle of Community law, given the references in *Montecatini* to the presumption of innocence,[34] which means that, irrespective of Regulation 1, it applies in national public enforcement cases on Article 81 EC.

Jurisprudence is not always characterised by the greatest lucidity. For instance, in *Volkswagen*, the Court of Justice explicitly connected its interpretation of the concept of agreement in Article 81(1) EC to the burden of proof and the principle of presumption of innocence, demonstrating an unwillingness to differentiate clearly between the concepts of agreement and burden of proof.[35]

The second presumption applied frequently in cartel cases is that of pursuant market behaviour once collusion has been established. This is a rebuttable presumption, according to the explicit wording of the Court. Further, the strength of

[30] Joined Cases C-204/00 P, etc *Aalborg Portland and others v Commission* [2004] ECR I-123, at para 84.
[31] *Hüls v Commission*, above n 24, at para 155.
[32] Case C-49/92 P *Commission v Anic Partecipazioni* [1999] ECR I-4125, at paras 95–96.
[33] Case C-235/92 *Montecatini v Commission* [1999] ECR I-4539, at para 181.
[34] *Ibid.*
[35] Case C-74/04 *Commission v Volkswagen* [2006] ECR I-6585, at paras 37–38.

the presumption can vary, depending on how durable and institutionalised the cartel has been.[36] In *Hüls*, this finding was connected to the burden of proof and the presumption of innocence.[37] The nature of the rebuttable presumption of pursuant market behaviour, once collusion is shown, is thus an interpretation of the burden of proof and a fundamental principle of Community law. As an interpretation of the concept of burden of proof, it applies in national Article 81 procedures in the Member States, whether public enforcement or private litigation; and as a fundamental principle of Community law, it applies in national public enforcement cases on Article 81 EC irrespective of Article 2 of Regulation 1 (a matter of importance for infringements that took place prior to the entry into force of Regulation 1). It must be said, however, that the Court of First Instance, when trying the *Carbonless paper* cartel, cross-read paragraphs 117 and 121 of *Anic*, and implicitly made the rebuttable presumption an interpretation of the concept of a concerted practice in Article 81(1) EC.[38] Identical reasoning was applied in *Zinc Phosphate*.[39] If the presumption is indeed a Treaty interpretation, the result is the same—it applies in all national Article 81 cases, regardless of whether they involve public enforcement or private litigation.

It is evident that the Court has not developed these rules in the context of national supervision and enforcement, but nevertheless the principles must be tested in relation to decentralisation.

Another contribution is that a parent company must rebut a presumption of responsibility for the actions of its wholly-owned subsidiary.[40] Perhaps we have not seen the last presumption yet.

Relying on the case law just mentioned makes the reasoning very legalistic, and this approach should be balanced against reasoning based on the purpose of Regulation 1. As was discussed in chapter two, Regulation 1 is based on considerations of uniformity and effectiveness. The problems addressed by the presumptions are not of a marginal nature but go to the core of most cartel cases. Arguments along the lines, 'certainly we took part in the meeting, but we only listened passively to the price-fixing decision while making mental reservations' and 'we certainly exchanged information, but we did not allow this to affect our decision-making process' can be expected to occur in the vast majority of national Article 81 cartel cases. It is difficult to see how uniformity and effectiveness can be achieved other than by making the presumptions developed by the Court of Justice applicable in national procedure—nothing is really gained by departing from these solid pieces of case law.

[36] *Commission v Anic Partecipazioni*, above n 32, at para 121.

[37] *Hüls v Commission*, above n 24, at paras 167–68.

[38] Joined Cases T-109/02, etc *Bolloré SA and others v Commission* [2007] ECR II-947, at para 291.

[39] Case T-62/02 *Union Pigments v Commission* [2005] ECR II-5057, at para 39.

[40] Case T-325/01 *DaimlerChrysler v Commission* [2005] ECR II-3319, at paras 218–20.

D. Standard of proof

The precise relationship between Community law and national law as regards the standard of proof in cartel cases is not yet settled. Of central importance here is whether national authorities and courts can set the standard of proof in accordance with their national law, or whether this is a matter for Community law. In the former case one can expect different standards in the (now) 27 Member States. If the standard of proof is to be determined by Community law, a unitary standard may be envisaged, ranging from manifest error, through to a balance of probabilities test (51 per cent), to a standard closer to that in criminal proceedings, in effect proof beyond reasonable doubt.[41]

Standard of proof is not mentioned in Articles 81 or 82 EC, nor in the provisions of Regulation 1. As explained, Regulation 1 does not affect national rules on the standard of proof, provided that such rules and obligations are compatible with general principles of Community law.[42] In the absence of Community rules, procedure is governed by the principle of national procedural autonomy, although national rules must not be less favourable than those governing similar domestic actions (the principle of equivalence) and must not render virtually impossible or excessively difficult the exercise of rights conferred by Community law (the principle of effectiveness).[43] Kerse and Khan consider this jurisprudence exhaustive: 'There is no Community rule and therefore national law applies subject to the general principles of effectiveness and non-discrimination'.[44] Collins advances a similar view: '. . . national courts remain free to apply their own rules of evidence and proof as before, notwithstanding Article 2'.[45] However, I must disagree. It is settled that where national legislation falls within the field of application of Community law, the national court must observe fundamental rights in order to assess the compatibility of that legislation with the fundamental rights.[46] If standard of proof is a fundamental principle of Community law, for instance a right of the defence, it will apply in national public enforcement of Articles 81 and 82 EC, and could in principle modify national procedure. In the *Steel Beams* cases, the Court of Justice held that in all proceedings in which sanctions, especially fines or penalty payments, may be imposed, observance of the rights of the defence is a

[41] Bailey, David, 'Standard of Proof in EC Merger Proceedings: A Common Law Perspective' (2003) 40(4) *CML Rev* 845, at 851.

[42] Regulation 1, preamble, at 5.

[43] Joined Cases C-222/05 to C-225/05 *van der Weerd and Others* [2007] ECR I-4233, at para 28 with references.

[44] Kerse, C S, and Khan, N, *EC Antitrust Procedure*, 5th edn (London, Sweet & Maxwell, 2005), at 300.

[45] Collins, Michael M, 'The Burden and Standard of Proof in Competition Litigation and Problems of Judicial Evaluation' (2004) *ERA Forum Scripta Juris Europaei* No 1, 66, at 69.

[46] Case C-159/90 *The Society for the Protection of Unborn Children Ireland Ltd v Stephen Grogan and others* [1991] ECR I-4685; Case C-299/95 *Kremzow* [1997] ECR I-2629, at para 15; Case C-94/00 *Roquette Frères* [2002] ECR I-9011, at para 25.

fundamental principle of Community law, which must be complied with even if the proceedings in question are administrative proceedings.[47]

Since the requirement to protect fundamental rights is binding on Member States when they apply Community law, it will be binding not only for national courts but also for all organs of the State, including national competition authorities.[48] National competition authorities (as well as courts and all organs of the State) are ultimately obliged to disapply national laws which contravene Community law, which entails an obligation to take all appropriate measures to enable Community law to be applied in full.[49] Private litigation remains unaffected, however.[50]

The following analysis of the relevant case law aims at extracting the nature of the standard of proof.

The Court of Justice has been reluctant to make any clear delineation between burden of proof and standard of proof. In *Hüls*, the presumption of pursuant market behaviour, once collusion has been established, was connected to the burden of proof, to the requisite legal standard and the presumption of innocence.[51] In *Cement*, the Court held undertakings liable when they had participated in cartel meetings, with reference to the Commission's obligation to 'prove *to the requisite standard* that the undertaking participated in the cartel' (emphasis added).[52] This in turn goes back to *Baustahlgewebe*, where the burden of proof and standard of proof seem intertwined, as

> it is incumbent on the Commission to prove the infringements found by it and to adduce evidence capable of demonstrating to the requisite legal standard the existence of the circumstances constituting an infringement . . .[53]

Was the Court referring to the burden of proof, the standard of proof, or both? From a linguistic perspective, both the burden and standard of proof are included in the wording of the judgments in *Cement* and *Baustahlgewebe*.

The Court of First Instance recognised the standard of proof as part of the principle of legal certainty in *Dunlop Slazenger*,[54] and went on to develop its view in *Seamless steel tubes*. There, it reasoned extensively and connected the standard of proof to the presumption of innocence, a fundamental right. More precisely, it held that where there is doubt as to the existence of an infringement, the benefit of that doubt must be given to the undertakings accused of the infringement, taking into account the presumption of innocence resulting in particular from Article 6(2) of the ECHR, a fundamental right protected in the Community legal order.[55]

[47] Case C-176/99 P *ARBED v Commission* [2003] ECR I-10687, at para 19; Case C-194/99 P *Thyssen Stahl v Commission* [2003] ECR I-10821, at para 30.
[48] *Roquette Frères*, above n 46, at para 28.
[49] Case C-198/01 *CIF* [2003] ECR I-8055, at para 49.
[50] Case C-60/92 *Otto* [1993] ECR I-5683, at para 17.
[51] *Hüls v Commission*, above n 24, at paras 167–68.
[52] *Aalborg Portland and others v Commission*, above n 30, at para 81 with references.
[53] Case C-185/95 P *Baustahlgewebe v Commission* [1998] ECR I-8417, at para 58.
[54] Case T-43/92 *Dunlop Slazenger* [1994] ECR II-441, at para 79.
[55] Case T-67/00 *JFE Engineering v Commission* [2004] ECR II-2501, at paras 177–78.

The Court of First Instance went on to explain that the Commission must produce sufficiently precise and consistent evidence to support the firm conviction that the alleged infringement took place. It emphasised that it is not necessary for every item of evidence produced by the Commission to satisfy those criteria in relation to every aspect of the infringement; it is sufficient if the body of evidence relied on by the institution, viewed as a whole, meets that requirement.[56] On appeal the Court of Justice upheld the findings of the Court of First Instance.[57]

Looking at the ruling from a legitimacy perspective, it seems that the Community courts are referring to the ECHR as justification. However, we can only guess how the European Court of Human Rights would assess a complex competition law case—it is unlikely that it will ever have the occasion to do so in practice. A line of cases where the standard of proof is developed should properly be labelled as an outright development of Community law, rather than as a replica of the law created under the ECHR.

In conclusion, standard of proof seems to be a part of, or possibly a corollary to, the presumption of innocence, which is a fundamental right. In addition, it is part of the principle of legal certainty. As explained, fundamental rights are binding for Member States, and the Member States must, as far as possible, apply national rules in accordance with the requirements flowing from the protection of fundamental rights in the Community legal order. This is not to say that national procedural law must be set aside altogether, but it may have to be modified. To my mind, this mean that the standard of proof developed by the Community courts applies *as a minimum standard* in national Article 81 and 82 EC cases. Given that the standard of proof is a corollary to the presumption of innocence, a national authority or court must, in public enforcement cases, require at least the same standard of proof as in settled Community jurisprudence. In addition, it is possible that undertakings may be able to rely directly on the protection offered by the ECHR, provided the Member State has acceded to the Convention, but this question will not be addressed here.

The idea that there is no uniform standard of proof seems prevalent. For instance, we can look at what the American Bar Association (ABA) said when commenting on the modernisation package. The ABA underlined that

> Consistent application of EC competition law is also a question of consistent procedural requirements and means to satisfy the burden of proof . . . relevant for NCAs and national courts reviewing NCA decisions . . . this is subject to non-harmonized national law of the Member States and outside the competence of the European Union to regulate, in contrast to the burden of proof itself, which is dealt with by the draft notices.[58]

[56] *Ibid*, at paras 179–80.

[57] Joined Cases C-403/04 P and C-405/04 P *Sumitomo Metal Industries and others v Commission* [2007] ECR I-729, at paras 45, 52.

[58] Joint comments of the American Bar Association's Section of Antitrust Law and Section of International Law and Practice on Draft European Commission Notice and Draft Regulation Implementing Regulation 1/2003, December 2003, at 4, available at http://www.abanet.org/antitrust/at-comments/2003/12-03/ecmodernization.html.

The ABA considered that in proceedings in national courts, national procedural law determined what was sufficient to demonstrate an allegation. The ABA stated that it would have been preferable if Regulation 1 had directly established a harmonised degree of proof for all proceedings involving the application of Article 81 EC.[59]

It has been demonstrated here that the ABA was working from incorrect assumptions on the mechanisms of EC competition law on evidence. Nevertheless, there is agreement in so far as the statement demonstrates the need for a common standard of proof, and how the crux of the question is at which level it should be regulated—Community law or national law.

Whether the standard set by the Community courts is also a maximum level is quite another matter. The protection a party can claim under fundamental rights in this regard is a minimum standard of proof which the competition authority must bring forward in order to win or defend its case. But employment of the standard of proof in Community cartel cases as a maximum level (national authorities and court not being allowed to apply a higher standard of proof) cannot reasonably be derived from fundamental rights which in this case derive from the presumption of innocence. According to Wils, 'National law could of course provide for wider procedural rights and guarantees than those flowing from the protection of fundamental rights in the Community legal order'.[60] Higher standards of proof can consequently be envisaged. Still, it seems possible that a common maximum level of standard of proof in Article 81 cartel cases may be derived from the principles of uniformity and effectiveness. Phrased differently, the question is whether Community law would intervene if a Member State applied a very high standard of proof, far exceeding that in Community jurisprudence, with the result that alleged cartel activities were seldom proved. In *San Giorgio*, the Court held that any requirement of proof which has the effect of making it virtually impossible or excessively difficult to secure the repayment of charges levied contrary to Community law would be incompatible with Community law. The Court made further specific references to presumptions or rules of evidence.[61] Apart from such extreme situations, however, it appears that the Member States enjoy a margin of discretion when it comes to standard of proof in cartel cases, provided the minimum level set by the Community courts is complied with.

E. Standard of legal review

The Community courts generally carry out a rather detailed review of the Commission's findings of fact, and a more limited legal review of any complex

[59] *Ibid*, at 18.

[60] Wils, Wouter P J, 'Powers of Investigation and Procedural Rights and Guarantees in EU Antitrust Enforcement: The Interplay between European and National Legislation and Case-law' (2006) 29(1) *World Competition* 3, at 22.

[61] Case 199/82 *San Giorgio* [1983] ECR 3595, at para 14.

economic assessments relied on by the Commission. This difference, often referred to in academic writing,[62] is, however, of less importance in cartel cases as a result of the low significance of economic analysis in these cases. For pragmatic reasons, I believe it will be superfluous in cartel law to analyse whether national procedural law on the standard of legal review will be modified by way of analogy from the Commission's margin of discretion on economic assessments and the Community courts' review of those assessments. As stated by Judge Legal of the Court of First Instance, 'it appears . . . that standards of proof and standards of review are not two separate notions but two aspects of a single control system'.[63]

Looking at the issue in principle, it was established in *Upjohn* that, when there are complex assessments, Community law does not require the Member States to establish a procedure for judicial review of national decisions which involves a more extensive review than that carried out by the Court of Justice in similar cases.[64] Nevertheless, any national procedure for judicial review of decisions of national authorities must enable the court or tribunal effectively to apply the relevant principles and rules of Community law when reviewing their legality.[65] Tridimas finds that the judgment 'promotes the internalization of Community law at the expense of uniformity . . . it opts for convergence from below rather than convergence from above'.[66] Going back to the rather intensive review of facts exercised by the Court of First Instance, it was explained in the previous section that the standard of proof is a minimum standard in national proceedings.

F. Preliminary conclusions

In the first part of this chapter I have taken the following views on the relation between Community law and national law on evidence in cartel cases:

a) The ascertaining of facts in cases on Articles 81 and 82 EC is a matter for national authorities and courts when such cases are initiated at the national level. But Community law ultimately determines what facts are relevant, through the interpretations given by the Community courts.
b) According to Article 2 of Regulation 1, the burden of proof in any national or Community proceeding is on the party alleging that an infringement of Article 81(1) or Article 82 EC has taken place. An analysis of the case law demonstrates that the presumptions developed by the Court of Justice in Article 81(1) EC cases, namely the opt-out principle for cartel meetings and the presumption of

[62] Prete, Luca, and Nucara, Allessandro, 'Standard of Proof and Scope of Judicial Review in EC Merger Cases; Everything Clear after Tetra Laval' (2005) 26(12) *ECLR* 692, at 696–97.

[63] Legal, Hubert, 'Standards of Proof and Standards of Judicial Review in EU Competition Cases' in Hawk (ed), *International Antitrust Law & Policy: Fordham Corporate Law* (New York, Juris Publishing, 2005) Ch 5, at 113.

[64] Case C-120/97 *Upjohn* [1999] ECR I-223, at para 35.

[65] *Ibid*, at para 36.

[66] Tridimas, above n 10, at 449.

pursuant market behaviour once collusion is shown, are interpretations of the concept of burden of proof, now regulated in Article 2 of Regulation 1. The direct applicability of the Regulation means that the presumptions apply in national Article 81 procedures, in both public enforcement and private litigation. Furthermore, those presumptions constitute general principles of Community law and form part of the rights of the defence.

c) Lastly, the standard of proof developed by the Community Courts is *a minimum standard* in national Article 81 or 82 EC cases, given that it derives from the presumption of innocence, a fundamental principle of Community law. However, one cannot presently discern a Community law maximum standard of proof. National authorities and courts have the discretion to apply higher standards of proof, provided such standards do not render virtually impossible or excessively difficult the exercise of Community law.

II. THE EMERGENCE OF A COMMUNITY LAW ON EVIDENCE IN CARTEL CASES

As discussed in part I of this chapter, there is a Community law on evidence in relation to Articles 81 and 82 of the Treaty. The content of the standard of proof in cartel cases developed by the Community courts will be examined further in this part of the chapter. This is an attempt to fill the gap in what has (for good reasons) been described as 'surprisingly little comment on the development of CFI's review of evidence in competition cases'.[67]

Admittedly, it is not easy to determine if a specific case, or line of cases, represents the minimum standard just mentioned. Further references to the Court of Justice will be needed to define more precisely the borders. Regardless, it seems that a thorough understanding of Community jurisprudence will be useful for national authorities and courts as a point of reference and source of analogy. That is because the Community courts have tried a significant number of cartel cases since the late 1960s, and have gained considerable experience in the field.

A. Principles—a discussion

It is submitted here that determination of the standard of proof in antitrust public enforcement cases must in principle be based on three different interests, which must be balanced and reconciled. The first (and perhaps, in EC law, the predominant) interest involves the avoidance of insufficient amounts of proof being found enough to hold companies liable for infringements of Articles 81 and 82 EC. This interest derives from the now accepted view that competition law sanctions are of a penal nature and that the principles enshrined in the ECHR apply to the

[67] Harding, Christopher, and Gibbs, Alun, 'Why go to court in Europe? An analysis of cartel appeals 1995–2004' (2005) 30(3) *EL Rev* 349, at 351.

proceedings. Adequate standards of proof are necessary to ensure correct outcomes and uphold confidence in the system.

The second interest, on the other hand, relates to ensuring procedural economy and, ultimately, enforcement efficiency. If the standard of proof is set at a level which corresponds to the highest requirements in penal law, it will be very difficult to prove infringements, or at least to prove them to their full extent. Furthermore, paperwork generated in each case will be voluminous. Authorities and courts alike will risk being clogged up, and the system will require massive resources to produce more than the occasional, symbolic decision.[68] To avoid those effects, we may have to live with lower standards of proof. On the other hand, we must preserve some standards (if nothing else) to keep litigants out of court; indeed, the interest of conserving judicial resources has been an element in the development in US law of summary judgment in conspiracy cases.[69]

Allowing authorities and private parties to bring proceedings on the basis of purely circumstantial evidence will overload the courts just as much as extremely high standards of proof. A solid argument can be made that procedural economy (and ultimately enforcement efficiency) is best served not by high or low standards of proof, but by adequate standards. A low standard of proof will risk being over-deterrent, in so far as it can induce businesses to avoid even actions that are pro-competitive.

The concerns regarding over-deterrence have been expressed in US law, where the interplay between business behaviour and regulation has been the subject of mature discussion.[70] The significance of the aim to avoid over-deterrence varies, however, depending on what type of infringement is suspected. It carries more weight in cases where the allegation is joint refusal to deal or joint predatory pricing, for instance, because we might want to conserve the unilateral right of traders to refuse to deal with problematic customers, or to lower their prices in response to competition. Over-deterrence concerns carry less weight in litigation on outright horizontal price-fixing or market sharing.[71]

Fears about over-deterrence illustrate the connection between standard of proof and substantive law. Over- or under-inclusiveness in the admission and evaluation of evidence will erode substantive law. For instance, mere parallel conduct (intelligent market behaviour) is lawful in EC law, but if evidence on market structure and parallel behaviour is used to *infer* the existence of an agreement even in the absence of evidence such as communication between the parties, the end result will be a *de facto* prohibition against mere parallel behaviour. In summary, a common view on standard of proof is necessary if we want the law to be the same in the EU.

[68] On the need to consider the total time spent by a competition authority on each case see Motta, Massimo, 'On Cartel Deterrence and Fines in the European Union' (2008) 29(4) *ECLR* 209.

[69] Levin, Nickolai G, 'The Nomos and Narrative of Matsushita' 73 *Fordham Law Review* 1627, at 1629.

[70] *Ibid*, at 1632, 1637, 1688 ff.

[71] *Ibid*, at 1690–91.

B. The standard of proof and general methodology for evaluating evidence in cartel cases

On standard of proof, Louveaux and Gilbert found in 2005 that 'European jurisprudence offers little concrete guidance on this issue'.[72] Although there is some merit in this view, the general understanding seems to be that the Community courts have come a rather long way in formulating what, as a matter of principle, is needed to prove cartel activities.[73] Much jurisprudence is of recent date, however. I have chosen to provide accounts of cases which seem significant in the sense that the reasoning is both transparent and accessible.

1. Evidence taken together

Of central importance for cartel cases is the guidance provided in *Cement*, where the Court held that evidence will normally be only fragmentary and sparse, so that it is often necessary to reconstitute certain details by deduction. In most cases, the existence of an anticompetitive practice or agreement must be inferred from a number of coincidences and indicia which, *taken together*, may, in the absence of another plausible explanation, constitute evidence.[74] These considerations correspond to what I have referred to above as the combined interest of procedural economy and enforcement efficiency. By accepting the difficulties in securing evidence, the Court ensures that cartels are at least detected and penalised.

The Community courts have acknowledged the difficulties in proving cartel activities, given that several years might have elapsed since the infringement took place and that a number of the undertakings might have decided not to actively co-operate in the investigation. While re-stating the Commission's burden of proof, they have considered that it would be excessive also to require the Commission to produce evidence of the specific mechanism of an illegal market-sharing agreement.[75] The Commission is required to produce sufficiently precise and consistent evidence to support the firm conviction that the alleged infringement took place, but it is not necessary for *every item* of evidence to satisfy those criteria in relation to every aspect of the infringement. It is enough if the body of evidence relied on by the institution, *viewed as a whole*, meets that requirement.[76]

[72] Louveaux, Bertrand and Gilbert, Paul, 'The Standard of Proof under the Competition Act' (2005) 26(3) *ECLR* 173, at 173.

[73] On standard of proof in cartel cases, see generally Arbault, Francois, and Sakkers, Ewoud, 'Cartels' in Faull, Jonathan, and Nikpay, Ali (eds), *The EC Law of Competition* (Oxford, Oxford University Press, 2007), at 8.508, 8.522–8.552; and Siragusa, Mario (ed), *EU Competition Law—Volume III Cartel Law* (Leuven, Claeys & Casteels, 2006), at 649–52.

[74] *Aalborg Portland and others v Commission*, above n 30, at paras 56–57.

[75] *JFE Engineering v Commission*, above n 55, at para 203, upheld on appeal in *Sumitomo Metal Industries and others v Commission*, above n 57, at paras 50–51.

[76] *Sumitomo*, above n 75, at paras 42, 45, 52.

The method of viewing the bulk of evidence as a whole rather than as separate pieces is well established by now,[77] and has been explicitly endorsed by the Court of Justice.[78] This is consistent with the experiences from the OECD's Global Forum on Competition, where it was concluded that a holistic approach is much preferable to a requirement that each item of evidence be linked directly to a specific agreement.[79] It also seems to correspond to US law, where, under the Sherman Act, 'plaintiffs should be given full benefit of their proof without tightly compartmentalizing various factual components and wiping slate clean after scrutiny of each'.[80]

Of central importance, furthermore, is the principle of the unfettered evaluation of evidence which, according to the Court of Justice, prevails in Community law.[81]

2. Direct versus indirect evidence

One single document may be sufficient to establish the existence of a cartel, as illustrated by the shipping cartel case *FETTCA*. There, minutes of one single meeting of the participating undertakings became decisive of the outcome. The Court of First Instance noted that the undertakings had not challenged the fact that there was a meeting, nor the content and wording of the minutes. The wording of the minutes left little to the imagination; it set out a decision that all parties should adopt a certain pricing policy.[82] As a matter of principle, however, the Court has held that the probative value of documents must be evaluated in the light of all the circumstances of the case.[83]

Similarly, a single statement from a person with direct knowledge of the facts may be decisive, provided the total body of evidence is sufficient to confirm that statement.[84] But this must not be over-construed: when one undertaking admits and other undertakings dispute cartel participation, the admission cannot be regarded as constituting adequate proof of an infringement committed by the other undertakings unless supported by other evidence.[85]

In *PVC II*, the Commission had based its finding of a quota system on a combination of documents, and on appeal the finding was confirmed by the Court of

[77] See especially *Bolloré and others v Commission*, above n 38, at paras 155, 238.

[78] Case C-105/04 P *Nederlandse Federatieve Vereniging voor de Groothandel op Elektrotechnisch Gebied v Commission* [2006] ECR I-8725, at para 96.

[79] OECD Global Forum on Competition, *Prosecuting Cartels without Direct Evidence of Agreement* (OECD, 2006, DAF/COMP/GF/(2006)7), at 9.

[80] *Continental Ore Co v Union Carbide & Carbon Corp* 370 US 690 (1962).

[81] Case C-407/04 P *Dalmine v Commission* [2007] ECR I-829, at paras 62–63.

[82] Case T-213/00 *CMA CGM and others v Commission* [2003] ECR II-913, at paras 131–40.

[83] Case C-113/04 P *Technische Unie v Commission* [2006] ECR I-8831, at para 93.

[84] *JFE Engineering v Commission*, above n 55, at paras 334–35, upheld on appeal in *Sumitomo Metal Industries and others v Commission*, above n 57, at paras 68ff.

[85] *Bolloré and others v Commission*, above n 38, at para 167; *JFE Engineering v Commission*, above n 55, at para 219, upheld on appeal in *Sumitomo Metal Industries and others v Commission*, above n 57, at paras 73–74.

First Instance. In order to establish the duration of the infringement, six of the documents were compared with a seventh document, a table found at Atochem's premises, which, according to the Commission, demonstrated that the quota system had continued at least until April 1984. The Court of Justice noted that the Commission, and indeed the Court of First Instance, had made cross-checks between the figures in the table and other information contained in three documents. It then rejected a plea alleging an incomplete examination of the facts.[86]

Clear and unambiguous documentary evidence can thus be conclusive in cartel cases. Statements by persons involved in the cartel carry considerable weight as well, but must be supported by other evidence, and consequently have a lower probative value. But this latter case law must not be transposed automatically to the national context, keeping in mind that the Community courts must rely on national enforcement if they hear witnesses who would face the penalty of imprisonment if they committed perjury.[87] (The Community does not have its own police force or prisons, so enforcement against persons who perjure themselves would ultimately have to be carried out nationally.)

If a person who was directly involved is heard under oath in a national court, and clearly explains the existence and mechanisms of the cartel, there is no reason why the value of that evidence should be less than that of documentary evidence. Indeed, the Court of First Instance has taken the position that adverse consequences which might arise under criminal law for a person who perjured himself in an inquiry, are circumstances which render such evidence more reliable than a mere statement.[88] Statements which run counter to the interests of the maker must in principle be regarded as particularly reliable evidence.[89] In *Cement*, a combination of documentary evidence and company statements was considered to be direct documentary evidence of the infringement.[90]

The position taken in EC law seems to correspond to that in US law, where the Court of Appeals, Seventh Circuit, has explained that direct evidence of collusion includes admissions or eyewitness accounts of agreement to collude.[91] A copy of the agreement, references to it or other documents indicating a quid pro quo will do as well: 'When the evidence is direct, unambiguous, and clearly reliable, it settles the conspiracy issue'.[92]

Under EC law there is a need to prove the participation of each undertaking in the cartel, and collective responsibility is not accepted.[93] In *PVC II*, the Court of

[86] Joined Cases C-238/99 P, etc *Limburgse Vinyl Maatschappij and others v Commission* [2002] ECR I-8375, at paras 369–405.

[87] See generally Arts 68, 71 and 72 of the Rules of Procedure of the Court of First Instance, OJ L/136 of 30 May 1991.

[88] *JFE Engineering v Commission*, above n 55, at para 312.

[89] *Ibid*, at para 211.

[90] *Aalborg Portland and others v Commission*, above n 30, at para 237.

[91] *In re Brand Name Prescription Drugs Antitrust Litigation* 186 F 3d 781 (1999).

[92] Areeda and Hovenkamp, *Antitrust Law—An Analysis of Antitrust Principles and Their Application*, 2nd edn (New York, Aspen Publishers, Wolters Kluwer Law and Business), Vol VI, § 1418, at 116.

[93] Joined Cases T-305/94, etc *Limburgse Vinyl Maatschappij and others v Commission* [1999] ECR II-931, at para 770.

First Instance started out with finding that there had been a cartel, and then proceeded to try whether each undertaking had participated (all the undertakings that appealed denied that they had taken part in the cartel, save for ICI which admitted participation).[94] By way of comparison, the US Court of Appeals, Ninth Circuit, has found that once the existence of a common scheme is established, very little is required to show that defendant became a party, and slight evidence may be sufficient to connect a defendant to it.[95]

3. *Parallel behaviour*

In the absence of any direct evidence, the position in Community law is that the existence of an agreement *can* be deduced from the conduct of the parties concerned.[96] Two types of evidence must be distinguished here: communications evidence, and parallel behaviour. The first category is widely considered most important in cartel cases and comprises evidence that the parties met, talked over the phone or engaged in other communication.[97] Secondly, the Court of Justice has declared its willingness to accept parallel behaviour as evidence of concerted practice if it leads to conditions of competition which do not correspond to normal conditions of competition.[98] But a cartel cannot be presumed where the parallel behaviour can be accounted for by other means.[99]

It is difficult to find any action based entirely on parallel market behaviour that has ever succeeded before the Community courts. On the contrary, the Commission has spectacularly lost three cases where the admissible evidence amounted only to parallel behaviour. The first of those was *CRAM and Rheinzink.*[100] The Commission had fined one French and one German zinc producer for, among other things, a joint refusal to supply products to an undertaking called Schiltz which re-exported the products into Germany. It was common ground that the two producers had both ceased to supply Schiltz, CRAM on 21 October 1976, and RZ a few days later on 29 October 1976. The Commission sought to explain this as a concerted practice aimed at protecting the German market. The evidence relied on was the fact that the cessations to supply occurred in close proximity, and a telex from RZ to CRAM in which RZ informed CRAM of a reduction of its prices on the German market by 3 per cent. The Court did not find the evidence sufficient and quashed the Commission's decision in this regard. According to the Court, CRAM had proved that it had encountered difficulties in obtaining payment from Schiltz before it ceased to supply zinc products. Further, the telex alone was not sufficient evidence. The Commission had not 'produced

94 *Ibid*, at paras 780–941.
95 *Safeway Stores v FTC*, 366 F 2d 795 (1966).
96 Joined Cases C-2/01 P and C-3/01 P *BAI and Commission v Bayer* [2004] ECR I-23, at para 100.
97 OECD Global Forum on Competition, above n 79, at 29, 193.
98 Case 395/87 *Ministère Public v Jean-Louis Tournier* [1989] ECR 2521, at para 24.
99 *Ibid.*
100 Joined Cases 29/83 and 30/83 *CRAM and Rheinzink v Commission* [1984] ECR 1679.

sufficiently precise and coherent proof to justify the view that the parallel behaviour of the two undertakings in question was the result of concerted action by them'.[101]

The second case where the Commission sought to infer agreements and concerted practices from parallel market behaviour was *Italian Flat Glass*.[102] The Commission's decision rested heavily on findings that the glass producers had applied identical prices, identical discounts and identical classification of the main customers by category and level. All those findings were quashed by the Court of First Instance upon a detailed examination of the documents used as evidence.[103] It did not exactly help the Commission's case that it had deliberately deleted or omitted certain passages of the relevant evidence.[104] At the end of the day the Commission had to rely on evidence of concertation between the producers; but that evidence, although incriminating, proved insufficient to uphold the decision in that regard.[105]

The third case where the Commission had to rely on mere parallel behaviour was *Woodpulp*.[106] In a decision addressed to 43 producers of bleached sulphate wood pulp, the Commission found that the producers had acted in concert on prices charged to customers inside the EC. Several different infringements were tried before the Court, one of them being a system of quarterly price announcements which, according to the Commission, in itself constituted an infringement of Article 81. This ground fell into two parts: first, the system had allegedly been introduced deliberately by the pulp producers in order to enable them to ascertain the prices that would be charged by their competitors in the following quarters; secondly, it had the effect of making the market artificially transparent. The Court rejected this since the price announcements were made to users and constituted market behaviour which did not lessen each undertaking's uncertainty as to the future attitude of its competitors.[107] But the Commission had submitted a second hypothesis: that the system of price announcements constituted evidence of concertation at an earlier stage. It relied on the parallel conduct of the pulp producers in the period from 1975 to 1981, and on different kinds of direct or indirect exchange of information. However, the Court dismissed the evidence on exchange of information on procedural grounds, and went on to examine whether the system of quarterly price announcements, the simultaneity or near simultaneity of the price announcements and the parallelism of price announcements amounted to sufficient evidence of prior concertation. The Court demanded 'a firm, precise and consistent body of evidence',[108] and accepted alternative explanations for the parallel market behaviour.

[101] *Ibid*, at para 20.
[102] Joined Cases T-68/89, T-77/89 and T-78/89 *Società Italiano Vetro SpA and others v Commission* [1992] ECR II-1403.
[103] *Ibid*, at paras 174–210.
[104] *Ibid*, at paras 90–91.
[105] *Ibid*, at para 232.
[106] Joined Cases C-89/85, etc *Ahlström Osakeyhtiö and others v Commission* [1993] ECR I-1307.
[107] *Ibid*, at para 64.
[108] *Ibid*, at para 70.

Agreements or concerted practices must apparently be the only plausible explanation if an action based on parallel behaviour is to succeed.[109] Still, the scope of this case law is limited. Subsequent developments have shown that the ability to refute allegations of cartel participation by bringing forward another plausible explanation is open only in cases where the evidence is limited to mere parallel market behaviour. If the Commission has produced documents which show that the practices were the result of an agreement or a concerted practice, the Court of First Instance will refuse to engage in examination of alternative explanations (such as normal market functions, etc).[110]

Under US law, agreements can be inferred from parallel behaviour, but only if the plaintiff can show the existence of 'plus-factors'. Plus-factors seem to fall into two categories:

a) industry structure factors which make collusion more likely; and
b) behavioural factors, such as acts against self-interest and inter-firm communication.[111]

Elhauge and Geradin, when discussing standards for finding a horizontal agreement or concerted action, find that 'both US and EC law focus on a distinction between (a) parallel separate action and (b) agreement/concerted action'.[112] Although the distinction between lawful intelligent market behaviour and antitrust violations has attracted much attention in scholarly debate, it is submitted here that this question is quantitatively not the focus of EC case law on cartels. It would be so if the Commission had insisted on bringing numerous actions against parallel market behaviour without attempting to demonstrate the existence of meetings or other communication between the parties; but while *CRAM and Rheinzink*, *Italian Flat Glass* and *Woodpulp* are leading cases, they are nevertheless from a quantitative perspective of less significance seen in relation to 150 or so EC cartel cases. The problems encountered in the vast majority of cases are not so much related to defences based on lawful unconscious parallelism. Normally the existence of a cartel and the illegality of it are not disputed as such. Instead, standard grounds for appeal include questioning the involvement or degree of involvement of the individual undertaking, or alleging legal or procedural errors in the Commission's handling of the case.[113]

[109] *Ibid*, at paras 126–27.

[110] *Limburgse Vinyl Maatschappij and others v Commission*, above n 93, at paras 722ff.

[111] Levin, above n 69, at 1681.

[112] Elhauge, Einer, and Geradin, Damien, *Global Competition Law and Economics* (Oxford, Hart Publishing, 2007), at 735.

[113] Harding, Christopher, and Gibbs, Alun, 'Why go to court in Europe? An analysis of cartel appeals 1995–2004' (2005) 30(3) *EL Rev* 349, at 352, 356.

4. Standard of proof for demonstrating a role as an instigator or a ringleader of a cartel

In *Vitamins*, the Commission sought to establish that BASF and Roche had jointly instigated a cartel; but the Commission's finding was reversed by the Court of First Instance, which, upon a detailed evaluation of the evidence, found that Roche had instigated the cartel alone.[114]

Here, the standard of proof for establishing leadership in a cartel was tried in detail. BASF had taken initiatives to be the first publicly to announce price increases relating to vitamins A and E, which was sufficient to show a leadership role.[115] Similarly, price increase initiatives on vitamin B5, combined with alerting competitors, proved sufficient for establishing leadership.[116] When, on the other hand, there were negotiations leading up to the joint establishment of quotas, it was impossible to show that one particular undertaking had been the leader.[117] The only undertaking which could conceivably be classified as a leader was then Roche, which organised a significant number of meetings, separately met competitors, represented certain competitors vis-à-vis others, collected and reported sales figures of the cartel members, and most often undertook to make proposals as to the operation of the cartel.[118]

5. Standard of proof for demonstrating participation in a complex infringement

As set out in chapter four, Community law operates from a combined notion of agreements and concerted practices in the assessment of complex cartels. But the link between separate anticompetitive measures and the larger cartel is not always easy to establish. The Court of First Instance has considered that the mere fact that there is identity of object between an agreement in which an undertaking participated and a global cartel does not suffice to render that undertaking responsible for the global cartel. In other words, just because one undertaking is useful to the global cartel does not mean it participated in the more extensive infringement. It is only if the undertaking knew, or should have known, when it participated in the cartel that in doing so it was joining in the global cartel that its participation in the agreement expressed its accession.[119]

Carbonless paper illustrates the point just made. Spanish companies Divipa and Zicuñaga argued that they were only part of a Spanish cartel, not an EEA-wide cartel.[120] The Commission could only establish that Divipa and Zicuñaga had participated in collusive meetings concerning the Spanish market, but asserted that

[114] Case T-15/02 *BASF v Commission* [2006] ECR II-497, at paras 323 ff.
[115] *Ibid*, at para 348.
[116] *Ibid*, at para 371.
[117] *Ibid*, at para 392.
[118] *Ibid*, at para 404.
[119] Case T-28/99 *Sigma Tecnologie v Commission* [2002] ECR II-1845, at paras 45 ff.
[120] *Bolloré and others v Commission*, above n 38, at paras 205 ff.

they must have understood that the cartel covered the whole territory that became the EEA in 1994. The Commission's cause of action had three limbs:

a) The general European cartel meetings and the national collusive meetings were inextricably linked.
b) Large European carbonless paper producers took part in collusive activities on the Spanish market.
c) Significant intra-Community trade flows in the carbonless paper sector were observed during the reference period.

Upon an examination of the facts, the Court of First Instance found that Divipa and Zicuñaga were necessarily aware of the wider framework, at European level, of which the meetings relating to the Spanish market formed part.[121] Concluding, the Court held that it was

> scarcely conceivable that . . . Divipa and Zicuñaga, which, at the meetings on the Spanish markets, rubbed shoulders with representatives of major European carbonless paper producers involved in the general cartel meetings, were unaware that, by participating in collusive agreements on that market, they were part of a European-wide cartel.[122]

But on the other hand the Court exonerated Zicuñaga from participation in a market-sharing practice on the French market, the existence of which Zicuñaga could not have known or reasonably foreseen.[123]

6. *Standard of proof for demonstrating duration*

It is not unusual for the evidence about a cartel to involve gaps, so that certain periods of the alleged cartel's operation must be inferred indirectly rather than through direct pieces of evidence. When the appeal against the decision on the Dutch *electrotechnical* cartel had reached the final instance, the trade association involved criticised the Court of First Instance for having ignored the absence of evidence of a collective exclusive dealing arrangement during certain specific periods. The Court of Justice held that this did not preclude the infringement from being regarded as established during a longer overall period than those periods for which evidence was available, provided that such a finding was supported by objective and consistent indicia.[124]

In *Methionine*, the undertaking Degussa claimed that there were two separate infringements: one in 1986–88, and another in 1992–97. The Commission had considered there was one continuing infringement from 1986–99. The Court of First Instance applied the presumption of innocence with reference to the ECHR by way of analogy as the legal basis for its reasoning. The evidence included

[121] *Ibid*, at para 213.
[122] *Ibid*, at para 215.
[123] *Ibid*, at para 238.
[124] Case C-105/04 P *Nederlandse Federatieve Vereniging voor de Groothandel op Elektrotechnisch Gebied v Commission* [2006] ECR I-8725, at para 98.

meetings during the years 1989, 1990 and 1991 between the participants, and additional meetings at a lower level during the years 1988–98. According to one of the participants, the object of those meetings was target prices and information exchange. An added objective was to find a way to deal with market entry by a new actor, and to discuss future market strategies. On the facts, the Court of First Instance ruled in favour of the Commission and found that the infringement had continued.[125]

In *Organic peroxides*, the Commission relied on a combination of evidence. The package included a document showing detailed sales and market share figures, both the 'theoretical' market shares agreed within the cartel and the 'deviations'. There were handwritten minutes of a meeting and some information from other undertakings on information exchange. The Court of First Instance reiterated that the duration of the infringement, which requires that the date on which it ended is known, is one of the essential elements which must be proved by the Commission. If there is no evidence directly establishing the duration of an infringement, the Commission should adduce at least evidence of facts sufficiently proximate in time for it to be reasonable to accept that that infringement continued without interruption between two specific dates. The Court then examined the evidence in detail, as well as the counter-arguments brought forward by the applicant, and upheld the Commission's findings.[126]

7. Standard of proof for cartel overcharges

It will be explained in chapter seven that a fining policy according to which a competition authority calculates cartel overcharges on a case-by-case basis is inappropriate. Under a deterrence model, cartel overcharges are often approximated, based on a proxy representing what would be normal in relation to the turnover in the cartelised products. Even so, a competition authority may decide to justify (at least in part) fines with reference to the overcharges generated by the cartel.

The standard of proof for finding that overcharges had occurred was tried in *Citric acid*. There, the Commission had not calculated the overcharges but had limited itself to finding that the participants had carefully implemented the cartel agreements and that, during the material period, their aggregate average world market share was over 60 per cent and their European market share around 70 per cent. The Commission had also observed that prices set by the cartel corresponded to a certain extent with those actually charged by the participants. The Court of First Instance found that 'the likelihood of a price and sales quota cartel being effective will rise in accordance with the size of the market share held by the members of that cartel',[127] and

[125] Case T-279/02 *Degussa v Commission* [2006] ECR II-897, at paras 113 ff, 149–53.
[126] Case T-120/04 *Peróxidos Orgánicos v Commission* [2006] ECR II-4441, at paras 50–75.
[127] Case T-59/02 *Archer Daniels Midland v Commission* [2006] ECR II-3627, at para 165.

> Moreover, the Commission was entitled to take the view that the weight of that evidence increases with the duration of the cartel. Having regard to the administrative and management costs associated with the sound functioning of a complex cartel concerning, like the one in this instance, price-fixing, market sharing and exchange of information, and taking account of the risks inherent in such unlawful activities, it was reasonable for the Commission to consider that the fact that the undertakings persisted with the infringement over a long period indicates that the cartel members made a certain profit from that cartel and, therefore, that it had an actual impact on the relevant market.[128]

The Court of First Instance continued:

> in the case of price agreements the Commission must find—with a reasonable degree of probability . . .—that the agreements have in fact enabled the parties concerned to achieve a higher level of price than that which would have prevailed had there been no cartel. Second, it follows that, in making its assessment, the Commission must take into account all the objective conditions in the relevant market and have regard to the economic context and, if appropriate, also the legislative background. It is clear from the judgments of the Court of First Instance in the cartonboard cartel case . . . that account should be taken of the existence of any 'objective economic factors' which indicate that, had there been a 'free play of competition', prices would not have developed in the same way as the prices which were actually charged . . .[129]

The standard of proof for demonstrating the existence of overcharges for price cartels (without actually having to quantify them) was consequently set by the Court of First Instance as a reasonable degree of probability, taking into account all the objective conditions in the relevant market and having regard to the economic context.

8. *Circumstantial evidence, indicia*

Circumstantial evidence is widely considered important by competition law enforcers, especially evidence which shows that the suspected undertakings communicated with each other through meetings, phone conversations, e-mail or otherwise.[130]

Must separate pieces of evidence correspond to some minimum standard? In other words, are there pieces of evidence that are so remote or insignificant that they have no value? And will several pieces of evidence, where the probative value of each is of a more remote nature, be sufficient as a whole?

Ruling on the Dutch *electrotechnical* cartel, the Court of Justice explicitly accepted indicia and coincidences as proof. A number of coincidences and indicia may, taken together and in the absence of another plausible explanation, constitute evidence of an infringement, not just regarding the existence of a cartel but also on the duration.[131]

[128] *Ibid*, at para 166.

[129] *Ibid*, at para 182.

[130] OECD Global Forum on Competition, above n 79, at 29, 193.

[131] Case C-105/04 P *Nederlandse Federatieve Vereniging voor de Groothandel op Elektrotechnisch Gebied v Commission* [2006] ECR I-8725, at paras 94–95.

Among circumstantial evidence accepted by the Community courts, the following examples may be given:

a) Being perceived by its partners as an undertaking whose opinion should be sought in order to establish a common position, is a factor which tends to prove participation in an anticompetitive agreement.[132]
b) A system of monitoring and penalties constitutes an indicator of the existence of an agreement.[133]

Whereas there is scope for development of theory-building in EC law on what is a circumstantial piece of evidence and how to use it, US law has come a bit further here. While an opportunity to conspire is insufficient, evidence of a conspiracy can include several matters. Unexplained meetings or other communications, secret meetings that cannot be explained with reference to legitimate objectives, cover-ups such as destruction of evidence and other suspicious behaviour, as well as false or incomplete explanations, are all relevant.[134] As the Court of Appeals, Ninth Circuit, held: 'It is, we think, well established that the proof and evidence in an anti-trust conspiracy case is, in most cases, circumstantial'.[135] But that statement was made in 1952. Given the success of modern leniency programs, the days when antitrust authorities were forced to rely on circumstantial evidence alone may well be over. Experiences with cases where there is overwhelming evidence, as a result of co-operation by defendants, may provide us with a better understanding of how cartels operate and what evidence they typically produce. This in turn can lead to refined standards for reliance on circumstantial evidence.

9. *Refusal to reply*

The Court of First Instance held in *PVC II* that a refusal to reply to requests for information, or the impossibility of replying to them, cannot in itself constitute proof of an undertaking's participation in an agreement. Such circumstances must be left out of account.[136] Similarly in *Valmont* (a State aid case), the Court of First Instance held that the Commission must exhaust its investigative powers before relying on incomplete answers from the defendants.[137] Presumably this is driven by fears that reliance on refusals to reply would contravene the ECHR.

Although I am not proposing that refusals to reply should be conclusive, I do suggest that they should at least be given some weight. This view is formed by reference to US law. In *Interstate Circuit*, it was held that

[132] Case T-56/99 *Marlines v Commission* [2003] ECR II-5225, at para 59.
[133] Joined Cases C-2/01 P and C-3/01 P *BAI and Commission v Bayer* [2004] ECR I-23, at para 83.
[134] Areeda and Hovenkamp *et al*, above n 92, § 1417, at 104–14.
[135] *C-O-Two Fire Equipment Co v US* 197 F 2d 489 (1952).
[136] *Limburgse Vinyl Maatschappij and others v Commission*, above n 93, at paras 489–90.
[137] Case T-274/01 *Valmont v Commission* [2004] ECR II-3145, at para 60.

production of weak evidence when strong is available can lead only to the conclusion that the strong would have been adverse, and silence then becomes 'evidence' of the most convincing character . . .[138]

The case is admittedly rather old, but the general proposition is still accepted. Areeda and Hovenkamp suggest that although any and every conspiracy cannot be inferred from silence, the policy that competitors should not get together without some legitimate reason requires some implementing sanction. This calls for alleged conspiracies to be 'held proved by a significant assemblage consistent with it as to which *no* testimony is offered'.[139] A package of evidence, together with the fact that an undertakings has refused to provide explanations, could then be conclusive.

C. Cartel cases where the Commission lost in substance

It seems near impossible to define in the abstract what type of evidence is needed to prove the existence of a cartel and, conversely, what evidence would be insufficient. Guidance can be found, however, in the cases the Commission lost on the merits. Admittedly there are only a few such cases: *CRAM and Rheinzinc*, *Italian Flat Glass* and *Woodpulp* concerned attempts to infer agreements or concerted practices from parallel market behaviour, and these have already been discussed above. Complete losses are otherwise rare, comprising only *Soda-ash*, *Wirtschaftsvereinigung Stahl*[140] and *Euro-zone currencies—Germany*.

Soda-ash concerned geographic market sharing.[141] It was set aside because of procedural errors, but the Court of First Instance indicated that the case was not as strong as the Commission had assumed. While not definitely ruling on the substance, the Court nevertheless made several observations to that effect, including that there were no documents relating to meetings with regard to the period in which the Commission had claimed the infringement had begun.[142] The Court considered that due to the weakness of the documentary evidence relating in particular to 1973 and the years immediately following it, the Commission should have provided an overall and detailed economic assessment, in particular of the relevant market and the size and conduct of the undertakings active on that market. It also criticised the Commission for not considering whether the practice of staying out of each other's market could be due to the abuse of dominance though loyalty rebates in which Solvay and ICI had allegedly engaged.[143] Given that the Commission had referred to regular meetings and information exchanges between

138 *Interstate Circuit v US* 306 US 208 (1939).

139 Areeda and Hovenkamp *et al*, above n 92, at 109.

140 Case T-16/98 *Wirtschaftsvereinigung Stahl and others v Commission* [2001] ECR II-1217.

141 Case T-30/91 *Solvay v Commission* [1995] ECR II-1775; Case T-36/91 *ICI v Commission* [1995] ECR II-1847.

142 *ICI v Commission*, above n 141, at para 84.

143 *Ibid*, at para 86.

Solvay and ICI in the later part of the period of infringement, the outcome would presumably have been different if the case had been tried today, and the significance of these cases is consequently low.

Euro-zone currencies—Germany, on the other hand, emerges as the borderline case where standard of proof is tested. The Commission had adopted a decision fining German banks for price-fixing on trade in banknotes.[144] The price-fixing was supposedly done prior to the permanent switch from national currencies to the euro. The Commission's decision was set aside on appeal for lack of sufficient evidence.[145] Why? Undisputedly, there was a meeting between competing banks on 15 October 1997, and some phone calls. Consequently this was no case of mere parallel behaviour. But there were some errors in the decision. The market shares of the parties were considerably lower than stated by the Commission, which affected the probability of the existence of a cartel. Furthermore, the legal background was given considerable importance by the Court of First Instance, which found that there were regulatory uncertainties as to the rules on transition to the euro. This justified some sort of industry action to clarify the situation. Next, the probative value was evaluated of five documents relating to the meeting on 15 October 1997 (one fax, one letter, three reports). All except one were drafted prior to the meeting. The one document drafted after the meeting was an internal report drafted by one of the participants. The reliability of this report was checked by the Court in relation to witness statements and evidence on pursuant market behaviour. The witness statements were deemed inconclusive and the pursuant market behaviour did not match the Commission's story. As a matter of principle the Court held that the

> fragmentary and sporadic items of evidence which may be available to the Commission should, in any event, be capable of being supplemented by inferences which allow the relevant circumstances to be reconstituted . . .[146]

It also reiterated the now well-established method for assessing the probative value of a document:

> regard should be had first and foremost to the credibility of the account it contains and, in particular, to the person from whom the document originates, the circumstances in which it came into being, the person to whom it was addressed and whether, on its face, the document appears sound and reliable.[147]

Partial Commission losses are not that frequent either if the analysis is limited to those that were due to insufficient evidence, leaving aside all losses due to procedural irregularities, incorrect calculations of fines and mistaken attribution of liability to members of groups and associations of undertakings. An account will be given here of the parts of *Cartonboard* and the *Haberdashery cartel* decisions that were set aside.

[144] *Euro-zone currencies—Germany* [2003] OJ L/15/1.
[145] Joined Cases T-44/02, etc *Dresdner Bank and others v Commission* [2006] ECR II-3567.
[146] *Ibid*, at para 64.
[147] *Ibid*, at para 121.

The infringement on the cartonboard market took place within a body known as the 'Product Group Paperboard', which comprised several groups or committees. One of them was the 'President Conference', in which almost all the managing directors in the industry participated, meetings being held twice a year. The Finnish undertaking Enso-Gutzeit had participated only in the President Conference.

According to Stora, a cartel participant which admitted its involvement, the President Conference pursued anticompetitive objects. But this statement was contradicted by several other undertakings, including Enso-Gutzeit, and Stora's statement was not regarded as adequate proof by the Court of First Instance in this part.[148] There was further evidence incriminating Enso-Gutzeit: documents referring to it, its membership in the Nordic Paperboard Institute and its actual pricing conduct. All those items were scrutinised by the Court with reference to their origin, content and reliability, and what conclusions could be drawn from them. None of them separately constituted evidence of Enso-Gutzeit's participation in the infringement, neither did they suffice as evidence taken as a whole.[149]

As for the *Haberdashery* cartel, the Commission had held the undertakings Prym, Entaco and Coats liable for a product market division on hard haberdashery products and a geographic market division on sewing needles. The parties had a history of minority cross-ownership which made the case slightly atypical.

On appeal, the Court of First Instance found that the manufacturers Prym and Entaco had indeed operated a cartel, but that Coats (manufacturer and distributor of needles in the wholesale and retail business) was not a full member of it.[150] While the Commission had found that the parties had all taken part in two joint anticompetitive meetings in 1993, the Court considered that the evidence was insufficient to establish that those meetings were cartel meetings.[151] Further, Coats did not attend any of the meetings concerning the day-to-day implementation of the market-sharing agreements between Prym and Entaco. The Court of First Instance noted that Entaco's cartel obligation was not self-enforcing and that, if Coats had intended to require Entaco to comply with its obligation, it would have needed to attend those meetings in order to check Entaco's compliance.[152]

The cartel was basically structured by a written agreement between Prym and Entaco, and Coats had obtained a copy of that agreement, the background being an 'ongoing collaboration between Coats and Prym, which started in the 1970s'.[153] Coats had taken steps to contribute to the market-sharing agreement by selling a business to Entaco, which amounted to a concerted practice on its part.[154] The Commission sought to prove that a cross-reading of the agreement under which Coats sold this business to Entaco, on the one hand, and the agreements between

[148] Case T-337/94 *Enso-Gutzeit v Commission* [1998] ECR II-1571, at paras 91–101.
[149] *Ibid*, at paras 152–53.
[150] Case T-36/05 *Coats Holdings and Coats v Commission* [2007] ECR II-110.
[151] *Ibid*, at paras 83 ff.
[152] *Ibid*, at para 94.
[153] *Ibid*, at para 112.
[154] *Ibid*, at paras 114, 117.

Prym and Entaco, on the other, demonstrated a tripartite cartel agreement. A detailed examination of the contract clauses led to the opposite conclusion, however, so that Coats was not party to the cartel agreements.[155]

In 1997 Prym brought the cartel to an end. Some aspects of the cartel were maintained by Prym and Entaco, but the Court of First Instance found that Coats was not part of those.[156] Coats had infringed Article 81 EC, but the fine imposed was reduced from €30 million to €20 million.

D. Evaluation of certain pieces of evidence

1. Whether the practice was in the company's interest

Undertakings have on several occasions tried to bring their actions outside the scope of Article 81(1) EC, or to raise the standard of proof by arguing that their actions were based on legitimate business reasons or, in the alternative, that a cartel arrangement was not in their business interest. The Community courts are unimpressed by these lines of argument, finding them entirely irrelevant.[157] Neither will arguments on the presence or absence of legitimate business interests change the standard of proof.[158]

In *Cement*, the Court of Justice stated that

> the fact that commercial reasons led Cementir to participate in the anticompetitive agreement is irrelevant when the agreement had the effect of restricting competition. Since its participation in the agreement is demonstrated, there is no need to examine whether it had any interest in participating in it.[159]

This was reiterated in *Seamless steel tubes*.[160] Conversely, in *District heating pipes*, an argument was raised as to whether an undertaking had an interest in participating in a boycott. The Court held that it was irrelevant whether the undertaking had an interest in any boycott of one of its direct competitors by other participants in the cartel.[161] And in *Seamless steel tubes* again, Nippon Steel's argument that the existence of a plausible alternative explanation for the conduct complained of—namely, the absence of a commercial interest—should have led to stricter requirements as to the evidence to be adduced, was held contrary to case law.[162]

155 *Ibid*, at paras 133–58.

156 *Ibid*, at para 121.

157 See Wickihalder, Urs, 'The Distinction between an "Agreement" within the Meaning of Article 81(1) of the EC Treaty and Unilateral Conduct' (2006) 2(1) *European Competition Journal* 87, at 92.

158 Opinion of A-G Geelhoed in *Sumitomo Metal Industries and Nippon Steel v Commission*, above n 57, at para 190.

159 *Aalborg Portland and others v Commission*, above n 30, at para 335.

160 *Sumitomo Metal Industries and Nippon Steel v Commission*, above n 57, at paras 44–46.

161 Joined Cases C-189/02 P, etc *Dansk Rørindustri and others v Commission* [2005] ECR I-5425, at para 147.

162 *Sumitomo Metal Industries and others v Commission*, above n 57, at para 45.

On the other hand, the Court in *Bayer* endorsed the view that some additional proof is required when 'such an agreement is not at first sight in the interests of the other party'.[163]

The Court of First Instance has time and again rejected submissions that alleged cartel practices can either be explained as legitimate, or be rebutted by reference to business interests. In *Seamless steel tubes*, Mannesmann argued that the conclusion of a market-sharing agreement was in its own business interest. The Court of First Instance rejected that argument, finding that even if that was true, it would not undermine the Commission's argument that the agreement was unlawful. It added: 'Anticompetitive practices are very often in the undertakings' commercial interest, at least in the short term.'[164] In *Speciality graphites*, Intech argued that the increases in prices by the cartel were against its own economic interests, which in fact called for the adoption of an aggressive price policy and an expansion of its market share. Presumably Intech was attempting to raise the standard of proof. The Court of First Instance, somewhat beside the point, found that a finding of an economic advantage was not necessary to establish participation in a cartel.[165] A similar conclusion was reached in *Mercedes*, where, since the undertaking's participation in the concerted practice had been established, it was not necessary to consider whether it and its branches had an interest in participating in it.[166]

The harsh attitude of the Community courts is in my view justified, since Article 81(1) EC constitutes public law. The provision cannot be modified by private law agreements between parties. Furthermore, every agreement between two parties entails that each of them sacrifices some of their immediate or long-term interests in order to arrive at an understanding; the fact that concessions are made is not unique to cartels but is standard practice in all commercial relations.

2. Whether some caution is called for in relation to evidence submitted under a leniency application

The race to the courthouse brought about by modern leniency programmes has changed the landscape in recent years. Undertakings will compete for total immunity or significant fine reductions by attempting to be the first to offer the Commission or national competition authority compelling evidence about the cartel. Apparently, some undertakings have considered that their competitors are incriminating them without cause in the process. The development has forced the Community courts to question whether some caution is called for as to the probative value of evidence submitted under leniency applications.

In *Organic Peroxides*, one undertaking took the view that the information and explanations provided by two competitors were not reliable, inasmuch as those

[163] Joined Cases C-2/01 P and C-3/01 P *BAI and Commission v Bayer* [2004] ECR I-23, at para 102.

[164] Case T-44/00 *Mannesmannröhren-Werke v Commission* [2004] ECR II-2223, at para 176.

[165] Joined Cases T-71/03, T-74/03, T-87/03 and T-91/03 *Tokai Carbon and others v Commission* [2005] ECR II-10, at para 81.

[166] T-325/01 *DaimlerChrysler v Commission* [2005] ECR II-3319, at para 211.

competitors were seeking to benefit from the Leniency Notice. To this end, they had a certain interest in submitting incriminating evidence against others. The Court of First Instance recognised that some caution is generally called for,[167] but still rejected the argument in principle. That was because any attempt to mislead the Commission could jeopardise the undertakings' chances of benefiting fully under the Leniency Notice. There was accordingly not necessarily an incentive for the other participants in the cartel to submit distorted evidence.[168]

3. Probative value of corporate statements made by representative who did not participate himself

The use of corporate statements as evidence in the Community courts has resulted in a discussion of the probative value of such documents. This must be seen in its proper setting, ie the fact that witnesses are seldom heard before the Community courts. In *Seamless Steel tubes*, one of the undertakings challenged the probative value of a corporate statement, pointing out that the person who had given it had no direct knowledge of the alleged cartel. The Court, following its Advocate-General, observed that the submission of such a statement entails considerable legal and economic risks for the company. It was held extremely unlikely that a company would implicate itself in the absence of information provided by employees in possession of direct knowledge of the facts. The Court upheld the Court of First Instance's attribution of probative value to that statement.[169]

On US law, Areeda and Hovenkamp consider indirect admissions and find that 'The report from one in a position to know of the existence of a conspiracy is relatively reliable, subject to the usual hearsay problems'.[170]

4. Anonymous informers

Yet another question is whether the Commission or a national competition authority can preserve the confidentiality of informers without infringing the rights of the defence of undertakings. This question was posed in one of the *Seamless steel tubes* cases.

Mannesmannröhren-Werke opposed the Commission's use of a document, the origin of which the Commission had refused to reveal. Two questions were raised:

a) Was such a document admissible as evidence?
b) If so, was the document's value as evidence lower as a result of its obscure origin?

The Court of First Instance found that the document was admissible, as a result of the Community law principle of the unfettered evaluation of evidence. However,

[167] Case T-120/04 *Peróxidos Orgánicos v Commission* [2006] ECR II-4441, at para 70.
[168] *Ibid.*
[169] *Sumitomo Metal Industries and others v Commission*, above n 57, at paras 101–03.
[170] Areeda and Hovenkamp *et al*, above n 92, § 1418, at 121.

its probative value was affected, and the credibility of the evidence was necessarily reduced.[171] This view was confirmed on appeal by the Court of Justice.[172]

III. COMPARISONS WITH COMMUNITY LAW PRINCIPLES ON EVIDENCE IN CASES ON HARD-CORE VERTICAL RESTRAINTS, STATE AID AND MERGER CONTROL

There are indications in case law that the Community courts are actually determining the standard of proof according to deterrence objectives. This may be observed when a comparison is made between, on the one hand, cartel cases and, on the other hand, vertical cases and State aid.

It has already been explained that the Court of Justice in *Cement* acknowledged the difficulties in proving cartel activities, and allowed the Commission to prove unlawful contact between traders using fragmentary and sparse evidence, following which the Court would have to reconstitute certain details by deduction. A cartel must, in most cases,

> be inferred from a number of coincidences and indicia which, taken together, may, in the absence of another plausible explanation, constitute evidence of an infringement of the competition rules . . .[173]

The Court of First Instance has also expressly recognised the Commission's difficulties in proving cartel activities, given that several years may have elapsed since the infringement took place and that a number of the undertakings may have decided not to co-operate actively in the investigation. It would be excessive in such circumstances to require the Commission to produce evidence of the specific mechanism of an illegal market-sharing agreement.[174] On appeal in the *Seamless steel tubes* case, the Court of Justice upheld this view in particular, pointing out that appraisal of the evidence is consistent with well-established case law.[175]

One may ask, then, whether the Community courts have decided on lower standards of proof for cartels, in response to the difficulties in gathering evidence. It certainly seems that such a deterrence approach is applied in combination with the more penal law-orientated reliance on the ECHR. In contrast, the Community courts have required documentary evidence in vertical relations cases, to accept a claim that wholesalers agreed to do what the supplier wanted them to do.[176]

The deterrence approach may be observed not only in cartel cases, but also in cases of State aid. In *Stardust Marine*, the Court considered the standards of proof for showing that a public authority has incited a public undertaking to give State aid to a recipient. Here, the Court pointed out that the close relation between the

171 *Mannesmannröhren-Werke v Commission*, above n 164, at paras 84–86.
172 Case C-407/04 P *Dalmine v Commission* [2007] ECR I-829, at paras 50–51.
173 *Aalborg Portland and others v Commission*, above n 30, at paras 55–57.
174 *JFE Engineering v Commission*, above n 55, at para 203.
175 *Sumitomo Metal Industries and others v Commission*, above n 57, at paras 50–51.
176 *BAI and Commission v Bayer*, above n 163, at para 122.

State and the public undertaking leads to a risk that State aid is granted using the public undertaking as an intermediary. Furthermore, the Court pointed out how difficult it can be for third parties to show that aid had been granted by a public undertaking as a result of instructions from the public authorities. The outcome was a lower standard of proof, or perhaps recourse to assumptions:

> it cannot be demanded that it be demonstrated, on the basis of a precise inquiry, that in the particular case the public authorities specifically incited the public undertaking to take the aid measures in question . . .[177]

Damien Neven has made a strong case that higher standards of proof are required in *ex post* control of collusion than in *ex ante* merger control. The reason may be that *ex ante* decisions are surrounded by more uncertainty than *ex post* decisions. The policy may be explained with reference to procedural economy, or in other words an applied deterrence approach.[178]

IV. SUMMARY, DISCUSSION AND CONCLUSIONS

When it comes to evidence, Community law accepts divergences that lead to non-identical administrative enforcement against competition law infringements. The analysis carried out in this chapter reveals that Community law will indeed accept variations in outcomes, provided that a minimum standard applies. There is complex interplay between national law and Community law on evidence, where national authorities and courts must be prepared to apply their national rules on evidence in a flexible manner, to achieve the objectives laid down in Community law.

More particularly, the ascertaining of facts in cases on Articles 81 and 82 EC is a matter for national authorities and courts when such cases are initiated at the national level; but Community law ultimately determines what facts are relevant, through the interpretations given by the Community courts.

Further, the presumptions developed by the Court of Justice in Article 81(1) EC cases, namely the opt-out principle for cartel meetings and the presumption of pursuant market behaviour once collusion is shown, must be considered as interpretations of the concept of burden of proof, now regulated in Article 2 of Regulation 1. The direct applicability of the Regulation means that the presumptions apply in national Article 81 EC procedures, in both public enforcement and private litigation. Furthermore, those presumptions constitute general principles of Community law and form part of the rights of the defence.

The standard of proof developed by the Community courts is, in my view, *a minimum standard* in national cases on Articles 81 and 82 EC, given that it derives from the presumption of innocence, a fundamental principle of Community law.

177 Case C-482/99 *France v Commission* [2002] ECR I-4397, at para 53.

178 Neven, Damien J, '"Collusion" under Article 81 and the Merger Regulation' in *Fighting cartels—why and how* (Stockholm, Konkurrensverket, 2001), at 63.

However, one cannot presently discern a well-defined Community law *maximum* standard of proof in cartel cases. National authorities and courts enjoy the discretion to require higher standards of proof, provided such standards do not render virtually impossible or excessively difficult the exercise of Community law. The content of the Community law minimum standard of proof in cartels cases was set out in part II of this chapter.

The legal-theoretical basis for the Community courts' jurisprudence on evidence is still in its infancy. It appears that the courts are drawing legitimacy from the ECHR, while at the same time the case law on evidence may be seen as deterrence-based. An open discussion on the need to balance the rights of the defence with deterrence concerns would make better sense and contribute to a transparent dialogue. For pragmatic reasons, not all Member State courts will be able to ask the Court of Justice for guidance in every cartel case. Hence, they must have a better theoretical basis available for their adjudication. Developments of explicit theory building in Community law are relatively recent, and it is too early to say whether it has gained acceptance yet. The Court of Justice has not gone to great lengths to draw the line between 'burden of proof' and 'standard of proof', and the rationality of the present law must be developed further. Similarly, some development is needed in order to set out the connection between facts and standards of proof—in other words, to define situations when the standard of proof is typically met and where it is not. On several points, however, we can observe that EC law has developed much in line with US law. It is difficult to tell whether this is a coincidence, or if it signifies a systematic interest in US antitrust law by the Community courts. A pooling of experiences can only be an advantage in these complicated cases, and a comparative approach seems desirable.

Moving forward, we can see that there is a certain amount of *input legitimacy* in so far as a rule regarding the burden of proof has been enacted through legislation, a process in which the Member States that existed in the early 2000s participated. On the other hand, the rule in Article 2 of Regulation 1 is only a codification of previous judge-made law; but the Community could have changed that law had it so wished, and by enacting Article 2 of Regulation 1, it created democratic legitimacy.

Looking at the presumptions applied in cartel cases, their creation in case law has not generated any outrage in the legal community, even if voices have been raised as to how difficult it is for an undertaking to avoid being swept up once it comes into contact with a cartel. By and large these presumptions have been accepted, and consequently vested with some degree of *empirical and normative legitimacy.*

Turning to legitimacy aspects of *enforcement*, the analysis reveals a considerable potential for divergent outcomes in similar cases, depending on what view the respective national authority or court takes on the standard of proof. It has been explained how over- or under-inclusiveness in the admission and evaluation of evidence can erode substantive law from within. My prognosis is that decentralisation will fail to result in coherent outcomes. Actually, the position on evidence in Regulation 1 indicates that the achievement of coherent outcomes was not an objective—it affects neither national rules on the standard of proof, nor the obligations of national competition authorities and courts of the Member States to ascertain the relevant facts of a case, provided that such rules and obligations are compatible with general principles of Community law.[179] This may be contrasted with the uncompromising requirements from the Court of Justice on the consistent application of substantive rules, an objective that was emphasised time and time again in the preparatory works to the legislation. Either the uniformity requirement is exaggerated, or the tolerance of various national solutions to the standard of proof is entirely uncalled for. In other words, uniformity in substance and national competence on standard of proof are opposing values that seem to be cancelling each other out. Clearly, this was not how the law was supposed to come out. Rather, the political objective of preserving national procedural autonomy led to confused legislation, a stereotypical situation where 'the battle among opposite and equally strong values at the political level results in empty legal categories and concepts'.[180]

This analysis gives an idea of the intricacy of the process of determining a common minimum standard. The argument must be raised that this is not a trivial matter for every national authority or judge to handle. An idea is put forward here that efficiency considerations require specialised authorities *and* courts, to create the prerequisites for pooling the necessary know how.

[179] Regulation 1/2003, preamble, at 5.

[180] Zamboni, Mauro, *The Policy of Law—A Legal Theoretical Framework* (Oxford, Hart Publishing, 2008), at 187.

6

Legitimacy and the Relation between National Competition Procedure and EC Law

LEGITIMACY IS AN undercurrent in all EC case law on fundamental rights and the rights of the defence, where the Community courts have drawn inspiration from the European Convention of Human Rights (ECHR) and the case law related to it. The inequality of arms between an individual accused of violating the law and the often more powerful legal institutions is a core issue. One can observe moral reasoning when it comes to competition law procedure. Whether or not to allow extensive defences, thereby tying up the resources of the courts and the plaintiffs, is not just a matter of procedural economy but also a question of morality. In essence, 'moral harm will trigger the exercise of the rights of the defence'.[1]

Supervision and the enforcement of Articles 81 and 82 EC have been decentralised, although without any harmonisation of the Member States' national competition procedures. When the modernisation was designed, fears were generally expressed that it would result in inconsistent application, a debate described in chapter two above. Most of the arguments, however, centred around the risk of inconsistent interpretation of Articles 81 and 82 EC as such, or the risk that a national authority or court would disregard a previous Commission decision on the very same issue. Nevertheless, the absence of procedural harmonisation was addressed in the debate.

Temple Lang highlighted the need to consider the harmonisation of powers and procedures of national authorities, and pointed at the connection between procedures and results.[2] According to Kon, basic harmonisation of powers and procedures was essential, since there was no good reason why national competition authorities

[1] Barbier de La Serre, Eric, 'Procedural Justice in the European Community Case-law concerning the Rights of the Defence: Essentialist and Instrumental Trends' (2006) 12(2) *European Public Law* 225, at 240.

[2] Temple Lang, John, 'General Report on the Application of Community Competition Law on Enterprises by National Courts and National Authorities', FIDE Congress 1998, available at http://ec.europa.eu/comm/competition/speeches/text/sp1998_027_en.html, at 35, 49.

> should each follow separate procedures in matters as fundamental as powers of search and seizure, rights of inspection, rights of defence, duration of procedures, interim measures, enforcement and fining powers . . .[3]

During the legislative process the Economic and Social Committee drew attention to the risk that the absence of a harmonised competition procedure would affect consistency.[4] Later on it even suggested harmonised procedural rules and a central appeal authority as a remedy.[5] The Commission did not respond to these concerns; nearly every aspect of national supervision and enforcement of Articles 81 and 82 EC is governed by national procedure.[6] In a 2005 survey, the OECD commented on the absence of any EU directives requiring substantive harmonisation of national competition laws. 'The net effect of decentralisation remains to be seen,' says the OECD, observing that 'The system is founded on the expectation that coherence will be achieved through common legal principles subject to supervision by the ECJ'.[7]

Given the impact that competition procedure has on the final outcome of a case, wide discretion left to Member States on procedural law may be expected to affect the chances of uniform application. The present analysis is carried out with reference to relevant principles of EC law, with a discussion, in each case, of whether national authorities and courts have discretion as regards the solution to these problems. Unlike available handbooks on competition procedure, the aim is not to provide a comprehensive picture of the competition procedure within the Commission and Community courts, but to set a framework for analysing the problems connected with transposition of the relevant case law to the national context. In other words, how much of the jurisprudence is relevant for national authorities and courts, and to what extent? This chapter is furthermore based on EC law, and does not cover any questions relating to possible wider protection for companies and natural persons pursuant to the ECHR.[8]

[3] Kon, Stephen, 'The Commission's White Paper on Modernisation: The Need for Procedural Harmonisation' in Hawk (ed), *International Antitrust Law & Policy: Fordham Corporate Law* (New York, Juris Publishing, 1999), at 252–53.

[4] Opinion of the Economic and Social Committee on the 'White Paper on modernisation of the rules implementing Articles 81 and 82 of the EC Treaty—Commission programme No 99/027' [2000] OJ C/51/55, at paras 2.3.2.2–2.3.2.3.

[5] Opinion of the Economic and Social Committee on the 'Proposal for a Council Regulation on the implementation of the rules on competition laid down in Articles 81 and 82 of the EC Treaty. . .' [2001] OJ C/155/73 at paras 2.10.6. and 2.14.1.

[6] COM(2000) 582 Final—Explanatory memorandum p 12, 5th paragraph: 'The present proposal is based on the premise that national competition authorities will apply Articles 81 and 82 in accordance with their respective national procedural rules. It is not necessary for the implementation of the reform to embark on a full-scale harmonisation of national procedural laws.'.

[7] OECD, *Competition Law and Policy in the European Union* (OECD, 2005), at 61.

[8] See esp on this topic Riley, Alan, 'Saunders and the power to obtain information in Community and United Kingdom Competition law' (2000) 25(3) *EL Rev* 264; Smith, Graham P, 'Competition law and the ignoring of human rights' [2001] *International Company and Commercial Law Review* 1–4; and Willis, Peter R, '"You have the right to remain silent . . .", or do you? The privilege against self-incrimination following Mannesmannrohren-Werke and other recent decisions' (2001) 22(8) *ECLR* 313.

I. EMPIRICAL LEGITIMACY OF EC ANTITRUST PROCEDURE

Regulation 17 (now replaced by Regulation 1) said little about procedural rights for undertakings subject to investigations or allegations. The Community courts had to create procedural principles and standards in order to fill the vacuum left by the legislator. The content of those principles will be explored at some length in this chapter, but as a preliminary point, it is interesting to note that the initiative of the Community courts in creating a sophisticated set of procedural rules is largely uncontested by the legal community. The discussion focuses on whether the Community courts have created standards that are compatible with the ECHR,[9] but there seems to be general consensus that the Community courts were right to introduce procedural standards in the first place. Lenaerts emphasises the legitimacy aspect: '. . . checks and balances which guarantee the legitimacy of the exercise of public authority both at the national and the European level'.[10]

When considering the *empirical legitimacy* thus observed, one should once again keep in mind that the Community courts created procedural law to fill the lacunae left by the Community legislator. The creation of procedural principles in EC law is thus unproblematic in relation to the Commission's powers, because there was no pre-existing law with which it could come into conflict. Conflicts manifest themselves on another level: the balancing of efficiency against the integrity of companies, the strength of Community institutions versus the capacity of undertakings to defend themselves in the context of administrative procedures.

On the other hand, there is no reason to believe that there is a vacuum when it comes to procedural law in Member States. General principles of Community law will, as a general rule, have to be measured against existing procedural law, and can occasionally come into conflict with prevailing national principles. While the Community courts have motivated their creative activity in this field with reference to principles that can be found at least implicitly in the legal traditions of Member States,[11] this does not mean that such creation was preceded by comprehensive studies which eliminate the possibility of conflicting national procedural principles. Moreover, we should keep in mind that several of the prevailing principles were introduced in the 1980s, when the number of Member States was less than half that of today.

Looking at the problems generated by multi-level enforcement of fundamental rights, reference must be made to van Gerven:

[9] Ameye, Evelyne M, 'The Interplay Between Human Rights and Competition Law in the EU' (2004) 25(6) *ECLR* 332; Andreangeli, Arianna, 'The Protection of Legal Professional Privilege in EU Law and the Impact of the Rules of Exchange of Information within the European Competition Network on the Secrecy of Communication between Lawyer and Client: one step forward, two steps back?' (2005) 2(1) *The Competition Law Review* 31; Cumming, G, 'Procedural comment: Privilege against self-incrimination' (2005) 26(7) *ECLR* 375; Riley, above n 8; Smith, above n 8; Willis, above n 8.

[10] Lenaerts, Koen, '"In the union we trust": Trust-enhancing principles of Community law' (2004) 41(2) *CML Rev* 317, at 342.

[11] *Ibid*, at 317.

> Coherence of enforcement is an even greater problem: at all these levels, courts (or committees) are in charge of enforcement, however with considerable differences regarding jurisdiction (constitutional, administrative or civil courts), plaintiffs (states, institutions, private persons and private legal entities), defendants (legislatures, administrations, private persons), procedures (direct procedures, preliminary procedures, summary proceedings), and kinds of relief (nullity, restitution, compensation, interim relief).[12]

Whilst it is encouraging to see that the Community courts' jurisprudence on procedural rights has been generally accepted in the legal community, this does not allow for a conclusion that the transposition of the very same principles to Member States will be considered legitimate in a deeper sense. Consequently, it is necessary to embark upon an evaluation of the applicable principles, in relative detail.

A. The references to national law in Regulation 1

Articles 1, 2, 3, 5, 6, 11, 12, 13, 15, 16, 20(8), 21(3), 22, 28 and 35 of Regulation 1 are addressed to Member States. These provisions include the following:

—Direct applicability of Articles 81 and 82 EC (Article 1)
—Burden of proof (Article 2)
—The relationship between Articles 81 and 82 EC and national competition laws (Article 3)
—Powers of national competition authorities (Article 5)
—Powers of national courts (Article 6)
—Co-operation between the Commission and national competition authorities (Article 11)
—Exchange of information (Article 12)
—Parallel proceedings (Article 13)
—Co-operation with national courts (Article 15)
—Uniform application of Community competition law (Article 16)
—Assistance by national judiciary when the Commission is carrying out investigations (Articles 20(8) and 21(3))
—Fact-finding measures carried out by a national competition authority on behalf of the Commission or another national competition authority (Article 22)
—Professional secrecy (Article 28)
—Withdrawal of block exemptions (Article 29(1))
—Designation of competition authorities of Member States (Article 35).

Nevertheless, a closer look at Regulation 1 reveals that numerous issues of great significance are still entirely regulated by national law. National competition

[12] van Gerven, W, 'Remedies for Infringements of Fundamental Rights' [2004] *European Public Law* 261, at 261–62.

procedure remains outside Regulation 1.[13] National law thus governs procedural aspects when Articles 81 and 82 EC are applied in national authorities or courts. This includes fact-finding powers of national authorities, as well as the imposition of fines or other sanctions by national authorities and courts. National laws also govern the basic rules on access to documents. Article 12 of Regulation 1 only addresses exchange of information between competition authorities, and Article 28 of the Regulation is limited to professional secrecy.

In essence, national laws govern nearly every procedural aspect of supervision and enforcement at the national level. However, it will be demonstrated that national law must occasionally be modified in order to conform to general principles of Community law. Such modification must be made by the legislator, or, if it fails, independently by the national authorities and courts.

II. NORMATIVE LEGITIMACY—UNIFORMITY, EFFECTIVENESS AND NATIONAL PROCEDURAL AUTONOMY

National law governs competition procedure in each Member State. According to settled case law, in the absence of Community rules it is for the domestic legal system of each Member State to designate the courts and tribunals having jurisdiction, and to lay down the detailed procedural rules governing actions for safeguarding the rights which individuals derive from Community law. This is provided that such rules are not less favourable than those governing similar domestic actions (the principle of equivalence) and that they do not render practically impossible or excessively difficult the exercise of rights conferred by Community law (the principle of effectiveness).[14]

For the purposes of applying those principles, each case must be analysed by reference to the role of that provision in the procedure, its progress and its special features, viewed as a whole, before the various national instances. In the light of that analysis, the basic principles of the domestic judicial system—such as protection of the rights of the defence, the principle of legal certainty and the proper conduct of procedure—must, where appropriate, be taken into consideration.[15] There is consequently *no absolute requirement of uniformity*—Community law accepts that national procedural law exerts an influence on the outcome of a case, within the limits just described, and does not expect identical outcomes.

As mentioned in chapter five, the principles just referred to seem slightly at odds with strong effectiveness cases such as *Simmenthal* and *Factortame*, where the norm is the *full effect* of EC competition law. National courts have been obliged to

[13] COM(2000) 582 Final, Explanatory memorandum, at 12, 5th para: 'The present proposal is based on the premise that national competition authorities will apply Articles 81 and 82 in accordance with their respective national procedural rules. It is not necessary for the implementation of the reform to embark on a full-scale harmonisation of national procedural laws.'

[14] Case C-526/04 *Laboratoires Boiron* [2006] ECR I-7529, at para 51.

[15] Joined Cases C-430/93 and C-431/93 *Van Schijndel and van Veen* [1995] ECR I-4705, at para 19.

set aside any provision of a national legal system and any legislative, administrative or judicial practice which even *might impair* the effectiveness of Community law.[16] Are there two different standards of effectiveness? Or is there a general erosion of the principle of national procedural autonomy, where we will see ever more stringent requirements that Community law is given full effect?[17] The Court of Justice has required that national courts interpret, as far as it is possible, the provisions of national law in such a way that they can be applied in a manner which contributes to what must be understood as effective implementation of Community law. When such an interpretation of national law is insufficient to solve the problem, the Court has referred to the full effect of Community law to set aside national procedural provisions which would otherwise frustrate the application of Community law.[18]

It seems that the 'full effect' doctrine is applied mainly to solve outright conflicts of law.[19] The 'other' principle of effectiveness—that national rules must not render virtually impossible or excessively difficult the exercise of rights conferred by Community law—is relied on when national procedure merely exerts an influence on the case, without actually frustrating the outcome. The further steps in this analysis of the interplay between EC competition law and national procedure will be based on such a reading of the case law. I will consequently proceed from an understanding that uniformity and effectiveness must be balanced against national procedural autonomy.

In *Cement*, the Court of Justice reasoned on the Commission's investigative powers with reference to effectiveness.[20] This implies that national procedure must be scrutinised with reference to EC law to see whether the investigatory powers granted to national authorities comply with the principle of effectiveness. Further support for this view may be found in *Commission v Greece*, where the Court held that infringements of Community law must be penalised under procedural conditions

> which are analogous to those applicable to infringements of national law of a similar nature and importance and which, in any event, make the penalty effective, proportionate and dissuasive . . .[21]

Not that the Commission's fact-finding powers must be duplicated at the national level, but rather that any weakness of investigatory powers can make the supervision and enforcement of Articles 81 and 82 EC practically impossible or excessively difficult, contrary to the principle of effectiveness.

[16] Case 106/77 *Simmenthal* [1978] ECR 629, at paras 21–24; Case C-213/89 *Factortame and Others* [1990] ECR I-2433, at paras 19–21.

[17] Accetto, Matej, and Zleptnig, Stefan, 'The Principle of Effectiveness: Rethinking Its Role in Community Law' [2005] *European Public Law* 375, at 396.

[18] Case C-119/05 *Lucchini Siderurgica* [2007] ECR I-6199, at paras 59 ff.

[19] Flynn, Leo, 'Enforcement of EC Law: Protection of Individual's Rights in National Courts' (2007) 10(2) *Europarättslig Tidskrift* 294, at 316: '. . . disapplication of national law is reserved for these situations where it was not possible to read the national law in conformity with the requirements of EC law'.

[20] Joined Cases C-204/00 P, etc *Aalborg Portland and others v Commission* [2004] ECR I-123, at para 61.

[21] Case 68/88 *Commission v Greece* [1989] ECR 2965, at para 24.

III. FUNDAMENTAL RIGHTS AND NATIONAL PROCEDURE

Where national legislation falls within the field of application of Community law, the national court must assess the compatibility of national legislation with fundamental rights.[22] This applies in public enforcement of Articles 81 and 82 EC. Requirements for the protection of fundamental rights are binding on the Member States when they implement Community rules, which mean that Member States must, as far as possible, apply those rules in accordance with those requirements.[23] This means that if the cause of action in a national procedure falls within the field of EC law, fundamental rights will automatically be applicable and must be observed by the national court.[24] In particular, the Court of Justice has established that in all proceedings in which sanctions, especially fines or penalty payments, may be imposed, observance of the rights of the defence is a fundamental principle of Community law which must be complied with even if the proceedings in question are administrative proceedings.[25] There is little specific guidance from the Community courts on the subject, but Tridimas argues that

> the rights of the individual should not differ depending on whether he or she is dealing with the Community or national authorities. Thus the general approach must be that the principles applicable to the Community administration must apply *mutatis mutandis* to the national administration unless there is a reason which justifies the application of different standards.[26]

Application of fundamental rights in national procedure when EC law applies is actually old news for academics: Temple Lang pointed out this connection convincingly in 1998, and concluded that

> insofar as national competition authorities are applying Community competition law they must comply with Community procedural standards, and these will have a harmonising effect in the long term . . .[27]

Tridimas finds yet another ground for application of fundamental rights in so far as Article 35(1) of Regulation 1 states that the Member States must designate the competent authorities responsible for the application of Articles 81 and 82 EC. It would then be

[22] See esp Case C-94/00 *Roquette Frères* [2002] ECR I-9011, at para 25.

[23] Case 5/88 *Wachauf* [1989] ECR 2609, at paras 17–19.

[24] See esp Case C-292/97 *Karlsson and others* [2000] ECR I-2737, at para 37: '. . . it should be remembered that the requirements flowing from the protection of fundamental rights in the Community legal order are also binding on Member States when they implement Community rules. Consequently, Member States must, as far as possible, apply those rules in accordance with those requirements'.

[25] Case C-176/99 P *ARBED v Commission* [2003] ECR I-10687, at para 19.

[26] Tridimas, Takis, *The General Principles of EU Law*, 2nd edn (Oxford, Oxford University Press, 2006), at 416.

[27] Temple Lang, John, 'General Report on the Application of Community Competition Law on Enterprises by National Courts and National Authorities', FIDE Congress 1998, available at http://ec.europa.eu/comm/competition/speeches/text/sp1998_027_en.html, at 26, 49, 50.

> incongruous and contrary to the notion of equal treatment if undertakings were subject to a lower level of procedural protection where proceedings are initiated against them by national competition authorities rather than the Commission . . .[28]

Since the requirement to protect fundamental rights is binding on Member States, it will be binding not only for national courts but also for all organs of the State, including national competition authorities.[29]

Fundamental rights are also connected to the principle of effectiveness. Tridimas observes that the principle of effectiveness bypasses national standards and prompts national courts to view the domestic rules on remedies from a different perspective.[30] But the connection to uniformity seems weaker, and for good reason. Although fundamental rights apply when national authorities and courts apply Article 81 EC, it is crucial to observe that there is *no automatic transposition of the Community competition procedure to national competition procedure.* Rather, the principle of effectiveness requires that national procedural law must be assessed with a view to achieving the objectives laid down in Community law. This follows from the methodology of analysis prescribed by the Court in *Van Schijndel* and other cases.[31]

The Court recently established, when interpreting a Community regulation, an obligation for national courts to interpret their national law within the limits set by Community law, in order to achieve the result intended by the Community rule in question.[32] When ruling in a case on a Community regulation in the agricultural sector, the Court accepted reliance on the rules of evidence of national law, *provided that the effectiveness of Community law was not undermined.*[33] A general observation is thus that national procedure must be applied in a flexible manner, and occasionally even be set aside. National judiciaries may have to take it upon themselves to fill out gaps in the national procedural system. National authorities and courts must consequently observe dual requirements: the rights of the defence to protect undertakings, and the principle of effectiveness to ensure the impact of EC law. Occasionally a balancing act must be carried out between Community law rights and principles of legal certainty common to the systems in Member States.[34] Provided that effectiveness of Community law is not undermined, the Court of Justice accepted the possibility of parallel application of Community law and national procedure in *Roquette Frères*, where it hinted at this as follows: '. . . without prejudice to the guarantees under domestic law . . . undertakings under investigation are protected by various Community guarantees . . .'[35]

[28] Tridimas, above n 26, at 395.

[29] Case C-198/01 *CIF* [2003] ECR I-8055 p 49.

[30] Tridimas, above n 26, at 423.

[31] See esp Joined Cases C-222/05 to C-225/05 *van der Weerd and others* [2007] ECR I-4233, at para 33.

[32] Case C-60/02 *Rolex and Others* [2004] ECR I-651, at para 59.

[33] Case C-279/05 *Vonk Dairy Products* [2007] ECR I-239, at para 43.

[34] *van der Weerd and others*, above n 31.

[35] *Roquette Frères*, above n 22, at para 46.

A. Rights of the defence

In the previous section it was explained that fundamental rights developed in EC law apply when national authorities and courts apply Articles 81 and 82 EC. Of central importance for competition law cases are the rights of the defence. So what is the content of these rights? The Court explained the rights of the defence *in principle* in *Thyssen Stahl*:

(i) the rights of the defence are infringed where it is possible that the outcome of the administrative procedure have been different as a result of an error *and*
(ii) an applicant undertaking establishes that there has been such an infringement where it adequately demonstrates, not that the decision would have been different in content, but rather that it would have been better able to ensure its defence had there been no error.[36]

Put in minimalist terms by the Court of First Instance in *Seamless steel tubes*, the rights of the defence are infringed by virtue of a procedural irregularity if that irregularity had a definite impact on the possibilities for the undertakings implicated to defend themselves.[37]

Whether a national court must apply the same burden of proof as the Court (requiring the undertaking to demonstrate that it would have been better able to ensure its defence) seems to be an open question—presumably the standard just referred to is a minimum standard and Member States are free to provide a higher level of protection to undertakings.

The rights of the defence form part of a more extensive body of case law of the Community courts based mainly on Articles 6 and 8 of the ECHR, essentially intended to protect individuals, including companies, against measures of investigation ordered by public authorities which can lead to administrative or criminal penalties.[38]

In *Internationale Handelsgesellschaft*, it was held that respect for fundamental rights forms an integral part of the general principles of law protected by the Court of Justice. Protection of such rights, whilst inspired by the constitutional traditions common to the Member States, must be ensured within the framework of the structure and objectives of the Community.[39] This was derived from the constitutional traditions common to the Member States and not from the ECHR. The Court then established in *Hoffmann-La Roche*, although still without making any reference to the ECHR, that observance of the right to be heard is a fundamental principle of Community law which must be respected in all proceedings in which sanctions, in particular fines or penalty payments, may be imposed, even if the proceedings in question are administrative proceedings.[40] This obligation was

[36] Case C-194/99 P *Thyssen Stahl v Commission* [2003] ECR I-10821, at para 31.
[37] Case T-44/00 *Mannesmannröhren-Werke v Commission* [2004] ECR II-2223, at para 55.
[38] Case C-60/92 *Otto* [1993] ECR I-5683, at para 16.
[39] Case 11/70 *Internationale Handelsgesellschaft* [1970] ECR 1125, at para 4.
[40] Case 85/76 *Hoffmann-La Roche v Commission* [1979] ECR 461, at para 9.

stated in *Michelin* to include rights of the defence in general.[41] In *Johnston*, the Court held that the principles on which the ECHR is based must be taken into consideration in Community law.[42] The judgments in *Hoechst*,[43] *Dow Benelux*[44] and *Orkem*,[45] all delivered in 1989, clarified the connection between the principles of the Convention and the rights of the defence further.

It may be added that, according to Article 6 of the Treaty on European Union (TEU), the Union is founded on the principles of liberty, democracy, respect for human rights and fundamental freedoms, and the rule of law, principles which are common to the Member States. Moreover, the Union shall respect fundamental rights, as guaranteed by the Convention and as they result from the constitutional traditions common to the Member States, as general principles of Community law.

The precise approach of the Community courts to the rights of the defence appears to have evolved over time, the tendency being towards a gradual reinforcement. In early judgments, such as *Hoechst* and *Dow Benelux*, the Court of Justice held fundamental rights to be an integral part of the general principles of law the observance of which the Court ensures, in accordance with constitutional traditions common to the Member States and international treaties, of which the ECHR is of particular significance.[46] In this connection the rights of the defence are pronounced as a principle of a fundamental nature.[47]

In 1998, the Court referred to the ECHR in *Baustahlgewebe*, holding that the right to a fair legal process was inspired by those fundamental rights.[48] The Court of First Instance found in *Mannesmannröhren-Werke*, in 2001, that fundamental rights form an integral part of the general principles of Community law and that the Convention has special significance in that respect. Reference was also made to Article 6.2 TEU.[49]

The wording is yet clearer in recent cases: in the judgment in *ARBED* (one of the *Steel Beams* cases), the Court held that in all proceedings in which sanctions, especially fines or penalty payments, may be imposed, observance of the rights of the defence is a fundamental principle of Community law which must be complied with even if the proceedings in question are administrative proceedings.[50] An identical statement was made on the same day in *Thyssen Stahl*.[51] Notably, the *Steel Beams* cases concerned the ECSC Treaty, which is probably the reason why the Court referred to its judgment in *Hoffmann La-Roche* and not to the ECHR. In *Cement*, the law was summarised as follows:

41 Case 322/81 *Michelin v Commission* [1983] ECR 3461, at para 7.
42 Case 222/84 *Johnston* [1986] ECR 1651, at para 18.
43 Joined Cases 46/87 and 227/88 *Hoechst v Commission* [1989] ECR 2859.
44 Case 85/87 *Dow Benelux v Commission* [1989] ECR 3137.
45 Case 374/87 *Orkem v Commission* [1989] ECR 3283.
46 *Hoechst v Commission*, above n 43, at para 13; *Dow Benelux v Commission*, above n 44, at para 24.
47 *Hoechst v Commission*, above n 43, at para 4; *Dow Benelux v Commission*, above n 44, at para 25.
48 Case C-185/95 P *Baustahlgewebe v Commission* [1998] ECR I-8417, at paras 20–21.
49 Case T-112/98 *Mannesmannröhren-Werke v Commission* [2001] ECR II-729, at para 60.
50 *ARBED v Commission*, above n 25, at para 19.
51 *Thyssen Stahl v Commission*, above n 36, at para 30.

> The rights of the defence are fundamental rights forming an integral part of the general principles of law, whose observance the Court ensures . . . drawing inspiration for that purpose from the constitutional traditions common to the Member States and from the guidelines supplied by international treaties for the protection of human rights . . . such as the European Convention for the Protection of Human Rights and Fundamental Freedoms.[52]

Moving from meta-theory to pragmatic terms, procedural irregularities relevant to the rights of the defence in competition law cases may typically consist of the following actions and/or omissions (the list is illustrative and not meant to be exhaustive):

a) The decision authorising an inspection or a request for information does not fulfil the requirements set down in case law. The whole inspection/request is thus unlawful.
b) When carrying out an inspection based on a lawful decision/authorisation, the authorities exceed their powers of inspection by going outside of the subject-matter of the decision, by asking incriminating questions of the staff, or by allowing themselves access to premises or documents not covered by the decision.
c) Following an inspection where documents were collected lawfully, the authorities try to rely on the documents as evidence of infringements that were not the subject-matter of the inspection.
d) When carrying out an inspection, the authorities do not respect an undertaking's right to a legal representative.
e) When carrying out an inspection, the authorities do not respect the right to legal privilege, but read or seize material that constitutes correspondence between lawyer and client.
f) In a request for information which an undertaking is legally obliged to answer, incriminating questions are asked.
g) When interviewing a natural person, the authorities ask incriminating questions in a situation where the person is legally obliged to answer.
h) Infringements of the adversarial principle, for example deficiencies in a statement of objections.
i) The party suspected of a cartel infringement is given insufficient access to documents.
j) The authority or court does not fulfil its obligation to state reasons.

As explained, the rights of the defence are infringed only if the procedural irregularity in question had a definite impact on the possibilities for the undertakings implicated to defend themselves.[53] The respective rights and possible infringements will be described and analysed in detail in section IV. below, to explore from, a top-down perspective, whether the case law of the Community courts will have an impact on national competition procedure.

[52] *Aalborg Portland and others v Commission*, above n 20, at para 64.
[53] *Mannesmannröhren-Werke v Commission*, above n 37, at para 55.

1. Non-applicability of the rights of defence in private litigation

It has already been explained that the rights of defence are fundamental principles that must be complied with where national legislation falls within the field of application of Community law, in all proceedings in which sanctions, especially fines or penalty payments, may be imposed.

It is settled case law that the rights of the defence are not applicable in private litigation. It would seem difficult to place contractual remedies, claims for damages and even injunctions on an equal footing with sanctions such as fines and penalty payments. In *Otto*, the Court held that proceedings concerning exclusively private relations between individuals involving application of Articles 81 and 82 EC cannot lead, directly or indirectly, to the imposition of a penalty by a public authority. For this reason, the rights of the defence were held not to be applicable.[54]

IV. THE EMERGENCE OF A COMMON SET OF RULES APPLICABLE IN COMPETITION PROCEDURE

For the reasons set out in the previous sections, fundamental rights distinguish themselves as a common set of rules applicable in all public enforcement of Article 81 EC, whether it be the Commission or national competition authorities that are taking the initiative. Once again, that is not to say that the Community competition procedure should be duplicated at the national level—there is no requirement under Community law to this effect. Rather, national procedural law must be assessed with a view to achieving the objectives laid down in Community law. The bottom line is that the national judiciary must acquaint themselves with the fundamental rights in EC law, and check continuously whether national procedure lives up to this standard. Moreover, the Court has reiterated that

> each case which raises the question whether a national procedural provision renders the exercise of rights conferred by the Community legal order on individuals impossible or excessively difficult must be analysed by reference to the role of that provision in the procedure, its progress and its special features, viewed as a whole, before the various national instances. In that context, it is necessary to take into consideration, where relevant, the principles which lie at the basis of the national legal system, such as the protection of the rights of the defence, the principle of legal certainty and the proper conduct of the proceedings.[55]

The common set of rules will be examined in this chapter, save for general principles applicable to fines, which will be analysed in chapter seven.

[54] *Otto*, above n 38, at para 17.

[55] Among other cases see *van der Weerd and others*, above n 31, at para 33.

A. Investigatory powers—Member State discretion

Pursuant to Regulation 1, an investigation may be carried out by the Commission, by national competition authorities or by both. The Commission's powers are regulated in Articles 17 to 21 of Regulation 1, while the fact-finding powers of national competition authorities are outside Regulation 1. Co-operation between competition authorities is envisaged in Article 22 of the Regulation. Under Article 22(1), national competition authorities may carry out inspections or fact-finding measures on behalf and for the account of another national competition authority. Further, under Article 22(2), national competition authorities are under an obligation to carry out inspections which the Commission considers necessary or which it has ordered by decision.

In all these cases, the investigations are to be made in accordance with the law of the Member State of the competition authority carrying out the measures. National law also regulates investigations which a national competition authority carries out on its own initiative. In effect, national law will always regulate fact-finding measures carried out by a national competition authority, while the powers of the Commission are regulated in Regulation 1.

As has been explained, investigations of suspected infringements of Articles 81 and 82 EC carried out by national authorities must comply with general and fundamental principles of EC law. This means that investigations carried out pursuant to national law will, as a matter of principle, have to be very similar to investigations carried out by the Commission, since otherwise the rights of the defence (see section III.A. above) will risk being violated. This follows not only from application of the fundamental rights doctrine, but also from the principle of effectiveness. Reference may be made to the Court of Justice's judgment in *Cement*, where it based the Commission's investigative powers under Regulation 17 on the objective to ensure effectiveness.[56] This reasoning should apply similarly when national authorities supervise and enforce Articles 81 and 82 EC.

A more detailed account of relevant aspects of fundamental rights will be given next.

1. Necessary inspections and investigations

Under Article 18(1) of Regulation 1, the Commission is empowered to require undertakings and associations of undertakings to 'provide all necessary information'. Article 20(1) empowers the Commission to conduct 'all necessary inspections'. It appears that the Commission enjoys nearly total discretion in deciding whether a request for information or an inspection is necessary. According to the Court's judgment in *Orkem*, 'it is for the Commission to decide . . . whether particular information is necessary to enable it to bring to light an infringement of the competition rules'.[57]

[56] *Aalborg Portland and others v Commission*, above n 20, at para 61.
[57] *Orkem v Commission*, above n 45, at para 15.

In *Dow Chemical*, the applicants claimed that the Commission decisions infringed the principle of legality because they were not based on evidence or indicia of such a nature as to justify the inspections.[58] This allegation was rejected by the Court on the basis that the applicants had in no way substantiated that claim.[59] There is nothing in the judgment to indicate that the Court made any assessment at all of the evidence on which the Commission based the decisions. The judgment was adopted prior to the establishment of the Court of First Instance, where a review of the evidence underlying such a decision would, today, be made, as happened with the Commission's decision in *SEP*.[60] In any case, it would have been more straightforward for the Court of Justice to state clearly that the Commission enjoys full (or almost full) discretion when deciding whether there is sufficient evidence to necessitate an investigation. The way the judgment is drafted, a principle is set down where the undertakings must provide evidence to substantiate that the Commission did not have evidence to justify an investigation. Such evidence is practically impossible to produce, given, among other things, that the Commission is under no obligation to disclose the facts on which it bases its decisions.[61]

In *Roquette Frères*, the Court held that the review carried out by the Community courts is limited to ensuring that an investigation decision has not been adopted *in the absence of facts* capable of justifying the investigation.[62]

Even if the Commission already has evidence or proof of the existence of an infringement, it is still entitled to undertake further investigations to enable it better to define the scope of the infringement, determine its duration or identify the circle of undertakings involved.[63] Transposed to the national context, it may be concluded that a wide discretion left to Member State authorities when deciding whether an investigation is necessary will not infringe fundamental rights.

2. *Right to legal representation*

The right to legal representation is one of the rights of the defence, and thus a fundamental principle of EC law which must be complied with in the context of investigations carried out by national competition authorities. The Court held in *Hoechst* that while certain rights of the defence relate only to the contentious proceedings which follow the delivery of the statement of objections, other rights,

[58] Joined Cases 97/87 to 99/87 *Dow Chemical Ibérica and Others v Commission* [1989] ECR 3165, at para 50.

[59] *Ibid*, at para 52.

[60] Order of the President of the Court of First Instance of 21 November 1990, Case T-39/90 R *SEP v Commission* [1990] ECR II-649, at para 21.

[61] *Dow Chemical*, above n 58, at paras 45 and 51; similarly, when the Commission seeks enforcement by national authorities, *Roquette Frères*, above n 22, at paras 62–70.

[62] *Roquette Frères*, above n 22, at para 55.

[63] *Orkem v Commission*, above n 45, at para 15.

such as the right to legal representation, must be respected as from the preliminary inquiry stage.[64]

When carrying out inspections, the Commission will allow the undertakings subject to inspections a short delay for the arrival of legal representatives or for consulting the lawyer over the phone.[65] What, then, is a legal representative? This question does not seem to have been subject to interpretation by the Community courts. In the Commission's view, it could be an in-house legal adviser, or a lawyer of the undertaking's choice.[66] The Commission does not consider itself under a duty to await the arrival of external counsel if there is an in-house lawyer present,[67] but will still normally wait until such counsel has arrived.

If the Commission's view is correct, there is thus no obligation to await the arrival of external counsel if there is an in-house lawyer present. Given the increasing specialisation within the legal profession, this view appears out-of-date. As highly-skilled and experienced an in-house lawyer may be, he or she may still have no knowledge of competition law in general and dawn-raids in particular. Moreover, the investigating authority will often bring a dozen or so lawyers, and the undertaking should be allowed to provide enough counsel to oversee the work.

3. *Duty to state reasons in decisions authorising investigations*

Pursuant to Article 18(3) of Regulation 1, the Commission's requests for information shall specify the legal basis and purpose of the request, and what information is required. Decisions authorising Commission inspections shall, pursuant to Article 20(3) and (4) of Regulation 1, specify the subject-matter and purpose of the inspection. The difference in language appears to be reminiscent of Regulation 17, although Regulation 1 has added the requirement that the Commission specifies what information is required in requests for information. It follows from case law that both written authorisations and decisions on inspections must specify both the subject-matter and the purpose of the investigation.[68]

The Court established in *Hoechst*[69] and *Dow Benelux*[70] that the Commission is required to specify the subject-matter and purpose of the investigation, that obligation being a fundamental requirement to show that the investigation is justified. It is clear from the judgments that this requirement constitutes a fundamental guarantee of the rights of the defence of the undertakings concerned.[71] Consequently,

[64] *Hoechst v Commission*, above n 43, at para 16.

[65] See esp Dekeyser, Kris and Gauer, Céline, 'The New Enforcement System for Articles 81 and 82 and the Rights of the Defence' in Hawk (ed), *International Antitrust Law & Policy: Fordham Corporate Law* (New York, Juris Publishing, 2004) at 566.

[66] Answer to Written Question No 284/92 by Mr Yves Verwaerde to the Commission [1992] OJ C/168/45; see also Kerse, CS., *EC Antitrust Procedure*, 4th edn (London, Sweet & Maxwell, 1998), at 148.

[67] *Ibid.*

[68] *Hoechst v Commission*, above n 43, at para 22.

[69] *Ibid*, at para 29.

[70] *Dow Benelux v Commission*, above n 44, at para 40.

[71] *Hoechst*, above n 43, at para 41; *Dow Benelux*, above n 44, at para 8.

the same applies when a Member State competition authority or court adopts decisions on investigations of suspected infringements of Articles 81 and 82 EC.

What, then, are the precise requirements under EC law for a sufficient specification of the subject-matter and purpose of an investigation? In *Dow Benelux* the applicant claimed that a Commission decision authorising an inspection must contain a correct definition of the relevant market, a geographical definition of that market, an adequate description of the presumed infringements and an indication as to the period during which those infringements were supposedly committed.[72] The Court rejected this reasoning, finding that it is not an indispensable requirement for such a decision to delimit precisely the relevant market, to set out the exact legal nature of the presumed infringements and to indicate the period during which those infringements were committed.[73] However, the Commission must clearly indicate the presumed facts which it intends to investigate.[74] The Court's reasoning effectively leaves the Commission with a considerable discretion—if it can presume the facts it intends to investigate. However, in *Roquette Frères*, the Court of Justice held that the Community judicature may be called upon to carry out a review for the purposes of ensuring that 'the investigation decision itself is in no way arbitrary, that is to say, that it has not been adopted *in the absence of facts capable of justifying the investigation*'.[75] It thus appears that some level of proof (unclear what level) is required to justify an investigation.

In *Hoechst* and *Dow Benelux*, the Commission had drafted its decision in very general terms. Nevertheless, the decision referred to information suggesting the existence and application of agreements or concerted practices between certain producers and suppliers of PVC and polyethylene (including, but not limited to, the product LdPE) in the EEC, concerning prices, quantities or sales targets for those products. As for legal classification, the decision stated that those agreements and practices might constitute a serious infringement of Article 85(1) (now 81(1)) EC. The investigation concerned the undertaking's possible participation in those agreements or concerted practices. While criticising the decision, which according to the Court might well have been more precise, the Court rejected the claim that the statement of reasons was insufficient.[76]

In *Roquette Frères*, it was held, on the basis of the rights of the defence, that the Commission must state as precisely as possible what it is looking for and the matters to which the investigation must relate.[77]

Advocate-General Jacobs suggested, in his Opinion in *SEP*, that the Commission must make the subject-matter of its enquiry clear when requesting information, since otherwise the undertaking will be unable to determine whether there are grounds for refusing to comply and for challenging the decision before

[72] *Dow Benelux*, above n 44, at para 6.
[73] *Ibid*, at para 10.
[74] *Hoechst*, above n 43, at para 41; *Dow Benelux*, above n 44, at para 9.
[75] *Roquette Frères*, above n 22, at para 55, emphasis added.
[76] *Hoechst*, above n 43, at para 42; *Dow Benelux*, above n 44, at para 11.
[77] *Roquette Frères*, above n 22, at para 48.

the Court of First Instance.[78] This reasoning was made part of the judgment of the Court of Justice.[79]

From this, the following conclusion may be made as regards the minimum requirements under EC law of a decision authorising investigations of suspected infringements of Articles 81 and 82 EC. The decision (whether adopted by the Commission under Regulation 1, or by a national court or authority under national law) must contain information on:

a) the subject-matter of the investigation; not just a vague reference to agreements or concerted practices or abuse of a dominant position, but a statement, as precise as possible, of what the authorities are looking for and the matters to which the investigation must relate, sufficiently clear to enable the undertaking to determine whether there are grounds for refusing to comply and for challenging the decision;
b) what type of products or services the suspected infringement concerns; and
c) the reason why the undertaking is required to submit to the investigation, for example because of suspicions that the undertaking is involved in the infringement.

Decisions that are less specific are erroneous and will lead to infringements of the rights of the defence, provided that the undertaking demonstrates that it would have been better able to ensure its defence had there been no error.[80]

4. *The undertaking's duty to co-operate*

There is no right for undertakings to remain passive when subjected to an investigation relating to suspected infringements of Articles 81 and 82 EC. In *Orkem*, an obligation to co-operate actively was established, according to which the undertaking must make available to the Commission all information relating to the subject-matter of the investigation.[81] This duty of active co-operation includes that the undertaking must be prepared to make available to the Commission any information relating to the object of the inquiry.[82] Transposed to the national context, it is clear that fundamental rights under EC law will not require that undertakings are given a right to remain silent or passive.

5. *Extent of the investigatory powers*

Once there is a lawful decision on investigative measures, the question arises whether the Commission or national authorities may request information that has any connection, however vague, with the subject-matter of investigation, or

78 Opinion of A-G Jacobs in Case C-36/92 P *SEP v Commission* [1994] ECR I-1911, at para 34.
79 *SEP v Commission*, above n 78, at para 21.
80 *Thyssen Stahl v Commission*, above n 36, at para 31.
81 *Orkem v Commission*, above n 45, at para 27.
82 *Aalborg Portland and others v Commission*, above n 20, at para 62.

whether there are further limitations on the investigatory powers. Primarily, the scope of the Commission's investigatory powers does not extend to documents of a non-business nature, that is to say, documents not relating to the market activities of the undertaking[83]; but it is not clear whether this limitation on the Commission's power forms part of the rights of the defence—the Court is referring to Community law 'guarantees'.[84]

In *Hoechst*, the question arose whether the Commission was limited to asking for documents or files which it could identify with precision in advance. The Court of Justice held that the right of access would serve no useful purpose if the investigatory powers were limited in this way, and said: 'On the contrary, such a right implies the power to search for various items of information which are not already known or fully identified.'[85] This particular case law seems, implicitly, to be driven by the objective of achieving effectiveness. Further, in *Cement* it was made explicit that the extent of the investigatory powers is aimed at ensuring effectiveness.[86]

It would be unlawful, however, for the competition authorities to require an undertaking to provide legal or economic assessments. The undertaking is able to limit itself to *answering questions of a purely factual nature* and to produce only *pre-existing documents and materials*, a right which applies as from the very first stage of an investigation.[87] This is based explicitly on the rights of the defence.

The extent of the investigatory powers was further tried in *SEP*, where the Commission adopted a decision requiring four Dutch undertakings in the electricity sector to produce certain documents. The Court held[88] that a mere relationship between a document and the alleged infringement was insufficient to justify disclosure. The Commission should be able reasonably to suppose, at the time of the request, that the document would help it to determine whether the alleged infringement had taken place.[89]

It is thus clear that the Commission cannot request the production of *any* document. However, there is no need to show that the document would *directly* support or reject the existence of an infringement. It is sufficient that the document has a direct causal connection with the facts under investigation.[90]

In *SEP*, the Commission requested a copy of a contract between SEP and Statoil, in spite of the fact that the subject-matter of the inquiry was another contractual matter—a co-operation code between SEP and Gasunie. The Advocate-General and the Court of Justice referred to the proximity in time between the Statoil contract and the Gasunie code, and noted as the decisive point that the conclusion of

[83] *Roquette Frères*, above n 22, at para 45.
[84] *Ibid*, at para 43.
[85] *Hoechst v Commission*, above n 43, at para 27.
[86] *Aalborg Portland and others v Commission*, above n 20, at para 61.
[87] *Orkem v Commission*, above n 45, at para 33; *Mannesmannröhren-Werke v Commission*, above n 49, at para 77; see also Reg 1, preamble, at 23.
[88] *SEP v Commission*, above n 78, at para 21.
[89] Opinion of A-G Jacobs, *ibid*, at para 21; the ECJ referred to the A-G's Opinion and made it part of the judgment.
[90] Opinion of A-G Jacobs, *ibid*, at para 23.

the Statoil contract led Gasunie to negotiate the co-operation code with SEP.[91] In doing so, the Court of Justice overruled the findings of the Court of First Instance. The Court of First Instance had held that there had to be only a sufficient nexus between the subject-matter of the inquiry and the requested document, such nexus being present if there was a correlation or connection between the request and the suspected infringement,[92] and had in addition required a proportionality test.[93]

The Court of Justice and the Advocate-General were not really clear on the legal basis for finding that the Commission must be able reasonably to suppose, at the time of the request, that the document would help it to determine whether the alleged infringement had taken place. While the Court of First Instance was discussing the issue with reference to the right to a fair hearing and the rights of the defence,[94] and also in relation to the principle of proportionality,[95] the Advocate-General (whose opinion was made part of the judgment by the Court) seems merely to be interpreting the necessity requirement in Article 11 of Regulation 17 (now Article 18 of Regulation 1). The *SEP* judgment in itself would seem insufficient for an inference that the rights of the defence would oblige national authorities and courts to apply the same standard.

Considering what the law ought to be, it is clear that it must balance different interests. It would be pointless to carry out inspections while not being able to obtain a full picture of the suspected infringement. On the other hand, the company that is being investigated has an interest in ensuring that not too much confidential information leaks out, especially given that the outcome of access to documents by competitors and other parties may be difficult to predict at the time of the investigation. If, indeed, a competitor or third party would gain access to qualified confidential information, it could produce anticompetitive effects, and possibly other adverse effects as well, for instance on the stock market or for the company's contracting parties.

Procedural economy is another important aspect. Every document seized must be handled by the authority that collected it, and later on considered for the purpose of access to documents. This implies that at least some self-restraint must be exercised by the investigating authority, although the law might even (normatively) prescribe a legal restraint precisely for that purpose.

Another point to be noted is that *SEP* concerned a request for information under Article 11 of Regulation 17 (now Article 18 of Regulation 1), which means that the Commission was making the request without having seen the document. In this author's view, the requirement of a reasonably supposition that the document would help to determine whether the alleged infringement had taken place must be interpreted differently in the context of an on-site investigation. During a

[91] *Ibid*, at paras 22–23.
[92] Case T-39/90 *SEP v Commission* [1991] ECR II-1497, at paras 25–29.
[93] *Ibid*, at para 51.
[94] *Ibid*, at para 25.
[95] *Ibid*, at paras 51–53.

dawn raid (in contrast to requests for information), the investigating authority is able to read the document and make a more precise assessment of whether a copy is necessary.

In summary, it is not altogether clear whether all the case law relating to the extent of the Commission's investigatory powers forms part of the rights of the defence or otherwise constitutes fundamental rights. At least, the rights of the defence entitle an undertaking to answer only *questions of a purely factual nature* and to produce only *pre-existing documents and materials.* This minimum standard is a fundamental right and applies across the board. Fishing expeditions are not accepted either, whether the investigation is carried out under national rules or Community procedural rules. This follows directly from Articles 28(1) and 22 of Regulation 1, and by way of analogy from Article 12(2) of Regulation 1. Save for this, one cannot say for sure whether the limitations imposed on the Commission (a reasonable supposition, at the time of the request, that the information would help it to determine whether the alleged infringement had taken place) would apply in the Member States, or if they have further discretion. My suggestion is that national judiciaries must not duplicate EC law on extent of investigatory powers as a package solution. Rather, national judiciaries should look at the totality of the interests that are to be balanced and how this is best done in relation to national law on access to documents, taking into consideration aspects of procedural economy.

B. Legal professional privilege

Protection of legal professional privilege in EC law derives from the principles and concepts common to the laws of Member States concerning the observance of confidentiality, in particular as regards communications between lawyer and client.[96] The protection of the confidentiality of written communications between lawyer and client forms part of the rights of the defence,[97] or constitutes an essential corollary to the full exercise of those rights.[98] Accordingly, the Commission is not entitled to examine written communications between lawyer and client, provided that:

a) such communications are made for the purposes of and in the interests of the client's rights of defence; and
b) they emanate from independent lawyers.[99]

This includes written communications exchanged after the initiation of the administrative procedure, and extends to earlier written communications which have a relationship to the subject-matter of that procedure.[100]

[96] Case 155/79 *AM & S v Commission* [1982] ECR 1575, at para 18.
[97] *Ibid*, at para 23.
[98] Order of the President of the Court of First Instance in Joined Cases T-125/03 R and T-253/03 R *Akzo Nobel Chemicals and Akcros Chemicals v Commission* [2003] ECR II-4771, at para 100.
[99] *AM & S v Commission*, above n 96, at para 21.
[100] *Ibid*, at para 23.

As to the meaning of 'communications between lawyer and client', the Court of First Instance in *Akzo* included preparatory documents, even if they were not exchanged with a lawyer or were not created for the purpose of being sent physically to a lawyer, provided that they were drawn up exclusively for the purpose of seeking legal advice from a lawyer in exercise of the rights of the defence. However, the mere fact that a document has been discussed with a lawyer is insufficient to give it protection.[101]

The undertaking is entitled to refuse to allow the investigating authorities to take even a cursory look at the documents which it claims to be privileged, provided that such a cursory look is impossible without revealing the content of the documents, and that the undertaking gives the Commission officials appropriate reasons for its view.[102] Such reasons may include information regarding the author of the document and for whom it was intended, an explanation of the respective duties and responsibilities of each, and references to the objective for which and the context in which the document was drawn up, as well as the context in which the document was found, the way in which it was filed and any related documents.[103] The procedure under Community law is to place a copy of the document in a sealed envelope and let the Community courts rule on the matter. Meanwhile, the Commission is not entitled to read the document.[104]

The precise nature of the concept of independent lawyers has been disputed. The Court in *AM & S* clearly intended this to cover only outside legal counsel, but the development of legal practice has forced the Community courts to reconsider whether communications with in-house legal counsel would also be protected.[105] The Court of First Instance observed, in an interim order in *Akzo*, that the solution in *AM & S* was based on an interpretation of the principles common to the Member States dating from 1982. On the other hand there were indications that, since then, a number of Member States had adopted rules designed to protect written communications with in-house lawyers, provided that that lawyer is subject to certain rules of professional conduct.[106] The order was set aside for reasons of lack of urgency.[107] When finally adjudicating in the case following some four years of litigation, the Court of First Instance found that the evolution of competition law since *AM & S* did not justify legal privilege being extended to in-house legal counsel.[108]

[101] Joined Cases T-125/03 R and T-253/03 R *Akzo Nobel Chemicals and Akcros Chemicals v Commission* [2007] ECR II-3523, at para 123.

[102] *Ibid*, at para 82.

[103] *Ibid*, at para 80.

[104] *Ibid*, at para 85.

[105] See esp Andreangeli, Arianna, 'The Protection of Legal Professional Privilege in EU Law and the Impact of the Rules of Exchange of Information within the European Competition Network on the Secrecy of Communication between Lawyer and Client: one step forward, two steps back?' (2005) 2(1) *The Competition Law Review* 31.

[106] Order of the President of the Court of First Instance in *Akzo Nobel Chemicals and Akcros Chemicals v Commission*, above n 98, at para 124.

[107] Case C-7/04 P (R) *Commission v Akzo and Akcros*, order of 27 September 2004, [2004] ECR I-8739.

[108] *Akzo Nobel Chemicals and Akcros Chemicals v Commission*, above n 101, at paras 170 ff.

Given that legal professional privilege constitutes, or is a corollary to, the rights of the defence, it will apply as a fundamental principle of EC law in national cartel procedures where Article 81 EC applies. The standard established by the Community courts will be a minimum standard, regardless of the protection offered in the Member State in question. However, Member States would remain free to apply a higher level of protection for undertakings, as long as the effectiveness of Community law is not undermined. This leaves us with the question of how effectiveness could fail to be undermined if an undertaking in a Member State were able to refuse to hand over incriminating documents simply by placing them with its in-house legal department.

C. Assistance by national authorities

Specific considerations apply when the Commission is assisted by national authorities in its fact-finding expeditions. The Court has recognised (reference is made here to *Roquette Frères*) the need for protection against arbitrary or disproportionate intervention by public authorities in the sphere of the private activities of any person, whether natural or legal. This constitutes a general principle of Community law.[109] The competent authorities of the Member States are required to respect that general principle when they are called upon to act in response to a request for assistance made by the Commission.[110]

Further, the Court has reiterated the reciprocal obligation for national authorities and Community institutions to co-operate in good faith.[111] When providing assistance to the Commission's officials, the Member States must ensure that the Commission's action is effective, while respecting various general principles of Community law.[112] The national judiciary's powers of review are, however, very limited in scope. The national court is entitled to assess only whether the envisaged coercive measures are arbitrary or excessive having regard to the subject-matter of the investigation,[113] as opposed to reviewing the need for the investigation as such, the lawfulness of which may be determined only by the Community courts.[114] This case law is codified in Articles 20(8) and 21(3) of Regulation 1.[115]

[109] *Roquette Frères*, above n 22, at para 27, with references.
[110] *Ibid*, at para 28.
[111] *Ibid*, at para 31.
[112] *Ibid*, at para 35.
[113] *Ibid*, at para 36.
[114] *Ibid*, at para 51.
[115] For criticism of the *ex post* legal review exercised by the Community courts, see McCurdy, Gregory V S, 'The Impact of Modernisation of the EU Competition Law System on the Courts and Private Enforcement of the Competition Laws: A Comparative Perspective' (2004) 25(8) *ECLR* 509, at 516.

1. Information obtained from Member State authorities

Article 12 of Regulation 1 enables exchange of evidence between the Commission and Member State competition authorities. They are empowered to provide one another with and use in evidence any matter of fact or of law, including confidential information. However, in *Seamless Steel tubes* another matter was raised, namely, transmission of information to the Commission by a national prosecutor. Notably, only exchanges between competition authorities are covered by Regulation 1. Here, the Court ruled that the lawfulness of the transmission of evidence from a national authority was a matter for national law. As for the admissibility of the evidence, the Court referred to the principle of the unfettered evaluation of evidence which prevails in Community law. Since the transmission of the evidence was not declared unlawful by the national court, those documents were admissible.[116]

D. Incriminating questions

1. What is an incriminating question?

Respect for the rights of the defence requires that certain of those rights be respected as soon as the preliminary investigation has begun:

> [I]t is . . . necessary to prevent those rights from being irremediably impaired during preliminary inquiry procedures which may be decisive in establishing the unlawful nature of conduct engaged in by undertakings.[117]

For the reasons set out previously in this chapter, fundamental rights bind national authorities and courts as well, in public enforcement of Articles 81 and 82 EC.

The Community courts have established that the obligation of companies to supply information pursuant to a request for information is limited to *answering questions of a purely factual nature* and to producing only *pre-existing documents and materials*, a right which applies as from the very first stage of an investigation initiated by the Commission.[118] The Commission is entitled to

> compel an undertaking to provide all necessary information concerning such facts as may be known to it and to disclose to it, if necessary, such documents relating thereto as are in its possession, even if the latter may be used to establish, against it or another undertaking, the existence of anticompetitive conduct.[119]

[116] Case C-407/04 P *Dalmine v Commission* [2007] ECR I-829, at paras 62–63.

[117] T-34/93 *Société Générale v Commission* [1995] ECR II-545, at para 73, with references.

[118] *Orkem v Commission*, above n 45, at para 33; *Mannesmannröhren-Werke v Commission*, above n 49, at para 77; see also Reg 1, preamble, at 23.

[119] *Orkem*, above n 45, at para 34.

Requests that are not limited to factual information may, on the other hand, undermine the rights of the defence. The fundamental rule laid down in *Orkem* is that the Commission may not compel an undertaking to provide it with answers which might involve an admission on its part of the existence of an infringement which it is for the Commission to prove.[120] The burden of proof for infringements of Articles 81 and 82 EC always rests on the alleging party or authority.[121] In *PVC II*, the Court of Justice held that the right of undertakings not to be compelled by the Commission to admit their participation in an infringement means that it must be determined whether a reply from the undertaking to which the question is addressed is in fact *equivalent to the admission of an infringement.*[122]

In *Graphite Electrodes*, the Court once again upheld the *Orkem* principle. The Commission had requested that a producer of graphite electrodes should describe:

a) the object of a number of meetings in which the undertaking SGL participated; and
b) what occurred at a the meetings; and also
c) the results/conclusions of those meetings.

This was held unlawful by the Court of First Instance. It furthermore held that the Commission was not entitled to request protocols of the said meetings, working documents and preparatory documents concerning them, handwritten notes relating to them, notes and conclusions pertaining to the meetings, planning and discussion documents, and also implementing projects concerning price increases.[123] The Court of First Instance's judgment was in this part set aside by the Court of Justice.[124] The Court held that the finding of the Court of First Instance misconstrued the scope of Article 11 of Regulation No 17, as interpreted by the Court of Justice, and therefore weakened the principle that undertakings subject to a Commission investigation must co-operate.

In *Orkem* the Court of Justice annulled questions concerning:

a) the purpose of the action taken and the objective pursued by certain measures; as well as
b) requests on clarification of every step or concerted measure which might have been envisaged or adopted to support such price initiatives;
c) details of any system or method which made it possible to attribute sales targets or quotas to the participants; and
d) details of any method facilitating annual monitoring of compliance with any system of targets in terms of volume or quotas.[125]

[120] *Ibid*, at para 35.

[121] Case C-185/95 P *Baustahlgewebe v Commission* [1998] ECR I-8417, at para 58, now codified in Art 2 of Reg 1.

[122] Joined Cases C-238/99 P, etc *Limburgse Vinyl Maatschappij and others v Commission* [2002] ECR I-8375, at para 273.

[123] Joined Cases T-236/01, etc *Tokai Carbon and others v Commission* [2004] ECR II-1181, at paras 407–09.

[124] Case C-301/04 P *Commission v SGL Carbon* [2006] ECR I-5915, at para 47.

[125] *Orkem*, above n 45, at paras 38–39.

In *Mannesmannröhren-Werke*, the Court of First Instance annulled not only a request that the undertaking should describe:

a) the purpose of the meetings it attended; and
b) the decisions adopted during them;

but also a question which, if answered, would require the undertaking to give its assessment of the nature of certain decisions.[126]

Nazzini considers that we can define directly incriminating questions as questions requiring the undertaking to confess guilt. Indirectly incriminating questions, on the other hand, are questions asked in such a way 'as to compel the applicant to acknowledge its participation' in activities prohibited by EC competition law'.[127]

The law seems settled in principle, but remains difficult to apply in practice. What, precisely, is a question of a purely factual nature? Asking the Head of Sales where he was and with whom during a certain day is a question of a factual nature. Asking about the purpose of the action taken is unlawful. The matter becomes even more complex if we consider that the investigating authority may nowadays have received an application for leniency even before it begins its investigation, consequently working from a strong information position.

2. *Legal consequences if incriminating questions are asked*

In *PVC II*, the Court of First Instance held that incriminating questions were unlawful when included in a decision requiring information based on Article 11(5) of Regulation 17 (equivalent to Article 18(3) of Regulation 1). The Court of First Instance nevertheless dismissed the plea, holding that the undertakings either had refused to answer the questions, or had denied the facts on which they were being questioned. This meant that the illegality of the questions had not affected the legality of the decision where the undertakings were fined for cartel participation.[128] As regards requests based on Article 11(2) of Regulation 17 (equivalent to Article of 18(2) Regulation 1), the undertakings were not under an obligation to reply, and were thus not compelled to provide answers which might involve an admission of an infringement.[129]

From the reasoning it seems unclear whether the rights of the defence have been infringed only if the unlawful questions affect the legality of the final decision,[130] or whether the rights of the defence may have been infringed at an earlier stage when unlawful questions are included in a request for information. No references

[126] *Mannesmannröhren-Werke v* Commission, above n 49, at paras 71–74.

[127] Nazzini, Renato, 'Some Reflections on the Dynamics of the Due Process Discourse in EC Competition Law' (2005) 2(1) *The Competition Law Review* 5, at 22.

[128] Joined Cases T-305/94, etc *Limburgse Vinyl Maatschappij and others v Commission* [1999] ECR II-931, at paras 451–53.

[129] *Ibid*, at para 457.

[130] *Ibid*, at para 453: '. . . the illegality of the questions does not affect the legality of the Decision'.

to the rights of the defence were made in this part of the findings. On appeal, however, the Court of Justice confirmed the findings as regards the request for information answers to which were voluntary, thereby accepting incriminating questions provided that the company is not obliged to reply.[131] Conversely, incriminating questions were held unlawful when the undertaking was obliged to reply.

The crucial factor in the *PVC II* case appears to have been whether a penalty can be imposed in the event of a refusal to reply. On a general level, the decisive factor was held to be the exercise of coercion against the suspect in order to obtain information from him.[132]

Further in *PVC II*, the Court of Justice rejected the plea relating to a decision requiring information, holding that LVM and DSM had failed to indicate any aspects of those answers which were in fact used to incriminate the addressees of the decisions or LVM and DSM respectively.[133] The reasoning demonstrates that questions that would lead to incrimination of third parties are illegal in the same way as self-incriminating questions.[134] It is consequently irrelevant whether an undertaking is induced to incriminate itself or another undertaking—the illegal nature of incriminating questions may be referred to by addressees as well as by third parties.

In addition, the reasoning in this part of the *PVC II* judgment confirms the view that the rights of defence are infringed only if illegal questions have some negative outcome. Accordingly, the decisive criterion is (in addition to coercion) the establishment of the existence of an actual interference with fundamental rights.[135] While important in principle, this statement did nothing to clarify when such interference was deemed to exist. However, one year later, in *Thyssen Stahl*, the Court of Justice explained that:

a) the rights of the defence are infringed where it is possible that the outcome of the administrative procedure conducted by the Commission might have been different as a result of an error committed by it; *and*
b) an applicant undertaking establishes that there has been such an infringement where it adequately demonstrates, not that the Commission's decision would have been different in content, but rather that it would have been better able to ensure its defence had there been no error.[136]

To conclude, questions are unlawful if:

a) a reply is in fact equivalent to the admission of an infringement; and
b) there is exercise of coercion against the addressee in order to obtain information from him.

131 *Limburgse Vinyl Maatschappij and others v Commission*, above n 122, at para 279.
132 *Ibid*, at para 275.
133 *Ibid*, at paras 289–92.
134 *Ibid*, at paras 284–91.
135 *Ibid*, at para 275.
136 *Thyssen Stahl v Commission*, above n 36, at para 31.

For the rights of the defence to be infringed, there is an additional third criterion, which is:

c) a potentially different outcome of the administrative procedure, which is deemed to exist if the applicant adequately demonstrates not that the decision would have been different in content, but rather that it would have been better able to ensure its defence had there been no error.

The Community courts have used several different terms to describe mistakes made by the Commission: errors, illegal questions, and unlawful questions. While the parallel use of the terms 'unlawful' and 'illegal' appears to be the result of inconsistent translation, it remains unclear whether an error (*irrégularité* in the French original) is something different from an illegal question.

The Commission had no right to interview natural persons prior to 1 May 2004, and will be able to do so now only if the person consents. No penalties can be imposed on natural persons. For this reason, it is not surprising that the case law of the Community courts is limited to self-incriminating questions addressed to undertakings. National competition authorities may, however, have powers under national law to interview natural persons, possibly under the threat of fines or other sanctions. If there is a legal obligation for a person to reply to questions asked by the competition authorities, there is a direct parallel with the case law in the *Orkem* line of judgments, which means that questions that incriminate an undertaking are unlawful.

If natural persons interviewed by the competition authorities are under no legal obligation to answer (or to be interviewed at all), it follows from the judgment in *PVC II* that questions may be incriminating without infringing the rights of the defence. There appears to be no limitation as regards the subsequent use in a procedure of answers given in reply to incriminating questions, provided that there was no coercion in order to obtain information from the persons interviewed. However, these conclusions presuppose that questions asked when interviewing natural persons are considered equivalent from a legal point of view to questions addressed to undertakings in requests for information. Arguments may be raised against such a position. The interests of the person who is interviewed do not necessarily coincide with the interests of the undertakings.[137] Even if the interests would coincide, a natural person cannot be expected to have the capacity to protect the undertaking's interests during the interview. However, an absence of a mutual interest (or even the existence of a conflicts of interests) may be observed in all investigations of suspected infringements. An undertaking that has infringed Articles 81 or 82 EC may, for example, choose to admit its own participation and inform about the actions of other undertakings in order to reduce its own fines.

[137] Another argument against placing interviews with natural persons on an equal footing with requests for information is that the latter procedure is written and provides the undertakings with a reasonable period of time in which to assess the legality of the questions asked, possibly with the assistance of a legal attorney. An interview situation does not provide the person who is interviewed with the same opportunity.

On the other hand, the undertaking may chose a restrictive line of conduct and provide the authorities with as little information as is legally possible. The Community courts are hardly unaware of the conflicting interests and various procedural tactics of undertakings, but nevertheless have decided that incriminating questions are allowed, provided that there is no element of coercion.

3. Information supplied voluntarily

Natural persons and undertakings occasionally contact the competition authorities on their own initiative to report infringements. This is an important source of information for the authorities, encouraged by the leniency programmes. What if the authorities ask incriminating questions in these situations? Provided that there is no coercion in the context of such informal contacts, it follows from *PVC II* that the authorities can ask incriminating questions without committing any errors.

In addition to what has been explained above on incriminating questions, the Court in *PVC II* regarded as unfounded a plea alleging undue interference by the public authority, in the absence of any evidence that the Commission went beyond the co-operation offered by the undertaking.[138]

4. Use of evidence collected in non-EU jurisdictions

A matter of some importance for worldwide co-ordinated cartel fighting is the authorities' ability to use evidence originating from other authorities across the globe. Exchange of information between the Commission and Member State competition authorities is governed by Article 12 of Regulation 1, but what about information obtained from other sources?

In *Citric Acid*, the Commission had relied on an FBI summary of an interview with an employee of Archer Daniels Midland (ADM) as evidence of ADM's leadership of the cartel. The summary was submitted to the Commission by a competitor of ADM, Bayer, which had also taken part in the cartel. ADM did not claim that the document had been obtained illegally by Bayer or by the Commission; it nevertheless submitted that by relying on the report, the Commission infringed the procedural safeguards provided under Community law. According to the Court of First Instance, there was no provision that prevented the Commission from relying on a document as evidence because the document was established in the context of a procedure which was not conducted by the Commission itself. However, the Commission had to safeguard the rights against self-incrimination according to the principles developed in *Orkem*. It should carry out an examination automatically if, prima facie, there was serious doubt as to whether the procedural rights of the parties concerned were complied with in the procedure during which they provided such statements. The Court of First Instance concluded:

[138] *Limburgse Vinyl Maatschappij and others v Commission*, above n 122, at para 254.

> If there is no such serious doubt, the procedural rights of the parties concerned must be deemed to have been adequately safeguarded if, in the statement of objections, the Commission clearly indicates, if necessary by annexing the relevant documents to it, that it intends to rely on the statements in question.[139]

If this assessment holds on appeal then Member State competition authorities should not be barred, by principles of Community law, from relying on information obtained from non-EU sources. This is provided they check that the procedure applicable in the country of origin does not raise serious doubts as to compliance with fundamental rights, as developed in EC law, and that the undertaking is given notice of the intention to use the evidence.

E. Use of unlawfully obtained evidence

Let us assume that evidence is obtained unlawfully. *Dow Benelux* and *PVC II* tell us that an undertaking's defence rights would be *seriously endangered* if the Commission were able to rely on evidence against undertakings which was obtained during an investigation but which was not related to the subject-matter or purpose thereof.[140] This principle is reiterated in Article 28(1) of Regulation 1. If the competition authorities find evidence of an infringement other than the one which is the subject-matter of the inspection, the way to proceed is to seek authorisation for another inspection concerning the newly-discovered infringement. Furthermore, if a decision authorising an inspection is annulled by the Community judicature, the Commission would be prevented from using any documents or evidence which it might have obtained in the course of that investigation.[141]

Infringements of the right to legal privilege will, as far as the Commission is concerned, be remedied by an obligation to exclude from the proceedings any evidence obtained unlawfully. This was established in *Akzo*, where the Commission furthermore accepted that it would be required to remove from its file the documents affected by that unlawfulness and would therefore be unable to use them as evidence.[142]

Transposition to the national context of the case law relating to use of unlawfully obtained evidence is discussed next.

1. Obligation to exclude evidence in national proceedings—the Steffensen principle

It should be noted that Article 12(2) of Regulation 1 contains a limitation on the use of information in evidence, to the subject-matter for which it was collected by the transmitting authority. This principle is reiterated in Article 28(1) of

[139] Case T-59/02 *Archer Daniels Midland v Commission* [2006] ECR II-3627, at para 265, on appeal Case C-511/06 *Archer Daniels Midland v Commission.*

[140] *Dow Benelux v Commission*, above n 44, at para 18; *Limburgse Vinyl Maatschappij and others v Commission*, above n 122, at paras 298–300.

[141] *Roquette Frères*, above n 22, at para 49, with references.

[142] Case C-7/04 P (R) *Commission v Akzo and Akcros* [2004] ECR I-8739, at paras 38–39.

Regulation 1, according to which information collected pursuant to Articles 17 to 22 shall be used only for the purpose for which it was acquired. Given that Article 22 concerns investigations by national competition authorities under national law, and since the Regulation is directly applicable, it follows that an undertaking can rely directly on Article 28(1) of Regulation 1 to prevent national courts or authorities from relying on evidence for purposes other than those for which it was acquired.

While Article 28(1) of Regulation 1 deals with the use of information for purposes other than those for which it was acquired, the Regulation is silent on the more general question of the use of unlawfully obtained information. The question addressed in this section is whether national authorities and courts are under the same general EC law obligations as the Commission and Community courts, to exclude as evidence documents, statements or other information obtained unlawfully.

The Court has not been entirely clear on the legal basis for preventing the Commission from using such materials. In *Roquette Frères*, it makes no explicit references to the rights of the defence when reiterating that the Commission is prevented from using documents or evidence obtained on the basis of a decision that is subsequently annulled.[143] However, the Court referred in *Roquette Frères* to the judgment in *Dow Chemical*, where the prohibition against improper use of information is explicitly based on the rights of the defence.[144] It might seem illogical to treat various forms of unlawful acts by the investigation authorities differently, and it could thus be argued that it follows from this line of cases that unlawfully obtained evidence must be excluded in national procedures in order to avoid infringements of the rights of the defence.

Further support for this view may be found in the *Steffensen* case. As has been discussed above, a distinction must be drawn between evidence obtained through requests answers to which are voluntary, and requests where the addressee is under a legal obligation to reply. The rights of defence can be infringed only in the latter situation. In *Steffensen*,[145] the Court considered the legal consequences when evidence is obtained through measures that may infringe fundamental rights.

The case concerned a manufacturer of veal and pork sausages. German administrative authorities took samples of the manufacturer's products from retail outlets, and had the samples analysed in laboratories. When taking the samples, the authorities left reference samples in the stores, although those samples never reached the manufacturer. It could not be established whether the manufacturer was notified about the taking of samples, or of the analyses. The outcome of the laboratory tests was that the quality of the samples failed to reach the standard required under the German legislation on foodstuffs. Mr Steffensen, who was responsible for product supervision within the company, was subsequently fined for infringement of national law, legislation based on an EC Directive. That

[143] *Roquette Frères*, above n 22, at paras 41–50.

[144] *Ibid*, at para 49; *Dow Chemical*, above n 58, at paras 17–18.

[145] Case C-276/01 *Steffensen* [2003] ECR I-3735.

Directive provided for the right of those subject to inspection to apply for a second opinion as regards analyses of samples. Notably, German law did not impose a general prohibition on the admission of evidence obtained through an improper administrative procedure.

The German Government claimed that principles of German procedural law, in particular those relating to *ex officio* investigations and the free evaluation of evidence, made it possible to challenge the results of irregular analyses, and that those principles were not contrary to the Community principles of equivalence and effectiveness. The Court found, however, that the Directive provision on a right to a second opinion had direct effect.[146] As regards the legal consequences, the national court had to decide whether admission as evidence was likely to give rise to an infringement of the adversarial principle and, thus, of the right to a fair hearing, in which case it would have to exclude the results of the analyses as evidence in order to avoid such an infringement.[147]

In its answer to the German court, the Court made a more general statement of principle, ruling that

> the national court must verify that the national rules on the taking of evidence applicable to such an action are not less favourable than those governing similar domestic actions (the principle of equivalence) and that they do not render practically impossible or excessively difficult the exercise of rights conferred by Community law (the principle of effectiveness). In addition, the national court must consider whether such evidence must be excluded in order to avoid measures incompatible with compliance with fundamental rights, in particular the right to a fair hearing before a tribunal as laid down in Article 6(1) of the European Convention for the Protection of Human Rights and Fundamental Freedoms.

There is thus no doubt about the legal consequences: if admission of evidence will lead to infringements of fundamental rights, the national court must exclude it from the proceedings. As discussed above, the rights of defence constitute fundamental rights. They may be infringed if evidence is obtained unlawfully (or erroneously) and the outcome of the administrative procedure might have been different as a result of the error, such a potentially different outcome being deemed to exist if the undertaking demonstrates that it would have been better able to ensure its defence had there been no error. In such a situation, the national court is obliged under EC law to exclude the evidence.

2. Rights of the defence can be precluded if an undertaking fails to use available legal remedies

As regards incriminating questions, it appears to be of crucial importance whether a request for information may be appealed as such. National law may be expected to provide for various rights of appeal in this respect. It may offer extensive rights

[146] *Ibid*, at para 41.
[147] *Ibid*, at para 79.

to appeal against a request for information, or may, on the other hand, contain limitations on rights to appeal, or even provide that such issues may be raised only in an appeal against a final decision or judgment.

In *Orkem* and *Mannesmannröhren-Werke*, the undertakings had appealed the Commission's decisions on requests for information, and the Community courts annulled the unlawful questions. A more complicated situation arises if a request that includes unlawful questions is not appealed but is challenged later in the context of an appeal against a decision on infringements of Article 81 or 82 EC. In *PVC II*, the Community courts assessed that situation.

On the basis of Article 11 of Regulation 17, the Commission had sent requests for information to a number of undertakings, among them LVM and DSM, the questions contained in the requests being identical to those annulled by the Court in *Orkem* and *Solvay*. LVM and DSM failed to appeal the requests for information, but later argued before the Community courts that the answers provided by them and by the undertakings ICI, BASF, Elf Atochem, Solvay and Shell should have been excluded from use as evidence. They asked that the *PVC II* decision be annulled, inasmuch as it was based on evidence obtained in breach of the privilege against self-incrimination. Those pleas were dismissed by the Court in relation to undertakings which did not bring actions against the decisions requiring information.[148]

It follows that the addressee of a request for information must be alert and use any right it may have to appeal a decision where unlawful questions are asked. An omission to appeal a request for information may bar the undertaking from raising the issue of unlawfulness in the further proceedings.[149]

Similar pleas were, on the other hand, tried in substance in *PVC II* when it came to incriminating information obtained from *addressees other than the appellants themselves*, given that only the addressees were allowed to bring actions against the requests.[150]

From *PVC II*, it is clear that undertakings are offered sufficient protection through a right to appeal the request for information. If there is no such right, or if evidence is used against an undertaking that did not have standing to bring action against the request for information at issue, other legal consequences must be considered in order to avoid infringements of the rights of defence.

3. *Confidentiality as to the origin of evidence*

Can the Commission or a national competition authority preserve the confidentiality of its informers without infringing the rights of the defence of undertakings? This question was posed in one of the *Seamless steel tubes* cases. Mannesmannröhren-Werke opposed the Commission's use of a document the origin of which the Commission had refused to expose. Two questions were raised:

[148] *Limburgse Vinyl Maatschappij*, above n 122, at paras 267–70.

[149] The same principle applied when an applicant had failed to use all remedies available in a request for access to documents: *Mannesmannröhren-Werke v Commission*, above n 37, at para 58.

[150] *Limburgse Vinyl Maatschappij*, above n 122, at para 268.

a) Was such a document admissible as evidence?
b) If so, was the document's value as evidence lower as a result of its obscure origin?

The Court of First Instance found that the document was admissible, although its credibility was necessarily reduced.[151]

4. Obligation to return unlawfully obtained documents and information?

The Commission might be under an obligation to return unlawfully obtained documents. Advocate-General Warner stated in *National Panasonic* that the Court may order the Commission to return to the undertaking any copies of documents obtained as a result of the investigation, and to refrain from using any information so obtained if the decision was unlawful.[152] However, this view has not been confirmed by the Community courts. Legally privileged documents must indeed be removed from the file,[153] but this does not extend to all documents. The Court of Justice has limited itself to holding that the Commission is prevented from using any documents or evidence obtained as a result of a decision which is subsequently annulled.[154]

5. Incriminating questions—statements by natural persons

How should the principle laid down in *Steffensen* (see section IV.E.1. above) be applied if the investigating authority has asked incriminating questions when interviewing natural persons (provided, as discussed above, there is a legal obligation to answer and no failure by the undertaking to use any rights it may have to appeal the request)? The answer would depend on how statements are used in the competition procedure at issue. The question does not seem to arise at all if the investigation has been made by the Commission pursuant to Regulation 1, since natural persons are obliged neither to be interviewed at all, nor to answer any questions. However, national competition procedure may give the authorities more extensive powers. For example, the Swedish Competition Act provides for the ability to summon natural persons on the penalty of fines, to be questioned by the national competition authority.[155] In addition, natural persons may be required to provide information, documents or other material.[156]

From the point of view of fundamental principles of EC law, the relevant questions are whether incriminating questions have been asked and whether there is a legal obligation to answer (ie an element of coercion). If the answers to both questions are affirmative, the incriminating questions are unlawful.

[151] *Mannesmannröhren-Werke v Commission*, above n 37, at paras 83–86.
[152] Opinion of A-G Warner in Case 136/79 *National Panasonic v Commission* [1980] ECR 2069.
[153] *Commission v Akzo and Akcros*, above n 142, at paras 38–39.
[154] *Roquette Frères*, above n 22, at para 49.
[155] Chapter 5 Sections 1 and 2 and Chapter 6 Section 1 of the Swedish Competition Act (2008:579).
[156] *Ibid*, and ruling 2001:23 of the Swedish Market Court.

To establish an infringement of the rights of defence, it must be demonstrated that the undertaking would have been better able to ensure its defence had there been no error. If any of the constitutive elements of an infringement of fundamental rights are absent, the use of answers made during the administrative procedure is lawful in relation to fundamental principles of EC law of the rights of the defence.

6. *Indirect use of unlawfully obtained evidence*

It is clear from *Steffensen* that Community law requires evidence to be excluded to avoid measures incompatible with compliance with fundamental rights. Even if such evidence is excluded, though, there may still exist in national competition procedure various ways of indirectly using unlawfully obtained evidence. The question thus remains whether compliance with the rights of defence requires that even *indirect use* of unlawfully obtained evidence is prohibited. On this point, it is difficult to find any explicit guidance in the case law of the Community courts, although there are cases in which similar issues have been dealt with.[157]

The first case is *Otto*, where the Court established that the Commission and national competition authorities are not allowed to rely on evidence obtained in proceedings where the rights of defence are not applicable, if the means of obtaining the evidence at issue would have been unlawful in proceedings that might result in penalties. Information obtained through incriminating questions in the course of national civil proceedings which exclusively concern private relations between individuals could not be used by the Commission or, for that matter, by a national authority.[158] The prohibition on using such information covered not only its use in the establishment of infringements of the competition rules in proceedings which might result in the imposition of penalties, but also use as evidence justifying the initiation of an investigation prior to such proceedings.

Otto has been overtaken by Article 12 of Regulation 1, according to which the Commission and the competition authorities of the Member States are empowered to provide to one another and use in evidence any matter of fact or law, including confidential information. Nevertheless, it still gives an indication of the legal consequences if evidence is obtained unlawfully.

In *Spanish banks*, the Court limited the right of a Member State's competition authority to use information. The Commission had obtained information from undertakings pursuant to Article 11 of Regulation 17, and forwarded it to the national authority pursuant to Article 10(1).[159] The Court held, first, that the authorities must take care not to disclose to other national authorities or third parties information covered by professional secrecy.[160] Secondly, such informa-

[157] On the jurisprudence under the ECHR, see Nazzini, Renato, above n 127, at 18–19.

[158] *Otto*, above n 38, at paras 17–21.

[159] Case C-67/91 *Asociación Española de Banca Privada and Others* ('*Spanish banks*') [1992] ECR I-4785, at paras 40–43.

[160] *Ibid*, at para 41.

tion could not be relied on by the authorities of the Member States, either in a preliminary investigation procedure or to justify a decision based on provisions of competition law, be it national law or Community law.[161] The information had to remain internal to those authorities and be used only to decide whether or not it was appropriate to initiate a national procedure.

The *Spanish banks* judgment has been overtaken by the introduction of Article 12 of Regulation 1. Article 12 confers powers on the Commission and national competition authorities to exchange and use in evidence any matter of fact or law, including confidential information, for the purpose of applying Articles 81 and 82 EC. Still, the reasoning in *Spanish banks* provides guidance on how the Court might consider various forms of indirect use of unlawfully obtained evidence.

F. Witness statements

As was explained at the beginning of this chapter, the rights of the defence under EC law are undoubtedly applicable in all national cases of public enforcement of Article 81 EC. What, then, is the position under EC law if incriminating questions are asked when a witness is heard under oath in national competition proceedings where Articles 81 and 82 EC apply?

It should be noted that the hearing of witnesses is connected with specific problems in Community competition procedure. The Commission is not a court and can hear witnesses only on a voluntary basis.[162] If an undertaking wishes to rely on witnesses in order to exculpate itself, it can at the most make its own employees attend interviews with the Commission; persons unconnected with the undertaking cannot be compelled to appear.[163] Witnesses may be heard under oath by the Court of First Instance, but criminal liability is a matter for the witness's national law.[164] Prior to the entry into force of Regulation 1, the Commission's decisions were almost exclusively based on written evidence.[165] This explains why EC case law on incriminating questions is related to requests for information during the administrative procedure and not to witnesses.

Taking as a starting point that witnesses or experts examined under oath are under a duty to provide full and truthful answers, the court must act against incriminating questions posed by the investigating authority. This follows from *PVC II*. The combination of incriminating questions and a legal obligation to answer will otherwise mean that the court violates the rights of the defence under

[161] *Ibid*, at para 42.

[162] Art 19 of Reg 1; Art 3 of Commission Regulation 773/2004.

[163] This problem is amply illustrated by Case T-9/99 *HFB and Others v Commission* [2002] ECR II-1487, at paras 373 ff.

[164] Arts 68–72 of the Rules of Procedure of the Court of First Instance of 2 May 1991, OJ L/136 of 30 May 1991, including amendments up to OJ L/127 of 29 April 2004, at 108.

[165] Witnesses were heard, however, in the *Steel beams* cases, Case C-199/99 P *Corus UK v Commission* [2003] ECR I-11177.

EC law of the undertaking charged with infringements of Articles 81 and 82 EC. It seems irrelevant whether incriminating questions are addressed to witnesses employed by the undertaking or to witnesses employed by third parties. Crucial is whether the witness is obliged by law to give evidence. Another question is whether the mere fact that a witness is summoned (possibly on the penalty of a fine) to appear for examination would constitute an element of coercion which means that the rights of defence are violated if incriminating questions are posed, even if there is no legal obligation actually to answer any questions? In *PVC II*, the decisive factor was held to be the exercise of coercion against the suspect in order to obtain information from him.[166] This implies that coercion in order to make a witness appear is acceptable, while coercion in order to make him or her answer incriminating questions is not.

It has been explained at length in this chapter that the rights of the defence are infringed only if there is a procedural error which has some negative impact on the undertaking's ability to defend itself. When it comes to examination of witnesses, it is difficult to see how admissions made as a result of incriminating questions could not have an adverse impact on the defence.

1. Right to cross-examine a witness

The question arose in *Cement* whether an undertaking has a right to be given the opportunity to cross-examine a particular witness and to analyse his statements at the investigation stage. The Court of Justice answered in the negative with reference to case law from the European Court of Human Rights.[167] However, there is nothing to prevent Member State competition procedure from affording a higher level of protection for undertakings accused of competition law infringements.

G. Unlawful procedural steps taken before 1 May 2004

As from 1 May 2004, national competition authorities and courts must apply Articles 81 and 82 EC pursuant to Article 3 of Regulation 1. This raises the question of how errors committed prior to 1 May 2004 by the Commission or national competition authorities or courts will be dealt with in the national competition procedure. For example, if evidence was collected erroneously prior to 1 May 2004, can it be used, or must it be excluded from the procedure?

As has been explained, the rights of the defence are fundamental rights which apply independent of Regulation 1. Violation of the rights of the defence requires, first, an error committed by the authority or court, secondly, a potentially different outcome of the procedure, which will be deemed to exist had the undertaking

[166] *Limburgse Vinyl Maatschappij*, above n 122, at para 275.
[167] *Aalborg Portland and others v Commission*, above n 20, at para 200.

been better able to defend itself in the absence of the error. There will thus be a violation if errors committed by authorities or courts are not cured during the competition procedure.

H. Statement of objections, applicability of Community case law in national procedure

Before the Commission adopts a decision imposing sanctions on undertakings pursuant to Regulation 1, a statement of objections must be sent to the undertakings. A statement of objections is a draft decision setting out the facts and legal assessments, as well as the evidence on which the Commission relies.

The Community courts have developed rather extensive law on how a statement of objections must be drafted.[168] The Commission is barred from basing the final decision on facts or entirely different legal assessments other than those presented in the statement of objections. If the Commission nevertheless does so, the decision may be annulled by the Community courts.

The statement of objections is a procedural and preparatory document drafted to enable the undertakings against which the procedure is initiated to exercise effectively their right to a fair hearing.[169] In *Cement*, the Court summarised the law and held that the undertaking concerned must have been afforded the opportunity, during the administrative procedure, to make known its views on the truth and relevance of the facts and circumstances alleged, and on the documents used by the Commission to support its claim that there has been an infringement.[170] The Court of First Instance has repeatedly held that the statement of objections must be couched in terms which, even if succinct, are sufficiently clear to enable the parties concerned properly to identify the conduct complained of by the Commission, giving undertakings all the information necessary to enable them properly to defend themselves, before the Commission adopts a final decision.[171]

The less elaborate levels of reasoning required in decisions authorising investigations may be brought to mind here as a contrast (see section IV.A.3. above). Implicitly, this means that the statement of objections is primarily a matter of jurisdiction, finally to establish that an infringement has taken place and to impose penalties.

Not all national competition authorities are empowered to impose fines and other sanctions. In a number of Member States, that power rests with the courts. This raises the question whether a statement of objections must be sent by the national competition authority prior to the initiation of court proceedings, or

[168] Kerse, C S, and Khan, N, *EC Antitrust Procedure*, 5th edn (London, Sweet & Maxwell, 2005), at 204 ff.

[169] Order in Joined Cases 142 and 156/84 *BAT and Reynolds v Commission* [1986] ECR 1899, at para 14.

[170] *Aalborg Portland and others v Commission*, above n 20, at para 66.

[171] Case T-213/00 *CMA CGM and others v Commission* [2003] ECR II-913, at para 109.

whether the court proceedings as such guarantee the same rights of the defence as are intended by the statement of objections. In other words, must the national procedure duplicate the Community competition procedure in this respect?

It could reasonably be assumed that the court procedures in most Member States are structured so as to provide for an adversarial principle. A court procedure might even be more transparent than the Commission's administrative procedure. Provided that the judgment is based only on factual circumstances as presented during the procedure, and that each party has been provided with the opportunity to comment on the other party's submissions, it would seem superfluous to require a statement of objections to precede litigation in court. Still, there might be borderline cases in which the judges would have to consider the possibility of raising of their own motion certain questions with the parties. Moreover, the court hierarchy system in some Member States would provide for a full re-examination of facts and law on appeal, which means that national procedure may provide the means to cure errors which would otherwise lead to violations of the rights of the defence.

I. Access to file

1. Access to file and the adversarial principle

In *Cement*, the Court of Justice held that the right of access to the file is a corollary of the principle of respect for the rights of the defence, which means that the undertaking concerned must be given the opportunity to examine all the documents in the investigation file which may be relevant for its defence. This includes both incriminating evidence and exculpatory evidence, save where the business secrets of other undertakings, the internal documents of the Commission or other confidential information are involved.[172]

From this reasoning it may be deduced that the same principle applies in national Article 81 and Article 82 EC proceedings. The exact extent of access to documents would, of course, have to be determined under national law.

Expanding on the right of access to documents, *Cement* shows that it is primarily related to the adversarial principle.[173] There had apparently been some confusion on this subject: in *TACA* and *Dutch electrotechnical*, the Court of First Instance considered that the right was there to ensure, in particular, that the right to be heard could be exercised effectively.[174] In *Sodium Gluconate*, adopted after *Cement*, it was described with reference to the general principle of equality of

[172] *Aalborg Portland and others v Commission*, above n 20, at para 68.

[173] *Ibid*, at para 70.

[174] Joined Cases T-191/98 and T-212/98 to T-214/98 *Atlantic Container Line and others v Commission* [2003] ECR II-3275, at para 334; Joined Cases T-5/00 and T-6/00 *Nederlandse Federatieve Vereniging voor de Groothandel op Elektrotechnisch Gebied and Technische Unie v Commission* [2003] ECR II-5761, at para 32.

arms.[175] Whether we pigeonhole this right under the adversarial principle, the right to be heard or elsewhere is in all likelihood irrelevant for the purpose of the present discussion: of primary importance is that it constitutes a general principle of Community law and a corollary to the rights of the defence.[176] The next section provides a brief examination of the legal consequences when the authorities fail to provide the undertaking with access to documents.

2. Consequences of failure to provide access to documents

Failure to communicate documents to the undertakings concerned will not lead to any automatic nullity of a decision imposing fines. On the contrary, the Court has distinguished between incriminating and exculpatory documents, with reference to the evidence's importance for the case.

In *Cement*, the Court outlined a method of analysis. For incriminating documents, the failure to communicate a document constitutes a breach of the rights of the defence only if the undertaking concerned shows, first, that the Commission relied on that document to support its cause of action concerning the existence of an infringement[177] and, secondly, that the infringement can be proved only by reference to that document.[178] If one incriminating document is inadmissible as evidence, a finding of an infringement may still be based on other documentary evidence of which the parties were aware during the administrative procedure.[179] To overturn the finding of an infringement, the undertaking must show that the decision would have been different if a document not communicated to it on which the Commission relied had to be disallowed as evidence.[180]

The matter was phrased slightly different in *Graphite electrodes*:

> [T]he mere failure to communicate a document constitutes a breach of the rights of the defence only if the undertaking concerned is able to show, first, that the Commission relied on that document to support its objection concerning the existence of an infringement and, second, that the objection could be proved only by reference to that document.[181]

For exculpatory evidence, the requirements on undertakings are lower; they need establish only that non-disclosure was able to influence, to the undertaking's disadvantage, the course of the proceedings and the content of the decision of the Commission.[182] It is sufficient for the undertaking to show that it would have been able to use the exculpatory documents in its defence, in so far as it would have been able to have some influence on the Commission's assessment in any decision it

[175] Case T-314/01 *Avebe v Commission* [2006] ECR II-3085, at para 66.
[176] Case T-5/02 *Tetra Laval v Commission* [2002] ECR II-4381, at para 89.
[177] *Aalborg Portland and others v Commission*, above n 20, at para 71.
[178] *Ibid.*
[179] *Ibid*, at para 72.
[180] *Ibid*, at para 73.
[181] Case C-308/04 P *SGL Carbon v Commission* [2006] ECR I-5977, at para 79.
[182] *Ibid*, at para 74.

adopted, at least as regards the gravity and duration of the conduct of which it was accused and, accordingly, the level of the fine.[183]

The case law just referred to aims to establish the final outcome of a proceeding when evidence may be inadmissible, but it does not clarify whether the evidence must be excluded in the first place. More recently, in *Carbonless paper*, the undertaking Koehler claimed that documents were used by the Commission as inculpatory evidence, without Koehler having had access to that evidence during the administrative procedure and without its being able to comment on it. The Court of First Instance stated that documents that have not been communicated to the parties concerned during the administrative procedure are not admissible in evidence.[184] It would be necessary, if it were proven that the Commission relied in the contested decision on documents that were not in the investigation file and were not communicated to the applicants, to exclude those documents as evidence.[185] The Court of First Instance was not entirely clear on the legal basis for this conclusion, and the case law referred to is somewhat ambiguous on this point. It then turned out that Koehler had failed to file a request for access to those documents, and was therefore barred from raising the argument that it had not had access to them.[186]

J. Right to be heard

It constitutes a general principle of Community law, inspired by Article 6(1) of the ECHR, that everyone is entitled to a fair hearing.[187] Closely linked to it is the right to be heard,[188] a fundamental principle of Community law which must be observed in all circumstances, in particular in all proceedings liable to give rise to penalties, including administrative procedures.[189] It forms part of the rights of the defence. This requires that the undertaking under investigation is given the opportunity during the administrative procedure to put forward its point of view on the reality and the relevance of the alleged facts, and also on the documents used by the Commission.[190]

The right to be heard extends to all the matters of fact and of law which form the basis for the decision-making act, although not to the final position which the administration intends to adopt.[191] More particularly, the Court of Justice held in *Graphite electrodes* that

[183] *Ibid*, at 75.

[184] Joined Cases T-109/02, etc *Bolloré SA and others v Commission* [2007] ECR II-947, at para 56.

[185] *Ibid*.

[186] *Ibid*, at para 59.

[187] Joined Cases C-189/02 P, etc *Dansk Rørindustri and others v Commission* [2005] ECR I-5425, at para 69.

[188] Case C-3/00 *Denmark v Commission* [2003] ECR I-2643, at para 46.

[189] *Nederlandse Federatieve Vereniging voor de Groothandel op Elektrotechnisch Gebied and Technische Unie v Commission*, above n 174, at para 32, with references.

[190] Case C-328/05 P *SGL Carbon v Commission* [2007] ECR I-3921, at para 71.

[191] Case T-15/02 *BASF v Commission* [2006] ECR II-497, at para 49.

> the obligation to hear undertakings subject to proceedings under Article 81 EC is fulfilled when the Commission states, in the statement of objections, that it will examine whether fines should be imposed on the undertakings considered and when it indicates the main matters of fact and of law which may result in the imposition of a fine, such as the duration and gravity of the infringement involved.[192]

The right does not extend to an absolute right to obtain the attendance of witnesses before a court; it is in principle for the national court to determine whether it is necessary or appropriate to call a witness.[193]

When there is a failure by the investigating authority to observe the right to be heard, this can result in the nullity of the decision adopted, although some negative effect on the undertaking's ability to defend itself has been required in competition law cases.[194] As for the transposition of this case law to national proceedings, reference is made to section III above: fundamental rights apply when national authorities and courts act within the scope of Community law.

1. Preclusion of the procedural right to dispute the allegations

In *Graphite electrodes*, the undertaking Nippon had co-operated with the Commission with a view to obtaining reductions in its fines. It made numerous admissions during the administrative procedure, and did not challenge the findings in the Commission's statement of objections. On appeal, however, it claimed that its participation in the cartel was of shorter duration than the Commission had found. The Court of First Instance referred to the burden of proof, but held, *a contrario*, that

> where the undertaking expressly, clearly and specifically acknowledges the facts: where it explicitly admits during the administrative procedure the substantive truth of the facts which the Commission alleges against it in the statement of objections, those facts must thereafter be regarded as established and the undertaking estopped in principle from disputing them during the procedure before the Court.[195]

Admissions made during the administrative procedure may consequently preclude an undertaking from utilising certain lines of defence.

K. Languages—specific problems arising from multinational cartel cases[196]

Multinational cartel cases require considerable resources in so far as several languages may be involved. For the Commission's procedure, a Council Regulation from 1958 applies. Article 2 of that Regulation provides that documents which a

[192] Case C-289/04 P *Showa Denko v Commission* [2006] ECR I-5859, at para 69.
[193] *Dansk Rørindustri and others v Commission*, above n 187, at para 70.
[194] Case C-194/99 P *Thyssen Stahl v Commission* [2003] ECR I-10821, at para 31.
[195] Case T-236/01 *Tokai Carbon v Commission* [2004] ECR II-1181, at para 108.
[196] I am grateful for the help received from Anna Tissot-Favre on the Commission's approach to language issues. Any mistakes remain my own.

Member State, or a person subject to the jurisdiction of a Member State, sends to institutions of the Community, may be drafted in any one of the official languages selected by the sender. The reply shall be drafted in the same language.[197] Article 3 of the same Regulation says that documents which an institution of the Community sends to a Member State, or to a person subject to the jurisdiction of a Member State, shall be drafted in the language of such State. While this is reassuring for the Community competition procedure, it does not actually say anything about language application in decentralised EC competition procedure.

It is not entirely clear what an undertaking accused of cartel participation may require from a national investigating authority—is there, for instance, a right to receive questions and provide answers only in the undertaking's own language? Given that national competition authorities can be expected to be less multilingual than the Commission, such a right would considerably diminish the possibility to allocate cases among national authorities. In *Graphite electrodes*, the undertaking SGL Carbon claimed that its right to be heard had been infringed because the Commission officials responsible for the investigation had insufficient knowledge of German.[198] The undertaking argued that the Commission's officials must be capable of understanding all the data relied on by the undertakings concerned, whether directly or by means of translations.[199] The Commission replied that all the correspondence exchanged during the procedure was in German, except the third request for information which was in English, but then SGL had not requested a translation and had merely replied in German.[200] The Court took the view that even on the assumption that certain officials responsible for the case did not have the necessary knowledge of the language, the knowledge of a member of the team responsible for investigating a cartel cannot in itself be decisive for the purpose of determining whether there was any breach of the rights of the defence.[201]

From the facts of the case and the reasoning of the Court, it appears that there is no right for an undertaking to require that all documents are translated into the undertaking's national language, or that the officials responsible have extensive knowledge of that language. Similarly in the *Pre-insulated pipe cartel*, the Court of First Instance found that there is no provision of Community law that obliges the Commission to provide a translation of documents which do not emanate from it (in that case, documents submitted by other undertakings).[202] Still, the procedure actually applied by the Commission and the Court of First Instance is relatively generous towards undertakings in this respect, and it should be noted that the Community institutions employ skilled translators on a permanent basis.

197 Regulation No 1 of the Council determining the languages to be used by the European Economic Community [1958] JO 17/385.

198 *SGL Carbon v Commission*, above n 190.

199 *Ibid*, at para 66.

200 *Ibid*, at para 69.

201 *Ibid*, at para 73.

202 Case T-9/99 *HFB and Others v Commission* [2002] ECR II-1487, at para 329.

The situation would, for practical reasons, be different if a Member State competition authority was in charge of a cartel investigation. Looking for an answer, the starting point is the principle of national procedural autonomy. Whether an undertaking has a right to employ its own language is primarily a question for national procedure; but can there be a right to be subjected to investigative measures and litigation in one's own language, according to general principles of Community law?

Kerse and Khan appear to consider the matter as one of human rights, since they refer to Article 6(3)(a) of the ECHR in connection with discussing language issues, although without explaining why.[203] The said article in the Convention includes a right for everyone charged with a criminal offence to be informed promptly, in a language which he understands and in detail, of the nature and cause of the accusation against him. Further, there is a right to have the free assistance of an interpreter if the accused cannot understand or speak the language used in court. As discussed previously in this chapter, fundamental rights in EC law have often derived from the ECHR. This right, if it applies in national competition procedure, would then override national legislation. If it does not apply then national procedure applies. There seems to be no authoritative statement by the Court of Justice here. Presumably, most Member States employ their own national language(s) and use translators only as a last resort.

Looking further at this intricate question, it is likely that the Community courts will operate with reference to the case law of the European Court of Human Rights.

In *Stenuit*, the French company Stenuit had submitted tenders for landscape gardening contracts. It was then accused of bid-rigging by the Minister responsible. After consultation with the French Competition Commission, the Minister subsequently imposed a fine of 50,000 FF on Stenuit. Stenuit appealed to the Minister to reconsider his decision, requesting application in its favour of an amnesty law. The Minister dismissed this appeal, inter alia, on the ground that the infractions committed had given rise to administrative fines rather than any criminal penalty. Only infractions which had led to a *criminal penalty* were covered by the amnesty law. The Conseil d'État dismissed Stenuit's appeal, taking the view that fines imposed on firms or corporate bodies were not criminal penalties. The matter was brought to the European Court of Human Rights, where the European Commission for Human Rights expressed the unanimous opinion that there had been a violation of Article 6(1) of the ECHR. The French Government then explained that it had changed the legislation. Stenuit withdrew the case from European Court of Human Rights, and the case was struck off the list.[204]

Öztürk concerned administrative fines for a person who caused a traffic incident by careless driving. The German court responsible had placed the costs of translation on the person charged with the infringement. The German Government

[203] Kerse and Khan, above n 168, at 88, fn 11; *ibid*, at 205, fn 6.

[204] Judgment of the European Court of Human Rights of 27 February 1992, *Société Stenuit v France*.

submitted that road traffic accidents were decriminalised and constituted mere regulatory offences. The European Court of Human Rights considered that if the Contracting States were able, at their discretion, by classifying an offence as regulatory instead of criminal, to exclude the operation of the fundamental clauses of Articles 6 and 7 of the ECHR, the application of these provisions would be subordinated to their sovereign will. It went on to explain that the notion of 'criminal' under Article 6 of the Convention had an autonomous meaning which would have to be ascertained with reference to the national law defining the offence in issue and the nature of the offence. Lastly, the Court held that the nature and degree of severity of the penalty that the person concerned risked incurring must be examined. The examination must have regard to the object and purpose of Article 6, to the ordinary meaning of the terms of that Article and to the laws of the Contracting States. After a lengthy discussion the Court found that the road traffic contravention in issue was 'criminal' for the purposes of Article 6 of the Convention. This meant that the decision under which the German court had made the person charged bear the costs of an interpreter at the hearing, violated Article 6(3)(e) of the ECHR.[205]

The significance of this line of cases (more particularly *Öztürk* and *Lutz*) has been recognised repeatedly by the Community courts,[206] although it cannot be said that they have accepted the application of the same level of protection in competition cases.[207]

Drawing from *Stenuit* and *Öztürk*, it seems possible, and even likely, that undertakings charged with administrative competition law offences may require that they are informed promptly, in a language which they understand and in detail, of the nature and cause of the accusation against them, and that they have the free assistance of an interpreter if they cannot understand or speak the language used in court. If this is indeed a general principle of Community law, it places a huge administrative burden on Member State competition authorities and courts in cross-border cartel cases.

Clearly, the burden is no greater than for the Commission and the Community courts, but at least these institutions are properly equipped to deal with this obligation. If it is difficult to build up competition law competence at 28 different authorities in the Community, it will be even more difficult to produce translation services at all 28 of these points and in the courts that are carrying out legal review. National competition authorities will to a certain extent be able to adjust for this problem by directing the action against undertakings present in the Member States' territory. In accordance with what has been said in chapter four, there is

[205] Judgment of the European Court of Human Rights of 21 February 1984, *Öztürk*, Series A No 73; see also judgment of 25 August 1987 *Lutz*, Series A No 123-A.

[206] Case C-235/92 P *Montecatini v Commission* [1999] ECR I-4539, at para 176; see also Case T-67/00 *JFE Engineering v Commission* [2004] ECR II-2501, at para 178, confirmed on appeal in Cases C-403/04 P C-403/04 P and C-405/04 *Sumitomo Metal Industries and Nippon Steel v Commission* [2007] ECR I-729, at para 52.

[207] Ameye, Evelyne M, 'The Interplay Between Human Rights and Competition Law in the EU' (2004) 25(6) *ECLR* 332.

considerable leeway as to the choice of which undertaking to bring action against within a group. Nevertheless, this requires careful pre-judicial considerations and steps by the investigating authority, if it wishes to avoid a situation where it will have to provide translation.

L. Duty to investigate exculpatory facts

The competent institution has a duty to examine carefully and impartially all the relevant aspects of the individual case. This follows from respect for the rights guaranteed by the Community legal order in administrative procedures.[208] In *TACA*, the duty was said to originate from the principle of sound administration.[209] The precise content of this duty, as well as the consequences flowing from it, are, however, difficult to ascertain. Reichel points out that the duty still lacks clear delineation:

> The principle of due diligence covers the widest span of legal situations. First, the principle can be used as a tool to require public authorities to maintain a high standard in handling cases and in carrying out other responsibilities, so that a private party can rely on the assumption that any mistakes made by the authority will not lead to negative consequences for the individual. Second, the principle can be used as a tool to influence the decision-making of the public authority itself, so that the organ may be required to consider facts and issues beneficial to the individual.[210]

M. Sound administration

The Community law principle of sound administration applies in Article 81 and 82 EC proceedings. Member States must be ready to accept that they can no longer decide unilaterally, in accordance with national principles, what constitutes sound administration.[211] The precise content of the principle and its impact on national procedure are, however, difficult to establish.

The principle of sound administration has manifested itself in various ways in Community competition law cases. In *FETTCA*, it was ground for finding that the Commission must act within a reasonable time when it adopts decisions.[212] In *TACA*, it was connected to the duty to examine carefully and impartially all the relevant aspects of the individual case.[213] In *Seamless steel tubes*, the Commission had lost the documentation relating to an international trade agreement between Japan and the EC, and this failure was held contrary to the principle of sound

[208] *Bolloré SA and others v Commission*, above n 184, at para 92.

[209] Joined Cases T-191/98 and T-212/98 to T-214/98 *Atlantic Container Line and others v Commission* [2003] ECR II-3275, at para 404.

[210] Reichel, Jane, *God förvaltning i EU och i Sverige* (Stockholm, Jure, 2006), at 592.

[211] *Ibid*, at 572.

[212] *CMA CGM and others v Commission*, above n 171, at para 317.

[213] *Atlantic Container Line and others v Commission*, above n 209, at para 404.

administration.[214] In *Vitamins*, the principle had an impact on the procedure applicable when an undertaking applied for leniency. The Court of First Instance held:

> If an undertaking makes contact with the Commission with a view to cooperating to an extent which may be rewarded under the Leniency Notice and a meeting is organised in that context between the institution and that undertaking, the minutes of such a meeting, recording the essential aspects of the assertions made at that meeting, must be drawn up or, at the very least, a sound recording must be made, pursuant to the principle of sound administration, if the undertaking in question so requests at the latest at the beginning of the meeting.[215]

Further, in the same case, the Commission's duty not to disclose to the press information on the fines it intended to levy was held to follow not only from the duty to respect professional secrecy, but also from the duty of sound administration.[216]

In *Choline chloride* (one of the *Vitamins* cases), there had been a meeting between Commission officials and representatives of the cartel participants BASF and Hoffman-La Roche, to discuss possible co-operation. The Commission did not draw up minutes from the meeting and made no sound recording. The Court of First Instance found that since BASF had not requested such recording or minutes, the Commission could not be criticised for breach of the principle of sound administration.[217]

Reichel finds that

> Regarding the content of the principle, it is mostly formulated as minimum requirements, leaving Member States room to adjust the Community requirements to national procedural traditions. Further, Community law does not seem to demand that national courts attribute any specific consequence or effect if a national public authority fails to uphold the principle correctly.[218]

From this we may conclude that the principle of sound administration applies in national proceedings on Article 81 EC, although its impact is of a softer nature.

N. Duty to act within reasonable time

The requirement that administrative procedures relating to competition policy are carried out within reasonable time constitutes a general principle of Community law.[219] Administrative procedures of excessive duration may have an effect on the future ability of the undertakings concerned to defend themselves, because the more time that elapses,

[214] *Mannesmannröhren-Werke v Commission*, above n 37, at paras 261 –62.
[215] *BASF v Commission*, above n 191, at para 502.
[216] *Ibid*, at para 604.
[217] Joined Cases T-101/05 and T-111/05 *BASF and UCB v Commission* [2007] ECR II-4949, at para 96.
[218] Reichel, above n 210, at 593.
[219] Case C-105/04 P *Nederlandse Federatieve Vereniging voor de Groothandel op Elektrotechnisch Gebied v Commission* [2006] ECR I-8725, at para 35.

> the more unlikely it becomes that exculpatory evidence relating to the infringements . . . can be obtained, owing in particular to the changes that may have come about in the composition of the managing boards of the undertakings concerned and to the movements affecting their other staff.[220]

This assessment must extend to the entire procedure, and be carried out by reference to its total duration.[221] Nonetheless, since the existence of a breach of the rights of the defence must be examined by reference to the specific circumstances of each particular case, it falls upon the undertaking concerned to bring forward arguments and facts to indicate how its defence rights were limited.[222]

In reality, the duty to act within a reasonable time influences the procedure rather than the final outcome of a case. The Court of First Instance said in *FETTCA* that

> the Commission may not defer defining its position indefinitely and . . . in the interests of legal certainty and of ensuring adequate judicial protection the Commission is required to adopt a decision or to send a formal letter, if such a letter has been requested, within a reasonable time.[223]

However, adoption of a decision establishing an infringement against Article 81 EC after the expiry of a reasonable period, is not such as to justify the annulment of a decision. It is clear from *Sodium gluconate* that unless it is established that the undue delay has adversely affected the ability of the undertakings concerned to defend themselves effectively, the decision will be upheld.[224]

O. Limitation periods

The Commission's power to impose fines is subject to a five-year limitation period pursuant to Article 25(1) of Regulation 1. According to Article 25(2), the time begins to run on the day on which the infringement is committed. For continuing or repeated infringements it begins to run on the day on which the infringement ceases. As set out in Article 25(3) of Regulation 1, any action taken by the Commission or by the competition authority of a Member State for the purpose of investigation or proceedings in respect of the infringement, interrupts the limitation period.

The imposition of penalties by national competition authorities or courts, as well as statutory limitation periods, remain outside Regulation 1 and thus are subject to national law. While national law may be modified by general principles of Community law, there are no indications that national legislators would have to

220 *Ibid*, at para 49.

221 *Ibid*, at para 50.

222 *Ibid*, at paras 56–59.

223 *CMA CGM and others v Commission*, above n 171, at para 317.

224 Case T-67/01 *JCB Service v Commission* [2004] ECR II-49, at para 40; Order of the President of the Court of First Instance in Case T-378/02 R *Technische Glaswerke Illmenau v Commission* [2003] ECR II-2921, at para 65.

duplicate the limitation periods in Regulation 1 in order to comply with Community law. The ultimate test is whether national law on limitation periods is consistent with the principle of loyal co-operation in Article 10 EC, and the principle of effectiveness.[225]

It is furthermore clear that fundamental principles of Community law apply.[226] Infringements of Article 81 EC must not be treated less favourably under national law, as regards limitation periods, than other infringements of national law of a similar nature and importance.[227] In addition, the requirements that the penalty be effective, proportionate and dissuasive will prevent any application of national limitation periods which hinders the effective application of Article 81 EC.[228] A national limitation period must be reasonable.[229]

In *Manfredi*, the Court warned that a

> national rule under which the limitation period begins to run from the day on which the agreement or concerted practice was adopted could make it practically impossible to exercise the right to seek compensation for the harm caused by that prohibited agreement or practice, particularly if that national rule also imposes a short limitation period which is not capable of being suspended.[230]

It would then be possible that the limitation period would expire even before the infringement was brought to an end.

Case law on limitation periods normally turns on the establishment of the start and end dates for the cartel. The Court of First Instance explained in *FETTCA* that in order to calculate the duration of an infringement, it is necessary merely to calculate the period during which the agreement existed. This means the time between the date on which the agreement was entered into and the date on which it was terminated.[231]

The duration of the infringement, which requires that the date on which it ended be known, is one of the essential elements of the infringement which must be proved by the Commission, also in relation to limitation periods.[232] As for the starting date, the conclusion of an agreement, even if it is to be implemented later, deprives the parties of their autonomy and consequently forms the beginning of the cartel's duration.[233]

Establishing an end date is somewhat more complicated. The Court of Justice has found that with regard to agreements which are no longer in force, it is sufficient, for Article 81 EC to be applicable, that they continue to produce their effects after they have formally ceased. That is because

[225] Case C-62/00 *Marks & Spencer* [2002] ECR I-6325, at paras 34 ff.

[226] Case C-85/97 *Société Financière d'Investissements SPRL (SFI) v Belgium* [1998] ECR I-7447, at paras 28 ff.

[227] *Commission v Greece*, above n 21, at para 23.

[228] *Ibid*, at para 24.

[229] *Marks & Spencer*, above n 225, at paras 34 ff.

[230] Joined Cases C-295/04 to C-298/04 *Manfredi and others* [2006] ECR I-6619, at para 78.

[231] *CMA CGM and others v Commission*, above n 171, at para 280.

[232] Case T-120/04 *Peróxidos Orgánicos v Commission* [2006] ECR II-4441, at paras 21, 52.

[233] Case T-241/01 *Scandinavian Airlines System v Commission* [2005] ECR II-2917, at para 184.

> the system of competition rules established by Article [81] . . . is concerned with the economic effects of agreements or of any comparable form of concerted practice or co-ordination rather than with their legal form.[234]

Nevertheless, this statement was made in the context of selective distribution of newspapers and periodicals, where there was no doubt about the ongoing contractual relation between publishers and their joint distributor. The Court of First Instance has held that, for cartels formally no longer in force, it is sufficient that they continue to produce effects.[235] The limitation period would thus start only when the cartel ceases to produce effects.

In *Cartonboard*, the parties announced a concerted price increase in October 1990, and the level of list prices agreed was still in force in April 1991 when the Commission carried out its dawn raid. April 1991 was established as the date when the infringement ended.[236] This is slightly at odds with what the Court of Justice found in *Cement*, where an agreement ended the last time a periodic information exchange was carried out, given that it underpinned the cartel agreement.[237] The most prevalent line of jurisprudence seems to be along this line. In *Choline chloride*, part of the Commission's case failed because it was held that the duration of an infringement must be appraised not by reference to the period during which an agreement is in force, but by reference to the period during which the undertakings concerned adopted conduct prohibited by Article 81 EC.[238]

In summary, the case law on duration of agreements and concerted practices seems to draw from Article 81 EC itself rather than procedural rules on limitation periods. This implies that national cartel cases should be adjudicated on the same basis.

P. Duty to state reasons

For the Community institutions, the duty to state reasons is stipulated in Article 253 EC. The duty is a matter of public policy, which must be raised by the Community judicature of its own motion and which, in consequence, may be invoked by the parties at any stage of the proceedings.[239] Nevertheless, the duty to state reasons has in addition taken on a life of its own and become a fundamental requirement of EC law, forming part of the rights of the defence.[240] It applies in Member States in order to secure the effective protection of a fundamental right.[241] The duty to state reasons is functionally related to the right to be heard.[242]

[234] Case 243/83 *SA Binon & Cie v SA Agence et messageries de la presse* [1985] ECR 2015, at para 17.
[235] Case T-59/99 *Ventouris v Commission* [2003] ECR II-5257, at para 182.
[236] Case T-327/94 *SCA Holding v Commission* [1998] ECR II-1373, at paras 95 ff.
[237] *Aalborg Portland and others v Commission*, above n 20, at paras 295–96.
[238] *BASF and UCB v Commission*, above n 217, at para 187.
[239] *Mannesmannröhren-Werke v Commission*, above n 37, at para 210.
[240] Joined Cases 46/87 and 227/88 *Hoechst v Commission* [1989] ECR 2859, at para 29; *Roquette Frères*, above n 22, at paras 47–48.
[241] Case 222/86 *Heylens and Others* [1987] ECR 4097, at paras 15–17.
[242] Reichel, above n 210, at 477.

In *Graphite electrodes*, the Court of First Instance reiterated the applicable criteria, according to which the statement of reasons

> must disclose in a clear and unequivocal fashion the reasoning followed by the institution which adopted the measure in question in such a way as to enable the persons concerned to ascertain the reasons for the measure so as to defend their rights and to enable the Community judicature to carry out its review.[243]

The Court of Justice expanded on the duty to state reasons in *Sytraval*, where it held that

> the statement of reasons required by Article 190 of the Treaty must be appropriate to the act at issue and must disclose in a clear and unequivocal fashion the reasoning followed by the institution which adopted the measure in question in such a way as to enable the persons concerned to ascertain the reasons for the measure and to enable the competent Community court to exercise its power of review. The requirements to be satisfied by the statement of reasons depend on the circumstances of each case, in particular the content of the measure in question, the nature of the reasons given and the interest which the addressees of the measure, or other parties to whom it is of direct and individual concern, may have in obtaining explanations. It is not necessary for the reasoning to go into all the relevant facts and points of law, since the question whether the statement of reasons meets the requirements of Article 190 of the Treaty must be assessed with regard not only to its wording but also to its context and to all the legal rules governing the matter in question.[244]

It follows that the more precise content of this duty can be established only with reference to the particular case at hand. Reichel analyses the principle in depth and finds that the duty to state reasons functions as an acknowledgement of the kind of investigation carried out by the institution and the conclusions reached.[245] She warns against an over-extensive interpretation of the principle, since this will lead to efficiency losses if there is an abundance of cases where the courts are forced to annul substantively correct assessments because of formal errors.[246] Further,

> the case law as it stands today allows the requirement of sufficiency to vary depending on the content of the measure in question, the nature of the reasons given and the interests the addressees or others may have . . .[247]

It seems that the duty to state reasons must exert an indirect influence on national competition procedure. It is far-fetched to expect that the Court of Justice, upon a reference for a preliminary ruling, would engage in an extensive review of the facts of a complicated cartel case, to see whether the national authority or court had complied with the duty to state reasons. One might rather expect the Court to reiterate its well-known formulae in such a case, only to explain that it is for the national court to ascertain whether the duty to state reasons has been complied with in the individual case. Even so, this principle may provide parties with

243 *Tokai Carbon v Commission*, above n 195, at para 149.
244 Case C-367/95 P *Commission v Sytravaland Brink's France* [1998] ECR I-1719, at para 63.
245 Reichel, above n 210, at 419.
246 *Ibid*, at 435–36.
247 *Ibid*, at 592.

additional firepower in national litigation, and it is quite possible that the Commission will take action under Article 230 EC against Member States where the national procedural legislation does not include guarantees to ensure that reasons are stated. Indeed, such a procedure was initiated against Sweden. This was a result of the absence of an obligation for the highest Swedish courts to state reasons when they decided on leave to appeal in connection with requests for references for preliminary rulings under Article 234 EC. A reasoned opinion was sent by the Commission to Sweden, urging the Member State to take corrective measures.[248] The matter was resolved when the national legislator moved to pass legislation to ensure that the highest courts would be under a duty to state reasons when they decided on requests for references for preliminary rulings.[249]

Q. Legitimate expectations and legal certainty

The principle of protection of legitimate expectations is one of the fundamental principles of the Community.[250] It forms part of the Community legal order and must be observed by the Member States when they exercise the powers conferred on them by Community Directives[251]; there is no reason to suppose that it would apply to a lesser extent in Article 81 EC proceedings in the Member States.

For cartels, legitimate expectations and legal certainty have considerable impact when it comes to transitional aspects, such as when Article 81 EC enters into force in a Member State. In *Reinforcing bars*, the Commission had fined a number of Italian undertakings for operating a cartel on concrete reinforcing bars. The decision was based on the ECSC Treaty, and it was common ground that the infringements were made when the ECSC Treaty was still in force. However, the ECSC Treaty expired on 23 July 2002, the Commission's decision being adopted a few months later, in December 2002. On appeal, the Court of First Instance set aside the Commission's decision and annulled the fines. This was because the Commission lacked competence since it had relied only on the expired ECSC Treaty when adopting the cartel decision. The nature of the *lex specialis* of the ECSC Treaty in relation to the EC Treaty did not lend any support to the Commission's contention that it retained competence to base a decision on the *lex specialis* after that Treaty expired.[252] In principle,

> substantive rules of Community law must be interpreted, in order to ensure observance of the principle of legal certainty and of legitimate expectations, as not applying, in principle, to situations existing before their entry into force . . .[253]

[248] Motiverat yttrande 2003/2161, C(2004)3899, Bryssel den 13/10/2004.

[249] Lag (2006:502) med vissa bestämmelser om förhandsavgörande från EG-domstolen, Prop. 2005/06:157 Vissa frågor om förhandsavgörande från EG-domstolen.

[250] Case T-65/98 *Van den Bergh Foods v Commission* [2003] ECR II-4653, at para 192.

[251] *Marks & Spencer*, above n 225, at para 44.

[252] Joined Cases T-27/03, etc *SP SpA and Others v Commission* [2007] ECR II-4331, at para 114.

[253] *Ibid*, at para 116.

On the other hand, procedural rules were held to be of direct application.[254] It was furthermore emphasised that the competence of an institution precedes the question of the applicable substantive and procedural rules.[255]

Apart from this, the principle of legitimate expectations has not been a prominent feature in cartel law. The Court held in *Alloy surcharges* that the principle of the protection of legitimate expectations may not be relied upon by an undertaking which has committed a manifest infringement of the rules in force.[256] Still, in cartel investigations, undertakings often enter into intense dialogue or discussion with the authorities, especially if there is an application for leniency. A legitimate expectation arises if the administration gives precise assurance to an undertaking, which assurance gives rise to reasonable expectations or hopes.[257] Nevertheless, it was made clear in *Graphite electrodes* that

> no one may plead infringement of that principle unless he has been given precise, unconditional and consistent assurances, from authorised, reliable sources, by the administration . . .[258]

On legal certainty, an argument was raised by BASF in *Choline Chloride* that the absence of a time-bar for increasing fines as a result of past infringements was contrary to legal certainty. However, the Court of First Instance found that the Commission had a discretion to take past infringements of the same Treaty provisions into account and increase fines with reference thereto. BASF had, between 1964 and 1993, been in flagrant breach of the competition rules for approximately 13 years, in three separate infringements. This justified a mark-up of 50 per cent when fines were imposed for further infringements that had taken place in the 1990s.[259]

V. SUMMARY, DISCUSSION AND CONCLUSIONS

As explained in section I. above, there is no harmonisation of Member States' national competition procedure, and no absolute requirement of uniformity under general principles of Community law. National rules applicable for the supervision and enforcement of Articles 81 and 82 EC must be no less favourable than those governing similar domestic actions (the principle of equivalence), and must not render practically impossible or excessively difficult the exercise of rights conferred by Community law (the principle of effectiveness). Community law accepts that national procedural law exerts an influence on the outcome of a case, within the limits just described, and does not expect identical outcomes.

[254] *Ibid.*

[255] *Ibid*, at para 117.

[256] Joined Cases C-65/02 P and C-73/02 P *Thyssen Krupp Stainless and others v Commission* [2005] ECR I-6773, at para 41.

[257] Joined Cases T-213/95 and T-18/96 *SCK and FNK v Commission* [1997] ECR II-1739, at para 80.

[258] Joined Cases T-236/01, T-239/01, T-244/01 to 246/01 and T-252/01 *Tokai Carbon and Others v Commission* [2004] ECR II-1181, at para 152.

[259] *BASF and UCB v Commission*, above n 217, at para 72.

Nevertheless, the principles of equivalence and effectiveness are only part of the story—national law is profoundly affected by fundamental principles of Community law, especially the rights of the defence. These rules serve as a common minimum standard in national procedure when Community law applies, in all proceedings in which sanctions, especially fines or penalty payments, may be imposed. This does not extend to a duty for Member States to duplicate the Community competition procedure, but it will have very similar effects given the relatively detailed case law developed by the Community courts.

Contrary to perceptions, there is a common set of principles governing national competition procedure in Member States. This raises concerns. The existence of various fundamental rights and general principles, and their application in national Article 81 and 82 EC cases, means that the national authorities and courts are facing a very challenging task. National judiciaries not only must know their national law, but in addition must be familiar with the general principles developed in Community law. A comparative approach is necessary, in which national procedure must continuously be evaluated in relation to EC law. If competition law cases are complex in the Community courts, at least there is only one set of applicable procedural rules; in national competition law cases where Articles 81 and 82 EC apply, there are two sets of rules, and a requirement to evaluate and adjust the national rules correspondingly. This is a know-how intensive exercise which requires specialist skills and a certain amount of time and resources. Tentatively, this calls for considerations about the composition of national authorities and courts, and the resources allocated to them.

Furthermore, there may be a duty for the national judiciary, under human rights law *and* Community law, to translate into the language of the accused undertaking at least the more important procedural documents and provide interpretation at no cost to the undertaking. Although this may to a certain extent be adjusted for, because an undertaking will often have a presence in the relevant Member State through a subsidiary or otherwise, it entails considerable pre-judicial assessments and planning to avoid the procedure being burdened by translation.

The law just referred to is reflected in unilateral adjustments of Member State legislation to the Community competition procedure. This has been described by Commission officials as a healthy imitation process within the European Competition Network, with a trend of gradual procedural convergence in Member States.[260] Nonetheless, given the breadth and depth of existing case law, my best guess is that Member States have converged on paper but not in practice. This analysis shows, though, that decentralised competition law control is not necessarily jeopardised by the absence of procedural harmonisation. On the contrary, jurisprudence has harmonised European competition procedure. This realisation may come as good news if there are Member States where protection of fundamental rights in administrative enforcement has been weaker. This line of case law

[260] Dekeyser, Kris, and Jaspers, Maria, 'A New Era of ECN Cooperation—Achievements and Challenges with Special Focus on Work in the Leniency Field' (2007) 30(1) *World Competition* 3, at 12.

may indeed provide additional legitimacy to EC competition law. However, there is a risk that increased legitimacy through a common minimum standard of protection will be outweighed by legitimacy deficits created by this very development. Considerable skills are required by national judiciaries to keep themselves informed about fundamental rights in EC law, to evaluate their national legislation and, if necessary, to set national law aside.

The burden placed on national judiciaries has occurred gradually through case law and without any legislative measures. Indeed, the situation was misrepresented in the preparatory works of Regulation 1 and its preamble, where one could easily obtain the impression that evidence and procedure were entirely left to national law.[261] Although there is a reference to general principles of Community law in the preamble of Regulation 1,[262] the legislator could have used some more ink to develop this. The bulk of the applicable case law has been developed without any attempt at analysing whether conflicts with national legal systems will arise. In case of conflicts, Community law prevails. This may come as a surprise to lawyers in Member States, and may result in considerations based on the absence of participation in this profound development of the law. Furthermore, legitimacy tensions may be expected to arise if the ECHR, to which all Member States have acceded, were to confer a higher level of protection than is afforded by Community law. There is indeed a lively academic discussion on this subject.[263]

In summary, jurisprudence which may appear at first sight as a solution to the lack of procedural harmonisation, actually produces deep-rooted legitimacy problems. On the bright side, the high level of *empirical legitimacy* which this judge-made law has acquired indicates that, on balance, there are chances that the general procedural principles will be absorbed and accepted at the Member State level too. At any rate, the infiltration of general principles of Community law into the procedural systems of Member States may be expected to bring about no more than what application of the ECHR would have brought about in due course. Given the early stage of decentralisation, it remains to be seen how awareness and compliance develop.

[261] COM(2000) 582 Final—Explanatory memorandum, at 12, 5th para: 'The present proposal is based on the premise that national competition authorities will apply Articles 81 and 82 in accordance with their respective national procedural rules. It is not necessary for the implementation of the reform to embark on a full-scale harmonisation of national procedural laws.'

[262] Preamble, at 5, *in fine*, and at 36.

[263] See esp on this topic Riley, Alan, 'Saunders and the power to obtain information in Community and United Kingdom competition law' (2000) 25(3) *EL Rev* 264; Smith, Graham P, 'Competition law and the ignoring of human rights' [2001] *International Company and Commercial Law Review* 1; and Willis, Peter R, '"You have the right to remain silent . . .", or do you? The privilege against self-incrimination following Mannesmannrohren-Werke and other recent decisions' (2001) 22(8) *ECLR* 313.

7

Legitimacy in Fines and Sanctions

I. ENFORCEMENT AND LEGITIMACY

LAWS ARE LEGITIMATE only if the State can guarantee average compliance. Enforcement is a way of communication. The methods and intensity of enforcement in a given field of law communicate the public commitment to the realisation of the goals expressed by legislation. Weak enforcement signals that the State is not serious about the legislation and consequently undermines the law's legitimacy. A high level of enforcement signals strong commitment, but may result in other types of legitimacy problems, especially if the enforcement authorities are vested with a large margin of discretion. Legitimacy is important when competition law infringements are penalised. On a deeper level, fairness and justice in the imposition of penalties serve to assure public confidence in the system. Strong enforcement must consequently be combined with a strong legal focus in order to preserve legitimacy. These questions will be explored in this chapter.

The chapter begins with an outline of the requirements of uniformity and effectiveness of sanctions in EC competition law enforcement. It will be clear that although sanctions must in principle be effective, proportionate and dissuasive, no detailed requirements applicable to Member States have been developed in EC law, where there is an amazing absence of generally applicable theory-building. Given the need for a law that can be explained rationally, the discussion will then proceed to efficiency, to consider the requirements of an efficient sanctioning system and whether decentralised EC competition law enforcement may be expected to generate efficient sanctions.

Legitimacy is discussed next. It will be demonstrated that the legitimacy of the Commission's fining policy has been openly challenged before the Community courts. While evidentiary rules and procedure have gained general acceptance in the legal community, the Commission's policy on sanctions prior to 2006 failed to achieve anything like legitimacy, and indeed has generated massive criticism. Moreover, the Community courts have refused to develop any doctrine whatsoever on how fines should be calculated. We are thus impoverished when it comes to theory-building that could form a bridge between the legal systems of Member States.

National competition authorities and courts are not bound by the Commission's fining policy when applying Articles 81 and 82 EC; sanctions imposed by national courts must be based on national law. On the other hand, there is an obligation under EC law that sanctions are effective and deterrent. At the dawn of decentralisation, there is reason for Member States to look for efficient approaches to sanctions. Given the policy shift in 2006 described above, the vitality of the case law of the Community courts is questionable here, and inspiration must be drawn from economic theory and analysis. There are recent developments with empirical studies on convicted cartels. Experiences of econometric methods for proving antitrust damages may also be of help. Nevertheless, there is a dilemma here in so far as studies of economic theory will prove inconclusive for solving the intricate problem of structuring an effective sanction system. At any rate, the ambition here is to provide an up-to-date study.

As a preliminary point, it is not self-evident that competition law infringements must, as a general rule, be sanctioned through public enforcement. Even if the public enforcers (against probability) attempt and manage to calculate and confiscate the illegal gains, they can at most achieve deterrence. However, fines will not compensate injured parties, who must take action at their own risk. So why not let the market self-regulate confiscation of unlawful gains through private litigation? Private parties may be expected to have a better understanding of market functions than the authorities, and to take notice of infringements at an earlier stage.[1] Information deficits for injured parties are not necessarily overcome by extensive investigatory powers of authorities; the establishment of efficient discovery procedures is a viable alternative. On the other hand, a strong argument for using public enforcement to erase (in particular) cartel profits is pulverisation of the wealth transfer over vast classes of customers or consumers, each of whom has insufficient economic incentives to take action. However, this problem can in principle be addressed in two ways—public enforcement, or establishment of effective collective remedies.

Even if there is some attractiveness about private enforcement, reasoning on establishment of discovery and collective action is still largely hypothetical, at least as it was documented in the Community environment of 2005, where the state of play for antitrust damages is 'total underdevelopment'.[2] At present, and given that private enforcement is governed by disparate national rules in the Member States, it is debatable whether it would be a reliable method of enforcement.[3] The motives for private parties and authorities to bring actions differ as well. Private parties may be expected to take action when there is a sufficient economic incentive, while authorities may focus on markets where competition is weakened and take action against the most severe restrictions on competition.[4] If optimal conditions for

[1] Wahl, Nils, *Optimala sanktioner inom svensk konkurrensrätt*, Konkurrensverkets uppdragsforskning 2006:3, at 48, available at www.konkurrensverket.se.

[2] COM(2005) 672, Green Paper, *Damages Actions for Breach of the EC Antitrust Rules*, 19 December 2005, at 4.

[3] Wahl, Nils, *Konkurrensskada* (Stockholm, JureCLN, 2000), at 404.

[4] *Ibid*, at 24–25; Wils, Wouter P J, 'Should Private Antitrust Enforcement be Encouraged in Europe?' (2003) 26(3) *World Competition* 473, at 482 ff.

private enforcement were to be established in the EU we might be able to spend fewer resources on public enforcement, but it seems unrealistic to consider anything of the kind for the time being.

II. THE RELATION BETWEEN NATIONAL LAW AND COMMUNITY LAW ON FINES AND OTHER SANCTIONS

When it comes to sanctions for EC competition law infringements, the Community legislator has not considered any harmonisation. Theoretically the Commission could have taken the initiative to propose such legislation, and (given political agreement) the Council could have adopted it following consultation with the European Parliament. No such measures have been taken, however. The Community courts have refused to fill the vacuum by engaging in any theory-building, and have effectively left the theories to the Commission and, as will be seen, to the Member States.

A. National law governs fines and sanctions imposed in Member States

Article 5 of Regulation 1 empowers national competition authorities to impose fines, periodic penalty payments or any other penalty *provided for in their national law*. As for the imposition of fines by national courts, that is outside Regulation 1, unless the court has been designated as a competition authority pursuant to Article 35 of Regulation 1, in which case Article 5 applies. As explained, Article 5 refers only to national law. This means that national law always governs the imposition of cartel fines in Member States. The fining provisions in Regulation 1 concern only the Commission.[5]

B. Effectiveness requirements

Community law does not provide for the harmonisation of cartel fines or other penalties to be applied in Member States. In this situation, the principle of loyal co-operation in Article 10 EC still requires the Member States to take all measures necessary to guarantee the application and effectiveness of Community law.[6] The Court held in *Commission v Greece* that this is a requirement where Community legislation does not specifically provide any penalty for an infringement or refers for that purpose to national laws, regulations and administrative provisions.[7]

5 Arts 23 and 24 of Regulation 1/2003.

6 Case 68/88 *Commission v Greece* [1989] ECR 2965, at para 23.

7 *Ibid.*

The choice of penalties remains within the Member States' discretion.[8] This is important, because of the range of sanctions available against competition law infringements. Methods employed throughout the world include fines, imprisonment, disqualification of directors, and collaborative compliance techniques where the participants will rectify infringements by offering commitments. Other options include the introduction of incentives and instruments for private parties to engage in cartel-busting activities.[9] Sanctions may be directed against companies, individuals or both (and against associations of undertakings).

Current case law does not allow for any conclusions on whether one particular type of sanction is indispensable in the enforcer's toolbox under EC law, but corporate fines constitute the primary method under national competition laws in Member States.[10] Further, the absence of fines against undertakings may have adverse consequences, such as giving firms incentives to encourage cartel activities provided only their employees are subject to sanctions, to look in the other direction and to be lenient with employees who break antitrust laws.[11]

European Community law requires Member States to

> ensure in particular that infringements of Community law are penalised under conditions, both procedural and substantive, which are analogous to those applicable to infringements of national law of a similar nature and importance . . .[12]

The Court confirmed this in *Paquay*.[13] The Member State must in any event make the penalty effective, proportionate and dissuasive.[14] The point on proportionality was further confirmed in *Ntionik and Pikoulas*, where the Court expanded somewhat:

> [T]he administrative or punitive measures must not go beyond what is necessary for the objectives pursued and a penalty must not be so disproportionate to the gravity of the infringement that it becomes an obstacle to the freedoms enshrined in the EC Treaty . . . It is, however, for the national court to determine, in the light of the foregoing considerations, whether the penalties provided for by the applicable national legislation are proportionate.[15]

Commission v Greece and the other judgments just mentioned comprise a line of cases commenced prior to the modernisation. Furthermore, although those cases were on Community law, they did not specifically address competition law. It seems possible that the amplified supervision and enforcement task entrusted to

[8] *Ibid*, at para 24.

[9] Riley, Alan, 'Beyond Leniency: Enhancing Enforcement in EC Antitrust Law' (2005) 28(3) *World Competition* 377.

[10] Dannecker, Gerhard, and Jensen, Oswald (eds), *Competition Law Sanctioning in the European Union* (The Hague, Kluwer Law International, 2004), at 83.

[11] Whelan, Peter, 'A Principled Argument for Personal Criminal Sanctions as Punishments under EC Cartel Law' (2007) 4(1) *The Competition Law Review* 7, at 30.

[12] *Commission v Greece*, above n 6, at para 24.

[13] Case C-460/06 *Paquay* [2007] ECR I-8511, at para 52.

[14] *Commission v Greece*, above n 6, at para 24.

[15] Case C-430/05 *Ntionik and Pikoulas* [2007] ECR I-5835, at para 54.

Member States through Regulation 1 will lead to more sophisticated requirements as to what constitutes 'effective, proportionate and dissuasive' competition law penalties. Still, it remains difficult to find any direct support for this view. Indirectly one may look at how the Commission's powers and responsibilities have been defined over the years. Much of the case law, however, concerns whether the Commission applied its own fining guidelines correctly, assessments which are of little or no relevance for determining what EC law requires from Member States' competition law penalties.

In *Musique diffusion française*, the Court referred to the Commission's task of supervision and held that

> in assessing the gravity of an infringement for the purpose of fixing the amount of the fine, the Commission must take into consideration not only the particular circumstances of the case but also the context in which the infringement occurs and must ensure that its action has the necessary deterrent effect, especially as regards those types of infringement which are particularly harmful to the attainment of the objectives of the Community.[16]

However, it is difficult to say whether this applies to Member States as well; the Court was referring not only to the Commission's supervisory task and its duty to investigate and punish individual infringements, but also to its duty to pursue a competition policy in accordance with the Treaty.[17] The Commission still has a central role in cartel enforcement, exceeding that of Member States, which makes it hard to tell whether its duties can automatically be extrapolated to Member States.

Temple Lang has highlighted another aspect of fines imposed by Member States. He suggests that when the Commission imposes no fine, or a reduced fine following a leniency application, national competition authorities in Member States have a duty to reduce their fine accordingly. That is because of the duty under Article 10 EC not to jeopardise the objectives of the Treaty, and because the Commission's leniency policy promotes competition policy. The Member States' duty to reduce fines would apply only to anticompetitive conduct disclosed to the Commission (ie to one and the same cartel) and not to other conduct.[18]

C. The purpose of fines

As explained, fines are not the only cartel enforcement option for a national legislator. However, the present analysis is of EC law, and given that the Commission has only had recourse to fines and stop-orders against cartels, the available case law has certain limitations. It will also be obvious from the following discussion that

[16] Joined Cases 100/80 to 103/80 *Musique diffusion française and Others v Commission* [1983] ECR 1825, at para 106.

[17] *Ibid*, at para 105.

[18] Temple Lang, John, 'The Implications of the Commission's Leniency Policy for National Competition Authorities' (2003) 28(3) *EL Rev* 430.

fines are a necessary tool in the enforcer's toolbox. The further analysis will consequently address only fines.

There are several cases in which the Community courts have explained the purpose of competition law fines. Once again, though, it is difficult to work out whether the principles developed relate only to the Commission's power to impose fines under Regulation 17 and Regulation 1, or whether the principles have general application in all Member States, or indeed to sanctions other than fines.

In *Zinc Phosphate*, the Court connected the Commission's power to impose fines to the task of supervision conferred on it by Community law, which included 'in particular suppressing illegal activities and preventing their reoccurrence'.[19]

In *Graphite electrodes*, the Court considered that

> fines imposed for infringements of Article 81 EC and laid down in Article 15(2) of Regulation No 17 are designed to punish the unlawful acts of the undertakings concerned and to deter both the undertakings in question and other operators from infringing the rules of Community competition law in future.[20]

This statement is interesting in three distinct ways. First, the Court endorses a combined retributive and deterrent approach, by saying that the objective is to punish and deter. These two objectives have also been emphasised by the Court of First Instance.[21] Secondly, the combined references to Article 81 EC and Regulation 17 may be seen as alternative rather than cumulative. In other words, the Court is not only interpreting Article 15 of Regulation 17, but is also making a statement in principle. Accordingly, an argument may be made that the purpose, when Member States impose fines and other sanctions on cartel participants, is to suppress illegal activities and prevent their reoccurrence, to punish and deter. This in turn is consistent with *Commission v Greece*, where the Court held that penalties must be effective, proportionate and dissuasive.[22] Thirdly, the reasoning on deterrence in *Graphite electrodes* shows that the Court endorses both individual deterrence (to prevent the cartel participants effecting future infringements of Community competition law) and general deterrence (to prevent other operators from effecting future infringements).

D. Significance of the economic impact of the infringement

Opinion among lawyers seems to be that cartel fines should, as a minimum, confiscate illegal gains. Whether one favours deterrence or retribution, information about cartel overcharges would seem to be an important point of reference or departure. But EC case law does not offer much in terms of guidance. Calculations are intrinsically difficult. This theme will be developed in the following subsections.

[19] Case C-76/06 P *Britannia Alloys v Commission* [2007] ECR I-4405, at para 22.
[20] Case C-289/04 P *Showa Denko v Commission* [2006] ECR I-5859, at para 16.
[21] Case T-329/01 *Archer Daniels Midland v Commission* [2006] ECR II-3255, at para 141.
[22] *Commission v Greece*, above n 6, at para 24.

1. *A line of cases playing down the importance of actual effects*

As a starting point, the Community courts have played down the relevance of the effects of cartels for the purpose of establishing fines. In *Steel beams*, the Court of Justice held that

> the effect which an anticompetitive practice has is therefore not a conclusive criterion for assessing the proper amount of a fine. Factors relating to the intentional aspect may be more significant than those relating to the effects, particularly where they relate to infringements which are intrinsically serious, such as price-fixing and market-sharing . . .[23]

Further, in *Lysine*, the Court quashed the view that fines must be proportionate to the undertaking's size on the product market in respect of which the infringement was committed; there is no such general principle of Community law.[24]

The Court of First Instance held in *FETTCA* that the Commission 'is not required, in order to fix fines, to establish that the infringement brought about an unlawful advantage for the undertakings concerned'.[25] Furthermore, the Commission is not required to take into consideration any lack of benefit from the infringement.[26] Even if it was established that an undertaking did not benefit from an infringement, this cannot preclude the imposition of a fine, since otherwise it would cease to have a deterrent effect.[27]

Transposing this case law to the national context, my conclusion is that EC law does not require national law on cartel fines to take into account whether the infringement brought about any gains, neither does it require that national authorities quantify such gains. On the other hand, a national fining policy according to which such estimations were actually made, would also be acceptable under EC law.

As will be shown in the following subsection, the Commission has attempted a few times to estimate the economic impact of cartels. Conversely, parties have tried to prove that the cartel in which they participated had no market impact, or at least that such impact was negligible. Such evidence has been assessed by the Court of First Instance and is perfectly workable (although, as will be shown, parties have not been particularly successful in relying on economic analysis). Indeed, the Court of First Instance referred in *FETTCA* to the Twenty First Report on Competition Policy, in which the Commission stated that wherever it can ascertain the level of the ill-gotten gains, even if it cannot do so precisely, the calculation of the fine may have this as its starting point.[28]

[23] Case C-194/99 P *Thyssen Stahl v Commission* [2003] ECR I-10821, at para 118.

[24] Case C-397/03 P *Archer Midlands Daniels and Archer Daniels Midland Ingredients v Commission* [2006] ECR I-4429, at para 101.

[25] Case T-213/00 *CMA CGM and others v Commission* [2003] ECR II-913, at para 341.

[26] *Ibid.*

[27] *Ibid*, at para 340.

[28] *Ibid*, at para 342.

2. New developments: a 'but for' approach

If effects are to be analysed for the purpose of determining fines, the Court of First Instance has devised a 'but for' approach in *Zinc Phosphate*. The only guidance provided in that case is that one must 'take as a reference the competition that would normally exist if there were no infringement'.[29] However, in *Methionine* the Court of First Instance set aside in part the Commission's reasoning on price-increasing effects on the market. It held that a finding of higher cartel prices would allow the Commission to impose higher fines. If such a 'but for' approach is applied, all the objective conditions on the relevant market must be taken into account, including the economic context and the legislative background.[30]

The 'but for' approach was revisited again in *Citric acid*.[31] There, the Commission had observed actual price increase decisions implemented by the cartel, as well as quotas. In this type of situation, the cartel participants may be inclined to argue that the prices would have been the same regardless of the cartel. Importantly, the Court of First Instance found that 'consideration of the impact of a cartel on the market necessarily involves recourse to assumptions'.[32] Moreover, in carrying out a 'but for' analysis, the Commission could rely on 'reasonable probability, which is not precisely quantifiable'.[33] The Court referred to effectiveness and held that the Commission is not required to quantify the impact or provide any assessment in figures.[34] The actual impact of a cartel on the market must be regarded as having been sufficiently demonstrated if the Commission is able to provide specific and credible evidence indicating with reasonable probability that the cartel had an impact on the market.[35] The Commission had based its decision on observations that the cartel members carefully implemented the cartel agreements, their market share, and how the data provided by the parties showed that the prices set by the cartel tallied to a certain extent with those actually charged by the cartel members.[36] The Commission's decision was upheld.

3. Economic analysis and fines

In *Carbonless paper*, the producer Zanders had commissioned a report from PricewaterhouseCoopers, seeking to show that the impact of the cartel during a period from January 1992 to Autumn 1995 was minimal or non-existent. The Commission rejected that argument, and its view was upheld on appeal.[37]

Another participant in *Carbonless paper*, AWA, submitted two expert reports, seeking to demonstrate for the purpose of fines that the prices resulting from the

[29] Case T-64/02 *Heubach v Commission* [2005] ECR II-5137, at para 106.
[30] Case T-279/02 *Degussa v Commission* [2006] ECR II-897, at paras 223–24.
[31] Case T-59/02 *Archer Daniels Midland v Commission* [2006] ECR II-3627.
[32] *Ibid*, at para 159.
[33] *Ibid*.
[34] *Ibid*, at para 160.
[35] *Ibid*, at para 161.
[36] *Ibid*, at para 162.
[37] Joined Cases T-109/02, etc *Bolloré and others v Commission* [2007] ECR II-947, at paras 104–07.

cartel could not have exceeded those which would have been observed under normal conditions of competition. This was all in vain, as the Court of First Instance wrote:

> The fact that the undertakings actually announced the agreed price increases and that the prices so announced served as a basis for fixing individual transaction prices suffices in itself for a finding that the collusion on prices had both as its object and effect a serious restriction of competition . . .[38]

If it is difficult to estimate the actual impact of a price-fixing scheme, it is even more difficult to estimate the impact of market-sharing. In *SAS and Maersk*, there was a market-sharing agreement between airlines, according to which Scandinavian Airlines System would cease operating two routes, and Maersk would cease to operate another route. There were consequently three routes that the parties to the agreement respectively abandoned in each other's favour. Scandinavian Airlines System tried to argue that they were making losses on these routes prior to the conclusion of the agreement, so that the agreements had no effect. All the amendments made by either of the parties to its traffic programming were justified on economic and commercial grounds, claimed the airline. The Court of First Instance held this argument to be irrelevant.[39] The market-sharing agreement 'had the effect of removing all real competition in those two markets'.[40]

Scandinavian Airlines System further relied on a study carried out by the Lexecon company, trying to show that the actual impact of the agreement on the fares for routes from Denmark was minimal. Nevertheless, the Court of First Instance found that

> it is sufficient to note that the infringement which was found consists in the sharing of markets, and thus does not directly concern the fares charged by parties to the agreement, and that the parties adopted a line of conduct in accordance with that marketsharing.[41]

The study was criticised for dealing only with the prices of one of the airlines and not with both, and the Court noted that 'Clearly, in the absence of an agreement, SAS would have been able to exercise a significant competitive constraint on Maersk Air'.[42] From this, it seems that the Commission does not have to demonstrate that a market-sharing practice has any specifically quantifiable price effect; further, such counter-evidence presented by the cartel participant will be met with scepticism. Apparently the standard of proof for demonstrating no or low impact of cartel activities is very high.

Another market-sharing case in which effects were assessed is *Graphite electrodes*. There, producers had applied a home market rule. The cartel participants referred to autonomous decisions, taken in their economic interest, to concentrate on their respective home markets. This did not make much of an impression on the Court of First Instance, which wrote:

[38] *Ibid*, at para 451.
[39] Case T-241/01 *Scandinavian Airlines System v Commission* [2005] ECR II-2917, at para 109.
[40] *Ibid*, at para 117.
[41] *Ibid*, at para 126.
[42] *Ibid*, at para 127.

> [W]hile it is always difficult to imagine what developments would have taken place on a given market in the absence of the cartel active on that market, such prognoses are particularly problematic where the markets are shared according to the 'home' producer principle, which obliges the members of the cartel to be passive in certain geographic areas . . . It cannot be precluded that, in the absence of the security conferred by the cartel, the 'home' producer would, under the simple threat of access to that market by other producers, have applied quite low prices so that those other producers would choose to remain outside the market in question and thus not acquire the slightest market share. In such a situation, the free play of competition would have been to the advantage of consumers, in the form of a price reduction, without market shares changing at all.[43]

Looking at these cases, it is questionable whether there has been any point at all in submitting economic analysis determining market impact in Community cartel cases. Following the adoption of the new Commission Guidelines for setting fines, however, there is a possibility that economic analysis on the actual impact of cartels will acquire higher significance. The key issue is whether undertakings will be able to rebut the proxy employed by the Commission. A proxy is a principle applied in fine setting, which allows an authority or court to presume that, once an infringement has been demonstrated, the fines should equal a certain level. The alternative would be that the authority must demonstrate actual effects on competition in every specific case. The proxy presently applied by the Commission allows for fines of up to 30 per cent of the turnover on the relevant market, plus certain mark-ups.

It may be recalled that the US Antitrust Modernization Commission recommends the Sentencing Commission to amend the Sentencing Guidelines to make explicit that the 20 per cent proxy employed in the US may be rebutted by proof by a preponderance of evidence that the actual overcharge was higher or lower.[44] The prospects under EC law are unpromising, though: the Court of First Instance has held that 'that the fact that an undertaking has derived no profit from the infringement cannot prevent it from being fined, as otherwise the fine would lose its deterrent effect'.[45] Nevertheless, if one distinguishes between, on the one hand, overcharges and, on the other hand, cartel profits, both views may be correct. As set out in chapter three in section I.C.6., overcharges are often translated into social costs—it is quite possible that a cartel participant has not derived any profits at all, since overcharges tend to go into costs for upholding the cartel and inefficiencies created by it. On the basis of economic theory, the Community courts are correct to hold that the Commission should not have to prove profits; but is it inconceivable that an undertaking should be able to produce evidence demonstrating that overcharges were in fact lower than the proxy employed by the Commission, and consequently have its fines reduced to some extent? Evidence on

[43] Joined Cases T-236/01, T-239/01, T-244/01 to T-246/01, T-251/01 and T-252/01 *Tokai Carbon and Others v Commission* [2004] ECR II-1181, at paras 211–12.

[44] Antitrust Modernization Commission Report and Recommendations April 2007, at 295, available at http://www.amc.gov/report_recommendation/toc.htm.

[45] *Bolloré and others v Commission*, above n 37, at para 671.

actual overcharges could increase our understanding about cartels and, in addition, give plaintiffs in follow-on damages suits some additional fire-power.

E. Member States' discretionary power equals that of the Commission

As explained, cartel fines imposed by Member States must be effective, proportionate and dissuasive in order to conform with Community law. However, this does not say much about the detailed design of a Member State's fining policy. When a Member State court is struggling to determine an appropriate fine for a cartel participant, can it expect to obtain guidance from the Court of Justice through an Article 234 EC reference? In other words, will the Court develop a line of case law on the level of fines or other sanctions imposed by national authorities and courts, following references for preliminary rulings?

A general observation here is that if the Court were to begin to develop principles in this field, such principles would also apply to Commission decisions, eroding the present case law on the Commission's wide discretion. It seems impossible that principles of Community law would apply only to Member States and not to the Commission. Until now, the Court of Justice has refused to engage in outright proportionality assessments of fines.[46] It has emphasised repeatedly that the Commission enjoys a particularly wide discretion. The view put forward here is that Member States enjoy at least as much discretion as the Commission in setting fines.

As mentioned above, it is settled case law that the Commission enjoys a wide discretion in setting fines, and that, furthermore, the Court of Justice will not second-guess the Court of First Instance. In *Hüls*, the Court held that it will not substitute, on grounds of fairness, its own appraisal for that of the Court of First Instance as to the amount of a fine imposed on an undertaking.[47] The same statement was made in *PVC II*.[48] Further, the Court of First Instance accepted in *Seamless steel tubes*, as a matter of principle, that the Commission is entitled to raise or adjust the level of fines at any time.[49] The development has been summarised by the Court as follows:

> [T]he Commission has a particularly wide discretion as regards the choice of factors to be taken into account for the purposes of determining the amount of fines, such as, inter alia, the particular circumstances of the case, its context and the dissuasive effect of fines, without the need to refer to a binding or exhaustive list of the criteria which must be taken into account . . .[50]

[46] Case C-359/01 P *British Sugar v Commission* [2004] ECR I-4933, at paras 45–48.

[47] Case C-199/92 P *Hüls v Commission* [1999] ECR I-4287, at para 197.

[48] Joined Cases C-238/99 P, etc *Limburgse Vinyl Maatschappij and others v Commission* [2002] ECR I-8375, at para 614.

[49] Case T-44/00 *Mannesmannröhren-Werke v Commission* [2004] ECR II-2223, at para 217.

[50] *Showa Denko v Commission*, above n 20, at para 36; Case C-3/06 P *Groupe Danone v Commission* [2007] ECR I-1331, at para 37.

According to the case law, the Commission's wide discretion extends to the acceptance or otherwise of mitigating factors. For instance, in *FETTCA* (a shipping cartel), Senator Lines had referred to its financial losses as a mitigating factor. The Court of First Instance underlined that the Commission was not required to take account of an undertaking's financial losses, since that would have the effect of conferring an unfair competitive advantage on the undertakings least well adapted to the conditions of the market.[51] Nevertheless, it allowed the Commission to decide 'not to impose a fine or to reduce its amount on account of the financial difficulties faced by the undertaking concerned'.[52]

Some more detailed guidance was given by the Court in *Cement*. The amount of the fine is set according to the gravity of the infringement and, where appropriate, its duration.[53] As regards the gravity of the infringement, that has to be determined by reference to criteria such as the particular circumstances of the case, its context and the dissuasive effect of the fines.[54] Further, the relative gravity of the acts of each cartel participant will be examined.[55] Further, the Court explained that

> the content and duration of the anticompetitive conduct, the number of incidents and their intensity, the extent of the market affected and the damage to the economic public order must be taken into account. The analysis must also take into consideration the relative importance and market share of the undertakings responsible and also any repeated infringements.[56]

Nevertheless, when reading *Cement*, due attention should be paid to the fact that the Court of Justice was *not* expressing this method for setting fines with reference to general principles of Community law. On the contrary, the Court referred to *Ferriere Nord*[57] and *Suiker Unie*,[58] and this demonstrates that the Court was interpreting (the now obsolete) Regulation 17 rather than developing general principles of law. Consequently, not even this rather general guidance applies to Member States. Naturally, this does not exclude the possibility that the Court would develop similar principles applicable to Member States, but this cannot be inferred directly from the present case law.

[51] *CMA CGM and others v Commission*, above n 25, at para 351.
[52] *Ibid*, at para 352.
[53] Joined Cases C-204/00 P, etc *Aalborg Portland and others v Commission* [2004] ECR I-123, at para 89.
[54] *Ibid*, at para 90.
[55] *Ibid*, at para 92.
[56] *Ibid*, at para 91.
[57] Case C-219/95 P *Ferriere Nord v Commission* [1997] ECR I-4411, at para 32.
[58] Joined Cases 40/73, etc *Suiker Unie and Others v Commission* [1975] ECR 1663, at paras 622 and 623.

III. EFFICIENCY: THEORIES AND EMPIRICAL OBSERVATIONS ON FINING POLICY

It has been explained that the case law of the Community courts leaves considerable discretion to Member States as regards competition law fines. The requirements of uniformity and effectiveness are not very pronounced here. But what may be considered an *efficient* fining policy? The survey undertaken here is an attempt to do what the Community courts have refused to do: to outline a model for reasoning on efficient penalties.

For reasons that will be set out in greater detail here, it is impossible to apply a 'pure' penal theory to competition law sanctions. Yeung explains this with reference to the complexity and uncertainty that arise at two levels: within the penal theories themselves, and with reference to how competition law infringements differ from traditional crimes.[59] Even so, an understanding of prevailing penal theories will be helpful as an analytical tool in the quest for efficient fines.

A. Deterrence

1. *The basic theory and available empirical support*

Deterrence is based on the notion that a sanction is justified in order to prevent infringements.[60] Prevention is thus at the core of the theory. It depends on the assumption of rational actors acting in the pursuit of self-interest in order to maximise their welfare.[61] Undertakings are assumed to weigh, on the one hand, the expected gains of an infringement against, on the other hand, the expected sanctions and the risk of detection. The fine should equal the cartel profits or harm caused, plus a mark-up for the risk of detection. Thus the model's openness to economic theory and analysis is fundamental. In principle, a fining policy based on deterrence is open to adjustments based on new knowledge derived not from legal practitioners, but from economists.

The Court of Justice has explicitly accepted that a deterrence multiplier may be used in the calculation of fines.[62]

In *Sodium gluconate*, the Court of First Instance wrote:

> It is reasonable to assume that when making financial calculations and management decisions, undertakings take account rationally not only of the level of fines that they risk incurring in the event of an infringement but also the likelihood of the cartel being detected.[63]

[59] Yeung, Karen, *Securing Compliance—A principled approach* (Oxford, Hart Publishing, 2004), at 85.
[60] *Ibid*, at 63.
[61] *Ibid*, at 64.
[62] *Showa Denko v Commission*, above n 20, at para 24.
[63] *Archer Daniels Midland v Commission*, above n 21, at para 141.

At the outset, it is important to realise that the assumed cost–benefit analysis, central to the deterrence model, is made not only when undertakings are considering whether to establish a cartel or not, but continuously through the operation of the cartel, and it determines whether a particular firm will stick with the cartel, cheat on its co-conspirators or deviate by reporting to the authorities. Leniency policies exploit this mechanism precisely in order to destabilise cartels.[64]

There are certain empirical foundations for the assumption that undertakings make cost–benefit analyses when considering cartel activity. The study by Clarke and Evenett, published in 2003, examined the international vitamins cartel with econometric methods. The evaluation, carried out country by country and continent by continent, supports the view that the cartel raised prices more in economies without active cartel enforcement regimes.[65] Further, Rodger's empirical study of corporate compliance programmes, published in 2005, provides support for the theoretical framework of deterrence based on rational choice. The author claims to have found only limited evidence to support the deterrence approach, but the study seems sound enough to justify a less cautious view. On fines, Rodger finds that

> There is certainly evidence from the interviews conducted in the various companies to support the view that the existence of fines in particular acts as a deterrent and motivates compliance efforts . . .[66]

Otherwise, perhaps the strongest support for the view that cost–benefit analyses are actually made lies in the success of leniency programmes—the prospect of stepping out of a cartel without incurring liability for fines is extremely attractive, possibly because it presents undertakings' with an opportunity to make a rational choice.

2. *The harm-based approach*

The deterrence model comes in two distinct forms: the harm-based approach, and the gain-based approach. Under the harm-based (or cost-based) approach, the sanction should equal the cost that the infringement imposes on society.[67] According to Posner, this is a criterion of efficiency—if the sanction is less than the cost to society, the potential infringer will calculate with a cost that is lower than the social cost. The consequence will be 'an excessive amount of unlawful activity'.[68] If, on the other hand, sanctions are higher than the costs of the infringement to society, the result is over-deterrence. One might intuitively ask whether cartels

[64] See esp Camilli, Enrico Leonardo, 'Optimal Fines in Cartel Cases and the Actual EC Fining Policy' (2006) 29(4) *World Competition* 575, at 586 ff.

[65] Clarke, Julian L, and Evenett, Simon J, 'The deterrent effects of national anticartel laws: evidence from the international vitamins cartel' (2003) *The Antitrust Bulletin*, Fall, 689.

[66] Rodger, Barry J, 'Competition Law Compliance Programmes: A Study of Motivations and Practice' (2005) 28(3) *World Competition* 349, at 358.

[67] Posner, Richard A, *Antitrust Law*, 2nd edn (Chicago, University of Chicago Press, 2001), at 267.

[68] *Ibid.*

can be over-deterred at all, especially in a system where exemptions can be granted to cartels that are, on balance, pro-competitive.

3. *The gain-based approach*

Gain-based sanctions base the calculation of fines on the expected gains of the infringement. Wils is in favour of the gain-based approach, and concludes:

> The minimum fine for deterrence to work thus equals the expected gain from the violation multiplied with the inverse of the probability of a fine being effectively imposed.[69]

The gain-based approach explicitly assumes that competition law infringements are inefficient and must be deterred, 'as it aims at deterring all antitrust violations, irrespective of whether the offender's gain exceeds the harm caused to consumers'.[70] Under the gain-based approach:

> Its aim of absolute deterrence follows from the premise that the unlawful conduct is either utterly without any redeeming social benefits, or the social benefits of unlawful conduct are always outweighed by its costs, so that total social costs are minimised by its complete elimination.[71]

However, this view is difficult to reconcile with the notion that certain infringements may on balance be pro-competitive, eligible for exemption under Article 81(3). In other words, if we proceed from the idea of deterring not because of the net cost imposed on society by an infringement, but on a pre-determined view of what is inefficient, we must be absolutely precise about the actions on which we impose fines or other sanctions. Otherwise the result is over-deterrence (certain efficiency-enhancing actions will be fined), or under-deterrence (for reasons of fairness, courts will refuse to impose fines, or impose low fines, on actions that are anticompetitive). By comparison, the harm-based version of the deterrence model seeks to 'deter only those violations whose costs . . . exceed the benefits to the actor',[72] and 'if the benefits *to society* of a particular activity outweigh the costs to society, then the activity is efficient and should be encouraged'.[73]

As explained above, the value of the deterrence model lies precisely in its openness to economics. Before we accept the gain-based approach we should ask whether we are able to conclude that we know once and for all what is efficient and welfare-enhancing, and what is not. As explained in chapter three, horizontal sales price-fixing, bid-rigging, market-sharing and quotas are always, or nearly always, harmful to society. It seems that such a fining policy could be employed for those

[69] Wils, Wouter P J, 'Optimal Antitrust Fines: Theory and Practice' (2006) 29(2) *World Competition* 183, at 191.

[70] *Ibid*, at 192.

[71] Yeung, above n 59, at 66.

[72] Bilmes, Jack, and Woodbury, John, 'Deterrence and Justice: Setting Civil Penalties in the Federal Trade Commission' (1991) 14 *Research in Law and Economics* 191, at 200.

[73] Yeung, above n 59, at 64.

hard-core infringements; but then a different fining policy must be devised for other restrictions.

More problematical, the gain-based approach is theoretically different from the balancing exercise carried out under Article 81(3), where pro-competitive and anticompetitive effects are balanced against each other to determine whether a practice may be exempted. Even cartels have exceptionally been exempted, and it has been explained in chapter three that no practice is inherently disqualified from an assessment under Article 81(3). Given that authorities and courts are to carry out such a balancing exercise under Article 81(3), it would be more coherent to use the harm-based approach, which is theoretically consistent with Article 81(3), rather than the gain-based approach. It will be easier to apply one theory instead of two.

However, if one accepts the gain-based approach in principle for calculating cartel fines, the difficulties in isolating cartel profits should be noted. Price increases by cartelists are not always equal to cartel profits. As suggested by Posner, monopoly profits tend to be transferred into costs, normally referred to as social costs.[74] Wahl emphasises the risk of under-prevention if cartel profits are used as a base.[75]

Still, the difference between cost- and gain-based calculations is, at the end of the day, more philosophical than anything else, given the difficulties we have in estimating either harm to society or the gain derived from the infringement. Posner indeed recognises that it can be quite enough to use the overcharge as a proxy.[76]

4. *Problems with the deterrence model*

There are three prevalent problems with the deterrence model in competition law. The first relates to the scarcity of input data,[77] and Bilmes and Woodbury discussed this in their 1991 study.[78] Even if science has made progress, it has not overcome this obstacle yet.

Only recently have we been enlightened as to the actual impact of cartels. It is worth repeating that the study by Connor and Lande in 2005[79] exposed a median cartel overcharge of 25 per cent. This was based on an analysis of 489 cartel episodes from the years 1780 to 2004. International cartels were more effective over time in raising prices: 30 to 33 per cent, as compared to 17 to19 per cent for domestic cartels.[80] For the 30 post-1990 observations in the study, the estimated

[74] Posner, above n 67, at 13–18, 299 ff.
[75] Wahl, above n 1, at 68–69.
[76] Posner, above n 67, at 270.
[77] Becker, Gary, 'Crime and Punishment: An Economic Approach' (1968) 76(2) *Journal of Political Economy* 169, at 194.
[78] Bilmes and Woodbury, above n 72, at 206–09.
[79] Connor, John M, and Lande, Robert H, 'How High do Cartels Raise Prices? Thinking Creatively About Remedies' (2005) 80(2) *Tulane Law Review* 513, at 519.
[80] *Ibid*, at 559.

overcharge was 24.5 to 26.2 per cent, possibly reflecting the increased enforcement against cartels worldwide. Unsuccessful cartels were rare, accounting for only about 7 per cent of the observations.[81] In a subsequent study, European cartel overcharges were found to be in the 28 per cent to 54 per cent range.[82] These studies can be of great help in designing proxies for cartel overcharges.

Moreover, it may be recalled that we still have no data available on the probability of detection, and that any attempt at systematically estimating *cartel duration* involves methodological problems.

Wils has illuminated another difficulty in calculating probability of detection, that of transposing the cost–benefit analysis to a collective infringement such as a cartel. Should the cost–benefit condition be fulfilled for each (potential) cartel participant, or for the group taken together? Wils finds that

> given that the success of the cartel is likely to require the participation of most if not all of the members, it may be sufficient for deterrence to work that for some of them the expected fine exceeds the expected gain . . .[83]

In principle, however, I would go somewhat further than Wils and suggest that the success of leniency programmes should increase the probability of detection both individually and at group level, and result in lower mark-ups for the risk of detection when fines are set.

The second problem with the deterrence model is that, rigorously applied, it will result in outcomes which will be regarded as excessive.[84] For instance, if the risk of detection is 10 per cent, the adjustment of the penalty for detection means that the fine will be 10 times the gain or harm. During the life-span of the cartel, a large proportion of the cartel overcharges will have been transferred to shareholders, employees and tax authorities; one cannot expect there to be money left for paying fines.[85] This is why the deterrence model must be coupled with a (retribution-based) proportionality test to avoid adverse effects such as bankruptcy of offenders.[86]

Bankruptcy is one risk, and although there is 'nothing necessarily wrong with a company going into bankruptcy', it may be argued that the lessening of competition when one market actor disappears would be negative for competition.[87] Moreover, a bankruptcy hits not only the undertakings but also its employees, creditors, customers and suppliers, as well as taxpayers at large.[88] The drawbacks of bankruptcy may, on the other hand, have been over-estimated. Motta suggests

[81] *Ibid*, at 544.

[82] Connor, John M, and Lande, Robert H, 'The size of cartel overcharges: Implications for US and EU fining policies' (2006) 51(4) *The Antitrust Bulletin*, Winter, 983.

[83] Wils, above n 69, at 202.

[84] Yeung, above n 59, at 71.

[85] Whelan, Peter, 'A Principled Argument for Personal Criminal Sanctions as Punishments under EC Cartel Law' (2007) 4(1) *The Competition Law Review* 7, at 31.

[86] Yeung, above n 59, at 89.

[87] Schoneveld, Frank R, 'Cartel Sanctions and International Competition Policy: Cross-Border Cooperation and Appropriate Forums for Cooperation' (2003) 26(3) *World Competition* 433, at 448–49.

[88] Whelan, above n 85, at 32.

that a market exit by a cartelist should be seen as resulting from inefficiency and the loss of unlawful cartel profits.[89]

Yet again, case studies indicate that heavy sanctions can give cartel participants incentives to enter into mergers and acquisitions, leading to excessive market concentrations.[90] These considerations carry some weight, but I personally find them less compelling than the more fundamental risk that the deeper legality of the system is undermined if fines are too high.

Going back to Posner:

> The correct fine under the assumption of risk neutrality is calculated by dividing the social cost of the violation by the probability of apprehension and punishment.[91]

Landes explains that the optimal fine should equal the net harm to persons other than the offender, modified with the probability of apprehension and conviction.[92] An advantage of the harm-based approach is that it becomes irrelevant how the cartel members spend their profits; the social costs for organising and maintaining the cartels will not affect the fines, and 'Information on profitability is relevant only insofar as it conveys information on net harm'.[93] However, this is paradoxically also a disadvantage from a policy perspective, since it ignores the possibility that cartels are often inefficient and spend a large proportion of their overcharges in organising and maintaining the cartel.[94]

From the viewpoint of the undertakings involved in the cartels, the harm-based approach will lead to excessive fines. Conversely, the deterrence model will lead to lower sanctions for those who repeatedly engage in cartel activity, because for them the probability of detection increases.[95] This might be perceived as unjust in the eyes of the public.

As will be outlined in the next subsection, criminology studies of cartels and white-collar crime demonstrate the complexity of motivational factors. Even so, cartels represent a type of offence where well-educated persons make choices following deliberate calculations. This makes an economic approach more attractive, since the likelihood of rational choices is far higher than for traditional crimes.[96]

5. *Criminology and cartel behaviour*

The deterrence model suffers from what might be referred to as the principal–agent problem. Consider as a point of reference that incapacitation through imprisonment is possible when punishing natural persons, but that a company will simply

[89] Motta, Massimo, 'On Cartel Deterrence and Fines in the European Union' (2008) 29(4) *ECLR* 209, at 217.

[90] Schoneveld, above n 87, at 453.

[91] Posner, above n 67, at 269.

[92] Landes, William M, 'Optimal Sanctions for Antitrust Violations' (1983) 50 *University of Chicago Law Review* 652, at 656–57.

[93] *Ibid*, at 665.

[94] Whelan, above n 85, at 12.

[95] *Ibid*, at 17, 31.

[96] *Ibid*, at 17.

hire another employee and continue. The other way around, fines hit the undertaking, but deterrence rests on the idea of rational choices made by actual persons. Presuming that the legislator manages to create a competition law sanctioning system that tips the balance over against infringements, one still cannot assume automatically that managers always act in the undertaking's interest.[97] They may act to promote their individual self-interests of obtaining bonuses or promotions, or they may be loyal to the local workforce rather than to the undertaking or group of undertakings as a whole. Wahl observes that actions by employees, contrary to the undertaking's interest, represent a factor which should be included in the design of optimal sanctions.[98]

The problem just outlined is traditionally overcome in the analysis by assuming that the company (threatened with fines) will discipline its employees[99]; but it is doubtful whether such disciplining is effective.[100] Absent optimal deterrence, there can also exist conflicting communications on what the company's interest is. Even if an employee understands the stick-and-carrot message of a competition law penal system, he or she may nevertheless submit to the pressure from senior executives to engage in cartel activity, because of the strong message inherent is such (poor) company culture. Bilmes and Woodbury highlight that firms are complex social structures with internal dynamics and unofficial norms. They question whether we can characterise firm behaviour as rationally equivalent to individual behaviour.[101]

So why would well-paid executives, well adjusted in society, systematically and in an organised manner break antitrust law? Legal studies normally focus on the applicable rules and not on the motives of the offenders. In an attempt to obtain a deeper understanding of the causes underlying cartel behaviour, I have consulted literature on criminology in order to provide yet another perspective.

It emerges that the culture created within an organisation may be a significant contributing factor, especially since it is generally agreed that white-collar criminals are psychologically normal.[102] Newly-employed executives are moved from one area to another and are forced to work long hours, which weakens the ties they have with the outside world. This process of socialisation and relative isolation can cause an indifference to morality—a moral numbness.[103] Conformist executives might be expected to be more likely to go along with an infringement demanded by the employer.[104] 'Fear of falling' is a recurrent theme among white-collar offenders, where fear of losing what one already has can be a major driving force.[105]

[97] Connor and Lande, above n 79, at 513, fn 37.
[98] Wahl, above n 1, at 13.
[99] Whelan, above n 85, at 24.
[100] *Ibid*, at 24, 27.
[101] Bilmes and Woodbury, above n 72, at 203.
[102] Coleman, James William, 'Motivation and Opportunity, Understanding the Causes of White-collar Crime' in Geis, Gilbert, *et al*, *White-Collar Crime, Classic and Contemporary Views*, 3rd edn (New York, The Free Press, 1995), at 361.
[103] *Ibid*, at 371–72.
[104] *Ibid*, at 362.
[105] *Ibid*, at 363.

Of particular interest is Geis's study of the heavy electrical equipment cartel cases of 1961.[106] A widespread cartel on the market for heavy electrical equipment was exposed, resulting in fines and jail terms for those involved, in particular executives of General Electric and Westinghouse. Seven defendants, including four vice presidents, two division managers and one sales manager, were imprisoned for 30 days. Geis analysed the reasons for the blatant conspiracies. Several executives expressed the view that their actions might have been against the law but had still served a worthwhile purpose by stabilising prices.[107] Fear of being transferred to other assignments by the employer unless one followed the established practices was another common explanation.[108] Their personal motives included promotion, security and large salaries for those who 'played the game'.[109] The drive for easily-acquired power was yet another explanation, since cartel behaviour could give the individuals involved the impression that they were controlling segments of the industry.[110]

In an anecdote about one of the offenders, Geis outlines the successful career of an executive who was heavily involved and who eventually was sentenced to 30 days in prison. Notable was his dramatic ascent from first employment to managerial ranks, and finally to vice president of General Electric. Shortly after his prison term he was employed by another large corporation, where he soon became president of the company.[111] When summing-up, Geis concludes that

> It seems apparent, looking at the antitrust offences . . . that the attractiveness of a secure market arrangement represented a major ingredient drawing corporate officers to the price-fixing violations. The elimination of competition meant the avoidance of uncertainty, the formalization and predictability of outcome, the minimization of risk.[112]

Simpson and Piquero analysed the *amino acid* and *citric acid* cartels of the 1990s.[113] They note that the conspirators apparently understood that their actions were unlawful, and that price-fixing appeared to be standard operating procedure for the participating company ADM.[114] Since ADM was making millions of dollars in losses every month on the products concerned before cartelisation, cost considerations were a major motivational factor, but the corporate structure, with fairly autonomous management teams, also contributed. The board of ADM was, in addition, stacked with ADM insiders, family and friends.

[106] Geis, Gilbert, 'The Heavy Electrical Equipment Antitrust Cases of 1961' in Geis, Gilbert (ed), *White Collar Crime* (New York, Atherton Press, 1968).
[107] *Ibid*, at 108.
[108] *Ibid*, at 109–10.
[109] *Ibid*, at 111.
[110] *Ibid*, at 111–12.
[111] *Ibid*, at 112–15.
[112] *Ibid*, at 116.
[113] Simpson, Sally S, and Leeper Piquero, Nicole, 'The Archer Daniels Midland Antitrust Case of 1996: A Case Study' in Pontell and Shico Eds. *Contemporary Issues in Crime and Criminal Justice: Essays in Honor of Gilbert Geis* (Old Tappan, NJ, Prentice Hall, 2001).
[114] *Ibid*, at 181.

Individual motivation for entering into the cartels was more difficult to ascertain.[115] While ADM appears to have been fairly lenient with several of the employees involved, the reaction in the legal community was one of intense pursuit and seriousness.[116]

Simpson and Koper published a study in 1992 on deterrence of antitrust violations, based on a sample of 38 corporations charged with antitrust violations in the US between 1928 and 1981.[117] They observed that industry characteristics had stronger effects on future illegality than the risk or consequence of formal sanctions:

> [A]pparently, how organizations are sanctioned for misconduct affects future illegality less than cultural and structural circumstances in which firms find themselves conducting day-to-day business . . .[118]

However, the study was made prior to the introduction of more efficient enforcement methods. The US stepped up its cartel enforcement in the 1990s following a long period of limited activity, introducing more severe sanctions and a successful leniency program.[119] Figures from the 1920s to early 1980s cannot be expected to tell the whole story. The authors indeed recognise the need for further studies, and highlight that

> Particularly, greater understanding is needed of how organizational goals, pressures, and rewards, are calibrated vis-à-vis threats to managers' self-respect, future employment, and approval from significant others . . .[120]

Lane concludes from a study of 275 shoe-manufacturing firms in the US (1936 through 1950) that violation of trade practices laws is related to economic decline.[121] He suggests a causal relationship between violation and decline before the event. Although Lane's findings have been debated,[122] his prediction is remarkably consistent with the much later economic study by Grout and Sonderegger, who find that cartel formation is nearly always preceded by industry decline.[123] Conversely, Lane finds pieces of evidence 'which tend to support the idea that the more profitable firms do not violate some laws as easily and quickly as the less profitable firms'.[124] Similarly, Simpson and Koper predict that

115 *Ibid*, at 182–84.

116 *Ibid*, at 185–86.

117 Simpson, Sally S, and Koper, Christopher S, 'Deterring Corporate Crime' (1992) 30(3) *Criminology* 347.

118 *Ibid*, at 368.

119 Klein, Joel I, Speech at the International Anti-Cartel Enforcement Conference, 30 September 1999, available at http://www.usdoj.gov/atr/public/speeches/3727.htm.

120 Simpson and Koper, above n 117, at 368.

121 Lane, Robert E, 'Why Businessmen Violate the Law', in Geis (ed), above n 106, at 91.

122 Coleman, above n 102, at 360, 375.

123 Grout, Paul A, and Sonderegger, Silvia, *Predicting cartels*, Economic Discussion Paper, March 2005, Office of Fair Trading, at 16.

124 Lane, above n 121, at 91.

> If antitrust offending represents an attempt to control uncertain markets and to increase or stabilize profits, firm or industry profitability should be negatively related to reoffending . . .[125]

However, Lane makes yet another striking observation: '. . . violation of recent laws is less related to the prosperity of the firms than violation of the older established (and accepted) laws'.[126] This in turn is consistent with the recent studies of Parker on enforcement of Australian competition law, where old industry habits clashed with the modern approaches of the regulator, resulting in confrontation and conflict about the moral significance of cartel conduct.[127]

Further, Lane finds some support for the differential association hypothesis, a doctrine 'based on the common view that men pick up most of their opinions and orientations from their associates'.[128] Geis's study reinforces the impression that cartel behaviour is to some extent a matter of corporate pressure and/or culture; most executives who participated in the heavy electrical equipment cartel were brought to cartel meetings by their superiors.[129]

The combined importance of the industry's economic situation and culture is cemented by Simpson and Koper:

> [A]mong the select group, the motivations and opportunities for crime apparently outweigh the costs incurred by firms as a result of offending in the first place. It seems that a firm's cultural and economic climate exert [*sic*] more influence toward reoffending than the legal environment exerts against reoffending.[130]

The complexity of motivational factors observed in the theory on white-collar crime contrasts sharply with the economic model often employed by lawyers and economists. Under the deterrence model, companies are presumed to be rational and weigh the expected benefits of a violation against the costs. Lane indicates that there are difficulties with this economic explanation, observing that

> Two firms with similar opportunities for breaking the law may show different records: One violated the law, another does not. Why? The simple explanation based on economic motivation does not tell us.[131]

Similarly, Braithwaite concludes that 'All organizations, capitalist or socialist, experience pressure to resort to illegitimate means of goal attainment when legitimate means are blocked'.[132] Coleman finds that 'A mere attraction to the rewards of criminal behaviour is not a sufficient motivation, since society also erects strong ethical barriers to restrain such behaviour'.[133]

[125] Simpson and Koper, above n 117, at 357.

[126] Lane, above n 121.

[127] Parker, Christine, 'The "Compliance" Trap: The Moral Message in Responsive Regulatory Enforcement' (2006) 40(3) *Law and Society Review* 591, at 613–14.

[128] Lane, above n 121, at 95.

[129] Geis, above n 106, at 109.

[130] Simpson and Koper, above n 117, at 367.

[131] Lane above n 121, at 89.

[132] Braithwaite, John, 'White Collar Crime' in Geis *et al*, above n 102, at 122.

[133] Coleman, above n 102, at 361.

Furthermore, there is apparently a gender issue in cartel behaviour, in as much as the majority of cartel offenders are men. Based on a study of 1989, Coleman finds that '98 per cent of those charged with antitrust and Securities and Exchange Commission violations were male'. The explanation lies in differences in opportunity, ie the gross under-representation of women in the higher circles of corporate decision-making. However, it is also possible that women are more closely supervised than men, and have less access to social networks.[134]

To sum up, the value of looking at criminology is that it provides a different perspective, where the focus is on the complex motivational factors of industry, individual employees and corporations. An assembly of factors such as the economic situation at industry level, the corporate culture, industry culture and the driving forces of individual employees is required to understand, on a deeper level, what causes and sustains cartels. These insights are indeed reflected in recent legal writing, where Parker recognises the motivational complexity in one of her studies of Australian competition law:

> The motivations evident for entering into cartels in the case studies analyzed . . . were often more complex and less dramatic than pure greed. They included the desire for stability in new market conditions . . . simply accepting market-sharing and price-fixing as an established part of the job . . . and the fear of retaliation and being driven out of the industry if one did not submit to a cartel.[135]

B. Retribution

1. The basic theory

Retributive penal theory, or 'just deserts' theory, does not try to explain sanctions with reference to prevention objectives, but is based on the premise that the offender gets what he justly deserves.[136] Notions of fairness, social balance and neutralising the advantage gained by the offence are commonly used as justifications.[137] The sanctions communicate moral blame or censure,[138] and the severity of the punishment should reflect the seriousness of the offensive conduct.[139]

Retributive approaches are present in the jurisprudence of the Community courts, although in combination with reasoning based on deterrence.[140] Thus in *Graphite electrodes*, the Court said that fines are designed to

[134] *Ibid*, at 378–79.
[135] Parker, above n 127, at 607–08.
[136] Yeung, above n 59, at 72 ff.
[137] Whelan, above n 85, at 9.
[138] Yeung, above n 59, at 72 ff.
[139] Bilmes and Woodbury, above n 72, at 198.
[140] Harding, Christopher, and Joshua, Julian, *Regulating Cartels in Europe—A Study of Legal Control of Corporate Delinquency* (Oxford, Oxford University Press, 2003), at 241.

> punish the unlawful acts of the undertakings concerned and to deter both the undertakings in question and other operators from infringing the rules of Community competition law in future . . .[141]

The Court of First Instance emphasised in *Sodium Gluconate* both the deterrent effect and the punitive effect of the fine.[142]

Fines may be imposed not only as a way to punish the infringement, but also against measures taken to conceal it. In *Graphite electrodes*, warnings to other undertakings that investigations were being carried out resulted in an 85 per cent increase in the fines, and this was upheld on appeal.[143]

2. *The problems with retributive theory*

It is widely accepted that the problem with retributive theory is that it fails to produce a specific measurable penalty.[144] Given that the source of the sanction is morality, regulators must aspire to translate moral consciousness into figures. It goes without saying that this exercise can lead to disparate results.

This objection is of central importance, since it targets the legitimacy of retributive penalty systems. Legitimacy in this context is understood as the perceived legality of the system, in the eyes of the public. Yeung explains that ' "anchoring" the penalty scale cannot be achieved on any principled basis, even if it were possible to devise an acceptable scale of relative offence seriousness,' and that 'There is no quantum of penalty that suggests itself as uniquely appropriate for competition law violations'.[145]

Furthermore, a retributive penalty system is, as a matter of principle, open to adjustments based on changes in the moral perception of the violation to which it relates. This means that the creation of a retributive penal system must comply with notions of input legitimacy. Which person, committee, institution or court will be vested with the authority to channel public perceptions of morality into a detailed fining policy, and how can we trust that they will get it right? What sort of democratic or judicial control is exercised, and how can we tell that the people involved have the necessary skills?

Since application of the retributive theory will not as such generate correct fines or other sanctions, the legal–political process becomes crucial in justifying the policy choices. It is here that another feature of EC and national competition law is encountered—the fact that not only the Commission but also several Member State competition authorities are empowered to design fining policies and impose fines on offenders, subject to court review. Thus the fining policies, as well as their application, are determined within the administration.

[141] *Showa Denko v Commission*, above n 20, at para 16.

[142] *Archer Daniels Midland v Commission*, above n 21, at para 141.

[143] Case C-308/04 P *SGL Carbon v Commission* [2006] ECR I-5977, at para 69.

[144] Bilmes and Woodbury, above n 72, at 198; Yeung, above n 57, at 76.

[145] Yeung, above n 59, at 77, 95.

Normally, we accept values transposed into politics because of the legitimisation carried out through the traditional legislative process.[146] For instance, we may accept that theft will be punished within a range of one to six years' imprisonment, the individual penalty being set by the court on the basis of the circumstances of the case. We accept this because of the democratic control exercised through the legislative process. Absent the legislative process, a competition law sanctioning system based on retributive theory runs the risk of being perceived as illegal in a wider sense. This is precisely what happened with the Commission's power to impose fines under Regulation 17. In *Citric acid*, the German undertaking Jungbunzlauer challenged this legislation for being contrary to the principle of legality. Jungbunzlauer claimed that the provision on fines was too vague as to how fines should be determined and left too much scope to the Commission. The Court of First Instance reasoned extensively on the subject, *inter alia* with reference to the ECHR, and found that the Commission's margin of discretion was not contrary to the principle of legality.[147]

Now, if a fining policy is to be adopted by legislation, the resulting system will not be particularly flexible; further, it will require new legislation to change it in response to new circumstances. Moreover, considerable discretion will inevitably have to be left to regulators and courts given the complexity involved, the specialised knowledge required and the exercise of judgment.[148] This may be what the Court of First Instance had in mind when writing:

> In addition, it must be added that, to avoid excessive prescriptive rigidity and to enable a rule of law to be adapted to the circumstances, a certain degree of unforeseeability as to the penalty which may be imposed for a given offence must be permitted.[149]

We turn to the question whether a retributive fining policy would be legitimate because of the *output legitimacy* it generates. Whereas the input legitimacy may be questioned (as explained above), perhaps we could still accept a retributive fining policy, provided it had the capacity to deter and punish infringements adequately. However, retributive systems are unable to accommodate new economic insights and knowledge, precisely because the level of sanctions is derived from morality, not from economics. Development of competition law is normally based on such new insights in economic theory and analysis; in an outright retributive system those aspects are invalid as input, whether for determining individual sanctions or for determining the sanction policy as a whole.

This demonstrates a rather self-evident problem: that a retributive competition law sanctioning system ignores the education and training of the addressees. Company managers, as well as competition lawyers, may be expected to understand reasoning based on economics. While moral aspects will often be relevant in

[146] Zamboni, Mauro, *The Policy of Law—A Legal Theoretical Framework* (PhD thesis, Stockholm, 2004), at 207 ff.

[147] Case T-43/02 *Jungbunzlauer v Commission* [2006] ECR II-3435, at paras 69 ff.

[148] Yeung, above n 59, at 38.

[149] *Jungbunzlauer v Commission*, above n 147, at para 84.

the decision-making process, reasoning based entirely on morality, detached from economics, will be foreign to them. Further, competition lawyers may be expected to be more inclined towards the law and economics school than lawyers in general. In effect, if a competition enforcement policy is based on retributive theory, not just the addressees but also the decision-makers are faced with the task of applying a system to which they feel little or no professional attachment. Furthermore, jumping from one theory base to another when moving from substantive law to sanctions will be difficult for all people involved, and may be expected to generate a certain amount of confusion. This aspect will be analysed in the next section.

3. *The Commission's 1998 fining guidelines*

The problems connected to retributive theory may be illustrated empirically with reference to the Commission's 1998 fining guidelines.[150] The guidelines themselves can plainly be placed in retributive theory. Different violations were singled out and price-tagged, without any attempt to relate the methodology to economics[151]—neither through individual assessments, nor through proxies. Camilli notes that

> the gravity was not explicitly linked to a quantitative measure of the effect of the infringement . . . in fact a qualitative criterion was claimed to be the most important element . . . the behaviour of the undertaking is taken into account, in order to accomplish the punitive aim of the sanction, on the basis of a retributive setting.[152]

Thus horizontal restrictions, such as price cartels and market-sharing quotas, were classified as very serious infringements which would generate likely fines above €20 million. Reference was made to the nature of the infringement committed, the effective economic capacity of offenders to cause significant damage to other operators, in particular consumers, and the geographic impact.

The requirements on large undertakings were higher since they were considered to have better capacity to keep themselves informed about competition law. Wils explains this with reference to fairness,[153] a typical retributive justification.

Mark-ups for duration were made without any attempt to relate the figures to the actual harm or gain caused by a cartel in a single year. This represented a major weakness, since it disregarded the assumption that every year generates full cartel profits for the participants (not just an additional 10 per cent), which gave incentives to continue the infringement.[154]

[150] *Guidelines on the method of setting fines imposed pursuant to Article 15 (2) of Regulation No 17 and Article 65 (5) of the ECSC Treaty* [1998] OJ C/9/3.

[151] Geradin, Damien, and Henry, David, 'The EC fining policy for violations of competition law: An empirical review of the Commission decisional practice and the Community Courts' judgments' (2005) 1(2) *European Competition Journal* 401, at 413.

[152] Camilli, above n 64, at 592–93.

[153] Wils, Wouter P J, *The Optimal Enforcement of EC Antitrust Law—Essays in Law and Economics* (The Hague, Kluwer Law International, 2002), at 81.

[154] Camilli, above n 64, at 602.

The method signified a departure from calculating fines on the basis of turnover in the relevant market,[155] and the Court of Justice described it in *District heating pipes* in the following terms:

> [T]he main innovation in the Guidelines consisted in taking as a starting point for the calculation a basic amount, determined on the basis of brackets laid down for that purpose by the Guidelines; those brackets reflect the various degrees of gravity of the infringements but, as such, bear no relation to the relevant turnover. The essential feature of that method is thus that fines are determined on a tariff basis, albeit one that is relative and flexible.[156]

As interpreted by the highest instance, the guidelines were thus understood as a tariff-based system, disconnected from turnover in the relevant products. However, Commission officials made clear references to deterrence theory when writing about the guidelines.[157] Arbault described how the optimal fine equals the unlawful profits multiplied by the probability that the infringement will be detected.[158] When describing the Commission's 1998 fining guidelines in particular, however, Arbault leaned on retributive theory by referring to the intrinsic gravity of the infringement. He argued that fining ranges for pre-defined categories of infringements were dissuasive, precisely because of the absence of a connection between the raised fine and the economic value of the market concerned.[159] Even so, the value of the market concerned was, as a matter of fact, used when fixing the basic amount.[160]

From this it may be deduced that the Commission, contrary to the guidelines, continued to rely on the turnover on the relevant market, not as a justification but as an internal working order. Killick finds that the Commission's approach was the result of a 'fundamental absence of a theoretical underpinning'.[161] I would rather characterise the 1998 fining guidelines as a deterrence-based system under the cloak of retributive theory. It may have worked wonders had the Commission only managed to apply it consistently. Lawyers might be ready to go along with muddled theory, provided that the system was predictable.

Attempts were made by Commission officials to explain how fines were actually set.[162] However, as demonstrated by several authors, predictability was precisely what was lacking in the application of the 1998 guidelines. Geradin and Henry

[155] Wils, above n 153, at 71–72.

[156] Joined Cases C-189/02 P, C-202/02 P, C-205/02 P to C-208/02 P and C-213/02 P *Dansk Rørindustri and others v Commission* [2005] ECR I-5425, at para 225.

[157] Wils, above n 153, at 71.

[158] Arbault, Francois, 'La politique de la Commission en matière d'amendes antitrust: recent développements, perspectives d'avenir' (2003) *Competition Policy Newsletter,* Number 2, Summer, 1.

[159] *Ibid,* at 3.

[160] *Ibid,* at 4.

[161] Killick, James, 'Is it now time for a single Europe-wide fining policy? An analysis of the fining policies of the Commission and the Member States' (2005) Working Paper Number 07, *Competition Law Scholars' Forum (CLaSF) Working Paper Series,* first presented at the CLaSF Workshop on 7 April 2005, at 13.

[162] Castellot, Miguel Ángel Pena, 'The application of the guidelines on fines: an overview' (2000) *Competition Policy Newsletter* No 3, October, 5.

analyse the fining policy of the 1998 guidelines in depth and comment on the difficulty of understanding the logic of the fines imposed by the Commission, where identical factual scenarios would be treated differently and different factual scenarios alike.[163] They conclude that the lack of clarity of the method used by the Commission, combined with the tendency of the Court of First Instance to reduce the fines, had generated massive litigation.[164] Veljanovski observed that the appeal rate in 1999 to 2006 was 85 per cent, and that the fines were reduced on appeal by an average 18 per cent. He concluded that the situation indicated serious problems with the way the fining guidelines were applied.[165] Killick found that 'Transparency and coherence remain illusive, in particular as between one cartel case and another'.[166] Camilli thought that

> the reference to the nature of the infringement and the overall size of the firm, rather than clearly to the impact and the gain derived from the behaviour, made the achievement of the deterrent effect a matter of chance . . .[167]

Joshua and Camesasca expressed serious concerns as well:

> Companies charged with antitrust violations in the EC are kept guessing up until the moment when the Commission issues its final decision, and while it is usually (but not always) easy enough to follow the steps in the Commission's calculations, the crucial initial figure chosen as the start point for the whole exercise is largely discretionary.[168]

Connor and Lande made the observation that the

> primary reason why EC fines are unpredictable is that the number of euros chosen as the 'start point' for the fine calculation appears to be almost arbitrary . . .[169]

In late 2006, the 1998 fining guidelines were replaced by new guidelines, where the basis for calculating fines is the value of the undertaking's sales of goods or services to which the infringement directly or indirectly relates in the relevant geographic area within the EEA.

4. *Conclusions on retributive theory in competition law*

In summary, retributive theories may correspond on a general level to popular notions of justice, but will fail to come up with methods for calculating competition law fines. Empirically, retributive theory was applied through the Commission's 1998 fining guidelines, with appalling results. It led to widespread criticism due to

163 Geradin and Henry, above n 151, at 403.

164 *Ibid*, at 472.

165 Veljanovski, Cento, 'Penalties for Price-fixers: An Analysis of Fines Imposed on 39 Cartels by the EU Commission' (2006) 27(9) *ECLR* 510.

166 Killick, above n 161, at 3.

167 Camilli, above n 64, at 604.

168 Joshua, Julian M, and Camesasca, Peter D, 'EC fining policy against cartels after the Lysine rulings: the subtle secrets of x', *The European Antitrust Review 2004* (London, Global Competition Review, 2004), at 5.

169 Connor and Lande, above n 82, at 999.

the absence of consistency, and to a questioning of the legality of the Commission's power to impose sanctions.

I believe that the 1998 guidelines were valuable in so far as they contributed to higher sanctions than the lower levels applied before 1998, but that objective could have been fulfilled through better methods. From the point of view of procedural economy, the retributive approach generated massive litigation about the level of fines, a result that must be seen as adverse in the extreme. Retributive penal systems are impervious to new insights generated from economists, and will thus be viewed with suspicion by antitrust practitioners who are used to basing their reasoning partly on economics. Legitimising a retributive competition law fining system through the traditional legislative process is unworkable. Deterrence-based reasoning is likely to come in through the backdoor, as was indeed the case with the Commission.

From an efficiency perspective the outcome is counter-productive. That is because considerable resources are spent on litigation, tying up the regulatory authorities and preventing them from pursuing other infringements. It is also quite possible that the authority must spend valuable time deciding, on a case-by-case basis, how to set and defend fines, instead of relying on well-established principles.

As if this were not enough, retributive penal systems in EC competition law suffer from the principal–agent problem, just like deterrence systems. That is because the punishment hits the undertaking and not the employees or representatives who, as a matter of fact, took part in the cartel.

C. Collaborative compliance techniques and trade associations

Article 9 of Regulation 1 has introduced commitment decisions as a remedy.[170] In this context it is worthwhile observing an alternative approach to cartel sanctions. Compliance program remedies, compensation undertakings and community service undertakings have been tried in Australia in response to competition law infringements, including price-fixing. Yeung describes how

> in one price-fixing case, the offenders admitted their unlawful conduct, submitted to consent injunctions and negotiated penalties, and also gave enforceable undertakings to the Commission to develop and implement comprehensive internal trade practices compliance programmes.[171]

The theoretical basis lies in the dialogue between the authority and the companies as a mode of resolving regulatory problems.[172] Only if co-operative strategies fail should more punitive approaches be utilised.[173]

[170] On commitments, see esp Temple Lang, John, 'Commitment Decisions and Settlements with Antitrust Authorities and private Parties under European Antitrust Law' in Hawk (ed), *International Antitrust Law & Policy: Fordham Corporate Law* (New York, Juris Publishing, 2005) Ch 13 at 265.

[171] Yeung, above n 59, at 205.

[172] *Ibid*, at 171.

[173] Parker, above n 127, at 592.

This type of enforcement is called responsive regulation, and it 'seeks to build moral commitment to compliance with the law'.[174] Commitments may be restorative (such as compensation of victims), but may on a more general level be seen as rehabilitative through transforming the offender's behaviour.[175] The advantage of collaborative compliance is that it targets, at least to a certain extent, the principal–agent problem. By internalising the compliance objective, the undertakings concerned can build a culture of competition and weed out old habits that might otherwise simply go into hibernation, only to revive once the authorities are looking in another direction.

This is not an attempt to analyse collaborative techniques from a legal theoretical perspective.[176] However, two of the problems with collaborative techniques in competition law have been demonstrated by Parker in her study of Australian responsive regulatory enforcement. First, with broad, informal and weak sanctions, the legislator signals weakness, and as a consequence the moral message of the legislation is not particularly strong. Parker concludes that

> The availability of criminal law and high penalties are important not so much because of their deterrent impact but because of their moral impact in legitimising the substantive content of the message at the bottom of the pyramid . . .[177]

Secondly, the delinquent undertakings are not overly enthusiastic about being rehabilitated and will be sensitive to a lack of political support for the moral seriousness of the law. They may even engage in lobbying to take away powers from the competition authority.[178]

As a further reflection, a prerequisite for efficient enforcement through collaborative techniques should be effective detection, but how does one accomplish this without a combination of high fines and leniency? No detection method has proved itself even half as efficient as leniency. Leniency is useful, though, only if the alternative is substantial sanctions. If there is no risk of incurring a high fine, the incentive is to continue with the cartel until the authorities detect it through their own efforts, and perhaps *then* assist the authorities.

Under a collaborative compliance model, the undertaking will (after having been exposed) enter into a negotiation with the authorities, which might lead to an internal legal audit and the introduction of a compliance program, measures which arguably should have been there in the first place. This is a disincentive to refrain from unlawful activities, because cartel participants can first reap cartel profits and then put in place a system which other undertakings that apply good governance established a long time ago.

The Court of First Instance has, in *Citric acid*, explicitly rejected the view that a compliance program could to any extent replace fines.[179] The same approach can

174 *Ibid.*
175 Yeung, above n 59, at 207.
176 Reference is made to Yeung's analysis.
177 Parker, above n 127, at 617.
178 *Ibid.*
179 *Archer Daniels Midland v Commission*, above n 31, at para 359.

be seen in *Vitamins* with regard to dismissal of senior executives and adoption of a compliance program.[180] Similarly, damages could not replace fines, as is clear from *Citric acid.*[181]

From an efficiency perspective it seems impossible to rely solely on collaborative enforcement techniques. Just threatening to impose high fines without imposing them systematically will not make much of an impression on a cartel-prone industry. Nonetheless, responsive regulation may prove a valuable tool in relation to those entities that cannot be subjected to adequate fines, in particular trade associations. It has been explained (chapter three at III.C.1) that trade associations have participated in approximately 40 per cent of the cartels discovered in the EU, and it will be explained later on (chapter seven at VII.C) that it is often impossible to impose appropriate fines on them because of the absence of turnover and assets. In addition to imposing fines on those member undertakings that can be linked to the cartel, it might be useful to require, as a commitment, that the trade association carry out an internal audit, introduce a compliance program and undertake structural measures to make the association more independent in relation to its members.

When it comes to the mingling of interests of the members and the association, the statement of the US Supreme Court in *Hydrolevel* is worthwhile to recall:

> [A] standard-setting organization . . . can be rife with opportunities for anticompetitive activity. Many . . . officials are associated with members of the industries regulated . . . Although, undoubtedly, most serve . . . without concern for the interests of their corporate employers, some may well view their positions . . . at least in part, as an opportunity to benefit their employers. When the great influence of [the trade association's] reputation is placed at their disposal, the less altruistic . . . agents have an opportunity to harm their employers' competitors through manipulation of [the trade association's] codes.[182]

D. Behavioural law and economics

The difficulty of equating the interests of the undertaking with those of its employees is present in both the deterrence model and the retributive model. Managers may act to promote their own interests rather than those of their employer. Furthermore, the perspectives derived from criminology suggest that people are not as rational as the rational choice model implies. Scepticism has also been voiced as to the undertakings' ability to discipline their employees effectively.

Strong support for the view that we are not perfectly rational may be found in behavioural law and economics.[183] Although the studies and theories presented under the heading of behavioural law and economics are of great interest, no

[180] Case T-15/02 *BASF v Commission* [2006] ECR II-497, at para 266.

[181] *Archer Daniels Midland v Commission*, above n 31, at para 352.

[182] *American Society of Mechanical Engineers v Hydrolevel*, 456 US 556 (1982).

[183] Gowda, Rajeev, and Fox, Jeffrey C (eds), *Judgments, Decisions, and Public Policy* (Cambridge, Cambridge University Press, 2002).

attempt will be made here to analyse them further. No coherent theory of how cartelists behave or how to design a cartel enforcement system has (to my knowledge) been presented in behavioural law and economics. There seem to be no claims that behavioural law and economics can generate actual figures for the purpose of designing a fining policy. Furthermore, it seems uncertain how much impact individual decision-making has in relation to market forces.[184]

Competition law scholars are not entirely adverse to behavioural law theories, and can even find them useful for their analysis.[185] Connor and Lande suggest that an alternative to ascertaining the actual probability of detection and conviction would be to focus on how the probable defendants perceive the probability of being caught and convicted. However, no reliable information on the issue is available.[186]

Wils has embraced these concepts, and has attempted to fuse them with deterrence theory. He suggests that the relevant measure for fines is the *subjectively* expected gain or harm, discounted by the *subjectively* expected probability that a fine would be imposed.[187] This presents problems both theoretically and practically. The practical aspect was identified by Connor and Lande: we have no information on how potential offenders perceive the probability of detection and fines. Wils accepts this too.[188] However, if, hypothetically, the risk perceptions could be measured, legal theory stands in the way. A policy based on risk perception among business people would be constantly open to revision based on changes of view among those very same people. Looking at it from the perspective of the rule of law, this proposition is unfeasible. A subjective view among potential offenders is not a source of law, and would be extremely difficult to measure and transpose for that purpose. If, on the other hand, one does accept as a matter of principle that behavioural law and economics should be allowed to influence the structure of a deterrence-based fining policy, it would seem necessary to take all relevant aspects of the former discipline into account. This has not been attempted, and I do not propose such a solution.

E. Conclusion: efficient competition law fines

I will temporarily leave aside detection, which will be addressed later on. Looking at fines only, it may be concluded that the deterrence model is preferable here, not because it produces correct results (as explained, there are several problems, not least with insufficient input data) but because of its openness towards new experience in economics. When compared to the retributive theory, it is less

[184] *Ibid*, at 235.

[185] Kordel, Guido, 'Behavioural Economic Analysis of Collective Bargaining Agreements under EC Antitrust Law' (2006) 27(1) *ECLR* 28.

[186] Connor and Lande, above n 79, fn 34.

[187] Wils, above n 69, at 207.

[188] *Ibid*.

static, theoretically more sound and may be expected to contribute in the long run to a better sanctioning policy. In comparison with retributive theory, it has the advantage of actually generating figures which can be explained. The basis for calculations will to a certain extent have to be based on assumptions—and those can prove to be incorrect over time, as is the case with the proxy applied in the US—but at least the deterrence model invites economics into the arena, and calculations are likely to improve gradually over time.

A fining policy according to which the competition authority must prove, on a case-by-case basis, the overcharges resulting from the cartel, seems inefficient. The authority does not have access to the market data of those suffering damages, and it might even be inappropriate for the authority to collect all those data. If cartel participants or competitors gain access to such documents, through the authority, this may do more damage than the cartel itself. Moreover, calculations will be work-intensive and may be expected to burden the procedure.

With the deterrence model, on the other hand, we can work with proxies (as in the EU and in the US), providing pre-determined approximations of likely fines, equalling a certain percentage of the affected commerce. We can choose to make the proxy an irrebuttable presumption (as in the US) or a rebuttable presumption (as suggested by the US Antitrust Modernization Commission). An irrebuttable presumption has the advantage of making the proceedings less heavy, because evidence will not be allowed that the actual cartel overcharge was lower than the proxy. A rebuttable presumption, on the other hand, makes the proceedings heavier but has the advantage of allowing the legal community to learn more about cartel overcharges, and may be expected to bring considerable resources into the area of research on this topic.

Arbault, when writing on the 1998 fining guidelines, referred to the need to avoid predictability in order to prevent undertakings from making cost–benefit analyses on whether to violate the law.[189] The fear that undertakings would make rational choices has been an undercurrent in the Commission's policy over the years.[190] It was also endorsed by the Court of First Instance in *Methionine*:

> [T]he objectives of punishment and deterrence justify preventing undertakings from being in a position to assess the benefits which they would derive from their participation in an infringement by taking account, in advance, of the amount of the fine which would be imposed on them on account of that unlawful conduct.[191]

Camilli criticises this line of reasoning, finding that 'Rather than a "Freudian" approach, only a clear and transparent policy can be deemed to be consistent with the cost–benefit analysis lying behind the deterrent objective'.[192]

Wahl finds that it is important that the level of sanctions can be calculated with some degree of accuracy. His reasoning starts from the premise that if the level of

[189] Arbault, above n 158, at 6.

[190] Gerardin and Henry, above n 151, at 407, fn 23.

[191] Case T-279/02 *Degussa v Commission* [2006] ECR II-897, at para 83, upheld on appeal in Case C-266/06 P *Evonik Degussa v Commission and Council* [2008] ECR I-81.

[192] Camilli, above n 64, at 593.

sanctions cannot be calculated with any accuracy then obviously undertakings will be unable to calculate whether an infringement will be profitable. However, this does not automatically mean that an undertaking will refrain from certain actions, since it may just as well assume that the action will be profitable and therefore act anti-competitively. Neither is the undertaking able, if the level of sanctions is uncertain, to see whether it will be advantageous to assist the competition authorities in their investigation. Total immunity is not always available, and the leniency rules providing mere reductions may be negatively affected if the undertaking believes that the sanction will increase in larger proportion than the reduction. Moreover, it is not only undertakings that are affected by uncertainty; the competition authorities run the risk of misallocating resources if they have difficulties in setting correct fines.[193]

At any rate, the idea that fines should be unpredictable is obsolete following the Court's judgment in *District heating pipes*: fines must be reasonably foreseeable.[194] On appeal in *Methionine*, the Court of Justice upheld the findings of the Court of First Instance, but refrained from endorsing the idea that difficulty in calculating fines in advance was justified for deterrence purposes.[195] Reasonably foreseeable fines is what EC law requires, but from an efficiency perspective I would go somewhat further and suggest that sanctions should to the greatest extent be foreseeable. This enables undertakings to make rational choices, and prevents unnecessary administration and excessive litigation. Calviño reasons along this line: 'Knowing the likely punishment for illegal activities is essential for deterrence purposes.'[196]

It should furthermore be observed that a deterrence system does not lend support for mark-ups in fines for repeat offending, the size of the undertaking or the phenomenon of 'entrance fees'. Those are retributive relics from the 1998 fining guidelines. It is clear that such mark-ups are legal under EC law[197]; the point here is to highlight that they are inconsistent with a deterrence-based policy, and suffer from all the theoretical and practical problems of retributive theory.

F. What type of bird is the Commission's 2006 fining policy?

According to the Commission's 2006 fining guidelines,[198] a proxy of up to 30 per cent of the value of sales to which the infringement relates is employed, and fines

[193] Wahl, above n 1, at 66–67.

[194] Joined Cases C-189/02 P, C-202/02 P, C-205/02 P to C-208/02 P and C-213/02 P *Dansk Rørindustri and others v Commission* [2005] ECR I-5425, at para 226.

[195] *Evonik Degussa v Commission and Council*, above n 191, at para 55.

[196] Calviño, Nadia, 'Public Enforcement in the EU: Deterrent Effect and Proportionality of Fines' in Ehlermann, C D, and Atanasiu, I (eds), *European Competition Law Annual 2006: Enforcement of Prohibition of Cartels* (Oxford, Hart Publishing, 2007), at 321.

[197] See, eg, Case C-3/06 P *Groupe Danone v Commission* [2007] ECR I-1331, at paras 36–37, and *Archer Daniels Midland v Commission*, above n 21, at para 142.

[198] *Guidelines on the method of setting fines imposed pursuant to Article 23(2)(a) of Regulation No 1/2003*, [2006] OJ C/210/2.

up to this level will be imposed for every year of the cartel's duration.[199] The guidelines rest on the theory of deterrence, but they also incorporate considerable elements of retribution. This may require some explanation.

The guidelines refer to the value of the sales of goods or services to which the infringement relates as a basis for setting the fine, and to the duration of the infringement.[200] So far the guidelines are compatible with deterrence theory, and one can in particular note that the 30 per cent proxy is in line with recent empirical studies of cartel overcharges. Nonetheless, retributive elements are present. There is an 'entrance fee' for cartels in so far as, 'irrespective of the duration of the undertaking's participation in the infringement', the Commission will impose fines of between 15 per cent and 25 per cent of the value of sales in order to deter undertakings from even entering into horizontal price-fixing, market-sharing and output-limitation agreements.[201] Entrance fees have no apparent relation to the costs to society of cartel activity. Neither have mark-ups for repeat offending, ringleaders or instigators, but those are employed as well.[202] Given that the actual sum relating to such mark-ups may be considerable, and even exceed the otherwise applicable 30 per cent proxy, the retributive elements are still significant and may be expected to generate litigation.

IV. EFFICIENCY THROUGH DETECTION—LENIENCY

The term 'leniency' refers to a system according to which an undertaking can obtain immunity or the reduction of fines (or other penalties) in exchange for reporting the infringement to the authorities. Leniency is a subject of great practical importance for enforcers, and it has generated a great amount of academic discussion.[203] In this work, however, leniency is primarily addressed with reference to the relation between national law and Community law.

An optimal sanctioning system may in theory be built on detection of only a few infringements, which are then heavily penalised. This keeps enforcement costs at a minimum while ensuring deterrence. In reality, however, it is not an option to multiply the harm or gain caused by a cartel several times to ensure deterrence. It

[199] *Ibid*, at 21.
[200] *Ibid*, at 5.
[201] *Ibid*, at 25.
[202] *Ibid*, at 28.
[203] Van Barlingen, Bertus, and Barennes, Marc, 'The European Commission's 2002 Leniency Notice in practice' (2005) *Competition Policy Newsletter* No 3, Autumn, 6; Blake, Stephen, and Schnichels, Dominik, 'Leniency Following Modernisation: Safeguarding Europe's Leniency Programmes' (2004) 25(12) *ECLR* 765; Leslie, Christopher R, 'Trust, Distrust and Antitrust' (2004) 82(3) *Texas Law Review* 515; McElwee, Donal, 'Should the European Commission adopt "Amnesty Plus" in its Fight Against Hard-Core Cartels?' (2004) 25(9) *ECLR* 558; OECD, 'Using Leniency to Fight Hard Core Cartels', *OECD Observer*, September 2001; Wils, Wouter P J, 'The Commission Notice on the Non-imposition or Reduction of Fines in Cartel Cases: A Legal and Economic Analysis' (1997) 22(2) *EL Rev* 125; Ysewyn, Johan, and Jordan, Eve, 'Cashing in on Cartels' (2003) 24(6) *ECLR* 235; Zane, Phillip C, 'The price fixer's dilemma: applying game theory to the decision of whether to plead guilty to antitrust crimes' (2003) 1 *The Antitrust Bulletin* 1.

has been explained in the previous section that such fines would be considered arbitrary and disproportionate, and could drive undertakings out of business. Statutory caps on fines represent another factor to take into account.[204] Further, for an undertaking that is unable to pay more than, say, 100, the threat of higher fines is not a deterrent because the undertaking will be unable to pay them.[205] Together these factors point in the direction of a high detection rate as a key cartel enforcement measure.

A. Relation between national law and Community law

It may be recalled that Member States must ensure that infringements of Community law are *penalised* under conditions, both procedural and substantive, which are analogous to those applicable to infringements of national law of a similar nature and importance, and which, in any event, make the penalty effective, proportionate and dissuasive.[206] This tells us something about penalties, but what about *detection*? More specifically, is there a duty for Member States to adopt and apply a leniency program?

There is no specific guidance so far to indicate such a duty, and one possible view is that Member States are at liberty to adopt, or refrain from adopting, their own leniency programs and to design their cartel detection as they find suitable. Leniency remains outside Regulation 1, so the uniformity issue does not arise. However, if leniency is employed in relation to infringements of national competition law infringements, the principle of equivalence[207] should result in application of the same regime for infringements of Articles 81 and 82 EC. On the other hand, the principle of loyal co-operation in Article 10 EC requires the Member States to take all measures necessary to guarantee the application and effectiveness of Community law.[208] Speculatively, perhaps a duty to design a national leniency program might be deduced from Article 10 EC.

B. Efficiency considerations

Efficiency considerations should, in my view, lead to unilateral adoption of leniency programs in Member States, even if there is no duty under EC law to do so. The specific problem related to cartel detection may be summarised briefly as follows. If a manufacturer imposes competition restrictions on its network of

[204] Bos, Iwan, and Schinkel, Maarten Pieter, 'On the Scope for the European Commission's 2006 Fining Guidelines under the Legal Maximum Fine' (2006) 2(4) *Journal of Competition Law and Economics* 673.

[205] Wahl, above n 1, at 45.

[206] *Commission v Greece*, above n 6, at para 24.

[207] Joined Cases C-222/05 to C-225/05 *van der Weerd and others* [2007] ECR I-4233, at para 28, with references.

[208] See *inter alia Commission v Greece*, above n 206, at para 23.

distributors, opposition or even a complaint to the authorities is a likely outcome, given that at least a few of the distributors will perceive the restrictions as contrary to their business interests. Similarly, customers and competitors are likely to react against abusive conduct by a dominant undertaking. But who is to report cartels? Customers may notice increases in prices; refusals to supply, resulting from market-sharing practices, may also occasionally be detected by customers; and boycotts may be reported by those that are affected. Nevertheless, there is still a difference in terms of the quality of the evidence which may be supplied by complainants. Distributors will often have access to 'smoking gun' evidence in the vertical relationship, since they are the direct addressees of the instructions or impositions of the supplier. Customers and competitors of a dominant undertaking may be well informed about market conditions, to the extent that they are able to detect and verify abusive conduct. Customers and other business partners of cartels, on the other hand, may be expected to provide only fragmented circumstantial evidence. Competition authorities are unlikely to undertake costly investigatory measures in every sector of the economy where prices increase, or where someone is denied supply from a non-dominant undertaking. Certain practices, such as bid-rigging, may continue undetected for many years. Boycotts and other exclusionary practices may be framed as resulting from legitimate business reasons.

When a competition authority is alerted about a suspected cartel, there is the matter of deciding whether to use part of the authority's budget for investigation. The Court of Justice underlined in *Cement* that

> since the prohibition on participating in anticompetitive agreements and the penalties which offenders may incur are well known, it is normal for the activities which those practices and those agreements entail to take place in a clandestine fashion, for meetings to be held in secret, most frequently in a non-member country, and for the associated documentation to be reduced to a minimum.[209]

To overcome the secrecy and secure evidence, enforcers must search the premises of all the suspected undertakings, including computers, archives, etc. This is all very expensive. Wils explains:

> [I]n particular for secret price cartels, the undertakings that committed the violations and their staff may be the only ones holding the information which the competition authorities need to detect and punish these violations.[210]

How, then, does a competition authority secure the co-operation of one or several of the cartel participants? The answer, in the context of administrative public enforcement, is leniency programs. Leniency is described as a way to break the code of silence and provide the authorities with first-hand insider evidence from the cartel.[211] Under the European Commission's leniency program, undertakings

[209] *Aalborg Portland and others v Commission*, above n 53, at para 55.
[210] Wils, Wouter P J, 'Self-incrimination in EC Antitrust Enforcement: A Legal and Economic Analysis' (2003) 26(4) *World Competition* 567, at 581.
[211] OECD, above n 203.

that co-operate in the investigation are rewarded by either full immunity, or reduction of fines.

Immunity is available for an undertaking which discloses its participation in a cartel, if the undertaking is the first to submit information to the Commission. The information should enable the Commission to carry out an inspection (ie a dawn raid), or find an infringement in connection with the alleged cartel.[212] Consolation prizes are handed out as well: reductions in fines are available for runners-up, if they can provide the Commission with evidence which represents significant added value to the evidence already in the Commission's possession.[213] Certain conditions must always be fulfilled, including full, genuine, continuous and expeditious cooperation.[214] In *Graphite electrodes,* the undertaking SGL had provided an incomplete and misleading answer when the Commission requested information on the companies which SGL had warned of the Commission's investigation. This behaviour showed, in the Court's view, that SGL's conduct did not demonstrate a genuine spirit of co-operation.[215]

The design of leniency programs is consistent with the game theoretic model of the so-called prisoner's dilemma.[216] A cartel participant may inform the authorities and obtain immunity from fines, while at the same time inflicting serious economic injury on its competitors, since they will be heavily fined for the infringement. The knowledge of this mechanism destabilises cartels. Leslie analyses this phenomenon at length in relation to the US leniency program, and concludes that

> the Leniency Guidelines have two effects: providing a direct incentive to confess and creating distrust among cartel partners, which provides an additional incentive to confess. The two effects work in tandem to make quick confession the rational decision for cartelists.[217]

Some long-term effects may be envisaged as well. A leniency application in one cartel should make it more difficult for an undertaking to join other cartels, because it will earn a reputation for deviating and incriminating others.[218]

Leniency is one of those rare theories that actually works in the real world. As described previously in chapter three, the Commission received over 200 leniency applications in four years following the adoption of its 2002 Leniency Notice. The US Department of Justice received more than one amnesty application per month after the adoption of its 1993 Leniency program. The US cartel leniency policy 'is believed to be the most successful program in US history for detecting large commercial crimes'.[219] Strong efficiency considerations thus support the view that

[212] The Commission's 2006 Leniency Notice, recital 8.
[213] *Ibid*, recitals 23–24.
[214] *Ibid*, recital 12.
[215] Case C-301/04 P *Commission v SGL Carbon* [2006] ECR I-5915, at paras 66–70.
[216] Zane, above n 203.
[217] Leslie, above n 203, at 642.
[218] *Ibid*, at 643.
[219] Spratling, Gary R, 'Detection and Deterrence: Rewarding Informants for Reporting Violations' (2001) 69(5/6) *George Washington Law Review* 798.

Member States should, regardless of what EC law may require, establish leniency programs in order to detect cartels. According to information available on the website of the ECN, 24 Member States operated leniency programmes in 2007.[220]

V. INTENTION/NEGLIGENCE

According to Article 23(2) of Regulation 1, the Commission may impose fines on undertakings and associations of undertakings where, *either intentionally or negligently*, they infringe Articles 81 or 82 EC. This provision replicates Article 15(2) of the now obsolete Regulation 17.

A. National law or Community law issue?

There are no references to intention or negligence in Articles 81 or 82 of the Treaty. Article 23(2) of Regulation 1 applies only to the Commission and not to Member States. With reference to the Treaty and Regulation 1, there are no indications that Member States must, in their domestic legislation, apply a test of negligence or intention. Such an obligation could, on the other hand, in principle be derived from two alternative sources: general principles of Community law, such as the rights of the defence, in order to protect undertakings; or the principle of effectiveness, to ensure the impact of Community law. Conversely, an overly wide requirement that the investigating authority demonstrate intent may infringe the principle of effectiveness, as shown in Volkswagen. There, the Court of Justice clarified that a demand that the persons be identified who had acted improperly within the undertaking, or who ought to have been held responsible for any defective organisation of the undertaking, would seriously impinge on the effectiveness of Community competition law.[221]

B. Case law of the Community courts

As for the substantive interpretation of the intention/negligence test, it has turned out to be a rather low threshold. It is not necessary for an undertaking to have been aware that it was infringing Article 81 or 82 EC for an infringement to be regarded as having been committed intentionally; it is sufficient that the undertaking could not have been unaware that the object of the conduct was to restrict competition.[222] In *FEG and TU*, the Court of First Instance considered price-fixing and boycotts, and concluded that the infringements were intentional because

[220] http://ec.europa.eu/comm/competition/ecn/documents.html.
[221] Case C-338/00 P *Volkswagen v Commission* [2003] ECR I-9189, at paras 97–98.
[222] Case 246/86 *Belasco* [1989] ECR 2117, at para 41.

> In view of the intrinsic seriousness of the infringements, the applicants could not have been unaware of the fact that their participation in such agreements, explicitly referred to in Article 81(1)(a) and (d) EC, was liable to distort or restrict competition within the Community.[223]

Further, one must not confuse the intention/negligence test with the elements in Articles 81 or 82 EC. The Court held in *General Motors* that 'proof of . . . intention is not a necessary factor in determining whether an agreement has such a restriction as its object'.[224]

The gravity of an infringement is not necessarily affected by its classification as either negligent or intentional. In the Court's words, 'infringements committed negligently are not, from the point of view of competition, less serious than those committed intentionally'.[225] Then again, a statement to the opposite effect was made in *Steel beams*, where intention was outlined as an important factor for assessing the proper amount of a fine.[226]

VI. GENERAL PRINCIPLES OF COMMUNITY LAW APPLICABLE WHEN MEMBER STATES IMPOSE FINES

In *Industrial and medical gases*, the Court of First Instance reiterated that when the Commission is fixing the amount of each fine, it has a discretion and cannot be required to apply a precise mathematical formula.[227] Nevertheless, one important qualification was made: the Commission's assessment must 'be carried out in compliance with Community law, which includes not only the provisions of the Treaty but also the general principles of law'.[228] General principles of Community law are important when fines are set. It has been explained at length in chapters five and six that general principles of Community law apply when Member States apply Articles 81 and 82 EC.[229] The case law of the Community courts on the general principles of law applicable to fines consequently applies to Member States as well. The content of those principles will be examined next.

A. Foreseeability and legal certainty

Fines imposed by the Commission have been tried by the Community courts on all the grounds one could possibly imagine. The Court of First Instance on several occasions found that the Commission was free to increase its general level of

[223] Joined Cases T-5/00 and T-6/00 *Nederlandse Federatieve Vereniging voor de Groothandel op Elektrotechnisch Gebied and Technische Unie v Commission* [2003] ECR II-5761, at para 397.
[224] Case C-551/03 P *General Motors BV v Commission* [2006] ECR I-3173, at para 77.
[225] Order in Case C-137/95 P *SPO v Commission* [1996] ECR I-1611, at para 55.
[226] Case C-194/99 P *Thyssen Stahl v Commission* [2003] ECR I-10821, at para 118.
[227] Case T-303/02 *Westfalen Gassen Nederland v Commission* [2006] ECR II-4567, at para 151.
[228] *Ibid.*
[229] See esp Case C-94/00 *Roquette Frères* [2002] ECR I-9011, at para 25, with references.

fines.[230] However, it was not until 2005 that the central notions of foreseeability and legal certainty were put to the test in the highest instance. This happened in *District heating pipes*,[231] where the Commission had allegedly raised its fines in relation to previous fining practices. The Court of Justice considered that a change in an enforcement policy, in this instance the Commission's fining policy pursuant to its fining guidelines, might have an impact as regards the principle of non-retroactivity.[232] Importantly, fining guidelines come within the principle of 'law' for the purposes of Article 7(1) of the ECHR.[233]

The Court found that the introduction of the Commission's 1998 fining guidelines represented a move to a tariff-based fining policy.[234] It went on to examine whether this new method of calculating fines was reasonably foreseeable at the time when the infringements were committed.[235] If not, the application of the guidelines would be contrary to the principle of non-retroactivity of legislation[236]; otherwise it would be acceptable. The Court analysed the matter in relation to the ECHR and concluded that

> it follows from the case law of the Court that the fact that the Commission, in the past, imposed fines of a certain level for certain types of infringement does not mean that it is estopped from raising that level within the limits indicated in Regulation No 17 if that is necessary to ensure the implementation of Community competition policy. On the contrary, the proper application of the Community competition rules requires that the Commission may at any time adjust the level of fines to the needs of that policy.[237]

The conclusion was that the introduction of a new method, which increased the level of the fines, was reasonably foreseeable for undertakings at the time when the infringements concerned were committed.[238] This was the case even though the Commission adopted its new fining guidelines *after* the infringements were committed.[239] In summary, there is a requirement of reasonable foreseeability, but a change in fining policy resulting in higher fines is considered a foreseeable development.

The Court expanded on this in *Belgian beer*. If there was any doubt before, the reasoning in *Belgian beer* shows that the *District heating pipes* rule on non-retroactivity and foreseeability is a general principle of EC law, applicable whenever EC law applies. This means that the legal order of the Member States must ensure non-retroactivity when cartels fines are imposed. Specifically, the Court held that

[230] See esp *Mannesmannröhren-Werke v Commission*, above n 49, at para 217; *Tokai Carbon and Others v Commission*, above n 43, at para 191; Case T-33/02 *Britannia Alloys & Chemicals v Commission* [2005] ECR II-4973, at 73.

[231] *Dansk Rørindustri and others v Commission*, above n 194.

[232] *Ibid*, at para 222.

[233] *Ibid*, at para 223.

[234] *Ibid*, at para 225.

[235] *Ibid*, at para 226.

[236] *Ibid*, at para 222.

[237] *Ibid*, at para 227.

[238] *Ibid*, at para 231.

[239] *Ibid*, at para 232.

> the principle that penal provisions may not have retroactive effect is one that is common to all the legal orders of the Member States and forms an integral part of the general principles of law whose observance is ensured by the Community judicature . . .[240]

In principle, judicial interpretation which produces a result which was not reasonably foreseeable at the time when the offence was committed, especially in the light of the interpretation put on the provision in the case law at the material time, may be contrary to Article 7(1) of the ECHR.[241] However, although this principle applies, it seems that the actual scope for a competition authority is quite extensive. Again in *Belgian beer*, mark-up of fines for repeated infringements was held acceptable in relation to the principle of legal certainty.[242] Moreover, in *Amino acids*, the Court emphasised again that 'the fixing of an appropriate fine cannot be the result of a simple calculation based on the total turnover'.[243]

B. Legitimate expectations

Closely related to the principles of non-retroactivity and legal certainty is the concept of legitimate expectations. Once again the leading case is *District heating pipes*,[244] where the Commission had allegedly raised its fining levels through the introduction of its 1998 fining guidelines. The Court of First Instance considered that the fact that the Commission, in the past, had imposed fines of a certain level for certain types of infringement, did not mean that it was estopped from raising that level if that was necessary to ensure the implementation of Community competition policy. The Court of Justice upheld this and underlined that the proper application of the Community competition rules requires that the Commission may at any time adjust the level of fines to the needs of that policy.[245]

Yet another argument was raised by the undertakings involved in the cartel. They submitted that their decision to co-operate with the Commission, pursuant to the leniency notice, was based on the fining practice observable at the time.[246] The argument was that the Commission could not give with one hand (by publishing a leniency notice) and take with the other (by raising fines for past infringements). Although ingenious, this argument failed. Perhaps the appellants tried too hard by claiming that undertakings

> should be able to assess the benefits of co-operating and should be in a position to calculate in advance the absolute amount of the fine payable, depending on whether or not they decide to co-operate . . .[247]

240 *Groupe Danone v Commission*, above n 197, at para 87.
241 *Ibid*, at paras 88–89.
242 *Ibid*, at paras 36–37.
243 *Archer Daniels Midland and Archer Daniels Midland Ingredients v Commission*, above n 24, at para 100.
244 *Dansk Rørindustri and others v Commission*, above n 194.
245 *Ibid*, at para 169.
246 *Ibid*, at para 184.
247 *Ibid*, at para 185.

The Court quashed the idea of fines that could be calculated with precision, and said that

> it cannot be inferred from the Leniency Notice that that notice could found a legitimate expectation that the calculation will follow a particular method or that the fines will be set at a particular level . . .[248]

To be sure, the leniency notice created legitimate expectations, but those were limited to an assurance that fines would be reduced by a certain percentage, and said nothing about the basic fines from which the calculation started.[249]

In *Amino acids*, the question of legitimate expectations was revisited. The Court repeated, with reference to *District heating pipes*, that undertakings do not have a legitimate expectation that the Commission will not exceed the level of fines previously imposed. Neither is there a legitimate expectation that a specific method of calculating the fines will be applied.[250]

Once in a while an undertaking has been successful in relying on published guidelines. For instance, in the shipping cartel case *FETTCA*, the Court of First Instance set aside a fine that had been in excess of what was laid down in the Commission's guidelines. Nevertheless, the reasoning shows that the Commission is not absolutely bound by its guidelines: once the Commission decides to apply in a particular case the method laid down by the guidelines, it is required to adopt that method in its calculations, and where it departs from the guidelines it must set out expressly the reasons justifying such a departure.[251] In *FETTCA*, the fines imposed on Maersk were incorrect because of an inadequate statement of reasons, not because of legitimate expectations.[252] Jurisprudence on legitimate expectations consequently reinforces the impression of a wide discretion left to Member States.

C. Individual assessment and non-discrimination

It has been explained that the Commission has a wide discretion in setting fines, and that it can increase the level of fines without infringing the requirement of foreseeability. Further, it has also been explained that Member States have at least the same degree of discretion as the Commission. Nevertheless, general principles of Community law require that there is some minimum level of consistency within *one and the same* penalty decision. This derives from the principles of individual assessment and non-discrimination.[253]

[248] *Ibid*, at para 186.
[249] *Ibid*, at para 188.
[250] *Archer Daniels Midland and Archer Daniels Midland Ingredients v Commission*, above n 24, at para 22.
[251] Case T-213/00 *CMA CGM and others v Commission* [2003] ECR II-913, at para 271.
[252] *Ibid*, at para 275.
[253] *Ibid*, at para 380.

The Court of First Instance explained in *Graphite electrodes* that the Commission is not required to apply a mathematical formula when setting fines. However,

> the fact remains that, where it deemed it appropriate and equitable to have recourse, at a certain stage of that exercise, to mathematical calculations, it must apply its own method in a manner which is correct, coherent and, in particular, non-discriminatory. Once it has voluntarily chosen to apply such an arithmetical method, it is bound by the rules inherent therein, unless it provides express reasons for not doing so, in regard to all members of the same cartel.[254]

The Commission must, if it has chosen a certain logic for the establishment of fines, proceed from that in relation to all participants.

In *FETTCA*, the Court of First Instance elaborated on the principle of non-discrimination when setting aside cartel fines. The Commission had divided the cartel participants into four groups according to their size, but the decision did not explain the method and the criteria used to define the four groups. During the court proceedings the Commission submitted that it had relied on the parties' worldwide turnover from maritime liner transport in 1994. In principle, the determination of an overall amount of fines to be imposed, and a subsequent spread of that total among the undertakings concerned by dividing them into groups according to the extent of their activities in the sector concerned, was held lawful.[255] However, the Court established that the Commission had been applying at least two different methods, and that 'the thresholds were not based on any objective criterion and lack consistency'.[256] Consequently the Commission's division of the cartel participants into four groups infringed the principle of non-discrimination.[257]

D. Statement of reasons

As set out in chapter six, the duty to state reasons is a fundamental requirement of EC law, forming part of the rights of the defence.[258] It applies in Member States in order to secure the effective protection of fundamental rights.[259] Consequently, this applies when fines and other sanctions are imposed in Member States as a result of infringements of Articles 81 or 82 EC.

Even so, the actual requirements for statements of reasons for fines (as opposed to statements of reasons for liability) have been very low. The only unconditional requirement for Commission decisions was set out as follows in *Cartonboard*:

> [T]he essential procedural requirement to state reasons is satisfied where the Commission indicates in its decision the factors which enabled it to determine the

[254] *Tokai Carbon and Others v Commission*, above n 43, at para 232.
[255] *CMA CGM and others v Commission*, above n 251, at para 385.
[256] *Ibid*, at para 426.
[257] *Ibid*.
[258] Joined Cases 46/87 and 227/88 *Hoechst v Commission* [1989] ECR 2859, at para 29; *Roquette Frères*, above n 229, at paras 47–48.
[259] Case 222/86 *Heylens and Others* [1987] ECR 4097, at paras 15–17.

gravity of the infringement and its duration. If those factors are not stated, the decision is vitiated by failure to state adequate reasons.[260]

Still, the Court of Justice proceeded to say that it would indeed be desirable for the Commission to go beyond those requirements, 'in order to enable undertakings to acquire a detailed knowledge of the method of calculating the fine imposed on them'.[261]

E. Principle of proportionality and equal treatment

The principle of proportionality applies when undertakings are fined for infringements of Articles 81 and 82 EC, but it is not entirely clear what this principle actually produces.

In *Amino acids*, the Court of Justice accepted a range of factors as determinants for cartel fines, including the total turnover of the undertaking, the size of the undertaking and of its economic power, and the proportion of that turnover accounted for by the goods in respect of which the infringement was committed.[262] Having said that, the Court then went on to establish that Community law contains no general principle that the penalty must be proportionate to the undertaking's size on the product market in respect of which the infringement was committed.[263]

On the whole, it seems that the principle of proportionality primarily has the effect of levelling out disproportionate outcomes between undertakings within *one and the same cartel*. This impression is reinforced by the fact that the principle often is paired with the principle of equal treatment.[264] Nevertheless, equal treatment is sometimes assessed on its own in cartel cases, for instance in *Amino acids*, where the Court of Justice held that if the Commission wants to depart from its fining guidelines, it must give reasons that are compatible with the principle of equal treatment.[265]

The principle of proportionality has not been employed as a way to decrease the level of fines in general. Attempts to rely on it have led to mixed results in Community jurisprudence. A successful example of reliance on the said principle was *Greek ferries*, where the Commission had imposed similar fines on those undertakings which participated in two infringements and those which participated in only one of them. This was set aside for reasons of equity and proportionality.[266]

260 Case C-279/98 P *Cascades v Commission* [2000] ECR I-9693, at para 43.

261 *Ibid*, at para 47.

262 *Archer Midlands Daniels and Archer Daniels Midland Ingredients v Commission*, above n 24, at para 100.

263 *Ibid*, at para 101.

264 See esp *Tokai Carbon and Others v Commission*, above n 43, at para 244; *BASF v Commission*, above n 180, at para 149.

265 *Archer Midlands Daniels and Archer Daniels Midland Ingredients v Commission*, above n 24, at para 91.

266 Case T-59/99 *Ventouris v Commission* [2003] ECR II-5257, at para 219.

In *Citric acid*, the Court of First Instance held that a 35 per cent mark-up of fines for ringleaders was not incompatible with the principle of proportionality.[267]

In *Zinc Phosphate*, the principle of proportionality did not stop the Commission from imposing fines which, by reference to turnover, varied between different cartel participants.[268] Further, in *Vitamins*, the principle of proportionality did not dictate that the starting amount of the fine should represent the same percentage of individual turnover for all the different members of a cartel.[269]

Spectacularly, in *Graphite electrodes*, the Commission had multiplied Showa Denko's fines 2.5 times with reference to its size and financial strength. The Court of First Instance started out by finding that

> an infringement committed by an undertaking with vast financial resources may, in principle, be sanctioned by a fine proportionately higher than that imposed in respect of the same infringement committed by an undertaking without such resources . . .[270]

However, the actual calculation was to Showa Denko's advantage, since the Court of First Instance found that the Commission had been inconsistent in weighing Showa Denko's strength in relation to another cartel participant. The multiplier was cut to 1.5, which, in the end, reduced Showa Denko's fines from €17 million to €10 million. The judgment was upheld on appeal.[271] Once again, this shows that Member States are relatively unrestrained by EC law when setting fines.

The present case law raises the question whether we need all-encompassing proportionality assessments carried out by the Community courts as well as by national courts. Save for in the enforcement of Articles 81 and 82 EC, fines are not often imposed by the Community courts. The possibilities of benchmarking are consequently negligible. National authorities and courts, on the other hand, may be faced with arguments where competition law fines are compared to other fining policies prevailing in the Member State, for instance on financial markets or in relation to environmental damages. If competition law fines are to stand that type of test, they must be rationally explicable.

F. Legality

Whether the Commission's fining powers comply with the principle of legality has been tried by the Court of First Instance in *Citric acid* and *Methionine*. Following an appeal in *Methionine*, the judgment of the Court of First Instance was upheld by the Court of Justice.[272] Member State authorities and courts should be prepared to deal with allegations that their national cartel fining rules and policies are

[267] Case T-59/02 *Archer Daniels Midland v Commission* [2006] ECR II-3627, at para 313.
[268] Case T-52/02 *SNCZ v Commission* [2005] ECR II-500574.
[269] *BASF v Commission*, above n 180, at para 149.
[270] *Tokai Carbon and Others v Commission*, above n 43, at para 243.
[271] *Showa Denko v Commission*, above n 20, at para 38.
[272] *Evonik Degussa v Commission and Council*, above n 191.

contrary to the principle of legality in Community law and as enshrined in the ECHR.

In *Citric acid*, Jungbunzlauer claimed that the provision on fines in Regulation 17 was too vague as to how fines should be determined, and left too much scope to the Commission.[273] The Court of First Instance reiterated that the principle of legality is a corollary to the principle of legal certainty, a general principle of Community law.[274] This includes the requirement that all Community legislation, in particular those provisions that enable the imposition of sanctions, shall be clear and precise, so that the persons concerned can, without ambiguity, discover the existing rights and obligations and act accordingly.[275] Further, the principle of legality derives from the constitutional traditions of the Member States and the ECHR.[276] Given that Community law is inspired by the ECHR, reference was made to the jurisprudence of the European Court of Human Rights. The Court of First Instance noted that vague terms do not necessarily make a law incompatible with the ECHR. Neither does the fact that a law confers discretionary powers violate the requirement of foreseeability, provided that the scope of this power and the way it is exercised are sufficiently clearly defined with reference to the legitimate aims in question. The purpose is to provide individuals with adequate protection against arbitrariness. Relevant here is not only the wording of the law, but also how the notions have been determined in settled and published jurisprudence.[277] In conclusion, the Court of First Instance found that, in order to prevent norms becoming excessively rigid, and to allow rules to be adapted to the circumstances, a certain degree of unforeseeability must be allowed in relation to the sanctions resulting from infringements. Fines that can vary between a minimum and maximum amount within sufficient limits, may be expected to contribute to the efficiency of the law's application and dissuasive effect.[278]

In *Methionine*, the same question was raised—whether the Commission's fining powers were too extensive.[279] The reasoning of the Court of First Instance is the same, although with one twist—it is stated more explicitly that the fact that undertakings are not able to calculate fines in advance with precision, is justified with reference to the objectives of suppressing and deterring serious infringements.[280] However, that particular passage was not explicitly endorsed by the Court of Justice on appeal.[281]

The judgments of the Court of First Instance in *Citric acid* and *Methionine* could be seen to be of relevance in connection with the debate on the Commission's

[273] *Jungbunzlauer v Commission*, above n 147.
[274] *Ibid*, at para 71.
[275] *Ibid*.
[276] *Ibid*, at para 73.
[277] *Ibid*, at para 80.
[278] *Ibid*, at para 84.
[279] *Degussa v Commission*, above n 191.
[280] *Ibid*, at para 83.
[281] *Evonik Degussa v Commission and Council*, above n 191.

investigatory and decision-making powers. The Court of First Instance had to decide in 1998, in one of the *Cartonboard* cases, whether the Commission's dual functions regarding investigations and the imposition of penalties were acceptable. There it accepted the institutional arrangements and held:

> It is also settled law that the Commission cannot be described as a 'tribunal' within the meaning of Article 6 of the ECHR (Musique Diffusion Française and Others v Commission, cited above, paragraph 7). The applicant's argument that the Decision is unlawful simply because it was adopted under a system in which the Commission carries out both investigatory and decision-making functions is therefore irrelevant. The Court emphasises, however, that the Commission is required, during the administrative procedure before it, to observe the procedural guarantees provided for by Community law.[282]

G. *Ne bis in idem*

Decentralisation leads to a risk that the same infringement of Article 81 or Article 82 EC will be punished more than once, because authorities and courts in more than one Member State may be involved. The case allocation within the ECN should mitigate this risk, but there is nevertheless a need for a default rule to avoid double penalties. Such a rule exists in Community law, commonly referred to as *ne bis in idem.*

Not only is this a rule to prevent double penalties, it also constitutes a fundamental principle of Community law,[283] and consequently applies when Member State authorities and courts apply the Treaty.

A definition of how the principle of *ne bis in idem* applies was laid down in *Cement.* The application of that principle is subject to the threefold requirement of:

a) identity of the facts;
b) unity of offender; and
c) unity of the legal interest protected;

so that 'the same person cannot be sanctioned more than once for the same unlawful course of conduct designed to protect the same legal asset'.[284]

An important distinction has been made for Community-wide cartels and global cartels. The principle of *ne bis in idem* does not apply to fines imposed in jurisdictions outside the Community. This follows from *Graphite electrodes*, where the Court of Justice held that

> the principle of *non bis in idem* does not apply to situations in which the legal systems and competition authorities of non-Member States intervene within their own jurisdiction . . .[285]

[282] Case T-348/94 *Enso Española v Commission* [1998] ECR II-1875, at para 56.
[283] *Showa Denko v Commission*, above n 20, at para 50.
[284] *Aalborg Portland and others v Commission*, above n 53, at para 338.
[285] *Showa Denko v Commission*, above n 20, at para 56.

Furthermore, 'there is no other principle of law obliging the Commission to take account of proceedings and penalties to which the appellant has been subject in non-member States'.[286] Undertakings can consequently be subject to double fines if they engage in international cartel activity; fines imposed by jurisdictions outside the EU will not work to mitigate fines imposed in the EU. Further, in *Amino acids*, the Court determined that

> where the sanction imposed in a non-member country covers only the applications or effects of the cartel on the market of that State and the Community sanction covers only the applications or effects of the cartel on the Community market, the facts are not identical.[287]

Wils has pointed out another question which arises under the principle of *ne bis in idem*: whether multiple prosecutions are allowed in the EU. There might, for example, be instances where a Member State authority brings a case against a cartel that affects trade between Member States, although the end result is inadequately low fines. Could the Commission or another national competition authority then bring proceedings against the same cartel? Wils suggests that the efficiency of the network of EU competition authorities would require a ban on multiple prosecutions. That would force the Commission and national competition authorities to make full use of the co-ordination mechanisms, 'so as to ensure that each case is dealt with by an authority capable of imposing the required penalties'.[288]

H. Conclusions on general principles applicable when Member States penalise infringements

It has been explained that, under Community law, sanctions imposed as a result of infringements of competition law must comply with the principles of foreseeability and legal certainty. Communications from an authority may create legitimate expectations. Fines must meet the requirements of individual assessment and non-discrimination. Reasons must be stated. Fines must comply with principles of proportionality and equal treatment, legality and protection against double penalties. All these principles have a direct bearing on the need for legitimacy.

It has been shown that this applies when Member States impose sanctions, but it is nevertheless clear that these principles will not generate any method of setting fines or other sanctions, and that their application has left considerable room for discretion.

[286] *Ibid*, at para 57.

[287] *Archer Midlands Daniels and Archer Daniels Midland Ingredients v Commission*, above n 24, at para 69.

[288] Wils, Wouter P J, 'The Principle of Ne Bis in Idem in EC Antitrust Enforcement: A Legal and Economic Analysis' (2003) 26(2) *World Competition* 131, at 146–47.

VII. OTHER PRINCIPLES OF RELEVANCE WHEN FINES ARE IMPOSED IN MEMBER STATES

A. How serious is a domestic cartel?

The classification of cartels as serious or very serious under the Commission's 1998 fining guidelines does not constitute a general principle of EC law and consequently does not apply to Member States. However, the assessments made in Community jurisprudence may still be interesting for Member States as points of reference and sources of analogy.

In *Interbrew and Alken-Maes*, there was a cartel on the Belgian beer market. The Court of First Instance examined whether the Commission was correct in classifying the cartel as very serious, given that only one Member State was affected. The Court found that the criteria generally applied when fixing fines in price cartel cases should lead the Commission to classify the agreement as very serious.[289]

Similarly, in *SAS/Maersk Air*, a market-sharing agreement on three air routes was considered very serious, and the Court emphasised that not only infringements effectively concerning most Member States may be classified as such.[290]

B. Ringleaders and instigators

The Community courts have consistently held that it is appropriate that ringleaders and instigators should be punished more severely than other cartel participants.[291] The reasoning derives from the fining provision in Regulation 17 rather than from general principles of law. It is not possible to imply at present that Member States are required to impose higher fines on ringleaders and instigators.

C. Trade associations

The Commission has not been systematic in imposing fines on trade associations, often confining itself to punishing the member undertakings. In the past the Commission has on several occasions found infringements committed by trade associations, but without fining either the trade associations or their members.[292]

Although there are many examples of trade associations being fined for cartel participation, the severity of enforcement varies considerably from case to case. In *Raw Tobacco Italy*, the professional association of Italian tobacco processors

[289] Case T-38/02 *Groupe Danone v Commission* [2005] ECR II-4407, at para 152.

[290] *Scandinavian Airlines System v Commission*, above n 39, at paras 87–89.

[291] See esp *Archer Daniels Midland v Commission*, above n 31, at paras 296–97, with references.

[292] Eg, *Publisher's association* [1989] OJ L/22/12; *Sugar beet* [1990] OJ L/31/32; *CNSD* [1993] OJ L/203/27.

(APTI) and the Italian confederation of associations of raw tobacco producers (UNITAB) were fined €1,000 each.[293] Symbolic fines were also imposed on Spanish industry associations in *Raw Tobacco Spain.*[294] A fine of only €100,000 was imposed on the Belgian Architects' Association for adopting a minimum fee scale.[295] On the other hand, six French federations in the agriculture sector were heavily fined in *French beef.*[296]

Going back to the 1990s, a Dutch association in the electrotechnical fittings sector, FEG, was fined with €4.4 million for price-fixing and collective exclusive dealing agreements.[297] Conversely, a symbolic fine was imposed in 1996 on Fenex, a federation of Dutch forwarding agents, for drawing up and circulating recommended tariffs.[298] Far from symbolic was the 11.5 million ecu fine imposed on FNK, an association of firms which hired out mobile cranes, in *Kraanverhuurbedrijf.*[299] Moreover, no fewer than 28 Dutch trade organisations in the building and construction sector were fined in ranges up to several million ecu each in *Building and construction industry in the Netherlands.*[300]

Eight trade associations were fined some 100,000 ecu each in *Cement,*[301] although the fines were annulled on appeal because the Commission had failed to state in its statement of objections that it intended to impose fines.[302] There, the Court of First Instance held:

> It is also normal practice for the Commission, where it finds that an association of undertakings and its members have participated in the same infringement, to impose a fine either on the undertakings which are members of that association of undertakings or on the association of undertakings. In the latter case, it may take the turnover of the members of the association as a basis for calculating the fine, at least where, by virtue of its internal rules, the association is able to bind its members.[303]

Over time, the fining policy in relation to trade associations appears random. Transposed to the national context, the crucial issue is whether considerations of dissuasion and effectiveness require that Member State competition authorities and courts impose fines on trade associations. The quantitative analysis presented

[293] *Raw Tobacco Italy* IP/05/1315.

[294] *Raw Tobacco Spain* IP/04/1256.

[295] *Belgian architects* [2005] OJ L/4/10.

[296] *French beef* [2003] OJ L/209/12, upheld on appeal in Joined Cases T-217/03 and T-245/03 *FNCBV and others v Commission* [2006] ECR II-4987, upheld on appeal in Joined Cases C-101/07 P and C-110/07 P *Coop de France Bétail and Viande v Commission* [2008] ECR I-0000, see particularly para 98.

[297] *FEG and TU* [2000] OJ L/39/1.

[298] *Fenex* [1996] OJ L/181/28.

[299] *Kraanverhuurbedrijf* [1995] OJ L/312/79, upheld on appeal in Joined Cases T-213/95 and T-18/96 *SCK and FNK v Commission* [1997] ECR II-1739.

[300] *Building and construction industry in the Netherlands* [1992] OJ L/92/1, upheld on appeal in Case T-29/92 *Vereniging van Samenwerkende Prijsregelende Organisaties in de Bouwnijverheid and others v Commission* [1995] ECR II-289.

[301] *Cement* [1994] OJ L/343/1.

[302] Joined Cases T-25/95, etc *Cimenteries and others v Commission* [2000] ECR II-491, at paras 478–88.

[303] *Ibid*, at para 485.

in chapter three shows that trade associations have been involved in approximately 40 per cent of the Commission's decisions against cartels. One might argue that there is no need to punish them since their members will incur fines; but such an approach disregards the organisational aspect. A trade association may have its own premises, its own staff and its own organisation, and a fine will have an impact on its operational capacity. If the trade organisation is to have an independent incentive not to function as a vehicle for cartels, it should be liable in the same way as its members. This view has been endorsed by the Court of Justice in *French beef*, where the need for deterrence was emphasised.[304]

Probably, the underlying rationale for instances of low or zero fines for trade associations is the absence of a capacity to pay. I have suggested in section III.C above that commitments could be utilised as a remedy—for instance, as to the establishment of a compliance programme and training—as well as structural measures to make the trade association more independent from its members.

D. Reference year for calculation of fines

Member States have discretion in the calculation of fines, not only in general but also on specific points such as reference year. In *Cement*, the Court of First Instance granted the Commission certain leeway in this respect. The 'preceding business year', within the meaning of Article 15(2) of Regulation No 17, refers to the last full business year of each of the undertakings concerned as at the date of adoption of the contested decision. However, it is open to the Commission to take into account, when determining the fines, the turnover relating to an earlier business year, provided that the fine calculated on that basis does not exceed the 10 per cent limit.[305] Most important, there seem to be no general principles of EC law governing the issue, as the reasoning was derived only from Regulation 17.

VIII. IS THERE A NEED FOR HARMONISED SANCTIONS?

The European Parliament wrote, when consulted on the modernisation package, that 'Under an EU wide application of competition law, it is important that the form and level of sanctions for breaches are harmonised'.[306] This opinion has been voiced in academic writing as well.[307]

It is quite obvious that the decentralised enforcement of Articles 81 and 82 EC does not provide for any harmonised system of sanctions. There are no such pro-

[304] *Coop de France Bétail and Viande v Commission*, above n 296, at para 98.

[305] *Cimenteries and others v Commission*, above n 302, at para 5009.

[306] *European Parliament Report on the Proposal for a Council Regulation on the Implementation of the Rules of Competition Laid Down in Articles 81 and 82 of the Treaty . . .* Committee on Economic and Monetary Affairs, A5-0229/2001 at 8.

[307] Killick, above n 161.

visions in Regulation 1 or elsewhere; further, there are no general principles of EC law to this effect. As explained, the only guidance so far is that sanctions must be effective, proportionate and dissuasive. The fact that the Community courts have allowed the Commission a wide discretion, under which fines can vary considerably from case to case, and from undertaking to undertaking within the same infringement, indicates that no unitary method of calculation will be developed in case law. The introduction of EC legislation (through a Directive or Regulation) would effectively make the Court of Justice the court of last instance in every Article 81 or 82 EC proceeding in the EU, since Member State courts could refer questions on preliminary rulings pursuant to Article 234 EC.

If fines are harmonised, leniency must be harmonised as well if the idea is to uphold a common standard.

Although I feel some sympathy for the idea of harmonised sanctions, it seems like an unworkable prospect. On the other hand, co-operation between the national competition authorities within the EU may informally contribute to a de facto harmonisation of sanctions, as a result of exchanges of experiences and best practices.

IX. SUMMARY, DISCUSSION AND CONCLUSIONS

There is wide support among scholars and enforcers alike about the need for efficient sanctions against hard-core antitrust infringements. It is the express ambition of the Community courts to pursue a deterrence-based approach in combination with retribution: to punish and deter. However, the Commission's fining policy and practice, as applied before 2006, has been considered illegitimate by the legal community and the business community. That is because it generated unforeseeable outcomes which varied from one cartel to another, and from one participant to another. We are thus facing a situation with a high level of normative legitimacy for efficient sanctions, but a low level of empirical legitimacy for the actual policy that was pursued. This outcome is not surprising given that economic theory has only recently begun to generate some hard figures that can be applied for the purpose of calculating fines. The frustrations in EC law are thus a mere reflection of the development in empirical observations about cartels.

The Commission's 2006 fining guidelines are more deterrence-based than the previous policies, but still rest to a considerable extent on a retributive theory. This reflects (at least to some extent) considerations in legal theory about the need to combine deterrence theory with perspectives of proportionate justice.

Looking in particular at the aspects of the 2006 fining policy based on deterrence theory (the method of calculating fines on the basis of turnover on the market), the Commission has not made any attempt to explain where it sourced its figures. This explanatory gap may be contrasted with the US experience, where the origin of the 20 per cent proxy is at least known. The value of knowing is that it allows for a revision of the law when new empirical data are established. This is what the US Antitrust Modernization Commission (the AMC) has suggested after reviewing the proxies of 10 per cent gain and 20 per cent of the volume of affected commerce. As a result, it has recommended Congress to encourage the Sentencing Commission to re-evaluate and explain the rationale for the use of the 20 per cent harm proxy.[308] The direction taken by the AMC seems to have been prompted by the insistence of qualified observers that the 20 per cent proxy was, and still is, unsupported by empirical data.[309] If the European Commission were to be clear on where its figures come from, the system would be more transparent and would gain some stability, instead of constantly being open to challenge on procedural grounds and grounds of proportionality.

National law applies when national authorities and courts impose sanctions for infringements of Articles 81 and 82 EC. The Member States' duty to co-operate under Article 10 EC applies. Sanctions must be effective, proportionate to the infringement and dissuasive. General principles of EC law apply, including the principles of legal certainty, legitimate expectations, individual assessment and non-discrimination, the principle of proportionality and equal treatment, the duty to state reasons, legality and *ne bis in idem*. However, although these principles will provide some outer limit to how fines may be imposed, they will not generate any specific method for setting fines. Given the wide discretion in setting fines granted to the Commission by the Community courts, national courts should not expect any detailed guidance from the Court of Justice.

It follows that Member States have a wide discretion to design and apply rules on antitrust fines. The requirements for uniformity and effectiveness are very low indeed. One might consider how this situation will affect legitimacy, or in other words public confidence in a decentralised EC competition law system. On the one hand, the absence of a harmonised system for sanctions will enable Member States to construct their sanctions in conformity with established principles that exist within each system. Looking at enforcement from a more limited national perspective, this might increase legitimacy (locally) because sanctions will be perceived as system-sound and foreseeable. On the other hand, such a development will risk detracting from what could be understood as an *efficient* fining policy. Will the freedom to create sanction policies realise the goals in society of reducing competition law infringements? For instance, the analysis carried out here has generated some very specific views on the choice between a deterrence-based system and a retributive system, on whether the harm-based approach is better than the gain-based approach, and whether proxies for antitrust harm should be employed. These conclusions could be contested, and there are certainly other positions represented elsewhere, as set out in this chapter; but at least there seems to be a common understanding, in available scholarly writing, of the need to treat antitrust sanctions as a separate field where the solutions must be tailored to their

[308] Antitrust Modernization Commission Report and Recommendations, April 2007, at 295, available at http://www.amc.gov/report_recommendation/toc.htm.

[309] AMC Criminal Remedies Discussion Memorandum of 4 May 2006, at 13–14, available at http://www.amc.gov/commission_documents.htm#may9.

purpose. It seems plausible that attempts at keeping sanctions consistent with other national solutions must give way, to avoid sub-optimal outcomes. This in turn can create tensions within the legal community and business community, when a set of unfamiliar rules is imposed, even if such imposition is done unilaterally by the Member State itself. National officials and courts may feel that they are being shoehorned into a new set of rules, unprecedented in their respective systems.

The lack of harmonisation can in addition give rise to indignation if undertakings perceive that the same infringement is, or similar infringements are, treated differently depending on which Member State brings proceedings. The experiences with the Commission's guidelines prior to 2006, and the reaction in the legal community to the fluctuations in the Commission's fining decisions, are telling here. The legal community challenged the Commission's practice openly with reference to its low predictability and problems with anchoring. Presumably this was due to the reactions legal counsel received when trying to explain the law to their clients. It seems likely that the opposition was generated from the business community. Further, the legitimacy of applicable provisions in Regulation 17 was challenged before the Community courts with reference precisely to legality. The events reflect concerns expressed in the preparatory works of modernisation, as well as those expressed by scholars, on uniformity. Foreseeability is obviously in great demand for those addressed by fines. Furthermore, detracting from uniformity when it comes to fines raises the question why we should be so meticulous in ensuring uniformity in other respects, such as the definition of agreements, concerted practices and undertakings. Is there any theoretical basis for allowing widely disparate outcomes when it comes to penalties, but not on substantive law? Even if it makes a difference for specialised competition lawyers, those that are penalised may fail to see the subtlety.

As set out above, the harmonisation of sanctions is not an option. It seems that EC law is unable to provide coherency in a system of fines against competition law infringements in a decentralised system. The preceding discussion points in one direction—central enforcement. Discrepancies will then at least be kept at a minimum.

8

Sourcing Legitimacy

MY ANALYSIS HAS been of the role of legitimacy in decentralised EC cartel control. Some conclusions may be drawn at this point.

Decentralisation sought to cure two types of legitimacy deficit. Prior to modernisation the Commission was unable to ensure average compliance as a result of its focus on vertical restraints and its administrative burdens caused by the former notification system. On the other hand, Member States were reluctant to take part in enforcement. Decentralisation has consequently *raised expectations* on average compliance.

At the same time, though, decentralisation has exposed some deeper problems. Legitimacy presupposes not only average compliance guaranteed by the State, but also that the norms that are enforced are legitimate.[1] A set of rules and principles that previously was applied almost exclusively by the Commission and the Community courts is now out to be tried by courts and authorities in 27 Member States. In the dialogue opened up between national authorities and courts, the Commission and the Community courts, the normative legitimacy of EC competition law will be tested. Are the rules theoretically sound, and have they been expressed in a way that is user-friendly and characterised by internal logic? Will the system work, given the interplay between national law and Community law?

I. WHERE TO FIND THE LEGITIMATE GENESIS OF THE LAW IN EC CARTEL CONTROL

A. The integration objective

'Regulation is . . . the sustained and focused attempt by the state to alter behaviour thought to be of value to the community.'[2] Competition is in itself considered valuable to society. On a meta-level, the primary purpose of competition regulation is to ensure the integrity of the competitive process to secure economic efficiency.[3] In EC competition law, however, the objective of protecting competition

[1] Habermas, Jürgen, *Between Facts and Norms* (Cambridge, Polity Press, 1996), at 448.
[2] Yeung, Karen, *Securing Compliance—A principled approach* (Oxford, Hart Publishing, 2004), at 5.
[3] *Ibid*, at 18.

is coupled with the objective of promoting integration between Member States.[4] Joshua and Jordan go so far as to find that

> The immediate object of protection is thus not the consumer or even the notion of 'competition' as such but the European 'vision' of a certain type of market organization . . .[5]

The Court of First Instance has held that cartels counteract the EC Treaty's main objective of integrating the Community market.[6] The Court of Justice's references to the integration objective in cases on effect on trade (see chapter four) may also be recalled.[7]

In EC cartel control the integration objective is primarily visible in the aggregate requirements of uniformity and effectiveness (see chapter two). Those requirements include what must be understood as uncompromising demands on substantive law, certain minimum evidentiary standards and fundamental rights, encompassing the bulk of procedural rules. Furthermore, it is clear that the effect on trade concept is to a large extent integration driven.

The combination of an extensive effect on trade concept and relatively detailed laws on substance, evidence and procedure, coupled with the principle of effectiveness, represents an integration through law policy. It has been shown comprehensively here, however, that integration through law is at the same time undermined by the absence of generally applicable rules in several areas. There are no common standards for building competition institutions. There are no common standards on enforcement priorities. Evidentiary standards are minimum standards, not absolute standards. National procedure will continue to have an impact on outcomes, regardless of the common standards created through fundamental rights. Fines can vary, nearly without limitations.

B. Reliance on precedents

The leading source of legitimacy in EC cartel control is reliance on earlier case law. On balance, though, there is an over-exploitation of precedents as a source of legitimacy. It is difficult to see how reliance on jurisprudence could be any greater than it is today.

Jurisprudence on EC cartel control represents stability rather than flexibility. There is, of course, great value in preserving an institutional memory, but the studies in this work have demonstrated that case law on cartels in fact shifts and develops over time. Nevertheless, this development is seldom highlighted in the cases; it may be observed only by reference to the study of a large number of cases

[4] See esp Wahl, Nils, *Konkurrensförhållanden* (Stockholm, Juristförlaget, 1994), at 58–66.

[5] Joshua, Julian M, and Jordan, Sarah, 'Combinations, Concerted Practices and Cartels: Adopting the Concept of Conspiracy in European Community Competition Law' (2004) 24(3) *Northwestern Journal of International Law and Business* 647, at 650.

[6] Case T-241/01 *Scandinavian Airlines System v Commission* [2005] ECR II-2917, at para 85.

[7] Joined Cases C-295/04 to C-298/04 *Manfredi and others* [2006] ECR I-6619, at para 41.

adjudicated over a longer period. The most obvious example is the development of the per se question, analysed in chapter four. An open discussion in the cases about what changes are actually taking place would contribute to more transparency and better understanding. The legal community seems to respond well to leaps in development, and there is no reason to assume adverse reactions.

C. Economic theory and empirical observations

There is an underlying trend of greater reliance on economics in EC cartel control, presumably because the integration objective is ill-suited to providing us with solutions to legal problems in competition law. All the solid arguments for having a prohibition against hard-core infringements and for allocating scarce public resources to enforcement are derived from economic theory and empirical observations. Indirectly, economic theory is reflected in adjudicative practices and in the Commission's policies. References are made by the Community courts to deterrence[8] and to price-fixing, to market-sharing and control of outlets as obvious restrictions of competition,[9] but the language and reasoning is not elaborate. A candid discussion about economic perspectives could increase the legitimacy of the law.

Economic theory is very much present in the *choice* of cases in which the Commission decides to take action. Where the theory is not rock-solid, as in single-brand dealer cartels, what to classify as a boycott, or how to approach buyer cartels, very few prohibition decisions emerge, and consequently even fewer cases go to court. Nevertheless, at the same time the opposite holds true, given the 20-plus Commission decisions on mixed horizontal and vertical cartels. There too, theory is ambiguous, but this has not stopped enforcement. On appeal, over a dozen decisions on mixed horizontal and vertical cartels have been upheld by the Community courts. Presumably this is due to the idea, prevalent in older case law, that there was no reason to distinguish between vertical and horizontal restrictions. Advances in economic and legal theory have made this view obsolete. Monopoly theory is prevalent in enforcement against naked horizontal restraints, whereas a balancing of pro-competitive and negative effects must be carried out for vertical restrictions. This is reflected in contemporary case law, where different treatment of horizontal and vertical restraints may be observed, in particular on the notion of agreement, rules on evidence and fining policy. The ambiguity is primarily visible in the treatment of mixed horizontal and vertical cartels.

[8] Case C-289/04 P *Showa Denko v Commission* [2006] ECR I-5859, at para 16.

[9] Joined Cases T-374/94, etc *European Night Services and Others v Commission* [1998] ECR II-3141, at para 136.

D. Legal theory

Legal theory seems to have been attempting to catch up with the bulk of case law, rather than the other way around. Until recently there was not much systematic discussion of cartel control in European scholarly writing. The new focus on cartels in published works should, however, be seen as a tendency for scholars to take the initiative in developing the law rather than (at best) documenting it.

It must be admitted that the Community courts are ahead of scholars when developing certain central concepts in cartel law, such as agreements and concerted practices, and procedural rules. The situation can best be understood as a result of the massive litigation in the Community courts. Many skilled practitioners are busy litigating, and the enormous volume of appeals and judgments has made it difficult to extract a comprehensive picture of the law.

E. Internal rationality of the law

There is a high level of awareness in the Community courts' judgments on the need to develop the law in a way that is internally rational; in other words, to avoid contradictions. Nevertheless, there are certain contradictions to be observed. The law on extraterritorial jurisdiction does not match the later developments of agreements and concerted practices. Such occurrences should not be seen as too problematic—the Community courts can iron out the creases in due time. What causes more profound concern is the tendency to jump between different theory bases depending on what is being analysed. Much of the central law is deterrence-based, but the theory on how to delimit the application of Article 81 EC is often based on free-movement thinking (as in effect on trade), or on the need to preserve coherency with the Treaty at large or with the Member States' systems. Procedure is based on notions of fairness and equality of arms. Case law on fines displays an often unconscious combination of deterrence and concerns regarding fairness.

The existence of several legal theories in parallel operation can be expected to make the law, as a whole, difficult to understand for lawyers in the Member States. This predicament will be difficult to resolve, but it can at least be addressed through a more open discussion about these issues in the case law.

F. Comparative law

Strong support for substantive EC law on cartels may be found in US antitrust law, as indicated in chapters three, four and five. Increased globalisation and international co-operation on enforcement against hard-core restraints have gradually amplified the comparative aspects of competition law. The arena has been opened up, and now includes in the dialogue lawyers (and ultimately the business community) in jurisdictions outside the EU. The scarcity of explicit reliance on analogies with US law is surprising. This is a source of legitimacy that is severely under-utilised in EC law.

G. Common legal traditions in Member States

The judge-made law on legal professional privilege (see chapter six, section IV.B.) represents an example of how common legal traditions in Member States have been used to gain legitimacy in EC law. Normally, though, EC competition law has been one step ahead in its development of competition law principles, and the possibility of sourcing from national law has consequently been limited.

H. International standards including the ECHR

The principles enshrined in the ECHR have been used to a great extent to legitimise the innovative activities of the Community courts within EC competition law procedure. As set out extensively in chapter six, this creativity has met with general approval, and acceptance is almost universal. The distance between the present bulk of EC jurisprudence and the judgments of the European Court of Human Rights must be said to have increased, however, given that only the Community courts are actually judging competition law cases regularly. Given the success of this creative policy, perhaps the Community courts could rely on the legitimacy that has been gained and openly recognise this case law as relatively free in relation to the ECHR.

The procedural principles may be expected to undergo more intense scrutiny when they have to be applied in Member States. The connection to the ECHR is important here, but not conclusive for legitimacy. Some over-exploiting of the Convention as a base for legitimacy may be seen when it comes to evidence—it seems that what is actually applied is a combined human rights and deterrence approach, and this could be more visible and add to legitimacy.

Other international standards are emerging, not least from the OECD which has been engaged in cartel policy over the last decade. However, this development is relatively recent, and must be said to happen in the back draft of US law and EC law.

II. DEMOCRACY, PARTICIPATION, TRANSPARENCY

A legislative process fulfils a communicative function where it gains legitimacy through dissemination of knowledge.[10] The working out, adoption and

[10] Wahlgren, Peter, *Lagstiftning—Problem, teknik, möjligheter* (Uppsala, Norstedts, 2008), at 52.

implementation of Directives and Regulations will normally fulfil this function because Member States are included in the process. By contrast, in EC competition law, the development takes place primarily through case law. This aspect calls for a conscious view about legitimacy through jurisprudence.

The dialogue between Member State courts and the Court of Justice in Article 234 cases may be seen as a strong provider of legitimacy. Legitimacy could be further increased here if the Community courts engaged in more open and transparent theory-building in their judgments.

Decentralisation has opened up an arena, previously dominated by the Community courts and the Commission, to more actors. In addition to the addressees of competition law decisions and the legal community, actors involved now include Member State courts and competition authorities. This necessarily expands the legal community in the arena as well, in so far as lawyers in all Member States will have an incentive to participate in the debate taking place not only before the Community courts, but now also before national authorities and courts, and (to a greater extent than before) in scholarly writing. This brings to mind Scharpf's view that the expert community should effectively fulfil a control function though their critique.[11]

III. ENSURING AVERAGE COMPLIANCE AS AN OUTFLOW OF ENSURING THE LAW'S RATIONALITY?

If the law has a legitimate genesis then the chances of ensuring average compliance will improve. But will the enforcement deficit, the problem that steered the decentralisation process, be fixed?

A. What exactly is renationalisation?

The Economic and Social Committee, when consulted on the modernisation proposal, expressed concerns about the risk of renationalisation. More precisely, the Committee expressed concerns about the danger of fragmentation of the single market and renationalisation of competition law, and said that very careful attention must be paid to the risk of the latter.[12] These concerns were soon echoed in the academic community.

Meanwhile, the Commission's worries were focused primarily on the risk that one and the same practice (or infringement) would be dealt with by both the Commission and a national competition authority or court, with potentially

[11] Scharpf, Fritz Wilhelm, *Governing in Europe: Effective and Democratic?* (Oxford, Oxford University Press, 1999), at 16.

[12] Opinion of the Economic and Social Committee on the 'White Paper on modernisation of the rules implementing Articles 81 and 82 of the EC Treaty—Commission programme No 99/027' [2000] OJ C/51/55, at paras 2.3.5.6 and 2.3.5.12.

different outcomes. To avoid this, it was enacted in Article 16 of Regulation 1 that national courts cannot take decisions running counter to a decision adopted by the Commission. In accordance with the same provision, the national courts must also avoid taking decisions which would conflict with decisions *contemplated* by the Commission. If anything, the discussion in the previous chapters will have shown that the Commission's concerns and Article 16 of Regulation 1 were a side issue, because the real problems are of a more fundamental and complex nature.

The idea that decentralisation of EC competition law supervision and enforcement could lead to renationalisation may now be evaluated on the basis of the previous chapters. If one accepts—at least as a working hypothesis—the extent of Community law set out in chapters four to seven, public administrative proceedings in Member States must reach a certain minimum level when it comes to application of the law, provided, of course, that there is an effect on trade.

As outlined in chapter four, the criteria in Articles 81 and 82 EC, such as the concepts of effect on trade, agreements, concerted practices, undertakings, object and effect, leave no scope at all for deviations from the interpretations made by the Court of Justice. Were Member States to grant themselves leeway in interpreting them, this would effectively constitute renationalisation.

The analysis in chapter five shows a complex interplay between national law and Community law on evidence in competition law cases. The ascertaining of facts is a matter for national law, but Community law determines what facts are relevant. Presumptions developed by the Community courts, such as the opt-out principle for cartel meetings, apply in two distinct ways when Member States enforce Article 81 EC: as interpretations of the burden of proof; and as general principles of EC law. The standard of proof developed in Community law is (in my view) a minimum standard which applies in Member States because it derives from the presumption of innocence, a fundamental principle of Community law. A maximum standard could in principle be envisaged if a Member State were to apply extremely high standards of proof which would render the exercise of Community law practically impossible or excessively difficult. The principle of equivalence, furthermore, requires that claims based on EC law are not treated any worse than similar claims based on national law.

Looking at procedure, analysed in chapter six, there is no harmonisation of Member States' national competition procedures, and no absolute requirement of uniformity under general principles of Community law. National rules applicable for the supervision and enforcement of Articles 81 and 82 EC must no be less favourable than those governing similar domestic actions (the principle of equivalence), and must not render practically impossible or excessively difficult the exercise of rights conferred by Community law (the principle of effectiveness). Community law accepts that national procedural law exerts an influence on the outcome of a case, within the limits just described, and does not expect identical outcomes; but the principles of equivalence and effectiveness just referred to are only part of the story—national law is profoundly affected by fundamental principles of Community law, especially the rights of the defence. These rules serve as a common minimum standard in national procedure when Community law applies, in all proceedings in which sanctions, especially fines or penalty payments, may be imposed. They do not extend to a duty for Member States to duplicate the Community competition procedure, but they will have very similar effects given the relatively detailed case law developed by the Community courts.

On fines and other sanctions, analysed in chapter seven, national law applies when national authorities and courts impose sanctions for infringements of Articles 81 and 82 EC. The Member States' duty to co-operate under Article 10 EC applies. Sanctions must be effective, proportionate to the infringement and dissuasive. General principles of EC law apply, including the principles of legal certainty, legitimate expectations, individual assessment and non-discrimination, the principle of proportionality and equal treatment, the duty to state reasons, legality and *ne bis in idem*. However, although these principles will provide some outer limit to how fines can be imposed, they will not generate any specific method for setting fines. It follows that Member States have a wide discretion to design and apply rules on antitrust fines. The requirements of uniformity and effectiveness are very low indeed.

It is thus possible to distinguish in Articles 81 and 82 EC a number of legal concepts where the requirements of uniformity and effectiveness are absolute, including the concepts of undertaking, agreements, concerted practices, restriction of competition, effect on trade and opt-out. Moving to evidence and procedure, it may be observed that although Community competition procedure need not be duplicated nationally, there are certain minimum standards as a result of fundamental principles of Community law. In addition, effectiveness requirements determine an outer limit to what Member States can do. The reality is that Member States are pushed, if not towards a duplication of the Community competition procedure, then at least to an alignment.

On fines, however, Member States enjoy, if not total discretion, at least a very wide discretion in the design of what sanctions to employ and how to structure their policies.

Anything less than the standards just outlined will be non-compliant with Community law and may, for the purpose of the present discussion, be referred to as 'renationalisation'.

To conclude, standards for uniformity and effectiveness have been developed, but those standards are not absolute. Community law does not require identical assessments and identical treatment in all respects when competition law infringements are assessed and penalised, although a minimum standard applies. European Community competition law combines, paradoxically, a range of requirements on uniformity, which vary from very high to very low standards, depending on whether we look at substantive law, evidence, procedure or fines. The precise extent of this standard is different from point to point of the law, and will have to be further defined through case law, as indicated throughout the previous chapters. This conclusion challenges the idea that there is something that can be labelled 'renationalisation'. It should rather be a matter of ensuring average compliance with EC law.

B. Evaluating the relation between uniformity, effectiveness and efficiency in EC competition law

The concepts of uniformity and effectiveness were discussed in chapter two, where it was explained that these are integration goals, not stemming from the economic theory we apply in competition law. There is a legal–political value in uniformity and effectiveness, and also some cost savings given that it can be less expensive for national institutions to inform themselves about EC law than for companies operating across borders to inform themselves about 27 different laws. Nevertheless, the cost-saving argument is specifically only valid for cross-border business of some substance.

Very precise requirements coexist with extremely imprecise requirements on uniformity and effectiveness in EC competition law. There are precise requirements on uniformity of substantive law and (to a large extent) procedure, with large amounts of case law; there are imprecise requirements on evidence and fines. National authorities and courts may be established and operated according to national preferences. This strange combination of exact and inexact standards corresponds to EC law in general. It imposes high burdens on national authorities and courts, while at the same it is evident that we will not achieve similar outcomes. As set out in chapters two and four, the requirements on uniformity and effectiveness, and effect on trade, have evolved along integration lines and not with reference to economic theory. This means we have an economic-based substantive policy on the need to detect and deter cartel activities (and, from a larger perspective, competition restrictions), but actual enforcement is to a great extent steered by objectives that are integration-based.

This exposes certain shortcomings. First, we cannot have everything at the same time. If we want uniformity and effectiveness, we must accept that this comes at a high cost for compliance. The law has developed with great complexity, and we cannot have identical, or even similar, adjudications unless some very substantive resources are allocated. Then again, this detracts from the efficiency goal. Above all, though, uniformity and effectiveness are goals that will not help us determine how to make valid competition law enforcement priorities.

It is submitted here that enforcement policy choices must be characterised less by ideals on uniformity and effectiveness, and more by empirical observations about how detrimental different infringements are. Cartels are undoubtedly detrimental to society, but the empirical observations indicate that some cartels are worse than others. In particular, worldwide cartels generate considerably higher overcharges than domestic cartels. The present focus on uniformity and effectiveness detracts from the need to consider what are, from a welfare perspective, the most detrimental infringements. The effect on trade concept makes no difference as such between a short-lived domestic cartel in a small Member State and a worldwide conspiracy lasting for decades.

C. The role of harmonised procedure

The road towards developing common procedural standards has been tracked in chapter six. The fundamental question on procedure is whether we need more or fewer common procedural standards. Here, the step-by-step evolution of procedural rules through case law illuminates several important aspects. Rules on substantive law will not do unless combined with relatively detailed rules on procedure. The EC has not been able to manage without such, and we should not expect Member States to do so either. If there is no uniform standard, each and every Member State must make a similar journey, as have the Community courts in defining applicable procedure. Existing national procedure may not be sufficient in all respects. Adjustments in each Member State would include duplication of resources by legislators and courts.

The jurisprudence of the Court of Justice and the Court of First Instance in this field is important for another reason. Given that the case law is openly based on the ECHR, undertakings will presumably consider their rights under the Convention to have been infringed unless they obtain the same minimum protection pursuant to national law, regardless of the reach of EC law. The Community courts' jurisprudence on competition procedure can thus be seen as an accumulation of knowledge, available to the legal community, in relation to the problems that will appear on procedure and (possibly) how to solve them.

Save for a few brief rules in the former Regulation 17, the law on procedure has been developed by the Community courts as a response to an absence of legislation. Further, the Commission has not been the engine in creating these rules—on the contrary, the Commission's default position has often been that as much discretion should be left as possible to the Commission. Cases on procedure have been driven by a demand expressed by those subjected to Articles 81 and 82 EC. There is actually a need for relatively detailed rules. In fact, the experience with litigation on fines indicates a need for an even higher degree of sophistication.

Undertakings accused of cartel activity have managed to gain acceptance for the idea that they are worthy of procedural protection. The need for procedural safety to uphold confidence in the system and ultimately legitimacy has been explained in chapter six. To look at it from the entirely opposite point of view, even if we considered cartelists not worthy of procedural protection, experience shows that they will indeed litigate until a certain level of protection has been established. The costs for cartel litigation are so high that we would normally prefer, from an efficiency perspective, to have the rules settled in advance. Denying procedural rights will, at the end of the day, not work if we consider that competition law forms part of the legal system. Systemically, we have procedural safeguards built in everywhere else, and we cannot reasonably create an exemption in cartel control.

In summary, it would clearly be possible to create (or maintain) legitimate competition procedure unilaterally in each Member State, but the cost and time required means that it might be more efficient to allow for a common standard.

D. The current system is implicitly based on a case-by-case approach

For efficiency, it is crucial to make sure that competition law enforcement is made a priority, not only for the Commission but also in Member States, and that procedures are established to ensure a reasonable detection rate. The current system somehow presupposes that this will be done, and is designed to allocate the resulting cases. However, can we be certain that national authorities will carry out any antitrust control at all? As a matter of fact we cannot, since there are no EC law obligations on Member States as regards their priorities and allocation of resources for this purpose. An example may be drawn from Sweden, where the fight against cartels has been very modest since 1993, totalling just seven cases.[13] Meanwhile, some 20 Swedish companies were found by the Commission to have engaged in cartel activities, in 14 decisions adopted from 1993 through 2007.[14]

Once there is information indicating the existence of an infringement, the current system presupposes that national authorities are equipped to deal with such cases. The analysis in chapters three through seven has demonstrated how very complex this task is, and raised considerable doubts as to the real potential of building 28 well-functioning enforcers in Europe (plus three more in the EEA States, Iceland, Liechtenstein and Norway). To this should be added the difficulties associated with ensuring that courts have the necessary competence and resources to carry out legal review. This situation is not new, however—it existed prior to modernisation as well. Decentralisation did not cause this efficiency deficit, it only amplified it.

E. An enforcement deficit identified

Against the background outlined, it seems obvious that if we make uniformity and effectiveness the primary goals, there is a systemic enforcement deficit in EC competition law control. The deficit ultimately derives from two sources:

a) the fact that competition law is very complex and requires expert skills; and
b) the principle of institutional autonomy, ie Member States' power to organise the implementation, application and enforcement of Community rules in accordance with their national legal systems, which undermines any systematic efforts to ensure that adequate structures are built nationally.

[13] On the period 1993–2004, see Simonsson, Ingeborg, *Konkurrensverkets domstolsprocesser 1993–2004—En utvärdering* (Konkurrensverkets uppdragsforskningsserie 2005:2), available at http://www.kkv.se/t/IFramePage____1500.aspx., at 77.

[14] *European producers of beams* [1994] OJ L/116/1; *Cartonboard* [1994] OJ L/243/1; *Cement* [1994] OJ L/343/1; *Alloy Surcharge* [1998] OJ L/100/55; *Pre-insulated Pipe Cartel* [1999] OJ L/24/1; *Trans-Atlantic Conference Agreement* [1999] OJ L/95/1; *SAS Maersk Air* [2001] OJ L/265/15; *Industrial and medical gases* [2003] OJ L/84/1; *Carbonless paper* [2004] OJ L/115/1; *Copper plumbing tubes* [2006] OJ L/192/21; *Industrial bags*, IP/05/1065; *Bleaching chemicals*, IP/06/560; *Road bitumen NL*, IP/06/1179; *Gas insulated switchgear*, IP/07/80.

Mechanisms introduced in Regulation 1 will not overcome this obstacle, although they put some pressure on Member States.

This is not to say that EC competition law is bound to be enforced inefficiently. The point is merely that success or failure is a question of the goodwill of the Member States, because of the direct relationship between resources and outcomes in the field of competition law control. However, if all Member States actively sought to build up the necessary competence, there would be competition among 28 regulators and innumerable national courts for the best competition lawyers—and this in competition with law firms and with the institutions responsible for competition law-related regulatory control. On the whole, there seems to be an intolerable degree of duplication of institutions and expert competence within the system. The structure appears almost counterproductive. The need to ensure the goodwill of Member States enhances the need for legitimacy.

F. Conclusion: not even increased rationality of the law will cure the enforcement deficit

Two problems may be outlined. First, on the assumption that competition authorities and courts in Member States will live up to the standards just described, can we then automatically assume that the result will be efficient enforcement? Secondly, in the case of the opposite scenario (popularly referred to as 'renationalisation'), what precisely can the Commission do to rectify the problem? These two problems are in fact closely connected, because if the Commission possesses the necessary remedies to correct Member States, this will have a disciplining effect on uniformity, effectiveness and efficiency alike. Conversely, if Member States realise that they are relatively free to apply competition law as they find suitable, there may be a downward spiral.

Since there is no absolute requirement of uniformity, we must expect that outcomes will differ. Even if (against probability) everyone involved understands the concepts in Article 81 EC in the same way, there is still a certain discretion as to evidence, procedure and fines. As a result of the jurisprudence of the Community courts the gap is closing—we should expect more convergence towards the same standards, not less—but even so, similar cases will have dissimilar outcomes depending on where they are judged, and this is perfectly compatible with EC law given the leeway left to Member States on evidence, procedure and fines. Evidence that is sufficient for proving an infringement in one Member State will be considered insufficient in another. Evidence that is dismissed in one Member State will be allowed in another. Procedures will be fast and efficient in one Member State, lengthy and inconsistent in another. Fines for equally serious infringements may vary considerably between Member States, and within one and the same Member State. One Member State will allocate considerable resources to its courts and authorities for cartel control, another will have different priorities. When we add the potential for misunderstandings about the law, outcomes will be even more diverse. Uniformity is consequently illusory.

However, we can still measure the success of decentralisation by looking at *how* much average compliance is ensured, in other words how the outcomes differ. There are various *degrees* of inconsistency. Quality can then be understood as keeping discrepancies to a minimum. But what are the welfare effects of this kind of sophisticated analysis? It has already been explained that uniformity is an integration goal, not an economic goal, and there is consequently reason to ask what exactly we are trying to achieve.

G. A definition of efficient EC cartel control

As difficult as it may be to measure efficient cartel control, an attempt must be made here, encompassing the aggregate of national enforcement and the Commission's enforcement. There is no reason to assume that fundamentally different conclusions would be reached for types of infringements other than cartels. For average compliance, it is of primary importance that infringements are pursued with a reasonable detection rate (see chapter seven). This presupposes that enforcement is made a priority, and that the Commission and Member States have the necessary tools for detection. Sanctions must ensure deterrence. Efficient competition law enforcement in the EU is thus a matter of how much aggregate supervision and enforcement is produced by the Member States and the Commission. It is submitted that quality should not be measured in terms of uniformity and effectiveness, but with reference to whether the infringements that generate the highest welfare losses are exposed and deterred.

H. Has the Commission pursued a legitimate enforcement strategy against cartels?

It follows from the reasoning set out in chapter three (at I and IV) that there is a strong imperative for a prohibition against cartels and for spending public resources on cartel control. It is equally clear that cartels come in many different forms, with varying degrees of injury caused to society. More particularly, there are strong indications in economic theory that cartels with large market shares and large geographic scope cause considerably more damage than smaller, domestic cartels. Furthermore, mixed vertical and horizontal cartels have at least on one occasion been seen to produce such efficiencies that they can be exempted. Another aspect is that certain victims of cartels, such as large multinational purchasers, may be more suited than others to penalising cartels through instituting private actions for damages.

A policy to pursue cartels is therefore entirely inconclusive as such. As long as enforcement resources are limited, conscious choices must be made on *which* cartels to pursue. Given the large number of leniency applications filed in recent years, this issue has gained importance.

Looking at the Commission's enforcement policy, the experiences just mentioned have not been reflected to any great extent in administrative decision-making over the years. As set out in chapter four (at IV.A.3), about one-third of the Commission's cartel decisions have been limited to domestic cartels. Meanwhile, the acceptability of export cartels, heavily criticised in scholarly writing (see chapter four at IV.A.5), has not been addressed much at all. Even in recent years, penalties have occasionally been imposed by the Commission on cartels that appear rather insignificant if we take turnover into account.[15]

What is of great concern is consequently the absence of a clearly articulated policy on what priorities to make in cartel enforcement. The Commission and the ECN should make a joint effort to produce such a policy, possibly together with their US colleagues.

I. Supervision and enforcement through best-performing national authorities

As mentioned above and in chapter four, about one-third of the Commission's cartel decisions since the 1960s have concerned domestic cartels where there was an effect on trade. A strong argument can be made for transferring at least cases like those to Member State competition authorities, thereby freeing up the Commission's resources. Detection has improved with the introduction of modern leniency programs, which means that an increasing number of domestic cartels should now be discovered, as compared to previous decades.

It seems appropriate that these cases should be handled nationally, provided, of course, that the national authorities rise to this challenge. The Network Notice is clearly based on this view, where an authority will be considered well placed to deal with a case if *inter alia* the practice has substantial direct actual or foreseeable effects on competition within its territory.[16] However, given the complexity of the law as outlined here, it is doubtful whether all Member States will be capable of ensuring uniform, effective and efficient pursuit of even their own domestic infringements. This is not a question of having misgivings about the new Member States: experiences from Sweden, which joined the EEA in the early 1990s and then the EU, show that the authorities[17] and courts are struggling to understand EC competition law,[18] and this in a Member State which has at least average resources for competition law supervision and enforcement.

[15] *Luxemburg Brewers* [2002] OJ L/253, at 21–41; *Industrial and medical gases* [2003] OJ L/84, at 1–16.

[16] Commission Notice on Co-operation within the Network of Competition Authorities [2004] OJ C/101/43, recitals 8 –10.

[17] Simonsson, above n 13.

[18] Simonsson, Ingeborg, and Öberg, Ulf, 'Bensinkartelldomen MD 2005:7—fördragsstridig tillämpning av EG:s konkurrensrätt?, *Svensk Juristtidning* 1/2006 s 23.

As for infringements that cover more than three Member States, the Network Notice is based on the idea that the Commission will handle those cases.[19] For the reasons set out, I take the position that the Commission has been over-optimistic—it is more likely that it will have to take charge in cases involving two or more Member States, and possibly even in cases involving just one Member State. This is because of the complexity of infringements. For instance, allowing two or three Member States to divide a cartel case between them and bring an action against the undertakings present in each territory, is terribly inefficient from the point of view of procedural economy, since it would lead to doubling or trebling of procedures, without any corresponding efficiencies. A cartel would then have to be brought to justice in two or three countries. It should be clear from the analysis of substantive law in chapter four that a cartel is in essence a joint conspiracy, and it is difficult to imagine how the legal proceedings relating to one and the same cartel could be divided between several jurisdictions without duplicating costs and procedures. Admittedly this already happens because of the concurrent jurisdictions of the EU, US and other counties, but there is no reason to introduce this problem within the EU.

It has been explained in the previous subsection that it is not desirable that all Member States seek to establish competence to handle all types of cases, because of the intolerable duplication and fragmentation of institutions to which this would lead. Rather, it would seem efficient for less resource-rich Member States effectively to outsource their competition law enforcement to the Commission or to other Member States. Such a strategy was scarcely conceivable before modernisation, but now it is perfectly possible because of the co-operation established through Regulation 1 and the ECN. Member States whose resources remain limited can at least carry out investigations on behalf of the Commission or another Member State authority pursuant to Article 22 of Regulation 1, or hand over evidence in accordance with Article 12 of the regulation. I consequently envisage EC competition law enforcement around a few hubs in Europe—the Commission and a limited number of national authorities which take the lead.

Why, then, would a national authority take on cases which geographically extend to one or several other Member States? Would this not lead to complaints about unfair distribution of the burden of this workload? It is worth noticing here that law enforcement normally comes at a net cost for taxpayers. We accept these costs because of the adverse effects of allowing certain unlawful activities to go on. Interestingly, competition law enforcement may be carried out at zero cost, or even with considerable surplus for the enforcer. Although case-handling is very costly and time-consuming for an authority, the possibility of imposing substantive fines alters the equation. For instance, DG COMP levied approximately €372 million in cartel fines in 2004,[20] by far exceeding its total budget which was €83

[19] Commission Notice, above n 16, recital 14.

[20] Rough estimation gathered from DG COMP's website, http://ec.europa.eu/comm/competition/antitrust/cases/index/by_event_2004.html.

million[21]; and this even though cartel control constitutes only a small part of DG COMP's activities.

Competition law litigation in particular generates considerable indirect income for a government through the legal industry surrounding these cases. If a Member State were to manage to create an environment in which follow-on damages suits would be brought systematically, that income could increase even more. Further, the pursuit of cartels, hard-core vertical restraints and abuse of dominance is prestigious, and gives the authority (and hence its government) an aura of power. (Interestingly, competition law has the capacity to provide enforcers with status and power through the visibility, attention and influence generated.[22])

A Member State which manages to take the lead in European competition law enforcement, and to have cases allocated to it through the Network, has a unique opportunity to tether an industry to its territory. If one or more Member States were to do this, there would be more than one European hub in competition law enforcement, reducing the pressure on the Commission. However, like many other business opportunities, only those that have the necessary resources will be able to grasp this one. A critical mass is required for efficient control, as a result of the required expert competence. Cases tend to have a minimum life span of several years (if there is an appeal, 10 years or more), so the authorities and courts must have a structure in place in terms of recruitment, salaries, etc, which enables them to retain competence on a sustainable basis. If a few Member States decide to take on this challenge we will see competition law enforced by a few European centres. Otherwise, the Commission will have to step in and take responsibility for the vast majority of cases.

The conclusions just reached are somewhat undermined, however, by the fact that certain enforcement activities are carried out at great cost but without any results in terms of fines and spectacular publicity. Legal assessments of production joint ventures, technology licensing and certain vertical distribution systems fall into this category. Merger control is for the most part carried out without charging the undertakings concerned for the control activity. Similarly, competition advocacy may be of great importance for compliance with applicable rules, but does not generate any headlines or fines. It might seem unfair to allow a few authorities all the prestigious cases, while leaving the other authorities with information-gathering and competition advocacy. There may be a certain need for cross-subsidisation between income-generating activities and net cost-generating activities, as well as between prestigious and low-profile cases. On the other hand, the costs for bringing cartel cases unsuccessfully are so prohibitive that this, alone, could justify leaving some cases to the highest-performing authorities.

[21] OECD, *Annual Report on Competition Policy Developments in the European Commission*, DAF/COMP(2005) 32/EC, at 15.

[22] See Gerber, David J, *Law and Competition in Twentieth Century Europe: Protecting Prometheus* (Oxford, Oxford University Press, 1998), at xiii.

J. The role of Member States in an efficient decentralised system

In a perfect world, public competition law control in the EC should be spread out evenly across Member States, leaving only the largest and most complicated cases to the Commission. The present analysis has demonstrated that such a solution is not feasible, though, because of the complexity of the law relating to detection, investigation and litigation. Considerable administrative and judicial resources would have to be built up in each Member State if the envisaged system was to work, and this would entail the creation of a public enforcement system in which scarce resources were undesirably duplicated and fragmented.

My proposition is that we should use the best aspects of decentralisation to create an efficient, although geographically uneven, enforcement system. This could be achieved if a few resourceful Member States were to step forward and take the lead regionally in EC competition law control, taking responsibility for cases beyond what is presently envisaged in the division of work principles of the ECN. I have furthermore outlined why such a development ought to be logical, with reference to the huge amounts of fines that could be captured by successful enforcers, the prestige involved and the potentially prosperous industry relating to follow-on damages. For the Member States that do not grasp this opportunity, their role should essentially be limited to assisting other Member States and the Commission with investigations.

On the other hand, serious doubts have been developed here about the viability of uniformity and effectiveness as steering goals in EC competition law. Instead, it is submitted that the steering mechanism should be a based on an understanding about how to establish enforcement priorities. A solution along these lines implies that the role of Member States and the Commission should be to develop such understanding jointly. Member States could then be a vital source of information on how various infringements impact their territories. This in turn could generate aggregate understanding about the effects of cartels and other types of infringements, which infringements are most problematic, and how to enforce best at the lowest cost.

IV. INTEGRATION OR COMPETITION AS A POLICY BASE

A. Decentralisation meant a shift in emphasis from integration policy to welfare economics

It is submitted here that the policy shift from control of vertical restraints to cartel control represented a downgrading of the integration objectives and a corresponding upgrading of the economic theory that has (at least in the US) been allowed to shape competition law.

Cartel control in the EU can to some extent be explained with reference to the capacity of cartels to destroy integration between Member States. Notably, cartels engage in market-sharing, including bid-rigging, and exclusionary practices. This deprives customers and consumers of a wider choice of supplies, and it creates obstacles to the existence and establishment of suppliers in Member States. Nevertheless, impediments to the movement of products and services across borders caused by market-sharing, bid-rigging and exclusion are incidental, and not central to the mainstream analysis of the dangers of cartels. The real concern, according to well-established theory, underpinned by empirical studies, lies in how cartels raise prices and reduce output. This in turn causes deadweight loss, redistributes incomes from customers and consumers to cartelists, and leads to slackness and other inefficiencies in the cartelised industry. Moreover, standard cartel behaviour includes price-fixing and output restrictions, where the cross-border integration aspect is even weaker than when we look at market-sharing, bid-rigging and exclusion.

Once again, EC competition law aims at promoting integration and protecting competition. While the protection of competition may be explained by reference to economic theory and empirical economic studies, integration is a political goal. In order to protect competition, competition law must accept economics as input. In order to protect integration, there must be an openness towards politics. There are consequently two different theory bases in parallel operation: economics and politics. Switching between these, or indeed reconciling them, is not an easy thing; and when the arguments are lined up, integration will typically be disadvantaged in relation to economics. That is because economics can provide figures and examples that explain the utility of a functioning economy to citizens. Welfare economics is not necessarily easy to understand, but it can at least be reduced to rules of thumb or practical examples which most of us can understand. Integration, on the other hand, is more difficult to translate into useful examples for citizens, in so far as it relates to transactions between undertakings encompassed by Articles 81 and 82 EC. This may be compared with the policy of the free movement of persons, which is easier to grasp. Most citizens would clearly see the advantage of being able to travel, study and work across borders in the EU, to have their exams or professional experiences acknowledged throughout the EU, to receive health care in any Member State and generally have access to a larger market. The value to citizens of business cross-border integration is less immediately obvious.

The Commission has made considerable efforts to explain the value of integration in one field—car prices. Since 1992, the Commission has regularly published extensive comparisons of car prices in Member States. According to the Commission, this initiative was taken following numerous complaints from consumers about differences in car prices between Member States, and about the obstacles placed in the way of those who wished to buy in another EU country.[23] The studies demonstrate, at least indirectly, the value for consumers of integration when prices are gradually levelled out throughout the Union. If low-price oppor-

[23] Available at http://ec.europa.eu/comm/competition/sectors/motor_vehicles/prices/report.html.

tunities in one Member State can be taken advantage of by consumers, this exerts a competitive pressure on the market as a whole, at least regionally.

On the other hand, the car price reports illustrate the severe difficulties with this kind of comparison. There are still several currencies in operation in the EU. There are different regimes for VAT and other taxes. There are a large number of different brands and different car models on the market (some 25 brands and 100 models), various consumer preferences (left-hand drive, right-hand drive, etc), and even difficulties in comparing prices over time given that products develop and the EU is enlarging. Synthesising the figures and making them comprehensible is a complex business. Explaining, measuring and evaluating integration in a meaningful way is consequently very hard for the purposes of competition policy. Only the most straightforward problems can be explained comprehensibly with reference to integration, such as absolute territorial protection where customers are entirely deprived of the chance to buy products cross-border. By contrast, economics have the clear benefit of being explicable.

Primarily, cartel control must be understood as a counter-measure directed at practices that threaten welfare and economic growth. Indirectly this affects integration, but it is submitted here, in opposition to the case law,[24] that the impediments to integration that cartels cause are not so much in a 'free movement way'. Rather, efficiency losses makes the EU less attractive, while conversely, welfare and economic growth will tend to make the EU more legitimate in the eyes of its citizens and thus indirectly promote integration. Not only citizens may be expected to respond, but also companies established outside the EU when considering market entry. Furthermore, cartels take it into their own hands to redistribute wealth from customers and consumers to the cartelists. Preventing this ought to correspond to deeper notions of justice and make the EU more legitimate in a deeper sense. The connection pointed out by Majone between effectiveness, legitimacy and systemic stability, and, ultimately, the economic performance of the EU, may be recalled.[25]

B. A modernised view of the role of integration in competition law

While the Court of Justice has required uniformity in the application of Articles 81 and 82 EC, the ratio for this was not explored in depth during the modernisation process. The Commission referred in the White Paper to the maintenance of conditions of competition that are consistent throughout the Community, and referred in addition to the primacy of Community law.[26] The Economic and Social

[24] *Scandinavian Airlines System v Commission*, above n 6, at para 85.

[25] Majone, Giandomenico, 'Legitimacy and Effectiveness: a Response to Professor Michael Dougan's Review Article on Dilemmas of European Integration' (2007) 32(1) *European Law Review* 70, at 75.

[26] White Paper, *Modernisation of the Rules Implementing Articles 85 and 86 of the EC Treaty* [1999] OJ C/132/1, at 101.

Committee feared that companies would be able to exploit inconsistencies and differences to the detriment of others.[27] In its proposal for a new regulation, the Commission made reference to the creation of a more level playing field, 'limiting the scope for inconsistencies caused by differences in national competition laws'.[28] The arguments are grounded in the objective of integration.

Perhaps the Committee on Economic and Social Affairs identified the most compelling reason when it considered uniform application crucial to the goal of furthering European *competitiveness* and to ensuring that *consumers in Europe receive a fair deal.*[29] This view signifies a move away from the integration objective towards competition as generator of welfare and growth. Looking at cartel control in particular, it seems plain that industry can develop bad habits and gradually become less competitive if there are areas in the EU where cartels are allowed to harbour and flourish. This could put European industry at a disadvantage in relation to other jurisdictions with more stringent enforcement. Conversely, there could be over-deterrence regionally if authorities were too hard on horizontal or vertical co-operation, in which case pro-competitive outcomes would be prevented.

A tendency to doubt the capacity of the integration objective to provide solutions to our problems may be observed in other areas of Community law. Majone points out, with reference to the Community legislator's failure to deregulate port services (and other similar experiences), that 'even the goal of economic, let alone political, integration, can no longer be taken for granted'.[30]

The reality of decentralisation is consequently a deeper policy shift—from explaining the need for one common competition law with reference to integration, to explaining it by reference to the capacity for a competitive economy to generate growth and welfare in society. The objective of integrating Member States seldom works as theoretical underpinning for cartel control. Economic theory is a more solid theory base, and it has been demonstrated that the central case law is deterrence-based. This should not be understood as a downgrading of the integration objective; rather, we should look at the potential for competition law to enhance welfare and thus make the European Union a more attractive option for citizens and business alike. Integration is consequently important in cartel control, but in a more roundabout way. The central issue is not identical outcomes, but detection and deterrence of the most detrimental infringements. In principle, the shift may be seen as integration through economic welfare, rather than as integration through law.

[27] Opinion of the Economic and Social Committee, above n 12, at 2.3.2.3.

[28] COM(2000) 582 Final, Explanatory Memorandum, at 7.

[29] *European Parliament Report on the Proposal for a Council Regulation on the Implementation of the Rules of Competition Laid Down in Articles 81 and 82 of the Treaty* . . . Committee on Economic and Monetary Affairs, A5-0229/2001, at 21, Explanatory Statement.

[30] Majone, above n 25.

V. DISCUSSION

If EC competition law is to be viewed as legitimate in a deeper sense, the law must have rational foundations (a legitimate genesis) and be efficient by ensuring average compliance.

This research shows that the policy switch, from enforcement towards vertical restraints to cartels, is firmly based in values shared by society. A policy where hard-core horizontal restraints are actively pursued corresponds to established economic theory and to deeper notions prevailing in society. There is also wide support theoretically for the need to employ efficient sanctions. Nevertheless, once the cartel concept is studied in detail, it emerges that it comprises a variety of different behaviours, not all of which are always (or almost always) viewed as entirely anticompetitive. This is not necessarily a problem. Comparative studies of US law demonstrate that we have little need for an absolute category of per se infringements, instead relying on a continuum of 'per se', 'quick look', and a more elaborate balancing of pro- competitive and anticompetitive aspects.

A closer look at EC law on cartels reveals two central themes. One is that the Community courts have prohibited price-fixing, market-sharing and quotas without providing any elaborate reasons for this policy choice. The other theme is that, when there is reasoning in the judgments to support the law, a number of different sources are used to obtain or increase legitimacy. Integration objectives make an appearance every so often. The most obvious pattern is heavy reliance on previous case law. These sources appear somewhat over-exploited, and one may ask whether legitimacy can be increased through active use of *other* sources.

The principles enshrined in the ECHR have been relied on, and very successfully, to find legitimacy for the development in case law of a sophisticated set of procedural rules and fundamental rights. The present level of sophistication, however, indicates that a breaking point has been reached where the measures must be seen as independent creations of the Community courts rather than outflows of the principles enshrined in the Convention. Further, the evaluation of the law on evidence indicates the necessity to balance a fundamental rights approach with an economic-based deterrence approach, and how this is actually done already by the Community courts.

Economic theory is used in an indirect way in EC cartel control, especially in the formation of policies and in the choice of what cases to bring action against. Reliance on economic theory as a legitimacy base in the judgments could greatly improve our understanding of competition law. I have tried to illustrate how use of a deterrence perspective can increase our understanding of how to attribute liability within a group of companies (chapter four at VI), the notion of effect on trade (chapter four at IV.B), and how an economic perspective does not detract from the goal of integration (chapter eight at III.B).

Legitimacy may also be found in comparative law, especially US antitrust law. If used actively, this source could increase legitimacy further. Substantive EC law on cartels has developed very much in line with US law, and this is hardly a coincidence. Unlike the law on abuse of dominance, where the differences between EC law and US law are frequently pointed out in scholarly writing, there seems to be no great discrepancy in principle between the systems when it comes to cartels. Nevertheless, we can see that the Court of Justice declined to follow US law on per se prohibitions in *Polypropylene.*

Most of all, a higher level of *participation* could be obtained if the judgments of the Community courts were more focused on an instructive dialogue with all Member States on the theoretical foundations of competition law. Increased legitimacy could be won here, regardless of whether the Community courts justify their assessments with reference to economic theory, legal theory or comparative law.

The analysis aimed at sourcing a legitimate genesis of EC cartel control at least shows how the legitimacy concern is addressed by the Community courts and the Commission, although efforts could be more active, systematic and imaginative. With reference to legal theory, we can see that the need for legitimacy and its role is increasing constantly in EC law.

On enforcement, there is an obvious legitimacy concern in so far as the requirements of uniformity and effectiveness (integration through law objectives), in combination with the great complexity of decades of case law, impose very high administrative costs for compliance at national level, or, in the alternative, may be expected to generate a legitimacy debate because of low compliance. Hypothetically, difficulties could be solved if Member States were to allocate some very substantial resources to their competition authorities and courts, to ensure the necessary level of know-how. However, there is no avenue through which the Community can accomplish such a strategy: the principle of institutional autonomy will prevent a central policy aimed at forcing Member States to organise their authorities and courts in certain ways, or at forcing them to make specific enforcement priorities. Furthermore, loyal implementation in Member States will have counterproductive outcomes, since it will lead to an even more intolerable fragmentation and duplication of resources. It is presently difficult to see how decentralisation will ensure average compliance, especially since the incomplete harmonisation of evidentiary standards will undermine efforts at producing consistent outcomes.

Distribution of work within the ECN could untie the knot. This requires a few Member States to step forward and take special responsibility for the EU's competition law enforcement, *or* the Commission will have to be the central enforcer, a task that will require more resources than are available today. A change in the institutional arrangements would not only remedy the malfunctions generated by the fragmented institutional structure maintained by the modernisation, it would also solve the deep-rooted problems with double procedural standards resulting from the combination of Community law and national procedure. Increased legitimacy as regards the 'roots' of the law through better reasoning in the judgments of the Community courts, and by the Commission, would in turn increase the likelihood that Member States would see cartel control as a priority.

Then again, what we really need is not so much an elaborate institutional arrangement, but a basic understanding of how to establish correct enforcement priorities in EC competition law. Empirical observations indicate that worldwide cartels represent the major problem from a welfare perspective, whereas domestic cartels are at least to some degree less problematic. The present case law on effect on trade is entirely unhelpful as a point of reference for enforcement priorities. It could be replaced by a deterrence-based effect on trade theory (see chapter four, section IV.B,), without compromising other Community law objectives. At least, we ought to work to obtain more empirically underpinned observations about which infringements are the most detrimental, and develop an awareness of how to focus enforcement.

While this study has concentrated on cartel control, it is of relevance to competition law decentralisation as a whole. Let us remember that hard-core horizontal restraints are supposedly the easy cases when it comes to legal assessment, as opposed to the delicate balancing of pro-competitive and negative effects and market power undertaken for joint production, intellectual property licensing and other agreements, and abuse of dominance.

VI. FINAL CONCLUSION

Law that is rational when applied by one central enforcer may make less sense when its application is outsourced to 27 Member States. Member State authorities and courts do not have the institutional memory established by the Commission and the Community courts, and must build up competence from scratch. European Community law on cartels, developed over a 40-year period, must in addition merge with national institutional and procedural law. As quantified in this work, the body of EC law applicable to cartels is vast, encompassing far more than a few principles flowing from Article 81 EC.

It has been demonstrated here that there are, in Community competition law, very high requirements on uniform application of the law, prevalent when we look at substance and procedural principles flowing from fundamental rights, in combination with certain minimum evidentiary standards. On the other hand, there are hardly any common standards at all on institutions and sanctions. This curious combination means that even if we assume loyal and correct application, cartel cases in Member States will generate dissimilar outcomes.

One may ask whether we need *more* common standards in order to obtain identical, or at least similar, treatment of comparable cases?

Conventional thinking places great emphasis on the need for EC competition law to be applied uniformly in all Member States. The goal of coherency (uniformity), coupled with the principle of effectiveness, is an integration objective, the traditional 'integration through law' approach. It has been shown comprehensively, however, that integration in this wide sense is an objective that comes into direct conflict with the need for efficiency in EC cartel control. As a result of the wide application of the integration-driven effect on trade concept and the very detailed requirements prescribed by EC law on both substance and procedure, quality, if measured with reference to uniformity, comes at a high administrative cost. If uniformity is the leading objective then we can expect less cartel control at a higher cost. Institutional arrangements provide for a considerable number of small authorities rather than the large-scale institutional vehicles necessary to take up the challenge presented by the complexity of the law.

Economic theory places emphasis on detection and deterrence to fight cartels, rather than on uniform application of the law. The time and effort spent on every case is important here—if authorities are bogged down with vast cases that last for a decade or more, fewer infringements will be addressed with available resources. Accordingly, efficiency concerns point in the direction of identifying the infringements that are most detrimental to society, and then letting the most sustainable and efficient competition authority (whether that is the Commission or a Member State authority) deal with them, rather than expecting every Member State to investigate and litigate cartel cases. Not only will such a strategy enhance detection and deterrence, but the chances of achieving consistent application of the law must also be expected to have a direct causal connection to the competence, capacity and sustainability of the authority in charge.

Put in terms of legitimacy, we have a paradoxical combination of high empirical legitimacy for uniform application of the law, but a shortage of normative rationality for uniformity. The law as it stands is too complex to allow uniform application in all Member States, so average compliance cannot be guaranteed if uniformity is its yardstick. It is unrealistic to think that the decentralisation should be amended, especially so soon after its entry into force—in the absence of legislative proposals by the Commission, even adjustments to the effect on trade concept are out of reach, given how settled the case law is—but we can use the available resources in a better way. One such way is to use the relative freedom that remains for authorities in setting enforcement priorities. This must be coupled with a very focused allocation of cases to the highest-performing authorities. Lastly, we must look for empirical data on the presence of the most detrimental competition law infringements, in order to direct enforcement against those.

This suggested model of enforcement, which places emphasis on the need to detect and deter the most detrimental infringements, contrasts theoretically with the prevailing view under which enforcement is supposed to be carried out locally to a large extent, and where uniformity in application of the law is of central importance. The model is on the other hand in line with contemporary views on the importance of ensuring legitimacy for the EU through common goals such as increased competitiveness.

Bibliography

ARTICLES

Accetto, Matej, and Zleptnig, Stefan, 'The Principle of Effectiveness: Rethinking Its Role in Community Law' [2005] *European Public Law* 375

Adhar, Rex, 'Consumers, Redistribution of Income and the Purpose of Competition Law' (2002) 23(7) *ECLR* 341

Alfter, M and Young, J, 'Economic Analysis of Cartels—Theory and Practice' (2005) 26(10) *ECLR* 546

Alexander, Barbara J, 'The Impact of Exchange Rate Levels and Changes on International Cartels: Implications for Liability and Overcharge' (2003) 70(3) *Antitrust Law Journal* 819

Amcham EU, Position Paper on the Modernization Package, 10 December 2003, available on http://www.eucommittee.be/Pops/competitionpop0304.htm

American Bar Association, Joint Comment of the American Bar Association's Section of Antitrust Law and Section of International Law and Practice on Draft European Commission Notices and Draft Regulation Implementing Regulation 1/2003, December 2003, available at http://www.abanet.org/antitrust/at-comments/2003/2003.shtml

Ameye, Evelyne M, 'The Interplay between Human Rights and Competition Law in the EU' (2004) 25(6) *ECLR* 332

Andreangeli, Arianna, 'The Protection of Legal Professional Privilege in EU Law and the Impact of the Rules of Exchange of Information within the European Competition Network on the Secrecy of Communication between Lawyer and Client: one step forward, two steps back?' (2005) 2(1) *The Competition Law Review* 31

Arbault, Francois, 'La politique de la Commission en matière d'amendes antitrust recent développements, perspectives d'avenir' (2003) *Competition Policy Newsletter*, No 2, Summer, 1

Ashenfelter, Orley, and Graddy, Kathryn, 'Anatomy of the Rise and Fall of a Price-fixing Conspiracy: Auctions at Sotheby's and Christie's' (2005) 1(1) *Journal of Competition Law and Economics* 3

Ashurst, Study on the conditions of claims for damages in case of infringement of EC competition rules, 31 August 2004, available on http://ec.europa.eu/comm/competition/antitrust/others/actions_for_damages/study.html

Aviram, Amital and Tor, Avishalom, 'Overcoming Impediments to Information Sharing' (2004) [55] *Alabama LawReview* Winter 231

Baer, William J, Frazer, Tim, Gyselen, Luc and Liss, Frank, 'International leniency regimes: new developments and their strategic implications' [2006] *Global Competition Review, The Antitrust Review of the Americas* 61

Bailey, David, 'Standard of Proof in EC Merger Proceedings: A Common Law Perspective' (2003) 40(4) *CML Rev* 845

Barbier de La Serre, Eric, 'Procedural Justice in the European Community Case-law concerning the Rights of the Defence: Essentialist and Instrumental Trends' [2006] *European Public Law* 225

Van Barlingen, Bertus, and Barennes, Marc, 'The European Commission's 2002 Leniency Notice in practice' (2005) *Competition Policy Newsletter* No 3, Autumn, 6

Becker, Florian, 'The Case of Export Cartel Exemptions: Between Competition and Protectionism' (2007) 3(1) *Journal of Competition Law and Economics* 97

Becker, Gary, 'Crime and Punishment: An Economic Approach' (1968) 76(2) *Journal of Political Economy* 169

Bernitz, Ulf, 'Gemenskapsrätten och lagförarbeten', *Juridisk Tidskrift* 2000–01 s 698

Bilmes, Jack, and Woodbury, John, 'Deterrence and Justice: Setting Civil Penalties in the Federal Trade Commission' (1991) 14 *Research in Law and Economics* 191

Bissocoli, Eugenio F, 'Trade Associations and Information Exchange under US and EC Competition Law' (2000) 23(1) *World Competition* 79

Black, Oliver, 'Per Se Rules and Rules of Reason: What Are They?' (1997) 18(3) *ECLR* 145

—— 'Concerted Practices, Joint Action and Reliance' (2003) 24(5) *ECLR* 219

—— 'What is an Agreement' (2003) 24(10) *ECLR* 50

—— 'Communication, concerted practices and the oligopoly problem' (2005) 1(2) *European Competition Journal* 341

Blake, Stephen, and Schnichels, Dominik, 'Leniency Following Modernisation: Safeguarding Europe's Leniency Programmes' (2004) 25(12) *ECLR* 765

Bos, Iwan, and Schinkel, Maarten Pieter, 'On the Scope for the European Commission's 2006 Fining Guidelines under the Legal Maximum Fine' (2006) 2(4) *Journal of Competition Law and Economics* 673

Braithwaite, John, 'White Collar Crime' in Geis *et al*, *White-Collar Crime, Classic and Contemporary Views*, 3rd edn (New York, The Free Press, 1995)

Broberg, Morten P, 'Access to Documents: A General Principle of Community Law' (2002) 27(2) EL Rev 194

Brown, Christopher, and Hardiman, Donogh, 'The Extent of the Community Institutions' Duty to Co-operate with National Courts—Zwartfeld Revisited' (2004) 25(5) *ECLR* 299

Bryant, Peter G, and Eckard, E Woodrow, 'Price Fixing: The probability of getting caught' (1991) 3 *Review of Economics and Statistics* 531

Burnley, Richard, 'Interstate Trade Revisited—The Jurisdictional Criterion for Articles 81 and 82 EC' (2002) 23(5) *ECLR* 217

Calvani, Terry, 'Devolution and Convergence in Competition Enforcement' (2003) 24(9) *ECLR* 415

Calviño, Nadia, 'Public Enforcement in the EU: Deterrent Effect and Proportionality of Fines' in Ehlermann, C D, and Atanasiu, I (eds), *European Competition Law Annual 2006: Enforcement of Prohibition of Cartels* (Oxford, Hart Publishing, 2007)

Camilli, Enrico Leonardo, 'Optimal Fines in Cartel Cases and the Actual EC Fining Policy' (2006) 29(4) *World Competition* 575

Capobianco, Antonio, 'Information Exchange under EC Competition Law' (2004) 41(5) *CML Rev* 1247

Castellot, Miguel Ángel Pena, 'The application of the guidelines on fines: an overview' (2000) *Competition Policy Newsletter* No 3 October 5

Clarke, Julian L, and Evenett, Simon J, 'The deterrent effects of national anticartel laws: evidence from the international vitamins cartel' (2003) *The Antitrust Bulletin*, Fall, 689

Coleman, James William, 'Motivation and Opportunity, Understanding the Causes of White-Collar Crime' in Geis *et al*, *White-Collar Crime, Classic and Contemporary Views*, 3rd edn (New York, The Free Press, 1995), at 361

Collins, Michael M, 'The Burden and Standard of Proof in Competition Litigation and Problems of Judicial Evaluation' (2004) *ERA Forum Scripta Juris Europaei* No 1, 66

Connor, John M, and Bolotova, Yuliya, 'Cartel overcharges: Survey and Meta-Analysis', draft 3 October 2005

Connor, John M, and Lande, Robert H, 'How High do Cartels Raise Prices? Thinking Creatively About Remedies' (2005) 80(2) *Tulane Law Review* 513

—— 'The size of cartel overcharges: Implications for US and EU fining policies' (2006) 51(4) *The Antitrust Bulletin*, Winter, 983

Connor, John M, and Helmers, C Gustav, 'Statistics on Modern Private International Cartels, 1990–2005', The American Anitrust Institute AAI Working Paper No 07-01, available at www.antitrustinstitute.org/Archives/11307.ashx

Coyet, Johan, Fellenius-Omnell, Caroline, and Landström, Charlotte, 'Modernizing EC Competition Law: Will a System of Parallel Application of EC and National Competition Laws Ensure Convergence' in Hawk (ed), *International Antitrust Law & Policy: Fordham Corporate Law* (New York, Juris Publishing, 2002)

Cumming, G, 'Procedural comment: Privilege against self-incrimination' (2005) 26(7) *ECLR* 375

Davidow, Joel, 'United States Antitrust Developments in the New Millenium' (2001) 24(3) *World Competition* 425

—— 'Recent US Antitrust Developments of International Relevance' (2004) 27(3) *World Competition* 407

—— 'Recent Developments in US Antitrust' (2005) 28(3) *World Competition* 299

Dekeyser, Kris and Gauer, Céline, 'The New Enforcement System for Articles 81 and 82 and the Rights of the Defence', in Hawk (ed), *International Antitrust Law & Policy: Fordham Corporate Law* (New York, Juris Publishing, 2004).

Dekeyser, Kris, and Jaspers, Maria, 'A New Era of ECN Cooperation—Achievements and Challenges with Special Focus on Work in the Leniency Field' (2007) 30(1) *World Competition* 3

Delicostopoulos, John S, 'Towards European Procedural Primacy in National Legal Systems' (2003) *European Law Journal*, Vol 9, No 5, December, 599

Desai, Kiran, 'Reverse Non-Competes under EC Competition Law' (1997) 18(3) *ECLR* 178

—— 'Limitations on the Use of Economic Analysis in EC Competition Law Proceedings: Part 1' (2002) 23(10) *ECLR* 524

Dimitrakopoulos, Dionyssis G, 'The Transposition of EU Law: "Post-Decisional Politics" and Institutional Autonomy' (2001) *European Law Journal*, Vol 7, No 4, December, 442

Dobson, Paul W, 'Buyer-Driven Vertical Restraints', *The Pros and Cons of Vertical Restraints* (Stockholm, Konkurrensverket, 2008), 102

Dougan, Michael,' "And Some Fell on Stony Ground"—A Review of Giandomenico Majone's Dilemmas of European Integration' (2006) 31(6) EL Rev 865

Dubrow, Ben, 'The Passing on Defence: An Economist's Perspective' (2003) 24(6) *ECLR* 238

Durand, Benoît, Galarza, Andrés Font, and Mehta, Kirtikumar, 'The Interface between Competition Policy and International Trade Liberalisation. Looking into the Future: Applying a New Virtual Anti-Trust Standard' (2004) 27(1) *World Competition* 3

Dutheil de la Rochère, Jaqueline, 'The EU and the individual: Fundamental rights in the draft constitutional treaty' (2004) 41(2) *CML Rev* 345

Dyekjaer-Hansen, Karen, and Hoegh, Katja, 'Succession of Liability for Competition Law Infringements with Special Reference to Due Diligence and Warranty Claims' (2003) 24(5) *ECLR* 203

Eilmansberger, Thomas, 'The relationship between rights and remedies in EC law: In search of the missing link' (2004) 41(5) *CML Rev* 1199

—— 'How to distinguish good from bad competition under Article 82 EC: In search of clearer and more coherent standards for anti-competitive abuses' (2005) 42(1) *CML Rev* 129

Eilmansberger, Thomas, and Thyri, Peter, 'Third-Country Antitrust Sanctions and EC Law—Comments on the Advocate-General's Opinion in C-308/04 P SGL Carbon/Commission' (2006) 27(7) *ECLR* 39

Epstein, Richard A, *Free Markets under Siege—Cartels, Politics and Social Welfare*, Thirty-third Wincott Lecture, 13 October 2003, The Institute of Economic Affairs

Erdal, Ugur, 'Burden and Standard of Proof in Proceedings under the European Convention' (2001) EL Rev 26 Supp (Human Rights)

Evans, David S. 'How Economists Can Help Courts Design Competition Rules: An EU and US Perspective' (2005) 28(1) *World Competition* 93

Evenett, Simon.J, Levenstein, Margaret C, and Suslow, Valerie Y, 'International Cartel Enforcement: Lessons from the 1990s' (2001) *World Economy*, Sept, 1221

Fisher, Franklin M, 'Economic Analysis and Antitrust Damages' (2006) 29(3) *World Competition* 383

Flynn, Leo, 'Enforcement of EC Law: Protection of Individual's Rights in National Courts' (2007) 10(2) *Europarättslig Tidskrift* 294

Forbes Pirie, Mia, 'The Complainant in EC Competition Law' (2000) 23(1) *World Competition* 107

Fortsakis, Theodore, 'Principles Governing Good Administration' [2005] *European Public Law* 207

Fox, Eleanor M, 'State Action in Comparative Context: What if Parker v Brown Were Italian?' in Hawk (ed), *International Antitrust Law & Policy: Fordham Corporate Law* (New York, Juris Publishing, 2003) 463

Funk, Patricia, and Kugler, Peter, 'Identifying Efficient Crime-Combating Policies by VAR Models: The Example of Switzerland' (2003) 21(4) *Contemporary Economic Policy* 525

Geradin, Damien, 'Development of European Regulatory Agencies', (2004) (11) *Columbia Journal of European Law* 1

Geradin, Damien, and Henry, David, 'The EC fining policy for violations of competition law: An empirical review of the Commission decisional practice and the Community Courts' judgments' (2005) 1(2) *European Competition Journal* 401

Gerber, David J, 'Consistent Application of Competition Laws Across System Borders: Rethinking the Issues' in Andersson (ed), *Parallel and Conflicting Enforcement of Law* (Stockholm, Norstedts, 2005)

Gerber, David J, and Cassinis, Paolo, 'The Modernisation of European Community Competition Law: Achieving Consistency in Enforcement: Part 1' (2006) 27(1) *ECLR* 10

Gerber, David J, and Cassinis, Paolo, 'The Modernisation of European Community Competition Law: Achieving Consistency in Enforcement: Part 2' (2006) 27(2) *ECLR* 51

van Gerven, W, 'Remedies for Infringements of Fundamental Rights' [2004] *European Public Law* 261

Giannakopoulos, Themistoklis, 'The Right to be Orally Heard by the Commission in Antitrust, Merger, Anti-dumping/Anti-subsidies and State Aid Community Procedures' (2001) 24(4) *World Competition* 541

Gilliams, Hans M, 'Modernisation: From Policy to Practice' (2003) 28(4) EL Rev 451

Glazer, Kenneth L, 'Concerted Refusals to Deal under Section 1 of the Sherman Act' (2002)70(1) *Antitrust Law Journal* 1

Grout, Paul A, and Sonderegger, Silvia, 'Predicting cartels', Economic discussion paper, March 2005, Office of Fair Trading

Guersent, Olivier, 'The Fight against Secret Horizontal Agreement in the EC Competition Policy' in Hawk (ed), *International Antitrust Law & Policy: Fordham Corporate Law* (New York, Juris Publishing, 2003) 43

Gustafsson, Magnus, 'What are the prospects for enhanced private antitrust litigation? A Swedish perspective' (2005) 30(4) EL Rev 490

Habermas, Jürgen, 'Towards a Communication-Concept of Rational Collective Will-Formation. A Thought Experiment' (1989) *Ratio Juris* (2) 144

Hanh Rosochowicz, Patricia, 'The Appropriateness of Criminal Sanctions in the Enforcement of Competition Law' (2004) 25(12) *ECLR* 752

Harding, Christopher, and Gibbs, Alun, 'Why go to court in Europe? An analysis of cartel appeals 1995–2004' (2005) 30(3) EL Rev 349

Henriksson, Lars, 'I kartell mot sig själv', *Juridisk Tidskrift* 2004–05 nr 2 s 432

Hildebrand, Doris, 'The European School in EC Competition Law' (2002) 25(1) *World Competition* 3

Hofmann, Herwig C H, 'Negotiated and non-negotiated administrative rule-making: The example of EC competition policy' (2006) 43(1) *CML Rev* 153

Holmes, Katherine, 'Public Enforcement of Private Enforcement? Enforcement of Competition Law in the EC and UK' (2004) 25(1) *ECLR* 25

Holmes, William C, *Antitrust Law Handbook*, Database updated January 2006

Hoseinian, Foad, 'Passing-on Damages and Community Antitrust Policy—An Economic Background' (2005) 28(1) *World Competition* 3

Hutchings, Michael, 'The Competition between Law and Economics' (2004) 25(1) *ECLR* 531

Høegh, Katja, 'Succession of Liability for Competition Law Infringements—the Cement Judgment' (2004) 25(9) *ECLR* 534

Jacobs, Francis G, 'The evolution of the European legal order' (2004) 41(2) *CML Rev* 303

—— 'Enforcing Community Rights and Obligations in National Courts: Striking the Balance' in Lonbay and Biondi (eds), *Remedies for Breach of EC Law* (New York, Wiley, 1997)

Jaeckel, Liv, 'The Duty to Protect Fundamental Rights in the European Community' (2003) 28(4) EL Rev 508

Jenny, Frédéric, 'Competition Law and Policy: Global Governance Issues' (2003) 26(4) *World Competition* 609

—— 'Cartels and Collusion in Developing Countries: Lessons from Empirical Evidence' (2006) 29(1) *World Competition* 109

Jones, Clifford A, 'Private Antitrust Enforcement in Europe: A Policy Analysis and Reality Check' (2004) 27(1) *World Competition* 13

Joshua, Julian M, 'Balancing the Public Interests: Confidentiality, Trade Secrets and Disclosure of Evidence in EC Competition Procedures' (1994) 15(2) *ECLR* 68

Joshua, Julian M, and Camesasca, Peter D, 'EC fining policy against cartels after the Lysine rulings: the subtle secrets of x', *The European Antitrust Review 2004* (2004 Global Competition Review)

Joshua, Julian M, and Jordan, Sarah, 'Combinations, Concerted Practices and Cartels: Adopting the Concept of Conspiracy in European Community Competition Law' (2004) 24(3) *Northwestern Journal of International Law and Business* 647

Kaczorowska, Alina, 'The Power of a National Competition Authority to Disapply National Law Incompatible with EC Law—and its Practical Consequences' (2004) 25(9) *ECLR* 591
Killick, James, 'Is it now time for a single Europe-wide fining policy? An analysis of the fining policies of the Commission and the Member States' (2005) Working Paper Number 07, *Competition Law Scholars' Forum (CLaSF) Working Paper Series*, first presented at the CLaSF Workshop on 7 April 2005
Klein, Joel I, speech at the International Anti-Cartel Enforcement Conference, 30 September 1999, available at http://www.usdoj.gov/atr/public/speeches/3727.htm
Kleis, Maria, and Nicolaides, Phedon, 'The Concept of Undertaking in Education and Public Health Systems' [2006] *European State Aid Law Quarterly* 3
Kokkoris, Ioannis, 'Purchase Price Fixing: A Per Se Infringement' (2007) 28(9) *ECLR* 473
Kon, Stephen, 'The Commission's White Paper on Modernisation: The Need for Procedural Harmonisation' in Hawk (ed), *International Antitrust Law & Policy: Fordham Corporate Law* (New York, Juris Publishing, 1999) 233
Kovacic, William E, 'Achieving better practices in the design of competition policy institutions' (2005) 50(3) *The Antitrust Bulletin* 511
Kristof, Milan, 'Developments in cartel case-law: Commission decisions and Court judgments of 2005' (2006) *Competition Policy Newsletter*, No 1, Spring, 57
Landes, William M, 'Optimal Sanctions for Antitrust Violations' (1983) 50 *University of Chicago Law Review* 652
Lane, Robert E, 'Why Businessmen Violate the Law' in Geis (ed), *White Collar Crime* (New York, Atherton Press, 1968)
Langenfeld, James A, and Silvia, Louis, 'Federal Trade Commission horizontal restraint cases: an update' (2004) 49(3) *The Antitrust Bulletin* 521
Lasok QC, K P E , 'When is an Undertaking not an Undertaking' (2004) 25(7) *ECLR* 383
Lefevre, Silvère, 'Interpretative communications and the implementation of Community law at national level' (2004) 29(6) EL Rev 808
Legal, Hubert, 'Standards of Proof and Standards of Judicial Review in EU Competition Cases' in Hawk (ed), *International Antitrust Law & Policy: Fordham Corporate Law* (New York, Juris Publishing, 2005) Ch 5
Leibenstein, Harvey, 'Allocative Efficiency vs. "X-Efficiency" ' (1966) 56 *American Economic Review* 392
Lenaerts, Koen, 'Fundamental Rights in the European Union' (2000) 25(6) EL Rev 575
—— '"In the union we trust": Trust-enhancing principles of Community law' (2004) 41(2) *CML REV* 317
Lenaerts, Koen, and Gerard, Damien, 'Decentralisation of EC Competition Law Enforcement: Judges in the Frontline' (2004) 27(3) *World Competition* 313
Leslie, Christopher R, 'Trust, Distrust and Antitrust' (2004) 82(3) *TexasLawReview* 515
—— 'Antitrust damages and deadweight loss' (2006) 51(3) *The Antitrust Bulletin* 521
Levenstein, Margaret C, and Suslow, Valerie Y, 'What Determines Cartel Success?' available at http://papers.ssrn.com/sol3/papers.cfm?abstract_id=299415
—— 'Contemporary international cartels and developing countries: Economic effects and implications for competition policy' (2004) 71(3) *Antitrust Law Journal* 801
—— 'The Changing International Status of Export Cartel Exemptions' (2005) 20(3) *American University International Law Review* 785
—— 'Cartel bargaining and monitoring: The role of information sharing' (2006) *The Pros and Cons of Information Sharing*, Konkurrensverket, 35–74, available at www.konkurrensverket.se

—— *Determinants of International Cartel Duration and the Role of Cartel Organization*, Ross School of Business Working Paper 1052, available at http://papers.ssrn.com/sol3/papers.cfm?abstract_id=936912

Levin, Nickolai G, 'The Nomos and Narrative of Matsushita' (2005) 73 *Fordham Law Review* 1627

Levy, Nicholas, and O'Donoghue, Robert, 'The EU Leniency Programme Comes of Age' (2004) 27(1) *World Competition* 75

Lienemeyer, Max, and Waelbroeck, Denis, case-comment on Case C-94/00, Roquette Frères SA (2003) 40(6) *CML Rev* 1481

Lind, Robert, and Walker, Mike, 'The (Mis)use of Profitability Analysis in Competition Law Cases' (2004) 25(7) *ECLR* 439

Louveaux, Bertrand, and Gilbert, Paul, 'The Standard of Proof under the Competition Act' (2005) 26(3) *ECLR* 173

Lowe, Philip, 'What's the future for cartel enforcement', speech presented at the conference *Understanding Global Cartel Enforcement*, Conrad Hotel, Brussels, 11 February 2003

—— 'Commission's enforcement record in 2006', Competition Policy Newsletter 2007 No 1, Spring

MacCulloch, Angus, 'Honesty, Morality and the Cartel Offence' (2007) 28(6) *ECLR* 355

Magney, John S, and Anderson, Reyn, C, 'Recent Developments in Criminal Enforcement of US Antitrust Laws' (2004) 27(1) *World Competition* 101

Majone, Giandomenico, 'Legitimacy and Effectiveness: A Response to Professor Michael Dougan's Review Article on Dilemmas of European Integration' (2007) 32(1) EL Rev 70

Marsden, Philip, and Whelan, Peter, '"Consumer detriment" and its Application in EC and UK Competition Law' (2006) 27(10) *ECLR* 569

Mateus, Abel M, 'Why Should National Competition Authorities be Independent and How Should They be Accountable?' (2007) 3(1) *European Competition Journal* 17

McCurdy, Gregory V S, 'The Impact of Modernisation of the EU Competition Law System on the Courts and Private Enforcement of the Competition Laws: A Comparative Perspective' (2004) 25(8) *ECLR* 509

McDonell, Brett H, and Farber, Daniel A, 'Are efficient antitrust rules always optimal?' (2003) 48(3) *The Antitrust Bulletin* 807

McElwee, Donal, 'Should the European Commission adopt "Amnesty Plus" in its Fight against Hard-Core Cartels?' (2004) 25(9) *ECLR* 558

McNutt, Patrick A, 'Taxonomy of Non-Market Economics for European Competition Law' (2003) 26(2) *World Competition* 303

Meese, Alan J, 'Farewell to the Quick Look: redefining the Scope and Content of the Rule of Reason' (2000) 68 *Antitrust Law Journal* 461

Meiklejohn, D Stuart, 'You can't legislate perfection: The virtues of experimentation in the design of antitrust enforcement regimes' in Hawk (ed), *International Antitrust Law & Policy: Fordham Corporate Law* (New York, Juris Publishing, 2003) 55

Montesa, Aitor, and Givaja, Ángel, 'When Parents Pay for their Children's Wrongs: Attribution of Liability for EC Antitrust Infringements in Parent–Subsidiary Scenarios' (2006) 29(4) *World Competition* 555

Monti, Giorgio, 'Article 81 and Public Policy' (2002) 39(5) *CML Rev* 1057

—— 'Anti Competitive Agreements: The Innocent Party's Right to Damages' (2002) 27(3) EL Rev 282

Monti, Mario, 'The Modernisation of EC Antitrust Policy, opening speech', in Ehlermann and Atanasiu (eds), *European Competition Law Annual 2000: The Modernisation of EC Antitrust Policy* (Oxford, Hart Publishing, 2001)

—— 'Why should we be concerned with cartels and collusive behaviour', *Fighting Cartels—why and how?* (Stockholm, Konkurrensverket, 2001), available at www.kkv.se

Motta, Massimo, 'On Cartel Deterrence and Fines in the European Union' (2008) 29(4) *ECLR* 209

Muris, Timothy J, 'The Rule of Reason after California Dental'(2000) 68 *Antitrust Law Journal* 527

Navarro Varona, Edurne, 'Interim Measures in Competition Cases before the European Commission and Courts' (2002) 23(19) *ECLR* 512

Nazzini, Renato, 'Some Reflections on the Dynamics of the Due Process Discourse in EC Competition Law' (2005) 2(1) *The Competition Law Review*, 5

—— 'Article 81 EC between time present and time past: A normative critique of "Restriction of competition" in EU law' (2006) 43(2) *CML REV* 497

Neven, Damien J, '"Collusion" under Article 81 and the Merger Regulation', in *Fighting cartels—why and how* (Stockholm, Konkurrensverket, 2001), available at www.kkv.se

Nordlander, Kristina, case annotation on Joined Cases C-189/02 P, C-202/02 P, C-205/02 P to C-208/02 P and C-213/02 P, *Dansk Rorindustri and other v Commission*, (2006) 43(2) *CML Rev* 571

Öberg, Ulf, Några anteckningar om användningen av förarbeten inom gemenskapsrätten, *Juridisk Tidskrift* 2000–01, s 492

OECD, Using Leniency to Fight Hard Core Cartels (*OECD Observer* September 2001)

OECD, 'Illustrative Cartel Cases by non-OECD Jurisdictions' (2004) *OECD Journal of Competition Law and Policy*, Vol 6, Nos 1 & 2

OECD *Annual Report on Competition Policy Developments in the United States from October 1, 2004, to September 30, 2005* (OECD, 2006, DAF/COMP (2006)7/07), 11, available at http://www.ftc.gov/bc/anncompreports.htm

OECD Global Forum on Competition, *Prosecuting Cartels without Direct Evidence of Agreement* (OECD, 2006, DAF/COMP/GF/(2006)7)

Odudu, Okeoghene, 'Interpreting Article 81(1): Object as Subjective Intention' (2001) 26(1) EL Rev 60

—— 'Interpreting Article 81(1): Demonstrating Restrictive Effect' (2001) 26(3) EL Rev 261

—— 'Interpreting Article 81(1): The Object Requirement Revisited' (2001) 26(4) EL Rev 379

—— 'A New Economic Approach to Article 81(1)' (2002) 27(1) EL Rev 100

—— 'The Role of Specific Intent in Section 1 of the Sherman Act: A Market Power Test?' (2002) 25(4) *World Competition* 463

—— 'Article 81(3), Discretion and Direct Effect' (2002) 23(1) *ECLR* 17

O'Loughlin, Rosemary, 'EC Competition Rules and Free Movement Rules: An examination of the Parallels and their Furtherance by the ECJ Wouters Decision' (2003) 24(2) *ECLR* 62

Parker, Christine, 'The "Compliance" Trap: The Moral Message in Responsive Regulatory Enforcement' (2006) 40(3) *Law and Society Review* 591

Patterson, Mark R, 'The Role of Power in the Rule of Reason' (2000) 68 *Antitrust Law Journal* 429

Piernas López, Juan Jorge, 'The Aggravating Circumstance of Recidivism and the Principle of Legality in the EC Fining Policy: Nulla Poena Sine Lege?' (2006) 29(3) *World Competition* 441

Pijetlovic, Katarina, 'Reform of EC Antitrust Enforcement: Criticism of the New System is Highly Exaggerated' (2004) 25(6) *ECLR* 356

Pitt, Edward, 'Markets are instruments not values' (2006) 27(1) *ECLR* 1

Posner, Richard A, 'The Social Costs of Monopoly and Regulation', *Journal of Political Economy*, August 1975, Vol 83, Issue 4, 807

Prete, Luca, and Nucara, Allessandro, 'Standard of Proof and Scope of Judicial Review in EC Merger Cases; Everything Clear after Tetra Laval' (2005) 26(12) *ECLR* 692

Radicati di Brozolo, Luca G, 'Antitrust Claims: Why Exclude Them from the Hague Jurisdiction and Judgments Convention?' (2004) 25(12) *ECLR* 780

Reynolds, Michael J, and Anderson, David G, 'Immunity and Leniency in EU Cartel Cases: Current Issues' (2006) 27(2) *ECLR* 82

Riley, Alan, 'Saunders and the power to obtain information in Community and United Kingdom Competition law' (2000) 25(3) EL Rev 264

—— 'EC Antitrust Modernisation: The Commission Does Very Nicely—Thank You! Part 1: Regulation 1 and the Notification Burden' (2003) 24(11) *ECLR* 604

—— 'EC Antitrust Modernisation: The Commission Does Very Nicely—Thank You! Part Two: Between the Idea and the Reality: Decentralisation under Regulation 1' (2003) 24(12) *ECLR* 657

—— 'Beyond Leniency: Enhancing Enforcement in EC Antitrust Law' (2005) 28(3) *World Competition* 377

Rodger, Barry J, 'Private Enforcement and the Enterprise Act: An Exemplary System of Awarding Damages' (2003) 24(3) *ECLR* 103

—— 'Competition Law Compliance Programmes: A Study of Motivations and Practice' (2005) 28(3) *World Competition* 349

Saarela, Anna, and Malric-Smith, Paul, 'Reorganisation of cartel work in DG Competition' (2005) *Competition Policy Newsletter*, No 2, Summer

Schinkel, Maarten Pieter, 'Effective Cartel Enforcement in Europe' (2007) 30(4) *World Competition* 539

Schønberg, Søren, and Frick, Karin, 'Finishing, Refining, Polishing: On the Use of Travaux Préparatoires as an Aid to the Interpretation of Community Legislation' (2003) 28(2) EL Rev 149

Schoneveld, Frank R, 'Cartel Sanctions and International Competition Policy: Cross-border Cooperation and Appropriate Forums for Cooperation' (2003) 26(3) *World Competition* 433

Serebrisky, Tomás, 'What Do We Know about Competition Agencies in Emerging and Transition Countries? Evidence on Workload, Personnel, Priority Sectors and Training Needs' (2004) 27(4) *World Competition* 651

Shulman, Daniel R, 'Proof of Conspiracy in Antitrust Cases & the Oligopoly Problem' (4) *Sedona Conference Journal* 1, Fall, 2003

Simonsson, Ingeborg and Öberg, Ulf, 'Bensinkartelldomen MD 2005:7—fördragsstridig tillämpning av EG:s konkurrensrätt?, *Svensk Juristtidning* 1/2006 s 23

Simpson, Sally S, and Koper, Christopher S, 'Deterring Corporate Crime' (1992) 30(3) *Criminology* 347

Simpson, Sally S, and Leeper Piquero, Nicole, 'The Archer Daniels Midland Antitrust Case of 1996: A Case Study', in Pontell and Shico Eds. *Contemporary Issues in Crime and Criminal Justice: Essays in Honor of Gilbert Geis* (Old Tappan, NJ, Prentice Hall, 2001).

Smith, Graham P, 'Competition law and the ignoring of human rights' [2001] *International Company and Commercial Law Review* 1

Spink, Paul M, 'Recent Guidance on Fining Policy' (1999) 20(2) *ECLR* 101

Spratling, Gary R, 'Detection and Deterrence: Rewarding Informants for Reporting Violations' (2001) 69(5/6) *George Washington Law Review* 798

Szoboszlai, Judit, 'Delegation of State Regulatory Powers to Private Parties—Towards an Active Supervision Test' (2006) 29(1) *World Competition* 73

Teece, David J, 'Information Sharing, Innovation, and Antitrust' (1994) 62 *Antitrust Law Journal* 465

Temple Lang, John, 'General Report on the Application of Community Competition Law on Enterprises by National Courts and National Authorities', FIDE Congress 1998, available at http://ec.europa.eu/comm/competition/speeches/text/sp1998_027_en.html

—— 'The Duties of Cooperation of National Authorities and Courts under Article 10 EC: Two More Reflections' (2001) 26(1) EL Rev 84

—— 'Compensation for Unjustified Administrative Procedures in Community Law' (2002) 23(10) *ECLR* 490

—— 'Commitments Decisions under Regulation 1/2003: Legal Aspects of a New Kind of Competition Decision' (2003) 24(8) *ECLR* 347

—— 'The Implications of the Commission's Leniency Policy for National Competition Authorities' (2003) 28(3) EL Rev 430

—— 'National Measures Restricting Competition and National Authorities under Article 10 EC' (2004) 29(3) EL Rev 397

—— 'Commitment Decisions and Settlements with Antitrust Authorities and Private Parties under European Antitrust Law' in Hawk (ed), *International Antitrust Law & Policy: Fordham Corporate Law* (New York, Juris Publishing, 2005) Ch 13

Townley, Chris, 'The Liner Shipping Block Exemptions in European Law: Has the Tide Turned?' (2004) 27(1) *World Competition* 107

Trebilcock, Michael J, and Iacobucci, Edward M, 'Designing Competition Law Institutions' (2002) 25(3) *World Competition* 361

Tuori, Kaarlo, 'Discourse Ethics and the Legitimacy of Law' (1989) *Ratio Juris* (2) 125

Vedder, Hans, 'Spontaneous Harmonisation of National (Competition) Laws in the Wake of the Modernisation of EC Competition Law' (2004) 1(1) *The Competition Law Review* 5

Veljanovski, Cento, 'Penalties for Price-fixers: An Analysis of Fines Imposed on 39 Cartels by the EU Commission' (2006) 27(9) *ECLR* 510

Venayre, Florent, 'Échanges d'informations: Les jurisprudence Française et communautaire à laune des predictions théoriques' (2004) 108(4) *Revue d'Économie Industrielle* 91

—— 'Les apports de la théorie économique à létude des accords d'échanges d'information' (2005) *Revue Lamy de la Concurrence* No 2, 122

Venit, James S, 'Brave New World: The Modernization and Decentralization of Enforcement under Articles 81 and 82 of the EC Treaty' (2003) 40(3) *CML Rev* 545

Wahl, Nils, 'To What Extent Has the Modernisation Reform Been Successful at the National Level?', *Europarättslig Tidskrift* No 3, 2006, 490

Walker-Smith, A, 'Collusion: Its Detection and Investigation' (1991) 12(2) *ECLR* 71

Werden, Gregory J, 'Economic Evidence on the Existence of Collusion: Reconciling Antitrust Law with Oligopoly Theory' (2004) 71(3) *Antitrust Law Journal* 719

—— 'The Effect of Antitrust Policy on Consumer Welfare: What Crandall and Winston Overlook' (2003) Economic Analysis Group Discussion Paper EAG 03-2, January 2003, available at http://papers.ssrn.com/sol3/papers.cfm?abstract_id=384100

Wesseling, Rein, 'The Draft-regulation Modernising the Competition Rules: The Commission is Married to One Idea' (2001) 26(4) EL Rev 357

Wessely, Thomas W, 'Case C-49/92 P *Commission v Anic*, [1999] ECR I-4125; Case C-199/92 P, *Hüls v Commission*, [1999] ECR I-4287; Case C-235/92 P, *Montecatini v* Commission, [1999] ECR I-4539; judgments of 8 July 1999 (together: Polypropylene appeal cases)' (2001) 38(3) *CML Rev* 739

Whelan, Peter, 'A Principled Argument for Personal Criminal Sanctions as Punishments under EC Cartel Law' (2007) 4(1) *The Competition Law Review* 7

Wickihalder, Urs, 'The Distinction between an "Agreement" within the Meaning of Article 81(1) of the EC Treaty and Unilateral Conduct' (2006) 2(1) *European Competition Journal* 87

Whish, Richard, 'The Enforcement of EC Competition Law in the Domestic Courts of Member States' (1994) 15(2) *ECLR* 60

Willis, Peter R, '"You have the right to remain silent . . .", or do you? The privilege against self-incrimination following Mannesmannrohren-Werke and other recent decisions' (2001) 22(8) *ECLR* 313

Wils, Wouter P J, 'The Commission Notice on the Non-imposition or Reduction of Fines in Cartel Cases: A Legal and Economic Analysis' (1997) 22(2) EL Rev 125

—— 'The Principle of Ne Bis in Idem in EC Antitrust Enforcement: A Legal and Economic Analysis' (2003) 26(2) *World Competition* 131

—— 'Should Private Antitrust Enforcement Be Encouraged in Europe?' (2003) 26(3) *World Competition* 473

—— 'Self-incrimination in EC Antitrust Enforcement: A Legal and Economic Analysis' (2003) 26(4) *World Competition* 567

—— 'The Combination of the Investigative and Prosecutorial Function and the Adjudicative Function in EC Antitrust Enforcement: A Legal and Economic Analysis' (2004) 27(2) *World Competition* 201

—— 'Powers of Investigation and Procedural Rights and Guarantees in EU Antitrust Enforcement: The Interplay between European and National Legislation and Case-law' (2006) 29(1) *World Competition* 3

—— 'Optimal Antitrust Fines: Theory and Practice' (2006) 29(2) *World Competition* 183

Ysewyn, Johan, and Jordan, Eve, 'Cashing in on Cartels' (2003) 24(6) *ECLR* 235

Zane, Phillip C, 'The price fixer's dilemma: applying game theory to the decision of whether to plead guilty to antitrust crimes' (2003) 1 *The Antitrust Bulletin* 1

Zimmerman, Jeffrey E, and Connor, John M, 'Determinants of Cartel Duration: A Cross-sectional Study of Modern Private International Cartels', available at www.agecon.purdue.edu/staff/connor/papers/

BOOKS

American Bar Association, Section of Antitrust Law, *Proving Antitrust Damages, Legal and Economic Issues* (USA, American Bar Association, 1996)

—— *A Primer on the Law of Information Exchange*, 2nd edn (USA, American Bar Association, 2002)

Andersson, Torbjörn, *Dispositionsprincipen och EG:s konkurrensregler* (Uppsala, Iustus, 1999).

Areeda and Hovenkamp, *Antitrust Law—An Analysis of Antitrust Principles and Their Application* (New York, Aspen Publishers, Wolters Kluwer Law and Business).

Arnull, Anthony, *The European Union and its Court of Justice*, 2nd edn (Oxford, Oxford EC Law Library, 2006)

Arnull, Anthony, and Wincott, Daniel (eds), *Accountability and Legitimacy in the European Union* (Oxford, Oxford University Press, 2002)

Ashurst, report prepared by Clark, Emily, Hughes, Mat and Wirth, David, 'Study on the conditions of claims for damages in case of infringement of EC competition rules', 31 August 2004, at 43ff, available on http://ec.europa.eu/comm/competition/antitrust/others/actions_for_damages/study.html

Van den Bergh, Roger J, and Camesasca, Peter D, *European Competition Law and Economics: A Comparative Perspective*, 2nd edn (London, Thomson Sweet & Maxwell, 2006)

Dannecker, Gerhard, and Jensen, Oswald (eds), *Competition Law Sanctioning in the European Union* (The Hague, Kluwer Law International, 2004)

Dougan, Michael, *National Remedies before the Court of Justice—Issues of Harmonisation and Differentiation* (Oxford, Hart Publishing, 2004)

Ehlermann, Claus Dieter, and Atanasiu, Isabela, *European Competition Law Annual 2000: The Modernisation of EC Antitrust Policy* (Oxford, Hart Publishing, 2001)

—— *European Competition Law Annual 2006: Enforcement of Prohibition of Cartels* (Oxford, Hart Publishing, 2007)

Elhauge, Einer, and Geradin, Damien, *Global Competition Law and Economics* (Oxford, Hart Publishing, 2007)

Faull, Jonathan, and Nikpay, Ali (eds), *The EC Law of Competition* (Oxford, Oxford University Press, 2007)

Geis, Gilbert (ed), *White Collar Crime* (New York, Atherton Press, 1968)

Geis, Gilbert, *et al*, *White-Collar Crime, Classic and Contemporary Views*, 3rd edn (New York, The Free Press, 1995)

Gerber, David J, *Law and Competition in Twentieth Century Europe: Protecting Prometheus* (Oxford, Oxford University Press, 1998)

Gowda, Rajeev, and Fox, Jeffrey C (eds), *Judgments, Decisions, and Public Policy* (Cambridge, Cambridge University Press, 2002)

Grossman, Peter Z (ed), *How Cartels Endure and How They Fail, Studies of Industrial Collusion* (Cheltenham, Edward Elgar Publishing, 2004)

Habermas, Jürgen, *Between Facts and Norms* (Cambridge, Polity Press, 1996)

Harding, Christopher, and Joshua, Julian, *Regulating Cartels in Europe—A Study of Legal Control of Corporate Delinquency* (Oxford, Oxford University Press, 2003)

Hettne, Jörgen, and Otken Eriksson, Ida (eds), *EU-rättslig metod* (Stockholm, Norstedts Juridik, 2005)

Hovenkamp, Herbert, and Areeda, Philip E, *Fundamentals of Antitrust Law* 3rd edn. (New York, Kluwer, looseleaf).

ICN Working Group on Cartels, *Defining Hard Core Cartel Conduct, Effective Institutions, Effective Penalties* (European Communities, International Competition Network, 2005)

Jephcott, Mark, *Horizontal Agreements and EU Competition Law* (Richmond, 2005)

Jones, Alison, and Sufrin, Brenda, *EC Competition Law*, 2nd edn (Oxford, Oxford University Press, 2004)

Jordan, Andrew, and Schout, Adriaan, *The Coordination of the European Union—Exploring the Capacities of Networked Governance* (Oxford, Oxford University Press, 2006)

Kerse, *EC Antitrust Procedure*, 4th edn (Thomson, 1998)

Kerse, C S, and Khan, N, *EC Antitrust Procedure*, 5th edn (London, Sweet & Maxwell, 2005)

Koeck, Heribert Franz, and Karollus, Margit Maria (eds), *The Modernisation of European Competition Law—Initial Experiences with Regulation 1/2003* (Linz, FIDE XXIII Congress 2008, facultas.wuv)

Lenaerts, Koen, Arts, Dick, Maselis, Ignace, and Bray, Robert (eds), *Procedural Law of the European Union*, 2nd edn (London, Sweet & Maxwell, 2006)

Lenaerts, Koen, Van Nuffel, Piet, and Bray, Robert (eds), *Constitutional Law of the European Union*, 2nd edn (London, Sweet & Maxwell, 2005)

Levenstein, Margaret C, and Suslow, Valerie Y, 'Studies of Cartel Stability: A Comparison of Methodological Approaches' in Grossman (ed), *How Cartels Endure and How They Fail, Studies of Industrial Collusion* (Cheltenham, Edward Elgar Publishing, 2004)

Lonbay, Julian and Biondi, Andrea (eds), *Remedies for Breach of EC Law* (New York, Wiley, 1997)

Majone, Giandomenico, *Dilemmas of European Integration* (Oxford Scholarship Online, 2006)

Marsden, Philip, *Exclusionary Anti-Competitive Practices, their Effects on Competition and Development, and Analytical and Remedial Mechanisms*, Report prepared for UNCTAD (Geneva, United Nations, 2005)

Micklitz, Hans-W, *The Politics of Judicial Co-operation in the EU* (Cambridge, Cambridge University Press, 2005)

Nazzini, Renato, *Concurrent Proceedings in Competition Law* (Oxford, Oxford University Press, 2004)

Nehl, Hanns Peter, *Principles of Administrative Procedure in EC Law* (Oxford, Hart Publishing, 1999)

Nicolaides, Phedon, *From Graphite to Diamond—The Importance of Institutional Structure in Establishing Capacity for Effective and Credible Application of EU Rules* (Maastricht, European Institute of Public Administration, 2002)

Nicolaides, Phedon, Geveke, Arjan, and den Teuling, Anne-Mieke, *Improving Policy Implementation in an Enlarged European Union—The Case of National Regulatory Authorities* (Maastricht, European Institute of Public Administration, 2003)

Odudu, Okeoghene, *The Boundaries of EC Competition Law—The Scope of Article 81* (Oxford, Oxford University Press, 2006)

OECD, *Hard Core Cartels* (OECD, 2000)

OECD, *Report on the nature and impact of hard core cartels and sanctions against cartels under national competition laws* (OECD, 2002, DAFFE/COMP(2002)7)

OECD, *Fighting Hard-Core Cartels—Harm, effective sanctions and leniency programmes* (OECD, 2002).

OECD, *Hard Core Cartels, Recent Progress and Challenges Ahead* (OECD, 2003)

OECD, *Hard Core Cartels*, Third Report on the Implementation of the 1998 Recommendation (OECD, 2005)

Ortiz Blanco, Luis, *Review of Shipping Conferences under EC Antitrust Law: Criticism of a Legal Paradox* (Oxford, Hart Publishing, 2007)

Posner, Richard, *The Problems of Jurisprudence* (London, Harvard University Press, 1993)

—— *Antitrust Law*, 2nd edn (Chicago, University of Chicago Press, 2001)

Reichel, Jane, *God förvaltning i EU och i Sverige* (Stockholm, Jure, 2006)

Rowley QC, J William, and Low QC, Martin, *Cartel Regulation 2006* (London, Global Competition Review, 2006)

Sakkers, Ewoud, and Ysewyn, Jordan, *European Cartel Digest* (The Netherlands, Wolters Kluwer, 2008)

Senden, Linda, *Soft Law in European Community Law* (Oxford, Hart Publishing, 2004)

Scharpf, Fritz Wilhelm, *Governing in Europe: Effective and Democratic?* (Oxford, Oxford University Press, 1999)

Simonsson, Ingeborg, *Konkurrensverkets domstolsprocesser 1993–2004—En utvärdering* (Konkurrensvekets uppdragsforskningsserie 2005:2), available at http://www.kkv.se/t/IFramePage____1500.aspx

Siragusa, Mario (ed), *EU Competition Law—Volume III Cartel Law* (Leuven, Claeys & Casteels, 2006)

Stendahl, Sara, *Communicating Justice Providing Legitimacy—The legal practice of Swedish administrative courts in cases regarding sickness cash benefit* (Uppsala, Iustus, 2003)

Sunstein, Cass R (ed), *Behavioural Law and Economics* (Cambridge, Cambridge University Press, 2000)

Tridimas, Takis, *The General Principles of EU Law*, 2nd edn (Oxford, OUP, Oxford EC Law Library, 2006)

Van Bael, Ivo, and Bellis, Jean-François, *Competition Law of the European Communities*, 4th edn (The Hague, Kluwer Law International, 2005)

Wahl, Nils, *Konkurrensförhållanden* (Stockholm, Juristförlaget, 1994)

—— *Konkurrensskada* (Stockholm, JureCLN AB, 2000)

—— *Optimala sanktioner inom svensk konkurrensrätt* (Konkurrensverkets uppdragsforskning 2006:3), available at www.konkurrensverket.se

Wahlgren, Peter, *Lagstiftning—Problem, teknik, möjligheter* (Uppsala, Norstedts, 2008)

Whish, Richard, *Competition Law*, 5th edn (LexisNexis, 2003)

Wils, Wouter P J, *The Optimal Enforcement of EC Antitrust Law—Essays in Law and Economics* (The Hague, Kluwer Law International, 2002)

Yeung, Karen, *Securing Compliance—A principled approach* (Oxford, Hart Publishing, 2004)

Zamboni, Mauro, *The Policy of Law—A Legal Theoretical Framework* (Stockholm, 2004)

—— *Law and Politics—A Dilemma for Contemporary Legal Theory* (Berlin Heidelberg, Springer-Verlag, 2008)

—— *The Policy of Law—A Legal Theoretical Framework* (Oxford, Hart Publishing, 2008)

OTHER PUBLICATIONS

'Antitrust Enforcement Activities Fiscal Year 2002—March 15, 2006', presented at the ABA Antitrust Section Spring Meeting 2006, available at http://www.ftc.gov/bc/anncompreports.htm

'Status Report: A Summary Overview of the Antitrust Division's Criminal Enforcement Program', available at http://www.usdoj.gov/atr/public/guidelines/202531.htm

AMC Criminal Remedies Discussion Memorandum of 4 May 2006, at 13–14, available at http://www.amc.gov/commission_documents.htm#may9

AMCHAM EU, Position Paper on the Modernization Package

American Bar Association, Joint Comments of the American Bar Association's Section of Antitrust Law and Section of International Law and Practice on Draft European Commission Notices and Draft Regulation Implementing Regulation 1/2003

Annual Report 2004, Proceedings of the Court of First Instance, at 89, available at http://curia.europa.eu/en/instit/presentationfr/index.htm

Antitrust Modernization Commission Report and Recommendations April 2007, available at http://www.amc.gov/report_recommendation/toc.htm

Commission Discussion Paper on the review of Regulation 4056/86 applying EC competition rules to maritime transport, para 183, available at http://ec.europa.eu/comm/competition/antitrust/legislation/maritime/

ICN Working Group on Cartels, *Defining Hard Core Cartel Conduct, Effective Institutions, Effective Penalties* (European Communities, International Competition Network, 2005)

Mandate for the ICN Cartels Working Group, available at—
www.internationalcompetitionnetwork.org

OECD Global Forum, *Information sharing in cartel investigations* (OECD, 2002, CCNM/GF/COMP(2002)1)

OECD, *European Commission—Peer Review of Competition Law and Policy* (OECD Country Studies, 2005), available at www.oecd.org

OECD, *Evaluation of the Actions and Resources of Competition Authorities* (OECD Policy Roundtables, 2005

OECD Global Forum on Competition, *Prosecuting Cartels without Direct Evidence of Agreement* (OECD, 2006, DAF/COMP/GF/(2006)7)

Statute of the Court of Justice, Article 16, available at http://curia.europa.eu/en/instit/txtdocfr/index.htm

United States Sentencing Guidelines, § 2R1.1. Bid-Rigging, Price-Fixing or Market-Allocation Agreements Among Competitors, Commentary

World Trade Organisation Working Group on the Interaction between Trade and Competition Policy, 'Provisions on Hardcore Cartels', WT/WGTCP/W/191, at 3, available at www.wto.org

OFFICIAL DOCUMENTS

'Status Report: A Summary Overview of the Antitrust Division's Criminal Enforcement Program', available at http://www.usdoj.gov/atr/public/guidelines/202531.htm

2394th Council meeting—Energy/Industry, Brussels, 4 and 5 December 2001, PRES/01/452, 4/12/2001

Answer to written question No 284/92 by Mr Yves Verwaerde to the Commission [1992] OJ C/168/45

COM (2005) 672 Green Paper, *Damages actions for breach of the EC antitrust rules,* 19/12/2005

COM(2000) 582 Final, Proposal for a Council Regulation on the implementation of the rules on competition laid down in Articles 81 and 82 of the Treaty and amending Regulations (EEC) No 1017/68, (EEC) No 2988/74, (EEC) No 4056/86 and (EEC) No 3975/87 ('Regulation implementing Articles 81 and 82 of the Treaty'), OJ C/365/E, 19/12/2000, 284–96

COM(2007) 699 rev 2, Proposal for a Regulation of the European Parliament and of the Council establishing the European Electronic Communications Market Authority

Commission Notice on co-operation between national courts and the Commission in applying Articles 85 and 86 of the EEC Treaty [1993] OJ C/39/6

Commission Notice on the non-imposition or reduction of fines in cartel cases [1996] OJ C/207/4

Commission notice on co-operation between national competition authorities and the Commission in handling cases falling within the scope of Articles 85 or 86 of the EC Treaty [1997] OJ C/313/3

Commission Notice on the application of the competition rules to access agreements in the telecommunications sector [1998] OJ C/265/2

Commission Notice, Guidelines on the method of setting fines imposed pursuant to Article 15(2) of Regulation No 17 and Article 65(5) of the ECSC Treaty [1998] OJ C/9/3

Commission Notice, Guidelines on the applicability of Article 81 of the EC Treaty to horizontal co-operation agreements [2001] OJ C/3/2

Commission Notice on agreements of minor importance which do not appreciably restrict competition under Article 81(1) of the Treaty [2001] OJ C/368/13, at 11

Commission Notice on immunity from fines and reduction of fines in cartel cases [2002] OJ C/45/3

Commission Notice on co-operation within the Network of Competition Authorities [2004] OJ C/101/43

Commission Notice, Guidelines on the effect on trade concept contained in Articles 81 and 82 of the Treaty [2004] OJ C/101/81

Commission Notice, Guidelines on the application of Article 81(3) of the Treaty [2004] OJ C/101/97

Commission Notice, Guidelines on the assessment of horizontal mergers under the Council Regulation on the control of concentrations between undertakings [2004] OJ C/31/5

Commission Notice, Guidelines on the method of setting fines imposed pursuant to Article 23(2)(a) of Regulation No 1/2003 [2006] OJ C/210/2

Commission Notice on immunity from fines and reduction of fines in cartel cases [2006] OJ C/298/17

Commission Discussion Paper on the review of Regulation 4056/86 applying EC competition rules to maritime transport, para 183, available at http://ec.europa.eu/comm/competition/antitrust/legislation/maritime/

Delivering on the crackdown: recent developments in the European Commission's campaign against cartels, SPEECH/06/595, 13/10/2006

Draft Commission Notice on the conduct of settlement proceedings in view of the adoption of Decisions pursuant to Article 7 and Article 23 of Council Regulation (EC) No 1/2003 in cartel cases, available at http://ec.europa.eu/comm/competition/cartels/legislation/settlements.html

European Parliament resolution on the Commission White Paper on modernisation of the rules implementing Articles 81 and 82 of the EC Treaty (COM(1999) 101–C5-0105-1999–1999/2108(COS)) [2000] OJ C/304/66

European Parliament Report on the Proposal for a Council Regulation on the Implementation of the Rules of Competition Laid Down in Articles 81 and 82 of the Treaty . . . Committee on Economic and Monetary Affairs

Konkurransetillsynet, Sanksjonering—er verdt prisen? Om sanksjonering under konkurranseloven, Skrifter fra Konkurransetillsynet 1/2001

Opinion of the Economic and Social Committee on the 'Proposal for a Council Regulation on the implementation of the rules on competition laid down in Articles 81 and 82 of the EC Treaty—Commission programme No 99/027 [2001] OJ C/155/73

Opinion of the Economic and Social Committee on the 'White Paper on modernisation of the rules implementing Articles 81 and 82 of the EC Treaty—Commission programme No 99/027' [2000] OJ C/51/55

Report on Competition Policy 2005, SEC (2006) 761 final

Report on the proposal for a Council regulation, Session document of the European Parliament 21 June 2001, A5-0229-2001

Rules of Procedure of the Court of First Instance of 2 May 1991, OJ L/136 of 30 May 1991, including amendments up to OJ L/127 of 29 April 2004

US Department of Justice, *An Inside Look at a Cartel at Work: Common Characteristics of International Cartels*, by James M Griffin, presented at the American Bar Association, Section of Antitrust Law, 48th Annual Spring Meeting

United States Sentencing Guidelines, § 2R1.1. Bid-Rigging, Price-Fixing or Market-Allocation Agreements Among Competitors, Commentary

White Paper on Modernisation of the Rules Implementing Articles 85 and 86 of the EC Treaty [1999] OJ C/132/1

XXXIInd Report on Competition Policy 2002, SEC (2003) 467 final

Commission Notice on the conduct of settlement procedures in view of the adoption of Decisions pursuant to Article 7 and Article 23 of Council Regulation (EC) No 1/2003 in cartel cases [2008] OJ C/167/1

OTHER COMMISSION POLICY DOCUMENTS

32nd Report on Competition Policy 2002—SEC(2003) 467 Final

Report on Competition Policy 2005 (European Commission, 2005)

Index